"Feeding To Win"

II

All Rights Reserved

ISBN 0-935842-00-4

Last printed 1999

P.O. Box 8618   Tyler, Texas 75711-8618
(U.S. & Canada) (800) 848-0225
(Other Countries) (903) 894-3818

Written by
research staff of Equine Research, Inc.

Special Chapters

Chapter 12 - Internal Parasites
courtesy of:
Richard L. Asquith, D.V.M. and Jan Kivipelto, M.S.

Chapter 13 - Drugs
edited by:
Thomas Tobin, M.V.B., M.Sc., Ph.D., M.R.C.V.S.

Research Editor
Frederick Harper, Ph.D.

Editor/Publisher
Don Wagoner

Additional Acknowledgments

Special editing and technical contributions:

Harold F. Hintz, Ph.D.
E.A. Ott, Ph.D.
William J. Tyznik, Ph.D.
Craig H. Wood, Ph.D.

Disclaimer

Although every effort was made to present scientifically accurate and up-to-date information based on the best available and reliable sources, it should be appreciated that results of feeding and caring of horses depend upon a variety of factors not under the control of the publishers of this book. Therefore, Equine Research Inc., assumes no responsibility for, and makes no warranty with respect to, results that may be obtained from the procedures described or ingredients discussed herein. Equine Research Inc., shall not be liable to any person for damage resulting from reliance on any information contained in *Feeding To Win II*, whether with respect to feeding, care, treatment procedures, drug usages and dosages, or by reason of any misstatement or inadvertent error contained herein.

Also, it must be remembered that Equine Research Inc., does not manufacture, package, ship, label or sell any of the drugs, feeds, supplements, or veterinary products discussed in this book. Accordingly, Equine Research Inc., cannot be responsible for the results that may be obtained with the use of any of those items.

The reader is encouraged to read and follow the directions published by the manufacturer of each product, feed, supplement, or drug which may be mentioned herein. And, if there is a conflict with information in this book, the instructions of the manufacturer—or of the reader's veterinarian—should, of course, be followed.

To insure the reader's understanding of some technical descriptions offered in *Feeding To Win II*, brand names have been occasionally used as examples of particular substances or equipment. However, the use of a particular trademark or brand name is not intended to imply an endorsement of that particular product, or to suggest that similar products offered by others under different names may be inferior. Nothing contained in *Feeding To Win II* is to be construed as a suggestion to violate any trademark laws.

Introduction

The purpose of *Feeding To Win II* is to furnish the best information available to people who are serious about caring for horses. The needs of breeders, trainers, veterinarians, students of animal science courses, and professional horsemen of all disciplines have been addressed. In addition, the book will also be used by earnest, eager-to-learn horsemen with less experience. Therefore, information is provided so as to be useful for readers of varied levels of knowledge. Because of this, you may find some text to be more basic than you require, or on the other hand, some data may be too technical for your immediate needs. Don't dismay, the level of information you are seeking will also be found.

If you find text, or a chart you feel is too technical to be of interest to you at this time, skip that area—but make a mental note of its existence. Knowing what resources are available may prove helpful in the future when you need detailed information on a certain subject.

Should you discover a problem of any kind with this book, or if you have recommendations you feel would improve the form or content of future editions—please contact us. We listen carefully, and we appreciate suggestions and criticisms as well as compliments!

FEEDING TO WIN II

Contents

9

10

11

ART and SCIENCE of FEEDING 297
(Expert Opinions and Practices)

14

1

THE EQUINE DIGESTIVE SYSTEM

Digestion is the process by which feedstuffs are broken down to their simplest forms. The resulting nutrients can then be absorbed into the bloodstream and provide proteins, vitamins, and minerals for growth and repair, or they can be stored for future needs. Digestion takes place through a

Fig. 1–1. Having general knowledge of the equine digestive system is important for feeding a horse to achieve its full potential.

complex process that involves *peristaltic* muscular contractions, enzymatic action, and bacterial fermentation (digestion of fiber by bacteria in the hindgut). The digestive process is completed when usable nutrients are assimilated and undigested feed residues and waste products are excreted. To feed a horse to achieve its full potential, a working knowledge of the digestive system is important. This chapter will discuss the structures and functions of the digestive system.

Note: This chapter is intended to explain the equine digestive system to those interested in nutrition rather than to students of physiology. For this reason, the digestive system has been considered from a functional approach. Anatomical details have not been explored more than necessary to understand needs of the system, and their relationship to feeds and diets. (Readers needing more detail may refer to a text on equine anatomy and physiology, such as The Illustrated Veterinary Encyclopedia For Horsemen, published by Equine Research, Inc.)

The digestive system of the horse consists of the mouth, pharynx, esophagus, stomach, small intestine, cecum, large colon, small colon, and rectum. It may be referred to as the digestive tract, the gastrointestinal tract, or the alimentary canal. The accessory organs which aid in digestion are the salivary glands, liver, and pancreas.

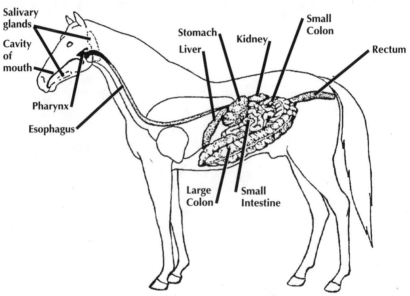

Fig. 1–2. This is a simple view of the digestive tract, showing various organs involved in digestion. As the cecum lies on the right side of the horse, it does not appear in this diagram. The pancreas is also obscured by other organs.

MOUTH

The digestive process in the horse begins in the mouth, which contains the teeth, tongue, and salivary glands. Feedstuffs are grasped and pulled into the mouth with the aid of the highly mobile lips. Upon entering the mouth, the feed is ground mechanically by the teeth and mixed with saliva to soften it.

Teeth

Healthy teeth play an important role in equine nutrition. The best diet will not be beneficial if the horse cannot chew it properly. The teeth break down feed into smaller sizes, producing more surface area for the digestive enzymes to come in contact with. This allows nutrients to be extracted more readily during the digestion process.

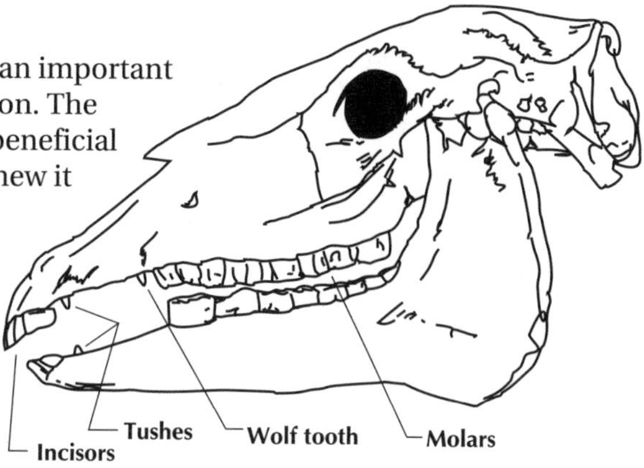

Fig. 1–3. These permanent teeth indicate the owner is probably a male. Mature male horses have 40 teeth, mares usually have 36.

The horse has two sets of teeth during its lifetime: *deciduous,* or milk teeth, and permanent teeth. Mature male horses have 40 teeth: 12 incisors, 4 tushes or canine teeth, and 24 molars. In most cases, mature female horses have 36 teeth: 12 incisors and 24 molars (mares may or may not have tushes). The teeth continue to grow throughout the horse's entire life, but the chewing action keeps the molars the same length.

The horse should have all of its permanent incisors by about four years of age. Either sex may have *wolf teeth,* which are small, vestigial teeth that erupt in the upper jaw. Wolf teeth are often removed to avoid bitting problems.

Equines have more difficulties with their teeth than any other domestic animal, and will encounter dental problems that require attention. Because the upper jaw is normally slightly wider than the lower jaw, the horse's circular chewing action causes the crowns of the molars to grind

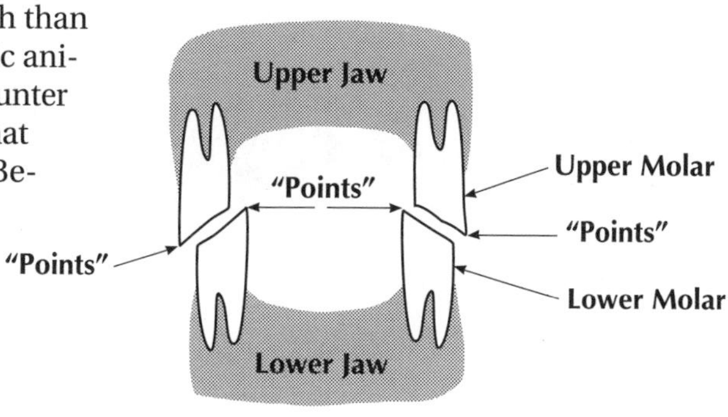

Fig. 1–4. The horse's chewing action results in sharp points on the outside of upper molars, and on the inside of lower molars. The points can lacerate tongue and cheek.

3

against each other. Eventually, this grinding action will cause sharp points to form on the edges of the molars, scraping and possibly cutting the tongue and the inside of the cheek. The sharp edges can cause problems with bitting and chewing, and the cuts can become infected.

The discomfort of the sharp points in the mouth will often hinder normal eating habits. The horse will sometimes extend its neck and turn its head sideways in an attempt to escape the pain in its mouth, or it will eat slowly and drop kernels of grain as it chews. As a result, feed intake will decrease, and the horse will lose weight and condition. In extreme cases, the horse may try to avoid chewing the grain and will swallow it before it is properly masticated and moistened. The gulping down of large *boluses* of improperly chewed feed can cause choke if they become trapped in the esophagus. These problems can be avoided by regular *floating* (filing) of the teeth, a common procedure normally performed by veterinarians.

Horses that are on pasture or that eat soft feeds exclusively, such as pellets, tend to require floating more often than horses fed a diet containing hard grains.

Horses that have sustained an injury to the mouth or jaw should be carefully observed. Dental care may be required if the effects of the injury are causing the teeth to grow or wear unevenly. In most cases, frequent floating is sufficient treatment, but sometimes removal of the problem teeth is necessary.

The horse may also have a *congenital* defect of the mouth that may require special care. The most common of these is "*parrot mouth,*" in which either the lower jaw is too short or the upper jaw is too long.

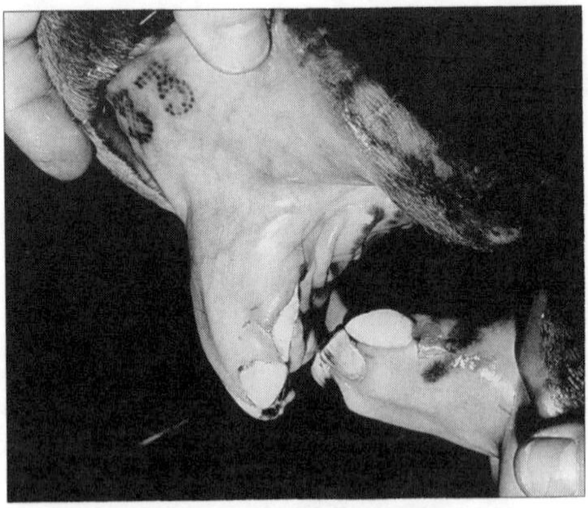

Fig. 1–5. A view of "parrot mouth."

The upper incisors are sometimes filed or trimmed to facilitate eating and bitting. Occasionally, the teeth grow to the point that the horse has trouble taking feed in. To avoid transmitting this congenital abnormality, parrot-mouthed horses should not be used as breeding stock. However, they can be used for performance, provided they receive adequate dental care.

A second genetic abnormality in the dentition of the horse is termed "*sow mouth*," which has the opposite appearance of parrot mouth. The sow mouthed (also called "monkey jawed," undershot jaw, or "bulldog mouthed") horse has a lower jaw that is too long, causing the lower incisors to protrude past the uppers, presenting problems very similar to those of parrot mouth. Sow mouth is also a congenital defect, and is treated in much the same way as parrot mouth.

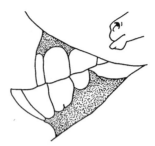

Fig. 1–6. Closeup of the incisors in a horse with "sow mouth."

A third abnormality is termed *shear mouth*, in which the upper jaw is wider than normal. This results in excessive angular wear of the molars, which produces extremely sharp edges. Teeth in the wider upper arcade wear on the inside edges, causing them to elongate to the cheek side. Teeth in the lower arcades will be worn on the outside edges, causing the inside edges to become sharp, near the tongue.

When the width difference is excessive, the molar crowns wear at such an extreme angle that the upper and lower teeth will slide past each other, much like the blades of scissors, causing severe damage to the soft tissue in the mouth. As there is no way to alter the width of the jaw or alignment of the molars, treatment is limited to frequent floating of the sharp edges. These horses should be treated as needed, but no less than twice yearly. As with parrot mouth and sow mouth, shear mouth is an inherited disorder, and horses afflicted with it should not be used for breeding purposes.

Tongue

Broad, flat, and spatula shaped, the tongue of the horse is very similar to the tongue of the human.

Located on the floor of the mouth, the tongue is supported in a sling formed by the *mylohyoideus* muscle. It is composed of three main parts: 1) a thick mucous membrane, 2) muscles, 3) salivary glands.

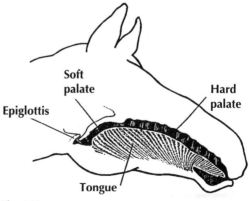

Soft palate

Hard palate

Epiglottis

Tongue

Fig. 1–7.

The muscular portion of the tongue contains many corresponding vessels and nerves. The tongue serves to move the feed around in the mouth and mix it with saliva, and its mechanical action also helps to break down the feed. Taste buds on the surface of the tongue, along with a keen sense of smell, help the horse to discriminate among various feedstuffs. When drinking, the horse uses its tongue in much the same manner as a person drinking from a straw.

After feedstuffs have been thoroughly chewed and mixed with saliva, they are moved to the back of the mouth, where the tongue pushes them into the pharynx.

Salivary Glands

Saliva is produced and excreted by three large pairs of salivary glands: the parotid, submaxillary, and sublingual. It is mixed with feedstuffs as they are crushed and ground by the teeth. Saliva contains small amounts of amylase, a digestive enzyme, but this enzyme is considered an insignificant part of the digestive process.

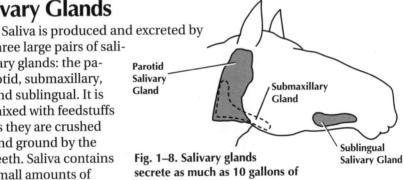

Fig. 1–8. Salivary glands secrete as much as 10 gallons of saliva a day.

The mature horse secretes as much as 10 gallons of saliva each day, or about 85 pounds. Unlike other species that salivate at the sight of feed, the horse must chew or have mechanical jaw movement in order for salivation to occur. The *alkaline* (basic) saliva is gradually neutralized by the acid in the stomach after the ingesta leaves the mouth, and its digestive action ceases.

PHARYNX

The pharynx is the muscular passage that connects the mouth and the esophagus. Air passes through the pharynx to the larynx, which is the upper part of the trachea. The soft palate is located at the back of the mouth, and it acts as a trap to prevent ingesta and air from returning to the mouth from the pharynx. It also, along with the epiglottis, prevents ingesta from entering the lungs. If the horse is unable to pass ingesta down the esophagus because of an obstruction, it will return through the nostrils rather than through the mouth.

After feedstuffs have been chewed and mixed with saliva, the tongue pushes boluses (balls) of ingesta into the pharynx, and from there it moves into the esophagus.

ESOPHAGUS

The esophagus is a tube, approximately five feet in length, that lies between the pharynx and the stomach. Material swallowed by the horse is moved through the esophagus by waves of muscular contractions called *peristalsis*. Ingesta that is being swallowed can be seen on the left side of the neck passing down just below the windpipe. It is important that the esophagus be located and observed when passing a stomach tube to ensure that the tube enters the esophagus and not the trachea. **Passage of a stomach tube should only be performed by a veterinarian.**

1- Path of stomach tube
2- Nostril
3- Nasal passage
4- Hard palate
5- Sinus cavity (upper)
6- Sinus cavity (lower)
7- Soft palate
8- Pharynx
9- Epiglottis
10- Trachea
11- Esophagus

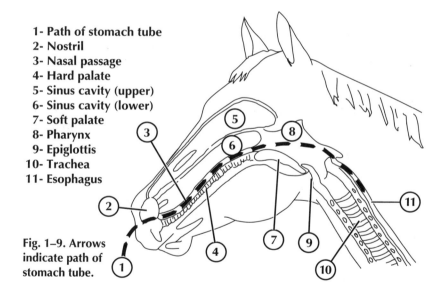

Fig. 1–9. Arrows indicate path of stomach tube.

The opening of the esophagus into the stomach is regulated by a very efficient *sphincter* (tight band of muscle) to prevent the return of ingesta from the stomach. For this reason, vomiting is not normal and occurs rarely in the horse, usually only in cases of extreme illness.

STOMACH

The stomach is a small, muscular, J-shaped sac in which the enzymatic digestive processes begin. Its relatively small capacity of 2 to 4 gallons (in the mature horse) is attributed to the nomadic, constant feeding habits the horse developed as it evolved. When considering this capacity, it must be remembered that saliva mixed with ingesta greatly increases the amount of contents. Because the horse can effectively digest only small amounts of ingesta at a time, there are definite advantages in dividing daily rations into multiple feedings.

After mastication, the feed is passed through the esophagus to the stomach, where it is acted on by digestive juices. The *gastric mucosa* (stomach lining) secretes the digestive juices, which are primarily hydrochloric acid and the enzyme *pepsinogen.* The hydrochloric acid breaks the pepsinogen down into pepsin, a protein digesting enzyme. Pepsin begins breaking down proteins into fragments, and hydrochloric acid begins dissolving the mineral matter in the feed, making the nutrients more available for absorption. The digestive process is then continued in the small intestine.

Enzymatic digestion is more efficient when the stomach is not completely full. If the horse consumes a large amount of feed at one time, the ingesta will quickly fill the stomach. Feedstuffs will then be forced into the small intestine before the enzymes secreted by the stomach can thoroughly break them down.

Unless feed is withheld for 24 hours or more, the stomach never completely empties, and ingesta may remain in the intestinal tract for as long as 96 hours.

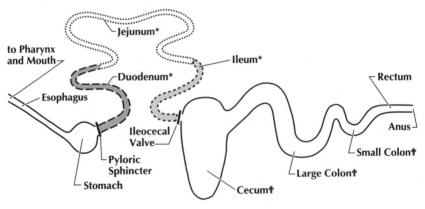

* Components of Small Intestine
†Components of Large Intestine

Fig. 1–10. Simplified diagram of horse's digestive tract.

SMALL INTESTINE

The *pyloric sphincter* regulates the juncture of the stomach and the small intestine by only allowing ingesta to pass through in one direction. The small intestine, which is located between the stomach and the cecum, is approximately 70 feet long and has a capacity of about 17 gallons. It is the major site of digestion.

The first section of the small intestine that is attached to the stomach is the *duodenum* (approximately 3 feet in length). The central portion is the *jejunum* (approximately 54 feet in length), and the final segment that connects with the cecum at the *ileocecal valve* is the *ileum* (approximately 6 feet in length).

When empty, its maximum diameter is only about 2 inches. This part of the digestive system is coiled, looped, and doubled back upon itself in many places. It is supported by a double fold of the *peritoneum* called the mesentery. The mesentery is strong and flexible enough to allow the peristaltic contractions to move freely along the length of the small intestine.

The small intestine is lined with thousands of tiny finger-like projections, called villi. It is through these villi that the digested feed nutrients are absorbed. Once absorbed, the nutrients enter the capillaries and lymph system to be carried throughout the body. The majority of the dissolved nutrients will be absorbed at this stage of the digestion process. The remaining ingested material, consisting mostly of fiber, is moved by peristaltic muscular action into the cecum and colon to undergo fiber fermentation.

ACCESSORY ORGANS

Apart from the functions of the major organs, digestion is made possible by the secretions of two major accessory organs, the liver and the pancreas.

The liver and the pancreas secrete, respectively, bile and pancreatic juice. The secretions are carried into the small intestine through a common duct, and it is in this part of the digestive tract (small intestine) that the major enzymatic breakdown of ingesta occurs.

Liver

The liver is the largest gland in the horse's body. Among its many functions, it secretes a continuous flow of bile, which aids in digestion of fats. The liver also serves as a storage facility for vitamin A (up to six months), energy (in the form of *glycogen)*, and iron. In addition, the liver has a very important role in processing many other vitamins and minerals. Unlike cattle and humans, the horse has no gall bladder for bile storage, so the liver must produce bile as it is needed for digestion.

Pancreas

The pancreas is a large, compound gland that secretes digestive enzymes. Each enzyme has a specific function in the digestive process, and acts on only one form of nutrient.

In the small intestine, bile and pancreatic juice combine to break down and extract remaining mineral matter, most fats, 65%–75% of the soluble carbohydrates, and 60%–70% of the proteins in the feed.

LARGE INTESTINE
Cecum

The *cecum* is a large pouch through which feed moves more slowly than through the rest of the digestive system. The cecum is about 4 feet long, and holds approximately 8 gallons. It has a somewhat comma-like shape, and has openings from the small intestine and to the large colon (openings not shown— the cecum is folded on itself and covered by other organs). Because its contents are predominantly liquid, the cecum is sometimes called the "water gut."

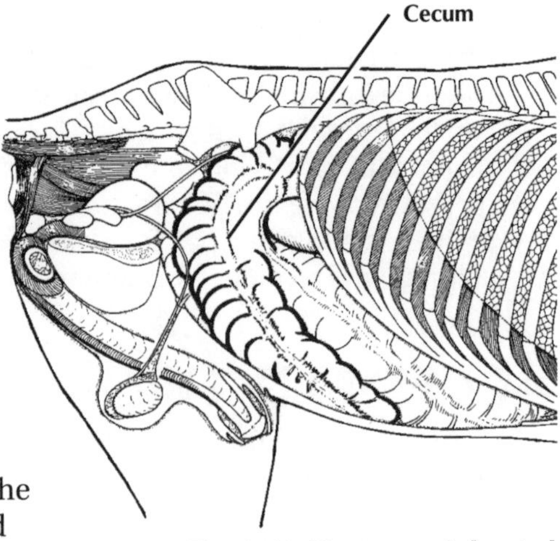

Cecum

Fig. 1–11. The cecum is located in the area of the right flank.

Fermentation by microbial action in the cecum helps to break down and digest fiber. It also helps to free a portion of the feed's fiber content for its nutrient value. Microorganisms in the cecum and part of the large colon synthesize B vitamins and amino acids, and break down fibrous carbohydrates and remaining soluble carbohydrates into volatile fatty acids (VFAs), which can be used as energy. Protein absorption is limited in the cecum, but there is considerable passive absorption of water-soluble nutrients. Because the presence of fermenting bacteria is required for fiber digestion, some of the energy absorption in the forage-fed horse takes place in the cecum. However, most of the bacterial fermentation, and consequently energy production and absorption, take place in the colon.

Large Colon

From the cecum, the ingesta passes to the large colon, where more moisture from the feedstuffs is absorbed. Further bacterial fermentation takes place here, and there is a small amount of nutrient absorption, primarily energy. The large colon is about 12 feet long, 8 to 10 inches in diameter, and holds about 20 gallons. It is usually distended with liquefied fibrous material.

Small Colon

The small colon is approximately 10 to 12 feet long and 3 to 4 inches in diameter, when not distended. It can hold up to 4 gallons, and it reabsorbs more of the water from the ingested material. The contents of this part of the intestine are mainly solid waste of indigestible or undigested feed, and it is here that the feces are formed. The small colon contains sac-like structures that form the undigested material into the horse's characteristic fecal balls.

Rectum

The rectum is a short straight tube about one foot in length, and it holds the waste material until it is passed out of the horse's body through the anal opening.

2

WATER

Fig. 2–1.

Water is a vital nutrient. It makes up 65% to 75% of the weight of an adult horse, and is the primary component of all body fluids. In a growing horse, where water deposits in tissues have not yet been replaced by fat, the proportion of water is from 75% to 80%.

Water controls and regulates body temperature, is an important component of every cell in the body, and is a vital member in all the chemical reactions of digestion, absorption, and metabolism. A horse can live up to 25 days without food, but only five days or less without water. The length of time a horse can survive will depend on many factors, such as ambient temperature and humidity, and intensity and duration of activities (work).

A horse can lose essentially all of the fat and up to half of the protein in its body and still survive. However, a loss of only 12% to 15% of body water is usually fatal.

Fortunately, while water is vital, it is also plentiful and inexpensive. There is no reason why the need for a pure, fresh, constant water supply should not always be met.

FUNCTIONS

1) Aids in production of saliva and other digestive juices.
2) Transports nutrients to, and waste products away from cells.
3) Acts as a body temperature regulator, evaporating as sweat.
4) Lubricates joints as a constituent of synovial fluid.
5) Fluid cushion for the nervous system in the *cerebrospinal fluid*.
6) Transports sound in the *perilymph* of the ear, and provides lubrication for the eye.
7) Necessary for life and shape of every cell, and is a major constituent of all body fluids.

REQUIREMENTS

Water requirements will vary, due to factors which include:

- age
- ambient (air) temperature
- size
- humidity
- activity
- type of feed consumed
- health status

Working horses, pregnant or lactating mares, and breeding stallions require more water than idle horses. Water requirements are also increased when the ambient temperature or humidity is high.

A general guide to follow is: the average healthy adult horse (1,100 lbs, or 500 kg) in light work, in a moderate ambient temperature and humidity environment, will consume about 6 – 10 gallons of water daily. Such a guide however is for information purposes only. Under normal circumstances, **a horse should be provided as much clean, fresh water as it will drink.** A horse over-heated from recent exercise is an exception. *(See "cooling out" later in this chapter.)*

Normal Water Needs	
Activity	Gallons per day
Non working	4 – 8
Gestation	7 – 9
Peak lactation	9 – 11
Medium work	9 – 15
Heavy work	12 – 15+

Fig. 2–2. Estimated needs of a 1,100 lb horse in 60° – 70° F. temperatures.

Special Considerations

Various types of stress, whether physiological or caused by man, may increase the amount of water required. Common instances in which extra water is required will be considered in the following material. Although each of these situations is discussed individually, any combination of them may additionally increase water requirements.

Pregnancy and Lactation

Pregnant mares will drink more water to serve fetal needs. Mares in last trimester of pregnancy will consume 8% – 10% more than usual.

Mare's milk contains about 90% water. An increase in water consumption by a lactating mare will vary from 50% – 70% above maintenance, depending on level of milk production. A lactating mare producing 30 pounds of milk per day will require an additional 5 gallons of water above maintenance amounts. Other factors such as temperature and humidity will also affect her water requirements.

Physical Exercise

As the horse's activity level increases, so does need for water. Moderate activity can increase water requirements by 60% – 80%. Hard work can increase water requirements by as much as 300%.

An average-sized (1,100 lbs, or 500 kg), adult, hard-working horse can lose 55 – 60 pounds in a few hours through sweating, especially with high ambient temperature and humidity. Body weight losses of 5% – 10% have been observed in endurance horses.

Extensive sweating produces significant electrolyte loss. Electrolytes lost in equine sweat are primarily sodium and chloride, along with a smaller, but still significant, amount of potassium. *(See more on electrolytes later in this chapter.)*

Fig. 2–3. Strenuous equine activity can increase water requirements by as much as 300%.

Cooling Out

When a horse has been exercising and is hot, it should receive water, but the **rate of consumption should be carefully monitored**. A hot horse ingesting large quantities of water and swallowing a lot of air can cause colic and/or founder.

A horse should be thoroughly "cooled out" before being offered free access to water. During the cooling out process, the horse should only be allowed to take a few swallows of water every few minutes. To cool properly, the horse should be covered with a light sheet (unless the ambient temperature is very high), then be walked until heart and respiration rates return to normal. Normal heart rate in an adult horse ranges between 30 and 42 beats per minute. Normal respiration rate should fall between 8 to 16 respirations per minute.

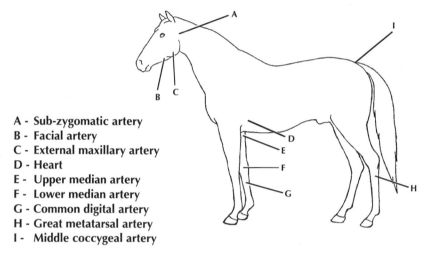

A - Sub-zygomatic artery
B - Facial artery
C - External maxillary artery
D - Heart
E - Upper median artery
F - Lower median artery
G - Common digital artery
H - Great metatarsal artery
I - Middle coccygeal artery

Fig. 2–4. Locations where pulse can be taken.

Following the return of the horse's heart and respiration rates to normal, it may be given free access to water.

If a horse is placed in a situation of long term physical exertion, such as endurance riding, ranch work, or long trail rides, it should be watered often, as long as it is kept moving and active after drinking.

Water and Feeds

Water content of feedstuffs is widely varied. For example, young, green grass is about 75% water, while dry, stored grain contains an average of 10% – 12% water. Consequently, water consumption may be affected to some degree by moisture content of the ration. Feedstuffs low in moisture and high in fiber, salt or other minerals, or containing a sweetener such as molasses, will increase thirst. Feeds high in protein and minerals will also increase thirst, as added water is needed for metabolism of these nutrients.

Horses are able to derive a small amount of water through the oxidation (breakdown) of carbohydrates, proteins, and fats during digestion. This is termed *metabolic* water.

Water Digestion and Excretion

Water is one of the few nutrients provided to horses in a pure form. It does not have to be simplified or processed.

Although the cecum is thought to be the main site for water absorption, a fair amount of water is also absorbed in the large intestine.

Water is excreted from the body in urine and feces, as water vapor from the lungs and as sweat from the skin. Water is also used and removed from the body in secretions such as milk, semen, and mucus.

In growing horses, some water is retained as a constituent of new tissue. As a result, the amount of water excreted will be slightly less than that ingested. In the mature horse, however, average water intake and average water excretion will be approximately the same, so total body fluid volume normally remains constant.

Dehydration

Dehydration is the extreme depletion of body fluids, resulting from insufficient water intake or excessive fluid excretion.

Dehydration will cause the horse's capillary refill time to increase, accompanied by a drying of *mucous membranes.* Urine will also become concentrated, darker in color and reduced in amount. After time, the dehydrated horse will become "tucked up" in the lower flank area and appear hollow or sunken eyed. The horse's hair coat will also develop a rough, dry appearance. Other symptoms of prolonged dehydration include drying and tightening of the skin and weight loss. These symptoms will generally be accompanied by a sharp decrease in work effort. Following long-term dehydration, kidneys may become sore and will soon malfunction if the horse does not begin to drink or is not adminis-

Fig. 2–5. The skin pinch test is a way of estimating dehydration. If the skin stays pinched over two seconds, dehydration is indicated. The longer it stays pinched, the more severe the dehydration that is indicated.

tered fluids. The degree of dehydration can be tested by pinching up a fold of skin on the neck. Normally the skin quickly slips back into place. In the dehydrated horse, the skin will remain pinched for two to five seconds before it returns to normal. In more severe cases, the skin may remained pinched for as long as ten seconds.

Simple dehydration is normally treated by supplying plenty of clean, fresh water and by observing the horse carefully to be sure it is drinking. In more serious situations, a veterinarian may administer water with a stomach tube. In severe cases, when dehydration includes mineral or electrolyte imbalance, extensive veterinary care will be required.

Decreased Water Intake

A decrease in water intake will usually be associated with decreased feed intake, as both situations often result from similar problems. For instance, mouth pain and certain illnesses may cause a decrease in feed and water intake. Decreased water consumption will affect feed digestion, as water is required in the digestion process to produce saliva and digestive juices.

A variety of situations may cause a horse to **refuse** to drink. It might be sick, or there could be an unpalatable contaminant present in the water supply. Water might be inaccessible because of an abnormal situation, such as faulty electrical wiring in a tank heater, which causes the horse to be shocked when it touches the water.

Other problems may cause a horse to be **unable** to drink, such as suffering from choke, an injury, or some type of disease. Whatever the situation, it must be corrected so that the horse can begin normal consumption of water as quickly as possible.

When a horse does not ingest water for an extended period, water will be used from sources within the body. Water will first be absorbed from the gut, then from the interstitial spaces surrounding the cells, and finally from blood plasma. Even though the horse's system is capable of using such water from within the body, it will deplete these reserves very rapidly. Only 3% of the body water must be lost before dehydration becomes visible, and it usually only takes a loss of 12% – 15% to be fatal.

Water and Digestion Impaction

Inadequate water consumption can cause ingesta to become impacted in the digestive tract, which can result in colic. Some horses are routinely fed a bran mash to help avoid impactions. The bran mash contains a high percentage of water, which increases the level of moisture in the digestive tract. However, the possible benefit of feeding large amounts of wheat bran should be weighed against the high level of phosphorus it contains. *(For information on phosphorus toxicity, see Chapter 4.)*

There is a theory that impaction can result if water is withheld from a thirsty horse until after it has eaten. Water will push the ingested material through the stomach too rapidly, causing ingesta to collect farther down the tract and becoming blocked there. Although no specific scientific data currently exists to support this theory, providing a horse with water before and after eating **is** recommended.

An impaction can be caused by feeding low quality forage. Poor forages usually contain high concentrations of fiber, and as a result are highly undigestible. They also normally contain a high percentage of dry matter, and consequently require a good deal of water for digestion and formation of feces.

Diarrhea

Diarrhea is the most common cause of excessive water loss in the horse. This section will discuss only nutritionally influenced reasons for diarrhea. *(For more information on other causes of diarrhea, refer to The Illustrated Veterinary Encyclopedia for Horsemen published by Equine Research, Inc.)*

Ingestion of feedstuffs with a high moisture content, such as young, green forages, can add significant amounts of water to the digestive tract. The water, along with the fiber content of the forage, then moves quickly through the tract, sometimes causing diarrhea.

Another nutritionally induced situation that may result in diarrhea occurs when a horse's ration is suddenly changed. Unfamiliarity with a new ration can alter the bacterial population of the intestinal tract, resulting in changes in pH (acidity/alkalinity balance). Changes in pH will lead to irritation, which often manifests itself as diarrhea.

When changing a ration, it is preferable to do so over a period of several days. Gradually increasing new ingredients at the rate old ingredients are being decreased allows for a smooth transition of changes in bacterial population. Gradual change produces a less traumatic effect on the digestive system.

Excessive intake of *concentrates* or legume hay can also result in diarrhea, as can allergic reactions to a specific protein. (The term "concentrate" denotes the portion of a ration that is primarily grains, but may also include non-grain components [e.g. soybean meal, corn oil, salt, commercial supplements, etc.].)

Many illnesses are characterized by diarrhea. Any horse, especially the young, showing symptoms of diarrhea should have access to clean, fresh water, and be examined by a veterinarian.

Overhydration

Overhydration (excess water) is not common in the horse. If it occurs, it may result from excessive fluid intake or from water retention.

Excessive fluid intake is not normally caused by voluntary over-consumption. It is usually a result of forced administration of water during a required related procedure, such as treating a case of choke. Forced administration may also be required for a horse whose water consumption has decreased to the point of dehydration. In these cases, water is administered by a veterinarian directly into the stomach with a stomach tube.

Overhydration may also result from water retention. Retention of water within the tissues is characterized by swelling in the legs (edema) and weight gain. When swelling is localized, it is usu-

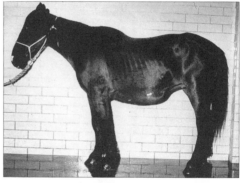

Fig. 2–6. Generalized edema indicates severe illness, and requires veterinary care.

ally a result of trauma or injury to a particular area. In addition, horses that stand in stalls for extended periods will sometimes develop localized edema in the lower legs due to prolonged inactivity.

When water retention is generalized, it is often a sign of serious illness. A **generalized** edema can be a sign of kidney or heart malfunction. It should be noted, however, that a **localized** edema in the ankle or lower leg is also a possible indication of kidney malfunction. A generalized edema is serious, and a veterinarian should be contacted.

WATER AND MINERAL INTAKE

After reaching the earth's surface in the form of rain, water begins to dissolve minerals in the soil and form a solution. The more minerals contained in water, the "harder" it becomes. Hence, "soft" water contains fewer minerals than hard water does. Hardness of water in a particular area depends on the mineral concentration of the soil through which the water filters. Usually, County Agricultural Agents can provide information on the mineral content of water in an area.

Although water hardness may affect the palatability of water, it does not affect its use as a drinking source. Since there is a difference in

Fig. 2–7. Show horses competing in different areas may need flavoring added to "new" water.

taste, a horse that is moved to a different location may refuse new water at first. The best way to accustom a horse to new water is to gradually mix water from old and new sources. If this isn't possible, intake should be monitored to avoid dehydration.

If traveling a great deal, such as with show or racehorses, there might not be time to accustom horses slowly to new water. Some trainers add a flavoring (e.g. molasses or a powdered drink mix) to water to mask the new scent and taste. Although not much is needed to be effective, flavoring should be added daily, begining a few days before the trip.

The horse utilizes some minerals from its water source. However, the amount of minerals obtained, even from hard water, is not normally considered significant. An exception exists in areas where soil contains high levels of limestone. The resulting calcium content of the water will be high enough to be considered a part of calcium requirements. *(See Chapter 4, for more information.)*

Harmful Mineral Intake

There are two situations where mineral content of water can be harmful. One is salty water, which contains a large amount of *sodium chloride* and is unsuitable. When salt water is ingested, it changes the electrolyte balance and intracellular pressure in the body. This pro-

Safe Upper Limit of Minerals in Water			
Mineral Element	Upper Limit (mg/liter)	Mineral Element	Upper Limit (mg/liter)
Arsenic	0.20	Mercury	0.01
Cadmium	0.05	Nickel	1.00
Chromium	1.00	Nitrate nitrogen	100.00
Cobalt	1.00	Nitrite nitrogen	10.00
Copper	0.50	Vanadium	0.10
Fluoride	2.00	Zinc	25.00
Lead	0.10		

Fig. 2–8.

duces a form of dehydration, which places a strain on kidneys. In the U. S., this problem is more likely to occur in areas of the West.

Another problem is the consumption of water containing high concentrations of fluorine. The result can be a case of fluorine toxicity. *(For a description of symptoms, see section on fluorine in Chapter 4.)*

Normally, horses may be given any water that has been tested and found to be safe, regardless of its hardness.

Safe Levels of Soluble Salts in Water	
Soluble salt content (mg/liter)*	**Comments**
Less than 1000	relatively low level of salinity; should cause no problems for any class of horses
1000 – 2999	should cause no problems; may cause mild diarrhea in horses not accustomed to it
3000 – 4999	should cause no problems; may cause temporary diarrhea or be refused by horses not accustomed to it
5000 – 6999	reasonably safe; avoid using higher levels for pregnant and lactating mares
7000 – 10,000	presents risks to pregnant or lactating mares, young horses, and to animals with heat stress or water loss
Over 10,000	not recommended for horses

Fig. 2–9.

Electrolyte Supplementation

In a hot or humid environment, oral electrolyte supplementation may be beneficial for heavily seating horses involved in lengthy activities. Need for supplementation is increased if the horse is particularly stressed or nervous.

There are several commercial electrolyte products available that are beneficial and easy to administer. Supplementation usually provides sodium and chlorine in roughly equal proportions. Proportion of potassium is normally about ⅓ to ½ that of sodium and chlorine, because that proportion is usually lost in sweat. Calcium and magnesium are sometimes added in small amounts. When supplementation is necessary, the amount given should not be excessive.

The objective should be to partially fulfill deficits until the lost electrolytes are replaced through normal consumption. If there is an immediate need for electrolytes and nothing else is available, human athletic drinks may be used. *(Chapter 7 discusses electrolytes in detail.)*

METHODS OF WATERING HORSES

There are two basic means by which a horse can obtain water—a natural source, such as a stream in a pasture, and human provision. The latter case has advantages of better inspection and control of quality and quantity. Also, consumption can be monitored, especially when watering by hand. As a sudden reduction in water intake usually indicates illness, the ability to gauge consumption is important.

Hand Watering

There are various methods by which man can provide water to horses, and since many similarities exist, only general methods will be discussed here. There are advantages and disadvantages to all systems, but any reasonable system will work, as long as it provides a constant source of clean, fresh water and does not pose any safety hazards.

Fig. 2–10. Buckets should be hung at the approximate height of the horse's point of shoulder.

Stabled horses are most commonly provided water in a bucket. The bucket should be made of a non-breakable material, have a flat side to hang against the wall, and be positioned at the approximate height of the horse's point of shoulder. If the water source is difficult to reach, the horse may not consume proper amounts. (It is important to remember this when watering a foal or small horse in a stall that was previously occupied by a taller horse.)

Buckets should be located conveniently for removal, so frequent inspection, cleaning, and disinfecting can be easily and quickly done. They should also be located far enough from feed troughs and hay sources to avoid dropped food particles.

Water buckets should be checked, emptied, and refilled several times per day. If this is not possible, then watering facilities need to accommodate circumstances. For example, a water bucket for an average size horse performing light work should hold at least 7 gallons if watering is only done twice daily. This ensures normal minimum water requirements are met. If for some reason the horse is consuming larger amounts of water, two buckets may be required, especially in hot weather. The horse should be receiving enough water that it **always has some left at regularly scheduled refills.**

Water buckets should be scrubbed daily and disinfected at least twice weekly. If a horse is sick, its water bucket should be scrubbed and disinfected daily to prevent re-infection and to minimize spreading of germs. In a group situation, a sick horse should be isolated from other horses, and it should be fed, watered, and handled last to avoid spreading disease. Water hoses should not be submerged in watering facilities when filling them, as they too, can spread disease.

When temperatures are below freezing, water buckets should be checked frequently to ensure they have not iced over.

Automatic Waterers

Automatic waterers are popular devices for providing fresh water on demand, both in stalls and in pastures. A problem with automatic waterers is the caretaker's reduced ability to monitor intake and to quickly notice if a horse has stopped drinking.

Fig. 2–11. Automatic waterers should be checked and cleaned frequently.

Automatic waterers require less labor than hand watering, but still need to be checked and cleaned. In cold climates, they should contain a temperature regulating mechanism to prevent freezng.

Pastured Horses

When watering horses from man-made facilities in a pasture, appropriate sanitation rules should be practiced. Facilities should be made of

Fig. 2–12. A water trough with no sharp corners helps to avoid injuries.

sturdy materials that do not rust or present danger of injury to horses. A round water trough, or at least one with rounded corners, helps to prevent injuries. It should be easy to drain and clean, and in a location that is readily accessible to the horses.

If possible, placing troughs in shade during summer months is recommended. Water will remain cooler and it encourages horses to drink more. During winter months, water troughs should be in sheltered locations and in the sun, if possible, to help avoid freezing. They should be checked frequently in freezing temperatures so ice may be removed.

Natural Sources of Water

When allowing horses access to a natural source of water, quality should be monitored closely. A sample should be tested periodically by a laboratory to determine any existence of water pollution.

Natural sources of water should have a constant fresh inflow and outflow to avoid stagnation. Horses do not consume stale or stagnant water as readily as fresh water. Stagnant water is also more likely to be polluted, and it provides a breeding ground for disease causing bacteria and pests such as mosquitoes. The level of a natural water source should be monitored frequently to ensure a sufficient supply. Natural water sources can also freeze in cold weather, so when temperatures drop below freezing, an alternate source of water may need to be provided.

3

VITAMINS

FUNCTIONS OF VITAMINS

A vitamin is a relatively complex organic substance necessary for normal body functions. Only small amounts of each vitamin are required. However, an absence or deficiency will eventually result in illness. Also, a number of problems from mild to severe, can be caused by excess supplementation of some vitamins.

The role of vitamins in the diet is complex and not completely understood. Among their general functions, vitamins play a part in the enzymatic actions of the body, specifically as *coenzymes*. Coenzymes are non-protein compounds that combine with proteins to form enzymes. Enzymes are responsible for bringing about many chemical reactions that are necessary for normal body functions, and they act as catalysts to accelerate chemical reactions. Vitamins are also essential components of body fluids.

Some vitamins are synthesized by *microflora* (bacteria and protozoa) in the intestine, or by the liver in sufficient amounts that a dietary source is not required. Other vitamins must be provided in the diet.

Fig. 3–1. Proper vitamin intake is essential for good health.

HISTORY OF VITAMINS

The first vitamin to be clearly recognized was vitamin A, in 1913. Since then, thirteen others have been identified, including:

- vitamin D
- vitamin E
- vitamin K
- vitamin B_1 (thiamine)
- vitamin B_2 (riboflavin)
- niacin
- vitamin B_6 (pyridoxine)
- choline
- biotin (sometimes called vitamin H)
- folacin (sometimes called vitamin M)
- vitamin C (ascorbic acid)
- vitamin B_3 (pantothenic acid)
- vitamin B_{12} (cyanocobalamin, also called cobalamin)

Vitamins B_1, B_2, niacin, B_3, B_6, choline, biotin, folacin, and B_{12} are known as the B-complex group. They were formerly considered different forms of the same type of water-soluble vitamin, called vitamin B. It is now known that they have different chemical structures and independent functions.

This chapter presents detailed information on vitamins. The following chart is offered as a brief overview of their functions.

Vitamins and Their Functions

FAT-SOLUBLE

Vitamin A - maintains integrity of epithelial tissue, eye function, bone development
Vitamin D - promotion of proper absorption, transportation, and metabolism of calcium and phosphorus
Vitamin E - an antioxidant at the cellular level
Vitamin K - involved in normal blood coagulation

WATER-SOLUBLE

B_1 **(Thiamine) -** required for carbohydrate metabolism and function of the nervous system
B_2 **(Riboflavin) -** energy metabolism and proper nervous system function
Niacin - essential in cellular respiration and metabolism
B_3 **(Pantothenic acid) -** part of a coenzyme, assists in protein, carbohyrate, and fat utilization
B_6 **(Pyridoxine) -** part of an enzyme system, involved in metabolism of protein, carbohydrates, and fats
Choline - metabolizes fat, transmission of nerve impulses
Biotin - coenzyme in the metabolism of protein, carbohyrates, and fats
Folacin - necessary for cell metabolism and normal red blood cell formation
B_{12} **(Cyanocobalamin) -** assists in production of red-blood cells, utilization of carbohydrates, fats, and proteins
Vitamin C (Ascorbic Acid) - formation of collagen, lysine, and proline

Fig. 3–2.

TYPES & MEASURES
Fat-Soluble Vitamins

Fat-soluble vitamins A, D, E, and K are defined as vitamins that dissolve in fat or fat solvents. They can be stored in the body for later use, either in the liver or the fat cells, so a deficiency will not occur immediately if they are not present in the diet. Due to this characteristic however, it is possible to build up excesses. So, oversupplementation can cause toxicity.

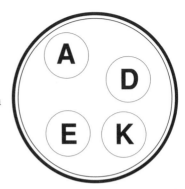

Fig. 3–3. Vitamins A, D, E, and K are stored in fat cells.

Water-Soluble Vitamins

The water-soluble vitamins are the B-complex vitamins and vitamin C (ascorbic acid). They dissolve in water and are stored in the body for only a short time. Because excess amounts are excreted in the urine, only a limited reserve of water soluble vitamins exists in the body. They must be provided in the diet, or manufactured in sufficient quantities by intestinal microflora or the liver to meet daily needs. Most water-soluble vitamins can be obtained from forages or are synthesized by intestinal bacteria in adequate amounts by the horse's body.

Methods of Measurement

Vitamin amounts may be measured in several ways. They may be listed in I.U. (International Units) or U.S.P. Units (United States Pharmacopeia Units). Both are equal in strength and are measures of effect (results accomplished in scientific tests), rather than of weight.

Vitamins may also be measured by weight in milligrams (mg), grams (g), and ounces (oz); or in parts per million (ppm), which is equivalent to milligrams per kilogram.

VITAMIN REQUIREMENTS

Vitamin requirements, like those of any other nutrient, will vary, depending on many factors. These factors include age of the horse, health and condition, work intensity and duration, and stresses such as illness, pregnancy, and lactation. For many of the vitamins, no specific dietary requirements have been set, because adequate amounts are synthesized by microflora in the horse's body.

If a horse is consuming a good quality, well balanced diet, it will most likely receive the required amounts of vitamins without a need for supplementation. An exception to this is vitamin E, which will be fully discussed later in this chapter.

The following chart provides an overview of vitamin requirements for different classes of horses:

Estimated Daily Vitamin Requirements				
	Mature Idle Horses	**Pregnant and Lactating Mares**	**Growing Horses**	**Working Horses**
Vitamin A	30 IU/kg of body weight	60 IU/kg of body weight	45 IU/kg of body weight	45 IU/kg of body weight
Vitamin D (horses w/daily sunlight)	Exact requirements not determined			
Vitamin D (horses w/no daily sunlight)	300 IU/kg dry matter	600 IU/kg dry matter	800 IU/kg dry matter	300 IU/kg dry matter
Vitamin E	50–80 IU/kg dry matter	80–100 IU/kg dry matter	80–100 IU/kg dry matter	80–100 IU/kg dry matter
Vitamin K	Exact requirements not determined			
Thiamine (B₁)	3 mg/kg dry matter	3 mg/kg dry matter	3 mg/kg dry matter	5 mg/kg dry matter
Riboflavin (B₂)	2 mg/kg dry matter	2 mg/kg dry matter	2 mg/kg dry matter	2 mg/kg dry matter
Niacin	Exact requirements not determined			
Pantothenic Acid (B₃)	Exact requirements not determined			
Pyridoxine (B₆)	Exact requirements not determined			
Choline	Exact requirements not determined			
Biotin	Exact requirements not determined			
Folacin	Exact requirements not determined			
Cyanocobalamin, Cobalamin (B₁₂)	Exact requirements not determined			
Vitamin C (Ascorbic Acid)	Exact requirements not determined			

Fig. 3–4.   IU/kg = *international units per kilogram*

FAT-SOLUBLE VITAMINS
Vitamin A

Vitamin A is converted from dietary *carotene,* a plant pigment. Vitamin A is produced by the horse's own *metabolism.* This means the body tissues, in particular those of the intestinal wall, *synthesize* vitamin A from the carotene provided in the diet. Large quantities of carotene can be found in green pastures and high quality hays. Vitamin A is one of the few vitamins that can be inadequate in diets fed to stabled horses. This is assuming limited grazing time and diets consisting of a high percentage of whole grains. In order for the stabled horse to receive adequate vitamin A, it should be fed high quality hay or a properly supplemented ration. In a case of short term vitamin A deficiency, the equine liver can provide up to a three month supply from stored reserves.

Fig. 3–5. Carotene is present in green pastures and high quality hays.

Functions

Vitamin A is necessary for maintaining the soundness of *epithelial* tissue in the respiratory, digestive, and reproductive tracts. It is important for proper eye function, healthy skin and hooves. Vitamin A also regulates the bone remodeling (growth and formation) process in young, growing equines.

Requirements

Only a small amount of scientific information on Vitamin A and carotene requirements exists for horses, so only estimates of their needs can be made.

Approximately 30 IU per kilogram of body weight (1,364 IU per 100 pounds of body weight) of vitamin A should be consumed daily for maintenance. Pregnant and lactating mares should consume 60 IU per kilogram of body weight (2,727 IU per 100 pounds of body weight) daily. Growing horses and all others should receive 45 IU per kilogram of body weight (2,045 IU per 100 pounds of body weight) daily.

Fig. 3–6. Colostrum provides foals with vitamin A and other vital nutrients. It is important that foals nurse soon after birth to receive colostrum.

During pregnancy and lactation, it is important for mares to have adequate vitamin A. This is due to increases in demand for vitamin A by the rapid growth of the fetus and the production of milk. Vitamin A requirements for gestating mares may be twice as much as maintenance requirements of an average adult horse. Unless the broodmare receives adequate levels of vitamin A, she may use nearly all of her stored vitamin A during the winter months, since fewer green plants are available during this time.

Colostrum (the first milk produced) is an important source of vitamin A and other vital nutrients for newborn foals. It is important that foals receive sufficient amounts of this "first milk" shortly after birth.

Vitamin A Supplementation

Vitamin A can be obtained in two different ways. It can be in the ration (either as carotene from feedstuffs or in a supplement), or it can be injected. Vitamin A injections are given intramuscularly or *subcutaneously*. Since they very quickly fill the storage capacity of the liver they should be administered only on advice of a veterinarian or qualified equine nutritionist .

Factors Which Influence Vitamin A Content

Carotene is found in green pasture forages and in high quality hay. The yellow pigment of this compound is masked by the green color of the *chlorophyll* in the plant. A mixture of these two pigments gives the plant a healthy green color, indicating a high carotene content.

High quality, green, leafy hay is a very good source of carotene and, therefore, vitamin A. Young plants contain the greatest amount of carotene, while those in late maturity will have the least. Most carotene is found in the leaves of the plant.

Harvesting and Storage of Feedstuffs

Several factors affect carotene levels in hay. Carotene is easily oxidized, and 80% of it can be destroyed in as little as 24 hours in the hot sun after cutting . The amount of carotene can also be reduced by 50% when stored for six months or more. Before purchasing hay, the cautious buyer should inquire about the history of the crop. Hay that is not properly cut and cured at the appropriate stage of maturity can be very low in carotene. When inspecting hay for quality, it should be bright green and have a high leaf to stem ratio. It should feel firm, but not stiff, to the touch and there should be a low percentage of bloom. The dust level should be low. Moldy hay or hay containing foreign objects is not acceptable.

Vitamin A added to feeds and supplements is easily destroyed by air, light, and heat. Proper storage of all feeds is essential to maintain adequate vitamin A levels. Feeds should be fresh and not stored for long periods, especially during hot or humid weather.

Fig. 3–7. Half the carotene content of hay can be lost after six months storage.

Vitamin A Deficiency

A deficiency of vitamin A can cause many problems in the horse:

- night blindness
- prolonged shedding
- progressive weakness
- photophobia (sensitivity to light)
- excessive lacrimation (tearing)
- impaired intestinal absorption
- impaired deposition of minerals into bone
- susceptibility to infection of the reproductive tract
- susceptibility to pneumonia and other respiratory infections
- rough, dry hair coat
- anorexia
- diarrhea
- decreased growth
- salivary gland abcesses

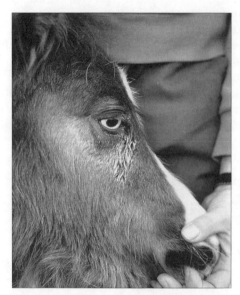

Fig. 3–8. An effect of inadequate vitamin A is excessive lacrimation (tearing).

Fortunately, most horses never experience a vitamin A deficiency, due to carotene in the forage portion of the diet and the horse's ability to store vitamin A in the liver and fat tissues.

Blood analysis is currently the only means of measuring vitamin A levels in the living horse's body. This is not, however, a true indication of the horse's vitamin A level, because the liver utilizes its stores to keep the blood concentration of vitamin A at a normal level. Therefore, the blood concentration of vitamin A appears normal, while the liver could be nearly devoid of its vitamin A stores.

If the blood level does indicate a low vitamin A concentration, veterinary treatment may include a sizable injection of vitamin A to bring the liver stores back to a reasonable level.

Vitamin A Toxicity

Excesses of vitamin A have been known to cause bone fragility, abnormal growth of bone tissue, and sloughing off of the epithelial tissue that lines the inner and outer body surfaces.

Experimentally induced vitamin A toxicity has been shown to cause unthriftiness, poor muscle tone, rough hair coat and depression. Prolonged toxicity (20 weeks) has caused loss of hair and periods of incoordination and depression. Both plasma and liver vitamin A concentrations became excessively high, and red blood cell concentrations began to decrease sharply.

The maximum recommended level of vitamin A is 16,000 IU per kilogram of dry matter in the diet (1 kilogram=2.2 pounds). Alfalfa pasture may have vitamin A concentrations very close to maximum recommended intake, but toxicity has never been known to occur from ingesting alfalfa. All known cases of toxicity from vitamin A seems to have been caused by excess supplementation.

Vitamin D

Functions

The primary functions of Vitamin D is thought to be promotion of proper absorption, transportation, and metabolism of calcium and phosphorus. This makes it critical for proper growth. It is soluble in fat, so a certain amount can be stored in the liver and fat tissues of the body. The liver and kidneys are active in the metabolism of vitamin D.

Sources

There are two main forms of vitamin D:

- D₂ (ergocalciferol), which is the form found in plant products
- D₃ (cholecalciferol), which is found in fish oils, irradiated milk, and in the skin after sun exposure

The two major sources of vitamin D for the horse are sunlight and sun-cured hay. Vitamin D found in sun-cured hay results from ultraviolet irradiation of *ergosterol*, which is synthesized in plants.

Fig. 3–9. Sunlight and sun-cured hay are the two main sources of Vitamin D for the horse.

Vitamin D is found in plants only after they have been cut and exposed to sunlight. *(Irradiation does not affect living plant tissue because the presence of chlorophyll is believed to screen out the necessary light.)*

Vitamin D derived directly from sunlight occurs because ultraviolet rays act on 7-dehydrocholesterol (a fat-related substance found in the animal's skin) and converts it into vitamin D.

Requirements

No scientific determination of exact requirements for vitamin D has been established for the horse. If a horse receives sun-cured hay as part of its ration, or is outside a few hours a day, a vitamin D deficiency is not likely. (An exact requirement of daily sunlight exposure has not been determined for the horse.)

The amount of dietary vitamin D is more critical to the stabled horse that has limited or no time outdoors. Horses that receive **no** sunlight and whose diets are suspected to be deficient in vitamin D should be supplemented with 300 IU/kg of dry matter for mature idle and working horses, 600 IU/kg dry matter for pregnant and lactating mares, and 800 IU/kg dry matter for growing horses.

Vitamin D Deficiency

Because deficiencies in a typical diet are not likely, vitamin D deficiencies have only been produced under experimental conditions. Horses that were experimentally deprived of vitamin D showed a reduced rate of growth, bone weakness, failure of bones to calcify normally, increased levels of bone demineralization, lameness, and loss of appetite. Studies also indicate that horses deprived of vitamin D excrete large amounts of calcium in the feces.

Vitamin D Toxicity

Excess vitamin D will cause improper calcium transport, allowing calcium to be deposited in the soft tissues. The result will be a loss of proper joint function, calcification (hardening) of soft tissues, and an enlargement of the skull and jaw. Supplementation of vitamin D should be done with caution and in compliance with the manufacturer's, veterinarian's, or equine nutritionist's instructions.

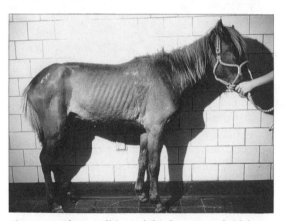

Fig. 3–10. The condition of this horse resulted from excess vitamin D. The tongue is partially calcified, which resulted in malnourishment and weight loss.

It should also be noted that ingestion of the *Wild Jasmine* plant (a member of the nightshade family and a noxious weed, also known as *Day-blooming Jessamine* and *Day Cestrum*) will result in symptoms similar to those of vitamin D toxicity. It is found in the southeast United States.

A maximum safe level of 1,000 IU vitamin D per pound of diet dry matter for long term feeding (over two months) has been suggested, based on information from studies of other species.

Vitamin E

Vitamin E, *tocopherol,* is required for normal cell structure. It can be found in green growing forages, good quality hay, cereal grains, and wheat germ oil. Immature forages that contain more leaves and less bulky, fibrous stem will contain higher levels of vitamin E. Accordingly, legumes such as alfalfa or clover will generally contain more vitamin E than a grass hay such as Bermuda or ryegrass. However, the vitamin E content will vary depending on methods of storage and processing. *(The effects of feed processing and storage on vitamin E are discussed in more detail in the Requirements section.)*

Functions

Through normal metabolism, cells form *oxides* (oxygen related compounds), which are waste products. These oxides are extremely toxic to cells. As an antioxidant, vitamin E serves to prevent the formation of toxic oxide compounds. This preventative action protects the cell membrane and its contents from severe damage and possible death. The role of vitamin E as an antioxidant is vitally important to every cell within the horse's body.

Vitamin E is essential for growth, proper muscle development and function, oxygen transport, and red blood cell stability. It is believed to have an important role in the equine immune system, as well. Its exact function within the immune system, however, is not yet understood.

Some horsemen believe supplemental vitamin E can enhance fertility by increasing conception rates and stallion semen quality. Although this theory is not backed by conclusive scientific evidence, a deficiency of vitamin E has been shown to impair fertility in other animals.

Vitamin E's Role in the Exercising Horse

Large amounts of oxides are produced in skeletal and cardiac muscle during periods of intense activity. Vitamin E prevents the formation of these toxic substances by combining with the oxygen before proteins or other vitamins can. Within the exercising muscle, vitamin E's role as an antioxidant is very important. An example of this is vitamin E's prevention of the formation of hydrogen peroxide.

If not eliminated, hydrogen peroxide is deadly to all cells, and red blood cells are especially sensitive to it. Vitamin E aids in the protection of these cells by combining with oxygen before the hydrogen can.

Vitamin E plays an important role as a *vasodilator,* a chemical compound that opens up the blood vessels so that blood can move more freely through tissues. This action will more readily enable nutrients and oxygen in the blood to enter working cells of the muscle.

Fig. 3–11. Racehorses have lower levels of serum vitamin E than broodmares and pleasure horses.

Researchers have found that racehorses exhibit lower levels of serum vitamin E when compared to broodmares and pleasure horses. Some researchers believe that greater quantities of vitamin E are used as an antioxidant, due to an increased accumulation of oxides associated with muscular activity. Therefore, supplementation of vitamin E may be advantageous for racehorses or any horses that encounter similar physical stresses.

Vitamin E Requirements

The minimum vitamin E requirement recommended by the National Research Council for maintenance is 22.7 to 36.4 IU per pound (or 50 to 80 IU per kilogram) of the total dry daily diet. In addition, it is recommended that working horses, pregnant or lactating mares, and foals be supplied a ration containing 80 to 100 IU of vitamin E per pound of total dry daily diet. It is recommended by some that high performance horses receive up to 2,000 IU of vitamin E per pound of total dry daily diet. However, to date, there is a lack of scientific evidence to support the need for levels this high.

Research has shown that a need for vitamin E supplementation is more likely than previously thought. Many factors contribute to this need. For example, vitamin E is easily destroyed by *peroxides* present in rancid feed. (Selenium, a mineral *[see Chapter 4]*, helps reduce the chances of this by removing peroxides from the bloodstream. However, selenium deficiencies are becoming more and more common, which eventually leads to vitamin E deficiencies.) Also, horses today spend more time in stables with less access than ever to green pastures, which are good sources of vitamin E. Another factor is the increased use of pelleted feeds. Intense heat used during the pelleting process lowers vitamin E content of a feed (unless it is replaced by the manufacturer).

If a horse is consuming a diet that is low in vitamin E, a supplement should be administered. Once supplementation is initiated, however, it should continue as long as the vitamin E-deficient diet is fed. If not, vitamin E concentrations that have been built up in the *serum*, liver, and muscle will rapidly decline.

Although vitamin E concentrations in blood plasma of healthy horses have been found to range from 1.67 to 9.5 milligrams per milliliter, the normal range is considered to be between 2 and 4 milligrams per milliliter. Any reading below 1 milligram per milliliter is considered a definite indication of deficiency.

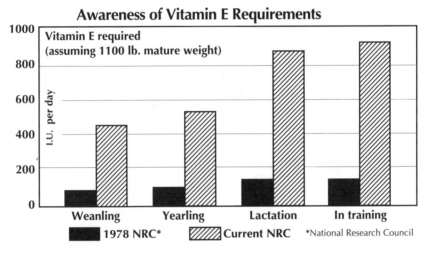

Awareness of Vitamin E Requirements

Fig. 3–12. This graph illustrates how further research has increased the awareness of vitamin E requirements.

Feed Processing

Normally, processing feeds will decrease vitamin E content. When kernels of grain are cracked or ground, the *unsaturated lipids* are exposed to air, promoting vitamin E breakdown and loss. If feeds are ground or rolled, it is recommended that processing be done just before feeding. A decrease in vitamin E content is not usually a problem in commercially pelleted feeds, because stabilized vitamin E is added to compensate for loss during processing.

When storing feeds, moisture should also be avoided. Moisture will promote fermentation and mold formation, which will not only decrease vitamin E content in the feed, but will also increase the possibilities of gastric disturbances.

Added Fat

When lipids (fats), such as tallow or corn oil, are added to the horse's diet in high quantities, more antioxidant activity will be required. For this reason, vitamin E supplementation may be beneficial to horses consuming over 10% fat in the total diet, unless synthetic antioxidants such as ethoxyquin are added to the feed in manufacturing.

Vitamin E Deficiency

Characteristics of a deficiency include swelling of the joints, fragmentation of the muscle fiber, and *ataxia* (loss of muscular coordination).

Deficiencies may also cause muscle degeneration, or *white muscle disease*. If it occurs, a *necropsy* will show that the muscle exhibits pale and diffuse linear patterns and the heart muscle is especially affected.

Vitamin E deficiency has also been linked to a form of *wobbler's syndrome*, a disease that affects the spinal cord and column, causing incoordination. However, the exact mechanisms are not yet known.

A deficiency of vitamin E is difficult to distinguish from that of selenium, due primarily to the close relationship they have with each other.

Vitamin E and Selenium

The relationship between vitamin E and selenium is very important. Vitamin E is destroyed by peroxides present in rancid feed. Selenium (discussed in Chapter 4) is involved in the formation of the enzyme *glutathione peroxidase*, which aids in removal of peroxides from the bloodstream, thus sparing vitamin E. To an extent, it is believed that vitamin E can be substituted for selenium in areas where the soil is low in selenium. Selenium cannot fully replace vitamin E, but it can reduce the amount required and prevent symptoms of vitamin E deficiency.

Vitamin E Toxicity

No documented signs of vitamin E toxicity have been produced in the equine. Based on studies of other species, vitamin E toxicity would theoretically interfere with other fat soluble vitamins.

Vitamin K

Functions

Vitamin K is fat-soluble, and has two primary functions: 1) promotion of normal blood coagulation, and 2) prevention of hemorrhage. Vitamin K is vital in the production of *prothrombin* (a substance that initiates blood clotting) in the liver. It is also required for growth.

The time required for the blood to clot is a reliable indicator of the horse's vitamin K level. Blood clotting time should always be determined before any type of surgery is performed.

The horse obtains vitamin K from three main sources:

1) *Phylloquinone* found in green, leafy plants.
2) Microflora (bacteria and protozoa), producer of vitamin K during hindgut fermentation.
3) Supplemental vitamin K_3 (usually provided in the form of *menaquinone* or *menadione)* converted into a nutritionally usable form by the liver.

Requirements

Dietary vitamin K requirements have not yet been determined for the horse. Considerable amounts of phylloquinone are found in pasture forage and high quality hay, and significant levels of vitamin K are synthesized by intestinal bacteria. It is presumed that the vitamin K requirements are met in all but the most unusual circumstances by dietary intake and microfloral synthesis.

If a horse has been ingesting antibiotics or has been ill, vitamin K supplementation may be necessary, due to destruction of intestinal microflora that might result from either of these situations.

Dicoumarol, a *mycotoxin,* is found in moldy sweet clover pastures and hay. Dicoumarol destroys vitamin K in the body, reducing the horse's blood clotting ability. To avoid effects of this mycotoxin, feedstuffs should be checked for mold, and if detected, the feedstuffs should be discarded.

If vitamin K content in a forage is questionable, supplementation may be necessary. Adequate vitamin K is especially vital at foaling, when hemorrhaging can occur if a mare's blood does not clot properly.

Deficiency

A deficiency of vitamin K is possible, but is not frequently seen. Equines that are lacking adequate vitamin K will show lower prothrombin levels and increased clotting time, and they will hemorrhage more easily than horses with normal levels of the vitamin.

Toxicity

Toxicity in relation to dietary vitamin K is very unlikely in horses. Though few experiments have been conducted, research shows that single intra-muscular and intravenous injections of vitamin K (menadione bisulfite) given to horses in amounts of 0.95 to 3.77 milligrams per pound resulted in acute renal failure.

WATER-SOLUBLE VITAMINS
B-Complex Vitamins

B-complex vitamins generally function as coenzymes, which are responsible for metabolism (chemical changes which provide energy for bodily activities) of carbohydrates, fats, and proteins.

Thiamine (B₁)

Functions

Thiamine (often referred to as thiamin) is required for carbohydrate metabolism and is useful in assisting with the proper function of the nervous system. It also serves as a vital component of the enzyme *erythrocyte transketolase* and is necessary for energy utilization.

Single doses of thiamine (1,000 – 2,000 mg) have been reported to have a calming effect on nervous horses, but it may also have a stimulating effect.

Requirements

Exact requirements for thiamine are not known, although NRC data suggests that 3 mg/kg dry matter daily should be sufficient for maintenance, growth, and reproduction. Many trainers advocate thiamine supplementation for race and other horses that are participating in strenuous activity on a regular basis. Normal recommendation for active horses such as these is five mg/kg dry matter daily.

Thiamine is available in good pasture forage and high quality, green, leafy hay. A considerable amount is also synthesized by microflora in the intestine. Cereal grains are a good source of thiamine as well, provided they have not been heated or cooked. Thiamine can be destroyed by high temperatures.

Horses that have poor appetites or receive poor quality rations will benefit from thiamine supplementation. Furthermore, consumption of certain plants such as *bracken fern, horsetail* and *yellow star thistle* will increase the

Fig. 3–13. Bracken fern contains thiaminases and antithiamin compounds which will induce thiamine deficiency.

need for thiamine supplementation. These plants contain *thiaminases* and *antithiamin*, which destroy thiamine, and can cause death.

Horses may have difficulty maintaining weight and condition as they begin to reach advanced age. This problem may be partially alleviated by feeding brewer's yeast, which contains a considerable amount of thiamine. Brewer's yeast increases a horse's appetite and ensures that tools necessary for energy utilization are present.

Brewer's yeast is widely used by racehorse trainers. Its success may be due to the presence of thiamine (and other

Fig. 3–14. Brewer's yeast is a popular supplement with racehorse trainers.

B-complex vitamins) necessary for energy metabolism. Thiamine may also be provided by adding thiamine hydrochloride or thiamine mononitrate to feed. The mononitrate form is usually preferred, due to low solubility in water. These substances are more expensive than brewer's yeast.

Certain parasites, such as *coccidia* and *strongylids*, will consume dietary thiamine in the intestinal tract, making it less available.

Deficiency

Deficiencies of thiamine are not common. Experimentally produced thiamine deficiencies have been shown to cause:

- localized muscular contractions visible under the skin
- *bradycardia* (abnormal slowing of heart rate)
- *ataxia* (muscular incoordination)
- periodic *hypothermia* of the extremities
- missing heartbeats
- appetite loss
- weight loss

Toxicity

Thiamine toxicity is very unlikely, due to the short time required for its removal from the body.

Riboflavin (B₂)

Functions and Requirements

Riboflavin, like thiamine, is essential for energy metabolism and nervous system function.

Riboflavin is contained in leafy, green hay (particularly legume hays) and good pasture forage, and it is synthesized by microflora in the equine intestine. Due to the intestinal microflora's ability to synthesize riboflavin in the horse's body, the dietary requirement is very small, no more than 2 milligrams per kilogram of dietary dry matter daily.

Deficiency of Riboflavin

Deficiency of riboflavin has not been described in the equine, but deficiency symptoms in other species include:

- rough hair coat
- *atrophy* (wasting away) of the outer layer of skin and hair follicles
- *dermatitis* (skin inflammation)
- *conjunctivitis* (inflammation of the transparent covering of the eyeball) with a discharge
- *photophobia* (abnormal sensitivity to light)
- excessive *lacrimation* (tearing)

Riboflavin deficiency is believed to cause *periodic opthalmia*, characterized by occasional periods of blindness. However, there is no scientific evidence to support this.

Riboflavin Toxicity

Riboflavin toxicity is very unlikely. Studies have shown that horses can consume dietary levels ten to twenty times the proposed requirement without creating problems.

Riboflavin excreted in the urine is close to the amount taken in by the horse, therefore little or no riboflavin is stored in the body.

Niacin

Functions

Niacin is a term used for two compounds with equal nutritional value: nicotinic acid and nicotinamide. Niacin is essential in cellular respiration and metabolism, and it is believed to be synthesized by bacteria located in the hindgut. However, an essential amino acid *tryptophan* is necessary for this synthesis to occur.

The amount of niacin synthesized will depend on the amount of tryptophan ingested, which in turn is dependent on the level of protein in the diet. Accordingly, a diet low in protein may result in low niacin concentrations. Pyridoxine (vitamin B6) is also required for *synthesis* of niacin to occur and should be provided in adequate amounts.

Requirements/Deficiency

No specific requirements of niacin have been determined. It is assumed that the horse's intestinal microflora can synthesize adequate amounts of niacin from a normal diet.

A niacin deficiency has not been described in the horse.

Toxicity

Toxicity of niacin is not described in the equine, but it has been observed in other species. In humans, a high intake of niacin has produced vasodilation (dilation of blood vessels), itching, sensations of heat, nausea, vomiting, headaches, and occasional skin lesions.

Pantothenic Acid (B₃)

Functions and Requirements

Pantothenic acid is a constituent of several important coenzymes, and it plays a part in protein, carbohydrate, and fat utilization. Pantothenic acid exists in two forms, D-pantothenic acid (which has nutritional value), and L-pantothenic acid (which lacks nutritional value).

In most cases, microfloral synthesis of pantothenic acid will meet the horse's requirements. A deficiency is unlikely if the horse consumes high quality hay or pasture forage.

Deficiency

Deficiencies of pantothenic acid are extremely rare, as it is synthesized in the horse's intestinal tract.

Supplementation

Microfloral synthesis of pantothenic acid is usually considered adequate. However, if supplementation of pantothenic acid is deemed necessary, it is available in calcium salt *(calcium pantothenate)*. This substance can be easily added to most feedstuffs and is often included in commercially produced feeds.

Toxicity

No documentation for toxicity of pantothenic acid exists for the equine. In addition, experimental results with other species indicate that an intake of 4.55 grams (approximately 0.16 ounces) per pound of body weight poses no danger.

Pyridoxine (B₆)

Functions

Pyridoxine functions as a vital part of an enzyme system and is very much involved in the metabolism of proteins, carbohydrates, and fats. Adequate pyridoxine is vital for proper function of the immune and nervous systems as well. The essential amino acid tryptophan, also depends on pyridoxine for its utilization.

There are two other forms of vitamin B₆: pyridoxal and pyridoxamine. Under most conditions, these two forms are equal in nutritional value to pyridoxine.

Fig. 3–15. Heavily worked horses may benefit from B₆ supplementation.

Pyridoxine Requirements

Adequate quantities of pyridoxine can be found in a wide variety of high quality grains and forages. Considerable pyridoxine losses will result from improper heat processing and storage of feedstuffs. In addition to its availability in the diet, large quantities are synthesized by microflora in the cecum and colon. In most cases, supplementation is not necessary. Nonetheless, an adequate presence of two other B-complex vitamins, riboflavin and niacin, is required in the diet in order for pyridoxine to be used nutritionally.

Heavily worked horses or those that are consuming poor quality pasture forages or hay may benefit from pyridoxine supplementation. The demand for pyridoxine does not appear to increase significantly during pregnancy and lactation.

If supplementation is advised, a dose of 25 milligrams per day is normally suggested. Of course, any vitamin or mineral supplement should be administered in accordance with the manufacturer's instructions.

Pyridoxine Deficiency/Toxicity

Neither deficiencies nor toxicities of pyridoxine have been documented in the equine. It should be noted that small quantities of pyridoxine can be stored in the liver for short periods of time. However, most excesses of water soluble vitamins are excreted in the urine.

Choline

Functions and Requirements

Choline serves to transport fat from storage in the liver to other parts of the body and to metabolize it into a more usable energy source. Choline also provides vital assistance for building and maintaining the structure of all cells and transmitting nervous impulses. Dietary need for choline is directly related to the level of methionine, a sulfur-containing essential amino acid. All natural fats contain some choline.

Deficiency

Choline deficiencies have not been documented in the equine, but in other species it is characterized by an accumulation of fat in the liver, poor body condition, muscular incoordination, a decrease in reproduction, and death of the young at birth. Intestinal synthesis of choline will most likely meet the horse's requirements. If supplementation is necessary, a dose of 500 milligrams per day is usually recommended for a 1,000 pound horse. Choline supplement is commonly given in *choline chloride,* which comes in both liquid and solid forms.

Toxicity

Although there is no data to reflect toxicity in the equine, excess choline should be avoided, due to a narrow margin of safety that exists between requirements and toxic doses in other species.

Biotin

Functions and Requirements

Biotin (sometimes called vitamin H) plays an important role as a coenzyme in metabolism of carbohydrates, fats, and proteins.

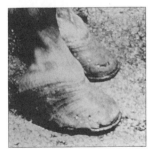

Fig. 3–16. Biotin supplementation may improve the condition of these hooves.

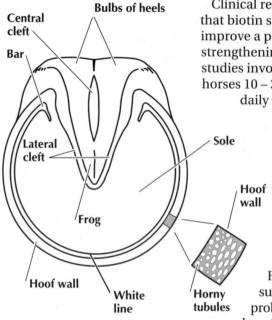

Fig. 3–17. Parts of the hoof.

Clinical reports have indicated that biotin supplementation will improve a poor quality hoof by strengthening the hoof wall. These studies involved feeding adult horses 10 – 30 milligrams of biotin daily for six to nine months. Other research has shown that when mature horses with good, healthy hooves were administered supplemental biotin, only 1% of it was absorbed. Most of this was excreted in the urine within 24 – 32 hours. Results indicate that supplemental biotin will probably not dramatically benefit a healthy horse being fed an adequate ration.

Although biotin levels can influence hoof growth, not all hoof problems are the result of a biotin deficiency. Horses must be provided with good quality, well balanced rations to ensure proper hoof growth and condition. Hoof growth and strength are highly inheritable as well.

The amount of moisture present in the hoof probably has a greater effect on hoof condition than nutrition. Too much moisture provides a favorable environment for *thrush,* or hoof rot to develop in the lateral and central clefts, and too little moisture will result in dry, cracked hooves.

Biotin Deficiency

Biotin deficiency is extremely rare and has never been documented in the horse, as considerable amounts of this vitamin are synthesized by intestinal microflora. However, if mold is present in the feed, it will tie up biotin and make it less accessible to the horse. It is very important that feedstuffs be stored in a moisture-free environment to prevent mold.

Biotin Toxicity

Biotin-related toxicity problems have never been documented in the equine. There should be no concern if the biotin level in the ration is slightly over suggested levels.

Folacin

Functions

Folacin (sometimes called vitamin M) is a group of related substances of which folic acid is the most nutritionally usable form. Folacin molecules contains the compound para-aminobenzoic acid (PABA). Some researchers think that PABA functions as a *precursor* (substance

Fig. 3–18. Green, leafy hay or pasture are good sources of folacin.

from which another substance is formed) of the folacin molecule, but it is not known if this is always true.

Folacin is necessary for cell metabolism and red blood cell formation, and it acts as a coenzyme for several enzymes involved in metabolism.

Requirements

Folacin appears to be synthesized by microorganisms in the cecum and large intestine of the adult horse. A good dietary source of folacin is green, leafy hay or pasture. If these are not available, supplementation of 20 milligrams of folic acid may be beneficial. It is also suggested that active stabled horses, particularly racehorses, require folic acid supplementation.

Deficiency/Toxicity

Folic acid deficiency has not been described in the equine, although a type of anemia that developed from a folic acid deficiency has been reported in other species .

No adverse reaction to the ingestion of excess folacin has been reported in any species.

B$_{12}$ (Cyanocobalamin, Cobalamin)

Functions

The primary function of vitamin B$_{12}$ is to assist in the production of red blood cells. It also plays a major role in utilization of carbohydrates, fats, and proteins from ingested feed. Furthermore, vitamin B$_{12}$ assists in the conversion of propionic acid, a primary volatile fatty acid produced by fermenting microflora in the gut.

Requirements

Vitamin B$_{12}$ is the only B vitamin not produced by plants. In most cases, adequate levels of vitamin B$_{12}$ are synthesized by microflora in the cecum and colon, and by cobalt, a mineral obtained from forages.

Exact requirements of vitamin B$_{12}$ have not been established. It is assumed that dietary requirement is met by microfloral synthesis.

No evidence of a B$_{12}$ requirement above that supplied by intestinal synthesis has been reported for horses in good health under normal circumstances . However, some supplementation of B$_{12}$ is advocated by many horsemen. Requirements have been estimated to be between 4 and 10 micrograms per pound of the total diet.

B$_{12}$ Supplementation

Horses that are in poor condition, anemic, or severely parasitized seem to respond positively to vitamin B$_{12}$ supplementation. Furthermore, it is believed by many horsemen that B$_{12}$ supplementation may be advantageous to the race or high performance horse, based on the belief that B$_{12}$ will build up the hemoglobin content of red blood cells. In turn, this would increase the oxygen transport capacity of the blood.

B$_{12}$ supplementation may be beneficial to horses heavily stressed by physical activity or other factors. It may also be helpful for those consuming poor quality forages that are low in cobalt.

Foals are provided with a great deal of B$_{12}$ through the mare's colostrum during the first 24 hours of life. Recommended supplementation for weanlings is a dose of 0.84 milligrams per day to keep pace with their rapid growth during this period.

Most excesses of water-soluble vitamins (like B$_{12}$) are only stored in the liver for a short time and then excreted in the urine. Consequently, when an injection of B$_{12}$ is administered, the majority will be lost in the urine. When supplementation is required, oral consumption of B$_{12}$ in the diet is likely to be more effective.

B₁₂ Deficiency/Toxicity

A vitamin B_{12} deficiency has not been reported in the horse, but other species have exhibited symptoms associated with deficiency. These animals experienced poor growth and reproductive performance, as well as anemia, hindquarter incoordination, unsteadiness of gait, poor appetite, weight loss, *hyperirritability*, and a rough hair coat. Neurologically-related problems have also been associated with vitamin B_{12} deficiency.

In experiments, horses on diets deficient in cobalt, and not supplemented with B_{12}, showed no decrease in serum B_{12} concentrations until after two years.

No toxic levels of B_{12} have been determined, but excessive levels should in any case be avoided.

Vitamin C (ascorbic acid)

Functions

Presence of vitamin C is essential for proper formation of *collagen* (a vital component of cartilage), *lysine* (essential amino acid), and *proline* (non-essential amino acid). Vitamin C is also believed to have interaction with iron and many B-complex vitamins. The impact and mechanisms of these relationships are not fully understood.

Fig. 3–19. Periods of high performance may create the need for vitamin C supplementation.

Requirements

Because vitamin C is synthesized by the liver and other body cells in adequate quantities, it is not considered a dietary essential for the horse. However, the body's ability to store vitamin C is limited. At present no specific requirements for the horse have been set for vitamin C.

Previous studies suggested that vitamin C supplementation decreased the incidence of *epistaxis* (bleeding from the nose), increased sperm quality, and improved breeding performance, but follow-up research has been unable to duplicate these findings. As a result, experimental evidence suggesting that vitamin C supplementation is beneficial is limited.

There may be a relationship between vitamin C synthesis, energy, vitamin E, and selenium. If this is so, it would indicate that any deficiency of energy, selenium and/or vitamin E could have a direct impact on vitamin C production and utilization.

Situations in which vitamin C supplementation may be beneficial:

- hot weather (due to loses of vitamin C through sweat)
- periods of stress (shipping, illness, injury, pregnancy, etc.)
- periods of growth
- periods of high performance

Deficiency/Toxicity

Vitamin C deficiency has not been reported in the horse, perhaps because the liver synthesizes adequate amounts.

Processing tends to decrease the amount of vitamin C present in the feed. This is especially true in pelleted feeds that are exposed to intense heat and moisture during manufacturing. However, most manufacturers take this into account and add vitamin C to the feed.

Toxicity of vitamin C has not been documented in the horse, but it has been reported in both humans and laboratory animals. Excess vitamin C is normally excreted in the urine.

4

MINERALS

Minerals are inorganic (non-living) compounds occurring naturally in the earth that are required in small amounts by the horse. They are essential to many body processes. They act as components of body tissues and as vital members of *catalytic enzymes,* which help trigger reactions within the body. Various minerals are also contained in hormones, vitamins, and amino acids.

MINERAL CONTENT FACTORS

The horse's mineral intake is affected by the mineral content of the water, plants, and soil in its area. However, grains and hays are not always grown in the same area where they are used as feedstuffs. Consequently, the mineral content of the soil where the feedstuffs were grown will affect the mineral content of the horse's ration.

Legume forages, such as alfalfa or clover, are generally higher in mineral content than grass forages. Hays and grains that are overly mature, weathered, or improperly harvested or cured will tend to be lower in mineral content. Poorly fertilized or badly maintained pasture may be deficient in some minerals or have toxic levels of others.

Fig. 4–1. Horses of varying ages, activity, or stress levels require different amounts of minerals.

REQUIREMENTS

Specific mineral requirements for the equine have not been determined. However, scientific research has provided recommended levels as a general guide for the horse owner. At present, there are at least 21 known minerals required in the diet. Horses of varying ages, stages of growth, activity, or stress levels require different amounts of minerals. Some minerals work in combination with others or with vitamins, while others have a completely independent action.

Mineral needs of specific horses in particular areas can be unique. Decisions concerning requirements and supplementation should be determined only after fully evaluating all relevant criteria. Therefore it is not possible in this book in most instances to offer exact recommendations. This chapter is offered to assist in understanding the necessary background information required to have good general knowledge. In medium to larger horse operations, laboratory analysis of some feedstuffs is sometimes beneficial. Consultations with veterinarians, equine nutritionists and County Agricultural Agents can also be helpful in establishing final plans.

A high quality, well balanced concentrate, from a reputable manufacturer, will usually supply the horse's daily mineral requirements. Some minerals however, such as sodium, are required in larger amounts, and under certain conditions, they must be supplemented.

If the concentrate portion of the ration consists only of one type of grain, such as oats, or if the horse is provided only hay or pasture, mineral supplementation will most likely be necessary. Because it is difficult to formulate one's own mineral supplement mixture, commercial mineral mixtures are available to round out the diet.

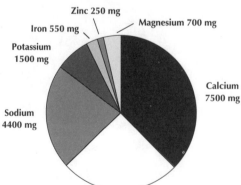

Fig. 4–2. Mineral components typical of a general vitamin/mineral supplement.

Zinc 250 mg
Iron 550 mg
Magnesium 700 mg
Potassium 1500 mg
Sodium 4400 mg
Calcium 7500 mg
Phosphorus 5200 mg

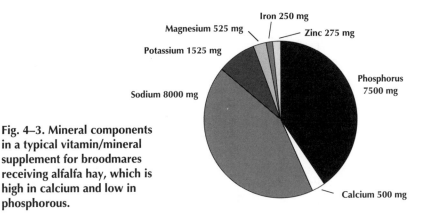

Iron 250 mg

Magnesium 525 mg

Zinc 275 mg

Potassium 1525 mg

Phosphorus 7500 mg

Sodium 8000 mg

Fig. 4–3. Mineral components in a typical vitamin/mineral supplement for broodmares receiving alfalfa hay, which is high in calcium and low in phosphorous.

Calcium 500 mg

There are many brands and types of mineral supplements, usually in the form of a trace mineralized salt and formulated according to specific needs. *(See Methods of Feeding Salt, later in this chapter for typical components of a mineral supplement.)* Minerals which are deficient in the diet vary greatly in different parts of the country, so no general mixture that will suit all circumstances can be recommended. The consumer should read the label carefully to determine if the mixture provides the needed amounts without excess. Because so little of each mineral is needed, amounts are expressed in grams, milligrams, and parts per million per kilogram of diet (ppm/kg).

Ensuring Proper Mineral Balance

To provide a well-balanced diet, both the forage and the concentrate portions of the ration must be of high quality and fed in proper amounts. A chemical analysis on the ration can be performed to determine if mineral supplementation is necessary. Soil tests, though not as accurate an indicator of nutrient content as chemical analysis, are useful in helping to produce proper hay, pasture, and crops. If the **ration** is deficient, it can be supplemented. If the **soil** is deficient, the pasture or crop field must be fertilized.

It is important that minerals be provided in correct **proportion**. A mixture should not include excessive amounts of one mineral to obtain sufficient amounts of another. Disease and weakness can be caused by both excesses and deficiencies of certain minerals. In most cases, requirements will be met by feeding a balanced ration. Some minerals will require supplementation, however. Refer to the discussions of each mineral for that infomation. The chart on the next page details the estimated daily mineral requirements for different classes of horses.

Daily Mineral Requirements

	Maintenance Requirements	Pregnant & Lactating Mares	Weanlings	Yearlings	2-Year Olds	Working Horses	Stallions (in breeding season)
Calcium	20g	35-37g Pregnant 36-56g Lactating	29-36g	27-36g	Not training 24g In training-34g	25-40g	25g
Phosphorus	14g	26-28g Pregnant 22-36g Lactating	16-20g	15-20g	Not in training 13g In training-19g	18-29g	18g
Potassium	25g	29-31.5g Pregnant 33-46g Lactating	11.3-13.3g	17.8-18.2g	Not in training 23.1g In training-32.2g	31.2-49.8g	31.2g
Sodium Choride (salt)	0.1% of total diet	0.1% of total diet	0.1% of total diet	0.1% of total diet	0.1% of total diet	0.3% of total diet	n/a
Magnesium	7.5g	8.7-9.4g Pregnant 8.6-10.9g Lactating	3.7-4.3g	5.5-8.6g	Not in training 7.0g In training-9.8g	9.4-15.1g	9.4g
Sulfur	0.15% of total diet	0.15% of total diet	0.15% of total diet	0.15% of total diet	0.15% of total diet	0.15% of total diet	n/a
Cobalt	0.1 mg/kg	0.1 mg/kg	0.1 mg/kg	0.1 mg/kg	0.1 mg/kg	0.1 mg/kg	n/a
Copper	10 mg/kg	10 mg/kg	10 mg/kg	10 mg/kg	10 mg/kg	10 mg/kg	n/a
Flourine	0.1 mg/kg	0.1 mg/kg	0.1 mg/kg	0.1 mg/kg	0.1 mg/kg	0.1 mg/kg	n/a
Iodine	0.1-0.6 mg/kg	0.1-0.6 mg/kg	0.1-0.6 mg/kg	0.1-0.6 mg/kg	0.1-0.6 mg/kg	n/a	n/a
Iron	40 mg/kg	50 mg/kg	50 mg/kg	50 mg/kg	50 mg/kg	40 mg/kg	n/a
Manganese*	40 mg/kg	40 mg/kg	40 mg/kg	40 mg/kg	40 mg/kg	40 mg/kg	n/a
Selenium	0.1 mg/kg	0.1 mg/kg	0.1 mg/kg	0.1 mg/kg	0.1 mg/kg	0.1 mg/kg	n/a
Zinc	40 mg/kg	40 mg/kg	40 mg/kg	40 mg/kg	40 mg/kg	40 mg/kg	n/a

*estimates based on research on other species   n/a = not available   g = gram   mg/kg = milligrams per kilogram total diet

Fig. 4-4.

MINERALS FUNCTION CHART

(The following chart offers an overview for readers not needing the extensive detail on mineral functions presented throughout this chapter):

Mineral	Functions
Calcium	• required for proper muscle and heart contractions and for normal blood clotting • necessary for normal nerve function, activation of several enzymes, release of certain hormones • makes up approximately 35% of the bone structure
Phosphorus	• makes up 14% – 17% of the skeleton • required for energy utilization • required for metabolism of phospholipids, nucleic acids, and phosphoproteins
Potassium	• influences muscle activity, especially the cardiac muscle
Sodium Chloride (Salt)	• acts as a buffer that helps maintain the acid-base balance of body fluids, osmotic pressure, and proper pH for efficient enzyme action • removes waste products from the cell • essential component of bile, which is necessary for fat and carbohydrate digestion
Magnesium	• essential constituent of bones and teeth • activates numerous enzyme-related activities
Sulfur	• important component of many compounds required by the body
Cobalt	• necessary component of vitamin B_{12}
Copper	• essential in the formation of hemoglobin, cartilage, bone, elastin, and pigmentation of the hair • plays major role in the utilization of iron
Fluorine	• essential for proper tooth and bone formation • helps to prevent tooth decay
Iodine	• essential for reproduction and the important thyroid hormone thyroxine
Iron	• component of hemoglobin, which carries oxygen to cells

Macro Minerals (Calcium through Sulfur)

Micro Minerals (Cobalt through Iron)

Manganese	• essential for utilization of carbohydrates and fats • essential for synthesis of chondroitin sulfate, a vital component of cartilage • necessary for proper bone development • plays important role in formation of many enzymes involved in growth, reproduction, and lactation
Selenium	• essential component of the antioxidant enzyme *gluta-thione peroxidase*, which aids in the detoxification of toxic *peroxides* • conserves vitamin E • constituent of cystine and methionine, amino acids that function as antioxidants and aid the immune system
Zinc	• essential component of many enzymes and hormones • plays an important role in the metabolism of proteins, fats, and carbohydrates • necessary for the immune system to function properly • needed to maintain healthy skin and hair

Fig. 4–5.

TYPES OF MINERALS
Macrominerals

Macrominerals include calcium, phosphorus, sodium, chloride, potassium, magnesium, and sulfur. Macrominerals are required by the horse in larger quantities than microminerals, and are commonly added to the equine ration.

Calcium

Calcium is one of the major minerals required by the horse. It has an important interrelationship with phosphorus, in which the amount of calcium must always be in correct proportion to the amount of phosphorus. Otherwise, bone deformities can occur. Calcium is also essential for bone mineralization.

Fig. 4–6. Regularly worked horses will require additional dietary calcium.

Functions

Calcium makes up approximately 35% of the mineral content of the bones and is involved in many body functions. It is primarily absorbed in the small intestine.

An estimated 98% of the calcium in the body is located in the bones and teeth. The other 2% is involved in other, critical functions. Calcium is required for proper muscle and heart contractions and for normal blood clotting to occur. The presence of calcium is also necessary for normal nerve function, the activation of several enzymes, and the release of certain hormones.

Calcium Requirements

The *absorption efficiency* of calcium is believed to decline as the horse ages, ranging from as high as 70% in young horses to 50% in mature horses. Normally, an 1,100 pound (500 kilogram) adult horse will require an average of 20 grams daily for maintenance.

Physical Exercise

Horses being worked regularly will require additional dietary calcium. However, the increased feed intake required by higher performance levels will usually meet the elevated calcium requirements.

Pregnant and Lactating Mares

Pregnant mares require a total of 20 grams of calcium per day during the first eight months of pregnancy. As a result of accelerated growth by the fetus, requirements will increase sharply to 35 – 37 grams during the last three months of pregnancy. (Figures are for maintenance and fetal deposition requirements for an 1,100 pound mare.)

Fig. 4–7. Growth of the fetus increases the pregnant mare's calcium needs.

Extra calcium is deposited daily into the fetus and *placenta*. If calcium provided in the diet does not meet the mare's requirements, her system will withdraw minerals from reserves in the bone to maintain fetus and milk production.

Lactating mares also have increased calcium requirements. Their bodies adjust milk secretion in accordance with the amount of calcium and phosphorus available, so it is important that lactating mares receive 36 – 56 grams of calcium in the diet daily.

Foals

If a lactating mare is deficient in calcium, the amount of milk produced will decrease, but the concentration of calcium in the milk will remain constant. The mare's body decreases her milk production in order to conserve remaining calcium stores. Consequently, although calcium and phosphorus levels of the milk may be adequate, there will not be sufficient amounts of milk to meet the foal's nutrient needs. It has been estimated that growing foals will require approximately 36 grams of calcium per day. An insufficient milk supply may result in a decreased growth rate and possibly a calcium deficiency.

Calcium Deficiencies Related To Other Minerals

There is evidence that a lack of calcium and phosphorus, along with deficiencies of copper and zinc, leads to a variety of *metabolic bone*

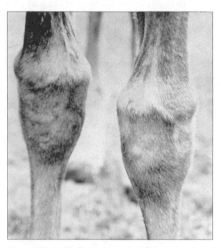

diseases (interrelated growth disorders of the bone). Some of these are *epiphysitis* (inflammation of the growth plate in bones of the limbs), *osteochondritis dissecans* (OCD-failure of cartilage to turn into bone), contracted tendons, and rickets. Rickets is characterized by poor mineralization of the bone, enlarged joints, and crooked long bones (cannon bones). In the mature horse, the condition is termed *osteomalacia*. Growing horses are particularly sensitive to mineral deficiencies and imbalances. For more information on the relationship between calcium and phos-

Fig. 4–8. A deficiency of calcium and phosphorus may lead to epiphysitis. Note enlarged upper portion of each knee.

phorus, see the *Calcium/Phosphorus Ratio* section in this chapter.

The body maintains *serum* calcium levels within a very narrow range. If the level of calcium in the blood starts to decrease, calcium is immediately removed from the bone to restore the normal calcium level of the blood. Therefore, the level of calcium in blood may not be an accurate indication of calcium levels in the body.

Calcium absorption is closely related to the intake of phosphorus, *oxalate* (a salt of *oxalic acid)*, and *phytate* (an organic form of phosphorus found in plants).

A study has shown that a ration containing as little as 1% oxalic acid reduced calcium absorption by as much as 66%. Oxalic acid is a compound found in several species of plants (including alfalfa, paragrass, buffel grass, pangola grass, and setaria grass). If the horse consistently eats only these plants, a calcium deficiency may result.

In the stomach, calcium will readily bind to the oxalic acid, forming an insoluble compound, *calcium oxalate.* In this form, the two cannot be separated. They will pass through the intestinal tract and be excreted in the feces. A horse can die from oxalate poisoning, caused by a secondary calcium deficiency *(hypocalcemia).* However, if a horse is suffering from a calcium deficiency, the addition of a dietary calcium supplement can correct the problem.

Cereal grains, such as oats, are high in phytate. The phytate content increases as the plant matures. Phytate binds to calcium, reducing the horse's ability to absorb calcium.

Calcium Supplementation

Many commercial calcium supplements are available. When selecting a supplement, the relationship between calcium and phosphorus must be considered. Ingredients of the overall diet must be calculated. For example, legume forages and hays, such as red clover and alfalfa, are higher in calcium than grass forages. *(See section on calcium/phosphorus ratio in this chapter for more information.)*

When both calcium and phosphorus are to be added to the diet, dicalcium phosphate is an excellent supplement. Bone meal is also a good source of calcium and phosphorus, and it contains many other minerals that may also need to be supplemented. However, bone meal is not very palatable to the horse and must be gradually introduced into the ration or mixed with a palatable carrier, such as molasses.

Common Calcium Supplements	
Ingredient	Calcium (%)
Limestone	38.0
Oyster shell	38.0
Calcite, high grade	34.0
Bone meal	31.7
Dicalcium phosphate	22.0
Dolomitic limestone	22.0
Gypsum	22.0
Wood ashes	21.0

Fig. 4–9.

The appropriate amount of supplement will depend on the concentrations and combinations of the various elements present in it. This will vary among different manufacturers.

Calcium Toxicity

The horse's body eliminates most excesses of calcium in the urine, and small amounts through sweat.

Horses have been fed experimental diets containing more than five times the required calcium without detrimental effects, **provided the level of phosphorus is adequate.** However, extreme excesses of calcium can interfere with magnesium, manganese, and iron utilization, and possibly with the utilization of zinc. It has also been suggested that *osteochondrosis* (improper maturation of bone) may be associated with excess calcium intake.

Phosphorus

Functions

Phosphorus makes up 14% to 17% of the mineral content of bones and is mostly absorbed in the large intestine. 80% of phosphorus in the body is found in the bones and teeth, and it is required for the synthesis of *phospholipids* (compounds that contain phosphorus and fat), *nucleic acids* (a component of genes necessary for heredity), and *phosphoproteins* (compounds that contain phosphorus and protein).

Requirements

Phosphorus Absorption and its Relationship to Age

The absorption efficiency of all nutrients should be considered when determining requirements for each class of horse. The estimated absorption efficiency of phosphorus in the horse ranges from 30% to 55%. The estimation varies with the age of the horse, as well as with the source and the concentration of dietary phosphorus. Accordingly, nutrient requirements will also vary with age. The level of phosphorus absorbed is likely to be higher in lactating mares and young horses, especially foals consuming milk, than in mature horses. In the adult horse, phosphorus absorption efficiency is approximately 35%.

Recommended maintenance requirement for an adult horse is 28.6 milligrams of phosphorus per kilogram (2.2 pounds) of body weight. Therefore, an 1,100 pound (500 kilogram) mature horse would require approximately 14 grams of phosphorus daily for maintenance.

Pregnant and Lactating Mares

For mares in late pregnancy, the growth of the fetus and *placenta* increase the mare's need for phosphorus beyond maintenance requirements. During the first eight months of pregnancy, the mare will require about 14 grams of phosphorus per day (the standard amount for an adult horse under maintenance conditions). During the last three months of gestation, this will increase to approximately 26 – 28 grams of phosphorus per day. These requirements are for the mare's maintenance, with fetal and placental needs combined. The fetus and placenta require 7, 12, and 6.7 mg/kg per day from the total requirements of the mare in months nine, ten and eleven, respectively, in an average 1,100 pound (500 kilogram) mare.

Daily Phosphorus Requirements of 1,100-pound Mares			
PREGNANT MARES	**grams**	**LACTATING MARES**	**grams**
9 months 26		Foaling to 3 months 36	
10 months 26		3 months to weaning 22	
11 months 28			

Fig. 4–10. The pregnant mare's phosphorus requirement will increase in late gestation and decrease in late lactation.

The lactating mare's phosphorus requirements will depend on milk production. As the level of milk production increases, the amount of phosphorus needed will also increase. Normally, mares produce more milk during early lactation (first three months). For example, an average mare may produce 15 kilograms (33 pounds) of milk per day during early lactation, and about 10 kilograms (22 pounds) of milk per day during late lactation. (Milk is represented in kilograms and pounds rather than gallons and liters, because the nutrients in milk are measured in units of weight, rather than liquid units.) Consequently, this mare will require approximately 36 grams of phosphorus per day during early lactation and 22 grams of phosphorus per day during late lactation. These are the combined requirements for maintenance and milk production for an average 1,100 pound mare.

Phosphorus concentrations in mare's milk will range from 0.75 gram per kilogram of fluid milk in **early** lactation to 0.5 gram per kilogram of fluid milk in **late** lactation (last three months).

(In order to avoid repetition, problems associated with excesses and deficiencies of phosphorus are discussed in the section titled "Problems Associated with Calcium and Phosphorus and their Interactions.")

Calcium/Phosphorus Ratios

Concentrations of calcium and phosphorus and their ratio to each other have major effects on health of the equine. Most diets containing both a grain and forage source provide a good calcium-to-phosphorus ratio. In general, grains are a good source of phosphorus, and hays and forages, especially legumes, are a good source of calcium.

Calcium and phosphorus comprise about 50% of the mineral content of the skeleton, and from 30% to 50% of the minerals present in mare's milk. These two minerals are essential for the horse's health, and they must remain in a close ratio to each other. However, the ideal ratio will vary according to the age of the horse. **It is critical**

Calcium to Phosphorus Ratios			
Class	Minimum	Maximum	Optimum
Nursing foal	1:1	1.5:1	1.2:1
Weanling	1:1	3.0:1	1.5:1
Yearling	1:1	3.0:1	1.5:1
Long yearling	1:1	3.0:1	2.0:1
Mature horse	1:1	6.0:1	2.0:1

Fig. 4–11. Suggested calcium/phosphorous ratios.

that dietary calcium never be lower than dietary phosphorus. *(Refer to Tables in the Appendix for mineral content of forages and concentrate components.)*

Proper utilization of calcium and phosphorus in the body is related to three main prerequisites:

1) adequate calcium and phosphorus intake
2) proper ratio between calcium and phosphorus
3) sufficient vitamin D to assist in absorption and utilization of calcium and phosphorus

Some researchers believe that if an adequate amount of vitamin D is present, the ratio of the two elements is less critical. *(See more on vitamin D in Chapter 3, Vitamins.)*

It is difficult to determine deficiencies of either of these minerals by a blood sample, because the body regulates the amount of these minerals in the blood. If the horse is not receiving the needed levels of calcium and phosphorus in its diet, it will remove them from the bone to keep blood levels normal.

Pregnant Mares

The fetus and placenta of the pregnant mare contain approximately 1.2% calcium and 0.6% phosphorus. To maintain this balance, approximately 16 grams of calcium and 9.4 grams of phosphorus will be required daily for fetal development during the last 90 days of gestation. It is estimated that during this period, 90% of fetal bone development occurs, which accounts for elevated calcium and phosphorus requirements.

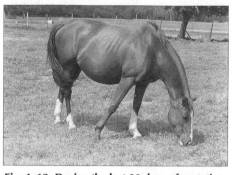

Fig. 4–12. During the last 90 days of gestation, pregnant mares need increased amounts of calcium and phosphorus.

For this reason, it is imperative that pregnant mares receive 35 – 37 grams of calcium and 26 – 28 grams of phosphorus daily in the total diet during the last three months of pregnancy. If the feedstuffs in the ration do not provide these amounts, a mineral supplement containing adequate amounts and a proper ratio of calcium and phosphorus should be added to the concentrate. There are also commercial concentrates formulated to provide required amounts.

Problems Associated with Calcium and Phosphorus and Their Interactions

Ailments such as osteomalacia and nutritional secondary *hyperparathyroidism* (also called miller's disease or "big head" disease) can result from feeding rations with low calcium or excess phosphorus. (Excess phosphorus in forages can be a direct result of using fertilizers that have a high phosphorus content.)

In studies, hyperparathyroidism developed in mature horses after being fed rations that had a calcium to phosphorus ratio of 0.8:1 (excess of phosphorus), for six to twelve months.

Whenever an inverted calcium to phosphorus ratio exists, excess phosphorus in the small intestine ties up calcium, so calcium cannot be absorbed. The parathyroid gland is activated to keep a constant level of calcium in the blood. The body withdraws calcium from bones to correct this imbalance. The calcium removed is replaced by a tough *connective tissue*, which causes a noticeable enlargement of the jaw bones, especially the upper one. It appears midway between the nostrils and the eyes, and is the origin of the common name, "big head disease."

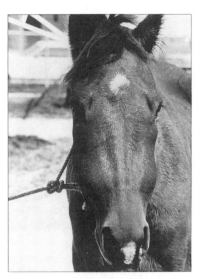

Fig. 4–13. "Big head," disease caused by an inverted calcium/phosphorus ratio.

Horses afflicted with hyperparathyroidism will also be lame, because their bones have weakened due to the removal of calcium.

When excesses of phosphorus are fed, the high concentration of serum phosphorus is perceived physiologically as a calcium deficiency. The body then responds by secreting *calcitonin* and *parathormone*. Calcitonin will prevent absorption of calcium by the bone.

Parathormone will initiate the removal of calcium from the bone. Both of these conditions can result in numerous metabolic bone diseases and related problems.

Phosphorus injections are often used in hopes of preventing metabolic bone diseases and related problems. However, routine injections of phosphorus can actually increase their chances of occurring.

A deficiency of either calcium or phosphorus can result in bone disorders. The extent of the resulting damage will depend on the age of the horse and the degree, as well as the duration, of the deficiency. In young horses, deficiency is characterized by poorly formed, soft bones, which may bend or bow. A deficiency of either calcium or phosphorus will also cause rickets in foals. In older horses, a deficiency can result in porous, fragile bones. It is extremely important to prevent deficiency, because total reversal of the effects is not possible.

Potassium

Functions

Potassium in the horse is found predominantly inside the cells. It is a major component in the acid-base balance and *osmotic pressure* of the cells. Osmotic pressure denotes the fluid pressures both in and outside the cells. Potassium is also found in extracellular fluid, and it influences muscle activity, especially the cardiac muscle.

Requirements

The daily potassium requirement for maintenance in the mature horse is estimated to be 50 milligrams per kilogram of body weight, or approximately 0.3% of the diet. Therefore, an 1,100 pound (500 kilogram) horse generally would require 25 grams of potassium daily for maintenance. However, requirements will vary with different stages of growth and activity.

Growing Horses

Foals six to twelve months old require 11.3 – 13.3 grams of potassium daily, yearlings require 17.8 – 18.2 grams daily, and two-year-olds not in training need approximately 23.1 grams potassium daily. A two-year-old in training will require 32.2 grams potassium daily.

The Pregnant Mare

During the first eight months of pregnancy, mares will **not** need potassium above maintenance levels. However, the pregnant mare will need additional potassium during the last three months of pregnancy, because the fetus and placenta will require increasing levels of potassium as birth approaches. Generally, an average 1,100 pound

(500 kilogram) mare requires 1.2, 1.7, and 2.2 milligrams per kilogram of body weight during months nine, ten, and eleven respectively.

Physical Activity

The required level of potassium is influenced by the activity level or work load of the horse. The estimated percentage of increase in the potassium requirement for working horses is:

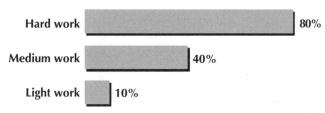

Fig. 4–14.

Potassium Deficiency

A horse can lose considerable amounts of potassium through sweat, stress, or illness, increasing the need for supplementation.

Diarrhea or kidney problems can cause a deficiency of potassium, and deficiencies will develop more rapidly in a young horse than in a mature one. A potassium deficiency can cause:

- reduced feed intake
- lethargy
- weight loss
- muscle weakness
- diarrhea
- ultimately, death

Blood serum potassium analysis is not an efficient indicator of potassium levels in the body. If a deficiency occurs, potassium is drawn from the cells to return the serum potassium level to normal. The potassium blood serum level might be normal, but the horse's system would be deficient. Permanent disorders of the heart or kidneys may result if potassium reserves become depleted and are not restored.

Potassium Supplementation

Forages are an excellent source of potassium, and a diet containing at least 50% forage should provide adequate potassium for maintenance. Molasses and oil meals (such as cottonseed and soybean meal) are also good sources of potassium. Potassium is readily absorbed from the feed and is excreted primarily in the urine. It is important to note that horses treated with *lasix* or other *diuretics* (substances which increase urination) will require additional potassium. Several commercial potassium supplements are available in the form of compounds. The following graph indicates the percentage of potassium in each compound:

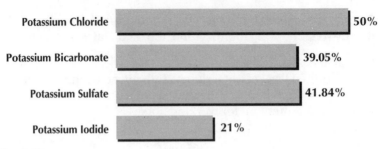

Fig. 4–15.

Potassium Toxicity

Potassium toxicity is rare in the horse, because excess potassium is readily excreted in the urine. However, if fed excess levels of potassium, some horses may develop *hyperkalemia,* an elevated level of potassium in the blood which can cause cardiac arrest. *Hyperkalemic periodic paresis,* a muscle weakness associated with hyperkalemia, has been reported in Quarter Horses. This condition can be treated by lowering the potassium intake of the horse and administering drugs that cause higher amounts of potassium to be excreted in the urine.

Sodium Chloride (Salt)

Functions

Sodium and chloride are two separate *electrolytes* provided to the horse bound together in the compound sodium chloride (NaCl), which is common salt. Sodium is primarily found outside cells, while chloride can be present inside and outside of the cell.

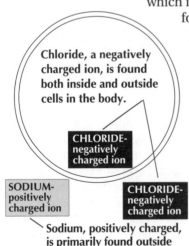

Chloride, a negatively charged ion, is found both inside and outside cells in the body.

CHLORIDE-negatively charged ion

SODIUM-positively charged ion

CHLORIDE-negatively charged ion

Sodium, positively charged, is primarily found outside the cells.

Fig. 4–16.

Electrolyte concentrations in extracellular body fluids are vital for maintaining proper flow of fluids and nutrients across cell membranes. If concentrations of either of these sodium and chloride electrolytes are drastically changed, serious consequences can result. Fluid may rush into cells, causing swelling or possible rupture, or fluid may rush out, causing them to shrink, or *crenate.*

Together, sodium and chloride act as *buffers* (chemicals that resist changes in pH) that help maintain the acid-base balance of body fluids, osmotic pressure, and proper pH for efficient enzyme action. Sodium and chloride also play a major role in bringing nutrients to the cell and removing waste products from the cell.

Sodium and chloride function as essential components of bile, which is necessary for fat and carbohydrate digestion. Muscle tissue also contains sodium, which functions primarily in aiding muscle contraction.

Chloride is also needed by the body for formation of *hydrochloric acid*, the major constituent of gastric juices.

Sodium Chloride Requirements

Sodium requirement for maintenance is about 0.1% of the total diet. When sodium requirements are met, it is assumed that chloride requirements are met as well. The salt content of most natural horse feeds is quite low, averaging 0.1%. However, most commercially processed feeds will have a slightly higher content.

It is a common practice to add 0.5 – 1.0% trace mineralized salt to the concentrate portion of the ration (10 – 20 lbs. of salt per ton of concentrate). This management practice helps to ensure adequate salt intake, especially for horses that do not consume adequate levels of salt when fed free-choice. The recommended amounts of salt required for growing and pregnant horses are the same as required for maintenance.

Physical Activity

If horses are involved in strenuous activity, or if the temperature and humidity are particularly high, the need for salt (and of course water) becomes very critical. For horses involved in moderate to heavy work, it is recommended that salt intake be increased to 0.3% of the total daily diet. This increased requirement is due to salt losses through sweat.

On an average, sweat contains 0.7% salt. Salt lost through sweating can range from 50 – 60 grams, depending on the level of intake and the amount of sweat. Additionally, a horse involved in moderate activity can lose an average of 35 grams of salt in its urine per day. The white foamy sweat seen on heavily worked horses indicates a high salt content in the

Fig. 4–17. For horses involved in moderate to heavy work, it is recommended that salt intake be 0.3% of the total daily diet.

sweat. However, this white, foamy sweat usually indicates a horse that is not physically fit. Once the horse is properly conditioned, its sweat becomes clearer and watery, because the body adapts and begins to conserve sodium.

Research studies have indicated that even an idle horse will lose *endogenous* salt (from sources within the body which are not a direct result of ingested salt) at rates of about 15 to 20 milligrams per kilogram of body weight per day.

Methods of Feeding Salt
Free-Choice

Horses are most commonly provided salt free-choice in a block or loose form. Because horses are "nibblers," not "lickers," it is usually considered preferable to provide salt to stabled horses in loose form. A small salt block may also be placed in a horses's stall, and large ones may be used in pastures. Method of choice will depend on the management situation and consumption levels of the horses.

If free-choice salt is being provided to a group of horses, management should ensure that each horse is consuming adequate salt. In the presence of an aggressive horse, a timid horse may not be able to eat enough salt to meet its needs. This is particularly a concern if the horses are being worked or if the weather is hot. Supplying salt sources at two or three different locations in the paddock or pasture should solve this problem.

In addition, salt should be protected from the weather whenever possible. This can be accomplished by placing it in covered feed troughs, a run-in shed, or an open barn. If these types of protection are not available, placing salt in a grove of trees will provide at least some protection.

Salt is usually available in three varieties: plain, iodized, and trace mineralized. Plain salt is sodium chloride (NaCl) with no other minerals added. Iodized salt, which contains iodine, should be provided in areas where iodine concentrations in the soil are low. *(See specific information on iodine later in this chapter.)*

Trace mineralized salt is highly recommended—it provides a simple means of furnishing salt and several trace minerals. Trace minerals required in significant quantities by the equine include copper, iron, cobalt, zinc, manganese, iodine, and selenium. This method is much easier and more economical than buying small quantities of each mineral and then trying to measure and combine them.

Most experimental results indicate a large variation in salt consumption among horses—even horses of the same breed, of similar size, and in the same environmental conditions. For this reason, feeding salt free-choice is recommended even if minimum required amounts are also provided in rations.

In The Feed

Salt may be added to the ration to cover minimum requirements in addition to, or in place of, free-choice salt. The levels to add vary according to the class of horse. *(See the requirements section.)*

Salt Deficiency

The equine body contains an average of 0.2% sodium, of which about 50% is stored in the bones. Even though much of the sodium is stored in the bones, only a small quantity of it is removed from bone tissue during periods of salt deficiency. A deficiency of chloride alone has not been reported in the horse.

A salt deficiency can be caused by dietary salt deprivation *(chronic deficiency)* or salt losses through sweat *(acute deficiency)*. The symptoms and circumstances of these two types of deficiencies are completely different.

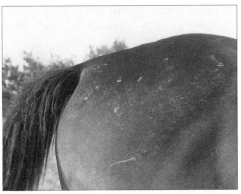

Fig. 4–18. Even non-working horses can lose significant amounts of salt through sweat. These salt deposits resulted from grazing on a hot day.

Chronic Salt Deficiency

A case of chronic salt deficiency occurs when a horse has been deprived of dietary salt over a long period. The salt-starved horse should be hand-fed salt in small quantities, while gradually increasing the amount over a period of time. When the horse begins to leave some of the salt behind, a free-choice salt feeding program may be initiated.

Typical symptoms of chronic salt deficiencies include:

- puffy appearance of the skin
- dramatic decrease in water consumption
- licking objects in surroundings (wood, metal, plastic)
- slowed rate of eating with eventual cessation
- rough hair coat
- decrease in milk production (mare's milk can contain concentrations from 161 to 364 parts per million [ppm] of sodium and from 300 to 640 ppm of chloride)
- decreased utilization of energy sources (fats and carbohydrates)
- decreased protein utilization
- decreased growth rate

Acute Salt Deficiency

A case of acute salt deficiency occurs when a horse is worked to the point of exhaustion and fatigue. Typical symptoms include:

- incoordinated muscular contractions
- irregular chewing
- walking with an unsteady gait
- a sharp decrease in serum concentrations of sodium and chloride
- a dramatic increase in serum potassium concentrations

Salt Toxicity

In a mild case of salt toxicity, allowing the horse free access to water is the recommended treatment. The only complication that could result is a loose bowel movement.

Severe salt toxicity occurs when a horse is unable to take in adequate quantities of water, making the excretion of sodium and chloride difficult. The horse will urinate frequently, appear weak and colicky, and even experience some paralysis of the hind limbs.

Water consumption will increase dramatically in response to excessive salt intake, and it will decrease when salt intake levels are lowered. Water is required to remove excess sodium and chloride from the body (in urine and sweat).

Horses seldom overeat salt, and in most cases it is safe to provide it free-choice without danger of toxicity. One exception to this rule is the "salt starved" horse that is suddenly allowed free access to salt.

Magnesium

Functions

Magnesium is an essential constituent of bones and teeth, and it activates numerous enzyme-related activities. It makes up approximately 0.05% of the horse's body mass and is absorbed primarily in the small intestine. Sixty percent of this amount is found in the skeleton in association with calcium and phosphorus. Most of the remaining magnesium is found in fluids and soft tissues.

Requirements

Horses can obtain magnesium both from dietary sources and from the bones. Magnesium requirements, depending on age and activities, will vary greatly.

The availability of magnesium from the bone decreases as the horse ages. In the mature horse it may be as low as 2%. Young horses, on the other hand, can mobilize as much as 33% of the required magnesium from their bones. This is especially important during periods of low magnesium availability. Therefore, it is important that young horses be fed enough dietary magnesium to meet their needs. Otherwise, in a period of magnesium deficiency, a young horse may draw upon magnesium from the bones, causing them to become weak.

It has been estimated that the endogenous (within the cell) losses of magnesium are approximately 6 milligrams per kilogram of body weight daily. The horse will excrete this amount of magnesium daily, even in a deficiency situation. This daily loss must be considered when formulating requirements for a ration or supplement. If the horse is experiencing a dietary magnesium deficiency, the endogenous loss will be taken from the bone tissue.

Absorption of magnesium from feedstuffs ranges from 40% to 60%. Using an absorption efficiency of 40%, daily maintenance requirement is estimated to be 15 milligrams per kilogram of body weight. An 1,100 pound (500 kilogram) horse needs approximately 7.5 grams of magnesium daily to meet the requirements of dietary magnesium.

As with most nutrients, pregnant mares require greater quantities of magnesium during the last three months of pregnancy. The fetus and placenta will require approximately 0.23, 0.31, and 0.36 milligrams of magnesium per kg. of the mare's body weight in months nine, ten, and eleven respectively. An 1,100 pound (500 kilogram) mare would require 287, 387, and 450 milligrams of dietary magnesium daily during months nine, ten, and eleven respectively to meet combined maintenance and fetal/placental requirements.

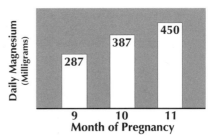

Fig. 4–19. Requirements for a 500 kilogram (1,100 lb) pregnant mare.

Magnesium requirements in a lactating mare will vary according to her stage of lactation. As milk production is generally higher in early lactation (first three months), the magnesium concentration averages 90 micrograms per gram of milk during this period, and 45 micrograms per gram during late lactation. Consequently, during early lactation, mares producing an average of 15 kilograms (33 pounds) of milk daily will require 3.4 grams of dietary magnesium daily in addition to maintenance requirements.

Magnesium Deficiency
A deficiency of magnesium will result in:

• nervousness

- muscle tremors
- damage to the heart
  and muscle tissue
- increase in the depth and rate of respiratory movements
- collapse
- convulsive paddling of the limbs
- sometimes death

Cases of magnesium deficiency in foals have resulted in calcification of the aorta. It has also been noted that horses suffering a magnesium deficiency may become aggressive and ill tempered. Because of this and magnesium's role in the nervous system, it is believed by some that feeding horses magnesium produces a calming effect.

Magnesium Supplementation

Most forages and grains contain 0.1% to 0.3% magnesium. Rations containing 50% forage will likely provide the unstressed horse sufficient magnesium, unless the forage is magnesium deficient.

Hard-working and highly stressed horses are a particular concern when a magnesium deficiency is involved. These animals consume greater amounts of grain, which is low in magnesium, to satisfy the energy demand, and consume lower quantities of hay and pasture, which are high in magnesium. The show or racehorse is sometimes high-strung and nervous, and although in many cases these traits will be temperament related, the possibility of a magnesium deficiency should not be disregarded. Some horsemen add ½ to ⅔ of the recommended daily magnesium to feed to help guard against a deficiency. Several magnesium supplements are available, as shown in the following graph with the percentage of magnesium they contain:

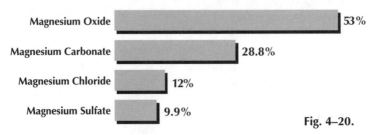

Fig. 4–20.

Magnesium Toxicity

No controlled studies of magnesium toxicity in the horse exist at this time. The maximum tolerable level has been assumed to be 0.3% of the total diet. However, this figure is derived from data obtained from other species.

Sulfur

Functions

Sulfur makes up approximately 0.15% of the horse's body weight, and the majority of it is contained in the hooves and the hair (2% to 3% sulfur). Sulfur is a very important component of many compounds required by the body. It is an essential part of:

- methionine (an essential amino acid)
- cystine (a non-essential amino acid)
- biotin and thiamine (two B-complex vitamins)
- heparin (a blood anti-coagulant)
- insulin (a hormone responsible for glucose metabolism)
- chondroitin sulfate (a constituent of cartilage)

Requirements

No exact requirements have been determined for sulfur. In most cases, when protein requirements are met, it is assumed that sulfur requirements are met. If an adequate level of quality dietary protein is provided, it will supply at least 0.15% of sulfur to the diet.

A small amount of sulfur-containing protein is produced by the microbial population in the hindgut, but very little of this sulfur is available to the horse for absorption.

Deficiency

A sulfur deficiency remains to be observed in the horse. To date, none has been reported or documented.

Toxicity

Maximum tolerable levels of sulfur have not yet been established. However, a report of twelve horses accidentally fed excesses of 200 to 400 grams of flowers of sulfur (greater than 99% pure sulfur) does exist. As a result, these horses experienced:

- lethargy
- colic
- a yellow, frothy discharge from the nostrils
- jaundiced mucous membranes
- labored breathing

Two of the twelve affected horses developed *cyanosis* (blue-tinted skin due to abnormally reduced *hemoglobin* concentrations in the blood), went into convulsions, and died. In another case, ponies fed excesses of sulfur refused to eat and lost weight. Long-term sulfur toxicity can result in liver dysfunction and other associated effects.

Microminerals

Microminerals (trace minerals) are required by the horse in much smaller quantities than macrominerals. The microminerals include cobalt, copper, fluorine, iodine, iron, manganese, selenium, and zinc. (As mentioned previously, these minerals can be supplied in commercially prepared trace mineralized salt mixtures. However, fluorine does not need to be supplemented in most cases.)

Chromium, nickel, silicon, vanadium, and tin have only recently been considered required microminerals. However, current findings indicate that it is extremely difficult to create a deficiency of these microminerals. They are of little practical concern in the study of equine nutrition and will not be addressed.

Cobalt

Functions

Cobalt is a micromineral that is required in very small amounts by the horse. Its only known function is as a necessary component of vitamin B_{12}, which is synthesized by the *microflora* (intestinal fermenting bacteria) in the cecum and colon.

Requirements

Cobalt requirements of the horse have not been studied specifically. It is estimated that the horse requires less than 0.1 milligram per kilogram of diet, and most diets will supply sufficient cobalt. Also, if a trace mineralized salt source that contains cobalt is provided, its needs should be met. However, these small requirements shouldn't be neglected. Cobalt is not stored in significant amounts in the body, and this small stored quantity is not easily utilized in B_{12} production. *(For additional information, see section on vitamin B_{12}, Chapter 3.)*

Deficiency

Cobalt deficiencies have not been observed in the horse. Horses have done well on pastures so low in cobalt that cattle (which require 0.1 to 0.2 milligram of cobalt per kilogram of diet) eventually died.

Cobalt Toxicity

Toxicity of cobalt has not been described in the horse. However, in other species, cobalt toxicity is known to cause *polycythemia*, characterized by an abnormally high red blood cell level. The assumed maximum tolerable level of cobalt in horses is 10 milligrams per kilogram of diet.

Copper

Functions

Copper is essential in the formation of hemoglobin, cartilage, bone, *elastin*, and pigmentation of the hair. Copper also plays a major role in the utilization of iron. It has not been determined to what extent copper is available for utilization.

Requirements

Copper requirements for the equine have not been conclusively determined. Requirements for maintenance, gestating, lactating, performance, and growing horses have been estimated to be 10.0 milligrams of copper per kilogram of diet. In addition, some nutritionists believe that extra copper may be beneficial in young, growing foals. This would involve supplementation of 30 milligrams of copper per kilogram (mg/kg) of the ration for lactating mares, and 40 mg/kg of the ration of young, growing horses. Since the horse can withstand a high level of dietary copper, supplementation at these levels would provide little risk of toxicity and possibly provide some benefits.

Other minerals and compounds are known to have negative effects on absorption and utilization of copper. These other substances are molybdenum, sulfate, zinc, selenium, silver, cadmium, iron, and lead.

High concentrations of these minerals are believed to tie up dietary copper, making it less accessible for nutritional utilization. Therefore, when they are present in large quantities, the amount of copper in the diet must be increased. For example, in areas with soils of high molybdenum content, it is recommended that the dietary copper for horses be four to five times the required amount.

Little is known about specific effects that sulfate, selenium, silver, cadmium, and iron have on copper requirements. Therefore, no set increase in copper can be recommended when high concentrations of these substances are present.

Deficiency

A deficiency of copper *(hypocupremia)* will cause the cortex of the bone to become thin and brittle. The horse will be weak due to poor

Fig. 4–21. A 3-month-old foal with osteochondritis dissecans, a condition associated with copper deficiency.

hemoglobin production, and anemia will result. Since copper is needed to produce *melanin*, the pigment found in hair, the coat will also fade due to the decrease in these iron-containing pigments. Decreased serum copper levels in older mares have been linked to the usually fatal rupture of the uterine artery. In suckling foals, copper deficiencies have been associated with osteochondritis. Additionally, foals have developed intermittent diarrhea as a result of a deficiency.

Copper Toxicity

A copper toxicity has not been described in the horse. Perhaps this is due to the fact that equines are very tolerant of high levels of copper, while most other species are not. Horses have been estimated to have a maximum tolerable copper level of 800 milligrams of copper per kilogram (mg/kg) of the total diet.

Fluorine

Functions

Fluorine is essential for proper tooth and bone formation, and it is also known to prevent tooth decay.

Requirements

An exact dietary requirement of fluorine has yet to be established in the equine. The estimated requirement for horses is about 0.1 milligram of fluorine per kilogram of diet. It should not require supplementation. as this amount is normally found in an average ration.

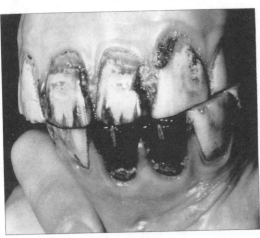

Fig. 4–22. Discolored, mottled teeth are one result of fluorine excess.

Deficiency

Fluorine deficiency is extremely rare in the horse and is not considered a problem.

Toxicity

Equines have been found to be more tolerant of excess fluorine than cattle. However, the esti-mated safe upper limit for horses is 50 milligrams of fluorine per kilogram of total diet. An excess can lead to toxicity and cause a variety of serious problems.

Fluorine has a high affinity for bone tissue—of the excess fluorine in the body, 99% will be retained in the bone. Once the bones have become saturated, the unabsorbed fluorine will produce effects of toxicity in the animal's body.

Moderate excesses of fluorine produce unthriftiness, even when the diet supplies adequate nutrition. The hair coat becomes rough and dry, the skin taut. Teeth become discolored and mottled, and they wear down, making chewing difficult, causing slobbering. After time, the horse becomes lame due to thickening of bones and excessive enlargement of fetlock joints.

Exercise or activity during this stage will worsen the lameness. Prolonged exposure to excess fluorine will cause teeth to break off, and abscesses may result when feed penetrates the pulp cavity of the tooth.

Conditions that May Result in Fluorine Excess

A case of fluorine excess can be caused by:

- forages grown and stored close to an aluminum smelter plant
- water sources containing high concentrations of fluoride
- supplements and mineral mixtures with excessive fluoride
- forages grown in soil containing high levels of fluoride

In these situations, there are steps which can be taken. Contaminated hay may be disposed of and replaced by hay containing a normal fluorine level. When the problem is not severe, excess fluorine may be diluted by mixing normal hay in with the fluorine-excessive hay. The resulting ration should contain no more than 50 milligrams of fluorine per kilogram of diet. In addition, it is usually a good idea to have a sample of the suspicious hay tested by a laboratory. Little or no grazing on affected pastures should be done during fall and winter months, when plants grow slowly.

If a horse is already suffering from fluorine toxicity, its hay may be chopped into smaller pieces and its drinking water heated slightly to lessen any tooth pain. However, the only known treatment for this condition is to reduce fluorine intake.

Iodine

Functions

Iodine combines with a non-essential amino acid called *tyrosine* and forms *thyroxine* (T_4), an important hormone. Thyroxine is made up of about two-thirds iodine and has an influence on almost every organ in the horse's body. It regulates metabolic rates, levels of oxygen utilized, amount of glucose absorbed, and protein metabolism in cells.

Requirements

The horse's body contains less than 0.00004% iodine and requires only 0.1 – 0.6 milligram of iodine per kilogram of diet daily. However, if this minute amount of iodine is not available, serious complications will result. Fortunately, the iodine provided in a normal ration, along with iodized salt, will usually provide adequate amounts.

An adequate presence of iodine is essential for reproduction and for thyroxine synthesis.

Iodine Deficiency

Deficiency symptoms of iodine are similar to toxicity symptoms, so it is very important to determine whether a horse is suffering from a deficiency or toxicity before treatment is initiated.

Iodine deficiency will usually result in the development of a *goiter,* an abnormal enlargement of the thyroid gland.

Goiters are formed when an iodine deficiency stimulates the *anterior pituitary* (a gland found at the base of the brain) to produce excesses of a thyroid-stimulating hormone. This hormone causes the thyroid to overwork, producing excesses of thyroxine in response to the increased stimulus. This causes the gland to swell. (There is a theory, although unproven, that a goiter may also be produced by an excess of calcium coupled with a borderline iodine deficiency.)

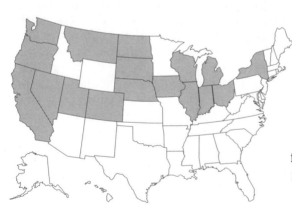

Some states have soils low in iodine. Those soils should be tested regularly when being used for pasture. The iodine concentration in forages and grains can range from 0 to 2 milligrams per kilogram depending on the soil's iodine content. A county Agricultural Agent can furnish accurate reports of iodine levels in the soils of a particular area. Feedstuffs can also be tested for iodine content.

Fig. 4–23. Shaded states may have inadequate iodine concentrations in the soil.

Broodmares and Foals

Broodmares deficient in iodine may exhibit abnormal *estrous* cycles. These mares may also exhibit goiters.

The iodine-deficient foal will occasionally be stillborn and/or hairless. If the foal is born alive, it will usually exhibit labored breathing, a rapid pulse, and, sometimes, a goiter. These foals will often be too weak to stand and nurse. No one treatment has been particularly successful once this condition occurs, and most foals with iodine deficiencies will die shortly after birth. If a veterinarian is called immediately, the foal may recover with treatment. However, those that do survive usually have deformed joints.

Fig. 4–24. Foals receive proper levels of iodine if their dams are provided sufficient amounts during gestation.

The dam of the iodine-deficient foal may not exhibit any symptoms of an iodine deficiency. The best way to prevent iodine-deficient foals is to ensure that the gestating mare is provided sufficient iodine.

Stallions

Some studies have linked iodine deficiency to a decline in sex drive and poor semen quality in the stallion. These are only indications at present and require further verification.

Iodine Supplementation

Supplementation of iodine with minimal risk of toxicity is best accomplished by feeding either an iodized or trace mineralized salt free-choice, in loose or block form. (By law, iodized salt must contain no less than 0.007% iodine.)

Other compounds can be used to supplement iodine—but only on the advice of an equine nutritionist or veterinarian. These include *potassium iodide*, which requires the addition of a stabilizer such as *calcium hydroxide*, or *sodium thiosulfate*. Compounds not requiring a stabilizer may also be used. These include *potassium* and *calcium iodate*, *pentacalcium orthoperiodate* (PCOP), *sodium iodide* and *ethylene diaminedihydroiodide* (EDDI).

Iodine Toxicity

The maximum tolerable level of iodine a horse can ingest has been set at 5 milligrams per kilogram of dietary dry matter, or 50 milligrams a day in a horse consuming 10 kilograms (22 pounds) of dry matter daily.

Supplements and feeds that contain kelp, a seaweed, may contain toxic levels of iodine. One kilogram of kelp can contain 1,850 milligrams of iodine. Overfeeding one of these supplements would most likely result in iodine toxicity, so caution is advised.

Toxicities have also resulted from the administration of excessive supplemental iodine, such as EDDI. This is routinely used by veterinarians to treat *dermatophilosis*, a skin disease.

Toxicity in Broodmares and Foals

Mares have given birth to iodine-toxic foals when consuming 3.5 – 4.8 milligrams of iodine per kilogram of daily diet. This greatly exceeds the recommended level of 0.1 – 0.6 mg/kg, but it is considered to be within the maximum tolerable level. It has not been determined why the foals were born iodine-toxic, but the results underscore the importance of feeding close to recommended amounts. These foals were weak, had goiters, and exhibited some skeletal abnormalities.

When a foal is born with iodine toxicity, an alternate source of milk must be provided. If the foal is allowed to nurse from its dam, it will receive even more iodine, which is readily secreted in the milk. The foal's condition will then worsen.

Mature equines are less likely to develop physical symptoms of iodine toxicity or deficiency than younger ones.

Iron

Functions

The primary function of iron is as a component of hemoglobin. Hemoglobin is a substance contained in red blood cells which serves to carry oxygen to the cells. Approximately 60% of the body's iron is contained in hemoglobin. Twenty percent is contained in *myoglobin* (oxygen transporting pigment of muscle tissue), and a very small amount is contained in enzymes. The body of an 1,100 pound (500 kilogram) horse contains approximately 33 grams of iron. Iron is primarily absorbed in the small intestine.

Red blood cells

Daily Iron Requirements (mg/kg diet)	
Maintenance	40
Pregnant and lactating mares	50
Growing horses	50
Working horses	40
Maximum tolerable level	1,000

Fig. 4–25.

(RBC's) are produced in bone marrow by a process known as *hemato-poiesis*. RBC's are constantly being destroyed and replaced, so the animal will require iron throughout its life. Horses require additional iron during periods of rapid growth. Increase in body size requires additional red blood cells to transport oxygen throughout the body. Pregnant and lactating mares will also need additional iron during late pregnancy.

Iron Requirements

Most equine feedstuffs will contain enough iron to meet most requirements. Forages and grains, on the average, contain 200 to 400 milligrams of iron per kilogram of diet (mg/kg).

Iron requirement is estimated to be 40 milligrams per kilogram of diet for mature, non pregnant, non lactating horses. Growing horses and pregnant or lactating mares require 50 milligrams per kilogram of diet. Approximately 37, 38, and 92 milligrams of iron are deposited daily in the fetus during months nine, ten, and eleven of pregnancy respectively.

The iron content of mare's milk ranges from 1.3 micrograms

Fig. 4–26. Foals store quantities of iron in their bodies before birth if their dams are provided adequate quantities during pregnancy.

per gram at foaling to 0.49 micrograms per gram four months after foaling. (Microgram = one millionth of a gram.) For early lactation, a mare producing 15 kilograms (33 pounds) of milk per day requires approximately 130 milligrams of iron daily. A mare in late lactation, producing 10 kilograms (22 pounds) of milk per day, requires 32.6 milligrams of iron daily.

Mare's milk is relatively low in iron when compared to the foal's needs. Unfortunately, the iron level of a mare's milk cannot be increased by feeding iron to the lactating mare. Therefore, there is a possibility of low or borderline iron intake in the foal if mare's milk is its sole source of nutrition. Fortunately, foals store iron in their bodies prior to birth and will consume solid feeds fairly early. The mare should receive adequate iron during pregnancy so the foal will be able to store adequate quantities for use after birth.

Nutritional availability of iron will decrease with higher than normal intakes of cadmium, cobalt, copper, manganese, and zinc. These substances are believed to tie up iron, making it less accessible for absorption and utilization.

Copper and iron have a special relationship. Without copper acting as a catalyst, the body cannot use iron to make hemoglobin. For this reason, it is important that adequate levels of both are provided.

Iron Deficiency

An iron deficiency will result in *microcytic* and *hypochromic* anemia. *Microcytic* anemia is recognizable by the shrinkage of the red blood cells. *Hypochromic* anemia is characterized by a loss of pigment in the red blood cells.

Blood loss due to wounds or heavy infestations of parasites is the most common cause of anemia. However, high dietary phytate (a source of phosphorus) levels have been shown to bind with iron and render it unavailable.

Concentration of *serum ferritin,* an iron-containing protein, is an accurate indication of a horse's iron level. Packed cell volume (pcv) is a less accurate measurement of iron in the horse's blood, because the pcv will change with the horse's attitude. Excess red blood cells are stored in the spleen. When the horse becomes excited or nervous (as when blood is drawn from the jugular), the spleen will contract, releasing more red blood cells into the bloodstream. This elevates the iron concentration in the blood, giving an inaccurate reading.

Young, milk-fed foals are susceptible to anemia resulting from iron deficiency. However, the body recycles iron derived from the breakdown of red blood cells and body constituents. Therefore, iron deficiency is not a common problem for horses of any age or activity level. However, young animals and mares in late pregnancy should be watched for any signs of iron deficiency (particularly anemia).

Iron Toxicity

It is known that iron toxicity will disturb phosphorus metabolism and decrease bone mineralization and growth rate. Few studies have been performed to determine levels of iron toxicity in the horse, but fatalities due to excess iron have been reported. Most of these horses died after being injected with iron compounds. Although it is very rare, some horses have an undefined hypersensitivity to injections of *iron dextran.* Fatalities resulting from supplemental doses of dietary iron are even more rare.

Iron toxicity is more dangerous to young equines. A number of foal deaths have been attributed to an oral dose of digestive inocula containing supplemental iron. These foals, treated in accordance with the manufacturer's instructions, received 350 milligrams of iron in the form of *ferrous fumarate* at birth and at three days of age. Before they died, the foals exhibited diarrhea, a *jaundice*-like condition called *icterus*, dehydration, and coma. Physiologically, the foals exhibited clinical signs that indicated erosion of the lining in the small intestine, lung hemorrhages, massive iron deposits in the liver, and liver degeneration.

In one study, a high concentration of supplemental dietary iron (500 and 1000 milligrams per kilogram of daily diet) was fed to a group of ponies. There was no apparent effect on feed intake, red blood cell count, daily weight gain, packed cell volume, hemoglobin count, serum iron, copper, or manganese. However, the excess dietary iron depressed the serum and liver zinc levels.

Due to a misconception that higher iron intake will increase stamina by increasing hemoglobin in the blood, it is a common practice to administer iron injections regularly to high performance horses. There is no evidence that these treatments are beneficial if the horse is already obtaining adequate iron. In fact, these injections could result in mild iron toxicity. These horses may experience appetite and weight loss, decreased growth, and even damage to their intestines and liver.

No toxic level of iron for horses has been determined, but 1,000 mg/kg of daily diet has been estimated.

Manganese
Functions
Manganese is essential for the utilization of carbohydrates and fats, and for synthesis of chondroitin sulfate, a vital component of cartilage. In addition to its role in cartilage formation, adequate manganese is necessary for proper bone development. Manganese plays an important role in the formation of many enzymes involved directly in growth, reproduction, and lactation.

Roughages will contain from 40 to 140 milligrams of manganese per kilogram of diet (mg/kg). Concentrates contain from 15 – 45 mg/kg manganese. This variation is dependent upon the manganese concentration of soils in areas where the feedstuffs are grown.

Manganese is predominantly stored in the liver, but some is stored in the skin, muscles, and bones.

Requirements

No exact requirement for manganese has been established in the equine. According to experimental results obtained from other species, 40 milligrams of manganese per kilogram (mg/kg) of the total diet is assumed to be adequate for maintenance purposes.

Manganese Deficiency

Effects of a manganese deficiency have rarely been observed in the equine. A manganese deficiency occurred in Oklahoma where a pasture was heavily limed to offset acidic soil conditions due to smelter effluence. Consequently, alfalfa grown on this soil contained twice as much calcium and two thirds less manganese than normal. A normal manganese level would be no less than 39 milligrams per kilogram of diet (mg/kg), and these pastures contained only 13 mg/kg. High calcium concentration severely debilitates manganese absorption.

Pregnant mares fed this alfalfa gave birth to foals that were deaf, had misshapen limbs and joints, shortened limbs, irregularly shaped skulls, and excessively curved spines. These foals were unable to stand and nurse due to the severity of these bone abnormalities, and subsequently died.

Horses grazing on pastures in sandy soil in southern New Jersey, or consuming hay grown on this soil, have, on occasion, developed cases of manganese deficiency.

An accurate indication of manganese deficiency is very difficult to detect in the living animal, because a liver biopsy is, at present, the most accurate test for this condition.

Manganese Toxicity

Manganese toxicity has not occurred in any species under natural conditions. Even in situations in which horses were ingesting large quantities of manganese for a long period of time, no toxicity symptoms were observed. However, excesses should be avoided, as they may disturb the utilization of other nutrients.

Selenium

Functions

Selenium is an essential component of the *antioxidant* enzyme *glutathione peroxidase*. This enzyme aids in detoxification of *peroxides*, which are toxic to cell membranes. If these toxins are not removed, the cell membrane's permeability will become impaired, making the cell very fragile. The result will be death of the cell. Selenium also conserves vitamin E. These two functions of selenium are important because any *rancidity* of feeds produce peroxides and vitamin E loss.

Selenium is also a vital constituent of methionine and cystine, two sulfur-containing amino acids. These amino acids also function as antioxidants and aid the immune system by protecting cells from diseases associated with selenium and vitamin E deficiency and toxicity. Thus, these amino acids have a sparing effect on selenium and vitamin E.

Selenium content in most feedstuffs ranges from 0.05 to 0.3 milligrams per kilogram of diet. These values depend on the selenium content and pH of the soil. On average, feedstuffs of plant origin contain more selenium than those of animal origin, such as bone meal.

Alfalfa meal and brewer's grains will usually have the highest availability of organic selenium. Furthermore, linseed meal will generally contain more selenium than soybean meal. Various newly refined chemical tests are available to test feedstuffs for selenium content. Absorption of selenium in the equine is believed to be about 77%.

Selenium Requirements

It has been estimated that 0.1 milligrams of selenium per kilogram of diet is adequate for maintenance. Providing this amount in a horse's diet will increase the blood level of selenium enough to avoid problems associated with a deficiency. Studies have revealed no apparent advantage to supplementation above maintenance requirements for the idle adult horse.

Fig. 4–27. There is no apparent advantage to selenium supplementation for the idle adult horse.

Selenium Deficiency

Soils in the eastern, northwestern, and Great Lakes areas of the U. S. are low in selenium. Forages and grains grown in these areas may contain less than 0.1 milligram of selenium per kilogram of diet.

A horse's level of selenium can be determined by measuring the selenium concentration of *plasma* or serum. Another method, which is fairly new and less expensive, uses a "rapid-screening, blood-spot test" which determines the concentration of the selenium-containing enzyme glutathione peroxidase.

If the concentration of selenium in the horse's blood falls below 60 nanograms per milliliter, a deficiency is likely. Also, because most plants do not depend on selenium for growth, even lush, green pasture or hay can be lacking in this mineral, causing a deficiency in horses consuming them. A selenium deficiency may be less likely if the horse's vitamin E level is adequate or above. *(The relationship between vitamin E and selenium is discussed in Chapter 3.)*

Young foals are more prone to selenium deficiency than mature horses. At birth, the foal's serum selenium concentration will normally be between 70 and 80 nanograms per milliliter. Serum selenium concentrations of 65 nanograms per milliliter or less indicate a deficiency in the foal, and may cause the foal to be prone to *white muscle disease.* White muscle disease is one of the main complications of selenium deficiency in equines of all ages.

Foals suffering from deficiencies of selenium will exhibit impaired movement, weakness, hair loss, dark urine, and respiratory distress. These foals will have difficulty nursing and swallowing as a result of this incoordination and unsteadiness. In severe cases, death will most likely result from respiratory and/or cardiac distress. The onset of these symptoms may occur following birth or after five to seven months.

A broodmare that is selenium deficient will experience serious complications, making her breeding efficiency decrease sharply. The selenium-deficient broodmare is characterized by frequent uterine infections, early embryonic death, abortions, and repeat breedings.

Supplementation of foals and gestating mares is beneficial in low-selenium areas. The recommended level for both is 0.1 milligram of selenium per kilogram of diet daily. Supplementation by injection in the pregnant mare is not recommended during early pregnancy. For the foal, selenium injections may be administered at birth, one, three, and six months of age. Selenium injections should be administered only on the advice of an equine nutritionist or veterinarian.

Selenium Deficiencies in Mature and Older Horses

A mature equine suffering from a selenium deficiency will exhibit symptoms such as weight loss, lack of appetite, loss of tail and mane hair, muscular weakness (primarily in the legs and jaws), rapid heart rate, and diarrhea.

Selenium Toxicity

Selenium toxicity is much more common than selenium deficiency. Toxicities have resulted from 5 to 40 milligrams of selenium per kilogram of feed. The maximum tolerable level of selenium is 2 milligrams per kilogram of the total diet.

The soils of South Dakota, North Dakota, Nebraska, Kansas, Colorado, Utah, Arizona, and New Mexico are known to have high concentrations of selenium. These concentrations may reach as high as 5 milligrams of selenium per kilogram of diet. Some believe that feeding high levels of protein, sulfur, and arsenilic

Fig. 4–28. Gray indicates areas with high concentrations of selenium in the soil.

acid will help prevent selenium toxicity. However, other problems associated with feeding high levels of these substances may be even more detrimental.

In horses suffering from toxicity, an abnormal enlargement of the liver, kidney and heart have been observed at *necropsy.*

Acute selenium toxicity will result in blind staggers, head pressing, sweating, abdominal pain, colic, diarrhea, elevated heart rate, lethargy, and increased respiratory rate.

A chronic case of selenium toxicity *(alkali disease)* is characterized by hair loss (predominantly around the mane and tail), and cracked hooves (mainly around the coronary band). Prolonged chronic selenium toxicity will cause paralysis, blindness, swollen eyelids, cloudy eyes, bloody frothy excretions from the nose, and eventually the hooves will slough off.

Certain plants collect and store selenium from the soil for their own use. These plants include milk vetch *(Astragaluses)*, woody aster *(Aster xylorrhiza)*, golden weed *(Oonopsis)*, and prince's plume *(Stanleya)*. These plants can provide as much as 1,000 to 10,000 milligrams of selenium per kilogram of diet, but 100 to 300 mg/kg is average. They are characterized by a sulphur-garlic odor and are unpalatable to the horse. However, if a pasture is overgrazed and the horse has nothing else to eat, it will consume these plants.

Some plants do not utilize selenium, but they may collect and store very high concentrations of it. These plants can produce dangerous selenium toxicity if eaten by the horse. They include:

- asters *(Machaeranthera)*
- four-winged salt brush *(Atriplex)*
- wheat grass *(Agropyron)*
- gum weed *(Grindelia squarrosa)*
- broomweed, snake weed, or matchweed *(Gutierrezia saraothral)*
- *Sideranthus*   • Comandra   • Castilleja

Horses experiencing toxicity symptoms should be removed from the suspect forage or grain at once. Their feedstuffs should then be replaced with feeds low in selenium.

Zinc
Functions
Zinc is an essential component of many body enzymes and hormones, and it also plays an important role in the metabolism of proteins, fats, and carbohydrates. Zinc is necessary for the immune

system to function properly. Zinc is also needed to maintain healthy skin and hair. In cases of stress or disease, zinc levels in the body will decrease. The highest concentrations of zinc can be found in the pigmented portions of the eye *(choroid, iris)*.

Moderate but lower concentrations are contained in the skin, liver, bone, and muscle. Small quantities of zinc are found in blood, milk, lungs, and the brain. Absorption of zinc depends on its concentration in the animal. In most cases, absorption will range from 5% – 10%.

Common equine feedstuffs will contain from 15 to 40 milligrams of zinc per kilogram of diet (mg/kg). Grains, on the average, will contain between 10 and 30 mg/kg zinc, while most plant-based protein supplements (such as soybean meal or cot-

Fig. 4–29. Stresses of training and showing may cause zinc levels to decrease, however supplementation is rarely needed.

ton seed meal) will contain 30 to 70 mg/kg zinc, and on the average, most common hays (including red clover and alfalfa) will contain about 30 mg/kg zinc.

Zinc Requirements
In most cases, 40 milligrams of zinc per kilogram of diet (mg/kg) will be adequate.

Mare's milk contains from 1.8 to 3.2 mg/kg zinc, meaning that an average foal, drinking 15 kilograms (33 pounds) of milk per day, will consume 27 to 48 mg/kg of zinc per day. The zinc found in mare's milk is assumed to be readily available when ingested.

The concentration of *phytin,* an organic phosphate compound found in plants, will have a direct effect on zinc absorption, and, subsequently, its requirement. Phytin will combine with zinc, forming zinc phytate, which is insoluble. As a result, the zinc will be unavailable during the digestion process.

Zinc supplementation is rarely needed. However, if it is deemed advisable by a veterinarian, several zinc supplements are available. They include:

- zinc sulphate
- zinc chloride
- zinc oxide
- zinc carbonate

Zinc Deficiency

Zinc deficiency in the equine has not been produced under natural conditions. Experimentally induced zinc deficiencies have caused a variety of problems. These include hoof lesions, hair loss, and dry skin, which begins on the legs and spreads upwards to the body and the face. Eventually, the skin will have a mange-like appearance and skin infections are likely to occur. Foals fed 5 milligrams of zinc per kilogram of diet (less than one-tenth of the minimal requirements) under experimental conditions exhibited:

- lack of appetite
- hair loss
- decreased growth rate
- dry skin
- decreased concentrations of serum and tissue zinc

Zinc Toxicity

Equines appear to be very tolerant of excess zinc when compared to other species. The maximum tolerable level of zinc in the total diet has been set at 500 milligrams of zinc per kilogram of diet. However, excesses of zinc have induced secondary deficiencies of copper and possibly calcium. The mechanisms which produce these secondary deficiencies have not yet been determined.

Foals fed 90 grams of zinc per day developed swollen joints, lameness, stiffness in gait, and increased zinc tissue concentration. In mature horses, zinc toxicity symptoms were similar, but were accompanied by anemia. The symptoms may resemble anemia due to zinc binding with copper.

Pastures that have been contaminated by nearby smeltering plants will exhibit extremely high concentrations of zinc. As a result, horses grazing on such pastures will likely develop toxicity-related problems. Zinc excesses can be determined with some degree of accuracy from plasma zinc concentrations; more than 2 milligrams of zinc per kilogram of diet present in the plasma indicates a possible toxicity.

5

ENERGY SOURCES

Energy is the fuel for the body systems. Its use is most commonly expressed through physical activity (work), growth, milk production, repair of body tissues, and the regulation of temperature in the body. Energy is provided in the horse's ration by three nutrient classes: carbohydrates, fats, and proteins. Energy is supplied primarily by carbohydrates because: 1) carbohydrates are readily available (they make up about ¾ of the dry matter in plants), and 2) carbohydrates include glucose, which is the chief source of fuel for maintaining body temperature and furnishing energy for body processes.

ENERGY

When planning a total ration, the amount of energy the horse requires and an efficient method of supplying that energy must be determined. The total amount of energy required by a horse is influenced by its age, health, body weight, breeding productivity, weather conditions and amount of daily exercise, or work performed. The critical factor in planning a balanced ration is measuring the *digestible energy* (DE), or usable energy, in a feed, rather than the total energy content in a feed.

Measuring Energy

It is necessary to know the amount of energy provided by a feed in order to formulate rations that ensure requirements are met. If a horse expends more energy than it receives, its productivity will decrease and it will lose weight. If it is provided excessive amounts of energy, the possibility of obesity, founder, and colic will increase.

The Total Digestible Nutrient System (TDN)

The TDN system has been commonly used for many years to measure the amount of energy contained in a feed. There are two steps in determining the TDN value of a feed:

1) The feed is divided into the percentages of crude protein, crude fat, crude fiber, and nitrogen-free extract it contains. Then each of those components is individually multiplied by the percentage of that component that will be digested. The number that results is the **digestible** amount of that nutrient contained in the feed. For example, if a certain feed contains 20% crude protein and 80% of that protein is digestible, then the digestible crude protein would be 16% (80% of 20% = 16%).

2) In the second step, the digestible amounts of each nutrient are added together to obtain the TDN:

> Digestible Crude Protein
> + Digestible Crude Fiber
> + Digestible Nitrogen Free Extract
> + Digestible Crude Fat x 2.25 *
> _____
> =Total Digestible Nutrients

* Fat has 2.25 times the energy of the other listed ingredients.

The TDN system is familiar to most horsemen due to its regular use in equine related literature, but it does have disadvantages. The TDN calculation accounts for energy lost in the feces, but it does not take into account energy lost in urine, gasses, and the process of digestion. Because of these inefficiencies, the TDN system is no longer used in scientific research. Instead, the caloric system of measurement is now used.

Caloric Measurement of Energy Values

Caloric measurement is more accurate than the TDN system in determining the energy content of a feed. Energy can be measured by the heat it forms. The amount of heat required to raise the temperature of one gram of water by one degree Centigrade is a calorie. A *kilocalorie* is equal to 1,000 calories, and a *megacalorie* is equal to 1,000,000 calories. Energy values are expressed as gross energy, digestible energy, metabolizable energy, and net energy.

- Gross energy is determined by placing a sample of feed in a *bomb calorimeter,* which is sealed and immersed in a known amount of water. The sample is then burned, and the amount of heat produced is expressed in calories. Due to losses of energy through normal body processes however, gross energy is not fully available to the horse.
- Digestible energy (DE) consists of the gross energy in the feed minus the amount of energy estimated to be lost in the feces.

- Metabolizable energy (ME) is DE minus the energy lost in urine and gas products of digestion.
- Net energy is ME minus the heat increment. The heat increment refers to increased heat produced by the process of digestion and the breakdown of nutrients.

DE is the value most commonly used to describe the energy content of feeds, because very little information is available on the metabolizable and net energy levels of equine feeds.

Digestible Energy and Fat Content of Common Feeds

Feed	Digestible Energy Mcal/kg	Mcal/lb	Fat %	Feed	Digestible Energy Mcal/kg	Mcal/lb	Fat %
ALFALFA				CORN (grain)	3.38	1.54	3.6
meal 15% protein	2.00	0.91	2.2				
17% protein	2.16	0.98	2.8	**BREWER'S GRAINS**	2.53	1.15	5.9
hay, sun-cured,				**ANIMAL FAT**			
early bloom	2.24	1.02	2.6	hydrolyzed	7.94	3.61	98.4
BAHIAGRASS							
hay, sun-cured	1.75	0.79	1.8	**FLAX SEED**	3.40	1.54	36.0
BARLEY (grain)	3.26	1.49	1.8	OATS (grain grade 1)	2.99	1.36	5.1
				hay, sun-cured	1.75	0.79	2.2
BEET (pulp)	2.33	1.06	0.5				
				RYE (grain)	3.36	1.53	1.5
CLOVER (hay, sun-cured)							
alsike	1.71	0.78	2.4	**TIMOTHY**			
ladino	1.96	0.89	2.4	hay, sun-cured			
red	1.96	0.89	2.5	early bloom	1.83	0.83	2.5
				late bloom	1.59	0.72	2.4
COASTAL BERMUDAGRASS							
hay, sun-cured				**VEGETABLE OIL**	8.98	4.08	99.7
(29–42 days growth)	1.96	0.89	2.4				
				WHEAT BRAN	2.94	1.33	3.8

Fig. 5–1.   Mcal/kg= megacalories of digestible energy per kilogram of feed
Mcal/lb = megacalories of digestible energy per pound of feed

The Body Condition Score System

Body weight can be used as an observable measure of the energy sufficiency of a ration. A body condition score system was developed by researchers at Texas A&M University which provides a uniform method for determining fat status and body condition.

The Body Condition Score System chart follows the next two Figures (5–2 and 5–3). These two Figures offer visual descriptions of the areas referred to in the chart.

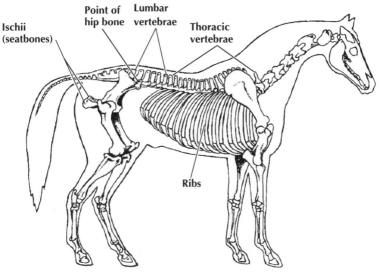

Fig. 5–2. Skeletal components which relate to the Body Condition Score System.

Fig. 5–3. The body condition score is judged by the amount of fat deposition in the shaded areas. *(See following chart.)*

Body Condition Score System

SCORE	DESCRIPTION
1 (Poor)	Animal extremely *emaciated; spinous processes* (upward projections) of lumbar and thoracic *vertebrae*, ribs, tailhead, point of hip bone *(tuber coxae)*, and seat bones *(ischii)* projecting prominently; bone structure of withers, shoulders, and neck easily noticeable; no fatty tissue can be felt.
2 (Very thin)	Emaciated; slight fat covering base of backbone; *transverse processes* (side projections) of lumbar vertebrae feel rounded; spinous processes, ribs, tailhead, point of hip bone, and seat bones prominent; withers, shoulders, and neck structure faintly visible.

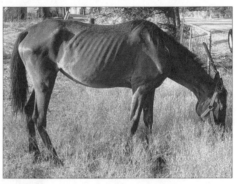

Fig. 5–4.

3 (Thin)	Fat buildup about halfway on spinous processes; transverse processes cannot be felt; slight fat cover over ribs; spinous processes and ribs easily seen; tailhead prominent but individual vertebrae cannot be identified visually; point of hip bone appears rounded but easily discernible; seat bones not distinguishable; withers, shoulders, and neck accentuated.
4 (Moderately thin)	Slight ridge along back; faint outline of ribs seen; tailhead prominence depends on conformation, fat can be felt around it; point of hip bones not seen; withers, shoulders, and neck not obviously thin.

5	**(Moderate)**	Back is flat (no crease or ridge); ribs not visually distinguishable but easily felt; fat around tailhead beginning to feel spongy; withers appear rounded over spinous processes; shoulders and neck blend smoothly into body.
6	**(Moderately fleshy)**	May have slight crease down back; fat over ribs spongy; fat around tailhead soft; fat beginning to be deposited along the side of withers, behind shoulders, and along the sides of neck.
7	**(Fleshy)**	May have crease down back; individual ribs can be felt, but noticeable filling between ribs with fat; fat around tailhead soft; fat deposited along withers, behind shoulders, and along neck.

Fig. 5–5.

8	**(Fat)**	Crease down back; difficult to feel ribs; fat around tailhead very soft, area along withers filled with fat; area behind shoulder filled with fat; noticeable thickening of neck; fat deposited along inner thighs.
9	**(Extremely fat)**	Obvious crease down back; patchy fat appearing over ribs; bulging fat around tail head, along withers, behind shoulders, and along the neck; fat along inner thighs may rub together; flank area filled with fat.

Fig. 5–6.

Energy Requirements

Energy requirements have been determined by the National Research Council (NRC) for horses of different body weights, growth stages, and activity levels. Maintenance energy requirements for each class of horse account for energy needed for normal body processes such as circulation and maintaining body temperature. It also accounts for energy expended by day-to-day activity, such as grazing.

Energy requirements are increased for pregnancy, lactation, growth, and work. Requirements will also be increased by extreme ambient temperatures. During hot weather energy is needed to eliminate body heat. This is critical for performance horses which must dissipate heat during work. In cold weather, energy in the form of heat keeps the horse warm.

The following is daily digestible energy requirements for a 1,100 pound (500 kilogram) horse in Megacalories (1,000,000 calories):

Digestible Energy Requirements for 1100 Pound Horse	
Maintenance	16.4 Megacalories
Stallions (breeding season)	20.5 Mcal
Pregnant mares	Ninth month: 18.2 Mcal Tenth month: 18.5 Mcal Eleventh month: 19.7 Mcal
Lactating mares	Early lactation: 28.3 Mcal Late lactation: 24.3 Mcal
Working horses	Light work: 20.5 Mcal Moderate work: 24.6 Mcal Intense work: 32.8 Mcal
Weanlings*	4 months: 14.4 Mcal 6 months: 15.0 to 17.2 Mcal[1]
Yearlings*	12 months: 18.9 to 21.3 Mcal[1] 18 months: 19.8 or 26.5 Mcal[2]
Two–year–olds*	18.8 or 26.3 Mcal[2]

* These are horses that should weigh 1,100 pounds (500 kilograms) when mature.

[1] Depends on rate of daily gain (growth).

[2] Lower figure is for horses not in training. Higher figure is for horses in training.

Fig. 5–7.

(For energy requirements for other specific weights of horses, refer to Nutrient Tables in the Appendix.)

Broodmares

A mare in early gestation (first eight months) requires energy intake similar to those of maintenance levels, unless she has a body condition score of five or less. Thin mares should have their energy intake increased 10% to 15% above the NRC maintenance requirement to increase body

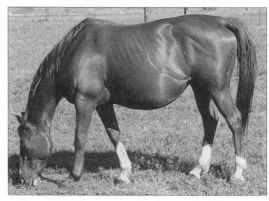

Fig. 5–8. Pregnant mares have increased energy requirements during the last three months of pregnancy, due to the accelerated growth of the fetus.

condition scores. During the last three months of gestation, energy requirements increase for pregnant mares, due to accelerated fetal growth. During months nine, ten, and eleven, mares' requirements for energy increase by 11%, 13%, and 20%, respectively.

Energy requirements in lactating mares will vary with the composition and amount of milk being produced. Mares of light horse breeds will generally produce an amount of milk equal to 3% of their body weight per day during early lactation (the first three months), and 2% of their body weight during late lactation (the last three months). Average milk production of a 1,100 lb mare ranges from 22 to 33 lbs. per day. A 1,100 lb. mare during the first 90 days of lactation needs 28.3 megacalories of digestible energy daily to meet high demands of milk production. From the third month of lactation to weaning, the mare's digestible energy requirement decreases to 24.3 megacalories per day.

Performance and Working Horses

Performance and working horses require large amounts of energy that can be utilized quickly. Horses in light, medium, or intense work need 25%, 50%, or 100% energy increase respectively, above maintenance requirements. Body weight and condition should be monitored to ensure proper energy reserves are maintained.

Fig. 5–9. Strenuous performance increases energy requirements.

Growing horses

Growing horses have the highest encrgy needs on a body weight basis—because growth requires energy. A 473 pound wean- ling, that will weigh 1,100 pounds at maturity, needs 15 megacalories of digestible energy per day for moderate growth, or 17.2 megacalories per day if the growth rate is rapid.

Fig. 5–10. Growing horses have high energy needs. A deficiency will retard growth.

Stallions

During most of the year, stallions will not require energy above the level needed for maintenance. Stallions during the breeding season, however, have an increased energy need of 25% above maintenance requirements. Some stallions are overly active and will pace the stall or paddock, and a heavy breeding season will place added stress on them. Stallions should be kept in good body condition, but not overweight. Obesity in stallions is discouraged, as it may lead to decreased sex drive, impaired mating ability, and a predisposition to laminitis and colic.

Fig. 5–11. This mare has received insufficient energy to support herself and her foal.

Energy Deficiency

An energy deficiency will result in reduced physical activity, general weakness, weight loss, insufficient lactation, slow growth, and poor reproductive performance. An energy deficiency is extremely detrimental to the young growing equine. It will retard growth and produce an unthrifty appearance.

Energy deficiencies occur in

mares during late gestation, due to rapid growth of the fetus, and also during lactation. Other energy deficiencies may result from lack of appetite, starvation, severe parasitism, or illness.

An energy deficiency can result in *hyperlipidemia* (elevated fat levels in the blood). It is characterized by lethargy, dullness, and general depression. Prolonged hyperlipidemia can lead to coma and death.

Energy Excess

When a horse is provided energy beyond its requirements, the possibility of obesity, founder and colic will increase. Excess body fat can impede performance and decrease milk production. In the young growing horse, skeletal problems may result. *(More detailed descriptions of these problems will be presented later in this chapter.)*

SOURCES OF ENERGY
Carbohydrates

Carbohydrates serve as the major source of energy for the horse and are necessary for the metabolism of fats. They are formed in plants during *photosynthesis.* In photosynthesis, *chlorophyll* in the plant utilizes energy from the sun to produce carbohydrates from carbon dioxide and water. Carbohydrates make up about three-fourths of the dry matter in plants. Carbohydrates also can be either simple or complex. Major carbohydrates in feedstuffs include:

- sugars   • starches   • *cellulose*   • *hemicellulose*
- *glycogen* (the form in which energy is stored in liver and muscle)

Simple (Soluble) Carbohydrates

Simple carbohydrates are found in the concentrate portion of a horse's diet. They are primarily digested and absorbed in the small intestine as glucose and other simple sugars. Simple carbohydrates include monosaccharides, disaccharides, and trisaccharides, along with starch and dextrin. (The term saccharide is used to denote sugars.)

Simple carbohydrates are broken down by *carbohydrases* secreted by the pancreas and intestinal mucosa. Carbohydrases found in the horse are lactase, sucrase, maltase, trehalase, and beta-galactosidase. Activity of these carbohydrases depends on the horse's age. At birth, there is little maltase or sucrase activity, but it peaks at six to seven months of age. Lactase activity, which breaks down lactose (a milk sugar), is high at birth but declines rapidly when the horse is 3 to 4 years old. Because older horses lack the ability to break down lactose, they are prone to intestinal disturbances if fed milk products.

When carbohydrates are digested, glucose and other simple sugars are absorbed into the bloodstream and carried to the cells for use as the primary energy source.

If simple carbohydrates are not fully digested in the small intestine, they will be fermented by microorganisms in the large intestine, resulting in the production of volatile fatty acids (referred to scientifically as VFAs). If large amounts of simple carbohydrates are digested in the large intestine, gastric disturbances may result. This is one of the reasons why it is better to divide the concentrate portion of the total daily ration into three or four meals, rather than one or two large ones.

Complex Carbohydrates (fiber)

Complex carbohydrates are found in hays and forages. They include hemicellulose, cellulose, and lignin. They form the cell wall in plants and provide fiber in the horse's diet.

Hemicellulose

Hemicellulose is the most digestible of the three complex carbohydrates, and in young growing plants it is the principle part of the plant cell wall structure. As the plant matures, the hemicellulose converts to cellulose, which is less digestible.

Cellulose

In more mature plants, cellulose is the major structural component of plant cell walls. Nutrients in plants are found inside the cell walls, and as the plant matures, the cell walls become harder to digest, making the nutrients less available.

Fig. 5–12. Mature plants have a high lignin content, which reduces the digestibility of cellulose and other nutrients.

Lignin

Prevalent in coarse stemmy feeds, large amounts of lignin are found in very mature pastures, hay, straw, and grain hulls. Although lignin is technically a carbohydrate, it is not considered a "true" carbohydrate because it is not readily digested and it has no nutritional value. However, it does provide bulk in the diet. Large amounts of lignin lower the digestibility of cellulose and other nutrients.

Digestion of Complex Carbohydrates

Complex and simple carbohydrates not digested in the small intestine are broken down into volatile fatty acids by fermenting bacteria in the hindgut. These volatile fatty acids can be utilized as energy. This energy source is very important for pastured horses and horses whose ration includes a high percentage of hay (because of the high level of complex carbohydrate intake).

The arrangement of the horse's digestive tract limits the amount of fiber (complex carbohydrates) that can be utilized. Fiber is digested by microorganisms in the hindgut, where fewer nutrients are absorbed. No maximum fiber requirements have been determined, but recommendations are that **minimum** forage intake, either in the form of hay or pasture, be 25% to 50% of total diet on a dry matter basis.

Newborns cannot efficiently digest the majority of crude fiber components in feeds, because there is an insufficient number of bacteria in the large intestine at birth. These bacteria increase in number as foals age, and their ability to digest fiber increases correspondingly. The suckling or weanling still requires a diet low in fiber, because the number of bacteria in the hindgut may still be limited.

Mature horses that are not under heavy stress should be provided higher levels of fiber than young horses. Fiber intake is reduced

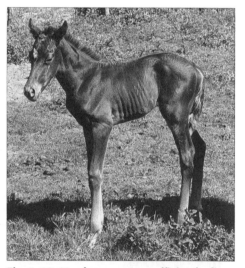

Fig. 5–13. Newborns cannot efficiently digest most crude fiber components in feeds.

slightly for horses in intense work, such as race training, so that more energy-dense concentrate can be fed.

Feeding low quality roughage, which is very high in fiber, is not recommended, because gastric disturbances and distension of the digestive tract are more likely to occur. In addition, as fiber in the ration increases, digestible protein will decrease.

Relationship of Feed Quality to Carbohydrates

As a general rule, the more soluble (simple) carbohydrates a feed contains, the higher its quality and digestibility will be. A mature forage crop contains more fiber (complex carbohydrates) and fewer soluble carbohydrates, making it less digestible.

Fig. 5–14. Pastures need frequent mowing to provide high-quality forage.

In order to provide high quality forages, pastures should be cut regularly and maintained so they are lush and green. Optimum cutting times will vary according to climate and species. Hay should be cut in early maturity when it is deep green in color and has a higher ratio of leaves to stem, because 80% of the nutritional value of forages is found in the leaves. Each type of forage plant has an optimum stage for harvesting. *(Refer to Chapter 9 for more information on hays and pastures.)*

Deficiency/Excess of Carbohydrates

Insufficient carbohydrate intake will directly result in an energy deficiency. Excesses of carbohydrates have been associated with a variety of health problems, including founder and colic. Excessive intake of simple carbohydrates (concentrates) have been linked to several types of metabolic bone diseases in young, growing horses. These diseases include *osteochondrosis, epiphysitis,* and bone deformities. For this reason, young growing horses, particularly weanlings, which are prone to bone abnormalities, should **not** be fed concentrate rations free-choice.

Fats (lipids)

Fats are contained in all feedstuffs in varying amounts, but the amounts are quite low, usually no more than 6%. Feedstuffs containing the highest amounts of fat include oats (5.1%), corn (3.6%), alfalfa hay (2.6%), and timothy hay (2.5%). Supplemental fat sources, such as vegetable oil and hydrolized animal fats, contain up to 98.4%.

Fats are an excellent source of energy because they contain 2.25 times more energy than carbohydrates and proteins. For example, one cup (8 oz.) of corn oil is equal in energy to 1.2 pounds of corn or 1.5 pounds of "sweet feed."

The term commonly used when discussing fats in feeds is *lipids.* This term includes not only fats, but also *glycerides, cholesterol, lecithin, chlorophyll, volatile oils, waxes,* and *resins.* All of these compounds are found in, and provide energy to, the growing plant. Chlorophyll, volatile oils, and resins are related to fats in their structure and have similar functions in the plant sources from which they are taken. All lipids contain carbon, hydrogen, and oxygen.

Fats are made up of *glycerol* (an alcohol) and *fatty acids.* There are two types of fatty acids: *unsaturated* and *saturated.* Unsaturated fatty acids are obtained from vegetable sources such as corn oil, soybean oil, canola oil, and blends such as soy/corn and coconut oil. These oils form unsaturated fat. Studies have shown these to be more easily digested than saturated fatty acids, which are obtained from animal sources such as tallow, and which form saturated fat. (Unsaturated fats are almost 100% digestible; saturated fats are 75% to 80% digestible.)

All unsaturated fats are liquid at room temperature (soft fats). They include the following fatty acids:

- linoleic acid
- palmitoleic acid
- linolenic acid
- arachidonic acid
- clupanodonic acid
- oleic acid

Unsaturated fats can become rancid. Feed manufacturers reduce the chances by adding *antioxidants* or synthetic vitamin E to feeds.

Most of the saturated fats are solid at room temperature (hard fats). They include the following fatty acids:

- butyric acid*
- caproic acid*
- caprylic acid*
- capric acid
- lauric acid
- myristic acid
- palmitic acid
- stearic acid
- arachidic acid
- lignoceric acid

* These are not solid at room temperature.

Functions of Fats

Fats are involved in several functions in the body, one of which is to aid in the absorption of fat-soluble vitamins. Also, they are the source of linoleic acid, linolenic acid, and arachidonic acid, dietary essential fatty acids which the body cannot synthesize on its own.

Fats and fat-like substances (chlorophyll, volatile oils, and resins) provide energy in a more concentrated form than other nutrients—more than twice the energy of carbohydrates and proteins. The energy content of fat is more than 9 kilocalories per gram, as compared to about 4 kilocalories per gram for carbohydrates and proteins.

The high energy factor of fat provides the same protein sparing effect that carbohydrates do, leaving protein available for muscle development and growth. When enough fats are present in the diet, they are used to meet the body's energy needs.

Fat Requirements

Exact requirements of fats in the equine diet have not been established. It is recognized that some fat is essential as a source of linoleic acid, to provide energy, and for absorption of fat-soluble vitamins. Generally, the amount of fats and fat-like substances in most quality feeding programs are considered adequate.

Most horse rations will generally contain 2% to 3% fat. Horses can readily utilize rations with up to 6% fat in the total diet, with the concentrate portion containing approximately 12% fat. While higher levels have been fed experimentally, there do not appear to be any advantages to exceeding these optimum levels. Also higher intakes of fat may produce diarrhea and a reduced feed intake in some horses.

Fat Supplementation

Feeding high levels of soluble carbohydrates (concentrates) as an energy source was previously considered a necessity for the high performance horse. However, because fat has more energy than carbohydrates and protein, horses that receive added fat as part of the ration will not need to consume as much feed to meet their energy requirements. Therefore, potential for health risks such as founder and colic will be reduced. Fat costs more per pound when compared to grain, but the fat that horses consume may be utilized more efficiently than grain.

Fig. 5–15. Fat can be used to meet the high energy requirements of performance horses.

The amount of fat in the horse's diet can be increased by top dressing the concentrate portion of the daily ration. For significant increases in energy for high performance horses, fat totalling 10 – 12% of the concentrate portion of the ration can be added. The horse's coat condition can be improved with small amounts of fat (e.g. a few tablespoons of vegetable oil added to the grain).

Broodmares

Pregnant mares in a controlled study that were fed 5% feed-grade *rendered animal fat* in their diets exhibited shorter periods of time from foaling to first *estrus*. In addition, it took them fewer cycles to conceive, and they had a higher pregnancy rate. Whether this was due directly to the fat or the positive energy balance it created is not clear.

Lactating mares that receive added fat in their rations will produce milk with a higher fat content. As a result, their foals may grow faster and gain weight more readily. In controlled studies, the protein content of mare's milk was unaffected by added fat in the diet. It should be noted, however, that excesses of energy should not be fed. Obese mares, when compared to mares in moderate body condition, were found to produce less milk.

Growing Horses

Growing horses that are in training will have a high demand for energy, approximately 26 megacalories of digestible energy per day, because they need energy for growth as well as work. Adding 10 – 12% fat to the concentrate portion of the diet will ensure energy for both.

While added fat may be advantageous, care should be taken to ensure that the diet remains balanced. Fat contains **neither vitamins nor minerals**, therefore its addition will dilute existing nutrients in the concentrate portion of the ration. If vitamin and mineral loss is not compensated for, the horse may show symptoms of mild malnutrition or skeletal problems when fat is added. A vitamin and mineral supplement should be used to rebalance the ration.

In a study on yearlings, they were fed a fat-supplemented diet in which the ration was rebalanced by adding proper amounts of vitamins and minerals. These yearlings were x-rayed periodically to determine if the added fat would produce skeletal abnormalities. In each case, no indications of skeletal abnormalities were discovered.

When young horses were fed a fat supplement without rebalancing the ration with vitamins and minerals, they were more likely to have skeletal abnormalities. This may have been due to the skeletal system not receiving adequate amounts of other nutrients. Rapid increase in growth, coupled with a lack of properly balanced nutrients, puts extensive strain on the skeleton.

Performance Horses

Addition of fat to the performance horse's diet has been shown to increase stamina. It is hypothesized that added stamina comes from glycogen being spared as fat is used for energy. Because there is more glycogen in the muscle, its stores are not depleted as quickly, so the horse has more stamina. Added stamina may also be due to the fact that conditioned horses utilize body fat very efficiently.

A study was conducted with fifteen Thoroughbreds under track conditions to determine if there were benefits to feeding added fat. Horses, which had been in training and were considered to be performing at their maximum potential, were first fed a diet containing 2% fat. While on this diet, their times at 1 mile were established. The group was then switched to a diet containing 12% fat and allowed three weeks to adjust to the change. They were then raced over the same distance. Thirteen of the fifteen horses ran, on average, 1.5 seconds faster on the 12% fat diet. They also exhibited improved endurance.

Deficiency of Fat

If a horse is fed a well-balanced diet, a deficiency of essential fatty acids should not occur.

Excess of Fat

Additional fat appears to be ineffective and possibly detrimental at amounts over 12% in the concentrate portion. Most horses find feed unpalatable beyond this point, and diarrhea becomes more likely.

It has also been determined that when horses begin consuming larger quantities of fat, their blood cholesterol levels increase as well. Therefore, it is possible that extreme excesses of fat will create very high cholesterol levels in the blood.

Palatability of Fat

A slightly increased fat content in feeds may increase palatability for most horses. If horses become accustomed to a feed with a higher fat content however, it may be difficult to return them quickly to a ration that is significantly lower in fat without a corresponding loss of appetite.

Protein

Proteins are essential to life for all plants and animals. They are found in the cell walls of plants and in the cell membranes of animals, as well as in hormones, enzymes, bones, skin, hair, and muscle.

Proteins are composed of *amino acids*, which are acid compounds that link together to form protein molecules. Amino acids contain nitrogen combined with carbon, hydrogen, oxygen, usually sulfur, and sometimes phosphorus and iron. Combinations of different amino acids are joined to form specific proteins. Each type of protein maintains the same specific proportions of amino acids.

The total amount of protein in a feed is called **crude** protein. Since crude protein is not fully digestible, the amount actually obtained is called **digestible** protein. *(For more information on protein content of grains and supplements, refer to Chapter 6.)*

Functions of Protein

Protein is important in building body tissue: skin, hair, hide, muscles, connective tissue, hooves, nervous system, and skeleton. It is also a vital component of blood, enzymes, and hormones, and is required for milk production. Protein is approximately 22% of the fat-free composition of a mature horse's body.

The presence of adequate protein is essential for growth, reproduction, lactation, resistance from disease, and for repair and replacement of all body tissues. Adequate protein intake, particularly in early life, is necessary to develop the muscle essential for high performance later in life. Protein is also essential for hypertrophy (enlargement of muscle), which occurs when nitrogen is removed from the protein source and is retained in the muscle. If quantity and quality of protein provided are not adequate, full growth potential cannot be reached. However, **excess** protein intake does **not** increase genetic growth and development.

Fig. 5–16. Feeding excess protein will not cause growth above genetic potential.

Protein is not generally used to meet energy needs, because it is not very efficiently converted to energy. Conversion of protein to energy produces three to six times more heat than carbohydrates or fats, which can lead to excessive sweating and heat exhaustion during work. However, if there is not enough energy (carbohydrates and fat) in the diet, protein will be removed from tissues to supply energy to the body— instead of being used to build and maintain tissues.

Protein Requirements

There are different views among researchers about exact protein requirements of the horse. Data from the National Research Council reflects a composite offering of many ideologies concerning feeding, contributed by nutritionists from around the United States. Some researchers feel that the resulting NRC recommended protein levels for each class of horse are conservative and should be considered as minimum amounts. Combined data from researchers at several leading universities indicate higher requirements than the NRC.

Daily Protein Requirements (% of diet)		
Class	NRC Data	Data From Other Research
Foals	n/a	16–18
Weanlings	13–13.1	14–16
Yearlings	11.3	12–14

Long Yearlings:
    In training
    Not in training
	
	10.8
	10.1
		
		12–14
		12–14

2-year-olds:
    In training
    Not in training
	
	10.1
	9.4
		
		12–14
		12–14

Stallions	8.6	12–14
Pregnant Mares	8.9–9.5	12–14
Lactating Mares	10–12	12–14
Mature Working	8.8–10.3	9–11
Mature Maintenance	7.2	9–11

Fig. 5–17. For a more detailed breakdown of different classes of horses, refer to the *Nutrient Requirements Tables* in the Appendix.

Growth

Because protein is used to build new tissues for growth and reproduction, a deficiency of protein will significantly impair growth rate. If protein is deficient in the diet, any amount taken from body tissues will be used to maintain body functions, and none will be available to provide fuel for growth.

Physical Activity

Prolonged heavy work and special stresses, such as racing, increase protein needs in the diet only slightly. In fact, it is the energy requirement that is greatly increased (and protein is not an efficient source of energy). If the **energy** requirement is met by increasing the concentrate intake, the protein requirements will be met as well.

Young horses in training are more sensitive to protein deficiency and must be fed sufficient protein to meet growth requirements (10.1% – 14% crude protein).

All requirements, as given, should be used only as a guide, and final adjustments must depend on the horse's appearance and condition.

Protein Quality

Amino Acids

More than 20 amino acids have been discovered. Each has unique characteristics, but can also fit into an almost limitless assortment of proteins. Growth, development, and almost every bodily function depend upon protein, and the quality of protein depends upon the correct supply of amino acids. In order for tissue formation to occur, all of the essential amino acids must be in the digestive tract simultaneously.

Amino acids are any of a class of organic compounds which result from protein hydrolysis. Amino acids are made up of nitrogen that is combined with carbon, hydrogen, oxygen, and occasionally sulfur, phosphorus, and iron. A short chain of amino acids is called a peptide. When many amino acids are joined together in a long chain, a protein is formed.

The study of amino acids is relatively new, even in the human body. New amino acids are being discovered, and as those already known are researched further, their therapeutic significance will become more evident. Selective use of amino acids can influence such physiological functions as detoxification of heavy metals and enhanced mental function through stimulation of neurotransmitters.

Essential Amino Acids

An essential amino acid is one which the body is unable to synthesize sufficiently for itself, and, therefore, which must be provided in the diet. There are ten essential amino acids (EAA) that can be synthesized to some degree in the cecum and colon, but not in the quantities needed to meet the horse's needs.

Based on studies which include research on other species, the essential amino acids for the equine are believed to be:

- lysine
- methionine
- tryptophan
- valine
- histidine
- phenylalanine
- leucine
- isoleucine
- threonine
- arginine.

(Each individual horse and circumstance will determine specific amino acid needs.)

Studies have shown that lysine is a limiting amino acid because its absence causes growth depression. It is also more likely than any of the other amino acids to be deficient, so it is termed the **first** limiting amino acid. Lysine is necessary in the diet of foals and young growing equines. Without it, the growth rate is slower than normal. The lysine requirement for weanlings is 0.55% of the daily diet.

Amino Acids and their General Functions*

Lysine	essential for growth, aids in formation of antibodies to control viral infection, important in fat metabolism
Methionine	antioxidant, relieves arthritic symptoms, detoxifies liver, essential for selenium bioavailability
Tryptophan	mood stabilizer, promotes sleep when combined with magnesium and vitamin B_6, pain killer, may help treat arthritis
Valine	vital for muscle coordination, mental and neural function, helps treat inflammation, normalizes nitrogen balance
Histidine	helps treat arthritis, necessary for growth, antioxidant, stimulates production of red and white blood cells
Phenylalanine	antidepressant, pain reliever, precursor of tyrosine, treats symptoms of rheumatoid arthritis
Leucine	decreases degradation of muscle protein
Isoleucine	assists in formation of hemoglobin, helps treat nervous system degeneration
Threonine	may be essential for mental health, required for digestive tract function, prevents fat accumulation in liver
Arginine	promotes growth, accelerates wound and burn healing, inhibits development of tumors
Tyrosine	antidepressant, aids in normal brain function, supplies neurotransmitters
Serine	involved in skin cell metabolism, moistening agent for skin
Carnitine	stimulates protein synthesis during stress, may accelerate fatty acid oxidation, which decreases lactic acid production
Citrulline	major component of urea cycle, antioxidant, treats fatigue, precursor of arginine
Alanine	aids immune system, metabolizes tryptophan and pyridoxine (B_6), may be used as a source of glucose
Glycine	synthesis of bile acids, may be useful for treating muscular, skin, and connective tissue degeneration when used with other amino acids
Glutamine	used by muscles to convert pyruvate to alanine, decreasing lactic acid production
Hydroxyproline	constituent of collagen (a protein), accelerates wound healing
Proline	component of muscle and connective tissue, accelerates wound healing, essential for skin health
Cystine	detoxifier, maintains health of hair coat, helps treat skin problems
Aspartic acid	protective functions for liver, detoxifier, relieves fatigue
Taurine	neurotransmitter, helps heart muscle function better, influences insulin and blood sugar levels

Fig. 5–18.   *Not necessarily specific to horses.*

Non-essential Amino Acids

Certain amino acids can be synthesized sufficiently from other amino acids and nutrients in the digestive tract, making it unnecessary to provide them in the diet. These are termed non-essential amino acids (NEAA). The following are some of the known non-essential amino acids:

- alanine
- aspartic acid
- carnitine
- citrulline
- cystine
- glutamine
- glycine
- hydroxyproline
- proline
- serine
- taurine
- tyrosine

Amino Acids and the Performance Horse

Studies have shown that specific amino acid supplementation can benefit the performance horse by increasing energy supplies, decreasing lactic acid concentrations, and lowering heart rates. This allows a higher level of work intensity and also delays onset of fatigue.

Research into the effects of amino acid supplementation is still in its infancy, but current findings indicate that it will be of increasing importance to the performance horse in the future. *(See more information in Chapter 7.)*

Fig. 5–19. Studies have shown specific amino acid supplementation can benefit the performance horse.

Protein Sources and Supplements

When formulating a ration, it is necessary to consider protein quality (amino acid makeup) as well as quantity in the feed. All feedstuffs do not supply the same balance of amino acids in their protein. For this reason, a ration containing only a few ingredients, such as hay and oats, may not contain a good **variety** of amino acids. It is advantageous to include several different grains and/or add protein sources, such as oilseed meals.

Oilseed meals are especially good sources of most of the essential amino acids. Of the oilseed meals, soybean meal contains the highest quality, followed by cottonseed meal and linseed meal. *(See Chapter 6 for detailed coverage.)*

Feed processing and handling methods can influence protein quality and digestibility. If the processing temperature is too high, the number of amino acids will be significantly reduced. Inadequate drying prior to storage may also reduce amino acid content.

Digestibility and quality of protein will vary with the source. For example, corn protein, due to its structure, is very difficult to digest. Milk protein, on the other hand (when fed to young equines), has been demonstrated to be of superior quality when compared to soybean meal, cottonseed meal, linseed meal, and brewers dried grains. However, horses over three years old lack the necessary enzyme to digest lactose (milk sugar). Feeding milk products to these horses will predispose them to gastric disturbances, such as colic.

A good quality protein will contain a wide variety of amino acids, including all the essential ones. In the diets of young horses, it is especially important for growth that protein contain the required amounts of lysine. Grains and linseed meal are known to be low in lysine, while soybean meal is considered to be a good source of lysine.

Essential Amino Acid Content of Common Grains						
	Oats	Corn	Barley	Wheat	Rye	Milo
Lysine	0.4	0.2	0.4	0.4	0.4	0.26
Methionine	0.2	0.1	0.16	0.2	0.16	0.5
Tryptophan	0.15	0.08	0.1	0.14	0.14	0.4
Valine	0.7	0.3	0.6	0.7	*	0.5
Histidine	0.2	0.2	0.2	0.2	*	0.2
Phenylalanine	0.7	0.4	0.6	0.8	*	0.3
Leucine	1.0	0.9	0.8	1.0	*	1.4
Isoleucine	0.7	0.4	0.5	0.7	*	0.6
Threonine	0.4	0.3	0.4	0.4	*	0.1
Arginine	0.7	0.4	0.6	0.7	0.5	0.4

Fig. 5–20.   * = not available

(High protein supplements are discussed in Chapter 6. For protein and lysine content of feeds and supplements, see Tables in the Appendix.)

Protein Deficiency

A protein deficiency in young horses will result in decreased growth rate and slow development. Prolonged deficiencies can actually stunt the growth of a young horse.

In a mature horse, protein deficiency will cause a decrease in appetite and feed consumption. After a certain period, the horse will lose weight, its hair coat will become rough and poor in appearance, and hoof growth will be retarded. In a case of prolonged deficiency, protein will be removed from tissues in the body. The result will be a wasted appearance similar to muscle *atrophy.*

A reserve supply of protein is not stored in the body to any great extent for later use, as are carbohydrates, fats, and some other nutrients. Therefore a prolonged protein deficiency is detrimental.

In the pregnant mare, a protein deficiency will impair fetal development, resulting in the birth of small, weak foals. Milk production will also decrease. Both situations impair growth and development of the foal. Broodmares whose diets are deficient in protein will also experience lower conception rates.

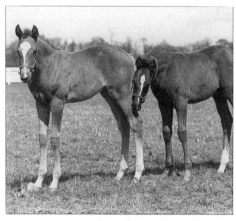

Fig. 5–21. Proper growth and development of young equines depend on adequate protein in their diet.

Sick foals often suffer from protein-calorie malnutrition, an imbalance of protein to calories caused by insufficient energy or protein. Adequate protein is needed for fighting infection and healing wounds.

Protein Excess

Excess protein can serve as a source of energy or can be stored as fat. However, it is expensive to feed protein to provide energy or fat. Also, conversion of protein to energy is not efficient and may be harmful.

Excess protein will increase the horse's water requirements because waste products of protein metabolism require large quantities of water when they are excreted in the urine. Because of this, some horsemen believe that excess protein will strain the kidney. No evidence exists to support the claim that kidney disease can be caused by protein excess if the kidney is initially healthy.

Extreme excesses of protein can cause increased stress on the horse's metabolic systems, because additional energy must be used to remove the waste products of protein metabolism from the body. In a study of endurance horses, excess protein caused an increase in heart rate, respiration rate, and sweating. Feeding excess protein to endurance horses is also known to increase losses of vital electrolytes and water through sweat and urine, which can impair performance.

Excess protein may cause increased urination of calcium, resulting in a calcium deficiency. In growing horses, this could lead to bone disorders such as epiphysitis and contracted flexor tendons.

6

GRAINS, HIGH PROTEIN CONCENTRATES, and OTHER ADDITIVES

GRAINS

Grains are the most common sources of energy fed to horses. Types of grains include oats, corn, barley, wheat, rye, milo, spelt, and triticale. They contain more simple (readily digestible) carbohydrates, and therefore more digestible energy (DE) per pound than forages. Grains are a good source of protein, although the protein is low in lysine (an important amino acid for growth) compared to forages.

Most grains can be fed to horses if fed in correct forms (some require processing) and proportions. To feed grains properly, it is important to measure by **weight,** because weights of different grains vary widely relative to volume (e.g. a quart of corn weighs more than a quart of oats).

Grains may be fed to horses alone or as part of a *concentrate.* The term "concentrate" denotes the non-forage portion of the ration which includes grains and any other component(s), such as soybean meal, molasses, vegetable oil, etc.

Grains should be free of mold and foreign materials to ensure high quality. Farms that purchase high volumes of grain or grow their own, often purchase a commercial grain cleaner to further improve quality.

High quality grains are characterized by high weight per bushel, low moisture content, and a very low percentage of damaged or discolored kernels. Grains are assigned grade numbers according to quality.

Oats

Advantages of Feeding Oats

Oats form the basis of many horse feeding programs because they are readily available, nutritious, palatable, and safe to feed. When compared to most other commonly fed grains, oats contain more protein, minerals, and fat.

Oats contain about 11% crude fiber, which is high compared to other grains. This makes them less energy dense, making them safer to feed. When the primary grain in a ration is oats, instead of an energy dense grain such as corn, horses will be less likely to founder, colic, or become obese. When switching from an energy dense grain however, more oats are required to meet energy demands.

Processed oats have good keeping qualities when compared to most other grains—and whole oats can be stored even longer.

Fig. 6–1. When the primary grain in a ration is oats, instead of an energy dense grain such as corn, horses will be less likely to founder, colic, or become obese.

Judging the Quality of Oats

Oats can be quite variable in quality. The best oats are plump, heavy, clean, ripe, and have a high proportion of kernel to hull. They should also appear bright in color. Oats are commonly white, but they may also be black or gray. Their color will depend on the area where they were grown and on the particular variety. Contrary to popular opinion, color does not affect the quality of the oat. A gray or black oat should not be considered inferior if that is its **natural** color. Bleaching oats may decrease their nutrient content.

Weight

Weight is a factor normally used when judging the quality of oats. The average weight of oats is 32 pounds per bushel. The heavier weight per bushel, the greater proportion of kernel to hull. Oats, on average, will contain about 30% hulls. Since the main nutrient content of oats is contained in the kernel, a heavier oat will contain more nutrients. Oats with a large percentage of hull are higher in fiber and lower in energy and protein. To increase weight per bushel, ends of the oats can be removed. This is called "clipping." In the clipping process, the points of the oat hull are cut off by machine and separated

Grades and Grade Requirements for Oats					
	Minimum limits		Maximum limits		
Grade	Pounds per bushel	Sound oats (%)	Heat-damaged (%)	Foreign material (%)	Wild Oats (%)
U.S. No. 1	36.0	97.0	0.1	2.0	2.0
U.S. No. 2	33.0	94.0	0.3	3.0	3.0
U.S. No. 3*	30.0	90.0	1.0	4.0	5.0
U.S. No. 4†	27.0	80.0	3.0	5.0	10.0

*Oats that are slightly weathered are graded no higher than U.S. No. 3.
†Oats that are badly stained or materially weathered are graded no higher than U.S. No. 4.

Fig. 6–2.

by a blast of air. Clipped oats are not considered "processed."

Top quality, very clean oats—which have a weight of 42 or more pounds per bushel—are often called "racehorse" oats. The name developed because racehorse trainers commonly use these heavy, high quality oats. The amount of energy compared to the fiber content makes them useful in feeding high performance horses. Oats weighing less per bushel can still be good quality oats—however, more fiber is ingested (by weight) relative to energy and other nutrients when compared to the heavier oat. Therefore, more oats by **volume** of the lighter varieties need to be fed to meet nutrient requirements.

Dust and Odor

Cleanliness of the oat is a factor in its nutritive value. Oats should be cleaned and recleaned at the mill until foreign materials, weed seeds, and broken or inferior kernels are removed. Dusty oats are of low quality, indicating that they were not properly cleaned or stored. They may also aggravate respiratory problems, such as *heaves.*

High quality grains will smell fresh—there should be no musty odor associated with them. Mustiness indicates age or the presence of too much moisture. Both factors represent poor keeping quality.

When choosing oats, it is best to buy the highest quality oats available, even if they must be shipped in. Specially ordered oats may have to be bought in bulk amounts to get reasonable prices. If finding a grain dealer who will handle this is not possible, forming a co-op with other horsemen is an alternative.

Top quality oats are palatable and have a high nutrient content. In any case, differences in price per ration will not be great. An increase in price when buying top quality oats (and heavier oats when needed) is usually a good investment in improved performance.

Forms of Oats

Oats may be fed either whole or processed. Different methods of processing include crimping, steam-rolling, and crushing. The merits of processed oats compared to whole oats have been debated for many years. While there are valid arguments for both sides, it is generally concluded that whole oats are more beneficial.

Whole oats are the natural form of a nutritious, easily digestible grain. They are palatable, nourishing, and have good keeping qualities in their natural state. Unlike other grains, such as barley, oats can be easily chewed and properly digested without processing.

Processing the oat breaks its outer coating and makes the kernel and nutrients more accessible to digestive juices. This reduces chewing requirements slightly, and may increase digestibility slightly. However, it also exposes nutrients to deteriorating effects of the air.

Fig. 6–3. On the left are crimped oats; on the right are whole oats with clipped ends.

The aging process is accelerated, and nutrients are lost more rapidly.

Extended storage should be avoided when feeding processed oats. Aging destroys vitamins and increases perishability. This can possibly cause the concentrate portion of a ration to become deficient in essential nutrients. Further, processed oats are more subject to fermentation and deterioration, with subsequent loss in palatability and quality. Whole oats can be stored for several months, whereas processed oats should be fed within two to three weeks after processing.

Unless grains are processed on the premises where they are fed, their freshness cannot be guaranteed. Also, processing increases their cost, and the increase in feeding value is slight.

Some processed oats are flavored with molasses. Since oats are highly palatable, this is unnecessary, and might serve to disguise the flavor of poor quality oats. *(Sweet feeds are a different situation. They have molasses added to reduce dust problems associated with the finer ground components.)*

Processed oats may be advantageous for:

- young foals
- older horses with poor teeth
- horses recovering from illness or surgery

If oats are processed, crimping is usually considered the best method. (As mentioned, clipped oats are not considered processed oats, and the clipping process does not reduce their nutrient value.)

Nutrient Value of Oats

Average good quality oats contain 12% crude protein (calculated by weight), and 5% fat. They contain about 70% TDN (total digestible nutrients) and 11% crude fiber. These figures will vary relative to weight per bushel. Laboratory analysis is useful in determining actual proportion of fiber in the hull when this information is required.

Oats contain about 1.3 megacalories of DE (digestible energy) per pound, and their carbohydrate content is about 60%. They are low in calcium and moderately low in phosphorus. Oats contain virtually no *carotene*, and are not a good source of B vitamins. If they are harvested when fully ripe, the moisture content is about 10%.

Other Facts

Oats are grasses of the cereal group. There are numerous varieties, and they may be grown throughout the world. The best varieties are grown in cool, moist climates, such as in Canada and the northern plains of the United States. Oats from these areas tend to be higher in weight and nutrient value than oats grown in warmer climates. Oats may be home grown easily, but unless the soil and climate are ideal, quality will be sacrificed. Adequate fertilization is also required.

Oats may also be grown for a hay crop. When grown for hay, oats should be cut in the soft-dough stage. This is the point at which the seeds are fully formed, but are not yet mature and hard. When grown for grain, oats should not be harvested until they are fully ripe and the straw is no longer green.

Naked Oats

A new high energy variety of oats, called naked oats, has been developed. These oats are lower in fiber than conventional oats, because they are grown without hulls. These oats offer a reduced transportation cost per unit of digestible energy, and they require less storage space than conventional oats.

A typeof naked oats, called Pennuda, has been developed at Pennsylvania State University. Research shows that Pennuda oats contain 42% more protein and only 46% as much neutral detergent fiber (NDF) as conventional oats, and they average 52 pounds per bushel. They also have higher digestibility of dry matter, energy, NDF, hemicellulose, and protein than conventional oats.

Digestible energy of Pennuda oats is about 20% more than regular oats. They are an excellent source of energy, but the same care should be taken when feeding naked oats as with any high energy grain.

Corn

Advantages of Feeding Corn

Corn is the most widely grown cereal grain in the United States. Corn can be easily produced for local use since it grows well almost anywhere and is a relatively inexpensive crop to maintain. It is second only to oats in its use as a feed grain for horses. (Mixing corn with oats to gain the advantages of both grains is a common procedure.)

An average bushel of shelled corn will weigh approximately 56 pounds. Corn contains a large concentration of soluble carbohydrates, making it a high energy feed. Because it is also very low in fiber, care must be taken not to overfeed corn, especially when it is first introduced into a horse's diet. It is recommended that small amounts be fed first, with gradual increases over a few weeks, in order to avoid founder, colic, and other gastric disturbances.

It is important that corn be fed by **weight,** not volume. A given volume of corn will contain twice the digestible energy as the same volume of oats. If this is not taken into consideration, overfeeding can occur which could cause digestive disturbances or obesity.

Judging the Quality of Corn

Corn is judged primarily on its moisture content and percentage of unsound kernels. Although there are several types of corn grown in the United States, the type usually fed to horses is dent corn. It is called this simply because the mature kernel has a dent in its surface when dry. Use of other types as feeds for horses is not common, because their kernels are either too hard after drying, or the starch has an undesirable texture and content.

Corn is the only common horse grain which contains significant levels of carotene, a *precursor* of vitamin A. Color of corn may range from white to yellow, and this does not affect quality as long as the corn is ripe and doesn't have a pronounced green color. Yellow corn does have a higher carotene content, however.

Grades and Grade Requirements for Corn				
		Maximum limits of		
		Damaged kernels		
Grade	Minimum pounds per bushel	Heat-damaged kernels (%)	Total (%)	Broken corn and foreign material (%)
U.S. No. 1	56.0	0.1	3.0	2.0
U.S. No. 2	54.0	0.2	5.0	3.0
U.S. No. 3	52.0	0.5	7.0	4.0
U.S. No. 4	49.0	1.0	10.0	5.0
U.S. No. 5	46.0	3.0	15.0	7.0

Fig. 6–4.

The higher the quality of corn, the fewer damaged kernels there will be. This can be easily determined by visual inspection of the unprocessed grains. Kernels of shelled corn should be plump and firm, but they should not be too hard. Very hard corn is difficult to chew and may pass through the digestive tract undigested. Kernels of ear corn (on the cob) should be separated slightly, not tightly packed together. Naturally, shelled corn requires much less storage space than ear corn, but it is more perishable and should be protected from light and moisture.

Musty odor indicates a high moisture content, which increases perishability. Corn which shows signs of mold or insect damage should not be fed. Moldy corn may contain toxins such as *fusarium*, which can cause brain damage, and *aflatoxins*, which cause liver and brain damage and possibly death. Symptoms of moldy corn toxicity include visual problems, disinterest in feed, and agitation. Horses afflicted with this toxicity may walk aimlessly into stationary objects. Since corn is high in starch, it can ferment rapidly and become toxic if damaged.

Forms of Corn

Corn may be fed as ear corn, whole shelled kernel corn, cracked, or crushed. However, it should **never** be finely ground, because it becomes excessively dusty. When corn is fed as whole ears, horses tend to chew it more slowly and mix it with saliva more thoroughly before swallowing. This increases the percentage of nutrients assimilated. Whole ears will also keep much longer than shelled or processed corn. Of course greater storage area is required for whole ear corn.

Since horses will eat shelled or processed corn more rapidly than whole ear corn, the tendency to colic may increase slightly. Aged horses with dental problems may be unable to chew and properly digest whole shelled or ear corn, so processing may be necessary.

Corn is often cracked (rolled) or crushed before feeding. This greatly increases digestibility, but it also lowers keeping quality. Of these two forms, cracked corn is better. Cracking corn is accomplished by rolling it lightly with heavy rollers. This cracks the outside of the kernel, which allows easier mastication and provides more surface area for penetration of digestive juices. Because kernels are not fully broken, they are not as likely to deteriorate as crushed corn.

When corn is crushed or ground, the particles are smaller than when cracked. This increases tendency towards rapid fermentation in the digestive tract and the possibility of colic. Unless a horse has very poor teeth or a digestive problem, cracked corn is sufficiently processed.

Occasionally, corn is ground and mixed with ground cobs. This increases fiber content, and lowers energy and overall nutrient value.

Fig. 6–5. Corn in ground, cracked and whole forms.

Nutrient Value of Corn

Composition of corn may vary among different regions of the United States, due to differences in the soil. If bought from a reputable, quality-conscious company, it is usually fairly standard in value. If it is home-grown, it should be laboratory tested to determine its nutrient content.

Corn contains only about 7% to 10% crude protein (about the same level of protein found in average to good quality grass forages). Protein in corn is also **low quality** because it is deficient in several essential amino acids, notably *lysine*, which is essential for growth.

The amount of crude protein in *hybrid* corn may be even lower, due to higher yields and heavier planting rates. Corn also tends to be sightly lower in calcium when compared to oats.

Corn can be a valuable ingredient in the total ration, but if it is used as the primary grain, a protein supplement or high-protein hay should always be fed. This is especially true for growing horses, for which protein requirements are high and protein quality is critical.

Corn contains about 2% crude fiber, making it highly digestible. It contains from 65% to 75% starch, which is a higher percentage than other cereal grains. It is high in energy, containing 1.8 Mcal of digestible energy (DE) per pound, and it has a TDN value of 80%. Corn contains about 3.6% fat. It supplies a moderate quantity of vitamin E, and it is a good source of thiamine, niacin, and riboflavin.

For many years, corn was considered a "hot" feed because it was believed that it caused a horse to overheat or sweat and should only be fed in winter. It is true that corn is high in energy, but this does not cause an increase in body temperature. In fact, corn gives off 41% of its gross energy as heat, while oats give off 66% gross energy as heat.

The major advantage of corn is its high energy content. Of course if an excess of energy is fed, it will cause weight gain (which can cause excessive sweating), and possibly digestive disturbances. *(Refer to Chapter 5 for more information on energy.)*

Barley

An average bushel of high quality barley will weigh about 47 pounds and contain about 78% TDN. In the U. S., barley is commonly grown, but the amount produced is only 5% of the amount of corn grown. Barley grown on the West Coast contains more fiber and is therefore lower in TDN. It is also lower in protein than barley grown in other regions.

Barley is used as a grain for many horses because it is inexpensive and plentiful in most areas of the United States, except in hot, humid climates. It also has good nutritional value. Barley has a low percentage of hull, and is therefore classified as a "heavy" feed. Barley is not as widely available as oats, and because of low fiber content (5% – 6%) it may cause digestive disturbances if not carefully fed.

Barley is more energy dense than oats, but less so than corn, and generally contains about 12% crude protein. It also contains 1.8% fat and 1.49 Mcal of DE per pound.

Grades and Grade Requirements for Barley

Grade	Min. limits of		Maximum limits of				
	Pounds per bushel	Sound barley (%)	Damaged kernels (%)	Heat-damaged kernels (%)	Foreign material (%)	Broken kernels (%)	Thin barley (%)
U.S. No. 1	47.0	97.0	2.0	0.2	1.0	4.0	10.0
U.S. No. 2	45.0	94.0	4.0	0.3	2.0	8.0	15.0
U.S. No. 3	43.0	90.0	6.0	0.5	3.0	12.0	25.0
U.S. No. 4	40.0	85.0	8.0	1.0	4.0	18.0	35.0
U.S. No. 5	36.0	75.0	10.0	3.0	5.0	28.0	75.0

Fig. 6–6.

Good barley should be clean, heavy, ripe, and free from weed seeds and foreign material. Hulls should be small and light, and the kernels should appear full and plump. Many nutrient values of barley resemble those of oats; however, barley is higher in niacin and is a fairly good source of this vitamin.

Barley is normally crushed or ground since it is a hard grain and is difficult to chew. When it is crushed or ground, it should be mixed with a bulkier feed, such as oats or corn; otherwise, it may cause a tendency to colic. The amount of barley in the concentrate portion of the ration should not exceed 50%.

Occasionally, barley is fed in a steam-rolled form and is often included as an ingredient in "sweet feeds," where it does not form a major part of the ration. Barley tends to be less palatable than oats, so it may be desirable to mix it gradually into a ration in increasing proportions until the horses become accustomed to it.

Barley may also be fed to horses in the form of dried brewers grains, brewers yeast, and dried distillers grains. (Distillers grains usually contain other grains in addition to barley.) These are by-products of brewing and distilling industries.

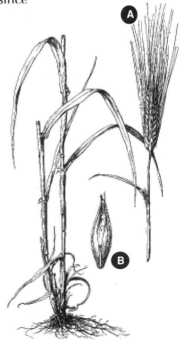

Fig. 6–7. (A) is the barley seed head, and (B) the individual kernel.

In the past, it was believed that brewers by-products had a low feeding value and nutrient content due to the heavy processing they undergo. It is now known that brewers by-products provide additional digestible energy, protein, minerals, and vitamins. Barley is also higher in lysine content than most grains. In addition, brewers yeast is an excellent source of the B-complex vitamins, notably thiamine. Generally, these products will contain about 27% protein, 7% fat, and 16% fiber, and can be used only on a supplemental basis. They should never be relied on exclusively as a feed.

Wheat

Wheat is a dense, small, expensive grain. Its use for horses is limited because it is generally processed for flour, and only its by-products are available as feedstuffs. Like barley, it is a "heavy" feed. An average bushel of wheat can weigh 60 pounds and contain about 80% total digestible nutrients. Its crude fiber content is 2.4%, fat content is 1.6%, its crude protein content is 11.4%, and it contains 1.55 Mcal of DE per pound.

Wheat fed to horses should be rolled, cracked, or steam flaked to improve digestibility. Wheat should **not be ground,** because it becomes gummy due to the presence of *gluten,* an elastic protein substance. Ground wheat will form a doughy mass in the stomach, which can lead to colic. When wheat is included in a ration, it should be combined with bulkier feeds, such as oats.

Wheat By-Products

Two forms of wheat used in equine diets are wheat bran and wheat middlings, both of which are by-products of the milling industry.

Wheat Bran

Bran is the shiny, dark-colored coating of the wheat kernel, in flake form. Because of its laxative qualities, wheat bran is often fed in small amounts to prevent constipation and impaction (usually about 5% – 20% of the concentrate portion of the diet).

Wheat bran contains about 67% TDN. It is high in organic phosphorus, containing about 1.13%. It contains about 15% crude protein, 3.8% fat, about 10% crude fiber, and 1.33 Mcal of DE per pound.

Wheat bran should never be considered a primary feed, and should form only a small part of the ration. It can be fed in the form of a mash or mixed with other feeds. Wheat bran mashes are considered useful because they cause water consumption to increase, which will in turn prevent feed from collecting in the digestive tract.

Wheat bran contains high concentrations of phosphorus, which, if fed in large amounts, may cause the calcium to phosphorus ratio to become inverted. This can lead to metabolic bone diseases. *(For more information on the calcium to phosphorus ratio, see Chapter 4.)*

Wheat Middlings

Middlings are fine particles of wheat kernels obtained in the milling process. They generally contain 7.8% or less crude fiber, depending on the variety of wheat. Since the husk portion is not included, they are higher in crude protein than whole wheat (16.4%), and they are a good source of niacin, thiamine, and riboflavin. They have a TDN value of 77.2% and contain 4.2% fat and 1.38 Mcal of DE per pound.

Because wheat middlings are fine and powdery, it is difficult to judge their quality by their appearance. Wheat middlings also tend to pack in the stomach and cause digestive disturbances. Therefore, they should be mixed with a coarser, bulkier feed. These factors, together with limited availability, are why wheat middlings are not more widely fed. It is possible to obtain the same nutrients more easily from other feed sources without the risks.

Fig. 6–8. (A) wheat seed head, (B) individual kernel.

Wheat Mill Run

Another by-product of wheat processing occasionally used in feeds is wheat mill run. The digestible energy content of wheat mill run in most cases is comparable to that of wheat.

Rye

Rye is grown as a crop for the milling industry and is a key ingredient in the production of flour and whiskey. In most cases, the only rye products available for feeding horses are mill by-products, and these are usually only available in milling areas.

Rye middlings are the most commonly fed form of rye. These are fine particles of the kernel left after the whole rye grain is milled into flour. Rye middlings have a crude fiber content of 5.2% and must be fed in a finely ground form. They contain 72% TDN, 16.6% crude protein, and 3.4% fat. Like wheat middlings, they must be mixed with a bulkier feed to prevent gastric disturbances.

Grades and Grade Requirements for Rye						
		Maximum limits of				
	Minimum	Foreign matter		Damaged kernels		Thin
Grade	pounds	Other than	Total	Heat-	Total	Kernels
	per bushel	wheat (%)	(%)	damaged (%)	(%)	(%)
U.S. No. 1	56.0	1.0	3.2	0.2	2.0	10.0
U.S. No. 2	54.0	2.0	6.0	0.2	4.0	15.0
U.S. No. 3	52.0	4.0	10.0	0.5	7.0	25.0
U.S. No. 4	49.0	6.0	10.0	3.0	15.0	–

Fig. 6–9.

Rye can be contaminated with *ergot,* a dark purple fungus which contains high concentrations of *alkaloids.* This fungus may induce abortion in mares, but this has not been scientifically proven.

Rye middlings are not a good source of any particular vitamins or minerals, and their **digestible** protein content (12% to 13%) can be matched by other more palatable and nutritious grains. If fed, it should not exceed 20% of the concentrate portion of the diet.

Milo

Milo is a variety of sorghum grain. Sorghum grains have composition and feeding values similar to corn. Milo and other sorghums of today, which have been improved through research, are more resistant to insects and more nutritionally valuable than old varieties. Milo is grown primarily in dry areas of the plains states and Texas.

Milo grows low to the ground and has heavy seed heads when it ripens. It is divided into classes based on the color of these seed heads, which may be yellow, white, or brown. Brown seeds may contain high levels of tannic acid, which cause unpalatability.

Crude protein content of milo varies from 8% to 16%, but it is usually around 11.5%. It is low in crude fiber (about 2.6%), and contains about 2.7% fat. Since it is high in carbohydrates (about 75%), it is considered to be a high energy feed. It has a TDN value of 79.4% and contains 1.46 Mcal of DE per pound, but is not a good source of vitamins or minerals.

On a nutritional basis milo is similar to corn, except that it contains less carotene. It is also slightly less palatable. Milo is a high energy feed and must be fed carefully to avoid colic and founder.

Unprocessed milo is difficult to chew. If milo is in a ration, it should be coarsely ground, rolled, or crimped. The amount of milo in the concentrate portion of a ration should not exceed 30%.

As mentioned above, some milo is relatively unpalatable to horses and should be tested for tannic acid before purchasing. A simple bleach test can be performed to determine the presence of tannic acid. Bleach is added to a small amount of kernels and heated, then rinsed with water and dried. If this yields white kernels with no brown color, there is no tannic acid present. If there is a brown tint, it has a low tannic acid content, but should not affect taste much. If the kernels are very brown, there is a high tannic acid content and they should not be fed.

Grades and Grade Requirements for Milo				
		Maximum limits of		
		Damaged kernels		Broken Kernels
Grade	Minimum pounds per bushel	Heat damaged (%)	Total (%)	foreign material and other grains (%)
U.S. No. 1	57.0	0.2	2.0	4.0
U.S. No. 2	55.0	0.5	5.0	8.0
U.S. No. 3	53.0	1.0	10.0	12.0
U.S. No. 4	51.0	3.0	15.0	15.0

Fig. 6–10.

Spelt

Spelt is a relative of wheat and is encased in a large fibrous hull. Spelt contains 9.1% crude fiber, and the amount of digestible energy it contains is slightly lower than that of oats. It contains 1.9% fat and 12.0% crude protein. Only a limited amount of spelt is produced.

Triticale

Triticale is a hybrid of wheat and rye. This cross was made to produce a plant with the quality of wheat and the hardiness of rye. Triticale contains 4.0% crude fiber, 1.1% fat, and 15.0% crude protein. Except in areas of the world where soils are poor, little of this crop is grown. The ergot fungus is also known to contaminate triticale.

Nutrient Composition of Common Grains and Grain Products

	Oats	Corn	Barley	Wheat	Wheat Bran	Wheat Middlings	Rye Middlings	Milo	Spelt	Triticale
Crude Protein (%)	12.5	9.10	11.7	11.4	15.4	16.4	16.6	11.50	12.0	15.0
Lysine (%)	0.44	0.25	0.40	0.34	0.56	0.68	na	0.26	na	na
Fiber (%)	10.8	2.20	4.90	2.4	10.0	7.8	5.2	2.60	9.1	4.0
Ash (%)	3.0	1.30	2.40	1.8	5.9	4.6	na	1.70	na	na
Calcium (%)	0.05	0.05	0.05	0.03	0.13	0.13	na	0.04	na	na
Phosphorus (%)	0.34	0.27	0.34	0.36	1.13	0.89	na	0.32	na	na
Magnesium (%)	0.12	0.11	0.13	0.12	0.56	0.34	na	0.15	na	na
Potassium (%)	0.38	0.32	0.44	0.35	1.22	0.98	na	0.37	na	na
Sodium (%)	na	0.03	0.03	0.01	0.05	0.02	na	0.01	na	na
Sulfur (%)	na	0.11	0.15	0.13	0.21	0.17	na	0.13	na	na
Fat (%)	5.0	3.6	1.8	1.6	3.8	4.2	3.4	2.7	1.9	1.1
TDN (%)	70.0	80.0	78.0	80.0	67.0	77.2	72.0	79.4	na	na
Carbohydrates (%)	60.0	65.0	na	na	na	na	na	75.0	na	na
Copper mg/kg	5.8	3.70	8.20	5.7	12.6	15.9	na	5.40	na	na
Iodine mg/kg	na	na	0.04	na	0.07	0.11	na	na	na	na
Iron mg/kg	83.0	31.0	73.53	40	145	90.0	na	57.0	na	na
Manganese mg/kg	37.0	5.00	16.0	32	119	114	na	12.0	na	na
Selenium mg/kg	0.20	0.12	0.18	0.04	0.51	0.74	na	0.41	na	na
Zinc mg/kg	35.0	19.0	17.0	34.0	98.0	97.0	na	27.0	na	na
Cobalt mg/kg	na	0.13	0.17	0.10	0.07	0.10	na	0.27	na	na
Digestible Energy mg/lb	1.3	1.8	1.49	1.55	1.33	1.38	1.46	na	na	na

na = data not available

Fig. 6–11.   Adapted from *Nutrient Requirements of Horses*

HIGH PROTEIN CONCENTRATES

In some cases, cereal grains and high quality hay will not provide enough protein for particular classes of horses. Examples are: growing horses, mares in the last three months of pregnacy, and lactating mares. For these horses, a concentrate should be provided that includes protein supplements. *(The term "concentrate" denotes the portion of a ration which primarily contains grains, but may also include non-grain components.)* Protein supplements, added to the concentrate ration, can be derived either from plant or animal sources.

Fig. 6–12. Protein supplementation is required to meet the needs of growing equines.

Protein supplements should be used in addition to good quality feeds when: 1) a ration lacks the amount of required protein, or 2) to provide a better variety of amino acids in an otherwise well balanced diet. Supplements should bring the ration's protein content and quality up to the level required for the class of horse being fed.

Many commercial supplements are available to raise the protein content of rations. There are methods for judging quality:

1) It should be a complete source of protein, not lacking any essential amino acids, including: lysine, tryptophan, methionine, valine, histidine, phenylalanine, leucine, isoleucine, threonine, and arginine. *(Recent research has indicated some specific amino acids can be supplemented to improve performance. See chapters 5 and 7 for more information.)*
2) Reputation of the company is as important as the ingredients.
3) Cost should be reasonable for amount of protein per pound when compared to other protein supplements.
4) It should not contain unnecessary ingredients.
5) It should be palatable.

Plant Sources of Protein Supplements
Oilseed Meals

Oilseed meals (also called oilmeals) are by-products of their respective industries. Oilseed meals contain 32% – 50% protein, but not all have a good variety of amino acids, and they are low in fiber. They can be fed to offset protein deficiencies and to balance rations, but they should never be fed as a major feed source. Because they are so high in protein, oilseed meals should be introduced to a horse's ration gradually to avoid digestive upsets.

Soybean Meal

The most commonly fed protein supplement is soybean meal, because it is rich in crude protein (44%) and contains high levels of lysine, methionine, and threonine. (These three amino acids are particularly beneficial in the diets of growing horses.) It is also a good source of phosphorus, a fair source of calcium, and provides moderate amounts of riboflavin and thiamine.

Soybean meal is highly digestible (80% TDN), low in crude fiber (3% – 7%), readily available, and economical in price per unit of protein. By adding it to a horse's diet in appropriate amounts, it will improve the protein quality of a ration. Soybean meal contains 1.4% fat, and 1.43 Mcal DE per pound.

Soybean meal should have a clean, light colored appearance and should not taste raw or bitter. It can be readily mixed into a feed in the amount necessary to balance the protein content of the ration. Since the texture of soybean meal is finer than cracked or whole grains, care should be used to thoroughly blend it in the ration.

In a study comparing two groups of mares and their foals, soybean meal was fed to mares during the last two weeks of gestation and the first seven weeks of lactation. Results showed the crude protein content of milk from soybean meal-fed mares was significantly higher than milk from mares that did not receive soybean meal. Protein content was 3.32 grams of protein per 100 grams of milk from mares fed soybean meal, and 2.53 grams of protein per 100 grams of milk from non-supplemented mares.

Foals of the soybean meal-fed mares grew about 10% more rapidly in height during their first seven weeks compared to foals of non-supplemented mares. Also, these foals did not suffer mid-lactation decline in plasma lysine concentration that foals of non-supplemented mares did.

Soybeans should **not** be fed to horses in their whole, raw state. They contain a trypsin inhibitor, which prevents the enzyme trypsin from digesting protein. The inhibitor is destroyed by heat used in the oil milling process.

Cottonseed Meal

Cottonseed meal ranks second to soybean meal in its use as a protein feed in the United States. Crude protein content of cottonseed meal varies from 34% to 50%, and fat content ranges from 1.5% to 6%. Cottonseed meal is usually higher in crude fiber than soybean meal, having a fiber content of about 12.2%. It is low in lysine and tryptophan, two essential amino acids, and it doesn't have the amino acid variety that soybean meal has. It is also known to be low in calcium, carotene, and vitamin D, but high in phosphorus. Its TDN value is 75%, and it contains 1.25 Mcal of DE per pound.

Cottonseed meal contains *gossypol*, a chemical substance which may be detrimental to horses when fed at higher than recommended levels. Most gossypol is destroyed by heat used in the oil extraction process. However, when cottonseed meal is fed to growing equines, it is recommended it be as low as possible in gossypol, because young horses are much more sensitive to its negative effects.

Because cottonseed meal is low in lysine (1.68%), it should be combined with a lysine rich source of protein, such as soybean meal. Inadequate lysine will limit growth in young horses.

Linseed Meal

Linseed meal is derived from the seed of the flax plant. It contains 34.6% crude protein and from 1% to 5% fat. Protein contained in linseed meal is low in several essential amino acids, notably lysine and tryptophan. Consequently, this protein source is lower in quality when compared to soybean meal and milk by-products. If linseed meal is used it should be fed in combination with other sources of protein.

Its crude fiber content is 9.1%, and it contains 81% TDN and 1.25 Mcal of DE per pound. Linseed meal is low in carotene. It contains fair amounts of calcium and B-complex vitamins.

In addition to being used as a

Fig. 6–13. Linseed meal may be slightly better for the hair coat than other oilseed meals.

131

protein supplement, there are other properties of linseed meal. It may have a laxative effect and
although it is less palatable, it may also be slightly better for the hair coat than other oilseed meals. This is thought to be due to *mucins* (*glycoproteins* mainly found in mucus) or fats contained in linseed meal.

Solvent-processed linseed meal, which is the form produced almost exclusively at present, has a fine and powdery consistency. However, many horsemen prefer to feed linseed meal in a pelleted form.

Sunflower Meal

Sunflower meal is high in quality, and when processed correctly will contain 41% – 45% crude protein. However, it contains only half the lysine found in soybean meal. As growing horses require lysine for proper growth, it should not be fed to these classes of equines without lysine supplementation. Sunflower meal contains 2.7% fat, 70.8% TDN, and 1.17 Mcal of DE per pound. It is less palatable than soybean meal and contains a great deal of crude fiber (approximately 25%) if the hull is not removed. If the hull is removed, fiber content will drop to about 11.7% and the quality and energy content will be higher.

Rapeseed Meal/Canola Meal

Rape, a plant with oil-rich seeds, is predominantly grown in colder climates, such as Canada, Northern Europe, Asia, and northern regions of the United States. Original varieties of rapeseed meal contained high levels of glucosinolates, which interfere with the *thyroid gland*, causing it to overwork and produce too much *thyroxine*. When large quantities of this substance are ingested, a *goiter* can result. Older varieties should not be fed to broodmares. Intake by other mature horses should not exceed 2 pounds per day.

Recently a new safe variety, which contains much lower concentrations of glucosinolates, has been developed in Canada. This new variety is commonly called canola meal. Horses have been fed diets containing up to 30% canola meal with no palatability problems.

Rapeseed meals (including canola meal) contain between 36% and 43% crude protein and about 2% lysine. They contain an average of 11% crude fiber. Fat content is 2.8%, the TDN value is 68.1%, and they contain about 1.28 Mcal of DE per pound. In a study, growing horses fed a diet containing 15% canola meal showed no difference in feed efficiency and gain when compared to growing horses fed 15% soybean meal.

Peanut Meal

Peanut meal is highly palatable, but its lysine content is quite low at 1.45%. It is also low in *methionine*, another essential amino acid for growth. Consequently, it is **not** a good protein feed for growing equines.

Peanut meal contains 7.7% crude fiber, 2.1% fat, 48.9% crude protein, and its TDN value is 77.3%. It also contains 1.36 Mcal of DE per pound.

Other Oilseed Meals

Other oilseed meals which are available, but rarely used :

- coconut (copra) meal—its quality and quantity of protein is considerably lower when compared to other oilseed meals
- safflower meal—high in fiber (about 15%), lower in digestible energy and palatability

Cull Peas

Cull peas, low in the amino acids lysine and methionine, should not be fed to growing horses, as these amino acids are necessary for growth. Containing 23.4% crude protein, they can be used to substitute part of the grain portion of a ration for mature horses. Cull peas contain 5.6% crude fiber, 0.9% fat, 79.1% TDN, and 1.4 Mcal of DE per pound.

Brewers Dried Grains

Brewers dried grains are somewhat palatable to the horse, containing 23.4% crude protein and 13.7% crude fiber. They also contain 5.9% fat, 67.1% TDN, and 1.15 Mcal of DE per pound. They are low in lysine, methionine, and tryptophan, three of the essential amino acids, when compared to other protein supplements. For these reasons, they should not exceed 10% of the ration for growing horses. A level of 20% can be used if it is supplemented with lysine or fed with high lysine feed.

Essential Amino Acids in Plant Protein Supplements					
	Soybean meal	Cottonseed meal	Linseed meal	Sunflower meal	Brewers Dried Grains
Lysine	2.9%	1.68%	1.16%	1.68%	0.88%
Methionine	0.6%	0.5%	0.5%	1.6%	0.4%
Tryptophan	0.6%	0.5%	0.5%	0.6%	0.4%
Valine	2.4%	1.8%	1.7%	4.2%	1.5%
Histidine	1.1%	0.9%	0.7%	na	0.5%
Phenylalanine	2.2%	1.9%	1.5%	na	1.3%
Leucine	3.4%	2.2%	2.0%	na	2.3%
Isoleucine	2.5%	1.5%	1.9%	na	1.5%
Threonine	1.7%	1.3%	1.2%	na	0.9%
Arginine	3.2%	3.3%	2.8%	na	1.3%

Fig. 6–14.   na = data not available

Animal Sources of Protein Supplements

Protein supplements obtained from animal sources are generally derived from materials inedible for human consumption. These materials include by-products from meat processing and surplus milk by-products. *(They do not, however, contain substances such as hair, hoof, horn, hide trimmings, manure, and stomach contents.)* These by-product protein sources provide large quantities of high quality protein because they contain many of the essential amino acids. They are also good sources of calcium and phosphorus.

Because animal-derived protein sources contain large quantities of fat, they have poor keeping qualities and can easily become rancid. They are also more costly and less palatable than plant sources of protein.

Meat/Bone Meal and Fish Meal

Meat/bone meal is a good source of lysine and contains a variety of other amino acids. It contains many vitamins and minerals, especially calcium and phosphorus. However, the nutritional value varies widely and it is expensive and low in palatability.

Fish meal, high in lysine and methionine, can be used as part of the protein supplement of a ration. It is expensive, however.

Milk By-products

Milk by-products are an excellent source of lysine, vitamins, and minerals, notably calcium and phosphorus. In addition, they are highly palatable and digestible. For these reasons they are excellent protein supplements for growing equines.

Most commercial feeds specially formulated for foals will contain milk by-products. However, they are expensive. For this reason, milk by-product protein sources are usually combined with soybean meal.

Mature horses may develop diarrhea and digestive upset when fed milk by-products. This is because mature horses lack the enzyme lactase, which is necessary for digestion of lactose (milk sugar). Mature horses should be fed other sources of extra protein, such as an oilseed meal, rather than milk by-products.

The more common milk by-products used as protein sources are:

- dried skim milk
- dried buttermilk
- dried whey
- dried whole milk
- *casein* (milk protein)

Essential Amino Acids in Milk By-Products					
	Dried Whey	Dried Buttermilk	Dried Skim Milk	Casein	Dried Whole Milk
Lysine	1.1%	2.4%	2.54%	7.0%	0.3%
Methionine	0.2%	0.7%	0.8%	2.7%	0.1%
Tryptophan	0.2%	0.5%	0.4%	1.0%	na
Valine	0.7%	2.8%	2.2%	6.8%	0.2%
Histidine	0.2%	0.9%	0.9%	2.5%	0.1%
Phenylalanine	0.4%	1.5%	1.5%	4.6%	0.1%
Leucine	1.4%	3.4%	3.3%	8.6%	0.3%
Isoleucine	0.9%	2.7%	2.3%	5.7%	0.2%
Threonine	0.8%	1.6%	1.4%	3.8%	0.1%
Arginine	0.4%	1.1%	1.23%	3.4%	0.1%

Fig. 6–15.   na = data not available

Other Concentrate Components

In addition to grains and high protein supplements, other substances may be mixed into the concentrate part of the ration for various reasons.

Molasses

Molasses contains about 54% TDN. It provides energy, increases palatability, and prevents separation of fine substances in the concentrate. It contains 4.3% crude protein, 0.4% crude fiber, 0.2% fat, and 1.18 Mcal of DE per pound. It is also low in phosphorus.

Feeds which contain high levels of molasses are likely to mold in hot, humid weather. For this reason, rations that will be stored should contain no more than 5% – 10% molasses during the summer months.

Cocoa Shells

Cocoa shells are the thin covering found on cocoa beans, which are used to make chocolate. These shells will generally contain 15% crude protein, 17% crude fiber, 3.0% fat, and 47.0% TDN. Cocoa shells are mainly used to improve the flavor of feeds.

Caution should be taken when feeding any cocoa-based product, as the cocoa plant contains a chemical called *theobromine*. Theobromine has physiological properties similar to caffeine, and it is used as a diuretic, a smooth muscle relaxant, a cardiac muscle stimulant, and a vasodialator. In the horse, this chemical is thought to increase urination and relax smooth muscles, such as those in the intestines. Others believe theobromine may increase cardiac output.

High intake of this chemical has resulted in diarrhea and a decrease in appetite. Even low levels of this chemical can be detected by simple urinary analysis.

Beet Pulp

Beet pulp is an excellent source of crude fiber (18.2%) and calcium, and it is easily digested. Its fat content is 0.5%, crude protein content is 8.9%, its TDN value is 68.7%, and it contains 1.06 Mcal of DE per pound. However, it contains low levels of phosphorus, carotene, and vitamin D.

Beet pulp, which is relatively dust-free can be used as a fiber source for horses with respiratory problems such as *heaves.*

Peanut Skins, Citrus Pulp, and Rice Bran

Peanut skins are a good source of crude protein, containing 16.3%. They also contain 23.9% fat, 11.8% crude fiber, and 61.5% TDN. Citrus pulp is high in calcium (1.7%), but low in crude protein (6.1%), carotene, and phosphorus (0.12%). Its fat content is 3.4%, crude fiber content is 11.6%, and it contains 1.16 Mcal of DE per pound. Both have been found to be highly unpalatable to most horses.

Rice bran contains 13% crude protein, 11.7% crude fiber, 13.6% fat, and 1.19 Mcal of DE per pound. Because the fat portion is highly *unsaturated,* it easily becomes rancid. It should be limited to no more than 5% to 10% of the concentrate part of the diet.

Hominy Feed

Hominy feed is similar to corn in nutritional value. Hominy feed contains approximately 6.9% fat that is highly unsaturated and unstable. Its crude protein content is 10.6%, crude fiber is 4.7%, and the TDN value is 83.9%. Hominy feed has a tendency to become rancid and increase the chances of gastric disturbances and should be fed with great care. If used, it should be limited to no more than 25% of the concentrate.

Other substances which have been known to be added to the concentrate portion of the ration include:

- peanut hulls
- mesquite beans
- vegetables
- soybean hulls
- oatmeal
- oat mill by-products
- rice polishings
- buckwheat

These substances are mainly fillers that provide bulk in the diet. They offer few, if any, nutritional contributions to the ration.

Nutrient Composition of High Protein & Other Concentrates

	Soybean Meal	Cotton-seed meal	Linseed Meal	Sun-flower Meal	Rapeseed Meal	Peanut Meal	Cull Peas	Dried Brewers Grains	Molas-ses	Cocoa shells	Beet Pulp	Peanut skins	Citrus Pulp	Rice Bran	Hominy Feed
% Crude Protein	44.4	41.3	34.6	45.2	37.1	48.9	23.4	23.4	4.3	15.0	8.9	16.3	6.1	13.0	10.6
% Lysine	2.87	1.68	1.16	1.68	2.08	1.45	1.65	0.88	na	na	0.54	na	0.20	0.57	na
% Fiber	6.2	12.2	9.1	11.7	11.0	7.7	5.6	13.7	0.4	17.0	18.2	11.8	11.6	11.7	4.7
% Ash	6.4	6.5	5.9	7.5	6.4	5.8	2.8	4.4	9.9	na	4.9	na	6.0	10.4	na
% Calcium	0.35	0.17	0.39	0.42	0.63	0.29	0.12	0.30	0.74	na	0.62	na	1.71	0.09	na
% Phosphorus	0.63	1.11	0.80	0.94	1.18	0.61	0.41	0.50	0.08	na	0.09	na	0.12	1.57	na
% Magnesium	0.27	0.54	0.60	0.65	0.55	0.15	0.12	0.15	0.31	na	0.26	na	0.16	0.88	na
% Potassium	1.98	1.30	1.38	1.17	1.22	1.18	0.95	0.08	2.98	na	0.20	na	0.70	1.71	na
% Sodium	0.03	0.04	0.14	0.03	0.01	0.03	0.22	0.21	0.16	na	0.18	na	0.08	0.03	na
% Sulfur	0.41	0.26	0.39	0.31	1.23	0.30	na	0.29	0.35	na	0.20	na	0.07	0.18	na
% Fat	1.4	1.5	1.4	2.7	2.8	2.1	0.9	5.9	0.2	3.0	0.5	23.9	3.4	13.6	6.9
%TDN	80.0	75.0	81.0	70.8	68.1	77.3	79.1	67.1	54.0	47.0	68.7	61.5	na	na	83.9
Copper mg/kg	19.9	19.5	25.7	3.7	77.0	15.0	na	21.2	48.8	na	12.5	na	5.6	11.0	na
Iodine mg/kg	na	na	na	na	na	0.06	na	0.06	1.56	na	na	na	na	na	na
Iron mg/kg	165	188	319	31.0	85.0	143	64.0	245	196	na	266	na	328	207	na
Manganese mg/kg	31	21.0	38	19.0	49.0	27	3.0	37	44	na	34.0	na	7.0	358	na
Selenium mg/kg	0.45	0.90	0.82	2.12	0.91	na	na	0.70	na	na	0.11	na	na	0.40	na
Zinc mg/kg	50	61.0	na	97.0	73.0	33.0	23.0	28	15	na	1.0	na	14.0	30.0	na
Cobalt mg/kg	0.11	0.48	0.19	na	na	0.11	na	0.07	1.18	na	0.07	na	0.17	1.38	na
Digestible Energy/lb.	1.43	1.25	1.25	1.17	1.28	1.36	1.40	1.15	1.18	na	1.06	na	1.16	1.19	na

Fig. 6–16. Adapted from *Nutrient Requirements of Horses.* All values are on an as fed basis.

na indicates that data was not available.
No data available on Meat/Bone and Fish Meal, or Milk Protein By-products.

7

SUPPLEMENTS, LABELS and FEED ANALYSIS

SUPPLEMENTS

There are many types of commercially available supplements. Some are simple, containing only salt and a few other minerals. Others are more complex, containing such ingredients as bee pollen, *bioflavonoids*, yeast, clays, seaweeds, and *ginseng*. Although many mixes and combinations are available, most supplements include one or more of the following:

- vitamins
- fat
- milk replacers
- amino acids
- DMG (dimethyl glycine)

- minerals
- live yeast cultures
- electrolytes
- octacosanol

- protein
- antibiotics
- enzymes
- mucopolysaccharides
- MSM (methylsulfonylmethane)

Supplements are widely and frequently used, but their uses and physiological impact are not always fully understood. Proper supplementation can increase performance and improve health. However, some horse owners believe that the more supplements a horse receives, the better its performance and health will be. This is normally untrue, and such a theory can cause decreased performance and even the possibility of health problems. Before a horse is given a supplement, the actual

need for that supplement should be determined. Both over-supplementation and improper supplementation can be detrimental.

Idle horses and horses used solely for pleasure riding usually do not need supplementation if they are receiving a well balanced ration. However, horses in stressful

Fig. 7–1. High performance horses may benefit from supplementation.

situations, such as intensive training, showing, racing, or lactation, may benefit from appropriate supplementation.

When a need for supplementation has been determined, ingredients and products should be chosen carefully. A manufacturer, or dealer may claim to have performed numerous studies to determine the benefits of a product. Even if the claim is true, the **quality** of the research should also be evaluated. The following questions should be considered:

1) Were the researchers properly qualified (i.e. educational background, research experience, reputation in the scientific community)?
2) Were the studies conducted in a proper, scientifically controlled environment?
3) Were the studies conducted on a sufficient number of horses?
4) Did the research span a sufficient period of time for the results to be meaningful?
5) Were the findings based on unbiased research?

Anyone can perform studies, and no matter how little value their results may offer, they can still claim that research was conducted. Also, if a supplement contains all natural ingredients, it is not considered a drug, so it is not government regulated. For this reason, supplements that provide no benefits can appear on the market.

When Supplements May Be Needed

Horses on pasture, not receiving grain, usually benefit when provided a mineral supplement. A salt and trace mineralized block is a common method of providing supplemental minerals to pastured horses. However, these blocks cannot always be relied upon exclusively to meet the needs of the horse, because they are consumed based on palatability rather than dietary need. If the pasture is of poor quality, or if it is late in the growing season when grasses are mature and lower in nutrients, horses may require supplemental feeding. A grain ration and possibly a good quality hay (depending on the amount of useful pasture forage available) may be needed to meet their nutritional requirements.

Horses that are involved in strenuous activities, such as racing, intensive showing, or endurance events may also benefit from supplementation, because they will deplete their nutrient stores more rapidly than a horse which is relatively idle.

Broodmares need high levels of nutrients because they must supply nutrients to the fetus during pregnancy and to the foal during lactation. Feeding a commercial grain mix which has been specially formulated for pregnant mares will usually provide them with the required nutrients, but supplementation may still be necessary.

Choosing A Supplement

When choosing a supplement, the needed nutrient levels it contains should be considered. A supplement should **balance** the ration by compensating for nutrient deficiencies; it should **not** supply nutrients already existing in adequate quantities. Nutrients from grains, hays, and any supplements should be added together. These totals should be compared to the daily requirements of the horse to be sure they are met, and that the amounts of any nutrients provided are not toxic.

Vitamins tend to break down and become lost from feeds and supplements during long storage periods. Therefore, the fresher the product, the more effective it will be. This should be considered when buying from a low-volume dealer who experiences slow merchandise turnover.

Fig. 7–2. Working horses may need supplements to make up for depleted nutrients.

Available Supplements

The following sections discuss general types of supplements available and why they may be needed. To avoid repetition, protein supplements are discussed in the section on *High Protein Concentrates* in Chapter 6.

Vitamins and Minerals

There is a wide variety of vitamin and mineral supplements available. Some contain many nutrients, and some contain only a few specific ones such as biotin or thiamine (B_1). They are available in liquids, blocks, pellets, or powders. The variety of forms makes them easy to add to any feeding program.

If a horse is believed to have a vitamin or mineral deficiency *(See Chapters 3 and 4 for symptoms.)*, the contents of its ration should be evaluated and any recognizable problems should be dealt with. If problems are not obvious, then an analysis of the ration should be performed. This analysis will determine the nutrient content of the different ingredients. After the problem(s) is determined, the ration should be reformulated to correct it. If this is not possible, then a proper supplement should be added to the diet.

In most cases, if a horse's diet is deficient in one nutrient, it will also be lacking in others. Since vitamin and mineral supplements are generally expensive for the amount of nutrients provided, it is usually more cost effective to switch to better quality forage and/or feeds.

Vitamin E

Supplementation of vitamin E may be advantageous to the high performance horse, as it is believed that intense exercise depletes vitamin E. Studies have shown that racehorses have lower levels of blood serum vitamin E than broodmares or pleasure horses. *(Refer to Chapter 3 for more information.)*

Iron

Providing excess iron will not increase *hemoglobin* content of the blood. Excess iron may actually cause anemia. An overabundance of iron creates deficiencies in zinc, manganese, copper, and possibly other minerals. Both iron and copper are needed to produce hemoglobin, so too much iron and inadequate copper may result in anemia.

Seaweed and Kelp

Products containing seaweed and kelp should be used with caution because they contain high levels of iodine. Horses which receive amounts of iodine exceeding their daily requirements have been known to develop a *goiter. (For more information refer to Chapter 4.)*

Selenium

Supplements containing high levels of selenium should be used with care. These should only be fed if the ration is deficient in selenium, or if the horse is grazing where the soil is selenium-deficient. Some areas of the country have high levels of selenium in the soil, and supplementation may cause a toxicity. *(See section on selenium in Chapter 4.)*

Chelated Minerals

Chelated minerals are becoming more and more common as additives to feed products. A chelated mineral is one that is bound to an easily digested organic molecule, such as a carbohydrate or protein, allowing increased absorption and utilization of the mineral. This can be beneficial when supplementing minerals, because under normal circumstances, extra amounts of one mineral can decrease availability of others. Sufficient research on equines is unavailable to offer much information at this time.

Supplementation for Specific Problems

Some vitamins have been shown to improve, in some cases, such conditions as *azoturia,* nervousness, and weak hooves. Before supplementation is used however, veterinary advice is recommended.

Vitamin E has been shown to aid some horses suffering from azoturia by helping to prevent formation of toxic substances in muscles during exercise. It is the build-up of these toxic substances that may lead to azoturia.

Nervous, high-strung horses may benefit from having thiamine added to their diets. Some fretful horses have become calmer when supplemented with thiamine, and in some cases, the resulting change in temperament was dramatic.

Horses fed supplemental biotin have shown improvement in weak hoof walls. *(See Chapter 3 for detailed information on these vitamins.)*

Hair Analyses

Hair analysis measures amounts of calcium, phosphorus, magnesium, sodium, potassium, iron, copper, manganese, and zinc in the hair. Although a popular method, at this time it is not considered to be very accurate. Hair analysis may be helpful when used in conjunction with other tests, but on its own it can be misleading. Results often are not true indicators of the amounts of minerals in the body. Test results will vary depending on hair coat color and time of year. Dirt on the hair alters true nutrient values, as can washing the hair, due to leaching action of water on the minerals. Hair analysis may become more accurate, but at this time its results should not be over-valued.

Fat As a Supplement

Fat is supplemented to diets for various reasons—primarily as a good source of energy. It contains 2.25 times the energy of carbohydrates and protein. Fat is also supplemented to improve the condition of the hair coat.

Added fat should not exceed 10% – 12% of the concentrate portion of a ration, or loose stools may result. Also, if fat is added to the ration in larger amounts, the feed will become unpalatable.

Many commercial supplements are available to improve the hair coat, and most work quite well. Similar results can also be achieved by adding 1 – 2 ounces (30 – 60 milliliters) of any vegetable-based cooking oil, such as corn oil, to the ration twice daily. Flaxseed is also used for this purpose. A handful of flaxseed is placed in a cup and covered with water. It is left to soak overnight, then is poured over the feed. This is usually done twice weekly. *(See Chapter 5 for more detailed information on fat.)*

Amino Acids

Studies on specific amino acids given to performance horses—with administration timed around exercise—suggest that they are effective in lowering the heart rate. This allows a higher level of work intensity and delays the onset of fatigue.

Strenuous exercise increases the rate of muscle protein degradation. Some of the amino acids that result from degradation are resynthesized to replace the lost muscle proteins. Most, however, especially the *branched-chain amino acids* leucine, isoleucine, and valine, are not resynthesized and are removed. Research suggests that an increased supply of glutamine, carnitine, and the branched-chain amino acids can benefit the racehorse.

Intensely worked horses appear to require a larger supply of carnitine for maximum fatty acid oxidation. (Fatty acid oxidation supplies energy.) Carnitine also seems to stimulate protein synthesis during the stress of intense exercise, which would help in post-exercise recovery.

Glutamine can be used by muscles to convert pyruvate (a salt of pyruvic acid) to alanine, thus decreasing the amount of lactic acid produced from pyruvate.

Only the surface has been scratched in studies of amino acid supplementation, but readers should watch for the results of future research. Current findings indicate that manipulation of the horse's metabolism during exercise by supplementation of amino acids will become an innovative and beneficial means of improving athletic performance.

Electrolytes

An electrolyte is a substance found in body fluids which conducts electricity in body functions such as nerve impulses, oxygen and carbon dioxide transport, and muscle contractions.

During physical exertion, horses lose such nutrients as calcium, sodium, potassium, and chloride through sweat. During prolonged exertion, these nutrients may reach a dangerously low level. Electrolyte supplements are made to replace these nutrients.

If a horse has low blood levels of calcium and potassium, it may exhibit muscle twitching, spasms, *tetany,* or *"thumps"*

Fig. 7–3. Electrolyte supplements replace nutrients lost during prolonged exertion.

(Syndronous diaphragmatic flutter). Thumps is a repeated contraction of the diaphragm in rhythm with heart beats.

Reduced levels of sodium, potassium, and chloride cause fatigue and muscle weakness. It should be noted, however, that such symptoms are not exclusively caused by reduced levels of the above nutrients. The horse may experience fatigue during exercise or competition even if these nutrient levels remain high. (Other issues may deserve consideration such as other nutritional deficiencies, lack of proper conditioning, conformational faults, or health problems.)

Electrolyte loss increases with length and intensity of work, as well as with an increase in environmental temperature and humidity. Amounts of electrolytes lost under similar conditions are different for all horses, so horses in intense work should be individually monitored.

Proper electrolyte supplementation—based on veterinary recommendation—is suggested for all horses that are performing any type of prolonged, stressful, or intense physical exertion. Supplementation may also be beneficial to horses that have a difficult time coping with higher temperatures of summer.

Other Performance Supplements

There are four substances which may be of significant benefit to horses in intense work:

- octacosanol
- DMG (dimethyl glycine)
- mucopolysaccharides
- MSM (methylsulfonylmethane)

Scientific research on the long term effects of these substances is virtually non-existent, and they are not FDA-approved for use in commercial horse feeds. They can, however, be obtained in a powdered form and added to the concentrate portion of the horse's ration.

Octacosanol

Octacosanol is a natural ingredient found in wheat germ oil, various vegetable oils, and alfalfa. It can also be purchased in its pure form as a white crystalline powder, but is usually supplied in wheat germ or cottonseed oil. In studies done on human athletes, octacosanol improved stamina, strength, and reaction time. It is also believed to help in human cardiovascular function and neurological disorders, and it may have the same effect in horses. Octacosanol generally takes four to six weeks to produce any effects.

Mucopolysaccharides

Mucopolysaccharides appear to help the body repair normal *articular* cartilage wear and tear that might otherwise lead to degenerative joint diseases. They also help prevent inflammation when connective tissue diseases occur, and they help regulate the immune system. *(Refer to Chapter 13 for more information.)*

DMG

Dimethyl glycine is believed to increase work output. Studies have shown it to cause lower post-exercise lactic acid levels and faster exercise recovery times. The horses used in the studies also exhibited increased aggression and appetite. Suggested but not yet proven effects of DMG are benefits in blood sugar metabolism, avoiding cardiovascular dysfunction and immune dysfunction.

MSM

Methylsulfonylmethane is a sulfur-rich organic compound that is derived from DMSO, an anti-inflammatory drug. It is a naturally occurring substance in the blood of the horse, though it is not present in large amounts. It is useful in preventing muscle soreness and in improving recovery time. *(Refer to Chapter 13 for more information.)*

Summary

The above four substances have not been rigidly tested under controlled research conditions. Although they may indeed be beneficial to performance horses, the data is not available to provide more support for their use.

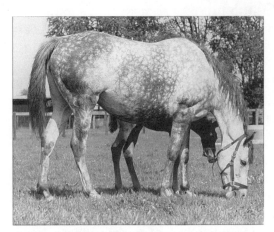

Fig. 7–4. Adding yeast culture to a mare's feed may increase the protein, energy, sugar, and concentration of lipids in her milk.

Live Yeast Cultures

Live yeast cultures are another type of dietary supplement given to horses. They have been shown to increase dietary hemicellulose and cellulose fermentation in the hindgut. Studies of yearlings, given yeast supplements, show an increase in the efficiency of nitrogen utilization and an increase in net nitrogen retention. However, it is not known if supplementation in mature horses produces these same results.

Another study has shown that lactating mares given live yeast culture in their feed produced milk with greater total proteins and amino acids, concentrations of lipids, sugars, and higher gross energy. Their foals averaged 21 kilograms (46.3 lbs) heavier and 11.2 centimeters (4.41 inches) taller at eight weeks of age, compared to foals whose dams were not supplemented with yeast culture.

Antibiotics

Antibiotics are not a common feed supplement for horses. The FDA has approved certain antibiotics at specific levels for growth promotion and for improvement of feed efficiency in equines **only** to the age of one year.

Antibiotics appear to be helpful to foals that suffer setbacks from infections, digestive disturbances, inclement weather, and other stress factors. It has been shown that poor health caused by low quality rations and questionable management practices were improved by the administration of antibiotics. However, antibiotics should **not** be used to replace good management and high quality rations.

Feeding antibiotics as a supplement to mature horses is not beneficial and may be harmful.

Antibiotics are known to be detrimental to the intestinal bacteria in the hindgut, which are responsible for fiber digestion and the synthesis of some vitamins.

Milk Replacer

Milk replacer is most commonly used for feeding a foal whose dam is unable to provide adequate milk. It is also used as a nutritional supplement for weanlings that are being fitted for show or sale. It is believed to help the weanling maintain its condition during this stressful time.

All supplements should be fed with great care to young, growing horses. Any imbalances in nutrients can create critical problems during this period. This is especially so in regard to the calcium-to-phosphorus ratio, which can affect proper growth. *(See Chapter 4.)*

Fig. 7–5. Milk replacer is sometimes used as a supplement for weanlings being fitted for show or sale.

Fruits and Vegetables

Fruits and vegetables can also be used as supplements, but the practice is not very common. More often, they are fed as treats. When evaluated on a **dry matter basis,** high water content tubers (such as carrots), fruits, and melons have almost the same nutrient value as cereal grains.

Due to their high water content, it takes seven pounds of carrots to equal the energy contained in one pound of oats. In some instances this high water content can be advantageous, because it allows carrots to act as a filler. The horse feels full but does not receive the added energy that the same volume of oats would provide. If carrots are fed, they should not replace more than 10% to 20% of the diet.

Other vegetables that are safe to feed in small amounts include:

• parsnips	• rutabagas	• pumpkins	• sugar beets
• turnips	• potatoes	• squashes	• melons

Enzymes

Enzymes are protein molecules that are naturally produced in the stomach, pancreas, and small intestine of the horse. They are catalysts in the digestion process of ingested feedstuffs, breaking down proteins into amino acids, carbohydrates into sugars, and fats into fatty acids. Amino acids, sugars, and fatty acids can then be absorbed into the bloodstream and utilized to produce energy.

Supplements containing enzymes can be fed to horses that have digestive or *metabolism* disorders which prevent them from properly digesting their feed. These enzymes may help improve digestive efficiency.

Sweeteners

Molasses, honey, and other sweeteners are not usually added to the feed because of their nutrient content. They are commonly mixed into the feed to increase palatability or cut down on dust. Sugar and honey provide few nutrients other than energy, because they are added in such small quantities to the ration. Molasses increases palatability of a feed, but also adds energy and minerals. Sweeteners are also used to keep fine textured feed components from being sifted out of the ration.

FEED BAG LABELS

When buying a commercial feed mix, the list of feed ingredients can be helpful in determining and choosing the proper feed. It is important to choose feed containing the best nutrients for the particular class of horse being fed. Requirements for each equine will depend on many factors, including its age, breeding activity, and work intensity.

HORSE FEED
Net Weight 50 pounds

┌ Guaranteed Analysis: ┐
Crude protein not less than......... 12%
Crude fat not less than................ 4%
Crude fiber not more than........... 10%

INGREDIENTS: Grain products, plant protein products, soybean oil, molasses, bone meal, dicalcium phosphate, salt, calcium iodate, copper sulfate, cobalt carbonate, zinc oxide, vitamin A supplement, vitamin B_{12} supplement, vitamin D_3 supplement, sodium selenite, choline chloride, vitamin E supplement.

Manufactured by **HORSE FEEDS, INC.** 123 North St., Anytown, USA 12345

Fig. 7–6. Feed bag labels can be helpful in determining and choosing feed that contains proper nutrients for the class of horse being fed.

What to Look for

By law, minimum percentages of crude protein, crude fat, and crude fiber must be listed on feed bag labels. Minimum and maximum values for calcium and phosphorus, as well as minimum amounts of each vitamin and mineral in feed may also be listed.

The purpose of nutrient analysis is to show that adequate amounts of nutrients needed are included without causing a harmful surplus. If feed is pelleted, the variety and amount of vitamins and mineral supplementation added to the feed by the maker must be sufficient to cover any lost in the pelletizing process. Supplementation must be sufficient to provide for the horse's needs.

Feed bag labels should show all the ingredients in the feed. According to USDA regulations, there can be no hidden components. This is primarily to ensure safety of the animal. If the horse has a reaction to a particular type of feed, the ingredients must be known in order to determine proper treatment. It also allows buyers to check for hazardous ingredients, low quality substances, fillers, and drugs.

Feeding instructions may be included on feed bag labels. Any possible hazards must be specified, as should emergency treatment for possible side effects.

Product name and net weight should be listed, with name and address of the manufacturer. If consumers have questions that the feed dealer cannot answer, the manufacturer can be contacted directly.

Quality or quantity of many ingredients cannot be determined to any great degree by the label. Consumers must rely on visual examination of the grains to verify that ingredients are fresh and of good quality. There should be no obvious damage, foreign materials, or mold. With pelleted feeds, however, such visual examination of grains is virtually impossible; more emphasis must be placed on feed bag labels and reputation and integrity of the manufacturer. Quality of a feed can also be determined by appearance, performance, and overall health of horses to which it is being fed.

Common Feed Terms and What They Mean

1) *Crude protein*–Percentage of protein contained in the feed.
2) *Crude fat*–Percentage of fat, oil, and related substances (such as waxes, resins, and pigments) which can be extracted in a laboratory with ether compounds.
3) *Crude fiber*–Percentage of complex (insoluble) carbohydrates, mainly cellulose and related substances of low digestibility.
4) *Dry matter*–Percentage of feed left after all moisture removed.
5) *Ash*–Percentage of mineral matter in the feed *(determined by the*

residue that remains after complete burning of the feed).

6) *Nitrogen-free extract* (NFE)–Percentage is determined by subtracting from 100 the sum of the percentages of moisture, crude protein, crude fiber, fat, and ash. Consists mainly of sugars and pentoses (monosaccharides), starches (polysaccharides), and non-nitrogen organic acids.

7) *Total digestible nutrients* (TDN)–Sum of digestibilities of all nutrients contained in the feed.

8) Terms such as "processed grains" or "plant products" indicate that   the manufacturer may change the formula to compensate for price changes of various ingredients.

(The first three terms must be listed on feed bag labels. The last five terms are not usually listed.)

FEED ANALYSIS

Book values for various nutrients in feeds provide only guidelines. There is a wide variance in nutrient content of any particular ingredient, such as oats. Therefore, when exact values are needed, the most accurate method of determining nutrients in a feed is by feed analysis.

When practical, especially in large operations, feed analysis should be conducted on each major feed ingredient on a routine basis to determine percentages of:

• protein • fat   • fiber   • copper
• moisture   • phosphorus
• calcium   • zinc
• *nitrogen-free extract* (NFE)
• carotene (*precursor* of vitamin A)
• Total Digestible Nutrients (TDN)

Supplements added to feeds for a particular purpose, such as increasing protein content, do not usually require analysis, unless their quality is in question.

Laboratory analysis services offered by state universities are usually inexpensive and are available to the public. *(Types of analyses are covered in Chapter 5.)*

Fig. 7–7. Appearance and condition of the horse being fed should also be used in judging the value of a feed.

8

COMMERCIALLY PREPARED HORSE FEEDS

Commercial feed companies purchase ingredients in large quantities, providing the potential for reduced costs. They also have nutritionists who determine feed formulas, and trained personnel to monitor ingredients. These measures ensure that the quality desired by the manufacturer can be maintained consistently. For some horse owners, buying commercial feeds is cost and quality effective. Others prefer to formulate their own rations and have them prepared by feed mills. Some operations prefer to formulate and prepare their own rations.

GRAIN MIXES

Commercial grain mixes include common grains such as oats, corn, barley, and milo. Many also contain vitamins, and minerals, and some contain high-protein ingredients. In addition, molasses is often added, and they are called "sweet feeds." When fed with good quality hay, properly prepared, high quality grain mixes usually provide adequate nutrients for each class of horse for which it is prepared.

Sweet feeds may be low in fiber, around 8%, or they may be high, up to around 20%, depending on the ingredients. Some sweet feeds include rice or peanut hulls, indigestible fillers that only provide added bulk to the diet.

Molasses is added to increase palatability, reduce dustiness, and prevent ingredients from sifting out of the mix. Molasses also contains beneficial levels of potassium. No more than 10% liquid molasses should be used in a mix or it will cake and become messy. In a hot, humid climate, no more than 5% should be added, to avoid mold.

Molasses can also be used to make poor quality feed ingredients more palatable. For this reason, when purchasing sweet feeds, a sample of the feed should be visually examined to ensure the grains are of desirable quality.

PELLETED FEEDS

Many commercially processed feeds are pelleted, and the number of pelleted feeds available has increased dramatically. Pelleted feeds are formed by processing a feed component such as hay, or even an entire ration, into round, oval, or most commonly, cylindrical pellets.

Pellets normally range in size from one-sixth of an inch to one inch in diameter, and one-eighth of an inch to three inches in length. Pellets require less storage space and can be accurately measured. They can be fed with little or no waste, and most are very digestible, although digestibility will vary with the ingredients. With hay, digestibility of protein and energy show no differences among cubed, pelleted, chopped, or loose forms.

Horses may ingest pellets at a faster rate than unpelleted and extruded feeds. Very rapid consumption is undesirable because it can increase the

Fig. 8–1. Pellets are compact and easy to store. They also prevent the horse from picking out ingredients.

possibility of gastric disturbances. The possibilities of problems occurring can be reduced by feeding only part of the ration in pelleted form. *(There are several reasons, discussed in the following material, why feeding non-pelleted hay is a good idea.)*

Types of Pelleted Feeds

Commercial pellets are widely produced, and may include many different feed ingredients in addition to common grains and forages. Some of these ingredients include:

- corn cobs
- corn plants
- cocoa husks
- carrot tops
- straw

- peanut hulls
- pangola hay
- torula yeast
- poultry litter
- apple pomace

- ryegrass straw
- almond hulls
- grape pulp
- pineapple bran
- tunafish meal

Pellets containing computer paper (25%) have been fed to horses **experimentally**. The paper did not contain significant amounts of protein, minerals, or vitamins, but it did contain a high level of digestible cellulose. Adequate quantities of minerals, vitamins, and protein were added to the paper. Energy content was found to be similar to that contained in alfalfa meal. Newspaper was not used because it contains large quantities of ink and lignin, which are not digestible. Glossy paper, such as that found in most magazines, contains substantial amounts of clay and is indigestible, as well.

Molasses is often used as a binder in pelleted feeds. 7.5% to 10% is commonly used. If more is used, pellets become soft and chewy; less will make them crumbly. Other materials such as *lignin sulfonate, sodium* or *calcium bentonite*, and *hemicellulose extracts* are often added to pelleted feeds to assist in the mixing and pelleting process. These agents help bind ingredients together. The amount of agent used will depend on the concentrations of the ingredients used. In most cases, they range between 0.5% and 2.55% of pellet contents.

Dewormers are now available in pelleted form, as are mineral, vitamin, and protein supplements. It is possible to feed entire rations in pelleted form, including hay. Many feed companies do, in fact, market feeds that contain a complete pelleted ration in one bag. *(The possible **disadvantages** of feeding completely pelleted rations are discussed later in this chapter.)*

Pelleted feeds may be derived from:

- forage sources only
- primarily forage sources with a smaller percentage grain (usually 10% to 25%)
- grain mixes only
- complete rations: grain and forage
- supplements of various types (mineral, vitamin, protein)

The first three types mentioned above differ from each other in crude fiber content. Crude fiber content provides an estimate of the energy content; its percentage can be found on feed bag labels. The lower the crude fiber *(complex carbohydrate)* content, the higher the feed's energy value. Pellets derived exclusively from forage sources will contain 27% or more crude fiber. Those that contain mostly forage and some grain will generally contain 18% to 26% crude fiber. Pellets that are derived exclusively from grains will usually contain less than 15% crude fiber. The energy content needed depends on the requirements of the horse being fed.

Alfalfa Pellets

High quality alfalfa in any form is known to be a good source of protein, minerals, and vitamins. Dehydrated alfalfa meal pellets are commonly fed. They are available with different levels of crude protein to meet the needs of different classes of horses. These levels generally range from 15% to 22% crude protein. Alfalfa pellets are easy to feed and convenient to store.

In one experiment, lactating mares were fed dehydrated alfalfa pellets for one year. They exhibited excellent body conditions, and their foals grew at the same rate as foals with dams on standard mixed grain and hay diets.

The Pelleting Process

A pelleting machine has a mixing and heating chamber, knives to cut the pellets, a cooling bin, and a shaker that removes the fines (small particles that did not bind during pelleting).

There are several steps in the pelleting process. First, ingredients are carefully weighed. Most companies have highly automated equipment that weighs exact amounts of each ingredient. This allows formulas to be controlled within a small tolerance range.

Second, the ingredients are carefully ground and thoroughly mixed, so that each pellet has a uniform content. Molasses may be added to produce a mixture of desired consistency, and the entire vat is then heated by a steam process, making the pellets resistant to mold and decay and enhancing their overall keeping quality.

This mixture is heated to approximately 212° F, after which it is forced through dies under high pressure. Friction created by this process increases the temperature of the pellet. As pellets are formed, they are dried by cool air and are cut automatically to desired lengths. They then pass over a shaker to remove fines and other components that did not bind. These components are put into a new mixture to be pelleted again.

Pellets can be improperly processed. They can be overheated (which destroys vitamins and protein), made too hard or too soft, or be poor in consistency. Pellets should not contain more than 5% fine particles. A quality problem with a pelleted feed can sometimes be visually noticed, however it is most accurately determined by laboratory analysis by the feed company.

Lab analysis assists in maintaining quality control. It also helps in ensuring uniform distribution of the ingredients in the ration. Even with modern technology, pelleting still remains a somewhat controversial method of processing feed. Arguments are delivered both for and against the use of pelleted feeds.

Advantages of Pelleted Feeds

Feeding high quality pelleted feeds is a safe method of ensuring a standard nutrient content within a ration. Those who mix their own feeds must deal with day to day variances within the ingredients used, whereas the nutrient content of pelleted feeds remains the same for every horse fed from a particular batch. Horsemen can be sure of the protein, vitamin, and mineral content being fed, and that the energy value of a ration will not vary. Each portion from a batch will equal the nutrient content specified on the label.

Horses that have trouble maintaining weight or adequate body condition may benefit from a pelleted feed, because feed wastage is reduced to such an extent that horses can consume more of their feed with improved efficiency. Horses that are aged and/or have poor teeth may benefit from having part or all of their forage source in a pelleted form, because less chewing is required. Impaction colic may be less likely to occur due to the less bulky nature of pellets.

Pelleted feeds containing quality ingredients are generally highly digestible. They are compact, easy to store, and are not subject to the spoilage problems of fresh ingredients. For these reasons pelleted feeds are considered a good choice by many horsemen.

Pelleted feeds reduce feed wastage, resulting in more efficient utilization by the horse. In addition, vitamins, miner-

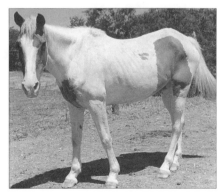

Fig. 8–2. Aged horses that have trouble maintaining weight may benefit by having their forage source in a pelleted form.

als, fats, and various other substances that are difficult to mix uniformly in a ration can be easily combined with feed into a pellet.

If pelleted feeds are well mixed, the taste of individual ingredients is not readily apparent. Consequently, finicky eaters cannot select their favorite ingredients and leave others uneaten.

Feeding pellets may help alleviate symptoms of *heaves* in some horses. Pellets are normally mold and dust free when processed correctly; therefore, they do not aggravate this condition, as dusty or moldy grains can.

Disadvantages of Pelleted Feeds

A problem often associated with feeding pellets to stabled horses, without also providing some loose forage, is that they may begin *cribbing* or chewing wood in an attempt to satisfy their urge to chew. This problem will most often occur with horses that have limited or no grazing time and are fed their entire ration in a pelleted form. This problem may be alleviated by providing hay in its natural form rather than including it in the pelleted ration.

Another problem is the highly concentrated form of pellets, because they tend to expand in the stomach when mixed with saliva. When horses are fed individually in measured amounts, this is not a problem. But when several horses are fed from the same trough, or if horses are fed a pelleted ration on a free-choice basis, overeating could occur, resulting in digestive problems.

Since pelleting involves a heat process that destroys some vitamins, any vitamin content analysis on feed bag labels should be carefully considered. Usually, feeds are supplemented during pelleting to make up for losses.

Selection of Pelleted Feeds

When choosing a pelleted ration, the portion of the ration to be fed in a pelleted form must be considered. Normally, total hay rations should **not** be in pelleted form. Hay in its natural state allows horses more chewing time, which has positive psychological advantages.

Another consideration when choosing a pelleted feed is to be sure it is suitable for the horse to which it will be fed. Pelleted feeds are often formulated for specific classes of horses, so nutrient contents vary.

Pellets cannot be visually inspected like grains, for quality and freshness. Reading the label, as well as considering the experience and reputation of the company, is very important. States have regulations regarding the labeling of feeds. Usually these regulations state that the minimum percent crude protein and crude fat, and the maximum percent crude fiber in the feed must be displayed on the bag. The reputation of the manufacturer must be relied on for freshness and quality control. It should also be remembered that even among reputable companies, all standards of quality are not the same.

Equine establishments responsible for a large number of horses may wish to formulate their own rations and have a commercial feed mill pelletize them. In this way, formulas can be processed to meet each class of horses' needs and owner preferences. This process should not be attempted without knowledge and experience, or without the assistance of a well quali-

Fig. 8–3. Pelleted feeds can be formulated to meet the specific needs of different age classes.

fied equine nutritionist, or a nutritionally knowledgeable veterinarian. And remember, feeds subjected to pelleting may require supplementation to maintain nutritional integrity.

Changing Rations

When considering a switch from regular rations to any pelleted feed, the change should be done **gradually.** Quick changes in diet can result in serious consequences. Digestive disturbances and other problems, such as founder, can result.

HAY CUBES

Alfalfa is the most common type of cubed hay, and the cubes are derived directly from sun-cured alfalfa hay. Cubes do not undergo any type of processing, as alfalfa pellets do.

Hay cubes are generally 1¼ to 1½ inches wide by 1 to 2 inches long and will have a bulk density of 30 to 32 pounds per cubic foot. Horses that are fed hay cubes (as opposed to pellets) are less likely to crib or chew wood, due to increased chewing time. However, chewing time is decreased compared to eating loose hay.

Some horsemen believe that horses fed hay cubes are more prone to *choke*. Experimental research indicates this is not true, unless the horse typically *bolts* its feed.

Horses fed cubes instead of loose hay have been shown to require less concentrate in their rations. During an experiment involving two groups of horses, those consuming loose alfalfa hay ate an average of 18.6 pounds of hay and 5.8 pounds of concentrate daily. After 65 days, these horses had lost an average of 19 pounds each. The other group of horses consumed 18.7 pounds of alfalfa cubes and 4.3 pounds of concentrate; at the end of the 65-day trial these horses had average gains of 31 pounds. The results of this study were thought to be due to less wastage by the horses consuming the cubes.

Although the use of hay cubes has increased in recent years, many horsemen still do not use them. The most common disadvantages usually mentioned are:

- difficulty in determining the quality of forage used
- possibility of foreign objects being cubed in the hay

From horsemen who use them, the advantages usually cited for their use are:

- hay processing is more efficient due to less wastage
- decreased storage and transportation costs (cubed hays need 75% less space than baled hays)
- decreased nutrient loss, due to fewer leaves lost in handling

EXTRUDED FEEDS

Extruded horse feeds are increasing in popularity. They are similar in appearance to dry dog food, and they are formed by processes that are similar to pelleting. The use of air and extreme pressure during processing gives extruded feeds a puffed-up appearance.

The Extrusion Process

There are several stages in the extrusion process. First, ingredients required to meet a specific need are determined. This will vary depending on whether the feed is to be used for foals, pregnant mares, performance horses, etc. Ingredients used to make an extruded feed should be fresh and of high quality. Reputable companies will perform a laboratory analysis of feed ingredients. Selected ingredients are then carefully weighed by computer scales.

After being weighed, mixed ingredients are steam pre-conditioned. This involves injecting water and steam into the feed mix at moderately high temperatures. Due to this process, it is not necessary to expose the mix for very long to the high temperatures of the extruder, and the vitamins and proteins are better protected. *(Not all manufacturers utilize steam pre-conditioning.)*

Fig. 8–4. Extruded horse feeds have a similar appearance to dried dog food.

Extrusion cooking is characterized by feed mixes being forced, under high pressure, through the extruder cooker. The extruder is a large, continuous flow pressure cooker which utilizes high volumes of steam under extreme pressures and high temperatures. The mix is then forced through a die, which determines its shape and diameter. After passing through the die, the nugget will "puff up," due to the sudden change in temperature and pressure from the heat in the extruder to the cold of the outside environment. Some moisture is removed from the extruded feed by evaporation, making it porous. The large nugget mass is then cut into the desired lengths by rotating knives.

At this point, the feed nuggets will contain 20% to 25% moisture. To prevent spoilage after packaging, 10% to 12% of this moisture must be eliminated. Feed nuggets are dried with hot air dryers, generally at 300° C for approximately 20 minutes. The nuggets are then passed through a cooler, reducing the heat level to room temperature, after which they are ready to be packaged.

Advantages and Disadvantages

Equines that may benefit from extruded feeds include:
- horses prone to colic or choke
- horses that bolt their feed (eat too rapidly)
- aged horses and horses that have poor teeth (however, smaller pellets may be even more beneficial to these horses)
- growing horses, particularly in group feeding situations

Extruded feeds have advantages similar to pelleted feeds, such as easier storage, less waste, less dust etc. One unique advantage they have is that their composition forces the horse to chew more thoroughly and eat at a slower rate. Digestive disturbances, such as colic, are less likely to occur, as is choke.

Slower consumption and more efficient chewing also results in more efficient digestion and absorption of nutrients. Because extruded feeds are "cooked," feed components that cannot be fed in their raw state (such as whole soybeans) can often be included in extruded feeds. This cooking process also helps to increase digestibility: when starch in grains is cooked, it is absorbed in the small intestine as glucose, which is converted to energy in an efficient manner. Uncooked grains, on the other hand, are converted to energy by bacteria in the hindgut, which is a far less efficient process.

The "*gelatinization*" involved in extrusion cooking may increase the availability of carbohydrates and, consequently, energy in the diet. This is thought to be caused by an increase in the conversion of complex polysaccharides (compounds consisting of chains of carbohydrates) into simple sugars. These are readily absorbed for energy utilization by the horse's digestive tract.

Some horsemen believe that extruded feeds lose less protein and fewer vitamins during processing when compared to pelleted feeds. However, no differences in nutrient digestibility have been proven between extruded and pelleted feeds.

A drawback to extruded feeds is they are more expensive than pelleted feeds, due to the technological processing techniques used.

SPECIAL FEEDS

Special feeds are formulated for particular types of horses. Examples are high level performance horses, aged horses, and horses with special health problems, such as heaves. They generally are designed to be fed with hay and water— some with specific types of hay. Some are meant to be fed with only water, such as for horses with heaves or allergies. Other formulas must be mixed with grain before feeding.

Special feeds are more expensive than regular grain mixes, but when needed they

Fig. 8–5. Some feeds are designed to meet the special nutritional needs of the high level performance horse.

are worth the extra cost. If a grain mix requires several supplements, the total cost of a regular mix plus supplements may equal or exceed the cost of a special feed.

Prices of special feeds will vary with the ingredients they contain. Ingredients that might be used are:

- wheat
- vegetable oil
- barley
- brewers yeast

- bee pollen
- vitamins
- electrolytes
- bran

- fat
- minerals
- beet pulp

Racehorses

Racehorse rations are sometimes supplemented with:

- vitamin E
- Octacosanol
- mucopolysaccharides

- probiotics
- Dimethylglycine (DMG)
- Methylsulfolnylmethane (MSM)

Vitamin E is believed to be depleted by intense exercise, so it is often supplemented to make up for losses. Octacosanol has improved stamina, strength, reaction time and cardiovascular function in humans. It is believed to have the same effect on horses, though this has not been determined scientifically. Mucopolysaccharides help the horse's body repair normal cartilage wear and damage that might otherwise lead to degenerative joint diseases. They also prevent inflammation in cases of connective tissue disease.

Fig. 8–6. Racehorse performance may improve through the use of certain supplements.

Probiotics are "friendly" bacteria such as *Lactobacillus* and *Streptococcus fecium.* These enhance the number and vigor of cellulose-processing microflora that normally reside in the horse's large intestine. DMG is believed by some trainers to enhance tissue oxygenation, which translates into increased stamina. MSM is a source of nutritional sulfur, and is widely used to relieve soreness and inflammation. DMG and MSM are at this time unapproved commercial feed additives, so they cannot be included in commercial feeds. They may be purchased for use as a supplement. An approved feed additive is one that has been reviewed by the Food and Drug Administration and found to be safe and effective for its intended use. *(See Racehorse section in Chapter 10 for more information on supplementing the racehorse.)*

Amino Acids

Studies have shown that specific amino acid supplementation can benefit racehorses.

(For further information on amino acids and their functions, refer to Chapters 5 and 7.)

Aged Horses

Fig. 8–7. Specially formulated rations can be beneficial for aged horses.

For aged horses, diets containing steam cooked, crimped, and flaked grains aid in digestion and absorption of nutrients. They also may contain chelated minerals and other ingredients beneficial for the older horse. These feeds can be fed dry or mixed with water to form a mash if the horse has dental problems.

Horses With Digestive Problems

Horses prone to colic can be fed special extruded grains, some of which contain yeast products, probiotics, and herbs. The combination is believed to have a calming effect on the horse's digestive system and improve feed utilization.

Other Special Feeds

Other special feeds include those formulated for specific classes of horses. For example, a special feed for broodmares will contain specific nutrients that broodmares require.

9

FORAGES

HAYS

There are two general types of hays—grass hays and legume hays. A major difference between legume and grass hays is legume hays have a higher protein content. Roots of legumes are covered with nodules containing bacteria that obtain nitrogen from the air *(nitrogen-fixing bacteria)*. Nitrogen is then converted to protein. Grasses do not have these nitrogen-fixing bacteria. Legumes are also higher in calcium, phosphorus, and vitamins than grass hays. There are also "mixed" hays containing both types, with grass usually making up a higher percentage.

Good quality hay contributes energy, protein, calcium, vitamin, and trace mineral content to the horse's ration. Sun-cured hay furnishes a primary source of vitamin D. The bulk of both grass hays and legume hays helps move other feedstuffs through the digestive tract by stimulating *peristaltic action.* Also, since equines are genetically predisposed to be grazers, hay provides the stabled horse something to satisfy its need for chewing time.

Fig. 9–1. Good quality hay contributes energy, protein, calcium, vitamins, and trace minerals.

163

Due to the horse's nutrient requirements and its somewhat delicate digestive system, hay needs to be of high quality, containing a great proportion of small, green leaves and tender stems. It should be free of weeds, foreign materials, and toxic substances. *(Refer to Tables in the Appendix for nutrient content of common hays.)*

Grass Hays

Grass hays include many species of grasses, and they vary greatly in nutritional quality according to species and areas where they are grown.

Grass hay is high in fiber and serves as the main source of roughage in diets of most stabled horses. Its protein content will differ according to the specie of grass and stage of maturity when cut. Grass hays cut at boot stage (when the seed head starts to emerge from the sheath), usually have the highest energy and protein levels. In well fertilized hay cut at this stage, the protein content will range from 6% to 13%. Energy and protein content decline as the plant matures.

Nutrient content of grass hays can be increased by seeding them with legumes to produce a mixed hay. This may also result in higher yields per acre because of the added nitrogen in the soil provided by the nitrogen fixing bacteria on the legume roots. When grasses and legumes are seeded together, the hay should be cut when the grass is in the boot stage.

There is little likelihood of overfeeding, colic, or founder from feeding grass hays. Of course there is a danger of health problems when any hay is fed that is moldy, fermented, or contains toxic compounds or foreign materials.

The following chart shows the basic components of commonly fed grass hays. Other characteristics are discussed under their headings. *(Detailed nutrient charts on all feedstuffs can be found in the Appendix.)*

Common Grass Hays								
	Bermuda-grass	Blue-stem	Brome-grass	Johnson-grass	Orchard-grass	Sudan-grass	Timothy	Wheat-grass
% crude protein	10.6	5.8	12.6	7.0	11.4	8.0	9.6	11.5
% crude fiber	26.7	34.0	28.0	30.4	30.2	30.0	30.0	33.0
% fat	2.4	2.4	1.9	2.0	2.6	na	2.5	0.6

Fig. 9–2.

Bermudagrass

Bermudagrass hay is plentiful and of good quality in southern regions of the United States. It grows well in these regions because it is heat and drought tolerant. Coastal bermudagrass is the most popular variety used for hay. It grows taller than common bermudagrass, which is too short for abundant yields. Bermudagrass hay may be cut four or five times in one year from the same stand. Second and later cuttings are generally higher in quality than the first.

Bermudagrass hay has a higher protein content than cereal grass hays. Its nutrient value can be further increased by seeding a legume crop in the same field.

Bluestem

Bluestem hays grow throughout the Northern Plains, dry hills, and open woods of inter-mountain regions. They perform well on sandy soils and soils that contain gravel.

A number of different grasses are included in this classification, but the two most common varieties used for hay are big bluestem and little bluestem.

Fig. 9–3. Big bluestem left, and little bluestem, right.

Bromegrass

Bromegrass is a very hardy hay that grows throughout the Great Plains region. Varieties most commonly used for hay are the smooth bromegrasses. Crude protein content of mid-bloom, smooth bromegrass hay is approximately 12.6%, declining to 5.6% by the mature stage. Crude fiber content of mid-bloom smooth bromegrass and mature smooth bromegrass is about 28%. Bromegrasses are frequently planted with legumes in order to provide a higher yielding, higher quality hay. Also, most horses find the bromegrass-legume mix more palatable than bromegrass alone.

Crested Wheatgrass

Crested wheatgrass is normally grown for pasture, but it is also used for hay. It is well adapted to cool dry areas of the Northern Great Plains, the inter-mountain regions, and higher elevations in the Rocky Mountain states.

This hay requires a moist climate for good growth, and it will stop active growth during hot dry summer periods. As it matures, it will become tough and fibrous and nutrient quality will drop sharply. It should be cut early, before the blooming stage.

Johnsongrass

Johnsongrass is commonly grown in the southern United States as a hay crop. It should be cut at the early bloom stage and may yield two or three crops of hay in one year.

Orchardgrass

Orchardgrass is grown in the northern areas of the United States. It produces early spring growth and is quite tolerant of drought and heat. If cut in the early bloom stage, it will be fairly high in quality, but if cut later, it is unpalatable and low in nutrients. It produces a much better quality hay when mixed with a legume.

Fig. 9–4. Orchardgrass seedheads and leaves.

Sudangrass

Sudangrass is easily grown throughout the southern portions of the United States. It grows well in warm climates and on most types of soil. Sudangrass produces two cuttings of hay per year if planted early, and may yield three cuttings in southern regions. To get maximum amount of nutritional value and palatability from sudangrass hay, it should be cut in the early bloom stage or slightly before.

There are a few drawbacks to using sudangrass. It requires large amounts of nitrogen in the soil for good growth, and it is difficult to cure as hay because of its heavy, juicy stems. There is also a slight risk of prussic acid poisoning when feeding sudangrass hay or grazing horses on sudangrass pasture. It is not recommended that horses be grazed on sudangrass pastures. *(See Problems of Johnsongrass Pasture for more information on prussic acid poisoning.)*

Timothy

Timothy is well adapted to the cool, humid regions of the northeast, the Lake States, the Corn Belt, the valleys of the Rocky Mountains, the coastal regions of the Pacific Northwest, and Alaska. It grows on a wide range of soils, tolerates cold weather, produces well in early spring, and is easy to establish.

Nutrient content and feeding value of early bloom timothy are similar to those of high quality bermudagrass hay. These two hays are often substituted for each other when transporting horses.

Timothy is highest in nutrient content, quality, and palatability during pre-bloom and early-bloom stages. Hay cut in late-bloom stage has a reduced crude protein content of 6.9% and a crude fiber content of 31.5%. If the plant has already gone to seed, protein content may be as low as 2%. Although yields in tons per acre are highest at full bloom or later stages, it produces fewer nutrients and is lower in palatability.

Timothy is usually mold-free, unless improperly cured, and it is relatively dust-free, making it a popular hay. Because of its mold- and dust-free characteristics, it is beneficial for horses that suffer from heaves.

Fig. 9–5. Timothy seedhead and leaves.

Timothy is frequently grown in a mixture with a legume crop, such as alfalfa or one of the clovers. Legume increases the protein content, and much of timothy's freedom from dust and mold is retained.

Other Grass Hays

Other grass hays which are used on a somewhat limited basis include bahiagrass, bluegrass, reed canarygrass, and pangolagrass. Their nutritional value varies depending on stage of growth and environmental conditions when harvested.

Tall fescue, a grass forage widely used for pasture in southern regions, is discussed further in the section, *Pasturing Horses.*

Prairie Hays

Prairie hays include many different varieties of wild native grasses. They are of greatest importance in the western states. If prairiegrass hay is cut in the early stages of growth, it is high in nutritional value and palatability. However, quality varies greatly, due to the many different grasses which may be included. On the average, high quality prairie hay contains from 5% to 7% crude protein.

Cereal Grass Hays

Cereal grass hays are made from the common cereal grain crops, such as oats, wheat, rye, and barley. They have a high nutrient value if the seed head is attached, but if the seed head is removed, only straw remains, which makes a poor feed.

Most cereal grass hays (rye being the exception) are very palatable to the horse. Oat hay is the most popular type fed, followed by barley and wheat. Cereal hays must be cut at an early stage, while still green, because the mature stems and leaves are coarse and unpalatable. The crude protein content of oat hay averages 8.6% and contains approximately 29.1% crude fiber. Crude protein content of barley hay is approximately 7.8 and contains approximately 24% crude fiber. Crude protein content of wheat hay is 7.7% and contains 26% crude fiber. Rye hay is low in palatability and quality. Crude protein content is about 6.7%, but it is not a high quality protein. Rye's fiber content is higher than other cereal hays, containing about 38%. The following chart shows the percentages of crude protein, crude fiber, and fat of the most commonly fed cereal grass hays:

Common Cereal Grass Hays			
	Oat Hay	Barley Hay	Wheat Hay	Rye Hay
% crude protein	8.6	7.8	7.7	6.7
% crude fiber	29.1	23.6	25.7	38.0
% fat	2.2	1.9	2.0	2.1

Fig. 9–6.

Legume Hays

Legume hays include alfalfa, the clovers, and lespedeza. As mentioned earlier, legumes differ from grasses because their roots are covered with nodules containing nitrogen fixing bacteria. These bacteria remove nitrogen from the air for the plant to use, instead of from the soil. Because these bacteria provide the plant with large amounts of nitrogen, which is a building block of protein, the protein level of legumes is higher than in grass hays. They also have higher calcium and phosphorus levels, and are good sources of vitamins A, B, and D. They also have a more laxative effect than most grass hays, especially when cut at an early stage.

There is a danger of diarrhea or colic if animals are given a legume hay free-choice when they are not accustomed to it. Horses should be allowed to accommodate themselves to legumes by gradually switching from grass hay to legume hay over a period of about three weeks.

Legume hays are generally higher yielding than grasses, but because they grow more densely, they can be harder to cure. Legumes are often seeded in mixtures with grass hays, because legumes enhance the nutritional value and grass keeps the mix from being too high in energy, protein, and laxative properties. The following chart shows percentages of crude protein, crude fiber, and fat of the most commonly fed legume hays:

Common Legume Hays						
	Alfalfa	Red Clover	Crimson Clover	Alsike Clover	Ladino Clover	Lespedeza
% crude protein	18.0	13.2	16.1	12.4	18.5	11.4
% crude fiber	20.8	27.1	26.3	26.2	21.6	26.2
% fat	2.6	2.5	2.4	2.4	1.7	2.3

Fig. 9–7.

Alfalfa

Alfalfa is the most widely fed legume hay. Good quality, bright green alfalfa is highly nutritious and is an excellent source of *carotene* (precursor of vitamin A) and calcium. When cut at early bloom stage, it contains 18% crude protein and 21% crude fiber. The phosphorus level is low, resulting in an improper calcium to phosphorus ratio (normally 6:1). Consequently, when feeding alfalfa without also feeding a concentrate, phosphorus supplementation is likely to be necessary—especially for young growing horses.

Some portion of the calcium in alfalfa may be unavailable to the horse due to the presence of *oxalic acid*. This acid combines with calcium to form *oxalate*, which cannot be absorbed from the intestines.

Generally, mature horses whose activities require only a maintenance diet do not need the high levels of protein and calcium in alfalfa. *(For more information, see the Calcium Deficiency section in Chapter 4.)*

Alfalfa is grown all over the U. S., although different areas may affect its quality to some degree. Some states that produce alfalfa in abundance are Wisconsin, Minnesota, California, Iowa, and Kansas.

Alfalfa is adapted to widely varying climates and soil, and it produces the highest yields of tonnage per acre and protein content per

Fig. 9–8. Idle mature horses that require only a maintenance diet do not normally need alfalfa.

acre of all the legumes. Alfalfa is capable of surviving periods of drought because of its extensive root system, but it is difficult to grow in hot, humid areas, such as Florida. However, new varieties are being developed which may be able to withstand these climates.

Quality of alfalfa is greatly influenced by moisture content at the time of baling. If the plant is too dry, leaf shattering may result. Leaves contain two-thirds of the energy, three-fourths of the protein, and almost all other nutrients present in the plant, so loss of leaves greatly reduces nutritional value. If hay is too wet when baled, it may mold or undergo a browning reaction in which protein is tied up by carbohydrates. It may even undergo *spontaneous combustion.* Improperly harvested alfalfa may also be quite dusty due to mold and fungus spores, which can be irritating to horses, especially those with respiratory problems.

Alfalfa should be cut just before flowering, in the bud stage, when the nutrients are at their highest level. Some growers prefer to wait until it is in full bloom in order to achieve higher yields. However, at that point the hay is lower in quality.

Alfalfa may produce up to three times as much hay per acre when compared to many of the grass hays. Under good conditions, eight cuttings can be made on the same field in one year.

Some horsemen believe that alfalfa should not be fed in summer because they think it causes horses to overheat and sweat more than normal. This only happens when alfalfa is overfed. It is easier to overfeed alfalfa than grass hays because of its high digestible energy content. If a horse is being fed a diet containing more energy than it needs, it is likely to gain weight in the form of fat. Excess fat increases body heat, and as a result, more sweat is produced. This is not due to the **source** of energy , but rather to an **excess** of energy.

Blister Beetles

Some alfalfa hay may contain blister beetles, which are deadly if ingested by the horse. Blister beetles range in size from ¼ inch to 1 inch in length. They may be black, black with orange-yellow stripes, gray, or yellowish brown with or without black spots. Blister beetles contain *cantharidin,* a powerful irritant and blistering agent which is toxic to all warm-blooded animals, horses being the most severely affected of domestic animals. When cantharidin is consumed, it causes severe irritation and hemorrhage of the intestinal tract. Upon

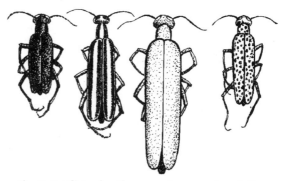

Fig. 9–9. Blister beetles come in several varieties, all of which can be deadly if ingested.

absorption by the intestinal walls, further damage occurs in the kidney and urinary tract.

Ingesting a few of these beetles can be deadly, whether the beetles are alive or dead. Even remains of dead blister beetles from previous year's hay can kill a horse. Levels of cantharidin varies in different species, and it's higher in male blister beetles than in females. The striped beetle is considered the most toxic.

Blister beetles prefer warmer climates and are most commonly found in bales of alfalfa that were grown in central and southern states, especially if the alfalfa was cut after midsummer. Blister beetles are crushed and killed in hay due to the modern practice of cutting and crimping alfalfa in a single operation. If alfalfa is cut without crimping and allowed to cure in the field, beetles will leave the hay.

Blister beetles produce one generation per year, and they are active from May until September. Their larvae (immature form) feed on grasshopper eggs, so the population may be higher if there is a large population of grasshoppers. Larger numbers of blister beetles may be found in irrigated alfalfa, because grasshoppers prefer dry areas and will live in areas around irrigated fields. In years following outbreaks of grasshoppers, there have been correspondingly higher levels of blister beetles.

Adult blister beetles feed in swarms, so some sections of a hayfield may be infested, while others are not. Blister beetles can be controlled with insecticides and by spraying around irrigated fields to limit the grasshopper population.

Symptoms

Symptoms of blister beetle poisoning include abdominal pain, fever as high as 105° F, increased pulse and breathing rate, muscle tremors, severe depression, sweating, dehydration, occasional soft feces, and *hypocalcemia* (low levels of calcium in the blood).

Treatment

Veterinarians often administer mineral oil to help speed the passage of the ingesta containing blister beetles through the digestive tract. The oil also coats the lining of the digestive tract, reducing absorption of the toxic compound. Large quantities (20 – 40 liters) of fluid can be given intravenously to combat dehydration and to excrete the toxin in a more dilute urine concentration. *Analgesics* and steroids may be helpful in controlling pain and shock.

Necropsies on horses that have died from blister beetle poisoning show sections of the first layer of the stomach lining *(epithelium)* missing, inflammation of the intestines, ulcerated lining of the urinary bladder, and severe heart muscle damage.

Alfalfa makes an excellent hay, but it should only be bought from a careful, reputable dealer whose crop is certified free of blister beetles.

Clover Hays

A common source of legume hays are the clovers. Included are:

- red clover
- crimson clover
- white clover
- alsike clover
- ladino clover

Clovers are usually slightly lower than alfalfa in total digestible nutrients and protein content. Because clover grows lower to the ground and its leaves tend to mat when they are cured, it is generally grown in a mixture with grass forages, particularly timothy.

White Clover/Ladino Clover

White clover is a low-growing legume that is not as productive as other clovers, and it is usually grown in a mixture with grass forages. Ladino clover is a larger variety of white clover. White and ladino clovers are usually grown for pasture, but if harvested for hay, they should be cut in early bloom stage. White clover may cause excessive salivation if it is moldy.

Fig. 9–10. White clover is commonly grown in a mixture with grass forages.

Red Clover

Red clover is the most important clover, yielding one or two hay crops in a season, depending on the variety. There are several varieties, all of which may be grown throughout the United States, but they are more commonly found in the northern regions. Red clover grows better than alfalfa on soils that are slightly acidic. It is also more winter hardy than alfalfa, but it does not handle drought as well. For highest quality hay, the crop should be cut at the early-bloom stage. Red clover contains 13.2% crude protein and 27.1% crude fiber.

Feeding moldy red clover may cause excessive salivation in horses, a condition called "slobbers." This condition is due to the presence of *Rhizoctonia leguminicola*, a soil fungus that produces the toxin slaframine, which plays a part in causing horses to drool.

Crimson Clover

Crimson clover is tolerant of humid weather, but not of severe cold. It is grown in the southeastern parts of the United States and does well on a variety of soils. It must be cut before mid-bloom, because as it matures, it becomes tough and unpalatable. Crimson clover contains approximately 16.1% crude protein and 26.3% crude fiber.

Alsike Clover

Alsike clover has thin stems that do not stand upright. It is usually grown with red clover or timothy to increase the total hay yield per acre. It tolerates land that is too wet or acidic for red clover, and it produces a high quality hay that is similar to red clover in nutrient content, containing 12.4% crude protein and 26.2% crude fiber.

Sweet Clover

Sweet clover is generally not recommended as a hay crop, as it has a high ratio of stems to leaves. The stems are thick and juicy, making the hay difficult to cure. It takes longer to dry in the field than the other clovers, so it is subjected to more nutrient losses by the environment. It may also suffer more leaf shattering, due to the leaves over-drying before the stem is dry. Moldy sweet clover is very dangerous to the horse, because it produces dicoumarol, an *anticoagulant*. When ingested, it causes the horse to lose its blood clotting capability, which can result in the horse's death. *(Refer to the section on vitamin K in Chapter 3 for more information.)*

Lespedeza Hay

Lespedeza is widely grown as a hay crop in the south. It grows well in poor soil, is drought-resistant, and because the price of its seed is low, it is economical to grow. However, lespedeza is not as mineral rich as other legumes, and some varieties are high in *tannin*, making them unpalatable. Lespedeza contains approximately 11.4% crude protein and 26.2% crude fiber. It should be cut at early-bloom stage.

Quality of Hay

Hay can be cut more than once during the growing season, but nutrient content varies for each cutting. It is difficult to determine which cutting is best, because quality of hay is dependent upon so many factors. The stage of maturity when cut is important. This is because as the plant matures, it becomes more stemmy, the amount of nutrients decreases, and digestibility decreases. The differences in methods of harvesting and curing also influence the nutrient content of forages.

Hay in the first cutting has the most nutrients, but it also has a higher moisture content and many weeds, which lower nutrient values. Weeds also may affect palatability and possibly even be toxic to the horse. Second to mid cuttings normally have the highest overall nutrient value.

Hay that grows during the hottest part of the growing season generally has more stem and fewer leaves, making it lower in quality. Hay also varies in quality based on management practices of the producer.

Good quality hay is characterized by:

- leafiness
- green color
- soft, fine, pliable stems
- no dust or mold
- fresh smelling, not musty
- no weeds or foreign materials
- leaves not too dry (should not shatter when touched)

Fig. 9–11. Hay should be examined closely before purchase. It should be green, leafy, have fine stems and be free of contaminates.

The inside of the bale should be checked. If discolored, it probably suffered weather damage, excessive heating after baling, or was too mature at cutting. All of these factors indicate a low level of carotene. The outside of the bale may be brown due to sun exposure, but if only the outside is brown, the quality is not lowered significantly.

If mold is present, moisture content (which should be no more than 13%) was probably too high when it was baled. Moisture can also cause hay to heat, ferment, or even undergo spontaneous combustion. Moldy hay should not be fed. It may contain *mycotoxins*, which can cause respiratory problems, abortion, and death.

Buying Hay

When buying hay, it is important to buy the best quality available. Nutrient values of hays mentioned in this text are given on the assumption that each variety is of high quality and is cut and baled under ideal conditions. "Textbook" nutrient values are only guidelines and should be considered useful only if **actual physical qualities of the hay are good.** The physical condition of hay indicates the nutrients which have been retained. Poor quality hay should never be fed.

Because availability of hay generally depends on environmental conditions and local suppliers, top quality hay may not be available. If storage space is available, it is advisable to buy large quantities when high quality, nutritious, palatable hay can be found. However, no more than one year's supply should be purchased, as hay does lose nutrients during storage.

Drying and Curing Hay

Proper drying of hay is very important. If hay is baled when moisture is too high, it can mold, making it worthless. There are several methods of drying hay, and they are often used in combination.

The easiest method is to cut the hay and allow it to sun-cure for two to three days. This method is used for grass hays and some legume hays. Water leaves the plant through the *stomates* (pores in the leaves), the *cuticle* (waxy covering on stems and leaves), and the point at which stems have been cut.

Hay exposed to the sun longer than two or three days starts losing nutrients and palatability. Also, if hay is rained on while curing, some nutrients will be washed out.

Most mowers have crimpers and crushers on them, devices which crimp or crack open the stems, allowing the plant to dry more quickly. These are often used on legume forages, which are harder to dry than grass hays, due to their thicker stems and matted leaves.

Drying Agents

Chemical drying agents are also used on legumes. The most effective of these drying agents is potassium carbonate. A mixture of potassium carbonate and sodium carbonate may also be used.

Chemical drying agents increase the drying rate by breaking down the waxy cuticle on the plant, allowing more water to be released. However, this method still depends on atmospheric conditions for optimum drying. If it is a cool or humid day, evaporation will be retarded and the plant will take longer to dry. If chemically treated plants are rained on, they will absorb more water than non-chemically treated plants. Plants rapidly dry out again, but lose valuable nutrients.

Preservatives

Preservatives such as propionic and acetic acids are also used. These are compounds that are normally found in the digestive tract of the horse. They allow the hay to be baled at a higher moisture content. They also help retain the hay's nutrient-filled leaves, inhibit mold growth, and decrease heat damage in stored hay. Treated hay is beneficial for horses that are prone to respiratory problems such as heaves. It dries more evenly, decreasing leaf shattering and alleviating dustiness.

There are problems associated with using preservatives. The preservatives' corrosive nature can ruin baling equipment. Also, preservatives must be applied uniformly; if not, pockets of mold may develop in the hay. If too much preservative is applied, vitamin levels may be diminished, causing the hay to turn brown.

Chemically treated hay should be introduced gradually into a ration, so the horse's digestive system can become accustomed to it. Treated hay tastes different than untreated hay, so horses may not initially accept it.

Drying After Baling

Hay may be dried after it has been baled. This is achieved by circulating air through the hay, but it should only be done to hay that has already been dried to a moisture content of about 25% before baling.

Fig. 9–12. Hay being sun-cured prior to baling.

If hay is to be dried by air or artificial heat, it must be stacked tightly, so air is forced through it, rather than through spaces between the bales. Artificial heat can be supplied by solar heaters in the roof. These evaporate water from hay, and fans then remove the evaporated water. Hay can also be stacked over grill-covered ducts. Fans placed at the open end of the duct force air through the hay, evaporating moisture.

Proper Storage

Hay should be stored in a dry, well ventilated area, and placing bales on pallets allows air to circulate underneath. Hay stored without proper ventilation can become heat damaged, moldy, or even undergo spontaneous combustion. If hay is stored in a loft, there should be small ventilator panels in the sides of the loft, under the eaves. Panels allow air to circulate, and cupolas in the roof allow the air to exit.

Storing hay above horses' stalls should be avoided. All hay, no matter how high in quality, can contain dust, pollen, mold spores, and fungus spores. Stabled horses that continuously breathe these irritants may suffer respiratory problems.

Fig. 9–13. Cupolas allow air to circulate out of a barn.

Danger of fire is a strong argument against storing hay near horses. Spontaneous combustion can cause just one bale to ignite, and the rest will be consumed very quickly. Many horses have lost their lives in fires that started in hay.

Where possible, hay should be stored in a separate building from horses. If this is not an option, ample ventilation to remove dust and spores should be provided and hay should be checked frequently for mold and heat, as a precaution against fire. *(All other fire prevention methods should be adhered to strictly as well. Any kind of stable fire usually has disastrous results.)*

Analyzing Hay

Having hay analyzed by a laboratory is a useful tool for determining its nutritional content and its contribution to a horse's daily ration. When analyzing hay, values for moisture, crude protein, energy, phosphorus, and calcium should be determined. Levels of some other minerals can be determined by analysis, including potassium, iron, magnesium, manganese, zinc, and copper. Levels of selenium, iodine, and vitamins can also be determined, but the process is usually more expensive than for other minerals.

"Wet chemistry" hay analysis, including *proximate analysis, in vitro digestion,* and the *Kjeldahl protein test,* determines values for amounts of dry matter, crude fiber, crude protein, and acid detergent fiber. They may also be used to estimate total digestible nutrients, digestible energy, and even net energy.

A newer method of analyzing hay is *near-infrared reflectance* (NIR). This yields comparable results in less time and at a lower cost.

NIR determines levels of:

- energy in megacalories per pound
- estimated digestible protein
- available fiber (neutral detergent fiber, or NDF)*
- unavailable fiber (acid detergent fiber, or ADF)**
- total digestible nutrients (TDN)
- crude protein
- dry matter

Neutral detergent fiber refers to fiber that fills the digestive tract and is slowly digested.

**Acid detergent fiber indicates the digestibility of a forage, as it has a high lignin content and is not readily digested.*

NIR also provides estimates of these minerals:

- phosphorus
- calcium
- potassium
- magnesium

In hay analysis, a core sampler is inserted 12 to 15 inches into the bale to obtain a sample. Several samples from different bales are taken and thoroughly mixed together in order to even out some of the variances in nutrients that naturally occur from bale to bale. These samples are placed in an air tight container to preserve the moisture level, and then taken to a testing laboratory for analysis.

PASTURE FORAGES

Good quality pasture has a higher energy, protein, vitamin, and mineral content than even early cut hay of the same variety. This is because even quality hay loses nutrients in the cutting, baling and storing stages.

In some instances, particularly in the spring, lush green grass pasture can be very rich, containing up to 15% crude protein, although in most cases it will range from 5% to 10%. Pasture forage is the best source of carotene available. It is also rich in B vitamins and vitamin E. Although pasture forage is not a good source of vitamin D, that is not important since grazing animals are exposed to sunlight, which enables them to synthesize vitamin D readily in the skin.

Although pasture is rich in nutrients, it is also moderately high in fiber (approximately 20%). Compared to hay, pasture forage has a higher TDN, but because its moisture content is higher than in hay, larger quantities must be consumed to obtain adequate nutrients.

High quality pasture, trace mineralized salt, and water can supply pregnant mares in early gestation and mature idle horses with their nutritional requirements. For other classes of horses, pasture alone will not be sufficient. Young, growing horses will need higher protein and TDN intake than pasture alone can furnish. This is also true for broodmares during the last three months of pregnancy and lactation, as well as performance or hard working horses.

Pasture that is not properly planted, fertilized and maintained should **not** be counted on to supply daily nutrient requirements. Also, during winter, pasture growth will be inhibited during cold months, and alternate nutritional sources (such as high quality hay and grain) will have to be provided. *(Nutritional analyses of forages used in pastures are in the Appendix.)*

Pasture grazing also provides horses with important psychological benefits. It allows horses to escape the confines of the stall, to relax, stretch, move around and visit with other horses. This is important for an animal that is naturally gregarious and genetically inclined to appreciate freedom.

Pasture grazing should of course be avoided if there is heavy parasite infestation, or when toxic weeds or minerals are present.

Fig. 9–14. Good quality pasture is an excellent source of essential nutrients.

Types of Pastures

Originally, pastures were composed of native grasses or grass/legume mixes. Native grasses grew naturally in areas to which they were adapted, so they were hardy and ideally suited to the land and climatic conditions. While there are still native grass pastures in use, many of them have become depleted by heavy grazing or by recurrent stands of grasses which have removed necessary minerals from the soil. For this reason, more and more horsemen have turned to improved, planned, and managed pastures.

Pastures may be permanent or temporary. Permanent pastures, when properly maintained, can provide high quality nutrients for several years. In many situations, permanent pastures are grown on land that is unprofitable for crops. These areas usually consist of rangeland where moisture content and soil fertility are limited.

Temporary pastures are generally utilized in a crop rotation system or to provide pasture at special times. They may be used for a short period of time, during seasonal periods when permanent pastures are relatively unproductive, or they may be grown for several years on land normally used for crops. This is done to help replenish the nutrients in the soil.

When planting pasture, a County Agricultural Agent can be consulted for information concerning plant varieties that grow best in the area. Bulletins containing information on pasture management are available through their offices.

The different varieties of forages planted should be compatible with each other, so that less hardy plants will not be crowded out. For example, if the pasture includes low-growing clovers and tall grasses, the tall grasses may shade the clovers and prevent them from developing properly. It is also important to choose grasses that are comparable in palatability and rate of growth, so that horses do not eat only certain plants and leave others.

Combination Pastures

Many pastures today are grass/legume mixes (e.g. bermudagrass/clover). Wherever possible, including legumes in a pasture mix is advantageous. Legumes obtain nitrogen from the air and add it to the soil, promoting life of the pasture and growth of other plants. They are also better protein sources than grasses.

Mixing different species has an additional advantage. If a pasture becomes infected by disease or infested by insects, all vegetation is not likely to be completely destroyed. Different species usually will not be affected equally (or at all) by the same problem.

Another advantage is that when species have different growing seasons, they can be seeded in the same pasture, so when one forage is ending its growing season, the other species is beginning to take its place. However, during the time of fresh new growth, pastures should not be heavily grazed, because the productivity of the plants may be decreased.

Fig. 9–15. A grass/legume mix pasture provides higher levels of nutrients than grass alone.

Native Grass Pastures

Every region of the country has native grasses that are well adapted for pasture in that region. Examples are Kentucky bluegrass, coastal bermudagrass in the south, the western mountain grasses, and the prairie grasses. These grasses should form an important part of the pastures in the regions where they grow well, and little, if any, reseeding will be necessary to maintain these native varieties.

Legume Pastures

Usually, fields which contain only legumes are not used for pastures, because they are worth more as as hay crop. If intended for grazing, legume pastures are often mixed with grasses.

Legumes are known for their long growing season. Because they can obtain nitrogen from the air, they generally contain higher quantities of protein than grass. Horses grazing on legume will require more water because they urinate more frequently. This is due to *urea*, the waste product of protein metabolism which requires water for its elimination.

Horses that are unaccustomed to legume pastures should be introduced to them by gradually increasing grazing time each day. If this is not done, loose stools and gastric disturbances may result. Combining grass forages with legumes will also reduce the possibility of problems occurring.

Legume forages which may be used for pasture include:

- alfalfa
- red clover
- ladino clover
- trefoil
- white clover
- crimson clover
- lupine
- lespedeza

Alfalfa
Advantages
- can be grown almost anywhere in the United States
- contains many vital nutrients essential for the equine
- long-lived when properly managed
- can be seeded with other pasture plants or by itself
- resistant to drought

Disadvantages
- has difficulty growing in acidic and non-fertile soils
- seeds are quite expensive
- may contain blister beetles
- insects such as the alfalfa weevil and the potato leafhopper can cause serious damage to pastures

In an effort to combat harmful insects without using stronger chemical pesticides, scientists have begun attempting genetic manipulation with plants. At Kansas State University, a sticky-haired alfalfa plant is being developed as a defense against the alfalfa weevil and the potato leafhopper. The fluid secreted by this plant traps and kills the newly-hatched insects as they emerge from the stems.

Crimson Clover
Advantages
- considered a winter legume, of which there are few
- provides winter forage in the south and spring forage in the north
- hard-seed perennial varieties have been developed which germinate in the fall

Disadvantages
- not productive in summer months
- regular crimson clover must be planted annually
- only adapted to warm climates
- cannot withstand severe winter temperatures

Ladino Clover
Advantages
- easily established
- very productive
- high in minerals, vitamins, and protein
- low in fiber
- more tolerant than alfalfa of wet soils common in winter
- re-establishes itself easily by natural seeding
- rapid recovery time following close grazing
- combines well with grasses

Disadvantages
- when planted too deeply, germination will be poor
- very susceptible to drought
- does not withstand continuous close grazing
- has a laxative effect when first introduced to the diet
- will die if it enters the winter months too long or too short

Lespedeza

Advantages
- grows well on soils which are not highly fertile
- high quality varieties can be easily obtained
- seed prices are relatively low
- yields are high when other forages are more or less dormant

Disadvantages
- contains fewer minerals when compared to other legumes
- productive growth is limited to warm summer months

Red Clover

Advantages
- produces high yields of nutritious forage one year after seeding
- grows better in acidic soils when compared to other legumes
- hardier during winter months when compared to alfalfa
- grows faster than white clover

Disadvantages
- is susceptible to disease, so may be short-lived
- must be re-planted about every two years
- more susceptible to drought than alfalfa, due to its shorter root system

Sweet Clover

Advantages
- grows well in areas which have 17 inches or more of rainfall a year, if the soils are well fertilized
- productive when many other pasture plants are dormant

Disadvantages
- moldy sweet clover may contain dicoumarol, a mycotoxin which destroys vitamin K in the body
- difficult to produce mold-free
- usually not eaten readily when horses are first introduced to it
- seedlings must be continuously grazed or they will become woody and overly mature
- requires well limed soils rich in phosphorus and potassium

White Clover
Advantages
- an excellent pasture legume
- combines well with orchardgrass, bluegrass, and tall fescue
- grows in a variety of soils
- re-establishes itself easily by using natural seeding
- can withstand close grazing
- highly nutritious

Disadvantages
- sensitive to drought
- seed is very small, making it difficult to establish a good stand
- yields less than Ladino clover

Grasses

Pasture grasses can either be *perennials*, which grow continuously year after year, or *annuals*, which germinate, grow, produce seed, and then die. Both are further classified by the time period of their maxi-

mum growth. They may either be cool-season, which begin growing in fall, or warm-season, which begin growing in the spring. Cereal grain grasses, such as tall oat grass, are generally annuals. Annuals do not necessarily have to be replanted each year, depending on how well they produce seed and the hardiness of the seed.

Fig. 9–16. There are many varieties of grasses available to meet different pasture needs.

Bahiagrass
Advantages
- uses heavy runners to spread and form dense *sod,* even when soil is drought stricken and/or sandy
- adapted well to the southern coastal plains, an area where many other grasses fail

Disadvantages
- cannot survive in even moderately cold temperatures
- difficult to establish stands which provide adequate grazing
- unfertilized soils have poor yields

Bermudagrass

Advantages

- grows extremely well during hot summer
- spreads by underground *rhizomes* (horizontal underground plant stems which produce new shoots and roots) and above ground *stolons* (similar to rhizomes except they project off the stem and are found above ground)
- properly fertilized improved varieties produce large quantities
- is a perennial, so does not require annual seeding

Disadvantages

- not hardy in cold weather
- coastal and midland varieties are very sparse seed producers, so expansion must rely on above ground stolons
- bermudagrass is very difficult to remove when no longer wanted

Special Problems

Some believe horses grazing on bermudagrass will be susceptible to impaction colic. However, **any** grass which becomes excessively mature will contain large quantities of *lignin*, a complex carbohydrate which is not readily digested and has no nutritional value. Lignin, when ingested in large quantities, can predispose the horse to impaction colic. It is also possible, during winter months when bermudagrass lacks growth, that grazing horses consume rhizomes and sand, causing impaction colic.

Bluestem

Bluestem is a native grass of the midwest. It has occasional rhizomes and is a perennial.

Advantages

- grows well in warm climates
- well adapted to the northern plains and valley regions
- tolerant of alkaline (basic) soils

Disadvantages

- not very palatable once seedheads form
- easily replaced by other grasses when heavily grazed
- forage production is limited to the warm season
- leaves are rough and narrow

Bromegrass

Advantages

- long-lived and does not require planting every year (perennial)
- adapted to regions with moderate rainfall and temperatures
- grows throughout the spring and summer

- highly palatable
- fits well into all legume mixtures

Disadvantages
- requires fertile soil
- cannot withstand long periods of hot, dry weather
- susceptible to many plant diseases

Crested Wheatgrass

Advantages
- a hardy perennial
- well adapted to the Northern Great Plains and regions around the Rocky Mountains
- root system penetrates deep into the ground
- can withstand drought, cold, and close grazing
- competes well with weeds
- has high yields and is very palatable
- begins growing in early spring

Disadvantages
- stops active growth during hot, dry seasons
- has a bunch-like growth pattern in which plants are not spread out evenly

Fig. 9–17. Crested Wheatgrass seedhead.

Dallisgrass

Advantages
- produces high yields during hot summer
- seldom produces dense sod, so combines well with other grasses
- maintains a good stand when well fertilized and managed
- produces good yields for many years

Disadvantages
- requires well irrigated soils that contain large quantities of *organic* matter (plant and animal wastes and debris)
- seed germination can be low, due to the presence of an *ergot* fungus, which destroys the seeds
- difficult to remove when unwanted
- very unpalatable when mature

Fig. 9–18. Dallisgrass seedheads and leaves.

Fescue

Fescue, a perennial, prefers cool seasons. It is also the dominant species on an estimated 35 million acres in the United States. It is a very aggressive and hardy forage. Many fields which were originally established with other forages are now primarily fescue.

Advantages
- well adapted to many regions
- can withstand close grazing
- has high yields
- combines well with clovers
- resistant to disease and drought
- in mild climates it will stay green throughout the entire winter
- easy to establish
- can grow well in wet soils

Disadvantages
- lower in palatability than other grasses
- requires careful management when mixed with legumes

Special Problems

Fescue infected with the fungus *Acremonium coenophialum* can cause numerous reproductive problems. Mares grazing on infected pastures will often experience prolonged pregnancy—an additional 30 days or more. *Dystocia* (difficult birth) can also result, as well as thickened and retained placentas. Difficult foalings and placenta-related problems can cause death of both foal and mare.

After foaling, a mare which has eaten infected fescue will often ex-hibit *agalactia*, a lack of milk production. The severity of this condi-tion will vary from limited milk let down to no milk let down. Either of these situations can be critical to the life of the foal. It is vital that the foal receive *colostrum*, which contains antibodies needed to build up the immune system, as well as many other important nutrients. Re-moving mares from infected fescue pasture two weeks before the de-livery date will eliminate most or all of the effects of the fungus.

Fescue pastures which are tested and found to be free of the fungus will not cause problems. This fungus is not found in soil and does not have the ability to spread from plant to plant. The only manner it can be introduced into a pasture is by an infected seed.

Existing fescue pasture should be tested by laboratory analysis to determine what, if any, percentage of the plants contains the fungus. Most fescue pastures located in the United States contain 70% fun-gus-infected plants. If a pasture is found to be infected, all of the ex-isting infected fescue seeds must be destroyed before planting new fungus-free seeds. Various herbicides are available for this purpose.

To combat these problems, fescue *hybrids* have been developed. The Johnstone Tall Fescue® variety is a hybrid formed with ryegrass and fungus-free fescue. This hybrid offers superior palatability, di-gestibility, and hardiness.

Fescue seeds which are used to form this hybrid are treated at temperatures of 120° Fahrenheit for seven days, killing any fungus present in the seed. Since the fungus can only be spread through the seed, this treatment works quite well.

Johnsongrass

Advantages
- hardy and roots spread well underground
- when grazed regularly, Johnsongrass produces high yields
- produces well during hot, dry months

Disadvantages
- may spread into areas where it is not wanted
- is difficult to eliminate
- may contain prussic acid

Special Problems
There is a slight risk of prussic acid poisoning when grazing horses on Johnsongrass. Prussic acid-yielding compounds are highest during periods of new growth or after stresses such as trampling, drought, or frost. When these situations exist, horses should be kept off the pasture for a few days to allow the prussic acid to break down.

Symptoms of prussic acid poisoning include abnormal breathing, trembling muscles, spasms or convulsions, nervousness, and respiratory failure. Prussic acid poisoning is rapid and often not detected in time to save the horse. Sodium nitrite is a recommended treatment, but usually cannot be administered quickly enough. Death can occur in one to two minutes after eating contaminated forage.

Fig. 9–19. Kentucky Bluegrass seedheads and leaves.

Kentucky Bluegrass

Advantages
- nutritious, rich in vitamins and minerals
- spreads by underground rhizomes and, as a result, is well rooted in suitable soil
- well adapted to northern and mountainous soils and cool southern regions
- grows well when combined with white clover or birdsfoot trefoil (a legume)
- grows naturally when soil conditions are favorable

Disadvantages
- becomes dormant during hot, dry periods, and will turn brown if it does not receive adequate water

> • requires soils which contain high concentrations of phosphorus and lime
> • yields are consistently low compared to other grasses

Orchardgrass

Advantages
> • very widely adapted
> • hardy and long-lived
> • does not require very fertile soils to grow
> • does well in shady areas
> • new growth begins in early spring
> • surpasses timothy and bromegrass in midsummer production
> • does well when combined with ladino clover and lespedeza

Disadvantages
> • careful management is required when maintaining legumes with orchardgrass
> • grows in bunches

Reed Canarygrass

Advantages
> • has a long growing season and is a perennial
> • produces sod
> • contains more leaves than the average grass forage
> • grows well during hot summer months
> • spreads well underground with its extensive root system
> • grows well on fertile, wet swampy soils
> • is very drought-resistant when compared to other grasses

Disadvantages
> • is unpalatable when mature
> • soils containing large quantities of clay and sand must be heavily fertilized with nitrogen or manure for proper growth
> • seed germination is low; summer weeds can create competition
> • seed is high priced when compared to other grasses
> • seed is very fragile and shatters easily in hot, dry, windy weather
> • contains *hordenine* when mature, a compound detectable in drug tests and can cause disqualification of performance horses

Ryegrass

Advantages
> • easy to establish
> • develops rapidly after seeding
> • seed is relatively inexpensive

Disadvantages
- does not have a long growing season
- if grown with slower growing grasses and legumes, it will use the nutrients which the slower growing plants need, making it highly competitive with them
- can become coarse and stemmy without irrigation

Sudangrass

Sudangrass and sorghum-sudan related hybrids are **not** recommended for use in horse pastures, as ingestion of these grasses during their growing stage can cause horses to develop *cystitis,* a bladder inflammation. Cystitis is characterized by frequent, strained urination, dribbling of urine, and general incoordination. It affects mares most often, causing them to appear to be in continuous heat. Horses seldom recover once they reach the stage of incoordination or dribbling urine.

Prussic acid poisoning can also result from grazing on sudangrass and its hybrids. For more information on prussic acid, refer to *Special Problems* in the *Johnsongrass* section earlier in this chapter.

Timothy

Advantages
- well adapted to cool humid regions, such as the northeast, corn belt, Rocky Mountain valleys, coastal regions of the Pacific Northwest, and the Lake States
- grows well with birdsfoot trefoil
- high quality seedlings are easy to obtain for planting
- seed is relatively inexpensive
- highly palatable

Disadvantages
- has lower yields when compared to orchardgrass, bromegrass, and fescue
- yields will decrease significantly during drought periods

Other Grasses

The following grasses can be used as pasture forage, but they generally are not as high in nutrients and lack many of the desirable characteristics of a number of grasses already discussed:

- blue grama grass
- redtop grass
- switchgrass
- buffalo grass
- meadow foxtail
- tall oatgrass
- pangola grass

The following chart shows common grasses and areas where they grow well:

Region	Grasses
Florida, southern Georgia, Gulf Coast region	pangola grass, bahiagrass, coastal bermudagrass
Middle Atlantic states	coastal bermudagrass, orchardgrass, fescue, white clover, red clover, bluegrass
Northeast	redtop grass, reed canarygrass, orchardgrass
Midwest	smooth bromegrass, buffalograss, bluestem grass, blue grama grass
Southwest	coastal bermudagrass, rye grass
Northwest	fescue, blue grama grass, bluestem grass, bentgrass, crested wheat grass
Far West	orchard grass, coastal bermuda grass, lovegrass, rhodes grass, fescue grass

Fig. 9–20.

Grazing Patterns and Livestock Rotation

It is impossible to suggest a minimum number of acres per horse for pasture without knowing exact specifications. (e.g. geographical area, amount of rainfall, management practices, etc.) A survey of horse farms in Kentucky found that an average of four acres of pasture per horse is common. That information is good for someone with average pastures in Kentucky. In some highly fertile areas, two acres might be sufficient—in other areas it might take fifty. For information in a specific area, County Agricultural Agents, local veterinarians and successful horsemen in the area can furnish suggestions. There are only two rules of thumb: "Use the best management practices, and more pasture is always better than less!"

Usually, horses will select the more palatable, tender grasses from the mixture within a pasture. Areas of the pasture which have unpalatable weeds or coarse, over-mature grasses may be completely avoided. For this reason, it is important to control weeds within a pasture, select forages which are comparable in palatability and maturity, and watch carefully for signs of selective grazing.

Fig. 9–21. Moderately grazed pastures have time to re-establish themselves between grazing periods.

If horses graze the same pasture continuously, forages may become depleted. Forages which are grazed down close to the roots cannot effectively maintain nutrient value and support new growth. Total nutrient yield of a pasture will be lower if it is over-grazed. Moderately grazed pastures have time to re-establish themselves between grazing periods. This is very important in spring, before forages are well established. If grazed too early in the life cycle, plants may soon die out. On the other hand, undergrazing is also a problem, because plants may become too mature and thus lower in quality.

Having multiple pastures allows rotational grazing. Rotational grazing provides a substantial advantage when controlling quality and productivity of pastures. In addition rotation is a useful method of reducing and controlling spread of internal parasites. Pastures used continuously, without rotation or rest may become heavily infested with worms, and the life cycle of the parasites will continue.

Rotating pasture use between cattle and horses is a useful management practice. Cattle will eat the longer, tougher, more mature portions of the grass which horses often leave behind. This reduces spot grazing and allows the pasture to be grazed more evenly. The rotation of cattle onto horse pastures will also break up the equine parasite chain, because the majority of equine parasites are unable to affect cattle and will die off. However, one type of stomach worm, *Trichostrongylus axei*, which is common in cattle and sheep, can also parasitize horses. If horses are grazed with cattle, or even on a pasture which was previously grazed by cattle, infestation by this parasite will be a problem unless effective deworming practices are followed.

In the spring, when pastures are green and lush, horses should be allowed gradual access to accustom them to the pasture and to prevent founder and colic. Allowing them to graze only a few hours each day for the first week is a good method. Also, providing plenty of dry hay prior to their first day of grazing is helpful.

Grass tetany can occur if horses are not given time to accommodate their systems slowly to lush pasture. This condition is associated with low magnesium and calcium levels in the blood. Symptoms include:

- muscle spasms
- tremors
- sweating
- heavy breathing
- general incoordination

Although somewhat common in the past, grass tetany is now a rare occurrence in the horse.

Pasture Maintenance

Good pasture maintenance includes fertilization, liming, weed control, reseeding, mowing, irrigation, and control of fecal matter. Pastures should also be kept free of objects which may injure horses. In addition, grazing during very wet weather should be avoided, as it damages the turf.

Fertilization, Liming, and Weed Removal

Fertilization and liming of pasture is necessary if it is to maintain strong, healthy plant growth. The soil should be analyzed at least every three years, before seeding, and whenever plants appear to be deficient or if mineral deficiencies are suspected in horses grazing on it. After analysis, proper fertilization is required to correct any deficiencies. If this is not done, the pasture will be of low quality and will become depleted of nutrients.

If legumes are grown, nitrogen in the soil is not likely to become depleted, but in a grass-only pasture, nitrogen fertilization is important to maintain high protein levels. Phosphorus and potassium are other substances likely to be required for pasture fertilization.

If soil is too acidic to support desired plants, lime may be added to neutralize it. The acidity of the soil is determined by testing its pH level.

Regular weeding of pastures can help remove weeds before they become established. Toxic weeds can become established in a pasture very quickly, and their effects may not be noticed until horses become ill. Unless it is an extremely large pasture, checking the boundaries is usually sufficient to note weed growth and ungrazed areas. If there are areas of desirable grasses which have matured and become unpalatable, to the point that they are being avoided, the pasture should be mowed. This will pave the way for young, tender new growth that will be readily eaten.

Poisonous Plants

Poisonous plants, which have a tendency to grow along fence lines and around ponds and lakes, should be carefully controlled. Many poisonous plants exist, however only a few are usually a problem in a specific geographical area. Knowing which ones to be alert for is important. This information is usually available from County Agricultural Agents. Some common varieties of poisonous plants that may appear in pastures are:

• Locoweed	• Brackenfern	• Wild cherry trees
• Milkweed	• Lantana	• Laurel
• Larkspur	• Buckeye	• Yellow star thistle

Avocado and yew poisoning are very dangerous and can result in death of the horse. They are not plants typically grown in pastures, but horses may still have access to them without the owner being aware.

Avocado Poisoning

Avocado poisoning is a significant problem encountered in southern California, and it can have serious effects. Leaves, bark, and fruit of the avocado tree are toxic to horses. Poisoning can even occur if wilted leaves are blown into a pasture and consumed. Symptoms of avocado poisoning include:

- depression
- appetite loss
- colic
- swellings around mouth and head, which can extend to neck and chest; these swellings sometimes resemble snake bites

Most horses survive avocado poisoning if they receive prompt veterinary treatment.

Yew Poisoning

Planting of yew around any horse operation is strongly discouraged. Yew poisoning can result in death after consumption of less than ten ounces (one or two bites) of the plant. Not a native plant, yew is often used as an ornamental shrub. It is often found along driveways or around houses and yards in many geographical areas. Usually, the horse dies before showing any obvious symptoms, but if any are evident, they will include shortness of breath, muscle tremor, weakness, and sudden collapse. Symptoms are similar to heart failure, because the toxin in yew has a strong depressive effect on the heart. There may also be inflammation of the digestive tract and bloody diarrhea. If the horse is discovered still alive, it may be saved, but only through intensive veterinary care.

Thistles

Thistles, which can cause havoc in horse pastures, are best controlled when they are young and vegetative. Thistles should be sprayed with a herbicide in early spring when the temperature is above 60° Fahrenheit. Horses should be kept off the treated pasture for the rest of the season. If only certain areas of the pasture are infested, spot spraying individual plants will control the spread of seeds. An alternative to using a chemical herbicide is to cut out thistles completely and burn them.

Safer herbicides that are sun activated and pose no threat to humans or animals are also available. These herbicides contain an amino acid called delta-amino-laevulnic acid. In laboratory testing, weeds sprayed with these herbicides were killed in 20 minutes. When the weed is sprayed with the amino acid, it begins producing large quantities of tetrapyroles. Tetrapyroles are light-sensitive compounds that normally form *chlorophyll* in plants. However, when large quantities of tetrapyroles are produced and accumulate in the weed, sunlight and oxygen present in the air cause a chemical reaction. This reaction creates an explosion within the weed which results in its death.

The amino acid used in this herbicide is not toxic and is metabolized by the plant in 24 hours. In addition, the tetrapyroles are removed in four hours of daylight. These sun-activated herbicides are considered to be quite safe.

Reseeding

Whenever quality of a pasture is dropping severely and cannot be brought back, the pasture should be plowed and reseeded. If this is not done, several things can occur:
- pasture yield will begin to drop sharply
- quality of forage will be low
- weeds will proliferate
- the soil will become depleted of essential minerals

Weeds can take over an entire pasture within a few years. Reseeding allows plants to remain evenly mixed. If the pasture is never reseeded, useful plants may be restricted to specific locations.

Whenever pastures are reseeded, the soil should be tested to determine if fertilization is necessary. Another benefit is to allow one year of rest for every two years of grazing within a pasture, so the soil does not become depleted of essential minerals too rapidly. Whenever a pasture is reseeded, it should not be grazed until the new plants are at least 3 inches tall, allowing them to become established and firmly rooted.

Grazing should not be delayed too long, as the plants may begin to grow very rapidly once they are established. In this case, horses may not be able to keep the plants grazed down enough, allowing the pasture to become tall and mature. If this happens, it should be mowed or cut for hay and allowed to grow again. Mowing pastures regularly will prevent overly mature plants from becoming predominant.

Mineral Supplementation

Good pasture management includes supplying an unlimited supply of clean, fresh water and salt sources when horses are grazed. High quality pasture can supply most essential minerals, but probably will not contain enough sodium and chloride. For this reason, trace mineralized salt in block or loose form is normally essential for pastured horses. In either form it should be appropriately protected from weather conditions.

Horses tend to graze more heavily in the areas where water and salt supplies are located, a fact that should be considered when choosing grazing locations. Placing the trace mineralized salt blocks a good distance from water will encourage the horses to move throughout the entire pasture, as will occasionally changing the location of the salt blocks.

Irrigation

Although installing an irrigation system is expensive, in dry regions the probability of losing large amounts of vegetation from an extended drought may be sufficient to justify the cost.

Control of Fecal Material

Controlling manure accumulation is an essential part of pasture maintenance, especially if there is a large number of horses per acre. Horses avoid grazing in areas where they defecate, resulting in patches of tall, unused grass. Chain dragging pastures scatters manure piles and avoids selective grazing. It also breaks parasite cycles and returns nutrients to the soil for plant utilization.

An even better management practice is to remove manure from pastures at least twice weekly. Parasite levels can be effectively reduced by this method. Manure can be removed manually (shovel, pitchfork) or by machine (vacuum pump). Harrowing is **not** advised, as it will spread parasite larvae in the grazing area and also damage the forage.

Manure taken from stalls should be composted and allowed to dry out before being spread on pasture. Fresh manure will infest the pasture with parasite eggs and larvae, and weed seeds.

Fig. 9–22. Removing manure from pastures is a good management practice.

10

FEEDING MANAGEMENT

GENERAL GUIDELINES
Feeding Time and Frequency

The horse is a grazing animal, genetically designed both physically and mentally to eat frequent small meals. An ideal feeding program for the stabled horse consuming fairly large amounts of concentrate—with limited or no pasture grazing time—would include dividing the concentrate ration into at least four feedings per day. The feedings should be separated by equal time spans during the 24 hour period. Hay would either be provided free-choice, or fed 15 minutes prior to the concentrate ration at each feeding.

If circumstances prohibit four or more feedings per day, dividing the concentrate ration into three portions, separated by equal time spans, is considered adequate for most horses. The same rules concerning the hay ration, mentioned above, should be observed.

Two feedings per day is a minimum requirement even for horses consuming small amounts of concentrate (i.e. horses not in heavy training or performance). If two feedings per day of concentrate is the program used, then feeding hay free-choice is strongly recommended. Otherwise, the horse may become bored between feedings.

Fig. 10–1. The stabled horse benefits mentally and physically from having its daily ration divided into multiple feedings.

It may resort to eating its bedding, cribbing, or coprophagy (eating feces), or other stable vices. Also, the availability of free-choice hay will help avoid possible digestive disturbances caused by infrequent feedings.

Feeding less than twice per day to the stabled horse is definitely not recommended. Such treatment will likely result in digestive changes which will be unhealthy or even life-threatening, and probably produce psychological problems as well.

Problems With Infrequent Feedings

A major concern with infrequent feedings is the large amount of concentrate that may be required per feeding. The equine stomach has a small capacity, so when large amounts of grain are consumed, they are forced through the digestive tract too rapidly. As the horse continues eating, the feed moves out of the stomach to the small intestine, and from there into the large intestine. Feed that is moved too quickly out of the stomach and small intestine is not properly digested, which will increase the tendency toward digestive upsets. It may also make the energy in the feed less available to the horse. When the daily ration is divided into smaller amounts and more frequent feedings, proper digestion can take place.

Infrequent feedings can also be detrimental to the intestinal bacteria. When the large colon is empty for long periods of time, the bacteria begin to die off, since they rely on a constant presence of feed for their survival. Bacteria are essential for proper fiber digestion, as well as for B vitamin and protein synthesis.

A study conducted at North Carolina State University compared the results of feeding six pounds of grain over a twelve-hour period to two groups of horses. One group was given one pound of grain every two hours. The other group was given only two feedings, one at each end of the twelve-hour period. The horses fed only twice per day experienced disruptions in their digestive tracts and circulatory systems. The documented problems were:

1) Large amounts of fluid were drawn from the bloodstream to generate saliva that accompanied the feed into the stomach.

2) Blood volumes fell and concentration of *blood solids* (red and white blood cells and *platelets*) became elevated, slowing delivery of oxygen to muscle and brain cells as blood thickened.

3) The endocrine system released hormones that raised the blood pressure and reduced blood flow to the digestive tract, and as a result:

    a. The circulatory system's ability to deliver oxygen and nutrients was hindered.

    b. Absorption of nutrients and electrolytes into the bloodstream was hampered.

    c. Cases of colic were more likely to occur.

4) Because of the large amount of concentrate fed, the small intestine was not given enough time to fully digest the feed, so large quantities of concentrate moved rapidly through it and into the *hindgut* (cecum and large intestine), improperly flooding it with soluble *carbohydrates*.

5) The hindgut was forced to react and adapt to an unnatural digestive rhythm and, as a result, there were fluctuating imbalances in electrolyte levels.

6) These events predisposed the horse to colic and gastric upset.

Horses fed at two hour intervals did **not** experience any of these abnormal physiological changes.

The shift in fluid volumes that occurs in the horse's body, due to ingestion of large amounts of feed in a short time, triggers a reaction from mechanisms that control blood flow. This reaction is usually seen only in extreme cases of blood loss, shock, or laminitis. It occurs under direction of several hormones (renin, angotensin, aldosterone) which aid in removing large quantities of fluid from the digestive tract in order to re-balance fluid distribution within the body. Removal of considerable amounts of fluid from the large intestine creates an opportunity for impaction colic. Therefore, the more concentrate a horse is fed, the more feedings per day its total ration should be divided into. And, ideally, each feeding should be spaced equally apart.

The Feeding of Hay

When frequent feedings are not possible, feeding hay free-choice, or providing extra hay, to stabled horses (or horses on poor pasture) is beneficial. If hay is not provided free-choice, it should be fed 15 minutes before the concentrate ration. The digestive process functions best when the stomach is about two-thirds full. Hay fills the stomach more quickly than grain and stimulates actions of the enzymatic juices, which will still be functioning fully by the time the high energy grain is consumed. Feeding hay first will also take the edge off a horse's appetite, making it less likely to bolt its grain.

Feed Changes

Any changes in type or amount of feed should be made gradually, to avoid mental and digestive system upsets. Microorganisms (also known as *microflora)* in the hindgut are responsible for fiber digestion. These fermenting bacteria will be affected negatively by sharp changes in diet, resulting in less efficient fiber digestion.

Horses should be fed at the same time every day, because failure to feed regularly and consistently can cause psychological as well as digestive problems. Horses anticipate feeding times and can become apprehensive and upset if the schedule is not consistent. This stress can lead to stall pacing, weaving, pawing, wall kicking, cribbing, and other stable vices.

Distraction and Digestion

The horse should not be rushed through a meal, or distracted with heavy activity in the stable. It is best to feed during quiet times of the day. It is also important the horse be given time to properly digest its rations before its exercise or work routine begins. (A minimum of thirty minutes before light exercise, and at least an hour before strenuous work.) Adhering to these important rules can make a significant difference in the horse's mental and physical health.

Equipment and Methods of Feeding

Feeding Stabled Horses

Normally, grain is placed in buckets, feed troughs, or in some cases, shallow rubber tubs on the stall floor.

Buckets should be made of non-rusting, non-porous, unbreakable material. Neither buckets nor troughs should have sharp corners or edges. They should also be designed to fit safely into the stall and be easily removed for cleaning.

Horses that *bolt* their grain can be discouraged from this habit by placing large rocks or salt blocks with the grain. This forces the horse to work around the objects to get its grain, causing it to chew more slowly. Spreading grain out so it is shallow in a container of large circumference will also help. This prevents the horse from getting a large mouthful at a time.

Hay may be fed in hay nets or in hay racks. In a clean, properly bedded stall, feeding hay on the stall floor may be alright if the horse eats its hay fairly quickly, without spreading it around. However, some horses will paw their hay, wasting part of it and possibly soiling it with manure. Other horses eat their hay slowly, walking on it as they move around the stall. The best feeding method for each horse is dependent to some degree on its eating habits.

Fig. 10–2. Grain may be fed in buckets, which should be made of an unbreakable plastic.

If hay is fed from a hay rack, the rack should be placed where the bottom is approximately level with the horse's point of shoulder. If it is placed too high, the horse will be forced to reach up, which is unnatural. It may also cause dust and hay particles to fall into the horse's eyes or be inhaled.

Hay nets are often used for temporary situations such as traveling to shows or tracks. They are a little difficult to deal with for regular use. If a hay net is hung at an appropriate level when full, it will hang quite low when empty. This produces the risk of the horse getting a foot entangled in it. The net should be removed as soon as the horse has finished eating the hay.

Feeding Horses In Groups

When feeding horses in groups, there is a potential for a few unique problems that must be recognized and properly managed.

Fig. 10–3. Horses fed from common troughs should be observed while eating.

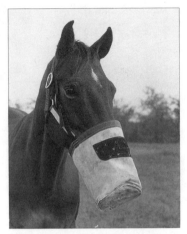

Fig. 10–4. Feedbags can help avoid problems in group feedings.

In group feedings, grain may be fed in buckets, individual or group feed troughs, or feedbags. Some horses are aggressive when fed in groups; tying them or stabling them at feeding time may be necessary. If horses are tied while eating, the rope should be short enough so they cannot become entangled. Also tied horses should not be fed from the ground for the same reason. If tying or stabling is not an option, individual feed buckets or troughs should be placed fifty feet or more apart.

If horses eat from common troughs, they should be closely watched to ensure each one gets its portion. Timid horses may be pushed away, giving bolder ones an opportunity to overeat. Also, a horse may show the first signs of illness by a lack of appetite. In unobserved situations this will go undetected.

Using feedbags to feed horses in groups ensures that each horse gets its own ration. Feedbags must be removed when they finish eating so they can drink.

Hay provided to pastured horses on the ground, can become mixed with dirt, sand, manure, and other foreign particles. This can be avoided by using large mats or hay racks. Racks should be large enough to accomodate the number of horses without crowding, and allow them to eat from both sides. If not, additional racks should be provided. Having rounded corners on hay racks and all other feeding and watering devices is a good safety measure to avoid injuries.

Round Baled Hay

When forage supplies are low, such as during a drought, it may become necessary to feed round bales of hay to pastured horses. Round bales are not normally recommended for horses because of quality problems caused by weathering. If the bale is of high quality and there is a large number of horses to eat it quickly, there usually isn't a problem. However, if the number of horses is small, the round bale may last long enough to become dried out and dusty, suffer serious nutrient loss, and possibly become moldy. Round bales should always be monitored closely and replaced with fresh bales when deterioration is noticed. The horse's digestive system will not tolerate low quality hay without the risk of health problems.

Cleaning Equipment

All equipment used for feeding and watering should be cleaned and disinfected regularly. Uneaten grain should be removed, as it may ferment if it has come into contact with saliva. Consumption of fermented grain can cause colic or poisoning.

When horses are to be fed from a trough also used to feed cattle, caution should be used. Some additives in cattle feed are toxic to horses, so a thorough cleaning of the trough is essential before horses are allowed to eat from it. *(Refer to page 239 for more information.)*

For stabled horses, water buckets should be cleaned and refilled several times a day and disinfected at least twice weekly. For pastured horses, watering facilities should be cleaned and checked frequently for leaks and foreign materials. Checking for ice during winter in some areas is important. Clean, fresh water should always be available. *(Refer to Chapter 2 for more information on water.)*

It is especially important to frequently clean and disinfect facilities from which a sick horse has been fed or watered in order to prevent re-infection and to minimize the spread of germs. When filling watering facilities, the hose should not be submerged in the water, as this will also spread disease.

FEEDING SPECIFIC TYPES OF HORSES
Breeding Stock Requirements
Stallions

During the non-breeding season, non-working stallions will require no more than a maintenance ration. Some stallions maintain their condition when provided only high quality forage, trace mineralized salt, and an unlimited supply of clean, fresh water. Others may require supplemental grain. *(For nutritional requirements of stallions, refer to Tables in the Appendix.)*

Stallions that have stable vices such as stall walking, weaving, or pawing are the most difficult

Fig. 10–5. To relieve boredom and expend nervous energy, stallions need daily exercise.

to keep in good body condition, because of energy expended during these activities. These behaviors often stem from nervous energy or boredom, which exercise and daily turnout can help alleviate. Regular dental care and deworming are also important for keeping stallions in optimum condition.

Stallions that are young, in regular intense work, or exposed to cold environmental temperatures will almost always require additional concentrate to fulfill their energy demands. Growing stallions will require more energy, protein, vitamins, and minerals when compared to their adult counterparts. Supplementation of vitamins A and E beyond the specified National Research Council requirements (which are dependent on age, work intensity, etc.) have not been found to benefit reproductive performance of the stallion.

Some horsemen recommend that stallions gain weight three to four weeks prior to the breeding season. This is thought to offset the initial stress and increased energy demand that the stallion may undergo. In moderation, this can be helpful. However, obesity is strongly discouraged, because it can predispose a horse to laminitis and other problems. Some reproductive problems associated with obesity are:

- decreased sex drive
- increase in breeding time
- impotency
- degeneration of sperm-producing tissue, caused by fat deposition in the scrotum which causes abnormally high temperatures
- decreased mating ability

In rare instances, *hypothyroidism,* a condition that is associated with a deficiency of the thyroid hormone in stallions, may produce obesity. This condition will cause delayed puberty, poor sex drive, decreased testicle size, and abnormal sperm production. Severe cases can result in reproductive failure. Similar complications can also occur in stallions that do not receive adequate nutrition.

Feeding Mares
Monitoring Body Conditions

Mares entering the breeding season and/or begining lactation in a moderate to fat body condition have a higher rebreeding efficiency. They are also more economical to feed during lactation, because they require less concentrate. In contrast, mares which enter the breeding season or begin lactating in a thin condition will have lower pregnancy rates, unless they are fed to increase their body condition. In addition, they will require increased amounts of concentrate to meet the demands of lactation and to regain any weight lost during pregnancy. Body condition of pregnant mares should be monitored closely throughout pregnancy and not be allowed to fall below a body condition score of 5. Pregnant mares exposed to very cold temperatures have been known to drop two body condition score points within a few days. *(Refer to Chapter 5 for a description of the Body Condition Score System.)*

Fig. 10–6. During the last 3 months of pregnancy, mares require increases of certain vitamins and minerals.

Feeding Pregnant Mares

Mares should be carefully provided proper nutrition throughout pregnancy. Studies have shown that good nutrition from the 18th to the 35th day of pregnancy aids in preventing early embryonic death. Mares receiving poor quality diets will likely have normal fetal development up to the 25th day of pregnancy, but reabsorption of the fetus can occur within the next six days. If the nutrient level is increased slightly on the eighteenth day after breeding and remains at that level until the 35th day, the incidence of fetal absorption is much lower.

If the mare is in good body condition, her nutritional requirements during the first eight months of pregnancy will be the same as those of an open mare. During the last three months, however, requirements for protein, calcium, phosphorus, and vitamin A will increase. *(Refer to Nutritional Requirement Tables in Appendix.).*

Mares increase their body weight approximately 15% during gestation. Also, during the last three months of gestation, the fetus undergoes the majority of its growth. If mares are not provided with adequate nutrition to support themselves and their fetus, the fetus has priority for nutrients and the mare will lose body condition.

Mares tend to lose their ability to consume their full ration during the last three months of pregnancy. This occurs because increase in fetal growth places pressure on the stomach and intestines, restricting their capacity. As a result, the mare will feel full though she may not have consumed a complete ration. Increasing energy density of the ration with added fat (e.g. ¼ cup of corn oil daily) can help alleviate this problem.

In a study conducted on broodmares, researchers compared a group of mares supplemented with 5% feed grade rendered fat, to a group of mares fed a general concentrate diet. The mares fed the added fat ate less concentrate, minimizing the risks of colic and laminitis, and their rebreeding efficiency was not affected.

Mares that are severely nutritionally deficient during pregnancy may give birth to foals that are not only smaller in size, but that may also suffer from:
- skeletal abnormalities, primarily due to inadequate calcium and phosphorus
- debilitated immune system
- increased incidence of disease
- decreased brain development
- decreased survivability

Studies have shown that obesity in mares will **not** cause *dystocia* (difficult birth), as previously thought. However, obese mares are more susceptible to laminitis and will produce less milk. *(Refer to Tables in the Appendix for nutrient requirements of pregnant mares.)*

It is very important not to graze pregnant mares on fescue pastures which are infected with the fungus Acremonium coenphalium *(see Chapter 9)*. This fungus has been shown to cause numerous reproductive problems, including prolonged pregnancy, *dystocia* (difficult birth), and thickened/retained placentas. It will also cause the mare to exhibit *agalactia*, a lack of milk production, following birth of the foal. This can have severe consequences for the foal, which may be prevented from receiving the vital colostrum. If pregnant mares are removed from the infected pasture at least two weeks before the expected delivery date, most or all of the effects of the fungus will be eliminated.

Feeding Mares in Lactation

With the exception of growth and intense work, no other function has higher energy demands than lactation. After foaling, the mare's energy requirements will increase by as much as 75% over mainte-

nance, due to demands of milk production. These demands are high because conversion of digested nutrients to milk is not a very efficient process.

Fig. 10–7. Lactating mares require increased levels of protein, calcium, phosphorus, and vitamin A.

Lactating mares will also require increased levels of protein, calcium, phosphorus, and vitamin A. These requirements are usually met when mares and foals are placed on a high quality, green pasture and supplemented with a high quality, energy-dense ration. Energy density of the diet can be increased by adding corn, corn oil or vegetable oil. Researchers have found that adding fat to lactating mares' rations increased the fat content of their milk. As a result, their foals received more energy and grew faster. These mares also consumed less feed because of the higher energy content of the ration. *(Refer to Appendix for nutrient requirements of lactating mares.)*

Peak milk production occurs during early lactation and then gradually declines until weaning. If the mare has stored adequate fat, she will be able to utilize some of it to meet the increased energy demands of lactation and will not require high levels of concentrate in her daily ration. She should not be allowed to lose much body condition during this time. If she is in a thin condition initially, her rebreeding efficiency will be impaired. It will also be impaired if she loses body condition.

If a lactating mare is not provided adequate nutrition, she will experience symptoms characteristic of progressive starvation:

- drowsiness
- muscle spasms
- diarrhea
- fluid retention (abdominal)
- possible death

Bowel movements of lactating mares should be monitored closely for indications of constipation. Regular exercise helps prevent this problem, but if it occurs, a laxative-type feed additive such as wheat bran or linseed meal is often recommended.

Feeding Young Growing Equines

No other topic concerning feeding of horses causes more controversy than that of the young horse. The period between birth and eighteen months of age is most critical, relative to increases in height, weight, and quality of skeletal development. Over 90% of mature height and 66% of mature weight are achieved during the first twelve months.

The rate and extent of growth are controlled by the following factors which work in unison: genetic growth potential, amount of feed consumed, and quality of the ration.

Optimum Growth Rate

Many horse owners try to achieve the maximum growth possible in a young horse. However, maximum growth rate and optimum skeletal development are often mutually exclusive. **Optimum** growth rate should be the goal, not **maximum** growth rate. The optimum rate helps to ensure a skeletal and muscular system that can withstand the rigors of early training and remain sound throughout the horse's life.

Developmental Orthopedic Diseases

Feeding excess amounts of concentrate to young horses has been suggested as a possible cause of *developmental orthopedic diseases* (DOD), such as *osteochondrosis, epiphysitis,* flexor deformities, and other hoof and limb problems. During growth, weight of the horse is borne on an immature skeleton. As force exerted on the limbs increases, the possibility of trauma to the *epiphysis* also increases. (The epiphysis is the small piece of bone which is separated from the cannon bone in early life by cartilage. The epiphysis eventually fuses to the cannon bone.) This is compounded if angular limb deformities are also present. Other conditions may also cause problems, such as nutritional imbalances or a genetic predisposition.

DOD can be caused by a copper deficiency, since copper is essen-

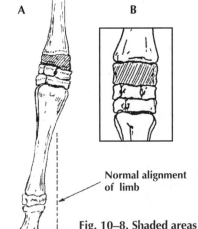

Normal alignment of limb

Fig. 10–8. Shaded areas denote the epiphysis; (A) illustrates bone deformity caused by epiphysitis, including misalignment and twisting of the bone; (B) shows normal epiphysis and carpal bone alignment.

tial for proper function and maintenance of elastic connective tissue. Research has suggested that copper supplementation in an equine that was previously copper deficient can help correct some damage caused by DOD. In a study, blood levels of copper, calcium, phosphorus, and zinc did not differ among copper-deficient foals and copper-supplemented foals. However, copper-deficient foals did show increased blood levels of a compound called osteocalcin, a protein incorporated into bone and released into the bloodstream during bone remodeling.

Flexor deformities, such as contracted flexor tendons, may result from epiphysitis, because foals alter the way they stand and move to relieve pain. However, flexor deformities may also be caused by a period of rapid growth that results in the cannon bones growing more rapidly than the tendons and other soft structures of the leg. This may be caused by confinement and lack of exercise during rapid weight gain, particularly if the foal has been under-fed and is then quickly placed on full feed.

Some horses are genetically predisposed to these problems; nutritional mismanagement and environmental factors can cause them to become evident. If epiphysitis or flexor deformities occur, concentrate intake should be immediately reduced or eliminated.

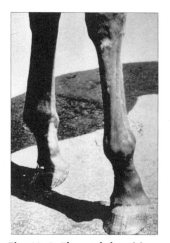

Fig. 10–9. Flexor deformities, such as contracted flexor tendons, may result from epiphysitis, or be caused by a period of too rapid growth.

Free Choice Feeding

At the University of Saskatchewan, Saskatoon, Canada, researchers examined the effects that free-choice feeding during the first two years of a horse's life had on its development. There were two groups of foals, nine in each group. Those in one group were fed measured amounts of a balanced ration, while those in the other group were allowed to eat as much of the same ration as they wanted.

The foals in the second group did well the first year. They gained in both height and weight, 23% to 30% faster than the first group. They also exhibited more aggressive behavior and engaged in more voluntary strenuous exercise.

As the horses approached two years of age, those fed free-choice were showing signs of structural unsoundness. Four had developed forelimb conformation faults and two developed hock lamenesses. The other three had a choppy stride, limited range of motion, and their limb angulation was too straight. It was determined that five of the nine had developmental orthopedic disease (DOD). In contrast, all of the foals in the group that had controlled feeding were sound and moved well. Based on these findings, it is recommended that the concentrate portion of the ration **not** be fed free-choice.

Foals

Proper feeding of the foal begins with a well-balanced diet for its dam. If a pregnant mare is lacking nutrients in her ration, the foal will likely be born with problems. *Goiters*, skeletal abnormalities, weakness, or debilitated immune systems are examples. Also the foal will not store adequate quantities of nutrients to sustain itself through periods of growth.

When the foal is two to three months old, its dam's milk will no longer contain sufficient amounts of nutrients required for growth, especially iron and copper. If the mare is provided adequate nutrition during pregnancy however, the fetus will store required nutrients for use when the mare's milk becomes nutritionally insufficient.

Fig. 10–10. A quality nutritional program for a foal begins by providing its dam with a well balanced diet during pregnancy and lactation.

Colostrum

Colostrum, the first milk, is vitally important to the foal, because it contains high levels of protein substances known as *immunoglobulins.* Immunoglobulins protect the body from disease and infection by combining with *antigens* to neutralize or inactivate toxins and bacteria. Failure to acquire immunoglobulins from colostrum may be the single most important factor causing infection and death in newborn foals. Colostrum has about five times the protein content and two times the energy found in normal mare's milk. It is also an excellent source of vitamin A.

Foals should nurse within one to two hours after birth, and should get 1 – 2 pints of colostrum within 24 hours. After that, the digestive tract of the foal changes and immunoglobulins cannot be absorbed.

After the foal has nursed, colostrum can be milked from the mare and frozen. This is in case it is required for some needy foal in the future. The colostrum (6 to 8 ounces) can be milked into and stored in a sterile plastic container. Glass containers are not used because they allow light to degrade or denature the proteins. Colostrum will last two years if stored in a freezer at -4° to -5° Fahrenheit. Stored colostrum is thawed and used to hand feed foals unable to receive it from their dams. It should be thawed slowly in warm water—**never** in a microwave oven, as this will destroy protein and immunoglobulins.

If the mare has dripped milk for an hour or more before the foal begins to nurse, most of the colostrum may have been lost. In such a case, the foal should be provided with colostrum from a previously stored reserve, or fresh from another mare if possible. Colostrum products are also available commercially.

The level of immunoglobulins in milk can be tested following foaling with a colostrometer or an agglutination test kit. Foals should be tested eleven hours after birth to determine if adequate levels of immunoglobulins were absorbed. If low, foals should be given more colostrum.

If a foal is unable to receive colostrum, a veterinarian may want to administer *plasma* from a male horse that has never received a blood transfusion. Mares which have foaled before or males that have had a blood transfusion may have *antibodies* that are capable of destroying the red blood cells in the foal. The foal should be given a minimum of 10 milliliters of plasma per pound of body weight (22 milliliters per kilogram of body weight), administered over a period of one to two hours.

Hemolytic Disease

Some mares may produce antibodies capable of destroying the red blood cells in her foal. This condition is called *hemolytic icterus, hemolytic disease,* or *neonatal isoerythrolysis.* It has been estimated to affect 1% to 2% of all foals born. It may occur if the mare receives red blood cells that are different from her own. These blood cells may be received by transfusion, antigen vaccination, or even by the passage of the foal's blood through an abnormal placenta into maternal tissues.

The antibodies that the mare produces against the red blood cells build up in the colostrum, and when the foal nurses, the antibodies pass into its bloodstream and destroy the red blood cells. The foal will become anemic within 12 to 36 hours and will probably die within a few days. Jaundice, a yellowish discoloration of the skin and membranes, will occur after 24 to 48 hours because of excess bile pigments in the blood that are deposited in the skin and membranes. If jaundice is present, a blood transfusion will be necessary.

The mare's serum can be tested during late pregnancy for the presence of these antibodies. Due to the low incidence of the disease, it is generally not practical to test all mares. However, if a mare has previously had a foal that was affected, she should be tested or her foal should be kept from nursing for thirty-six hours and be fed colostrum from another source.

Shaker Foal Syndrome

Shaker foal syndrome, which research has indicated is a form of equine *botulism*, is a problem in central Kentucky. Cases have also occurred in New York and New Jersey. It is caused by ingesting *Clostridium botulinium*, a microorganism found in soil. Symptoms of this condition include frequent urination, stiff legged gaits, muscle tremors, and difficulty swallowing.

Shaker foal syndrome most commonly affects rapidly growing foals between two and six weeks of age. It is estimated that 80% to 90% of these cases do not recover.

The Michigan Department of Public Health has developed a toxoid vaccine for shaker foal syndrome that is given to the dam during pregnancy. This vaccine causes antibodies to be produced, which the foal receives through the colostrum. So far, it has proven 100% effective.

Creep Feeding

Creep feeding supplements nutrients provided by mare's milk, and it allows foals to become accustomed to grain before weaning.

Fig.10–11. Creep feeders allow foal access only.

Mares fed in groups may fight over feed and pay little attention to foals. It is safer to have foals separate from their dams at feeding time, but close enough they can see each other.

If building an enclosed creep feeder is not an option, individual feed troughs with bars across the top can be used. These bars should be spaced so that the foal's muzzle fits easily between them, but the dam's muzzle cannot.

Foals can be creep fed within the first week of life, but at this age they may eat little, if any of the grain. Creep feed is usually offered when the foal shows interest in its dam's feed. It should never be offered free-choice, as that may result in overeating and cause bone abnormalities.

Foals may gain up to 4 pounds per day during the first month of life, doubling their weight by the end of the first month. From the first month to three and a half months of age, the foal again almost doubles its weight. By six months, the foal will have attained about 83% of its mature height. Creep feeding will provide foals with the nutrients demanded by such rapid growth. A pelleted creep feed may be preferable to loose grains to prevent the foal from sifting out ingredients.

By 3 months, the foal should be consuming about 1 pound for every 100 pounds of body weight per day. At weaning, it should be eating 5 to 8 pounds of creep feed per day. A creep ration should be a high energy feed containing 14.5% – 16% crude protein, and be fortified with required levels of vitamins and minerals. Foals should also have access to trace mineralized salt, either in loose or block form.

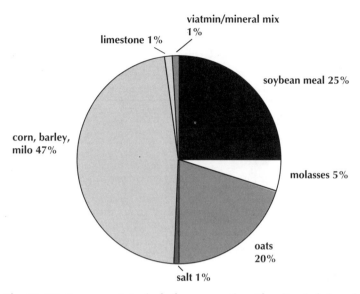

Fig. 10–12. Components typical of a creep ration. The vitamin/mineral mix contains vitamins A, D, E, and K, and dicalcium phosphate.

Weaning

Foals are often weaned at six months of age. Sometimes it is preferred at four months, as early weaning may prevent excessive loss of condition by the mare. Also, by the fourth month of lactation, the mare's milk production will have declined in both amount and nutrient content. However, if the foal is weaned earlier then six months, it should be provided a starter ration including 14.5% – 16% crude protein, 15% fat, and no more than 0.5% crude fiber.

Situations in which early weaning (at four months of age or before) might be necessary include:

- sickness or death of the mare
- mare is a poor milker
- injury to mare's udder
- training or showing of the mare

When possible, very early weaning should be avoided. A study was performed on 28 foals of approximately the same weight and expected **mature** weights. Half of the foals were weaned at three months of age and the other half continued nursing until six months of age. Both groups received a creep ration. Comparisons between the two groups showed similar height and weight gain, but the foals weaned at three months required more feed per day during the study. A summary of the results of the study is as follows:

Age at weaning	Average daily gain	Growth at withers	Amount of feed per foal per day	Weight at 6 months of age
3 months	2.3 lbs.	3.9 in	13.2 lbs.	458 lbs.
6 months	2.5 lbs.	3.7 in	4.6 lbs.	448 lbs.

After weaning, diet changes should be introduced gradually by mixing new ingredients in the creep feed. The amount of creep feed is reduced as amounts of new ingredients are slowly increased.

Fig. 10–13. Safe solid fencing is required when separating dams and foals during the weaning process.

Foals which are not provided creep feed while nursing may suffer setbacks at weaning time. They lose weight and body condition while adapting to the loss of their dam and adjusting to a grain diet.

Some breeders feel that weaning should be done abruptly, while others prefer a gradual method. Abrupt weaning is very stressful to the foal and may result in lower resistance to disease, injuries, and weight loss. In the gradual method, foals are separated from their dams by a solid fence. They are allowed to see, smell, and hear their dams, but they can't nurse. These foals are quieter, less stressed, and tend not to suffer post-weaning weight loss.

Orphan Foals

If orphaned at birth, the foal must obtain colostrum from another source. In such situations, having stored, frozen colostrum available is a valuable resource. Using colostrum from another mare who has recently foaled, or buying colostrum commercially, are two other alternatives. Once colostrum has been consumed, orphan foals can be trained to drink milk (mare's, cow's, or goat's) from a bucket. Five gallons daily is usually sufficient. Milk replacement pellets should be offered to these foals on the seventh day after birth.

A better alternative is to provide orphan foals a nurse mare until they can be weaned or placed on a supplemental milk replacer. Pony mares are high milk producers and are often used to nurse orphan foals. If it is impossible to find a nurse mare, nanny goats can be used. Common breeds used for this purpose are Toggenburg, Saanen, or French Alpines. Goats readily accept foals, and they can be trained to stand on ramps to allow the foal to nurse more easily.

Fig. 10–14.

Feeding Weanlings

The period between weaning and one year of age is an important time. Weanlings grow rapidly and develop considerable bone and muscle. Studies show that most light horse breeds reach 46% of their mature weight at six months of age, 66% at twelve months, and 81% at eighteen months. On the average, they reach 83% of their mature height at six months, 91% at twelve months, and 95% at eighteen months.

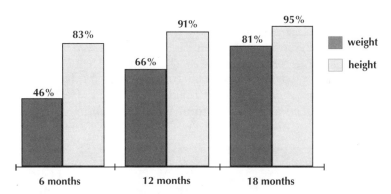

Fig. 10–15. Height and weight increases in weanlings expressed in percentages of their mature size.

Type and amount of feed will vary depending on the age at which the foal was weaned, and on the purpose for which it is being raised. Some owners prefer a faster rate of growth than others. A study, conducted on six-month-old colts, showed an increased rate of gain when they were fed increasing amounts of protein, from 10% to 19%.

Fast growth rates, however, may result in physical deformities.

A well balanced diet supplies correct amounts of energy, protein, vitamins, and minerals. Properly prepared, high quality commercial feeds usually provide necessary nutrients, but some owners prefer to formulate rations on their own.

Weanlings that receive a diet composed primarily of cereal grains and grass hay may not obtain enough protein or calcium and can have an inverted calcium to phosphorus ratio. A change in rations, or proper supplementation will be necessary. *(Refer to Tables in the Appendix for nutrient requirements of weanlings.)*

Dominance hierarchies will begin to appear at the weanling stage. Weanlings of similar disposition should be grouped together, and may even need to be fed individually to ensure they receive correct amounts of feed. They also should be fed at least twice a day. A good weanling diet should be about 30% – 35% forage and 65% – 70% grain.

Weanlings should be turned out for grazing and self-exercise. This helps strengthen bones and aids in proper development. Confinement and excessive forced exercise can cause skeletal problems.

When designing a feeding program, frequent changes in the diet should be avoided. Such changes do not allow evaluation of the efficiency of nutrients and they can cause digestive upsets as well.

Feeding Yearlings

If proper nutrition is provided during the suckling, weanling, and yearling stages, proper growth should occur. The rate of growth will decrease during the yearling stage, but as the horse is still growing at that point, it will continue to require a diet high in nutrient content. *(Refer to Tables in the Appendix for nutrient requirements of yearlings.)*

The ratio of concentrates to forages fed to yearlings depends to some extent on how rapidly one wishes yearlings to develop and how well they are responding to the diet being fed. Yearlings being developed for high performance activities should be fed a higher level of concentrates relative to forages. This helps produce bone

Fig. 10–16. Proper growth rates require a high quality diet for yearlings.

and muscle more rapidly. Yearlings raised for pleasure may be fed a higher level of forages because they do not need to develop as rapidly.

Yearlings should be fed 1 – 1½ pounds of forage and 1 – 2 pounds of concentrate per 100 pounds of body weight per day. To increase the energy level for yearlings intended for racing and other high intensity work, a fat source such as corn oil can be added to the ration. The fat can make up 5% – 10% of the concentrate portion of the ration.

Yearlings should be allowed to exercise at will. Forced exercise on an automatic walker is not recommended. Abnormal pressure of being forced to go in a tight circle for extended periods places stress on the legs. Ponying is a better alternative if free exercise is not possible.

Anabolic Steroids

Anabolic steroids should not be given to yearlings (or any other age class) unless the horse is sick or debilitated and a veterinarian prescribes their use. Studies conducted on anabolic steroid use have shown no benefits in terms of increasing muscle mass or growth. However, negative results have been seen in studies. Examples include: stallions two to four years of age had reduced testicular size, sperm production, number of sperm per ejaculate, and sperm motility after being given anabolic steroids. In fillies, anabolic steroids suppressed estrus and ovulation, induced male-like behavior, enlarged the clitoris, and upset the normal hormonal balance and fertility.

Feeding Two-Year-Olds

A University of Florida study has shown that maximum bone strength is not reached until horses are four to seven years old. Two-year-olds must receive a well-balanced diet to ensure that maximum skeletal development is accomplished. Also, two-year-olds in training require a higher level of nutrients than those not in training. *(Refer to Tables in the Appendix for nutrient requirements of two-year-olds.)*

Since the rate of bone maturity in young horses cannot be increased, over-training should be avoided so as not to compromise the long-term soundness of the horse. It is recommended that knee x-rays and a veterinary examination be conducted to determine skeletal maturity before intense training is begun with a two-year-old.

Training should not be forced to the point of fatigue. The skeleton cannot withstand such stress, and the young horse may be temporarily or permanently crippled. However, there is evidence that natural stress on the skeleton, which is associated with free exercise, will increase bone density. It has been found that horses raised on hilly terrain develop stronger bones than horses not raised in those conditions. Forced exercise does not seem to produce these same benefits.

Feeding Performance Horses

There has not been extensive research addressing nutritional needs created by specific equine performance events. However, the National Research Council has developed recommended levels of nutrients for different levels of work intensity. *(Refer to Tables in the Appendix for nutrient requirements of working horses.)*

Fig. 10–17. Performance horses must be fed according to the intensity of their work.

Body condition, hair coat, and performance are good indicators of a horse's nutritional and health status. Lethargy, depression, or lack of effort in performance may be related to inadequate nutrition or illness. Liver disease, *anemia*, infections, heart and lung related problems, all can cause similar symptoms to vitamin, mineral, energy, and protein deficiencies.

The horse's body condition is an excellent means of monitoring its energy intake. Stable environment, temperament of the horse, management practices, and activity level will also have an impact on each horse's energy needs.

Horses that are high-strung or that pace or weave in the stall will require more energy to maintain good body condition. In addition, horses that have rigorous competition schedules will require more energy than those competing less often or less rigorously. It has been estimated that horses will use 70 times more energy for racing a certain distance than they would walking the same distance. (This does not mean that racehorses need 70 times the normal amount of nutrients.)

All performance horses must receive sufficient energy to maintain endurance. A lack of energy and oxygen will lead to fatigued muscles, a lower level of performance, and injuries.

Equine athletes in good condition will utilize muscle glycogen, free fatty acids, and stored fat as energy much more efficiently than unconditioned horses. Conditioned horses will also exhibit lower heart rates and blood lactate levels after intense exercise. (High blood lactate levels have been observed to be associated with the development of fatigue.)

Corn may be used to increase the energy density of the diet. However, care should be taken not to overfeed any high energy grain, because colic and founder can result. Adding fat to the performance horse's diet will also increase the energy density of the ration. Incorporating 10% – 12% fat into the concentrate portion of the ration is considered about maximum. Higher levels will decrease palatability, become rancid more easily, and possibly cause diarrhea.

Increasing the energy density of the ration with added fat will decrease the quantity of concentrate needed and minimize possibilities of colic and founder. Some studies indicate that adding fat to the diet increases glycogen stores in the muscle, delaying the onset of fatigue. Other studies suggest that fat has a glycogen sparing effect on muscle (fat is used for energy first, allowing glycogen to be saved). The exact mechanisms of how the added fat creates these advantages are still being researched. *(For more information on fat, refer to Chapter 5.)*

Exercise has also been shown to influence the body's calcium. It decreases urinary excretion of calcium and increases its retention and deposition into the bone by 15% to 20%.

Salt and trace minerals should be provided free-choice to performance horses. Losses of these nutrients during intense activity are considerable, especially under conditions of high temperatures and humidity.

Although this section discusses performance horses in general, the following information discusses racehorse and endurance horse needs because their nutritional requirements exceed those of the average performance horse. Any horse in high intensity work, such as polo for example, will have requirements similar to race and endurance horses. *(See Chapter 7 for information on supplementation for performance.)*

Feeding Racehorses

A significant number of young horses in race training never reach the track, and many that do have difficulty staying sound after a year of racing.

The earlier in life racehorses begin training, the more susceptible to injury they are. This is because the skeleton is not fully mature. Consider this comparison: The average human life span is 77 years and the

Fig. 10–18. Racehorses should be trim and well-muscled for best performance.

average equine life span is 22 years. Many horses begin training and racing at two years of age. This is comparable in many respects to a seven-year-old human in training. Also, horses do not achieve maximum bone strength until they are between four and seven years old.

A horse that is moved frequently from track to track is exposed to additional stress. Forcing a fatigued horse to continue training and racing will almost always result in injury. Allowing any horse too little time for self-exercise and grazing may cause boredom and stable vices. It is highly beneficial to the equine's physical and psychological well-being to be allowed time to relax and relieve stress.

Inadequate nutrition for the level of performance involved can make the racehorse susceptible to injuries. High energy demands make it important to provide a high quality feeding program.

The NRC recommends 32.8 megacalories (Mcal) of digestible energy (DE) per day for horses in intense work. However, other research has shown that higher levels, averaging 35 – 50 Mcal DE/day can be utilized. Adding fat to the ration has become a popular method of increasing the energy content of the ration without overloading the digestive system with carbohydrates. A study conducted at Texas A&M University showed that racehorses fed added fat (in the form of feed grade rendered animal fat) sustained their speed longer in 600 meter (approximately 3 furlongs) sprints than horses not fed added fat.

The racehorse's body condition should be closely monitored, as it must be lean but not thin, and it should be well-muscled for optimum performance. When lean, the racehorse is better able to dissipate body heat. Also, extra weight can interfere with speed and endurance.

The average racehorse eats 10 to 15 pounds of hay and 15 to 16 pounds of grain per day. The required protein level depends on the age of the horse. Horses that are still growing while in training will need higher amounts of protein than mature horses in training. Studies from Australia suggest that two-year-olds thrive when consuming a diet with 12% protein, which is higher than the level recommended for the mature performance horse.

Studies on the use of excess protein have produced varied results. A study was conducted at Thoroughbred racetracks in which racehorses were fed varying amounts of excess protein. The study revealed that the amount of time horses took to finish a race increased 1 – 3 seconds for every 1000 grams of crude protein fed above NRC recommended requirements. (These are **very** high levels and would not normally be fed.) Another study, conducted at Cornell University, revealed no negative results from feeding 24% protein, which is well above recommendations by the NRC. *(Refer to Chapter 5, Energy Sources, and the Tables in the Appendix for protein requirements.)*

Feeding Endurance Horses

Endurance horses are among the most highly stressed performance horses, as they must exert themselves over very long distances. They are subject to excessive fatigue, muscle spasms and cramps, dehydration, and exhaustion, due to the large amounts of body fluids and electrolytes that are lost through sweat. Endurance horses may lose large quantities of sodium, potassium, chloride, and calcium in sweat during competition. In addition, the pH of the blood may increase almost to the point of *alkalosis* (an increased blood bicarbonate level) as the ride progresses. However, even if blood pH levels become high enough to indicate alkalosis, no clinical signs may be observed. Even after thirty minutes of rest following a long ride, the blood pH, carbon dioxide, and bicarbonate content may still be higher than normal. This occurs even in mild temperatures, such as 70° to 80° Fahrenheit (F).

Fig. 10–19. Endurance horses are among the most highly stressed performance horses.

Extensive energy is needed by endurance horses. However, the practice of feeding easily digestible simple carbohydrates, such as those in cereal grains, a short time before the ride is not recommended, and may be detrimental to the horse's performance. Carbohydrates increase blood sugar concentration which, in turn, causes secretions of hormones. This decreases the body's ability to mobilize body fat, glycogen, and protein. Most of the energy needed during endurance activity is derived from body stores, so a decrease in the horse's ability to use them will hasten the onset of exhaustion and fatigue.

The amount of grain fed by weight to endurance horses should not exceed the amount of roughage fed. Endurance horses should be provided with good quality pasture if possible, and hay containing 8% to 14% protein. The hay can be grass or a legume/grass mix. A common practice is to increase grain by 1 to 2 pounds and decrease forage by 3 to 4 pounds two days before a race. This decreases the ingesta in the digestive tract, and thus, decreases the weight the horse must carry.

The NRC recommends 10.3% protein for horses in intense work, but this figure is often considered conservative. Levels of 10 – 12% in the total diet is generally recommended for endurance horses.

A condition called "thumps" sometimes occurs in the endurance

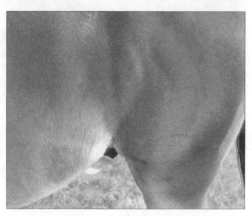

horse. This condition is characterized by a spasm of the diaphragm in time with the heart beat. "Thumps" usually results from an electrolyte imbalance, particularly a decrease in calcium and potassium. When mild spasms occur, the horse should be allowed to rest. If the "thumps" are audible, the problem is severe and a veterinarian should be called.

Fig. 10–20. The left flank is the area in which diaphragmatic spasms are visible.

Electrolyte supplementation in endurance horses can be beneficial, particularly in times of heat stress and fluid loss. Feeding electrolytes prior to an event will not build up stores, but they can be fed during and following long rides to replenish losses. Excessive supplementation should be avoided. *(Refer to Chapter 2 and 7 for more information.)*

Potential for dehydration is a problem in endurance horses. Horses should be allowed to drink as often as they wish during the ride, and most horses will require about 1 gallon of water each hour. Horses that are not properly conditioned will sweat more and require more water than a well conditioned horse. After competition, the horse should be given a few sips of water every few minutes while it is being hand walked and properly cooled down.

Feeding Pleasure Horses

The quantity of feed provided the pleasure horse should be adjusted to maintain optimum body condition. When work frequency and/or duration increase, the feed allowance will have to be increased as well. Individual temperaments and metabolisms will also play roles in ration requirements and maintenance of body condition.

Adding small amounts of fat (2 or three tablespoons of corn or vegetable oil) to the pleasure horse's diet will only slightly increase energy density, but will improve hair coat quality.

Managing Stress Problems

Horses are exposed daily to a variety of stresses. When these stresses are severe, or occur in combination with each other, the performance and overall health of the horse will be compromised.

Situations that can cause stress include:

- fear
- injury
- poor training
- noise
- isolation
- parasitism
- pain
- poor nutrition
- strange environment
- disease
- confusion
- allergies
- intense training/competition
- foaling
- travel
- rough handling
- bad weather
- erratic feeding/watering
- prolonged confinement
- weaning (mare and foal)

When stressed, the body responds by secreting steroid hormones called *glucocorticoids*. When small quantities of these hormones are present in the horse's system, they assist in healing by reducing inflammation and tissue swelling. However, during periods of extreme stress, large quantities of glucocorticoids will be produced. The level of white blood cells, which fight infection, is reduced, the production of antibodies is blocked, and healing of injuries is delayed. This can result in a depressed immune system and a predisposition to illnesses.

Glucocorticoids are also known to cause the release of a hormone called *prostaglandin*. This hormone inhibits the production of *progesterone,* which is a hormone necessary to maintain pregnancy. Pregnant mares in stressful situations may benefit from progesterone supplementation up to the 60th day of pregnancy.

In order to prevent or alleviate stressful conditions:

- Horses should be dewormed and immunized regularly.
- They should be provided plenty of fresh, clean water and a high quality balanced diet.
- Daily exercise is vital; prolonged confinement should be avoided.
- Contact with other horses; long isolation should be avoided.
- If free exercise is not possible, then relaxed sessions of hand walking in quiet areas with occasional stops for grazing.
- Adding variety to training sessions along with occasional pleasure riding will also help reduce stress.
- Ill or injured horses should not continue training/competition.

Dealing With High Temperatures and Humidity

Impact of environmental temperature and humidity can be determined by adding ambient temperature (F) to the relative humidity (%). If the sum is 130 or less, most horses will not be adversely affected. If the sum exceeds 150, with the humidity being 75% or greater, sweating will not provide enough heat removal to prevent heat stress. If the sum is 180 or greater, the body's cooling mechanisms will be ineffective, leading to dangerously high body temperatures. Obese horses in particular are stressed by hot, humid environments. Fat retains heat.

Anhidrosis

Anhidrosis (the inability to sweat) is common among horses in tropical-like, humid areas, especially if they originally came from cooler areas. This condition will debilitate their performance during the summer months. Symptoms of anhidrosis include:

- elevated temperature—up to 106° F
- hair loss, particularly over the face
- decreased appetite
- rapid heavy breathing
- weight loss

Anhidrosis can occur in any breed, although it is often associated with the Thoroughbred. It is rarely seen in horses under one year of age. Blockage of sweat glands, resulting from a lack of response from *epinephrine* stimulation, is theorized as a reason for its occurence, but the exact cause is still being researched. The only treatment appears to be to move the horse to a cooler, less humid climate.

Dealing With Cold Weather

Fig. 10–21.

Very cold weather will increase energy demands. Canadian studies have indicated that mature horses in good body condition will require 15% to 20% more feed for each 10° the temperature falls below 30° F.

Research also indicates digestible energy requirement of growing horses increases approximately 1% for each degree the temperature drops below 32° F. For example, weanlings exposed to 10° F will require about 3 pounds more feed each day than weanlings exposed to 32° F. Failure to meet additional requirements will result in weight loss and slowed growth.

In cold weather, energy demands will be further increased by:

- wind chill
- precipitation (rain, ice, sleet, or snow)
- poor body condition (little or no stored body fat for insulation)
- thin hair coat

Cold weather will cause the hair coat and skin to thicken. As horses age, their skin and hair will thicken even more during cold weather.

Roughages produce more body heat than do concentrates (per unit of weight) during digestion and metabolism. Oats produce more heat during digestion and metabolism than corn because oats contain more fiber. However, because corn occupies less space in the digestive tract, feeding it allows space for more heat-producing roughage to be fed.

It is difficult to fatten a thin horse during the winter. Horses should enter the winter season in moderate to fleshy condition and should maintain that body condition throughout the winter. Horses with thin hair coats should be kept in a fleshy condition; the excess fat will provide additional insulation to compensate for the thin hair coat. *(Refer to Chapter 5 for a description of the Body Condition Score System.)*

Three-sided sheds with the opening facing the prevailing cold winter wind can provide some protection to pastured horses. When large numbers of horses are pastured together, the sheds should be big enough to accommo-

Fig. 10–22. A three-sided shed provides protection to pastured horses during severe weather.

date all of them safely, or additional sheds should be provided. If the structures are too small, or there is not enough of them, injuries may result from crowding, or aggressive horses may fight and prevent more timid horses from entering.

Breeders who use artificial lighting to encourage their mares to cycle earlier in the breeding season must take into consideration the coat shedding which will occur. The unnatural hair loss will increase the mare's energy demands during winter months. Maintaining good body condition of the broodmare during winter months is critical to rebreeding efficiency.

Horses in heated barns will be better protected from harsh temperatures, but proper ventilation is essential. Heated barns with poor ventilation may have increased bacterial growth, which will predispose horses to respiratory problems. Recommended temperature range during cold weather is 45° F – 55° F. Increasing the temperature above 55° F is unnecessary and will cause unwanted shedding of the winter hair coat. This loss of protection from the cold can have negative effects when horses go from the warm barn to the cold outside temperature. Horses that have naturally short hair coats should be blanketed in pastures or in barns where temperatures are below 45° F.

Hot bran mashes are often fed in winter based on the theory they will somehow warm the horse. They do not provide a great deal of heat during digestion. However, they do increase water consumption, and this can be helpful. During the cold temperatures of winter a horse might consume inadequate quantities of water. This will likely cause feed consumption to decrease. This will result in a loss of body condition and weight, and consequently, the horse will have less protection from cold. So, due to increased water provided by mashes, the end result may be helpful. In addition, impaction colic is less likely to occur. *(For more information see Chapter 2.)*

Installing heated waterers will help water consumption, as horses are usually reluctant to drink very cold water. (Some decrease in water intake is normal, because the amount lost through sweat is decreased during cold weather.) If heaters are used, the water temperature should be maintained at 45° to 65° F (7° to 18° C). Electric heaters should be checked frequently due to the possibility of shorting out in the water. In most cases, the shock will not be dangerous, but it will discourage drinking.

Stresses of Transportation

When horses are to be transported long distances, the following steps can reduce stress:

1) Horses should be in good physical condition prior to shipping, as they may lose body condition rapidly during long trips.
2) Vacuum out all dust, debris, and old hay in the trailer or van.
3) The trailer, van, or the cargo area of a plane should be well ventilated, and exhaust pipes on a towing vehicle should be directed away from the trailer.
4) High strung, nervous horses may benefit from a veterinarian administering a gallon of mineral oil, by stomach tube, immediately prior to departure, to prevent impaction and gas buildup. Administering a tranquilizer may also help.
5) Horses benefit from being unloaded and walked around, every four hours. However, if this is not feasible, they should at least be allowed access to water every few hours.
6) Manure and urine-soaked bedding should be removed and replaced with fresh clean bedding during rest periods.
7) Provide familiar hay and feed; the taste of unfamiliar water can be disguised with a flavoring to encourage consumption.
8) When transporting horses by plane, long ground delays should be avoided. Air circulation in the plane is poor and bacterial counts, heat and humidity may become high.
9) Horses should have their temperatures monitored upon arriving from a long trip to see if they are developing "*shipping fever.*" If so, a veterinarian should be contacted. (52% of horses shipped long distance contract shipping fever.)

Stresses of Foaling and Rebreeding

Foaling and rebreeding stresses can be minimized by the following:

1) Allow mares to foal in a quiet and familiar place.
2) Introduce mares to an unfamiliar stud farm at least 30 days prior to foaling. This gives them the chance to develop antibodies against different bacteria and viruses.

Stresses of Injuries and Illnesses

Injured and ill horses should be allowed to rest quietly. If they have been on antibiotics for a long period, they may benefit from B vitamin supplementation, because antibiotics will kill the gut *microflora* (bacteria and protozoa) which normally produce B vitamins. Yeast and enzyme products can also help reestablish the gut microflora.

Seriously ill horses that are unable to eat can be fed through naso-gastric tubes. The soft silicon tubes, inserted by a veterinarian, are smaller in diameter than stomach tubes used for deworming. They can be left in place up to ten days without causing damage, and they provide an easy method of feeding small, liquid meals. The diets contain highly digestible carbohydrates, fats, and proteins. Providing these vital nutrients will promote healing and tissue replacement, and can make the difference between recovery and lengthy illness, or even death.

The naso-gastric tube feeding method costs less than intravenous feeding. It also keeps the digestive system slightly active, so when the horse recovers, solid feed will not be as much of a shock to the digestive tract.

Feeding Aged Horses

Activities and conditions of older horses vary, but in general, older horses will require more attention.

Changes that can affect feeding:

- elongation of incisors
- general wearing and deterioration of teeth
- decrease in digestion efficiency
- loss of lower lip elasticity
- loss of weight and body condition
- obesity, caused by less activity
- loss of mobility, due to arthritis

Horses over twenty years of age will require feeds which have higher quality protein and more digestible energy sources, because their ability to digest feed and absorb nutrients lessens as they age. They will also require higher levels of vitamins and minerals. Rations designed for yearlings, in terms of protein, energy, vitamin, and mineral content, appear to meet their needs. Special feeds formulated specifically for older horses are also available. Feeding excessive amounts of vitamins is not recommended, because metabolism of the older horse limits its ability to handle such excesses.

Trace mineralized salt and clean water are important in the diet of older horses. Lukewarm to tepid water is preferable to cold water, because it increases consumption and aids in efficient digestion.

Some older horses will tend toward obesity due to less activity. Obesity can be very detrimental to aged horses and should be avoided. It can predispose older horses to many problems, including arthritis, navicular disease, laminitis, and lung and heart diseases. Obesity can also cause fatty tumors, called lipomas. These tumors are non-cancerous, but they can interfere with normal digestion and blood circulation. Overfeeding can also result in kidney, liver, and heart damage.

On the other hand, because digestion efficiency decreases in the older horse, it may be necessary with some horses to increase the overall ration by 10% to 20%. Each situation must be individually assessed. Aged horses that are particularly hard keepers may benefit from top dressing the concentrate with ¼ to ½ cup of corn oil per day. The addition of the corn oil will increase the energy density of the ration and enable the horse to maintain a good body condition more efficiently. In most cases, aged horses should have at least a half-inch of fat between their skin and ribs. The ribs should be easily felt but not visible.

Aged horses should be fed small, frequent meals, and they should be fed separately from more aggressive individuals to prevent competition for feed. If older horses are pastured in herds, they should be watched closely to ensure that they are eating enough to maintain a good body condition.

Pastured horses often become more sensitive to weather stresses as they age. For these reasons, aged pastured horses should have access to shelter that will keep them dry and warm in cold weather and provide a source of shade in hot weather. Heat stress in particular is hard on older horses. In addition, if these horses are worked in very hot or cold weather, extra care should be taken to warm them up thoroughly prior to exercise and cool them down properly afterwards.

Teeth of the older horse should be monitored closely. Frequent floating may be necessary to maintain their ability to chew efficiently. Signs which indicate the need for floating and possibly more extensive dental care are:

- grain spillage from the mouth while eating
- undigested grain kernels in the manure
- loss of weight and body condition

- increase in amount of ration or energy density not resulting in weight gain
- discomfort when eating or drinking
- foul breath, which can indicate the presence of an abscessed tooth or gum infection

Fig. 10–23. The incisors of aged horses become elongated and tend to angle outward.

As the horse ages, some teeth may fall out or break off. Processing grains (cracking or crimping) and providing hay in a chopped, cubed, or pelleted form will help horses with these problems. In severe cases, grain mashes or pellets soaked in water may have to be fed. If pellets are fed, about 1½ to 2 pounds of pellets per 100 pounds of body weight is generally adequate.

Caring for the Malnourished Horse

A horse can become *malnourished* as a result of many situations. Some of the more common causes are:

- neglect
- dental problems
- overgrazed pastures
- disease
- metabolic disturbances
- low quality rations
- caretaker's lack of knowledge about proper nutrition

Malnourished horses in rehabilitation should have their teeth examined, as poor teeth may have been one of the initial causes of the horse's problems. Minor tooth problems may be solved with frequent floating, but if the problems cannot be corrected, horses may be fed pellets soaked in water to make them easier to chew. Less severe cases may benefit from cubed hay or pellets

Fig. 10–24. The malnourished horse requires substantial care and attention.

229

as the source of roughage.

A veterinarian should examine the malnourished horse and take a blood sample, which can determine if an illness or metabolism dysfunction is present. Internal tumors, liver, and kidney diseases are some of the problems which can lead to malnutrition.

Another important step in the rehabilitation of the malnourished horse is deworming. A mild product should be used when deworming the malnourished horse for the first time, because strong ones, such as ivermectin, will result in massive worm kill and major intestinal problems. At the second deworming, ivermectin may be used.

Transport and Stall Preparation for the Malnourished Horse

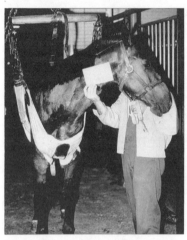

Fig. 10–25. A hoisting sling may be needed to raise and support a severely malnourished horse.

Severely malnourished horses are extremely weak and will go through considerable stress during transport. It is not uncommon for emaciated, weakened horses to fall while being transported. Unless a horse is in a dangerous position, it is usually best to leave it down. Forcing it to rise will lead to repeated falls and additional injuries.

Because the stress of being transported will further weaken the horse, it may go down again once it is in a stall. It should be allowed to rest before being encouraged to stand. In some cases, a hoisting sling may be required to raise and provide support. A sling is meant to support, not suspend, and its misuse can be very painful. Veterinary assistance is recommended when a hoisting sling is to be used.

The malnourished horse's stall should be clean, dry, and well bedded, so it can lie down comfortably. In cold weather, it should be kept warm, in order to conserve calories. Blankets and loose wool leg warmers may be placed on the horse to help retain heat. Massaging the horse's legs will also help.

Emaciated horses will be susceptible to skin sores, because they have minimal cushion between the skin and bones to provide protection. Fleece-lined halters and blankets made of soft materials will help prevent skin irritation.

Feeding the Malnourished Horse

High quality grass hay, a trace mineralized salt block, and a bucket of clean, fresh water should be made available. Because weak, malnourished horses spend so much time lying down, the hay should be placed on the stall floor where it can be easily reached.

Severely malnourished horses may be reluctant to drink, so adding a powdered drink mix to the water may encourage them to do so. If this is unsuccessful, using a turkey baster or similar object to squirt small amounts of water into the horse's mouth can be helpful, but it should not be forced. Providing the horse salt will increase its desire to drink.

A sweet feed formulated for broodmares and foals is a good concentrate for malnourished horses. The concentrate should be introduced slowly, as doing so too quickly can result in excessive gas production and colic. A severely malnourished horse should be given 1 – 1½ pounds of concentrate every three hours. Vegetable oil can be added to the concentrate in small amounts and slowly increased over time (too much oil to the malnourished horse's diet can result in diarrhea). Adding the vegetable oil will increase the energy density without the risk of carbohydrate overload.

Once the horse is eating adequate grass hay, *probiotics* (desirable intestinal bacteria) can be administered to help establish a beneficial balance of digestive microorganisms. Probiotics are commercially available in paste form, and can usually be found in feed or tack stores. They will improve the horse's digestive capability.

After the horse has started eating grain, some legume hay (no more than 25% of the hay ration) can be substituted for 25% of the grass hay.

When feeding legumes, loose stools should be watched for. If the horse develops diarrhea, the amount of legume should be reduced by mixing in additional grass hay.

Normally, intestinal microflora produce adequate quantities of B-complex vitamins, but because a malnourished horse may lack these microflora, B-complex vitamin supplementation may be necessary. These horses have limited fat tissue to store fat soluble vitamins A, D, E, and K, so supplementation of these vitamins may also be necessary. Supplemental vitamin C may aid the immune system and help avoid infections. Electrolytes may be helpful, but they should only be used on the advice of a veterinarian. To supplement all of the vitamins discussed above, a well balanced vitamin mix can be fed orally.

Sugar cubes, molasses, and injections of glucose and dextrose should not be given to the malnourished horse. It is not accustomed to them, and could go into "sugar shock." The result can be a coma or death. The small percentage of molasses found in sweet feeds should not cause a problem if the concentrate is introduced slowly.

Exercise for the Malnourished Horse

Once malnourished horses have regained most of their strength, they may begin a light exercise program. In good weather, turning them out in a paddock or pasture will encourage self-exercise. Hand walking or turning them loose in an indoor arena is preferable in cold or inclement weather.

Grooming the Malnourished Horse

Fig. 10–26. Cleaning around the eyes with sterile gauze and sterile saline spray.

Malnourished horses will benefit from frequent, thorough grooming. Brushing will increase circulation, remove debris, and allow inspection of the hair coat and skin. Cleaning of the hooves will reveal *thrush* or *grease heel*, common ailments of horses which have lived in filthy conditions.

Malnourished horses tend to attract more flies than usual, especially around the eyes. Oil-based insecticides have a prolonged action and tend to penetrate and build up in the body of the horse, making them especially toxic to these horses. Natural water-based repellants are the best to use on malnourished horses. The ears and areas around the eyes should be cleaned, using sterile gauze and sterile saline spray for the eyes. Water-based repellent may also be wiped on ears and around the eyes.

OTHER FACTORS WHICH CAN AFFECT NUTRITIONAL NEEDS

Easy and Hard Keepers

An easy keeper successfully maintains good weight and healthy condition on a normal ration and is not prone to digestive disturbances. The hard keeper, on the other hand, loses weight easily and may suffer digestive disturbances from even a slight change in rations. Even when fed high quality grain and hay, the hard keeper is difficult to fatten and maintain in good body condition.

Although it is difficult to determine easy or hard keepers on the basis of appearance alone, the easy keeper will normally appear sleek, healthy, and well nourished. The hard keeper may be underweight or poorly nourished, even though it is consuming the same quantity and type of ration.

If the hard keeper is experiencing no other difficulties, such as parasite infestation or dental problems, it can be assumed that the condition is related to its metabolism. It is probably inherent, so little can be done to alleviate the problem. However, the condition of the hard keeper can be improved by providing a well-balanced diet, deworming regularly, and by periodically checking its teeth and floating them as needed.

Increasing the energy density of the ration may also benefit hard keepers, particularly the "picky" eaters. The easiest way to increase the energy density of the ration is to replace high fiber grains (such as oats) gradually with more energy dense grains (such as corn or barley) and top dress the grain with a fat source (such as corn oil). Energy density should be increased slowly to avoid digestive problems. Discussing the plan with an equine nutritionist or a veterinarian before proceeding with a high energy-dense ration is recommended.

Stable Vices

Horses, particularly those which are stabled, can pick up numerous annoying habits or vices, some of which can be detrimental to their health. Stable vices make it difficult to keep a horse in good condition. They also cause the horse to require increased feed to meet energy demands. Most stable vices usually result from one or more of the following:

- boredom, from lack of exercise/grooming, free time outside, etc.
- too few feedings per day, and/or irregular feeding schedules
- insufficient long roughage

Cribbing

Cribbing is a vice that can cause health problems, and it is considered an unsoundness. The cribber rests the upper teeth on an object, draws back the upper lip, and arches the neck. It then depresses the tongue and bears down with the teeth, pulling backward and upward and swallowing air.

Cribbing causes the edge of the upper, outer surfaces of the front teeth to wear away. In horses that have cribbed for a long time, the upper teeth may be worn to the gums. The cribber may be identified by examining the upper front incisors for the characteristic wearing.

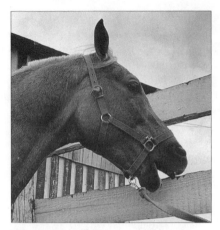

Fig. 10–27. Cribbing is considered an unsoundness.

Cribbers will usually be underweight. They tend to be "hard keepers" and at times will pay little attention to their feed, perhaps caused by a false feeling of fullness from the ingested air. The air in the stomach can also predispose the horse to gastric disturbances.

The exact cause of cribbing is not always identifiable. The vice probably begins as the result of too few feeding times per day, irregular feeding schedules, and/or boredom, and may be continued strictly from habit. Boredom usually results from too much stall time and insufficient exercise, grooming time, free time outside, etc. It may also result from insufficient chewing time if long roughage is not provided in adequate amounts.

Cribbing may sometimes be controlled with the use of a neck brace or strap that prevents the horse from holding its neck in the proper position to suck in air. There are also muzzles which allow the horse to eat and drink, but will prevent cribbing.

Wood Chewing

Wood chewing is commonly seen in non-pastured horses and is usually attributed to a lack of sufficient roughage. It may also result from boredom or lack of proper mineral intake.

Eating roughage satisfies the horse's natural urge to chew. If the horse is not provided enough roughage to satisfy this urge, it will chew items in its surroundings. Any wooden object is a likely target, including fence posts, gates, stall doors, etc.

Diets consisting only of pellets may encourage wood chewing. The horse on a completely pelleted ration finishes its meals quickly, since pellets do not require as much chewing as roughages do. The urge to chew is not satisfied, and coupled with boredom, the horse is tempted to start the wood chewing habit.

Horses that chew wood can get cuts in their mouths from the splinters. Some horses may even swallow the wood splinters, which can lead to very serious consequences if the intestinal tract becomes irritated or punctured.

Wood chewing can be discouraged by treating the wooden surfaces in the horse's surroundings. Commercial substances designed specifically for such purposes are available. Also, most horses can be discouraged from chewing wood when the only wood available to them is very hard, such as oak, or if the edges of exposed wood are covered with a metal trim.

Preventative measures are: 1) good quality pasture, or providing good quality roughage for non-pastured horses, 2) free-choice trace mineralized salt, 3) plenty of outside "free time" for stalled horses.

Weaving, Stall Walking, and Pawing

Weaving (rocking back and forth on the front legs), stall walking, and pawing are habits that usually result from nervous energy or boredom. These habits can be physically detrimental to the horse. Weaving and stall walking place stress on the horse's joints and expend energy. Pawing can lead to concussion-related problems in the hoof and limb, such as bruising. If the horse is shod, pawing may cause the shoe to become loose or wear out prematurely.

Turning a horse out in a pasture or paddock as much as possible, providing more grooming time, and exercise are ways of preventing or

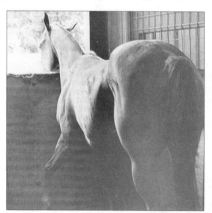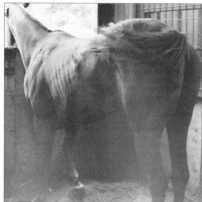

Fig. 10–28. Weaving places stress on the horse's joints.

alleviating these problems. Also, providing a stall mate, such as a goat, may alleviate the problem with some horses.

Another useful distraction is to hang a plastic bottle or tether ball in the horse's stall, over the area where the horse weaves or paws. As the horse plays with the hanging object by batting it with its nose, it will work off nervous energy that might otherwise be spent developing a stable vice. With stall walkers, the plastic bottles or balls should be hung in several locations around the stall.

A horse that has developed one of these habits in an isolated environment may be helped by putting it in a stall where it is able to see other horses. However, if the horse shows no signs of quitting the vice, it will unfortunately need to be put back in isolation, because these vices are easily picked up by other horses.

Horses with stable vices are likely to be underweight, nervous, and hard keepers. It may be helpful to provide free-choice hay and incorporate a fat source, such as corn oil, or replace some grains with more energy dense ones, like corn. If this is done, the ration will contain more energy, and less concentrate will have to be consumed. This makes it easier for these horses to maintain their body conditions.

Exercise

Before the horse was domesticated, it ran free and exercised at will. Confining horses to stalls is a direct contradiction to their natural state. Exercise and free pasture or paddock time have beneficial psychological effects for the horse. The stabled horse receiving insufficient exercise and free time is much more likely to develop stable vices.

Exercise is also a facet of good nutrition. A horse receiving insufficient exercise will have a reduced appetite and will not efficiently utilize the energy portion of its ration. Fit horses utilize stored energy sources more efficiently. Also, exercise allows for proper muscle development and tone.

Stabled, non-working horses should be allowed a minimum of one hour of exercise or free time per day. They enjoy being out in a paddock or large pasture where they can run, play, and enjoy freedom. This self-exercise provides minimal strain on the skeletal system and assists in the relief of stress.

Sometimes mechanical walkers, longeing or small round pens are used as methods of exercise for stabled horses. However, research has shown that forcing a horse to travel in a tight circle can predispose it to injuries of the soft

Fig. 10–29. Regular self-exercise will benefit the horse both physically and psychologically.

tissue and bone, which may lead to contracted tendons. Young, growing horses are particularly likely to be affected.

If self-exercise is not an option, there are forced exercise alternatives which are less stressful on the horse's skeleton than walkers or longeing. These include riding, hand walking, free longeing, and ponying. With larger operations, the use of treadmills and specially designed swimming pools are good options for some horses.

Ideally, riding for exercise purposes should be done in a large area such as a pasture, or on a trail, to offer the horse a change of scenery. If this is not possible, and an arena or paddock situation is the only choice, using the largest one available is preferable.

When being hand walked, the horse should be allowed to move freely and cover ground, rather than being led in circles. Free longeing should be done in an area large enough that the horse has plenty of room to move around. When ponying, the lead horse should be well behaved and remain calm.

Grooming

An essential part of good management is regular grooming. While racing and show horses require extensive grooming, even pleasure horses should be groomed at least once daily.

Daily grooming offers valuable close inspection of the horse. This allows injuries and changes in coat quality and body condition to be detected. Grooming is also believed to provide psychological benefits, and it is may even be an appetite stimulant.

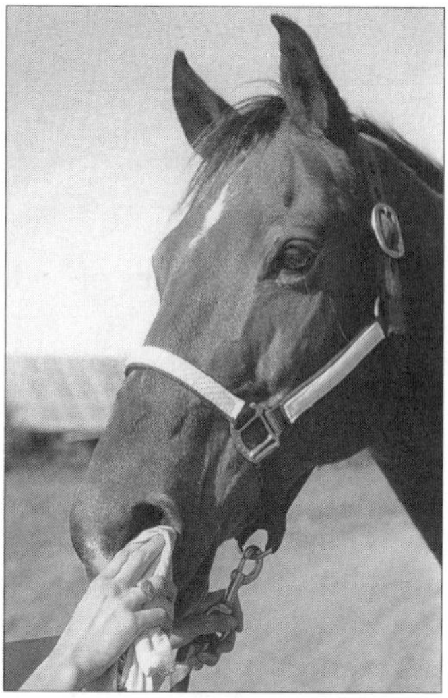

Basic equipment for thorough grooming consists of a rubber curry comb, a soft bristle brush, a slightly stiffer bristle brush, several cotton or wool rags, and a hoof pick. More elaborate systems may include an electric vacuum cleaner.

Fig. 10–30. Proper grooming includes cleaning the nostrils.

The rubber curry comb and stiffer brush should be used to remove any mud and dirt. The stiffer brush should not be used on the more sensitive skin of the face.

Next, a soft bristle bush should be used all over the horse. This brush removes any surface dirt that the stiff brush did not. It is also very good for brushing the face.

A brush of medium stiffness is preferable to one with very stiff bristles or a comb for brushing the mane and tail. The stiffer brush and the comb are more likely to pull out mane and tail hairs, or break them off. The best method of grooming the mane and tail is to first use one's fingers to carefully untangle and smooth the hair.

Hooves should be cleaned and checked to make sure there are no puncture wounds, *thrush*, or other foot problems. Finally, the grooming procedure should include careful wiping of the areas around eyes, nostrils, and the anal and genital areas with a clean rag. Brushes and rags should be cleaned frequently, as they can spread disease and infection.

The Stable

Barns should be well ventilated in order to prevent respiratory problems. If the barn does not have adequate ventilation, dust, mold spores, and ammonia will build up, leading to respiratory problems.

The Stall

The size of the stall is important. If the stall is too small, the horse may become *cast* when it rolls. Also, horses in small stalls will suffer psychologically and will have an increased likelihood of developing stable vices. A 12' x 12' stall is normally considered adequate for a 15 to 16 hand horse, but larger horses will need more room.

Bedding

The best types of bedding are clean bright straw or wood shavings. Rice hulls, sawdust, shredded paper, and peanut hulls are occasionally used for bedding. Dirt and sand are not recommended, because a horse bedded on such material may ingest it and develop impactions in the cecum and large intestine.

Bedding should have a fresh smell, be as dust-free as possible, and contain no foreign materials that could be harmful to the horse. It should be dry, warm, comfortable, and clean at all times.

When using wood shavings it should be noted that laminitis can result from bedding horses on fresh black walnut shavings. Black walnut shavings contain a toxic compound that induces founder in most horses within 24 hours of contact. The toxin responsible has not yet been isolated, but it is believed to be a compound called juglone.

Manure should be removed two or three times a day if the horse spends most of its time in the stall. Once per day is considered minimum under any circumstances. Wet bedding should be picked out and replaced with clean dry bedding at the same times manure is removed.

Pest Control

Controlling pests such as flies and mosquitos, is an important aspect of good management. These pests impair hair coat and skin quality, cause unthrifty conditions and decreased vitality, and may even hinder development of foals. They are also an annoyance to the horses. The best protection against these pests is sanitation, as they use manure as breeding areas. The use of insecticides around buildings and manure piles will also help. Automatic fly spray systems release a measured amount of repellent at set intervals. Horses may also be sprayed or wiped down with fly repellents.

Immunization

Horses should be vaccinated on a regularly scheduled immunization program. Because needed immunizations vary according to the diseases prevalent in a particular area, a veterinarian should be consulted when choosing a vaccination program.

Avoiding Toxic Feed Additives

The following feed additives are **not** intended to be fed to horses. However, because they may be accidentally ingested by the horse or inadvertently fed, knowledge of their dangers is an important part of good feeding management.

Rumensin (Monensin sodium)

Rumensin is an antibiotic widely used in the cattle industry. It is highly toxic to horses, and may inadvertently be present in grain mixes fed to horses. Horses should not be pastured with cattle being fed a ration containing rumensin, nor should they be fed out of a trough that has been used to feed cattle rations containing rumensin.

Horses that ingest low concentrations of rumensin may show decreased feed intake and uneasiness resembling mild colic. Symptoms at higher levels include posterior weakness, staggering, profuse sweating, and inability to rise after going down; blindness and absence of muscle twitching may also be present. Death may occur 12 to 24 hours after the onset of symptoms. Minimum lethal intake is 1 milligram per kilogram of body weight, and 2 to 3 milligrams per kilogram is fatal 50% of the time.

There is no known treatment for this toxicity other than administering drugs and mineral oil to speed passage of the feed through the digestive system. Horses that survive may have an abnormal *heart rhythm* (pattern of heart beats), and increased heart and respiratory rates. They can die during physical exertion years after rumensin poisoning.

Salinomycin

Salinomycin is a growth-promoting substance commonly fed to feedlot cattle. It is also very toxic to horses. Just 0.6 milligram per kilogram of body weight can cause death 50% of the time. Horses that ingest salinomycin experience symptoms of colic, muscle spasms, incoordination, and dehydration.

Lincomycin

Rations formulated for swine often contain lincomycin. This antibiotic is used to increase rate of gain and feed efficiency. In horses, lincomycin can cause founder, diarrhea, and inflammation of the colon, usually resulting in death.

Deworming

A well planned deworming program is one of the most important procedures in proper feeding management. See Chapter 12 for a complete discussion of internal parasites and methods of controlling them.

11

DIGESTIVE DISTURBANCES

Results of digestive disturbances in the horse can range from mild discomfort to death. Digestive disturbances can be caused by a variety of factors, but many of them are related to improper feeding management or internal parasites. Knowing the nature and cause of common digestive disturbances is basic and important information for anyone caring for horses.

Fig. 11–1. Proper feeding management and a good parasite control program can help to avoid many digestive disturbances.

One of the reasons the equine is predisposed to problems of the digestive tract is because toxic compounds and spoiled feeds cannot be regurgitated back up the esophagus and out through the mouth. This is prevented by the strong *sphincter* between the esophagus and

241

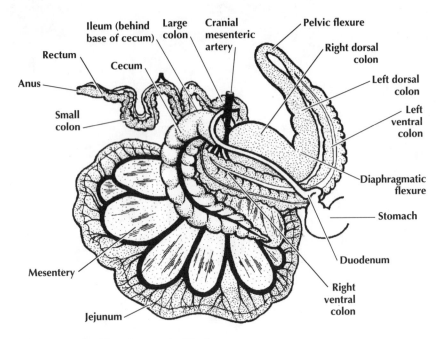

Fig. 11–2. The digestive tract of the horse.

stomach, and by peristaltic contractions, which move ingesta from the mouth into the stomach, not in the opposite direction. If a horse does attempt to vomit, a rare occurrence, the ingesta will come up the esophagus from the stomach. However, because the soft palate blocks its return to the mouth, the ingesta will come out the nostrils. Some of it may be forced into the *trachea* (wind pipe) and the lungs.

COLIC

Colic can be broadly defined as any abdominal pain. Since this is a book on equine nutrition, colic only as it is related to digestion will be addressed. *(For a detailed look at all types of digestive distur-bances and their treatments see The Illustrated Veterinary Encyclope-dia for Horsemen, and Veterinary Treatments and Medications for Horsemen, both published by Equine Research, Inc.)*

The length and configuration of the equine digestive tract predis-poses the horse to colic. The tract suddenly enlarges, narrows, twists, and turns in several places along its length, making intestinal block-age and partial obstruction a fairly common problem.

Places where changes in intestinal diameter occur are:
1) the muscular junction, or sphincter, between the stomach and duodenum
2) the junction of small intestine and large intestine
3) the pelvic flexure, where the left ventral colon becomes the left dorsal colon
4) the junction of the large colon and small colon

Types of Colic
Sand Colic

Sand colic occurs mainly in coastal and desert regions where the soil contains large quantities of sand. It results from sand accumulation in the intestines. Horses suffering from sand colic may appear sluggish, experience weight loss and diarrhea, and stand in a stretched-out position, similar to the male urination stance.

A simple test can be performed to determine the amount of sand in the feces. Place six fecal balls in a jar filled with water, mix, and allow to stand for three to five minutes. Pour the liquid off and measure the remaining sand. More than a tablespoon of sand is an indication of a potential for sand colic. The majority of ingested sand is not passed out in the feces, but remains in the digestive tract. Necropsies of fatal sand colic cases have revealed up to 100 pounds of sand in the intestinal tract. Horses grazing in sandy areas should always have easy access to plenty of clean, fresh water. Pastures that are overgrazed increase any existing potential for sand colic.

Bran mashes and oils are sometimes administered in an attempt to remove sand from the intestinal tract. However, bran mashes tend to pass right over the sand, leaving it behind.

Enterolith-Related Colic (intestinal stones)

Enteroliths are stones composed of ammonium, magnesium, and phosphate, which form in layers around a central body called a nidus. The nidus can be a nail, pin, needle, pebble, coin, piece of cloth, nylon webbing, or even horse hair. *Ascarid* (round worm) eggs have also been reported as a nidus for enterolith formation.

In most instances, only one enterolith will form around the nidus. Enteroliths usually range from two to six inches in diameter and weigh between one-half to five pounds. However, enteroliths weighing up to 26 pounds have been documented. True enteroliths usually are not found in horses under five years of age. The majority of the cases occur in horses five to ten years of age with a history of mild recurring colic.

Small enteroliths can be passed in the feces, but large ones may block the intestine, leading to serious problems. Providing mineral supplementation beyond the horse's requirements may add to any predisposition it may have to enterolith development.

Gas Colic and Intestinal Torsion (twisting)

Sometimes a digestive disturbance will develop into a case of intestinal torsion, or twisting. Excessive gas production can result in portions of the large intestine floating upward like a balloon and causing it to twist around itself and other organs.

Gas colic may result from cribbing, due to ingestion of excessive air. However, the most common cause of gas colic is gas production resulting from overeating, or from a large intake of rich, rapidly fermentable feeds. The horse's stomach is relatively small, so when large amounts of concentrates are consumed quickly, it fills and becomes distended. Ingesta will pass too rapidly through the small and large intestines, causing excessive gas production. Gas will generate pressure in the intestine, and consequently, colic. Excessive gas production can also be caused by feeding wet, partially fermented grain, or by feeding spoiled, moldy grain.

A horse may: 1) roll to relieve pain due to gas or an impaction, or 2) have the *mesentery* that supports the intestine tear due to trauma. Both situations can cause the intestine to twist, resulting in blockage and interruption of blood supply to that portion of the intestine. Lack of blood supply results in intestinal muscle spasms, followed by muscle relaxation. As muscles relax, gas produced by intestinal microorganisms cause the affected part of the intestine to distend. The lack of blood and distension of the intestine is very painful to the horse.

If a twisted intestine is diagnosed early, surgery can be performed and the horse's life may be saved. Without surgery, a twisted intestine is usually fatal.

Stabled horses are more likely to develop intestinal twisting than pastured horses. It may be caused by the fact that stabled horses eat only at specific times during the day, which is less natural for their digestive systems than the continuous grazing of pastured horses. Dividing the concentrate rations into several feedings per day instead of a few large ones, is a very important step in avoiding colic. Also, feeding the stabled horse hay free-choice, or providing hay 15 minutes before each concentrate ration is fed, are very helpful in preventing colic.

Internal Parasites

If large numbers of worms are present in the intestinal tract, they may cause an impaction. Large strongyles, commonly called blood-worms, can block intestinal arteries, resulting in portions of the intestine having little or no blood supply. This situation results in severe pain and intestinal cramping, which leads to colic. If the condition is not corrected, affected portions of the intestine will eventually die due to lack of blood, often resulting in death of the horse. *(See Chapter 12 for more on internal parasites.)*

Gallstones (choleliths)

Although horses lack gall bladders, they can still develop gallstones *(cholelithiasis)*. Gallstones occur predominantly in middle-aged and older horses. Gallstones generally form in bile ducts and can create blockages, preventing bile secretion. Bile is necessary for proper digestion, and its absence may lead to an impaction and, eventually, colic. Symptoms of this type of colic include *jaundice.*

Spasmodic Colic

Spasmodic colic results from an overly active and intensely contracting intestinal tract, which most often occurs in response to trauma. Severe thunderstorms and pre-competition nervousness are typical situations that can result in the horse suffering spasmodic colic. High-strung, nervous horses with excitable temperaments are particularly susceptible. It is characterized by frequent attacks that last for a few minutes and then pass.

Colic Caused by the Cockspur Hawthorne Tree Seed

The Cockspur Hawthorne tree can grow as far north as Canada, as far south as North Carolina, and as far west as Kansas. Its branches grow low to the ground and are covered with thorns. In summer, its leaves are dark green, and in fall they turn a dark red. The fruit resembles a small red crab apple and remains on the tree until late fall.

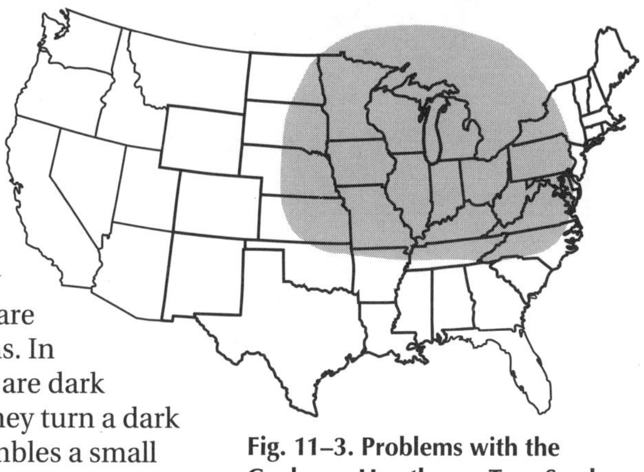

Fig. 11–3. Problems with the Cockspur Hawthorne Tree Seed are possible in the shaded area.

It is the fruit that can cause problems in the horse. The fruit's seed structure contains a bony *endocarp* (inner covering) which makes it extremely hard and dense. These seeds are virtually impossible to chew and digest. Seeds may be difficult to distinguish in manure because they appear similar to a large kernel of undigested wheat. Horses suffering from seed impaction colic will experience symptoms similar to sand colic.

Other causes of colic

Giving large amounts of water to hot horses or horses that have been deprived of water for a lengthy period may result in colic. Abrupt changes in type of feed, especially from a low energy diet to a high energy diet, may also result in colic, because intestinal bacteria do not have adequate time to adjust to new feed and will not digest it properly. Working a horse intensely too soon after a meal can lead to colic. Feeding coarse, low quality forage can cause colic and it is even more likely to happen if adequate clean, fresh water is not provided.

Symptoms of Colic

Symptoms of colic may appear gradually. The horse will become restless and may turn its head toward its flanks. As pain becomes more acute, the horse may try to kick at its belly. Other indications of a colic attack include pawing the ground, alternately getting up and lying down, rolling, and profuse sweating. Body temperature, respiration, and pulse rates will also increase. Dehydration and mucous membrane discoloration may be apparent as well.

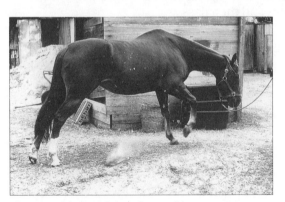

Fig. 11–4. The pawing and stretching out stance associated with colic.

The horse may attempt to defecate frequently, but may pass only a small amount of manure, or none. Horses suffering from colic often have an abnormal stance, stretching out in a position similar to the male urination stance. They will appear depressed and show little interest in feed or water.

What To Do

At the first sign of colic, a veterinarian should be called. The veterinarian can perform a rectal examination, monitor the horse's vital signs (temperature, pulse, respiration), and treat symptoms early, which may prevent more serious problems.

If colic is severe, transportation of the horse to a clinic for advanced treatment may be recommended. An *abdominal tap*, the removal of fluid from the abdomen for laboratory analysis, may be performed if the horse is brought to a clinic; ruptures of the intestines can be detected in this manner. Intermediate treatment involves trying to make the horse comfortable and preventing it from injuring itself. The horse may be allowed to lie down as long as it does so quietly and does not try to roll. If necessary, the horse should be walked to prevent rolling and decrease restlessness. In cold weather, a sheet or light blanket should be placed on the horse.

While waiting for the veterinarian's arrival, the vital signs should be checked. Normal body temperature is 99.5° – 101.5° F, normal pulse is 30 – 42 beats per minute, and normal respiration is 8 – 16 breaths per minute. The gums should also be examined. Normal healthy gums are pink in color and moist to the touch. If the gums appear white, purple, or deep red in color, the horse is seriously ill.

Medications should not be given unless recommended by the veterinarian, and feed should be withheld to prevent further disturbances in the intestinal tract. Water, however, should be available at all times. Strong pain killers, such as *phenylbutazone* and *banamine*, should **not** be given unless advised by the veterinarian, because they will mask signs of a more serious problem. Usually, colic can be relieved within 12 to 24 hours with prompt treatment by a veterinarian.

LAMINITIS (FOUNDER)

Laminitis, or founder, appears as soreness in the hooves due to inflammation and separation of the *laminae* in the hoof. The laminae are the thin layers of tissue in the hoof which attach the hoof wall to the coffin bone.

Research has indicated that laminitis is a *peripheral vascular* disease which affects the outermost blood vessels and results in decreased blood flow within the foot. *Arteriovenous shunting* usually occurs, in which a small vessel is formed that allows blood from the arteries to pass into the veins without fully circulating through the entire foot. This results in a decrease of capillary spread within the foot: blood will go to the heel area, but generally not the toe area. This causes a reduction in the supply of oxygen and nutrients to the tissues, which are essential for survival of the laminae in the toe area.

Inevitably, the laminae will die, due to lack of blood and oxygen; swelling, bleeding, and gas formation will then occur under the hoof wall, in the toe area. The buildup of gas, the weakening of the laminae, and the pull of the deep flexor tendon all play a part in causing the *coffin bone* to rotate downward. Laminitis most often occurs in the forefeet, but the hindfeet may also be affected.

Horses that are "easy keepers" and have a tendency to become obese are prime prospects for developing laminitis. Also, horses turned out onto rich pasture without adequate time to adjust are at risk. Stallions are also susceptible, due to insufficient exercise and the large quantities of concentrates they are commonly fed.

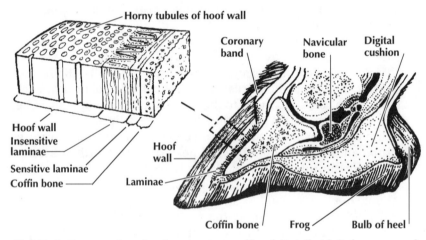

Fig. 11–5. Cross-section showing structures of hoof. Detail at left shows normal laminar attachment.

Causes of Laminitis

There are many causes of laminitis, including:
- overeating
- obesity
- drinking large amounts of water before being properly cooled down after strenuous exercise
- overexertion
- severe systemic infections, often due to a retained *placenta* or severe pneumonia
- eating large amounts of green pasture when unaccustomed to it

- concussion from being ridden on hard surfaces (road founder)
- allergic reactions to feed
- being transported long distances

Laminitis resulting from overfeeding concentrates is believed to result from a high intake of carbohydrates. When large quantities of carbohydrates overwhelm the hindgut, bacterial balance in the cecum and large intestine is altered.

Fig. 11–6. Note the changes in hoof structure between the normal hoof on the left compared to the hoof on the right suffering from chronic founder.

There is an increase in the number of lactic acid-producing bacteria, primarily *Lactobacillus* and *Streptococcus*. The result is an increase in the concentration of lactic acid, and consequently a decrease in the pH of the intestinal tract. The ensuing acidic environment causes the cell walls of the bacteria to break apart, releasing toxic compounds called *endotoxins*. These substances are absorbed through the intestinal wall and produce harmful effects. Changes in lactic acid and endotoxin levels in the cecum occur within three hours after carbohydrate overload. However, visible effects of laminitis usually do not appear for 16 to 24 hours.

Laminitis can also result from bedding horses on fresh black walnut shavings. Black walnut shavings contain a toxic compound that will induce founder in most horses within the first 24 hours of contact. The toxin responsible has not yet been isolated, but it is believed to be a compound called *juglone*.

Symptoms of Laminitis

Laminitis has three phases: developmental, acute, and chronic.

The developmental phase occurs between the time the horse first contracts the cause of laminitis and the first sign of lameness.

The acute phase begins as soon as lameness is apparent. There will be heat present in the hoof and at the coronary band. As laminitis progresses, the hoof becomes cold, due to the lack of blood, but heat can still be felt in the coronary band. The horse will have an increased digital pulse, increased respiration, anxiety, and trembling of the musculature from pain, depending on the severity of the founder. It may be reluctant to move, standing with the hind feet tucked up

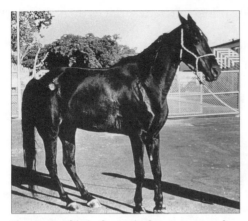

Fig. 11–7. This is the typical stance caused by a severe case of founder.

under the body and the front feet stretched forward. Diarrhea and colic may also be present.

The chronic phase of laminitis begins when lameness is continual for more than 48 hours, or when there is evidence of rotation of the coffin bone.

Rotation may be mild, with the horse still able to lead a useful life, or it may be severe enough to limit the use of the horse. In an extremely severe case, there will be extensive separation of the sensitive laminae from the insensitive laminae, and on the bottom of the foot there will appear a semicircular separation of the sole. Separation of the sole is an indication that the tip of the coffin bone has begun to penetrate it. If this has occurred, there is little chance for recovery, and the horse will usually have to be destroyed.

The chronic phase is characterized by intermittent or continual lameness and growth rings on the hoof wall.

What to Do

If it is known that a horse has consumed an abnormally large amount of grain, or if other conditions are present that might cause laminitis, preventative treatment should begin immediately, even if no symptoms of laminitis are evident. Laminitis is considered a medical emergency, and a veterinarian should be contacted immediately.

Emergency procedures by veterinarians include administration of laxative substances that lubricate the intestinal tract and speed up the passage of ingesta. This will aid in the removal of excessive or harmful substances from the body. A common practice used to be to stand the foundering horse in cold water. Current veterinary medical recommendation does not advise this, because it further reduces the blood supply to the foot.

The horse should be exercised lightly, about ten minutes every hour for the first 24 hours, unless it is in pain. At the first sign of lameness, exercise should be **stopped**; otherwise, it may aid in the separation of the coffin bone from the hoof wall.

Once lameness begins, analgesics should be administered to relieve pain. Pain triggers a release of hormones that cause further constriction of the blood vessels. There may also be increased coagulation of blood within the vessels of the foot. This can cause an increase in the blood pressure, which may remain elevated for up to six months. The analgesics help prevent constriction of the peripheral blood vessels and subsequent increase in blood pressure that will follow.

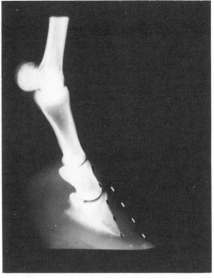

Fig. 11–8. This case of laminitis resulted in a rotation of the coffin bone. Note angle of the coffin bone to the angle of the hoof wall. They should be parallel.

The horse should be in a stall bedded with loose, unpacked sand. This helps support the exterior surface of the sole, and it allows the horse to stand more comfortably.

Current recommended treatment does not include using drugs that decrease inflammation, such as antihistamines and corticosteroids. It has been found that antihistamines are of little value if the body has already released *histamines* (protein compounds that cause enlarged capillaries and decreased blood pressure). Also, corticosteroids will increase effects of *dopamine, norepinephrine,* and *epinephrine,* compounds which stimulate the sympathetic nervous system, causing constriction of the blood vessels. Constricted blood vessels will allow even less blood flow to the hoof.

Fig. 11–9. A hoof wall resection. Some veterinarians recommend drilling small holes in the hoof wall to release gas pressure.

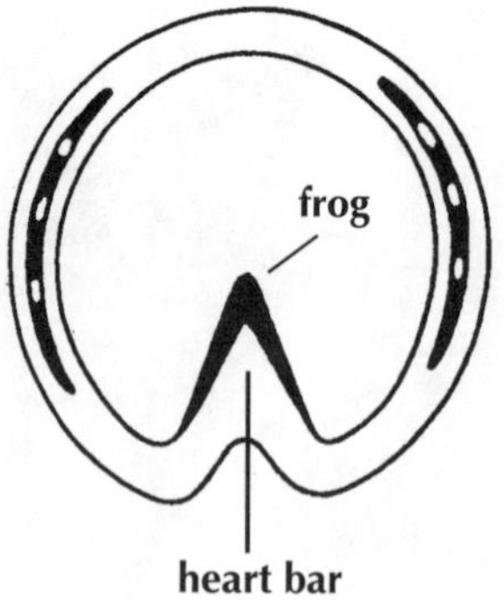

Once the horse enters the chronic phase of laminitis, treatment consists of minimizing pain and preventing further rotation of the coffin bone. If the coffin bone penetrates the sole, euthanasia is often recommended, because prognosis is usually unfavorable. If there is only slight rotation, prognosis is more favorable. However, such horses may be subject to infections in the foot due to separation of the hoof wall at the *white line*. The horse will also require special shoeing, possibly for the rest of its life.

Fig. 11–10. A heart bar shoe is used to support the sole of a foundered horse's hoof.

Further rotation of the coffin bone may be caused by the gas pressure building up in the foot. Also, dirt and debris may accumulate between sensitive and insensitive laminae if there is a separation at the white line on the sole of the foot. Dirt and debris force the coffin bone away from the hoof wall.

A resection (removal of a section of the hoof wall from the toe region) may be performed by a veterinarian or farrier in order to release gas pressure and prevent dirt and debris from packing between the laminae. Up to 40% of the total wall may be removed. The horse must then be shod with a heart bar shoe in order to support the sole. Exposed tissue must be kept clean and regularly painted with antiseptic.

Some veterinarians do not recommend complete removal of the toe section. They advocate drilling several small holes in the hoof wall to release gas pressure. However, dirt and debris must not be allowed to gain access into the area between the hoof wall and the laminae.

The horse should not be exercised until it is recommended by a veterinarian.

CHOKE

Choke is a partial or complete blockage of the esophagus. It frequently results from the horse *bolting* its feed. It does not, however, cause asphyxiation in the horse, as it does in humans.

Causes

A mass of dry grain or other feed may become lodged in the esophageal passage and cause choke. This problem occurs most often in older horses, since they may be unable to chew feed thoroughly. It may occur repeatedly in horses that have a malformed esophagus. Medications in the form of a bolus or tablet have also been known to cause choke.

Symptoms

Horses that develop choke will appear restless, often making repeated movements of the head and neck. The neck will be arched at times with the chin pressing against the chest. Constant pacing may also be observed. Horses suffering from choke will often drool, and a mixture of saliva and feed may come out of the nostrils.

What to Do

Salt blocks, bricks, or large rocks can be placed in the feed trough or bucket to force horses that bolt their feed to slow down. Bolters should not be fed hay cubes or other bulky feeds that can become easily lodged in the esophagus. Feeding in large, shallow containers reduces a horse's ability to gulp mouthfuls of feed and will help prevent choke. Older horses with poor teeth should be fed rations that require less chewing. *(Refer to the section on Aged Horses in Chapter 10 for more information.)*

If choke occurs, a veterinarian should be called at once. The horse should be kept calm and uneaten feed should be taken away. A stomach tube through which water or mineral oil is passed is usually inserted by the veterinarian to aid in dislodging the mass. The tube may also be used to gently push the mass of feed into the stomach.

12

INTERNAL PARASITES

Fig. 12–1. A well-nourished horse is less susceptible to heavy parasite infestation.

The horse that is heavily infested with internal parasites is not healthy and cannot perform to its capabilities. A well-nourished horse is less susceptible to heavy parasite infestation than a horse whose diet is of lower quality. It is less likely to become anemic and its stomach lining is more resistant to penetration by parasites.

Internal parasites can have a significant effect on the horse's digestion. They can reduce appetite and produce colic. They can also damage the liver, lungs, blood vessels, intestines, stomach, and cause blood loss. These factors will cause a significant loss of digestion efficiency, and the horse's stamina and performance can be impaired.

Scientific investigation over the years has resulted in an increased understanding of parasite life cycles, improvement in pasture management techniques, and the development of many new and highly effective deworming products. Despite extensive research in this area, most horses never remain completely free of internal parasites. However, parasite infections can be minimized with adequate control measures. The first step towards this goal is understanding the route of infection and the life cycles of some common equine parasites.

Horses are susceptible to almost 100 different species of internal parasites, including worms, fly larvae, and *protozoa*. The most commonly known are those referred to as large and small strongyles, ascarids, pinworms, intestinal threadworms, and bots. Lesser known, but potentially of equal importance, are the tapeworms. While a young horse is susceptible to certain parasite species not found in the adult horse, including *Parascaris equorum* and *Strongyloides westeri*, parasites such as tapeworms and strongyles are found as often in adult horses as in the young.

Current research indicates a significant reduction in the number of certain previously abundant parasites, including *Strongylus vulgaris* and bots. These reductions are likely due to the effectiveness of new deworming compounds. Unfortunately, along with reduction in numbers of some parasite species, increased resistance to deworming compounds has been noted. Also, increased *pathogenicity* (ability of a microorganism to produce disease) is being observed among other species, such as small strongyles and tapeworms.

TYPES OF PARASITES
Strongyles

Strongyles are the most prevalent of the equine internal parasites, with 56 known species of *Strongylidae* found in the horse. These parasites are commonly grouped according to their developmental differences and are referred to as either "large" or "small" strongyles. Whereas the terms large and small are technically correct (the large strongyles averaging 1 to 2 inches in length and the small strongyles usually less than 1 inch), better descriptive terms are "migratory" (for the large) and "non-migratory" (for the small) strongyles.

Large strongyles follow migratory routes through the organs and circulatory system during developmental stages. As adult parasites, large strongyles attach to the *mucosa* of the cecum and large colon and are bloodsuckers, thus the common name, "bloodworms."

Small strongyles include 36 species of worms from the subfamily *Cyathostominae* and are a totally different *genera* (scientific classification) than large strongyles. These small strongyles do not normally migrate through the organs and circulatory system during the developmental stages. As adult parasites, they feed on the *mucosa* in the large intestine and are not bloodsuckers.

All strongyle eggs are similar, and large or small strongyles cannot be differentiated during routine fecal egg per gram counts (EPGs). To establish the presence of large or small strongyles, a larvae *incubation* test must be run. This test allows strongyle eggs to develop into infective third stage larvae. At this stage, parasites can be differentiated and identified on the basis of number of intestinal cells.

Large Strongyles
Strongylus vulgaris

    S. vulgaris was, until recently, a very common and dangerous parasite in the horse. Scientists are now seeing a significant drop in numbers of these parasites. This is probably due to an increased level of deworming by horse owners, as well as development of dewormers which are effective against immature migrating forms of these parasites.

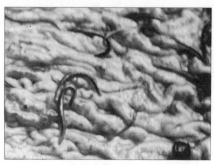

Fig. 12–2. Large strongyles in the intestine of a horse. Immature larvae migrate through the small arterioles, causing severe damage.

    S. vulgaris eggs are laid in the large intestines of the horse and passed out with the feces. Eggs hatch in the dung pile, then develop into second and third stage larvae. This developmental process takes from five to ten days, depending on climate and environmental conditions. The third stage larva is the infective form of this parasite.

    Third stage larvae migrate from the dung pile to blades of grass and are ingested by the grazing horse. Once ingested, larvae travel to the cecum and colon, where they *encapsulate* under mucosal membranes and undergo a *molt*. After about eight days, fourth stage larvae emerge and migrate into the small *arterioles*. They crawl along the innermost layer of the arterial wall, creating inflammation and fibrous deposits. Paths of these migrating larvae meet at the cranial mesenteric artery (the stem trunk that connects the abdominal artery with the branch arteries supplying the intestines with blood). These larvae cause inflammation that can result in formation of a *thrombus*, a blood clot within the vessel. *Emboli*, which are portions of the thrombus, can break off and block a branch of the artery, causing death to that part of the intestine. These larvae can also cause an *aneurysm* (abnormal dilation of the blood vessel wall) to form. If enough pressure is placed on the aneurysm, it can rupture, with fatal consequences to the horse.

    Larvae eventually return to the large intestine by the same route as they came, the small arterioles. Back in the intestine, they molt to fifth stage larvae (immature adult stage), mature sexually, and reproduce. Approximately six months after the horse first ingested the infective third stage larva of *S. vulgaris*, the parasite passes eggs onto the pasture in the feces of the horse and the life cycle begins anew.

    S. vulgaris can cause considerable damage long before it can be clinically detected through fecal examination. Fortunately, there are dewormers available (certain benzimidazoles and the avermectins) which are effective against the migrating forms of this parasite.

Strongylus edentatus

Another variety of large strongyles is *Strongylus edentatus*. These parasites may reach 1 – 1½ inches in length at maturity. After infective third stage larvae are ingested by the grazing horse, they burrow into the cecum or colon walls in much the same way as *S. vulgaris*. From this stage, larvae migrate through the blood stream to the liver, where they molt to the fourth stage. The third month after infection, larvae leave the liver and go to the connective tissue layer that lies underneath the *peritoneal lining* of the abdominal cavity. Here, larvae can cause bleeding and tissue death. Larvae return to the large intestine where they form a *nodule,* which bursts to release the fifth stage larva into the *lumen* of the large intestine. Here the parasite reaches sexual maturity approximately eleven months after initial infection.

As with *S. vulgaris*, this parasite can cause tissue damage before it can be clinically diagnosed by fecal examination. Use of effective dewormers, especially during the first year of a horse's life, can prevent, or reduce, tissue damage caused by migration of this parasite.

Strongylus equinus

The third variety of large strongyles is *Strongylus equinus.* This variety is rare and not considered a significant problem in the U. S. Its life cycle is similar to that of *S. edentatus* except that it forms a nodule (small solid swelling) when leaving the intestine to migrate to the liver. This parasite migrates to and from the large intestine via the abdominal cavity.

Developmental stages of this parasite, from ingestion of the infective third stage larvae through sexual maturity and egg laying of the adult parasite, take about nine months.

Small Strongyles

Small strongyles (also called cyathostomes) consist of 36 different species and are the most common parasite found in the horse. The adult small strongyles are slightly smaller than the large strongyles and are yellowish in color, rather than the reddish color of the large strongyles.

Small strongyle larvae do not migrate through the organ systems of the horse during development, as the large strongyle larvae do. They are, however, a serious problem and have been demonstrated to be a cause of worm-induced colic. When they occur in large numbers, inflammation and digestive upset of the horse can result. Some small strongyle larvae *encyst* in the mucosa membrane of the colon and

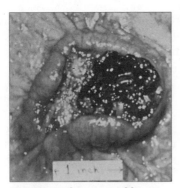

Fig. 12–3. Ulcer caused by an encysted small strongyle.

cecum during their development; dewormers are ineffective against these encysted stages. Developing larvae can remain in this encysted state for up to 2½ years.

Some small strongyle species have developed resistance to certain deworming compounds of the benzimidazole class of dewormers. To determine infection of a given horse or herd with parasites resistant to a specific dewormer, an EPG (fecal egg per gram count) must be run on the horse's feces before deworming. This should be done again approximately two weeks after deworming. Ideally, the deworming compound should reduce pre-treatment EPG by at least 90%. If after treatment with a deworming compound, the EPG is reduced by less than 60%, there is a resistance problem with that deworming compound and another product should be used.

Small strongyles require two to three months to develop in the lumen, or cavity, of the large intestine before maturing sexually and passing eggs in the feces of the horse. These eggs then hatch and develop to the infective stage on the pasture, just as discussed in the section on *S. vulgaris.* The most favorable climatic conditions for development of larvae in the pasture are mild, consistent temperatures with moderate sunlight and moisture. Excessive heat or cold and direct sunlight can be fatal to all species of strongyle larvae, both large and small.

Pinworms

Oyxuris equi, the seat or pinworm, is not as critical a problem in horses as the strongyles. While it does not usually cause serious illness, the parasite's presence in the anal area of the horse during egg-laying is a discomfort. In an effort to relieve itching, affected horses will rub against objects such as doors, fences, and trees, causing hair loss and skin irritation.

O. equi are several centimeters long and are found in the large

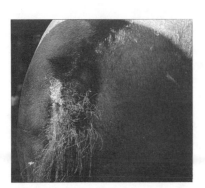

Fig. 12–4. Tail rubbing is a sign of pinworm infestation.

intestine. Mature females migrate down the intestine to lay eggs on the skin of the anus and the area immediately around it. It is these eggs, deposited in a sticky, yellowish-gray fluid, that cause itching and subsequent rubbing of the horse's tail head. Within four or five days after they are deposited, the egg masses flake off, contaminating the horse's environment. These eggs

Fig. 12–5. Male (left) and female (right) pinworms.

are inadvertently ingested by the horse, after which they hatch in the cecum and large intestine.

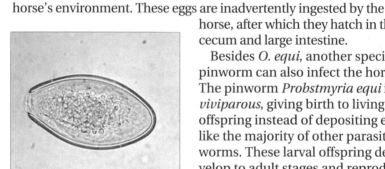

Fig. 12–6. Magnified *Oyxuris equi* egg.

Besides *O. equi*, another species of pinworm can also infect the horse. The pinworm *Probstmyria equi* is *viviparous*, giving birth to living larval offspring instead of depositing eggs like the majority of other parasitic worms. These larval offspring develop to adult stages and reproduce without ever leaving the horse. This is known as auto-infection.

Ascarids (round worms)

The horse ascarids, *Parascaris equorum*, are mainly a parasite of foals and young horses and are rarely seen in adults. Ascarid eggs can first appear in the feces of foals as soon as ten to twelve weeks after birth. As the horse matures, usually between twelve and eighteen months of age, the infections become lighter and less common. It appears that horses become immune to this parasite as they grow older. At about six months of age, there is a marked decline in the proportion of migrating larvae that reach the small intestine, or

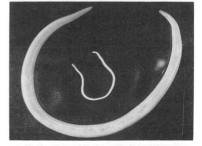

Fig. 12–7. Fourth stage larva (center), and adult ascarid.

259

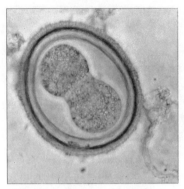

Fig. 12–8. The ascarid egg has a shell that protects it from desiccation, heat, and cold.

become established there. Ascarids are rarely found in horses over two years of age.

Infection occurs when ascarid eggs are ingested by the foal. Infective larvae contained in the eggs hatch inside the foal. *P. equorum* larvae are highly migratory. Larvae enter the bloodstream from the small intestine and migrate to the liver. While in the liver, they enter the *hepatic* veins and are carried to the lungs, where they enter the alveoli (tiny air sacs), and molt. While in the lungs, larvae can cause respiratory difficulties and pneumonia. From the lungs, they are coughed up into the pharynx and swallowed. Once back in the small intestine, this parasite develops to an adult form which can be 5 to 15 inches in length. Eggs are returned to pasture in manure and reach infective stage in one to two weeks.

Ascarids are sometimes responsible for an unthrifty appearance in young horses. In severe cases, the small intestine can actually rupture, due to the large number of adult worms present.

Ascarids may be difficult to eliminate from a farm, because the eggs can remain viable for years on pasture. The eggs have a thick protective shell which protects them so completely that they can withstand desiccation (dehydration), heat, and cold.

The egg has a sticky outer covering which causes it to stick to stall

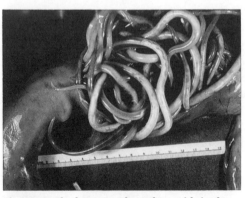

Fig. 12–9. The large number of ascarids in the above intestine resulted in its complete blockage and subsequent rupture.

walls, water buckets, and other items in the horse's environment. If it is suspected that there is a problem with this parasite in the barn or stable area, all surfaces should be washed with a disinfectant, using a high-pressure sprayer. Three cups of Clorox® to a gallon of cool water works well. The disinfectant will strip off the sticky outer coating of the ascarid egg, allowing it to be washed away.

Strongyloides

Strongyloides westeri is another parasite to which horses seem to develop immunity with age. Eggs of this parasite are rarely found in the feces of foals over six months of age and are almost never seen in fecal samples from adult horses.

Strongyloides species are unique in that they have both free-living and parasitic generations. The free-living generation has both male and female worms which reproduce sexually. The parasitic generation has no males, only *parthenogenetic* females. The parthenogenetic females carry out reproduction by the development of their own unfertilized egg (gamete); no male sperm is required. These eggs give rise to offspring of two types. They can develop into either infective parasitic larvae (*homogenic* life cycle) or they can become free-living males and females (*heterogonic* life cycle). The free-living generation lives in the soil and reproduces sexually. Their offspring can then become infective to the horse. How a particular egg from the parthenogenetic female will develop is both genetically and environmentally predetermined.

A foal can be infected with *S. westeri* in two ways:

1) Infective larvae enter the foal by penetrating the skin or oral mucous membranes. Larvae then enter the blood stream and travel to the lungs. They make their way up the *trachea* to the *pharynx* and

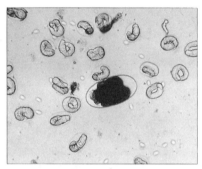

Fig. 12–10. The small eggs are *Strongyloides westeri;* the large egg is a strongyle type.

are swallowed into the small intestine, where they mature sexually and produce eggs.

2) Infective larvae accumulate in the mare's tissues and migrate to the mammary gland during lactation. They are then transferred to the foal through the milk, beginning approximately four days after foaling. (Infective larvae are not known to pass in the *colostrum.*)

Foals will often begin shedding eggs of *S. westeri* in their feces ten to fourteen days after birth.

Bots

Bots are larval stages of the botfly, of which there are several species. The three most common North American species are *Gastrophil-*

us intestinalis (common bot), *G. nasalis* (throat bot) and *G. haemorrhoidalis* (nose bot). These species differ slightly in the first stages of their life cycles.

Gastrophilus Intestinalis (common bot)

Gastrophilus intestinalis generally lays its yellow-colored eggs on the hairs of the horse's shoulders and forelimbs.

Fig. 12–11. Gastrophilus intestinalis lays eggs on the forelimbs and shoulders of the horse.

These eggs undergo a five day incubation period and then readily hatch when the horse rubs its mouth against them. Larvae enter the horse's mouth and burrow into the tip of the tongue. From there, they migrate toward the root of the tongue, creating airholes. After about three weeks, they transfer to the spaces between the molars and undergo the first molt. When the larvae emerge, they are about 6 – 7 millimeters long. They then attach to the root of the tongue for a short time before being swallowed.

Once in the stomach, they attach to the white, non-glandular portion of the *gastric mucosa* and remain there for approximately nine months. While in the stomach, bot larvae undergo another molt and develop into third stage larvae. They cause irritation and bleeding, and can even penetrate the stomach or intestinal wall, causing *peritonitis* (inflammation of the membranous lining of the abdominal cavity).

In the spring or early summer, these larvae detach from the stomach wall and are passed out with the feces. Once in the ground, they *pupate*, forming an outer covering. Inside this covering they develop into an adult insect, much like a caterpillar changes into a butterfly. After several months, the adult flies emerge. The adult fly cannot feed and generally lives only about five days, but during that time it can lay thousands of eggs.

Gastrophilus Nasalis (throat bot)

In this species, the female lays yellowish-white eggs in the space

Fig. 12–12. Bot larvae attached to the stomach wall of the horse.

between the jawbones of the horse. Larvae hatch spontaneously within five to six days and burrow through the skin to enter the mouth. They burrow between the molars and develop into second stage larvae which emerge and are swallowed.

G. nasalis larvae attach themselves to the *pylorus* and *duodenum* rather than to the actual stomach, and at this site they undergo a final molt to third stage larvae.

After spending about ten months attached to the intestinal tract, larvae are passed out in the feces. Once outside, the larvae pupate in the soil and hatch into botflies within 2 to 3 months. The adult botfly then lays eggs on the horse, and the cycle begins again.

Fig. 12–13. First, second, and third stage larvae of the bot.

Gastrophilus Hemorrhoidalis (nose bot)

In this species, the female botfly lays black eggs on the short hairs along the lips of the horse. These eggs incubate for two to four days, after which, upon contact with moisture, they burrow into the *epidermis* of the lips and proceed into the mucous membranes of the mouth. From this point, the life cycle is like that of *G. nasalis*, except that *G. haemorrhoidalis* sometimes attach temporarily to the rectum before being passed in the feces. This can cause irritation and straining by the horse during defecation.

Tapeworms

Three species of tapeworms are known to affect the horse: *Anoplocephala magna*, *Anoplocephala perfoliata* and *Paranoplocephala mamillana*. Each species has been diagnosed by microscopic fecal examination in foals as young as two months of age.

With tapeworms, a routine fecal examination would detect very few eggs, even in a heavily infected animal. This is because tapeworm eggs in EPG tests do not float in the solution used to test the feces as well as other parasite eggs, and they are also present in fewer numbers.

There does not appear to be an acquired immune response (immunity developed over time) to these parasites, and adult horses are infected as often as foals.

The life cycle and method of transmission for tapeworms is different from those of other parasites. All equine tapeworms require an

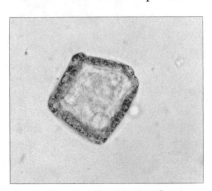

"intermediate host" for transmission of their infective form to the horse. An "intermediate host" is a host in which the parasite must undergo development before it can become infective to the final host, the horse. Horse tapeworms require an *oribatid* mite as their intermediate host. An oribatid mite is a free living pasture mite found on all established pastures, and it ingests tapeworm eggs passed in the feces of infected horses. Grazing horses ingest the mites along with the grass. Once

Fig. 12–14. A tapeworm egg. They are difficult to detect because they do not float as well as other parasite eggs.

the ingested mite reaches the stomach of the horse, it is digested, and the infective form of the tapeworm is released into the small intestine and cecum.

Mild infections often show no clinical signs; consequently, not much attention has been given to tapeworm infection in the horse. However, it is recognized that heavy tapeworm burdens in other animals, man included, can and do create *enteritis*, general unthriftiness, and poor growth. Case reports suggest obstruction by tapeworms of the ileocecal valve can be a cause of colic in the horse.

Research has indicated that up to 54% of all horses in the Kentucky area may well be infected with tapeworms. At this time, no dewormer in the United States has label approval for use against tapeworms in the horse. However, investigators have reported good effectiveness from a doubled dose of pyrantel pamoate.

Protozoa

Eimeria leuckarti is a member of a major protozoan group known as coccidia. These parasites invade the mucosa of the small intestine of young horses but do not appear to cause much damage. The egglike *oocyst* (encysted fertilized form) of this parasite is occasionally found during routine fecal examinations. However, because they are especially dense and do not float as well as the eggs of other parasites, the oocysts are not routinely seen, even in heavily infected animals.

These parasites are not affected by dewormers used against other parasites in the horse, and methods of treatment for it have not been extensively investigated. Fortunately, infections appear to be self-limiting, because the cells of the protozoa become unable to reproduce, due to an immunity response by the horse.

DANGERS OF WORM INFESTATION

Internal parasites are so common that prevention of all infections is almost impossible. They are especially a problem in moist, temperate climates. Parasite infections can produce weakness and disability in some animals, but horses hosting a large worm population may not exhibit signs of poor health if they are adequately nourished.

Blood values of a heavily parasitized horse often show very little variation from normal values, with the exception of elevated white blood cell counts and a slight anemia. There can, however, be digestive disturbances, diarrhea, and a predisposition to colic. In severe cases, internal *hemorrhaging*, peritonitis, or arterial and intestinal blockage can eventually result in death. Although not all horses with parasite infections show symptoms, any horse with a large worm burden cannot perform at its highest capabilities.

METHODS OF PARASITE CONTROL
Deworming

The use of dewormers which are **effective** against the parasites infecting a horse is an essential part of parasite control. As a general rule, adult horses should be dewormed every two months. When a horse is effectively dewormed, most of the adult parasites are killed and, subsequently, the number of parasite eggs passed in the feces is reduced. Depending on the effectiveness of the dewormer, parasite egg output by the horse should be reduced for four to eight weeks after treatment. If the dewormer does not significantly reduce the number of parasite eggs being passed in the feces (as determined by an EPG test), a different product should be used.

Parasite infection in the foal can be controlled very effectively by keeping the mare as parasite-free as possible both during pregnancy and after birth of the foal. Deworming the mare with an effective product in the last month of *gestation* can effectively control the transmission of *Strongyloides westeri* from the dam to the foal. (See section on *S. westeri*).

Because foals are susceptible to numerous parasites beginning as early as two weeks of age, they should be started on a deworming program at one to two months of age. Monthly deworming should continue through the first six months of life, or even throughout the first year if the parasite situation warrants. While it has been widely speculated that such a rigorous deworming regime might inhibit the development of an acquired immunity against such parasites as *S. westeri* and *P. equorum*, research findings do not substantiate this.

Fig. 12–15. Regular deworming of mares during gestation will help limit transmission of internal parasites to foals. Deworming foals monthly, starting at one or two months of age, will help prevent large infestations of parasites.

Even when dewormed monthly, the foal is still exposed to parasitic infection through its exposure to the pasture, paddock, or drylot environment. Through this exposure, the foal will be able to develop usual immunity to these parasites.

The main advantage of deworming foals monthly is the patent infection of the parasites (the egg laying phase) is minimized, if not eliminated altogether. This limits the number of parasite eggs foals deposit into their environment, which reduces pasture contamination and risk of infection to future generations of foals.

Whereas most veterinary parasitologists agree that it is important to rotate the use of various classes of dewormers, there are different schools of thought on how this should be carried out. At this time, there are eight different classes of anthelmintics (dewormers) to choose from, and they are listed in the following chart:

Classes of Anthelmintics	
Anthelmintic Class	**Generic Name**
Avermectin	**Ivermectin**
Benzimidazoles	**Febendazole, Mebendazole, Oxfendazole, Oxibendazole, Thiabendazole**
Phenylguanidines	**Febantel**
Imidothiazole	**Levamisole**
Organophosphates	**Dichlorvos, Trichlorfon**
Piperazines	**Piperazine**
Pyrimidines	**Pyrantel**
Others	**Phenothiazine, Carbon disulfide**

Fig. 12–16.

There are different methods of rotating classes of anthelmintics. "Fast rotation" involves choosing an anthelmintic from a **different class** each time the horse is dewormed during a given year. Because an adult horse would be dewormed six times during a twelve month period, rotation would include six different anthelmintic classes. A possible method would be to go straight down the list in the anthelmintic table and rotate using an avermectin in January, a benzimidazole in March, a phenylguanidine in May, an imidothiazole in July, an organophosphate in September, and a piperazine product in November. A "slow rotation" involves using the same anthelmintic class for an entire year, then switching to another class the following year. For instance, an avermectin would be used six times the first year, a benzimidazole six times the second year, and a pyrimidine six times the third year, and so on.

Other methods of anthelmintic rotation are now being investigated. Some parasitologists feel that when effective methods of pasture management are utilized, it may be possible to control parasite infections with only two or three "strategic" dewormings during the year. It is an established fact that parasite EPGs in the horse rise considerably in the spring and fall. During these periods, it is especially important to deworm using an **effective** anthelmintic. As previously discussed, some parasites have developed resistance to certain anthelmintics. When this occurs, that particular anthelmintic should not be used again on the farm which demonstrated the resistance, because that anthelmintic will not be effective.

The most commonly used classes of anthelmintics and the parasites they are effective against are in the following chart:

Anthelmintics	Parasites
Avermectins	strongyles, ascarids, strongyloides, pinworms and bots
Benzimidazoles	strongyles, ascarids, strongyloides, pinworms (Some small strongyles may be resistant to certain anthelmintics in this class.)
Organophosphates	ascarids, pinworms, and bots (Note: Organophosphates are very toxic and should not be given to foals or pregnant mares.)
Piperazines	mainly strongyles and ascarids
Pyrimidines	strongyles, ascarids, and tapeworms*

Fig. 12–17.   *A doubled dose must be used to be effective.

A complete deworming program that is universally applicable cannot be given, because anthelmintic treatments and intervals will vary with worm population, climate of the region, and pasture management practices. In all cases, a veterinarian should be consulted to devise a complete parasite control program. However, there are several guidelines which can be successfully applied by horse owners:

l) All horses within an age or pasture grouping should be dewormed at the same time with an anthelmintic to target specific parasites.

2) New arrivals at the farm should be isolated and dewormed before introducing them to the pasture.

3) Fecal egg per gram counts (EPGs) should be run to determine the effectiveness of the deworming program. (EPGs will determine the types of parasites present in the horse. They are **not**, however, good indicators of the **number** of parasites present .)

4) If possible, pasture should be rested at least once a year for two to six months. This helps reduce the number of some infective forms of certain parasites. Strongyle larvae, for example, cannot survive indefinitely on a pasture and will eventually die if not ingested by a horse. In the southern United States and other warm climate areas, however, strongyle eggs can survive on pastures for more than six months due to mild fall and winter months. Ascarid eggs, as discussed earlier, can survive in a pasture for years, regardless of climatic conditions.

5) Avoid overcrowding pastures.

6) Do not spread fresh manure on pastures that are being grazed. Manure should be composted at least two weeks before spreading, **if** it must be put on the pasture.

7) Label directions on dewormers should be carefully followed.

8) Method of administering a dewormer is not important as long as instructions are followed and the full dose is given.

While some anthelmintics are "larvicidal," meaning they are effective against migrating larval stages of various parasites, most are not. The avermectin class has good larvicidal effects against migrating larvae of large strongyles as well as later larval stages of *P. equorum* found in the intestinal lumen. Certain dewormers in the benzimidazole class are also larvicidal.

Methods of Administering Anthelmintics

Stomach Tube

Stomach tubing was once the most common method of deworming a horse. In this procedure, a flexible tube is passed through the horse's nostril, down the *esophagus,* and into

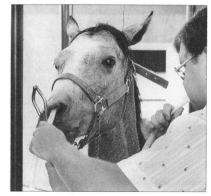

Fig. 12–18. Stomach tube deworming.

269

the stomach. A liquid dewormer is then pumped through the tube directly into the stomach. This is a dangerous procedure if not done properly, and it should only be practiced by a veterinarian.

Due to the effectiveness of paste dewormers on the market today, the practice of tube deworming is seen less often. Paste dewormers are becoming more and more accepted as being equally effective, provided the full recommended dose is ingested.

Pastes and Liquids

Pastes and liquids are effective only if administered properly. Liquids can be administered through a stomach tube as described previously or they can be placed in the back of the mouth with a syringe. Pastes can be

administered at the very back of the mouth as well, or in the cheek area.

With both pastes and liquids, it is helpful to wash out any feedstuffs from the mouth prior to deworming. This helps ensure the horse will not expel the dewormer from its mouth along with the feedstuff residue. It is also helpful to administer the dewormer as quickly as possible before the horse has a chance to resist. If unsure how to properly administer a paste or liquid dewormer, the owner should have a veterinarian demonstrate the proper method.

Fig. 12–19. Paste deworming is now widely accepted as being as effective as tube deworming, if the horse receives the recommended dose.

Pelleted Dewormers

Dewormers are also available in powdered form or as a component mixed into alfalfa pellets. These dewormers, made with low doses of deworming compounds, are designed to be fed on a daily basis. They are usually palatable and safe for horses of all ages, including foals, pregnant mares, and horses in training.

There are some shortfalls to this method of deworming:

    1) Horses may sort out and eat around the medication.

    2) The effectiveness of the drug may be reduced if it takes an extended period of time for consumption.

    3) Uncertainty that the horse always ingests a full therapeutic dose of the dewormer.

Despite these drawbacks, many veterinarians recommend their use (particularly those containing pyrantel tartrate) because of their palatability and safety.

Because most daily dewormers are not effective against large strongyles and bots, another class of dewormer, such as an organophosphate, carbon disulfide, or an avermectin must be used every six months to eliminate them. **Neither organophosphates nor carbon disulfide should be given to foals or pregnant mares,** particularly mares during late gestation (the last three months). Organophosphates and carbon di-sulfide are very toxic and can lead to serious complications in a pregnant mare and the fetus. Avermectin products should be used to remove bots and large strongyles in pregnant mares and foals.

Common Errors in Deworming

In this chapter, a wide range of topics related to parasite control in the horse has been discussed. The importance of deworming and pasture management programs cannot be stressed enough. However, even horse owners/managers with the best intentions can find their parasite control programs falling short of desired effectiveness. In this section, some common causes of ineffective deworming will be discussed.

First, the dewormer must be effective against the parasites infecting the horse. With a tapeworm problem, results should not be expected from any anthelmintic class except the pyrimidines (see tapeworm section), and those are only effective in a double dosage. Only dewormers containing avermectins, organophospates, and carbon disulfide are effective against bots. Certain dewormers, several in the benzimidizole class, are no longer effective against small strongyles, due to resistance. Resistance problems can only be determined by pre- and post-treatment EPGs *(see Small Strongyle section)*.

Errors in deworming may be made by misreading the dosage instructions on the label of the deworming container. Whereas the toxicity levels of the different deworming classes vary dramatically, there are wide margins of safety for most of these drugs. Occasionally, a horse may appear to have an idiosyncrasy in toleration of certain deworming compounds. However, accidental slippage of the knurled ring on deworming paste syringes can deliver an excessive dosage which usually causes no ill effect other than economic wastage. Exceptions to this are dewormers containing any of the organophosphates, carbon disulfide, or phenothiazine. These products **can produce toxicosis** at dosages only slightly over those recommended by the manufacturer.

Occasional overdosing with a dewormer is not a major problem, but continual underdosing can be. Repeated underdosing results in an ineffective deworming program which does not control parasite infections and invites resistance to the drugs being used.

Most horses are underdosed simply because of an inaccurate estimation of its weight. Dr. Richard L. Asquith and others at the of the University of Florida reported that the weight of adult horses is underestimated 80% of the time.

Numerous weight estimation tapes and formulas are available for use in estimating the weight of individual animals. One such formula was published by Dr. Frederick Harper from the University of Tennessee and has been shown to be particularly accurate. The heart girth is measured in inches and multiplied by itself, then multiplied by the number of inches in body length (measured from the point of shoulder to the point of hip). The resulting figure is divided by 330, which produces a good estimate of the total body weight in pounds.

$$\frac{\text{HEART GIRTH (in inches)}^2 \times \text{BODY LENGTH (in inches)}}{330} = \text{BODY WEIGHT in lbs.}$$

In an article discussing anthelmintic resistance in the horse, Dr. Craig R. Reinemeyer, of the University of Tennessee, stated that no method of anthelmintic dosing is any worse than another in causing resistance. Management practices such as half-dosing and frequent dosing with deworming compounds, however, do contribute to the development of resistance.

The same article lists dewormers to which small strongyles have developed resistance. These include cambendazole (no longer on the market), febendazole, oxfendazole, thiabendazole, phenothiazine, and febantel. All of these products are in the benzimidazole class of anthelmintics with the exception of febantel, which is a phenylguanidine, and phenothiazine, which is classified as an "other."

Pasture Management for Parasite Control

Another important method of parasitic worm control is good pasture management. Several methods commonly used are pasture rest, rotational grazing, segregated pastures, manure removal, chain dragging, harrowing, and plowing.

Pasture Rest

Pasture rest consists of alternately grazing and resting a pasture at six month intervals. During the resting period, some of the infective worm populations in the pasture can be killed off by sunlight, heat, cold, and lack of hosts to be infected. When horses are returned to that pasture, there should be fewer infective forms of parasites. This measure is especially useful if the pasture can be left ungrazed for up to nine months. This period needs to include either winter in the north or summer in the south. (Parasite larvae are killed off by very cold winters and hot summers.)

Rotational Grazing With Cattle

Rotational grazing with cattle is a variation of pasture rest that allows the pasture to be put to use during the rest period. Equine parasites generally cannot complete their life cycle in cattle, and vice versa. Therefore, rotating pasture use between horses and cattle will allow the equine parasites to die out while cattle are grazing.

It should be noted that the small stomach worm, *Trichoslrongulus axei*, is a parasite which can infect both horses and cattle. There are other parasites normally found in cattle, which may infect horses, but they are rare and not ordinarily of any medical significance.

Segregation

Segregation of pastures implies that weanlings and yearlings will be grazed in separate areas from mature horses. If broodmares are dewormed within a month before foaling and parasites are carefully controlled while the mares are nursing their foals, parasites will be less likely to pass from dams to their foals. Since foals are born parasite-free, chances of them developing significant internal

Fig. 12–20. Broodmares should be dewormed within a month before foaling.

parasite infections are greatly reduced if they are grazed on clean pasture away from other infested horses.

Fecal Control

To control parasites, removal of manure from pastures and stables should be performed as often as possible. If manure is collected from pastures at least twice a week, the number of infective larvae on the pasture will be reduced, and parasite infections will not be as readily spread. This involves more actual physical effort than other control measures, but it should always be considered worthwhile. In fact, it is probably the most effective way to control parasites in the pasture.

Pasture vacuums are being developed for manure removal on horse farms. These machines simplify manure removal and ensure optimum grazing conditions with minimum labor.

Chain dragging of pastures has some benefits in worm control. Dragging chains behind a tractor breaks up manure piles and exposes them to sunlight. It is most effective when done during hot, dry weather, because such conditions are detrimental to the parasitic larvae. This helps reduce the worm population. While not the best method of parasite control, chain dragging is preferable to harrowing, and plowing of pastures. Also, plowing and using harrows with spikes or disks disrupts pasture vegetation.

Fig. 12–21. Frequent removal of manure is probably the most effective method of controlling parasites in pastures.

Spreading **fresh** manure over the pasture, especially manure obtained from cleaning stalls, is not advised. It is likely to spread both parasite eggs and larvae, as well as weed seeds. If spread, manure should first be composted by piling it together in one area and allowing to sit for several weeks.

13

DRUGS

This chapter offers a simple overview of certain drugs of interest in the equine world. The chapter was included because the use of drugs (proper and improper) has an influence on the overall health of the horse and therefore can affect the results of nutritional programs. Readers needing more detailed information on equine drugs can contact Equine Research, Inc. for information on comprehensive books that are available on the subject. *(Toll free telephone number is listed in front of this book.)*

Drugs are used to treat lameness, cuts, wounds, upper respiratory tract infections, viral infections, and bacterial infections. Studies of racehorses in training show that 6% of the time, they cannot be worked. This 6% breaks down into: lameness 68% of the time, respiratory infections 21% of the time, and wounds and other infections 12% of the time. Approximately 80% of all positive drug tests in racing result from deliberate administrations of drugs in order to treat injury or sickness or restore performance, or from inadvertent administration of drugs due to error or ignorance.

Some trainers do not understand the long-term health dangers caused by some drugs. The *pathological* toxic effects of some drugs may irreparably damage parts of the body; performance drugs often damage the liver and kidney. *Genotoxic* effects involve alterations to the building blocks of the body, the *DNA*. The alterations are believed to be the basic cause of cancer. Some drugs are not toxic in their original form, but once the body breaks them down, their *metabolites* (by-products) may be toxic.

It should also be noted that illegally manufactured drugs have no guarantee of purity. They can have terrible side effects in horses, including seizures, muscular rigidity, intestinal spasms, diarrhea, intense pain in muscles and bones, cardiovascular collapse, and death.

There are many classes of drugs that may be beneficial in certain circumstances when administered or recommended by a veterinarian. Some examples are: the nonsteroidal anti-inflammatories, steroidal anti-inflammatories, local anesthetics, bronchodilators, antibiotics, muscle relaxants, diuretics, and others.

NONSTEROIDAL ANTI-INFLAMMATORY DRUGS

Nonsteroidal anti-inflammatory drugs (NSAIDs) are considered performance-restoring drugs. They do **not** speed up the healing process. They do, however, reduce the development of inflammation in injured tissue by blocking the formation of prostaglandin, which cells produce. These prostaglandins are released when a cell is damaged, causing swelling, increased blood flow, loss of function in the injured area, and hypersensitivity to pain and heat. Prostaglandins are also involved in the generation of fevers. Thus, nonsteroidal anti-inflammatory drugs are also known as antipyretics (anti-fever).

The use of nonsteroidal anti-inflammatory drugs is permitted in specified concentrations by some racing commissions. It is also allowed in some other equine sports, such as jumping. The argument for allowing the use of nonsteroidal anti-inflammatory drugs is that they are only preventing inflammation, thereby restoring the horse to, but not pushing it beyond, its physiological limits. However, some authorities hold that these drugs increase the risk of breakdowns due to the pain and inflammation-blocking effect. In addition, excessive doses of nonsteroidal anti-inflammatory drugs may lead to ulcers in the mouth, stomach, and intestines, depression, loss of appetite, and changes in the blood constituents.

Nonsteroidal anti-inflammatory drugs are acidic in nature and do not show up in saliva tests. The drugs tend to become concentrated in the stomach, small intestine, and kidneys.

Nonsteroidal anti-inflammatory drugs will not prevent the horse from feeling pain, nor will it prevent the horse from being aware that its leg is in a certain position or carrying a certain amount of weight. The more common types of NSAIDs are discussed below.

Phenylbutazone

Phenylbutazone ("bute") is the most common nonsteroidal

anti-inflammatory drug. When injected intravenously, it takes about 30 minutes to begin blocking the formation of prostaglandins. Phenylbutazone administered orally will take longer to be effective. However, since there will already be large amounts of prostaglandins in the inflamed area, the phenylbutazone does not appear to take effect until these levels are reduced, usually three to four hours later.

It may take up to twelve hours for the full pharmacological actions of phenylbutazone to become apparent, but swelling, heat, and hypersensitivity to pain will begin to decline as the levels of prostaglandins drop. Likewise, as blood levels of phenylbutazone drop, the levels of prostaglandins increase again.

Phenlybutazone is considered a safe drug when used at the recommended doses and periods of time.

Naproxen (Equiproxen®)

Naproxen is used to relieve pain, inflammation, and lameness in horses that "tie-up." It is also used to treat soft tissue diseases in the horse.

Naproxen is commonly administered orally, twice a day. There is little tendency for the drug to accumulate in the horse's body, because it is rapidly broken down and excreted. However, the drug is easily detected in the urine of the horse, and it requires at least 60 hours to clear.

Naproxen is a safe drug to use. In experiments, horses have been given three times the recommended dose for up to 42 days with no apparent side-effects. (This should not be done as a normal course of treatment.) A veterinarian's instructions should be followed closely.

Flunixin Meglumine (Banamine®)

This drug is characteristic of the nonsteroidal anti-inflammatories in that individual members of this group are more effective than others in improving some conditions. Flunixin has been very useful in the treatment of colic. It rapidly alleviates the pain and discomfort associated with colic, sometimes in as little as fifteen minutes. The drug is effective in controlling pain for six to eight hours.

Flunixin tends to be more potent than other nonsteroidal anti-inflammatory drugs. It only requires 1.0 milligram per kilogram of body weight to produce good clinical effects. Phenylbutazone, on the other hand, must be administered at 4.4 milligrams per kilogram of body weight to produce the same effects. Flunixin is a very safe drug when administered at the recommended levels.

Meclofenamic Acid (Arquel®)

This drug is very slow acting. It may take as long as 36 to 96 hours before improvement in the horse is seen.

Meclofenamic acid is useful in treating horses with osteoarthritis, navicular disease, and laminitis. A study was conducted on 304 horses, all suffering from these conditions. The results showed that meclofenamic acid improved 61% of the horses with osteoarthritis, 78% of the horses with navicular disease, and 76% of the laminitis cases. It is also useful in the treatment of musculoskeletal disease.

The usual dose rate is 1 milligram per pound of body weight daily, for five to seven days. At this dose it is considered a safe drug. However, if the dose is increased to 6 to 8 milligrams per pound of body weight, mouth ulcers, depression, edema, loss of appetite and weight will occur.

Non-Steroidal Anti-Inflammatory Drugs	
Benefits	**Drawbacks**
• **fever reduction** During bacterial and viral infections, prostaglandins are released into fluid surrounding the brain, which causes elevated body temperatures. NSAIDs prevent production of these prostaglandins. • **pain relief** NSAIDs reduce levels of prostaglandins in tissues, reducing pain hypersensitivity. • **prevention of inflammation** By preventing production of prostaglandins, NSAIDs stop development of inflammation in injured tissue.	• **production of ulcers** Ulcers will form when NSAIDs accumulate in the stomach, kidney, and small intestine. • **selective pain relief** NSAIDs only relieve pain associated with inflammation; they have no effect on pain associated with muscle fatigue or lactic acid buildup during intense exercise. • **no acceleration of healing** NSAIDs merely prevent inflammatory response to an injury. • **delayed healing** Horses treated with NSAIDs and which continue to race may increase their injuries and delay healing and repair.

STEROIDAL ANTI-INFLAMMATORY DRUGS

Steroidal anti-inflammatory drugs (SAIDs), are another class of drugs. They are broken down into three groups, the glucocorticoids (affect protein and carbohydrate metabolism), mineralocorticoids (aldosterone, gives rise to sodium and water retention), and the adrenal sex hormones (such as testosterone).

Steroidal anti-inflammatory drugs may be naturally occurring in the body (cortisone, corticosterone, aldosterone) or they may be synthetic analogs (based on cortisol, the major hormone produced by the adrenal glands). The synthetic analogs are more commonly used because natural cortisol causes water and sodium retention in the horse's body.

The main purpose of the steroidal anti-inflammatory drugs is to reduce inflammation. If injected locally, they will have a local effect. If injected systemically, they will affect the whole body, including the cardiovascular system, kidneys, skeletal muscle, nervous system, and other organs and tissues. If used in large amounts, or over a long period of time, they delay healing and reduce the body's ability to fight parasitic or viral infections.

When used for long periods, steroidal anti-inflammatory drugs may damage the adrenal glands, cause muscle wasting, and predispose the horse to ulcerations of the digestive tract. They may lead to demineralization of the bone, which results in osteoporosis and compression fractures.

Horses may suffer withdrawal symptoms if they have been given large doses of a steroidal anti-inflammatory drug over time (such as during racing or showing season), and are suddenly taken off of them. These horses may show symptoms of unthriftiness, dullness, and depression, even if they are receiving adequate nutrition. The horses suffer this withdrawal because their adrenal glands, which produce the natural corticosteroids, waste away while being given steroids. The body needs a certain level of these steroids to function normally. After a period of time, depending on the extent of damage to the adrenal glands, the body will again produce the natural corticosteroids.

The popular practice of injecting corticosteroids into "problem" joints should be avoided. These drugs slow the healing process and reduce the protective nature of joint fluid, which can lead to total collapse of the joint in the long term. These drugs suppress pain but in no way remove the cause of the lameness. A horse with an injected joint may appear sound, but the joint will continue to deteriorate at the same rate, or even faster **if the horse is not rested** after being injected.

Anabolic Steroids

Anabolic steroids are chemically and pharmacologically related to testosterone, a male hormone. When administered to **sick or debilitated horses,** they are known to improve appetite, weight gain, protein metabolism, hair coat, performance, and condition.

Some horsemen believe that anabolic steroids increase growth rates in young horses. In fact, anabolic steroids cause premature closure of the growth plates, resulting in a horse not reaching the full height of which it is genetically capable. Due to the belief that anabolic steroids increase muscle mass, many halter horses are fed steroids, but current studies indicate that they provide no such benefits. They actually can cause irreversible harm.

The consequences of anabolic steroid use on a young stallion's fertility can be quite costly. Studies show reduced testicular size, reduced sperm production, and reduced sperm motility. All of these are symptoms of testicular degeneration, a condition which under normal circumstances usually only affects aged stallions.

When used on mares and fillies, anabolic steroids induce stallion-like aggressive behavior and suppress estrus and ovulation, which can sharply decrease fertility. Studies show that in some cases, fillies' hormones become so unbalanced that an enlarged clitoris develops. This is characteristic of *hermaphrodites* (horses that have both male and female organs). They also become sterile.

Use of anabolic steroids should be avoided, particularly on breeding prospects, unless it is on the advice of a veterinarian.

Steroidal Anti-Inflammatory Drugs	
Benefits	**Drawbacks**
• **reduced inflammation and its accompanying symptoms (heat, redness, pain, and loss of function of injured area)** - SAIDs appear to prevent production of prostaglandins by preventing the release of a precursor molecule from damaged tissue. By reducing inflammation, the accompanying symptoms are also reduced.	• **delayed healing** - Inhibit cells responsible for healing tissue. • **immunosuppressive** - Reduce the body's ability to fight infections. • **damage causing** - In excess, can damage adrenal glands, cause muscle wasting, and predispose gastrointestinal tract to ulcers. • **treat symptoms only** - Do not remove the cause of the disease.

OTHER ANTI-INFLAMMATORY DRUGS

There are many other anti-inflammatory drugs that are not related structurally or pharmacologically to the nonsteroidal anti-inflammatory drugs or the steroidal anti-inflammatory drugs.

Dimethyl Sulfoxide (DMSO)

DMSO is a colorless liquid that is applied to the skin over the injured area. Its chemical characteristics enable it to penetrate quickly through cell membranes. Because DMSO accelerates the movement of other substances through the cell membranes, it is often used to increase absorption of other drugs through the skin, such as corticosteroids.

It has several other effects as well, including anti-inflammatory actions, local anesthetic properties, and antibacterial effects. It even has effects on diuresis (increased urination) and dilation of the blood vessels. It has been shown through studies to be helpful in treating inflammation of the joints, arthritis, and bucked shins. (However, it does not change the requirement for rest in the case of bucked shins.)

The use of DMSO is easy to detect because it produces a distinct garlic like odor in the urine. Most racing jurisdictions do not test for it, but its use in conjunction with topical applications of benzocaine or corticosteroids may lead to increased blood or urine levels of these drugs, and thus to positive tests for these agents.

DMSO should only be used in the medical or pure form, at a strength of 80% to 90%. The toxicity of DMSO is minimal, but no more than 100 milliliters a day should be used on a horse.

Orgotein (Palosein®)

Orgotein is a copper and zinc containing protein compound. It naturally occurs in the body as an intracellular enzyme called *superoxide dismutase*. This enzyme is part of the body's defense against the toxic oxides. These oxides are usually found within the superoxide radical, a highly reactive toxic compound, which is produced by *phagocytes* (a type of cell that engulfs bacteria), such as the white blood cells, during their killing attacks on bacteria. However, this radical can also kill the phagocytes. It is thought that the superoxide dismutase scavenges the excess radicals and prolongs phagocyte life.

When injected into a joint, orgotein preserves or restores the viscosity of the *synovial fluid*, the fluid contained in the sac-like structures, called bursa, which cushion the joints. It is "poorly anti-genic," meaning the body does not produce antibodies in an attempt to destroy it.

During a study, orgotein was injected into the joints of horses with noninfective traumatic arthritis, and beneficial results were pro-duced. These results were higher in the horses that had been lame for less than two months. Orgotein is essentially non-toxic and is consid-ered a safe drug to use.

Chondroprotective Agents

Chondroprotective agents are used in the treatment of joint dis-ease. They appear to slow cartilage breakdown, stimulate cartilage regeneration, neutralize any free radicals produced during exercise, and act as lubricants. They include:

- glycosaminoglycan sulphate (Adequan®)
- sodium pentosan polysulphate (Anarthron H®, Cartrophen Vet®)
- hyaluronic acid (Hyalovet®)
- superoxide dismutase may also be considered a chondroprotective agent

These drugs are usually injected into injured joints, sometimes in combination with a steroidal anti-inflammatory agent. An equivalent amount of synovial fluid is removed before the drugs are injected so as not to overfill the joint capsule.

Most horses will show improvement after being injected, but not all become sound. Horses with bony changes in the joint or that have had prior treatment with corticosteroids may show little improvement.

ANTIBIOTICS

An antibiotic is a substance that is selectively toxic to microorgan-isms, but not to the horse. This selectivity is achieved because of the basic biochemical difference between the horse and the bacterium. For example, penicillin destroys bacteria by acting on the fibrous cell walls of the bacteria. Since the cell walls in horses are not fibrous, penicillin has almost no toxicity in the horse.

Antibiotics must be used correctly if maximum benefits are to be obtained. Before any antibiotic is used, the causative organism must be sampled and cultured to determine its identity and to ensure that antibiotics will be useful against it. Once this is determined, the ap-propriate antibiotic can be chosen.

For antibiotic therapy to be beneficial, it is imperative that as much infected material, bacteria, debris, and foreign bodies be removed from the infected site as possible. Abscesses should be drained and injured areas should be kept clean. If catheters, bone plates, or other mechanical items are causing the infection, they should be removed if possible.

Using a combination of antibiotics is not recommended unless a special circumstance requires it. An example of a special circumstance would be a mixed bacteria infection, which occurs with *peritonitis* (inflammation of the lining in the abdominal cavity).

Bacteria can become resistant to drugs. The use of low levels of antibiotics encourages resistance because a few marginally resistant bacteria may survive the low levels. As a result, a new, more resistant strain will develop. Consequently, low levels should **not** be used, especially for extended periods of time.

Groups of Antibiotics

There are several groups of antibiotics that will be briefly discussed. However, the two general types of bacteria will be clarified first. Bacteria can be classified as gram-negative or gram-positive. These two types of bacteria differ in terms of the composition of their cell walls. Because certain antibiotics are only effective against gram-negative or gram-positive bacteria, it is important to determine what type of bacteria is involved in an infection before choosing the antibiotic. This is determined by the Gram's Stain procedure, in which a crystal-violet stain is placed on the bacteria. The bacteria are then rinsed with ethanol (diluted alcohol). A gram-positive bacteria will retain the crystal-violet stain after the rinse, and a gram-negative bacteria will not. The gram-negative bacteria will stain with sarafin. This staining procedure is done in a laboratory and the cells must be observed under a microscope.

Penicillins

Penicillins were the first of the true antibiotics to be introduced into medicine. They remain the most potent and effective antibiotic. The penicillins originally were not active against gram-negative organisms. However, broad-spectrum penicillins have been developed, such as ampicillin, which are effective against these organisms.

Penicillin blocks the formation of the cell wall by binding to the cross-linking enzyme and stopping it from performing its function, which is to build the cell wall. Without this tough cell wall, the bacteria ruptures, due to the osmotic (fluid) pressures in the body.

Penicillins are categorized as *bactericidal* drugs because they cause bacterial death rather than simply stopping the growth of the bacteria. A *bacteriostatic* compound stops growth.

Penicillins are relatively safe, but large doses of potassium penicillin should not be given intravenously, because the added potassium ion may depress the heart. Also, procaine penicillin should not be used if the horse will undergo drug tests. Procaine is a banned substance, because it is a local anesthetic and a central nervous system stimulant. It can show up in urine two or more weeks after a dose of procaine penicillin is given, resulting in a positive drug test.

Procaine is combined with penicillin because it makes the penicillin longer acting. When this substance is injected intramuscularly, it is slowly dissolved in the muscle fluid, and then slowly released into the circulatory system.

Aminoglycosides

The aminoglycosides have high water solubility and low lipid solubility, and consequently are poorly absorbed into cells. They also are not distributed throughout the body when injected intramuscularly. Instead, they enter the bloodstream and are eventually excreted in the urine, mostly unchanged. These characteristics make them useful in treating urinary tract infections, metritis (inflammation of the uterus) in mares, and genital tract infections in stallions.

Aminoglycosides are considered bactericidal, because they block the bacteria's ability to form proteins necessary for life. They are active principally against gram-negative bacteria, and are useful in the treatment of *Pseudomonas* infections when used in conjunction with carbenicillin (a penicillin-derived compound).

The most important and commonly used aminoglycoside is gentamicin. Care should be taken when using gentamicin on young foals because it can cause kidney failure and tubular damage in the kidney.

Sulfonamides

The sulfonamides are actually synthetic chemicals, but they have substantial antibacterial actions. They are active against both gram-positive and gram-negative bacteria. However, they are bacteriostatic, in that they stop the growth of the bacteria, but do not destroy it. Sulfonamides block the formation of *folic acid* (one of the B-complex vitamins) in the bacteria. The bacteria are dependent on the presence of folic acid for growth.

There are three general groups of sulfamides. The first group includes sulfaguanidine, sulfasuxidine, and sulfathaladine. They are administered orally, and because they are not readily absorbed, their action is in the digestive tract. The second group includes the systemically active sulfonamides. They are administered intravenously, and are widely distributed throughout the body. In addition, they are one of the few antibiotics that only need to be administered once a day. A third group, which includes sulfisoxazole, is rapidly excreted from the body via the urine, so there is a high level of the drug in the urinary tract. These are used to treat urinary tract infections.

Because the sulfonamides tend to be irritating and painful if given intramuscularly, they should be administered intravenously. If a large dose is required, it should be injected slowly, as staggering, tremors, and collapse may occur if it is injected rapidly. In addition, horses should have free access to water and be kept well hydrated to avoid any possibility of kidney damage, which may occur with certain types of sulfonamide drugs.

Nitrofurans

The nitrofurans are synthetic chemicals. They are active against gram-positive and gram-negative bacteria. Nitrofurans are applied topically, and the danger of toxicity is essentially nonexistent.

LASIX

Lasix is a controversial drug that is commonly used in racing. It is believed that lasix stops exercise-induced pulmonary hemorrhage (EIPH), also called *epistaxis* ("bleeding"). Virtually all horses will show some evidence of this problem following intense exercise, because the stress associated with racing leads to high blood pressure and increased blood *viscosity*. However, in most horses, the bleeding is minute and the horse's nasal passage must be scoped to detect the condition. EIPH is known to be detrimental to the horse's performance, and that is the reason for the popularity of lasix.

Most studies have shown no improvement in performance due to lasix. However, the results of a University of Pennsylvania study showed that when lasix was administered to horses that were not bleeders, there were improvements: Thoroughbred geldings had a 5.4 length improvement in a mile, mares and fillies improved 2.1 lengths, and colts less than ½ length. Lasix also showed an improvement in bleeders: geldings 2.8 length improvement, and fillies and mares a 1.2 length improvement. However, colts showed no improvement.

In the study, lasix failed to stop bleeding in 62% of the bleeders treated, and failed to prevent 26% of non-bleeders from becoming bleeders. Overall, the study when compared to others, has caused a bit of confusion in the racing community. The need for more research in this area is obvious.

Lasix produces an increase of fifty times the normal amount of urine excreted. It produces this effect within minutes after intravenous or intramuscular injection. This makes lasix useful in the treatment of horses that tie up, because it keeps muscle pigments from building up in the kidneys, and thus reduces the possibility of kidney damage caused by these pigments.

However, this tremendous loss of body fluid in the urine can add more stress to the already stressed racehorse, particularly if the weather is hot and humid. The fluid loss creates a decrease in the plasma (fluid portion of the blood) volume of the blood. This results in an increase in the total blood plasma solids of about 10%, and an increase in the concentration of red blood cells by about 5%. It causes a drop in the plasma potassium of 25%. The blood will then become more viscous, making it difficult for it to move freely through the blood vessels. All of these factors create additional stress on the racehorse. These effects occur within 10 to 30 minutes of dosing, and all values generally return to normal within two hours after dosing.

Lasix action in the horse tends to be short lived, although it can easily be detected in the urine for up to 72 hours after a 10 milliliter dose. Lasix is longer acting when administered intramuscularly, rather than intravenously. After an intravenous injection, lasix reduces blood pressure in the lungs within minutes, but it does not reduce blood pressure in the general circulation.

Lasix does not flush drugs out of the bloodstream. While it may reduce the urinary concentration of certain drugs, these drugs can still be detected in the blood.

STIMULANTS

The use of stimulants in an attempt to improve the performance of the horse is illegal and dangerous. This section is intended only to provide the reader with general information on stimulants and how their effects are produced.

General Stimulants

These stimulate without producing any clear behavioral characteristics. Their action appears to increase the level of excitability in the horse.

Different horses tend to react in different ways to the same dose of a stimulant. With some stimulants, if too large a dose is given, the horse will become dull and depressed.

Amphetamines, Methamphetamines, and Ephedrine

Amphetamines stimulate the brain by causing the release of *norepinephrine* and *dopamine* (two neurotransmitters) from the nerve endings. Both of these are stimulants which affect specific areas of the body, such as the brain or the heart. They also tend to delay the onset of fatigue.

Amphetamines tend to cause a slight restlessness in horses, and they may also show muscle tremors, increased motor activity, agitation, and sleeplessness. Blood pressure will rise due to amphetamines, and exercised horses may have an irregular heart beat. They also increase the diameter of the airways by relaxing the bronchi muscle, but not enough to warrant using the drug for this effect.

The methamphetamines are very closely related to amphetamines and ephedrine. Ephedrine is a synthetic compound that causes much the same effects as epinephrine, a stimulant. They both have marked effects on the brain at small doses, and larger doses will affect the heart and blood vessels.

Ephedrine is related pharmacologically to the amphetamines. It causes the release of norepinephrine from the nerve terminals, just like amphetamines and methamphetamines. It also acts like norepinephrine, producing the same stimulation in the body.

Ephedrine has less of a stimulating effect on the brain, and more of an effect on the heart, blood vessels, and lungs when compared to amphetamines and methamphetamines. All of these drugs are easily detected in the urine.

Cocaine

Cocaine causes the level of norepinephrine to increase near the norepinephrine receptors. This results in an increased level of brain stimulation, causing an increase in the restlessness of the horse.

At small doses, cocaine may depress the heart rate, whereas a higher dose may stimulate it. Blood pressure will rise due to an increased heart rate and vasoconstriction. Cocaine will increase the body temperature, and when administered to horses in warm climates prior to competition, it may cause heat stroke.

Cocaine is a local anesthetic when applied topically at low doses. As with other stimulants, horses vary in their sensitivity to the drug. In a study performed to determine the effects of cocaine on horses, one horse responded to a dose of 4 milligrams, but another horse required 300 milligrams to produce the same response. Doses as low as 600 milligrams have been reported to cause toxic effects in horses.

Cocaine is easily detected in the urine.

Caffeine

Caffeine produces a general brain stimulating effect. It also increases the amount of work that muscles can do before fatigue sets in.

In a study performed on racehorses, caffeine enhanced the running performance of all horses in the study. However, all the horses had an increased heart rate after exercise, and it took longer for them to return to normal, when compared to exercise without caffeine.

The metabolites of caffeine may be detected in the urine for up to nine days after an intravenous dose.

Opiate Narcotic Analgesics

These drugs are chemically and pharmacologically related to morphine. In humans, the opiate narcotic analgesics produce a sedative effect. However, in the horse, they produce the opposite effect, causing it to continuously trot or gallop around in its stall or paddock until the effects of the drug wear off.

Narcotics have the ability to increase the appetite. During studies, if a low dose was given, the horse would stand and eat hay continuously. When a higher dose was given, the horse would trot around the stall and grab mouthfuls of the hay as it passed by.

A horse on a high dose of narcotics has a glazed appearance to its eyes, and seems largely unaware of its surroundings. When used together and in the correct amount, narcotics and tranquilizers produce a good *analgesic* (pain blocking) response, and good sedation can be attained. This is useful in veterinary medicine. However, muscle tremors may be a side effect.

The horse's body also produces its own opiates. Leucine and methionine, two essential amino acids, are involved in acupuncture-induced analgesia and anesthesia.

It has been speculated that the stimulation effect in horses caused by the opiate narcotic analgesics evolved because the horse uses escape as a major defense mechanism. Studies indicate that the opiate receptors in the brain enable the horse to ignore pain and start moving rapidly. This is especially beneficial to horses in the wild that are injured and must escape from predators.

Opiate narcotic analgesics are easily detected in urine samples.

Fentanyl

Fentanyl was once a fairly commonly used opiate narcotic analgesic. This is no longer true, as it is easily detected in urine samples.

In a study, 8 milligrams (the maximum dose that should be given) of fentanyl were injected into a vein , and the horse began to trot around the stall within two minutes. The effect of the drug peaked at about four to six minutes after administration, at a rate of 100 steps every two minutes. After about an hour the horse was back down to the control level. When lower levels of the drug were given, the horse peaked at fewer steps. When the dose was increased above 8 milligrams, the number of steps the horse took did not increase. Instead, the horse became incoordinated, staggered, and nearly fell.

Fentanyl produces a highly repeatable reaction. The horses in the study would peak at about 100 steps every two minutes each time they were injected intravenously. Poor responses were received when the drug was given intramuscularly. Fentanyl can be detected in the urine up to four days after a dose is given.

Morphine

Morphine is another opiate narcotic analgesic. The trotting response produced by this drug peaks at about three hours after intravenous injection. It remains effective for up to fourteen hours. However, once the test horses reached between 80 – 100 steps every two minutes, they tended to become dazed and uncoordinated. Morphine is also easily detected by urine analysis.

Dilaudid®, methadone, anileridine, and pethidine are drugs which have effects that are similar to morphine. These drugs are often interchanged with morphine to prevent addiction to morphine. They also produce the trotting response and other similar effects. They are easily detected by urine analysis and their potencies fall between fentanyl (most potent) and morphine (least potent).

Dopamine Mimicking Drugs

Dopamine is a neurohormone that stimulates the horse, and drugs are made which mimic its actions. The drugs are very powerful running stimulants, but they are also easy to detect in urine samples.

Apomorphine was the most commonly used of these drugs before its popularity decreased as a result of easy detection. Apomorphine is obtained from morphine by a chemical process. During studies, when injected into the horse, it produced a very specific running pattern, due to the direct stimulation of the dopaminergic receptors. The response was not always reliable: sometimes the horse would respond to a given dose, and other times it would not. However, if the horse does respond, it is generally dramatic. Horses on the drug appear apprehensive and uncomfortable in the presence of an onlooker. They pace back and forth along the wall furthest from the observer, sometimes lunging upward in the corners. They may also emit a typical snort during the period that the drug is active.

Apomorphine is a very potent drug, and only 0.1 milligram per kilogram of body weight is needed to produce a running response. The onset and decline of action is very rapid— the horse can go from 130 steps taken in two minutes to five steps taken in two minutes, all within a very short period of time. There is no sign of incoordination.

TRANQUILIZERS

A tranquilizer is basically any drug that allows a horse to remain conscious and standing, but enables treatments to be performed which would otherwise be difficult.

Tranquilizers are used for many reasons. Often they are used to keep horses calm during air transport or when using clippers on young horses or horses that are afraid of them. Veterinarians use tranquilizers on horses that need medical attention, such as stitching cuts. Farriers may use tranquilizers on young, unhandled, or uncooperative horses. These horses are sedated just enough that they are aware of what is being done, but are not likely to resist as violently. In this way, shoeing does not become a frightening experience, as it may if the horse must be forcibly held in order to handle its feet.

Phenothiazine Tranquilizers

All of the phenothiazine derivatives appear to produce part of their effects by blocking the dopaminergic receptors in the brain. These are the receptors upon which apomorphine and the narcotic analgesics act to produce the trotting response. In male horses, they cause extension of the penis, so they are often used when cleaning and debeaning the sheath and penis of horses that resist this procedure.

The phenothiazines also have an effect on the hypothalamic or brain stem area, which controls body temperature and respiration rate, among other things. They markedly reduce the respiratory rate, both in the unexercised and the exercised horse. They also affect body temperature in such a way that it tends to move toward the ambient temperature.

These tranquilizers reduce blood pressure and **should not** be used in horses suffering from shock.

Acetylpromazine (Acepromazine®) is the most commonly used phenothiazine tranquilizer in equine medicine. At a dose rate of 0.05 to 0.1 milligrams per kilogram of body weight (2 to 4 milligrams per 100 pounds of body weight) it will begin to take effect within fifteen minutes. Giving a larger dose does not cause tranquilization to occur any faster, but the effect will be more profound.

Some horses may react violently after being given as little as 0.5 milligrams of acetylpromazine per kilogram of body weight, although it is rare at this dose. These horses will sink backward on their hocks, and then lunge forward in an uncoordinated manner. Others may sweat, tremble, and show general restlessness.

Horses tranquilized with phenothiazine tranquilizers may awaken suddenly, so caution is recommended when they are used.

Longer Acting Tranquilizers

These tranquilizers' effects last for longer periods of time or may be used over long periods.

Reserpine

Reserpine can produce considerable biochemical and behavioral effects in the horse by depleting the amount of neurohormones in the brain. Neurohormones stimulate the brain, so until they are replaced by the horse's body, the horse will be more subdued.

Reserpine lowers the blood pressure, slows the heart rate, and causes diarrhea at low doses (5 milligrams per horse). At higher doses, such as 10 milligrams, the horse will begin sweating over the shoulders, back, stifle, and between the legs about two hours after dosing. The horse will then pass gas and develop diarrhea, which will continue for two to three days. The horse appears dazed after eight hours. If particularly sensitive to reserpine, the horse may exhibit signs of acute colic and will remain depressed for up to 48 hours.

Methamphetamine is an antidote to reserpine. It acts in the same way as the neurohormones depleted by the use of reserpine.

Periwinkles and the *Vinca herbacea* and *Vinca rosea* plants contain reserpine. These plants are common in the southeastern portions of the United States. There are also about ten species of the Apocynaceae growing in the southeastern United States that are reported to contain reserpine.

Minor Tranquilizers

Librium® (chlordiazepoxide) and Valium® (benzodiazepine) have distinct anti-anxiety properties when administered in low doses. At higher doses, these drugs are powerfully anti-convulsant and are used in animals that have seizures. If the dose is increased further, they produce sedation and muscle relaxation. These drugs do not have any analgesic effects at any dose.

Horses may become shaky, have muscle tremors, labored breathing, and be generally uncoordinated when first given valium.

Horses with epileptic conditions or obscure central nervous system syndromes may benefit from being given valium. In one case, a horse suffered from recurrent bouts of colic. Clinical examination and exploratory *laparotomy* produced no explanation for the colic. The horse was given 100 milligrams of valium every other day, in the belief that it might have been suffering from abdominal epilepsy. Once this therapy was started, the colic episodes ceased. The dose was later dropped to 50 milligrams every two days, and eventually treatment was stopped altogether. The horse did not show signs of colic again.

Xylazine Hydrochloride

Xylazine hydrochloride, or Rompun®, is a rapidly acting tranquilizer. In controlled tests, when 1 milligram per kilogram of body weight was given intravenously, the onset of action took two minutes, and peak effect was at about seven and a half minutes. The sedative effects were usually about 50% reduced in 34 minutes. When the same amount was given intramuscularly, it took about five minutes to begin acting, and it peaked at about fifteen minutes. The effects were about 50% reduced after 50 minutes.

When given xylazine, a horse will lower its head and neck, the lower lip will hang loose, the penis will extend, and the horse will generally rest a hind leg. Some may have difficulty standing or walking. The blood pressure will increase and cardiac arrhythmia (irregular heartbeats) may develop. These will pass and are of little concern. The respiration rate will also decrease, and depth of breathing will increase.

When horses must undergo painful procedures, a local anesthetic should also be used. Usuallly, administration of xylazine will make a horse safe to work with around the head and neck, but care should be taken when working around the hindquarters.

LOCAL ANESTHETICS

Local anesthetics are used to deaden pain in a specific area; they are also central nervous system stimulants if given in high doses. They may be applied topically or injected, but are most commonly injected into the nerves of the lower leg to deaden pain due to navicular disease or other soreness. They may also be injected into joints, tendons, tendon sheaths, bursa, etc. Usually, these blocks last a only few hours. Veterinarians use them to determine the location of pain in the foot, since the blocks are not permanent.

Procaine, which is a synthetic analog of cocaine, is an example of an anesthetic that produces a short block. It also stimulates the central nervous system. When small doses are given, the horse may begin blowing deeply; at higher levels, pacing and excitation may be observed.

Pure alcohol and quinine are sometimes used to produce longer acting nerve blocks. These substances cause substantial damage to the nerves, which require a considerable amount of time for regeneration.

Cryosurgery is also a means of blocking a nerve. A metal disk is placed in liquid nitrogen and cooled to a temperature of about -196° Celsius. It is then placed on the skin over the nerve. This will usually block the nerve for a number of weeks. Horses that have been "nerved" in this way will have white hairs growing in the area in which the procedure was done.

It may be dangerous to work horses that have been blocked. They may no longer feel pain, but the cause of the pain is still present. If the pain was caused by a deteriorating joint, the joint will continue to deteriorate, with possible fatal consequences to the horse and rider if it gives out.

Horses also lose *proprioception* in the blocked area. This means that they cannot determine where they are placing that part, how much pressure is on it, the amount of tension in the muscles, etc.

Locally injected anesthetics are detectable in urine tests.

BRONCHODILATORS, MUCOLYTICS, and COUGH SUPPRESSANTS

These are used to help clear up respiratory infections in horses. However, these drugs are banned in racing.

Clenbuterol is one of the common bronchodilators used in veterinary medicine. However, while it is approved in Canada, Australia, New Zealand, and many European and South American countries, it is not approved for veterinary use in the United States.

It causes relaxation of the muscle in the walls of the bronchi and bronchioles, thus enlarging the airway passage. It also appears to aid in the clearance of mucus from the lungs and reduce the frequency of coughing. Some believe it may even aid in the prevention of exercise-induced pulmonary hemorrhage. Many veterinarians recommend its administration by using a nebulizer, which creates a fine mist that is breathed directly into the lungs.

Bromhexine is the most common mucolytyic used in horses. Mucolytics reduce the viscosity of mucous in the lungs, allowing rapid clearing of this material from the lungs.

There are a number of cough suppressants that are used for horses, most of which contain ambroxol and even antihistamines, mucolytics, and decongestants.

It should be noted that mucolytics and cough suppressants do nothing more than reduce the symptoms of respiratory disease. They do not speed up recovery from the infection.

MUCOPOLYSACCHARIDES (MPS)

Mucopolysaccharides (MPs) are compounds that occur naturally in elastic connective tissues such as tendons, cartilage, and ligaments. One very common MP, which is an important component of cartilage, is chondroitin sulfate. MPs aid in maintenance of the structure of connective tissues by literally helping to hold the cells together. They react with collagen and elastin (the protein components of connective tissue) in forming the structure of the connective tissue. For these reasons, their presence is vital in maintaining the normal function and structure of bodily structures that rely heavily on connective tissue, such as the joints, arteries, heart, brain, and skin.

MPs may also have the ability to decrease inflammation in the tissues, because they coat the cell membranes. They may aid the immune system as well. MPs help give synovial fluid its viscosity, making it better able to do its job of protecting the joints.

Another interesting finding about MPs is that their concentration will decrease with age, and the pattern that they exhibit within the connective tissue will change. These events are believed to be part of the physical changes that increase the occurrences of joint, tendon, and ligament injuries in older horses. The effects of the decrease of MPs due to age is very evident in human skin. The human skin progressively loses its elasticity and will begin to sag.

Due to the important role MPs play in joint protection and function, many veterinarians successfully use them for prevention of joint related problems, and the treatment of existing joint problems.

DRUGS IN FEEDS

Horses are grazing animals and will tend to nibble at a whole range of interesting plants, trees, and herbs, some of which may contain substances that will cause positive drug tests. Even horse feeds may inadvertently contain substances that will result in positive tests. These include salicylic acid, arsenic, theobromine, hordenine, and lupine. Also, poppy seed bagels, which have reportedly been fed to horses, may contain morphine and cause positive test results.

Salicylic acid is a nonsteroidal anti-inflammatory agent. It is present in most grasses, including the cereals. It is a major component of aspirin. The maximum level allowed to be present in the urine by Texas, the United Kingdom, Ireland, and France, is 750 micrograms per milliliter.

Arsenic has shown up in racehorse samples, although a cause for this has not been found. The maximum level of arsenic allowed in the urine by the state of Texas, the United Kingdom, Ireland, and France is 0.2 *micrograms* per milliliter.

Theobromine is a metabolite of caffeine, and is also a drug in its own right. It is the main alkaloid present in cocoa beans, which may be included in feed. Horses in Ireland, France, and the United Kingdom frequently test positive for theobromine for this reason. These countries have set a maximum threshold level of 2 micrograms per milliliter in the urine. Texas is the only state in the U. S. that tests for theobromine; the maximum threshold level is also 2 micrograms per millititer in the urine. This level is below that which would affect a horse's performance, and it is consistent with the level that results from contaminated feed. Theobromine has some diuretic action, and is also a cardiac and very mild central nervous system stimulant.

Hordenine has properties similar to adrenaline. It is present in germinated cereal grains, especially barley.

BLOOD DOPING

Blood doping is the practice of withdrawing blood from a horse, collecting the red blood cells, and then reinfusing these cells back into the same horse at a later date (usually close to a race or other type of event). This is an **unnecessary and harmful** procedure!

Horses are equipped with a built in blood doping mechanism, the spleen. The purpose of this organ is to store a large number of red blood cells. When adrenaline is released in the horse due to fear, exercise, etc., it causes the muscle of the spleen to contract, releasing the stored red blood cells into the circulatory system. This greatly increases the amount of red blood cells in circulation. At rest, red blood cells account for about 35% of the blood volume, and during exercise, they account for over 60%.

If blood doping is practiced on a horse, it will increase the number of red blood cells even further. This will cause the blood to become abnormally thick, affecting its ability to deliver oxygen to the muscles.

MILKSHAKES

Milkshakes, or *drenches*, contain mainly sodium bicarbonate. However, they may also contain glucose, sodium chloride, and potassium chloride dissolved or suspended in water. B-vitamins, Vitamin E, and methylsulfonylmethane (MSM) are also sometimes included.

Milkshakes are used in the belief that sodium bicarbonate will buffer lactic acid produced in muscles during strenuous exercise. Lactic acid is partly responsible for muscular pain and fatigue during exercise. Some horses show improvement and relief from chronic tying up when they are given sodium bicarbonate. However, in scientifically trained horses (horses trained by monitoring the heart, respiration rate and blood gas composition), the bicarbonate administration is unlikely to improve buffering capacity of muscle.

A horse can quickly remove excess bicarbonate from the body via the kidneys, which filter it from the blood and through the lungs. It is then breathed off as carbon dioxide.

These drenches can have a detrimental effect if they contain a concentrated level of electrolytes, especially if the horse does not have access to water. The horse will be prone to dehydration, because body fluids are used to dilute and excrete the excess electrolytes. The bicarbonate can alter the horse's body chemistry to such an extent that these horses will be unable to cool themselves off by normal means, sweating. This is evidently due to an altering of the body's perception of temperature. Prolonged use of milkshakes is considered very harmful to the equine athlete.

Bicarbonate supplementation should not be given to endurance horses, because they become *alkalotic* during the ride. It may also be dangerous to combine bicarbonate supplementation with lasix administration, because the fluid and electrolyte loss caused by the diuretic effects of lasix may increase the alkalotic effects of the bicarbonate supplementation to a dangerous level.

14

ART and SCIENCE of FEEDING
(Expert Opinions and Practices)

There are many different feeding practices, and just as many opinions on which practice is best. However, regardless of the class of horse, its value, or the amount of work that it does, the basic element of a sound feeding program is always the same—proper nutrition.

Examples of different feeding programs are presented in this chapter in the form of interviews conducted with a wide variety of well known trainers, breeders, veterinarians, professors, authors, equine nutritionists and breeding farm managers from major farms. The interviewees were chosen not on the basis of their particular opinions or practices, but because of their successes and their respected positions in the equine scientific, breeding or performance worlds.

The reader should evaluate answers in the inverviews carefully. Many answers are based on specific geographical areas; caring for specific classes of horses; using different management techniques; having different types of hays, grains and pasture forages available; dealing with unique seasonal differences, etc. All important possible variables should be considered before using anyone's ingredients or techniques in their own nutritional program. (e.g. Knowing someone feeds "twice a day" doesn't mean anything unless it is known:
- Is that concentrate only, or is that concentrate and hay?
- Is the horse pastured, stabled or a combination of both?
- Is hay provided free choice, or in measured amounts?
- Is it a high performance horse eating lots of concentrate, or a relatively idle individual eating small amounts?
- Etc., etc.)

Gary D. Potter, Ph.D.

Dr. Gary D. Potter received his Ph.D. in Animal Nutrition, Biochemistry, and Physiology from the University of Kentucky in 1968. Since 1978, he has been a professor of Animal Science and Nutrition, as well as the Equine Program Leader at Texas A&M University. Dr. Potter is involved in graduate and undergraduate teaching, as well as coordination of equine teaching, research, and service programs in the Department of Animal Science. He works closely with the students, acting as advisor to graduate students and the TAMU Horsemen's Association, as well as coaching the TAMU Horse Judging Team. Dr. Potter is in charge of the Horse and Equestrian Centers, comprising over 200 acres of land and 175 animals.

Dr. Potter has earned many awards and honors, including the Leadership Award from the National Horse Judging Team Coaches Association, the Superior Service Award from the Texas Agricultural Extension Service, and the Amoco Foundation Award for Outstanding Teaching at Texas A&M University. He is also an approved judge for the American Quarter Horse Association, the American Paint Horse Association, the Pinto Horse Association, the Palomino Horse Breeders Association, and the American Miniature Horse Association.

Dr. Potter has published almost 300 scientific and technical articles. His current research includes nutritional requirements for growth in horses, effects of nutrition on physical fitness and performance in horses, and nutrient metabolism in horses. He is also involved in many organizations, including the Equine Nutrition and Physiology Society, the American Society of Animal Science, and the North Central Region Equine Research Committee. Dr. Potter is also a member of the Committee on Horse Nutrition for the National Research Council, and he serves on the editorial boards of the *Journal of Animal Science* and *Modern Horse Breeding*. He was also a major editorial contributor to the original *Feeding To Win*.

The interview...

Grains

When would you recommend using processed grains as opposed to natural grains?

The only time I ever recommend using a processed grain is if the horse is very old, very young, or has bad teeth. I'll also recommend processed grains for creep feeding foals, and maybe for feeding weanlings. However, if the horse has good teeth, data indicates that the improvement in digestive efficiency is not great enough to offset the cost of processing the grain.

Are certain methods of processing superior to others?

If grains are going to be processed, it is better if they are coarsely processed, rather than finely ground. This is because the horses need to chew in order to salivate, and the coarser the grain is, the better they chew it. If it's finely ground, there are data that indicate that they don't chew as much per unit of dry consumption; therefore, you get drier feed ingested and entering the stomach, and that can be a problem. As far as the procedures used to coarse process a grain, I doubt one is better than the other.

What are the advantages and disadvantages of feeding corn versus feeding oats?

As far as advantages, corn is a more energy dense feed when compared to oats. If you have horses that require a high energy level in their feed, such as athletic horses, lactating mares, or rapidly growing young horses, corn allows you to get more energy into them in a smaller amount of feed when compared to oats. There's no real disadvantage, but when you feed corn to a horse, you obligate yourself to more management. You have to be careful and feed it by weight, not by volume. Regulating the amount of feed the horse gets relative to its requirements is also important. The biggest risk in feeding horses corn relative to oats is overfeeding them, particularly with people who are accustomed to feeding by the bucket full. There's a lot more energy in a bucket full of corn than a bucket full of oats.

Are racehorse oats worth the extra expense for the average horse?

For the average horse? No.

What should the minimum weight be for a good quality oat?

There's no way to answer that question. The biggest difference bushel weight makes in terms of feeding is—if you have a low bushel weight, you have to feed more of those oats. A low bushel weight does not mean that the digestible fraction of those oats is of any less value than the oats with the higher bushel weight. There is just more indigestible fiber. If you have a high bushel weight, you've less fiber, and the digestible fraction of the feed is larger.

Are there any particular geographic regions that excel in the production of grains?

No, the quality of the feed is more a reflection of the agronomic practices of the farmer than it is the geography of the country.

Commercially Prepared Horse Feeds

What are the advantages and disadvantages of feeding a commercially prepared feed?

The main advantage of feeding commercially prepared feeds, as long as they're prepared by a reputable company, is that the diets are already balanced. The companies can do as good a job as the individual feeder in balancing the diet, and often they do a better job. There is no disadvantage to feeding quality commercial feeds.

When is it worthwhile to mix your own feeds?

If a person has a large storage capacity and a strong knowledge of equine nutrition, he can save some money by buying ingredients in bulk and mixing them on the farm. The small producer cannot buy the individual ingredients and mix the feed any cheaper than the feed companies can mix it for him, because he can't buy in bulk. There is no advantage to mixing on the farm, from a nutritional point of view, if you're dealing with a reputable feed company. However, if you're not dealing with a reputable company, or if the company that is preparing the feed doesn't have a quality control program, then mixing feed on the farm is better.

Is sweet feed a poor feed in summer months?

The only disadvantage of feeding sweet feed in the summer is that it draws flies. There's no truth to the myth about it causing horses to get hot and sweat in the summer.

Are there any advantages to feeding pelleted feeds?

There are two major advantages to feeding pelleted feeds. The first is that every pellet is a balanced diet and the horse can't sort through the ingredients. This is particularly important for young foals, yearlings, or for any other horse that's prone to sort out ingredients. The second advantage is that by-product ingredients, which are nutritionally just as good as oats and corn, can be included in the pelleted feeds without any problems of acceptability, palatability, or anything else on the part of the horse. The use of by-products cheapens up the diets quite a bit. Of course, there are other advantages. There's less of a dust problem, less of a storage problem, and they're easier to handle. The only disadvantage—and it really isn't a disadvantage—is related to management. Pellets are very dense and they need to be fed by weight. It takes less of a pelleted feed to get the same results as a grain mix type feed. People need to pay attention to how much they feed. The other thing that a person wants to be sure of when he feeds pelleted feeds is that the pellet is firm, but not hard, so that the horse has to chew to break them up. If it's a soft, crumbly, mushy pellet, it can cause some digestive problems.

Are pelleted forages an adequate substitute for loose forage (such as pasture or hay)?

No. You could feed a so-called "all-in-one-feed," where you have the hay and everything ground up in the pellet, but the problems that you run into by doing this are numerous. If you run these horses together they'll eat each other's manes and tails. If they're exposed to wood, they'll eat it; they'll also eat the bark off trees. If you're going to feed pellets, horses are generally better off if they're fed the concentrate portion of the ration in a pelleted form and then fed the hay in some long form, such as baled hay, or given access to pasture.

What is the best method for horsemen to judge the quality and usefulness of a commercial horse feed?

The best information that horsemen have available to them is on the tag. You can't tell much about the nutritional value of the feed by looking at it. You can have one feed that looks one way and another that looks another way and the nutritional value will be the same. If there's not enough information on the tag to evaluate the feed, then ask the feed dealer for a complete nutrient analysis of that feed.

What is your opinion on extruded feeds?

The extrusion process has the advantage of allowing you to add ingredients, such as fat, to the ration at higher percentages than you normally could. It also increases the bulkiness of the feed, and there is some indication that horses eat extruded feeds slower than they do pelleted feeds. There's no good data to show that extruding enhances the digestibility of the feed, at least over the whole digestive tract. It might enhance digestibility in the upper part of the tract, but we really don't know that yet. The only disadvantage to extruded feeds right now is that they're expensive.

What are the advantages and disadvantages of feeding hay cubes?

The only advantage to using cubed hay is to standardize quality if you live in an area of the country where it's hard to get baled hay, or if the quality of the baled hay is very variable or consistently bad. Some people recommend cubed hay for a horse that has a respiratory problem and is irritated by the dust in hays. If you happen to have dusty hay, then feeding cubes may be advantageous. Another place where the use of hay cubes can really help is with people who are hauling horses on the road. If you can't get the kind of hay you want, or you can't haul enough hay, roughage can be provided with cubed forage products.

Forages

Hay

Which cutting of hay provides the highest quality?

A certain cutting cannot be singled out because the quality of the hay is determined by the stage of maturity of the plant when it is harvested. You can have good quality first cutting hay, and you can have bad quality last cutting hay. Generally, the later cuttings will be cleaner, because they'll usually have fewer weeds in them. But it is wrong to assume that third or fourth cutting hay is always higher in quality than first cutting hay.

How long should hay be cured before feeding?

Hay doesn't have to be cured before it's fed. The only requirement for curing hay is to get it dry enough so you can bale it and store it in the barn. If it gets dry enough to bale and put up, you can feed it to the horses that day.

Do you recommend feeding hay free-choice or in measured amounts?

It depends on management. If you have broodmares, idle horses, or horses that are not being fed anything except hay, and they're kept in confinement, they should be fed hay free-choice. Hay should be fed free-choice during the winter when the pastures are dormant and don't supply enough standing forage for the horse. Horses that are in training don't have to be fed hay free-choice if you are balancing the diet. You can feed them a given amount of hay and then balance the diet with the rest of what is fed. In these cases, I generally recommend feeding somewhere in the range of .75% to 1% of their body weight per day in the form of hay, to be sure the normal gut function is maintained.

What are the advantages of mixing grasses with legumes in hay?

There aren't any nutritional advantages to mixing grass hay with legume hay. If you have really high quality legume hay and its nutritional composition exceeds the requirements of the horses, then you can feed some grass hay with it. But other than that, there's not any advantage to doing it.

In your area, what varieties of hay would you recommend in terms of nutritional value?

It doesn't make any difference where you are. The nutritional value of the hay is reflected by the quality of the forage. This in turn is determined by the stage of maturity at which the hay is harvested. Generally, legume hays are higher in quality than grass hays simply because they have a higher leaf to stem ratio. But that's not always the case. You can have samples of bermuda grass that are higher in quality than samples of alfalfa.

What is the best method of feeding hay?

There is no best method. If you want to feed it on the ground, in a hay net, or an overhead feeder, that's fine. Anything you read about one way being better than another is pure speculation. When you talk about the best way to feed hay, it is relative to the whims of the feeder or the manager, not the nutrition of the horse. It doesn't make a bit of difference to the horses how it's fed, just as long as they have access to it.

Pasture

How do you determine how many acres per horse is minimal?

By determining the stocking rate capacity of the pasture you will be using. The stocking rate will be dependent on the innate fertility of the soil, the amount of fertilizer applied, and the amount of rain fall and/or irrigation it gets. Stocking rates will vary all the way from one horse per acre in some places to one horse per 50 or 60 acres in other places.

Supplements

Vitamin and Mineral

Do all horses need trace mineralized salt or just a salt source?

They all need salt. If there's a suspicion of trace mineral deficiencies in the forages or feeds it would be a good idea to use a trace mineralized salt.

Should salt be fed free-choice or added to the feed?

For pasture horses, it should be fed free-choice. For stabled horses, it should be added to the feed in measured amounts.

Explain the importance of the calcium to phosphorus ratio.

The diet should always contain more calcium than phosphorus. The total diet—the hays, the grains, the pasture, everything the horse eats—should contain about one and a half to two times as much calcium as phosphorus. The thing you have to remember if you are mixing feed on your own is that forages generally contain more calcium than phosphorus, not always, but generally. Grains will always contain more phosphorus than calcium. This means you have to be careful when you mix . Be sure that you wind up with a total ration that has about twice as much calcium as phosphorus. If you happen to get three times as much calcium as phosphorous, that's not going to be a real problem. But if you turn it the other way around where you have twice as much phosphorus as calcium, then you have real trouble. The high phosphorus diet causes a metabolic disturbance that results in calcium being removed from the bone. You absolutely should not allow that situation to occur. The calcium to phosphorus ratio is important. But it's more important that you provide more calcium than phosphorus than it is to worry about exactly how much calcium you have.

Why has the use of vitamin E supplementation become more popular for performance and racehorses?

Because of the role vitamin E has in maintaining membrane stability and other functions in the body. It is involved in many processes related to the immune system and the antioxidant systems. Since performance and racehorses become so highly oxidized while processing all the energy that they metabolize, they need more vitamin E than the non-working animal.

Can vitamin E supplementation enhance performance?

I don't know whether it enhances performance, but it will help avoid bad performance. I don't think you can take a horse that can run a certain speed, give it vitamin E, and make it run any faster. But it can help to keep the horse from running slower.

Are injectable supplements superior to oral supplements?

No.

What are the disadvantages of administering injectable supplements routinely?

You run the risks of abscess from the injection, particularly if you're injecting anything that's suspended in oil. The oil will produce a significant amount of trauma to the muscle at the injection site. The only time you need to use an injectable anything is if you can't get it to the animal any other way. If you have an oral alternative, then the oral alternative is a better route.

Do you feel most horsemen oversupplement their horses?

There are many cases where they add supplements that the horse doesn't need, but there are also cases where the horse needs supplements and doesn't get them. Typically, the scenario is people adding unneeded vitamin or mineral supplements to commercially prepared feeds. The feed company has already added vitamins and minerals. When people do this, they take a feed that was balanced, and they unbalance it. If you're feeding home-grown grain or if you're buying grain and mixing your own diets, there will be places where you do need vitamin and mineral supplements. So it really depends on the situation. It's not fair to say that there's no place for vitamin or mineral supplementation, they do have a place, but there are instances of overuse.

Protein and Protein Supplements

When should protein supplements be added to equine diets?
They should be added to the diets of horses that need them. You have to add protein supplements to grain mixes for creep diets, weanlings, yearlings, and lactating mares for sure. If you're feeding adult horses good quality hay and grain, they probably don't need protein supplementation. Adult performance horses don't need protein supplements either. But a horse that's growing, or any lactating mare, is going to need protein supplements.

Can excess protein be harmful and negatively affect performance?
Yes, it can. If you have more protein in the body than the horse can use, he has to excrete the nitrogen by way of the kidney, and that's an active energy-requiring process. It creates a metabolic load on the horse, and it causes him to drink more water. Consequently, he has to excrete the extra water.

Does protein supplementation increase muscle mass, as some believe?
No, not beyond what the animal is genetically capable of. If an animal is fed a balanced diet and he's getting all the protein he needs, more protein will not increase muscle mass. Now, if you're feeding a horse a diet that does not have enough protein, then adding protein will increase muscle mass.

Added Fat

How can performance horses benefit by having fat added to the diet?
Adding fat to the diet won't make an inferior athlete a better athlete, or make a slow horse run fast, but it will keep a horse from slowing down. Putting fat in the diet allows the horse to have more stamina because he becomes metabolically adapted to the use of fat for slow work. This spares his glycogen stores, which are used for really intense work.

Can pregnant and lactating mares benefit by having fat added to their diets?
There are some potential benefits for pregnant and lactating mares. In the pregnant mares, if you put fat in the diet, they'll

maintain themselves at a lower level of feed intake. This reduces some of the risks of digestive dysfunctions that you might encounter if you are supplement feeding mares on pasture. In a lactating mare, it enhances milk fat content. This tends to increase the rate at which the foals grow. It also appears that there may be some positive effects on reproductive efficiency.

How much fat would you recommend adding in terms of percentage of the total diet?

There are two ways to answer that. The total diet—hay, grain, and anything else—should be formulated so that 18% to 20% of the calories come from fat, or 10% of the grain mix by weight should be in the form of fat. The percentage of fat in the total diet, after supplementing it with added fat, is going to vary relative to the ratio of grain to hay, but it should be somewhere around 7% to 8% by weight.

What is the easiest way to add fat to the diet?

Buy a source of fat, such as a commercially available dry fat product, and top dress the ration with it. If you have a small number of horses, that's the easiest way to do it.

Management

Feeding

Are there any advantages to feeding cooked rations?

No.

What should one do to determine why a horse is a "hard keeper"?

First, you should check the horse's teeth to make sure that they are not causing a problem. Also, if a horse is a chronic hard keeper, it's a good idea to get some blood work done to see if there's anything clinically wrong with it. If you find out that there isn't, then being a "hard keeper" is related to the metabolism of the horse, and there is nothing you can do about it. Some horses simply require more feed compared to others to maintain the same body condition.

How many times per day should the stabled horse be fed?

It depends a lot on the amount the horse is being fed. If a horse has to eat more than .75% of his body weight per feeding, then the feeding frequency needs to be increased. When feeding stabled horses, it is critical that the feedings be spaced out evenly over a 24 hour period. Most horses can be satisfactorily fed every twelve hours, but if they're fed a lot of feed, they need to be fed three times a day. This needs to be done at eight hour intervals—not morning, noon, and night.

How long should you leave feed in front of a horse if it is not eaten?

It depends on the horse. Some horses eat their feed in a matter of minutes, and others take hours to eat the same amount of feed. I don't have a recommendation about how long you should leave the feed in there. If you're trying to teach a horse to eat in a hurry, then obviously you put it in, leave it a while, than take it out. Some horses can be taught to eat their feed in a shorter period of time than they normally would, but I don't know why anybody would want to teach a horse to eat fast. It's really not good for a horse to eat in a hurry.

What changes should be made in the horse's diet when the activity level is decreased?

If the activity level is decreased, the feed should be decreased accordingly, or the horse is going to get fat. Also, if you're working a horse a lot, and then you lay him off for a few days, the level of the feed needs to be decreased. If you keep feeding him the same amount of feed, and then put him back to work, you may end up with muscle problems (azoturia or tying-up).

What changes should be made in the horse's diet when it is sick?

If you have a horse that's ill, one of the first things he'll do is go off feed. Then other things start happening to him because he has lost his nutrient supply. Anything you can do to encourage a sick horse to eat, you need to be doing. Take him out and let him eat green grass, or feed him high quality, fresh hay. A sick horse will eat grass if it will eat anything. Then by trial and error, find out what he will eat. If the horse won't consume enough nutrients to maintain itself, you may have to actually dose the horse, either with preparations in paste form or by IVs. The main thing is to encourage the horse to eat any way possible.

How can one encourage the horse to drink more water if it is consuming inadequate amounts?

If a healthy horse is not consuming enough water it's possible the water is contaminated or has a high salt or mineral content, but more likely it's just because the water troughs are dirty. If you're talking about hauling horses on the road and they won't drink, the best way to deal with that is to mask the water before you leave. In other words, put something in it like Coca Cola® or Kool Aide® for several days before you leave home and get the horse accustomed to that taste. Then you can mask the water's taste when you go to the new location by putting the same thing in it.

What precautions should be taken when watering a hot horse?

The only thing you need to do is make the horse drink slow so that it doesn't swallow a lot of air. The idea of not letting a hot horse drink is incorrect. If a horse is dehydrated, he has to become rehydrated to cool himself. So allowing a hot horse to drink is, in fact, a good thing to do. However, you need to watch the **rate** of consumption. A hot horse that's really thirsty will drink fast, and as a result, may swallow a lot of air. This may cause it to become colicky. The best thing to do is to let the horse drink a little, then make him stop a minute or so to catch his breath and then do this again. Let him drink, because he needs to become rehydrated, but at a slow and steady rate.

Parasite Control

Would you recommend the dewormers that are fed on a daily basis?
I don't have any reason not to recommend them. If they work, they work, and there are indications that they do.

Is it essential that horses get tube dewormed, or are there other methods that are just as effective?
They don't have to be tube dewormed. Other methods are just as effective as long as the horse ingests all the deworming medicine.

How frequently do you recommend deworming?
Horses need to be dewormed at least twice a year. But in situations where the horses are exposed to a lot of manure, they are probably going to have to be dewormed every two months. So, I'd say somewhere between twice a year and six times a year, depending on the intensity of the management, and the cleanliness and sanitation of the facilities.

What is the most practical method for preventing the spread of parasites in pastures?
Rotational grazing, and the rotating of horses and cattle to break the life-cycle of the parasite. Also, dragging with a harrow to break up the fecal piles and, if possible, managing the pastures so there's enough forage that horses don't have to graze close to the ground.

General

Where would you like to see more research in equine nutrition?
There are many areas, but we really need to know more about the exact nutritional requirements of the severely stressed exercising equine athlete, such as racehorses, cutting horses, polo ponies, event horses, etc. We also need to know more about what the nutritional requirements are for sound, maximal bone growth in the young horse. Research needs to be done on skeletal development, and what the dietary requirements are for maximizing the rate of bone mineralization in the young horse.

Do most horsemen have good knowledge of equine nutrition?

No, I'd say most of them don't. Most have some knowledge of horse nutrition, and more and more people are becoming more knowledgeable than they used to be. But there's a lot of people in the horse business that do not have an in-depth knowledge of the intricacies of horse nutrition.

What is the most worthwhile use of laboratory testing to determine if the horse is receiving necessary nutrients?

If you are trying to determine nutritional adequacy in a herd of horses, by far the most useful information is the nutritional analysis of everything the horse consumes. This includes all the forage, grain, supplements, and water. This is a lot more reflective of nutritional adequacy than analyzing hair or blood.

Stephen G. Jackson, Ph.D.

Dr. Stephen G. Jackson received his Ph.D. in Equine Nutrition at the University of Kentucky, and since 1990 has part-owned, operated, and served as vice-president of research and marketing for Kentucky Equine Research. KER is an international research, consulting, and product development company specializing in nutrition, exercise, and growth physiology. The company works with feed manufacturers and horse farms in the development of feed and feeding management programs. Research emphasis includes nutrition for broodmares, young horses, performance horses, and growth physiology. KER's clientele includes farms such as Lanes End, Pin Oak, Denali, Buckram Oaks, Stonereath, and many others throughout the U.S. and sixteen foreign countries. Dr. Jackson has done nutritional consulting in the U.S., Ireland, Germany, France, Australia, New Zealand, Poland, and Russia.

Dr. Jackson has done considerable research on nutrition of the young, rapidly growing horse. From 1986 to 1990, while Associate Professor of Animal Science at the University of Kentucky, he directed research on the factors that lead to development of nutrition-related growth disorders and which limit athletic performance of the racehorse. He has directed seventeen theses and dissertations and has published more than 40 articles in scientific journals and conference proceedings. He has also made numerous presentations before professional societies, including the Irish Veterinary Association and the Mid-America Association of Veterinary Practitioners. He is the current president of the Equine Nutrition and Physiology Society.

Dr. Jackson and his wife, Debbie, own and operate Jackson Purchase Farm in Versailles, Kentucky, where they breed mares for the yearling market and raise horses to hunt, event, and show. He is an avid foxhunter, steer roper, and amateur steeplechase jockey.

The interview...

Grains

Number the grains below in order of palatability (based on your personal opinion) with 1 being the most palatable:

1 Oats   2 Corn   3 Barley   4 Wheat   5 Milo   6 Rye

To which classes of horses do you recommend feeding processed grains, as opposed to natural grains?

Foals, aged horses, sick, debilitated horses, and horses with poor teeth.

What method of processing do you recommend for oats, corn, barley, and milo?

For oats–crimped; Barley–steam flaked or crimped; Corn–cracked; Milo–micronized or steam rolled.

What are the advantages and disadvantages of corn and oats?

Corn is very energy dense, inexpensive, and available. The main disadvantage is that it can contain aflatoxins or fusarium if it is moldy. Oats contain a good amount of fiber and easily digested starch, and they are palatable. However, in most instances, they cost more per pound of total digestible nutrients than other grains.

Are racehorse oats worth the extra expense for the average horse?

No. The cost per pound of total digestible nutrients or any other nutrient for "heavy" racehorse oats is not economically feasible. Also, there tends to be an inverse relationship between test weight and protein content.

How valid are the USDA standards for judging grains?

They are fairly valid, but not fully descriptive of nutrient content.

How quickly can grains be fed after harvest?

Grains can be fed immediately following harvesting. If the moisture content of the grain is higher than 13% or 14%, they need to be artificially dried before they are mixed into a commercial feed.

Commercially Prepared Horse Feeds

What are the advantages and disadvantages of feeding sweet feed?

Sweet feed is palatable and easy to manage. It also allows for easy mixing in of medications. The disadvantages are that some horses sort out certain ingredients, and storage time is limited.

How much molasses should sweet feed contain?

It should contain between 5% and 10% molasses.

What are the advantages of pelleted feeds?
They are uniform, so horses can't sort out ingredients. There is less waste when they are fed outside, and they are stable, so they can be stored longer.

Are pelleted forages an adequate substitute for loose forage (such as pasture or hay)?
Not generally, although they may suffice if offered to the horse in adequate amounts. The fiber length in the pellet is important.

How important is the size of the pellet?
The size of the pellet is not that important, but I would recommend ¼ inch to ½ inch pellets.

Are horses which are fed pelleted feeds more prone to choke, crib, or chew wood?
They are not prone to choke. They also are not prone to crib or chew wood **if** adequate fiber is fed in addition to the concentrate.

Have you found commercial feed mixes from reputable companies to be consistently high in quality?
Yes.

What is the best method for horsemen to judge the quality and usefulness of a commercial horse feed?
How the horse looks and performs, laboratory analysis, and the nutrient specification of the feed.

When is it worthwhile (in terms of cost) to have a commercial mill prepare your own feeds to your formula?
It is worthwhile if a mill is available at a cost-competitive rate and the services of a competent equine nutritionist are available.

What is your opinion on extruded feeds?
They are good feeds, but are generally not worth the added cost when compared to pelleted or textured feeds.

Are extruded feeds more digestible?
Yes, somewhat, but the added digestibility does not offset the additional cost.

What are the advantages and disadvantages of feeding hay cubes?
The disadvantages are that they are difficult to eat and fiber length is not adequate. The advantages are uniformity and storage ability.

Which classes of horses benefit most from cubed hay?
Those with chronic pulmonary disease, otherwise known as "heaves."

What about the use of medicated feeds?
There is not adequate data to fully judge.

Forages

Hay

Which cutting of hay provides the highest quality?
The cutting is not a particularly good criterion. Nutritive value, maturity of the plant when cut, and curing conditions are the important things to consider in determining quality.

Do you prefer feeding hay free-choice or in measured amounts?
Free-choice if it is feasible, liberal allowance if it is not.

What proportion of hay to concentrate is best in the equine diet?
This varies, but the higher the percentage of forage in the diet, the better. Horses are continuous grazers!

What are the advantages of mixing grasses and legumes together?
In pastures it increases the nutritive value of the sward and nitrogen fixing, resulting in reduced fertilizer costs. In hay it increases digestible energy, protein, calcium, phosphorus, vitamin A, etc. It is also a better quality feed!

In your area, what hays are most nutritious and palatable?
Alfalfa and alfalfa mixed with timothy, brome, or orchardgrass.

What types of behavioral and gastric problems can arise if a horse does not receive adequate forage?
In terms of behavioral problems—wood chewing, cribbing, stall walking, weaving, etc. In terms of gastric problems—increased incidence of colic, laminitis, enterotoxemia, etc. There are also greater changes in cecal pH when more grain and less forage is fed.

What is the best method of feeding hay?
I prefer feeding hay in a manger if the horse is in a stall. If the horse is outside and in a clean grassy area, then I feed hay on the ground.

Pasture

How important is pasture to the equine of today?
Pasture is very important. It need not even be good quality pasture to be beneficial, but it is certainly a positive if it is.

How do you decide the best types of pasture to plant in your area?
Grasses and cultivars of legumes that are adapted to one's area of the country. Avoid species such as fescue and klein.

For pastured horses, how many acres per horse is minimal?
This can vary from one to fifty acres, depending on moisture and fertilization.

Is there much danger from toxic weeds if pastures are well cultivated?
Not much. Toxic weeds are more of a problem when pasture availability is limited.

Which pasture plant varieties grow best in your area of the country?
Bluegrass, white clover, and orchardgrass.

Supplements
Vitamin and Mineral

If a horse is receiving a high quality well balanced diet, is vitamin or mineral supplementation necessary?
No!

Do all horses need a trace mineralized salt source or just a plain salt source?
Plain salt is probably adequate, but there is no problem with trace mineralized salt.

How do you prefer feeding trace mineralized salt?
I prefer that trace mineralized salt be fed free-choice in a block form. In a loose form, it should be added to the ration at mixing time, generally 0.5% of the concentrate.

Explain the importance of the calcium to phosphorus ratio in layman's terms.
The total diet should **always** contain more calcium than phosphorus.

What do you feel is the optimum ratio for the adult equine?
The optimum Ca:P ratio is 1.2 – 1.6:1 in the total diet. However, it can range from 1:1 up to 6:1.

What can happen in an adult and in a foal if this ratio becomes imbalanced?
In an adult, nutritional secondary hyperparathyroidism, demineralization of the bone, and, in extreme cases, osteomalacia. These same things occur in a foal, and in extreme cases, rickets.

What is vitamin E's function in the body?
It is a biological antioxidant, and it maintains membrane integrity.

Why is vitamin E more important to the performance horse?
Exercise increases metabolic rate and nutrient intake, as well as decreasing cellular and extra-cellular pH, therefore the requirement for vitamin E is increased.

Can vitamin E supplementation enhance performance and fertility?
If it is given to a deficient horse, yes. If the horse is already receiving adequate vitamin E, no.

Are injectable supplements superior to oral supplements?
  Generally, no.

What are the risks and disadvantages of administering injectable supplements routinely?
  Anaphylaxis (shock) and local reactions. This is particularly true with selenium-vitamin E injections.

Do you feel most horsemen oversupplement or undersupplement their horses?
  Over!

Protein and Protein Supplements

Which oilseed meal protein supplement do you prefer?
  I prefer soybean meal, because the protein quality, or balance of essential amino acids, is superior, especially lysine content.

Is the use of commercial protein supplements worthwhile?
  Yes, if utilized as a part of the balanced diet. If they are simply top-dressed, with no consideration of total dietary intake of protein, then I don't agree with their use.

Should protein supplements be added to the diet routinely or only under special circumstances?
  The protein concentration of the total diet should be appropriate for the class of horse being fed, whether accomplished with supplements or base feed and forages.

What classes of horses will generally require protein supplement-ation, and why?
  Foals, lactating mares, and weanlings, because, in general, feed grains are inadequate in total protein and lysine. Supplementation also depends on pasture quality and availability.

Indicate the level of protein in the total diet that you would recommend for the classes of horses listed:

Pregnant mare	12%	*Two year old*	12%
Lactating mare	13%	*Stallion*	10%
Foal	15%	*Racehorse*	10% – 12%
Weanling	14%	*Endurance horse*	10% – 12%
Yearling	13%	*Mature idle*	9%

Can excesses of protein be harmful and negatively affect performance?
  Probably, although all the data is not in.

Does protein supplementation increase muscle mass?
  Not if it is given in addition to the requirement.

Added Fat

> *How can performance horses benefit from having fat added to the diet?*
> Fat increases the energy density of the diet and energy intake without increasing carbohydrate intake. Added fat also spares muscle glycogen utilization.

> *Can pregnant and lactating mares benefit from having fat added to their diets?*
> Yes, for the same reasons as above.

> *How does the added dietary fat improve performance?*
> Fat may be metabolized at low intensity work/aerobic work, and during idle periods. It is thought to spare glycogen, in both the muscle and liver, for use during high intensity anaerobic work, when fat is not metabolized to any great extent.

> *How much fat would you recommend adding?*
> The grain mix should contain 5% added fat, minimum. For example, there should be 50 pounds of added fat in one ton of grain.

> *What sources of fat are best to top dress the ration?*
> Corn oil and soybean oil, or blends of soy-corn and coconut oil.

Management

> *What factors are most important in planning and preparing a balanced ration?*
> The horse's age, physiological state, and intended use.

> *What can be done to increase the palatability of a ration?*
> Use fresh, high quality feed ingredients.

> *Is there any value in cooked rations?*
> NO!

> *What common problems can cause a horse to be a "hard keeper"?*
> Poor teeth, a nervous disposition, parasitism, and other stresses.

> *How many times per day should the stabled horse be fed?*
> If feed intake is less than 10 pounds a day, the horse may be fed only twice a day. If feed intake is between 10 and 14 pounds a day, three feedings are necessary. If the feed intake is over 14 pounds a day, it should be split into four feedings.

> *How long do you leave feed in front of a horse if it is not eaten?*
> Until the next feeding.

> *What changes should be made in the horse's diet when its activity level is increased or decreased?*
> The energy intake should be changed accordingly.

What about when the horse is ill or injured?
In most cases, the fibrous portion of the diet should be increased. However, some cases, such as pleurisy, may require significant increases in energy density.

Is it better to change the feed ration routinely or stick with a proven formula?
Stick with what works, by all means!

What management practices would you recommend to avoid colic and laminitis?
Maximize forage intake, increase feeding frequency, and decrease meal size.

How can one encourage the horse to drink more water if it is consuming inadequate amounts?
Make sure that it is fresh and clean at all times, and that the water temperature is not extreme.

Are there special times when water should be withheld from the horse?
When they are very hot, it should be offered in measured amounts, rather than free-choice.

What precautions should normally be taken when watering a hot horse?
Give small drinks frequently until they are cool.

Parasite Control

How does good nutrition relate to problems of parasitism?
A horse in good condition is generally less susceptible to damage from parasitism.

Would you recommend dewormers that are fed on a daily basis?
Sometimes. Generally, they are not worth it if the horse is on a good deworming program.

Is there is a danger of parasites building up a resistance to these dewormers when low doses are fed on a daily basis?
Not according to the data that has been presented at this time.

How frequently do you recommend deworming, and by what method?
Every 30 to 60 days with a **paste** dewormer.

Is it essential that horses get tube dewormed periodically?
No! Horses do not have to be tube dewormed! Paste, if properly administered, is just as good.

What is the most practical method of preventing the spread of parasites in pastures?
Routine deworming of the horses that inhabit the pasture.

General

What areas of equine nutrition do you feel most need further research?
Nutritional components of developmental orthopedic disease, nutrition of the high performance horse, mineral metabolism, and antagonisms.

What are the physical characteristics that a well fed horse displays?
Healthy appearance of eye, hide, and hair, and adequate body condition.

What are the danger signs that show an inadequate feeding program?
Poor condition, poor hair and hide quality, and lethargy, among many others.

Do most horse people have a good knowledge of equine nutrition?
Definitely **not**.

What is the most worthwhile use of laboratory testing?
Forage analysis.

What do you think about the average level of equine nutrition today?
It's very good, although some "good horsemen" are behind the times, as if they think no progress has been made in the last 50 years.

Philip Swann, Ph.D.

Dr. Swann studied chemistry at Melbourne University in Victoria, Australia, where he graduated with First Class Honors. He also received an Honors Degree in science and a Doctorate of Philosophy. For the past 30 years, his major interest has been in physiology and pharmacology of human and racehorse conditioning and exercise.

Since 1968, Dr. Swann has been training racehorses, and he has trained and driven winners at one of Australia's leading racetracks. In 1985, he was appointed to the position of Chief Executive of a State Government Racing Code. Two years later, he was awarded the "Personality of the Year Award" for his work in performance drug control and outstanding contribution to the racing industry. Dr. Swann's work was a major factor in the establishment of the Victorian Government Racing Analytical Laboratory in 1989, and he was appointed Director of the Laboratory.

Dr. Swann has written three books, each of which has won the Australian racing industry's highest literary award, as well as "Australian Best Book of the Year." These books are *Racehorse Training and Feeding, Modern and Scientific Conditioning Methods*; *Racehorse Training and Sportsmedicine-The Factors that Destroy Race Performance*; and his latest, most popular book, *Performance Drugs in Sport.* (Contact Equine Research, Inc. for information on these books.)

The interview...

Grains

Number the grains below in order of palatability (based on your personal opinion) with 1 being the most palatable:

1 *Oats* 2 *Corn* __*Barley* __ *Wheat* __ *Milo* __ *Rye*

I don't recommend the feeding of the other grains in large quantities because of the cheap availability of oats and corn here, and because of the digestive problems that can occur with the other grains.

When would you recommend using processed grains as opposed to whole natural grains?
Only when you are able to do processing immediately before feeding. Research indicates that processing only improves the digestibility approximately five percent, whereas the effects of storage on processed grain can reduce its value by more than five percent.

What method of processing would you recommend for oats, corn, barley, and milo?
For all grains, I would recommend sieving and cleaning to remove dust and grit. Cracking, rolling, and crimping are satisfactory if done immediately before feeding. I would not recommend steam flaking or extruding.

What are the advantages and disadvantages of corn and oats?
Corn costs less and has a higher digestible energy content. However, it can cause digestive and mental problems in some horses when it is fed in large amounts. Oats are safer in terms of feeding problems and management for best performance, but they cost more.

What should the minimum weight be for a good quality oat?
Weight is deceptive as a measure of quality. Rather than specifying a minimum weight, I feel the appearance of the oat should be examined. An oat should be full bodied and fat, rather than thin and long. The hull should be removed and the inner grain examined. They should be clean and free of dampness, mold, and fungus. If horsemen want a hard measure, then they should have the digestible energy value of the oats measured, rather than using weight.

Are there any particular geographic regions in Australia that excel in the production of certain grains?
Not really. In fact, the seasonal variation and differences in the agricultural management ability of individual farmers outweigh any regional advantage.

Commercially Prepared Horse Feeds

Have you found commercial feed mixes from reputable companies to be consistently high in quality?
No, their quality varies with the seasons. They do, however, tend to be more uniform than the Stock Merchant feeds, especially when the individual is not selective in choosing his supplier.

What is the best way to judge the quality of a commercial horse feed?
Have it regularly analyzed for digestible energy and digestible protein by a reputable laboratory. An analysis should also be done to determine levels of the main vitamins and minerals.

When is it worthwhile to have a commercial mill prepare feeds to your own formula?

The advantage of commercial milling is overrated, because the main problem is getting high quality base materials. If high quality grains and hays are not available, then you have problems whether or not a commercial mill is involved, and whether or not additives or supplements are included by the commercial mill.

Are pelleted feeds advantageous to feed?

Pellets have management advantages because they are uniform and easy to handle. However, there can be serious digestive problems due to variations and errors in the processing, and because of the "binder" used in the processing.

Are pelleted forages an adequate substitute for loose forage (such as pasture or hay)?

Not if high quality forages are available. If low quality forage is the only option, then pellets with roughage can be an improvement. In general, high quality forage is superior to pellets, and it also can have psychological advantages.

What are the advantages and disadvantages of feeding hay cubes?

They have the same advantages and disadvantages as pellets.

Are there any advantages to feeding extruded feeds?

The extrusion process, in theory, allows a higher quality product with some feed types. However, the advantages of these newer feeds are overrated and outweighed by the disadvantages, which are the digestive problems that occur because of process variations and errors by some manufacturers.

Forages

Do you recommend feeding hay free-choice or in measured amounts?

It depends on the individual horse, but generally free-choice is recommended.

In your region of the world, what varieties of hay are highest in nutritional value and palatbility?

Lucerne hay and Oaten hay.

What types of problems can arise if a horse does not receive adequate forage (hay or pasture)?

The major problem is in terms of reduced performance. This shows in a barely measurable reduction in stride length due to "myopathy" or "tying up" problems. These problems occur long before behavioral and gastric problems. Too little forage, particularly for fillies and mares, is a major cause of poor performance.

Behavioral problems will show by excessive chewing of any material, particularly wood. Gastric problems show as generalized colic.

What is the best method of feeding hay?

It depends on the environment. If the ground is clean, then ground feeding is best. In general, the higher the feed placement, the more likely for problems to develop.

What proportion of hay to concentrate is generally best?

At least one percent of the horse's body weight of hay per day is essential. However, free-choice is better, as it allows those individuals that need more roughage to obtain it.

How many acres per horse is minimal for pasture?

It depends on the quality of the pasture. But it should provide at least one percent of the horse's body weight in dry matter a day if no other forage is provided.

Supplementation
Vitamin and Mineral

If a horse is receiving a high quality, well balanced diet, is vitamin or mineral supplementation necessary?

Depends on the training and work stresses. Extremely intense interval workloads in hot humid climates will create the need for supplementation. In general, though, minimal supplementation is necessary when high quality feeds are given.

Do all horses need trace mineralized salt or just a salt source?

Depends on the training and work stresses and the trace minerals present in the salt source. A mineralized salt source is good protection for a performance horse. I prefer feeding trace mineralized salt free-choice.

What is vitamin E's function in the body?

It is a component of the body's antioxidant defense system and its function may be to protect the body's cells against reactive oxygen, such as free radicals. It may be important in both the body's immune defense system and in helping the body combat the adverse effects of intense exercise.

Is vitamin E particularly important to the racehorse?

Intense performance involves the oxidation of fuel compounds and Vitamin E had been said to help the horse combat the destructive effects of intense exercise. Since it is not a banned drug, and it may help race and endurance horses, trainers react positively to it, as it may give them an edge for better performance.

Can vitamin E supplementation enhance performance and fertility and benefit the highly stressed horse?
No one definitely knows the answer to this, but since it does no harm that we know of in moderate doses, and since it may help, it is worth using in high performance horses.

Can excesses of vitamin E be harmful?
Yes, excess vitamin E will interfere with the body's ability to use other fat soluble vitamins, such as vitamins A, D, and K.

Are there any supplements particularly beneficial to the racehorse?
The very high performance horse should have available a multi-vitamin and mineral supplement to ensure that deficiency problems do not arise.

Are injectable supplements superior to oral supplements?
No, they are not, and in fact, injectable supplements are dangerous because of pyrogens, which are toxic substances.

What are the risks and disadvantages of administering injectable supplements routinely?
Pyrogens in injectable supplements cause allergic reactions, infections, depression, loss of appetite, and loss of performance. They also carry some risk of direct physical injury, especially to nerves.

In your opinion, do most horsemen oversupplement or undersupplement their horses?
The majority of horsemen massively oversupplement their horses.

Electrolytes

Is electrolyte supplementation helpful before and/or after a race?
Prior to a race, buffer electrolytes help combat the destructive effects of lactic acid. After a race, the normal saline mixes help recovery from the adverse effects of intense exercise.

If used, how should a horse be provided with electrolytes?
Oral supplementation of important electrolytes is the only safe method of administration.

Can electrolyte supplementation ever be harmful?
Yes, especially when injectables or drenches are used.

What steps can be taken to prevent any harmful effects of electrolyte supplementation?
Use oral administration, quality ingredients, and targeting principles (small doses of the needed electrolyte, rather than large amounts of broad spectrum mixes).

Protein and Protein Supplements

Which oilseed meal protein supplement do you prefer and why?

Soybean meal. It has a high protein level and it is the safest of the available supplements.

Is the use of commercial protein supplements worthwhile?

If high quality Lucerne hay is available, then, for mature horses, protein supplementation is not valuable or worthwhile. Young horses need higher protein levels, but again this should be provided by high quality Lucerne hay, rather than supplements.

Can excesses of protein be harmful and negatively affect performance?

Yes, it can.

Does protein supplementation increase muscle mass?

Training increases muscle mass, and a well balanced diet will provide sufficient protein for muscle development.

Added Fat

Do you feel adding fat to the equine diet is beneficial?

High performance horses can benefit from added fat in their diet, provided the fat is not rancid, and if the **total** fat in the diet does not exceed 15% (this would mean that the **added** fat would equal no more than 10% of the diet). Soybean oil or corn oil appears to be two of the best methods of adding fat.

How can a horse benefit from having fat added to the diet?

Fat is a concentrated source of energy. It benefits both the available stores of, and the conversion of, blood glucose during strenuous exercise.

Drugs

Are drugs being abused in horse racing (in Australia)?

Yes, and this adversely effects both the public confidence and the product integrity (thus betting is less). It also has harmful effects on the animals.

Does Lasix really help bleeders?

Yes, and it also helps non-bleeders perform better.

Do you recommend blood testing on racehorses?

Yes, both pre- and post-race testing.

What is looked for in a blood test?

Computer controlled Mass Spectrometry should be used to screen blood samples for all drugs of abuse, especially designer drugs and endogenous drugs.

How do stimulants affect a horse's health and appetite?
Stimulant covers a wide group of substances, from opoids to simple caffeine. The effects depend on the specific stimulant and its dosage.

Management
Feeding

Does the training stress placed on racehorses greatly increase their need for protein, energy, vitamins, and minerals?
Yes, the amounts of each vary with the age, fitness stage, and health of the individual animal. For example, a young horse in training needs higher protein than a mature horse, which needs higher energy.

How are the additional energy needs of a racehorse met?
By controlling and measuring the amount of training stress using scientific training methods (such as the use of a heart rate meter) and adjusting the specific foods being given on a daily basis. For example, on high intensity days, more grain is fed, and on aerobic days, less grain is fed and more roughage, etc.

Do you recommend certain changes in the feeding program as a race draws nearer?
You must feed according to the work load, or the training stress. As you taper off training towards a race, you accordingly adjust the feed. Some trainers recommend glycogen loading. However, this can cause massive problems for mares, fillies, and young horses. Therefore, it is not normally recommended.

What factors are most important in planning and preparing a balanced ration?
The most important factor is the individuality of the horse. Each horse is unique and must be trained and fed as an individual. The next factor to consider is the training stress placed on the horse.

What can be done to increase the palatability of a ration?
This depends on the individual horse, but generally, using fresh, unprocessed feed of the highest quality will solve most palatability problems. Also, allowing the horse access to fresh pasture can produce results.

Where no dental or health problems are involved, what correctable problems can cause a horse to be a "hard keeper"?
Bad training methods or overtraining. (Overtraining being defined as the training stress at one particular time [race or training session] being greater than what should be given for that particular fitness level.) Thus, overtraining can occur at any stage of the conditioning process.

Up to 70% of racing horses suffer performance problems due to overtraining, and this most often shows up in feeding problems. Other minor problems relate to too much feed, or poor quality feed in terms of nutrient levels, cleanliness, fungus, or mold, etc.

Are there any special feeds or supplements you feed "hard keepers"?
Hard keepers' problems are solved as their training stress is measured (by heart rate meter, etc.) and the feed is adjusted to the work load.

Ideally, how many times per day should the stabled horse be fed?
Four or five times, with access to hay at all times.

Should changes be made in the horse's diet if its activity level is increased or decreased, or if it is ill or injured?
Yes, the energy level of the feed should be adjusted in both cases.

Is it better to change the feed ration routinely, or is it better to stick with a proven formula?
The ration should be adjusted daily to suit the work load, and it should be balanced so that it covers all nutrient requirements.

How long should you leave uneaten feed in front of a horse?
This indicates a problem, and most feeding problems are caused by overtraining or bad training. First, correct the basic problem. However, it is advisable to remove the concentrate after two hours.

How can one encourage the horse to drink more water if it is consuming inadequate amounts?
Make sure water is available at all times. If water consumption is inadequate, it may indicate a serious problem. Thus the major action is to determine and correct the problem, not try to stimulate the horse to drink more.

What management practices would you recommend to avoid colic and laminitis?
These problems can be avoided by measuring the amount of training stress, and adjusting the specific foods being given on a daily basis. For example, on high intensity days more grain is fed, on aerobic days, less grain and more roughage, etc.

Training

What is a scientific training program?
In the simplest terms, it is measuring training stress in every session and controlling the recovery period to allow maximum biological adaptation. The level of training stress is then changed for the next session to optimize the conditioning process. It also involves designing the correct mix of highly specific aerobic and anaerobic activities for the training process that are appropriate for that individual horse.

Do more horses remain sound when trained scientifically?
Yes, without a doubt.

Do scientifically trained horses require fewer nutrients than traditionally trained horses?
The nutrient level is adjusted to the horse's needs, rather than over or underfeeding it.

Why do you think people are slow to begin training their horses scientifically?
Until recently, the essential equipment, such as the memory heart rate meter, was not available, and the knowledge of stress levels, recovery rates, and specific programs was not known or available. Also, trainers who religiously used interval training without the proper knowledge or scientific equipment did a lot of damage to horses. This created bad public images and made many sensible trainers cautious.

Do you recommend that horses be rested prior to a race? If so, how long?
They should be rested from anaerobic exercise at least 48 hours prior to a race and should have only limited aerobic exercise.

Parasite Control

Would you recommend the dewormers that are fed on a daily basis?
At this time, no. Not enough is scientifically known about their long term effects.

Do you think there is a danger of the parasites building up a resistance to these dewormers when low doses are fed on a daily basis?
Yes.

How frequently do you recommend deworming, and by what method?
On a weekly basis, fresh manure should be sent for analysis to determine the presence and number of worm eggs. This should determine when oral deworming is needed. However, irrespective of results, the horse should be dewormed at least every six months. The resulting manure should be examined under a microscope for the presence of worms and eggs.

Is it essential that horses get tube dewormed?
Oral methods with the newer chemicals are better, as tubing can have disastrous results.

What is the most practical method for preventing the spread of parasites in pastures?
The aim should be to have your pastures thoroughly ploughed and resown. Then, when the pasture is established, only worm-free horses should be grazed on it. On a weekly basis, fresh manure

327

should be sent for worm egg analysis to monitor the situation. If ploughing is not possible, the pasture should be low cut and thoroughly harrowed repeatedly. It should be left ungrazed for several months, and then only worm-free horses should be allowed to graze on it.

General

Do rations commonly fed in Australia differ from those fed in the United States?

Yes, there are fewer high quality processed feeds available here, and fewer choices of cheap alternative grains. Also, the hay is very variable in grass types and quality.

What areas of equine nutrition most need further research?

The link between overfeeding of grain and subsequent growth, development, and performance problems, particularly in the young horse. Also, the true links between mineral and vitamin levels and performance.

What physical characteristics does a well fed horse display?

Excellent mental and physical health (willing, competitive attitude, shiny coat, etc.).

What are the danger signs that show an inadequate feeding program?

First, mental problems (lack of interest in training, aggression, etc.), then physical problems (poor racing performance, problems with eating, etc.).

Do you have any ideal complete rations to recommend for different ages and classes of horses?

Although rations differ with the age and class of horse, it should be remembered that the most important factor is the individuality of the specific horse, as every horse is a unique individual, and therefore must be trained and fed as an individual. In other words, feeding should be designed around the training and growth requirements of each individual horse.

J. Warren Evans, Ph.D.

Dr. J. Warren Evans received his Ph.D. in physiology from the University of California, Davis, in 1968. He began teaching animal science and physiology at U.C.D. as an Assistant Professor in 1968. By 1985, Dr. Evans was Associate Dean in the College of Agriculture and Environmental Sciences, Professor of Animal Science and Animal Physiology, and a physiologist at the Experiment Station, University of California, Davis. He's been a Professor of Animal Science at Texas A&M University since 1985. In 1991, he also became Assistant to Deputy Chancellor for Resource Development.

While at U.C.D., Dr. Evans worked on numerous teaching committees, including the Instructional Development Committee for Animal Sciences Subject Matter Area. He was the Master Advisor for Animal Science Majors from 1976 – 77. While holding this position, he set up the advising program and the advising center, and he was also responsible for the curriculum.

At Texas A&M, Dr. Evans is involved with several organizations, including the Institute of Equine Science and Technology and the Rodeo Association.

In the horse industry, Dr. Evans has been very active in various events and organizations, including the Annual Texas A&M University Equine Symposium Horse Breeders School. He is also an international consultant for Thoroughbreds, Arabians, and Quarter Horses in England, France, Germany, Spain, Poland, Russia, Australia, and Morocco. He is an active member of the Equine Nutrition and Physiology Society, the American Society of Animal Science, and the North American Riding for the Handicapped Association. He has received research grants from the Morris Animal Foundation, United States Department of Agriculture, Ethyl Corporation, American Quarter Horse Association, NASA, and the Sandstone Center.

He teaches therapeutic riding and equine reproduction, and his research interests include hippotherapy (the relationship of equine movement to human movement) and reproductive physiology of the mare and stallion.

The interview...

Commercially Prepared Horse Feeds

Is it necessary to purchase or formulate a feed for a specific class of horse, such as foals, weanlings, or broodmares, or can oats and corn supply the needed nutrients?

For the types of horses mentioned, oats and corn need to be mixed with other feedstuffs to achieve a balanced ratio. Each class of horse needs a certain amount of each nutrient, and the appropriate ratios of the nutrients change with each class. Proper use of a commercial feed that complements the hay being fed will keep most horse owners out of trouble, as long as they don't add supplements to the feed.

When are pelleted feeds advantageous to feed?

Pellets keep horses from sorting out and only eating certain ingredients. They keep dust to a minimum and are good when hauling horses to a show.

Are pelleted forages a nutritionally adequate substitute for loose forage (such as pasture or hay)?

Yes. Horses consume them and are able to utilize the nutrients. I fed alfalfa cubes for several years without any problems.

Are horses that are fed pelleted feeds more prone to choke, crib or chew wood?

They are more likely to crib and chew wood.

Have you found commercial feed mixes from reputable companies to be consistently high in quality?

Yes, as long as the company is reputable.

What is the best method for judging the quality and usefulness of a commercial horse feed?

Quality and usefulness are best judged by the feed ingredients and nutrient analysis. The reputation of the company is also important.

When is it worthwhile (in terms of cost) to have a commercial mill prepare your own feeds to your formula?

Normally, one must be feeding a fairly large group of horses to make "mixing your own feed" economical.

Forages

Which cutting of hay provides the highest quality?

It depends on the type of hay and on management practices used to grow it. Each situation should be considered individually.

Should hay be fed free-choice or in measured amounts?
In measured amounts to maintain desired body condition.

How many acres per horse is minimal for pasture?
This depends on the type of pasture and if the horses are kept on it all day or for limited periods. In general, I would say 1.5 acres per horse, with good management, is adequate in many areas.

What types of behavior and gastric problems can arise from a horse being provided inadequate forage?
Behavior problems can arise in the form of wood chewing, weaving, stall walking, and irritability. As far as health problems, gas and toxin production can occur as a result of digesting simple carbohydrates (from concentrates) too fast.

What is the best method of feeding hay?
I prefer a manger for ease of feeding and reduction of waste.

Supplementation
Vitamin and Mineral

If a horse is receiving a high quality, well balanced diet, do you think vitamin or mineral supplementation is necessary?
No! A balanced diet means all vitamin and mineral requirements are met if the horse consumes the required amount of feed.

Do horses need a trace mineralized salt source or just a salt source?
A salt source. I prefer that the feed contains .5% salt and that the horses have salt blocks available to them free-choice.

What is the optimum calcium to phosphorus ratio for adult equines?
The optimum Ca:P ratio is 1.1:1, but it can range to 4:1.

What can happen if this ratio becomes imbalanced?
An imbalance will influence absorption of the minerals.

Do most people oversupplement or undersupplement their horses?
Most oversupplement their horses.

Protein and Protein Supplements

Which oilseed meal protein supplement do you prefer?
I prefer soybean meal because it contains a better balance of essential amino acids.

Which classes of horses require protein supplementation?
Pregnant and lactating mares, foals, weanlings, and yearlings. During growth, these horses need a higher amount of protein than would be supplied in normal feeds.

Does protein supplementation increase muscle mass?
Not if the horse is already receiving adequate protein in his normal ration.

Can excesses of protein be harmful and negatively affect performance or reproduction?
It can negatively affect long, sustained performance because of the necessity to rid ammonia from the body. It doesn't affect reproduction.

Added Fat
Can pregnant and lactating mares benefit from having fat added to their diets?
Yes. It provides a good source of energy.

How much fat would you recommend adding?
Approximately 5%.

What sources of fat are best to top dress the ration?
I usually use a vegetable oil because of availability.

Management
Parasite Control
When mares are grazed with their foals during lactation, what can be done to limit parasite infestation in the foal?
Deworm the mare and foal regularly with ivermectin. Be sure that all the horses are dewormed before they are turned out on a pasture, and maintain the pasture to limit parasite eggs.

Would you recommend the dewormers that are fed on a daily basis?
I have had no experience with them.

Is there a danger of the parasites building up a resistance to these continuous dewormers when low doses are fed on a daily basis?
Eventually, they probably will.

What method of deworming and deworming compound are best to use with pregnant mares, lactating mares and foals?
Ivermectin paste.

Is it essential that horses be tube dewormed, or are there other methods as effective?
I would never allow anyone to tube deworm any horse that I have responsibility for, because of the potential risk to the horse and to the people involved. Paste deworming is just as effective, it is more economical, and you can do it yourself.

Reproduction and Nutrition

Does poor nutrition contribute to a lack of cycling in the mare?

Yes, if the mare is in poor condition. It is particularly noticeable during the transition period as the breeding season starts.

Is there any aspect of nutrition that can be used to enhance reproductive performance, beyond feeding a well balanced high quality diet?

Be sure they maintain a body condition score of 6 or 6.5.

Do you see more overweight or underweight stallions?

In my experience, I have seen more overweight stallions.

What effect does obesity have on the stallion in terms of reproductive performance?

This is not easy to answer because there is a high degree of variation among stallions. Some may have decreased libido in a hot, humid climate.

During each trimester of pregnancy, what factors determine how much concentrate the mare will need to be fed?

Growth of the fetus, physical exercise, and lactation status.

Do obese mares have more trouble foaling?

Our research indicates that this is not the case.

Are obese mares poor milkers?

Possibly, but more research is needed to be certain.

Does "flushing" mares enhance fertility?

No.

What aspects of nutrition are most commonly neglected on breeding farms?

Many farms group feed too large a group and don't remove mares that need individual attention, i.e., timid and "boss" mares. Thoroughbred owners seem to want the mare to be poor at the start of breeding season. Also, foal nutrition is often neglected.

General

What factors are most important in planning and preparing a balanced ration?

Nutrient requirements of the horse to be fed, availability of potential ration ingredients, and cost of ingredients.

What can be done to increase the palatability of a ration?

Use good quality ingredients, and sometimes a little molasses in the ration will increase consumption.

Is there any value in cooked rations?
Possibly for a sick horse.

What are the most common correctable problems that can cause a horse to be a "hard keeper"?
Bad teeth and a heavy parasite load.

How many times per day should the stabled horse be fed?
Three to four times a day is ideal, but sometimes circumstances make twice a day more practical.

What special precautions should be taken when feeding weanlings in groups?
They should all eat at about the same rate. The fast and slow eaters, and the "boss" and timid horses need to be removed and fed individually.

How long should you leave uneaten feed in front of a horse?
From one feeding period to the next.

How can one encourage the horse to drink more water if it is consuming inadequate amounts?
This is not easy. Make sure the water is cool. The addition of Jello® or a similar flavoring will sometimes help. Be sure that the water is palatable to them.

What management practices would you recommend to avoid colic and laminitis?
Feed adequate roughage and don't overfeed concentrates. Don't let the horse consume the concentrate too rapidly or drink too much cold water when it is hot.

Are there special times when water should be withheld from the horse?
When the horse is extremely hot from exercise, give him sips of water, but don't allow him to drink too much, too fast until he cools down.

What are the physical characteristics that a well fed horse displays?
A well fed horse should have a body condition score of 6, a good hair coat, be alert, and have adequate energy to perform.

What areas of equine nutrition do you feel most need more research?
Mineral metabolism and interactions.

Do you feel that breeding farms have improved their feeding methods and management practices when compared to past years?
Generally, yes.

W. L. Anderson, D.V.M.

Dr. William L. Anderson received his D.V.M. from Texas A&M University. He is a very active and successful equine practitioner who has gained great respect through the years from members of his profession and by many loyal clients.

Dr. Anderson owns the Veterinary Hospital in Addison, Texas and the Lake Country Animal Hospital in Frisco, Texas. He is past president of the Texas Veterinary Medical Association and the Dallas County Veterinary Medical Association. He is a member of the American Veterinary Medical Association, the American Association of Equine Practitioners, the American Animal Health Association, and the Texas Academy of Veterinary Practice.

Dr. Anderson served as president of the American Veterinary Medical Association, and was for years a member of the Texas Board of Veterinary Medical Examiners. He has also served as a member of the Texas Animal Health Commission, representing the veterinary profession.

The interview...

Grains

What are the advantages and disadvantages of corn?
Few people know how to properly feed corn today. It has a high calorie content. Because of this, there are more dangers of colic and laminitis compared to the use of oats.

When would you recommend using processed grains?
The only time I like to use processed grain is in older horses, and then I'd rather have it incorporated into pellets.

Are racehorse oats worth the extra expense for the average horse?
I think they're worth the money. They generally weigh in the area of forty pounds per bushel, and the quality of content is normally quite consistent.

Commercially Prepared Horse Feeds

Are there advantages and disadvantages to feeding sweet feed?

I think it has its advantages, provided it is made with high quality ingredients. Sometimes, undesirable or poor quality grains are incorporated into the mixture. This results in an inferior product. In addition, anytime sweet feed has over five percent molasses, you can have problems during hot weather.

Are horses that are fed pelleted feeds more prone to choke, crib, or chew wood?

Well, I think it's possible. I only like to feed pelleted feeds to older horses, but I still mix grain in with the pellets. Hay should also be fed with pellets in all instances. I think feeding pelleted feeds without providing sufficient forage can result in boredom for the horse. Properly used however, pelleted feeds are all right.

What is your opinion on extruded feeds?

They're all right, provided the actual content of the feed is known, and that recognized grains were used to make it.

What about the use of medicated feeds?

Generally, I don't like medicated horse feeds. It is difficult to stereotype the ingredients and the feed that each horse will need. For instance, the need for electrolytes will vary depending on the location and time of the year. As far as antibiotics in feed, they can be dangerous.

Forages

What types of problems can arise for the stabled horse that does not receive adequate forage (hay or pasture)?

The horse's digestive tract was designed to utilize forages. Problems can develop if a stabled horse does not receive good quality hay. Among these problems are vitamin deficiencies and colic due to stasis (diminishment of the flow of ingesta) of the gut. Also, stable vices can develop.

Hay

Which cutting of hay provides the highest quality?

Probably the second cutting. However, this varies with the time of year, rainfall, temperature, and the amount of fertilization used.

Should hay be fed free-choice?

In some instances. I don't think racehorses or show horses should have it free-choice due to the need for monitoring proper intake. Instead, these horses should be fed hay two to three times per day.

Can cubed hays be useful in some cases?

I think good quality alfalfa cubes can be used successfully, provided they have enough stem. You have a similar situation with pellets. I don't like the small smooth pellets that are commonly fed. I'd rather have the larger pellets that have a higher fiber content.

In your region of the country, what varieties of hay are highest in nutritional value and palatability?

In this area, we use coastal–bermuda quite a bit, but I don't think one should feed coastal exclusively. I think it should be supplemented with alfalfa to provide the minerals and vitamins (and in some cases protein) that the horse needs. Coastal here is usually palatable, provided it's clean and doesn't contain many weeds. The prairie grasses are excellent, but there are not many virgin prairies left in this area.

What is the best method of feeding hay?

I don't think it really makes a whole lot of difference. In many instances, especially with babies, I like to feed the hay on the ground. I think this is more natural for the horse.

Pasture

How many acres per horse is minimal for pasture?

This varies with the fertility of the soil, the parasite control program, the grasses, climate, and rainfall. If one has excellent soil and provides a parasite control program that will satisfy the situation, one horse per two acres may be fine. However, all factors must be considered before an exact figure can be recommended.

Supplements

Vitamin and Mineral

If a horse is receiving a high quality, well balanced diet, is vitamin or mineral supplementation still necessary?

This is affected by many factors. Some horses must have supplements to overcome anemia and other problems that they can't control, hypothyroidism for instance. If the horse doesn't have enough thyroid activity, he'll need supplements. Some horses tend to have poor hoof walls, and need to be supplemented with biotin, thiamin, or a combination. Mares in many instances need to be supplemented with soybean meal to provide the amino acids needed for the foal. So, I think supplements are needed in individual instances. In addition, a parasite control program is very important in order to allow the horse to utilize nutrients properly.

Do horses need a salt or trace mineralized salt source?

Yes. However, I don't think salt blocks are adequate in providing the horse with salt and trace minerals. It's difficult to determine how much is being utilized by a horse. The blocks that most people use are all right for cattle, but the horse is different. He doesn't have the prehension of the tongue that allows him to eat enough salt from blocks. I think trace elements should be provided in some form, either as a supplement or mixed in the feed, if you have control over its production. Whatever method is used, the minerals in the diet must be balanced, or problems can result. When balancing the ration, keep in mind that hays and grains vary in nutrient levels, depending on where they are grown.

Would you explain the importance of the calcium to phosphorus ratio in layman's terms?

The calcium to phosphorus ratio is important, but I feel that if good feeds are used, the calcium to phosphorus ratio will usually stay about normal. I don't think it has to be exactly 2:1, but I'd like to see it that way.

High phosphorus and low calcium levels occur when the horse is being fed too much grain and not enough good quality hay. The opposite (high calcium and low phosphorus) occurs when the horse is being fed a hay that has a high calcium level and is receiving an inadequate amount of grain.

Why does current research indicate vitamin E is more important to the performance horse than in the past?

We're going through a period where the value of vitamin E is being emphasized again. Vitamin E has always been a very important vitamin, but it has been neglected. Vitamin E is found in most grains. However, inferior grains, sweet feeds, and pellets may not have the vitamin E content that is needed. Selenium is also important because there is an interaction between vitamin E and selenium. If proper amounts of selenium are present, vitamin E can be utilized properly, especially for muscle metabolism.

Can excesses of vitamin E be harmful?

Yes. Just like any other vitamin, there are advantages with a normal level, but excess levels can be harmful. For example excess vitamin E supplementation can cause heart problems.

Are injectable supplements superior to oral supplements?

No. I don't particularly care for injectable supplements except in certain required circumstances, such as anemia, or with foals that were born without an adequate level of vitamin A stored in their bodies. Also, some horses that exhibit symptoms caused by a lack of vitamins may benefit from injectable supplements. I think it's advantageous to have the proper nutrients in the feed so that these vitamins can be obtained naturally. Sometimes, we (veterinarians) see inferior feeds, grains, and hays being used that do not have the needed vitamin content, so then we may have to supplement with injections.

Are there many problems with owners injecting supplements routinely?
I think so. Many people incorrectly feel that an injection has to be given before a horse can perform properly.

Do you feel many horsemen tend to oversupplement their horses?
Yes. I think the need to supplement should be decided by their veterinarian in the form of blood chemistries and blood counts to determine if supplementation is needed.

Protein and Protein Supplements

Which oilseed meal protein supplement do you prefer?
I prefer soybean meal.

Should protein supplements be added to the diet routinely or under special circumstances?
Only under circumstances where the class of horse being fed requires more protein than is being supplied in the ration. I think many people have a tendency to oversupplement with proteins, just like other nutrients. However, I do not see this problem as much as I did a few years ago.

Can excess protein be harmful and negatively affect performance?
Yes, it definitely can. Proteins are certainly essential, but the needs of the individual animal vary with the metabolic rate, temperature, and the degree of parasitism, among many other factors. Parasitism is a problem that is not taken as seriously as it should be.

Does protein supplementation above normal nutritrion requirements increase muscle mass?
No, and if it did, abnormally large muscle mass could lead to bone, joint (epiphysis problems), and other problems.

Added Fat

Many people are incorporating fat into their horses' diets. What do you think about this?
I think that we'll see more fat in feeds. It has a place economically and nutritionally, and I think that it can be utilized by the horse if fed properly. However, you should consider the horse's use to determine if it will need supplementation with fat.

What sources of fat are best to top dress the ration?
At this time I think that corn oil has advantages. I think later we're going to see animal fat also has a place.

Management
Feeding

Is there any value in cooked rations, such as bran mashes?

I think bran mashes are fine. The bran mash has a tendency to act as a laxative, and I think this is often needed. One should know how to use a bran mash. You can also get the addition of salt to the ration through bran mashes, if they are properly mixed.

How can one recognize the poorly nourished horse that appears fat?

There are many ways to determine whether a horse is receiving adequate nutrition. You can do blood testing and examine the mucus membranes and the hair coat. The hair coat should look excellent. The horse's performance will also show whether he is getting proper nutrients. I think a good nutritional program also requires proper exercise. A horse that shows a great deal of fat and no muscularity is certainly not in a nutritionally adequate condition.

What changes should be made in the horse's diet when the horse is ill or injured?

It varies with the illness, or type of injury the horse suffered. For instance, if the horse was an athlete, and performed regularly, the amount of feed should be reduced greatly when it is ill or injured. Bran mashes should be used to keep the horse's digestive tract functioning normally. Adequate protein should also be given if the horse underwent surgery or had a laceration. Plenty of clean fresh water should also be available.

Is it better to change the feed ration routinely, or is it better to stick with a proven formula?

I like to get with one program and stay with it as much as possible. That goes for hays and grains. I don't like to change feed often because the horse's system has to adapt, his bowel movements may change and the amount of grain or hay necessary may also change.

How can one encourage the horse to drink more water if it is consuming inadequate amounts?

Addition of salt in a bran mash can sometimes help. This doesn't always work; some horses just fail to like water. In cold weather, water may be painful to their teeth and mouth. In this case, you have to warm the water to get them to drink. If you have a horse that refuses to drink, it could end up with kidney problems because the urinary tract is not properly flushed due to lack of water consumption. Refusing water can be due to a variety of things. I would do a blood count and blood chemistry. Then I would try to supplement accordingly to alleviate the problem. Balanced electrolytes are sometimes needed.

What precautions should be taken when watering a hot horse?
When a horse is hot, you should not let him drink too much, because he can founder. A horse should be allowed to drink, say a gallon, over a period of three or four minutes. Keeping the animal moving will also help cool him off properly. Of course horses tend to drink more during the summer as compared to winter months. Still, it's very important to let the hot horse drink just a little bit at a time to avoid drastic problems.

Parasite Control

Would you recommend the dewormers that are fed on a daily basis?
I do, provided that the right one is used. There's only one that I know of that can be fed daily, and it is Strongid C®. However, I still think it is very important to tube deworm at six month intervals to kill the bots and the large strongyles that these continuous dewormers miss.

Is there is a danger of parasites building up a resistance to these dewormers when low doses are fed on a daily basis?
Oh, there's a possibility. All dewormers that are used daily have had this problem. It appears however, that there is no resistance right now to the product that Strongid C® contains.

What is the most practical method for preventing the spread of parasites in pastures?
I think the continuous feeding of Strongid C® is probably the most efficient means of stopping the spread of parasites in the pasture. Chain dragging and the utilization of cattle or small ruminants to break the life cycle of equine parasites is important. Of course, removal of all the manure would be ideal.

General

What areas of equine nutrition do you feel most need further research?
The mucopolysaccaharides in feeds and the utilization of fat. Also, possibly developing a pellet that has an adequate level of fiber. I think many of the pellets do not provide the fiber necessary for the horse. Also, the nutritional aspects of bone development in young horses need more research.

Do you think most horsemen have a good grasp of equine nutrition?
Well, compared to ten or fifteen years ago, it's better, but I think the average person has little knowledge of equine nutrition.

What steps, in terms of feeding management and nutrition, can horse owners take to increase the overall health of their horses?

They need to check their teeth regularly or have their teeth checked by their veterinarian, and they need to feed them correctly. Many people fail to realize that horses are natural foragers and require hay or grasses, and that they cannot survive strictly on grains. I think this fact needs to be strongly emphasized to the public. Also, overfeeding of the horse can be a problem.

What about use of hair analysis to determine the mineral levels in the body?

I think overall, it has been a disappointment. There are few people that can perform it properly.

Do you prefer to use blood analysis?

Yes.

William E. Jones, Ph.D., D.V.M.

Dr. William E. Jones received his D.V.M. from Colorado State University in 1957, and his Ph.D. from Oregon State University in 1970.

Dr. Jones practiced veterinary medicine in Wyoming and Colorado after graduation. Then he taught college for six years. Currently, he publishes veterinary material, including *The Journal of Equine Veterinary Science, Equine Veterinary Data,* and *The Large Animal Veterinary Report.* He has been writing freelance veterinary material for the past 20 years and is former editor of *Horse and Rider.* He has written a monthly column for *The Quarter Racing Journal* since its inception.

His first book, *Genetics of the Horse,* was published in 1971 and twice revised. Other books he has written are *The Care and Breeding of Horses, Nutrition for the Equine Athlete,* and *Sportsmedicine for the Racehorse.* He is also editor of the book *Equine Sports Medicine. (Contact Equine Research, Inc. for information on obtaining these books.)*

Interview...

Grains

What are the advantages and disadvantages of the more common grains fed today?

Corn has been "bad mouthed," probably more than it should be. There's a great deal of energy in corn, more than oats when compared by weight. A performance horse, especially the racehorse or endurance horse, needs more energy than oats can supply. You can pack more energy into less feed when using corn. I suppose the reason it's gotten a bad name is that people try to compare it straight across with oats. They say it makes the horse high, but he simply has more energy because he has more calories coming to him from the corn.

Do many people still feed by volume instead of by weight?
I think so, and it causes problems.

When would you recommend feeding a grain or concentrate source?
The horse that's just out there standing in the pasture really doesn't need any grain, as long as the pasture is good quality. If we only consider broodmares, growing foals, and horses in training (or those who are worked every day), then you'd need a grain or concentrate supplement. Often, straight grain such as oats or cracked corn mixed with oats is fine. I think that if you have a high performance horse or a growing foal, you would probably get more for your money by buying a pre-mixed commercial grain such as Omolene®. Even though you're paying a little more, you're doing a better job for your horse. On the other hand, some horsemen know enough about feeding that they can have their grain mixed to their own formula by a feed mill, and they are able to save money.

Are racehorse oats worth the extra expense for the average horse?
I believe that buying the best feed pays off in the long run.

Commercially Prepared Horse Feeds

When are sweet feeds advantageous?
A performance horse needs a grain supplement, and in the winter, people tend to gravitate more towards the sweet feeds like Omolene®. The only reason I can see for this is that people realize that a horse will need more energy to stay warm in the winter, and sweet feed can provide this energy.

When are pelleted feeds advantageous?
Pelleted feeds are advantageous for horses with chronic obstructive pulmonary disease (COPD, or heaves), which is often caused by sensitivity to dust in the hay, particularly low quality hay.

Are horses that are fed pelleted feeds more likely to crib or chew wood?
Yes, I think they probably are, so with some horses you have to decide what's worse—cribbing or heaves.

What is the best method for horsemen to judge the quality and usefulness of a commercial horse feed?
The feed bag label is a good tool. It tells you the amount of protein and the grains that are in the feed. It's hard for horsemen to judge all aspects of a commercial feed by looking at the label. You also have to go by feeding it for awhile and seeing what it does for your horses.

Which classes of horses would benefit most from cubed hay?
An aged horse or one with bad teeth would do better with cubed hay. I had a stallion who could not keep his weight up, even

though I fed him free-choice high quality alfalfa. I went to some
cubed alfalfa and his weight did increase.

Forages

*Does a lack of adequate forage contribute to gastric disturbances and
stable vices?*

Yes. There have been quite a few studies showing that stable vices
start from boredom, and once they start, they are very hard to stop.
Research shows that the more hours during the day that you provide
horses with something to eat, the less they are inclined to crib.

Hays

Which cutting of hay provides the highest quality, and why?

It depends more on the maturity of the plant, rather than the cutting. In terms of alfalfa, it is best to cut it before the bloom stage.
Studies have found that the blooming alfalfa is really past its prime
because the nutritive value goes down once it starts to bloom.

*In your region of the country, what varieties of hay are highest in
nutritional value and palatability?*

I think that in all regions alfalfa is definitely the highest in nutrient
value. As far as palatability is concerned, that might vary a little bit. I
think that any good grass hay is palatable and that horses like it.
However, poor grass hay is not as palatable as, perhaps, even poor alfalfa hay. Palatability is also a good indicator of the quality of the hay.

What is the best method of feeding hay?

I like having bunks, or those hay racks that have a trough around it
that will catch the leaves. I think that's important. You definitely
do not want to feed it on the ground. That's not only wasteful, but
the horse also picks up worm eggs and larvae.

Should hay be fed free-choice or in measured amounts?

This depends on the horse, what you are using it for, and what
you're feeding along with the hay.

Pasture

How many acres per horse is minimal for pasture?

Well, it's difficult to suggest an exact minimum because the value
of the pasture varies depending on the location.

*Is there much danger from toxic weeds if pastures are well cultivated
and managed?*

If it's a well-managed pasture, there shouldn't be much danger,
but it depends on where you are. Sometimes, toxic plants are the
first things to grow in the spring. This, coupled with a horse

starved for something green and maybe a little bit underfed, can lead to serious consequences. Many times the owner of the horse really doesn't know what is growing in the pasture. They just say "Hey, look at all that green stuff, let's turn them out." When this happens, all the horse really has to eat is the toxic plants, so he ingests more than he would otherwise. Now if the pasture is not overgrazed, and there is plenty of grass for the horses to eat, they'll more than likely avoid the toxic plants.

Are there advantages to mixing grasses and legumes in pastures?
I think that mixing legumes, such as alfalfa or trefoil, with grasses in the pasture is a good idea.

Supplements
Vitamin and Mineral

If a horse is receiving a high quality, well balanced diet is vitamin or mineral supplementation necessary?
Well, you can't draw general conclusions. Horses differ in their individual needs. Also, different regions of the country and the nutrients in the hay affect the needs of the horse. The vitamin, mineral, protein, and total digestible nutrient content of the ration need to be to looked at to determine if supplementation is necessary.

Do all horses need a trace mineralized salt source?
I think it's good insurance to provide them one, especially if you're not feeding a supplement. And, I think feeding the trace mineralized salt free-choice is a good idea.

Would you explain the importance of the calcium to phosphorus ratio in layman's terms?
Calcium and phosphorus go together in that the absorption of one affects the absorption of the other. If the ratio is very far off, you're going to affect how much of one or the other is in the body, and that can cause problems. This goes for a lot of other minerals as well. Research is finding that other minerals such as zinc, cobalt, and copper all seem to affect one another. If you get too much of one mineral, then it's going to inhibit the absorption of another mineral, creating deficiencies and problems.

Why is vitamin E so important to the performance horse?
Performance horses are under a great deal of stress, and vitamin E helps the body put up with the stress that is associated with intense performance. It has also been discovered that individual horses have different needs for vitamin E. Some seem to have less of an ability to absorb or metabolize it, so they need more vitamin

E. In fact, horses that don't have adequate levels of vitamin E can develop a central nervous system problem that makes them very uncoordinated, and we're beginning to see this more and more. At one time, these problems were being confused with inherited types of diseases such as cerebellar hyperplasia (underdevelopment of the cerebellum). Now we're beginning to realize that this may be a result of a vitamin E deficiency.

Can excesses of vitamin E be harmful?
Extreme excesses of anything can be harmful, but the horse tolerates and, in many cases, even needs more than previously thought.

Are injectable supplements superior to oral supplements?
Not overall, but if one mineral interferes with the absorption of another in the digestive process, an injectable might be better. Another point is that some oral supplements are not absorbed well in the intestine, and so injectables would be better. However, I think the routine injection of supplements is overdone on the racetrack.

Protein and Protein Supplements

What percentages of protein are required in the equine diet?
The young, growing horse will require 18% – 20% protein. Once they've stopped growing and matured they don't need that much. All the mature horse really needs is around 12% protein.

Does protein supplementation increase muscle mass?
No, I don't think that supplementing protein is going to do much in terms of building up muscle. But, of course protein is needed for the body to build muscle. Feeding a high percentage of protein will not stimulate muscle build-up in the normal sedentary horse.

Added Fat

What about adding fat to the horse's diet?
We're going to be seeing more and more of it because you can cut down the amount of grain needed by increasing the fat content of the diet. This helps minimize the chance of founder or colic occurring.

How much fat would you recommend adding?
In recent research from 4% up to about 20% has been used. As long as it's palatable, I don't think you can add too much.

What sources of fat are best to top dress the ration?
There have been a variety of fats used, including actual animal fat (like meat trimmings), which are ground up and made into a dry type fat. Once it is processed, it is solid in this form. I think corn oil probably is used more often than the other types, but I think more research needs to be done to know what is the best type.

Management

Feeding

What can be done to increase the palatability of a grain ration for a finicky or picky horse?

If a horse refuses to eat the grain that you have, you're probably feeding a low quality grain. Switching to a higher quality grain should solve your problem.

Is there ever any value in cooking rations?

I've heard that some people do that. I can't figure out how it could help anything. Maybe they are just trying to take poor grain, or a lot of bran, and get it into a form that the horse will accept better. If it's a palatability thing, they should buy a better feed.

Ideally, how many times per day should the stabled horse be fed?

The more the better. You can't overdo it in terms of how many times you feed. However, the feedings should be broken up evenly over a 24 hour period.

Is it better to change feed rations routinely, or is it better to stick with a proven formula?

I don't see any reason for a routine change. I think that changes should come about because of some change in the horse's activity, such as a broodmare during the stages of pregnancy.

Are there special times when water should be withheld from the horse?

Medical reasons, such as surgery, and if the horse is hot after a ride. A horse can founder if he drinks too much cold water when he's really hot.

Can mucopolysaccharides (MPs) be helpful to the racehorse?

Yes. The number one MP is actually classified as a drug (known as Adiquan®). It's a poly sulfated mucopolysaccaride and it is an injectable. There are also several companies that sell MP feed additives, which they claim are digestible. They are put on the feed and end up as nutrients in the cartilage. That's what these products are basically for, to increase the health of the cartilage in the joints. Often, in racehorses and other heavily used horses, the joints wear out, just like people involved in sports. There's a lot of evidence that mucopolysaccarides will help longevity of the joint cartilage.

Parasite Control

Would you recommend the dewormers that are fed on a daily basis?

Yes, I think Pfiser's Strongid C® is an effective product.

Do you think there is a danger of parasites building up a resistance to this dewormer?

It has been shown that parasites, especially small strongyles, can build up a resistance to most of the dewormers. Parasitologists are even concerned with resistance to ivermectin, although it has not been demonstrated. The resistance problem has been mostly with a group of drugs known as the benzimidazoles.

Is it essential that horses get tube dewormed periodically?

No, the paste dewormers are just as effective as long as you get it in the horse. Studies have shown this to be true. The reason that many vets advocate tubing a horse at least once a year is it gives them an opportunity to see the horse. If horsemen did their own deworming the year round, it might be two or three years before a vet would actually see a horse. An experienced veterinarian can usually spot potential problems in the early stages. These problems can then be treated, before they become serious. So from that point of view, rather than for the effectiveness of the deworming, it's a good idea to have them tubed dewormed once a year.

General

What areas of equine nutrition do you feel most need further research?

Minerals–the amount of minerals that horses need, and how the form in which they are fed affects the way they are absorbed, metabolized, and used. Also the interactions that minerals have with each other need a great deal of research, particularly in light of the problems associated with mineral deficiencies such as osteochondrosis, which seems to be on the rise.

Describe the physical characteristics of a well-fed horse.

I'm not sure that you can, really. It's a false assumption to just look at the horse and say it's getting a good balanced diet just because it has a nice, shiny coat and is in pretty good shape. If a horse is fat, it does not necessarily mean that it is getting a well balanced diet.

What about a poor feeding program?

In terms of whether or not the horse is getting enough calories, you can definitely tell by looking at the horse. I think this is something the experienced horseperson does naturally, and doesn't even think about. They mentally note if the horse is losing or gaining and regulate the amount fed. If you keep increasing the amount of feed and the horse doesn't gain the proper amount, then another problem should be considered. It could be several things; maybe the feed isn't good quality, or maybe the horse has a disease or a dental problem.

Is the condition score system an adequate means of measuring the body fat on the horse?

Yes, I think it is.

What types of laboratory tests can be the most helpful?

It depends on what your horse is doing. If you have an athletic horse in training, you might want to test for one thing, but if it's a growing foal, you might want to test for something else. I think some of the problems revolve around how you test for some of these things. For example, hair analysis is something that's often used and reported to be a good indication of what minerals are in the body. But there's a lot of controversy over it. Personally, I believe that with some experience, you can use hair analysis to get an idea of some of the mineral imbalances that are occurring in the horse's body. It's a little tricky sometimes to look at the ion content, or the mineral content of the serum, and try to relate that to what the horse has overall. Mainly because the horse has several mechanisms, as do people, for maintaining certain mineral levels in the blood by removing minerals from storage areas in the body. There's sort of a buffering system working within the horse's body. In feed analysis, checking the protein level is important. Also, the amount of total digestible nutrients should be determined.

What steps, in terms of feeding management and nutrition, can horse owners take to protect the health of their horses?

Study and learn a little bit about hay and the difference between good quality and bad quality hay. This would go a long way. Second, learn about proper feeding. There is a broad spectrum of horse owners out there. On one end of the spectrum, you have a group that tends to underfeed their horses. At the other end, and usually these are show people or people raising horses for sale as yearlings, they tend to overfeed them. In the latter situation, we get what has been termed overnutrition, which basically refers to too much grain, too much supplement, and that sort of thing. There's a great deal of evidence that this leads to osteochondrosis, epiphysitis, contracted tendons, and other related problems. This occurs because they're pushing too much high energy, high protein, and so forth, into these horses. Either end can be dangerous, but the overnutrition is more dangerous to the total life expectancy of the horse than the underfeeding.

Do you feel most horse people have a good grasp of equine nutrition?

No, I don't think so.

Charles W. Graham, D.V.M.

Dr. Charles W. Graham, an alumni of Texas A&M University, is a licensed veterinarian in Texas, Oklahoma, and Louisiana. He owns the Southwest Stallion Station in Elgin, Texas, and the C-Bar ranches. He is co-owner of the Elgin Veterinary Hospital, the Heritage Place Sale Complex in Oklahoma, the Graham Land and Cattle Company, and several other businesses.

Dr. Graham's past academic achievements include serving as President of the Central Texas Veterinary Medical Association, Who's Who in American Colleges and Universities, and "Outstanding Junior Class Student."

He is an Adjunct Professor of the Department of Large Animal Medicine and Surgery at the College of Veterinary Medicine, Texas A&M University. He has also earned the Distinguished Alumni Award from this college. In 1985 he was voted Horseman of the Year by the Texas Quarter Horse Association, and in 1986 he was voted the Equine Practitioner of the Year by the Texas Veterinary Medical Association, and Horseman of the year by the Texas Thoroughbred Breeders Association.

Dr. Graham is a past president of the Texas Quarter Horse Association, the Texas Thoroughbred Breeders Association, and the Tenth District of the Texas Veterinary Medical Association. He is also former director of the American Association of Equine Practitioners. He has published articles for trade and scientific journals, and has presented numerous papers to equine associations and scientific organizations.

The interview...

Grains

Would you recommend using processed grains, such as rolled or steamed?

No, I don't feel there is a need unless a horse has bad teeth or is old.

What method of processing would you recommend for oats and corn?

I don't recommend any processing for oats, I prefer whole oats.
For corn, I would recommend cracking it.

What are the advantages and disadvantages of corn compared to oats?
I don't feel that there are any advantages to corn, it can cause colic. Oats are a very good feed, without any disadvantages.

What should the minimum weight per bushel be for a good quality oat?
Thirty-eight pounds.

Are there any particular geographic regions that excel in the production of grains?
North and South Dakota.

Commercially Prepared Horse Feeds

Have you found commercial feed mixes from reputable companies to be consistently high in quality?
Yes.

What is the best method for horsemen to judge the quality and usefulness of a commercial horse feed?
The appearance of the horse. The coat should be in good condition.

When is it worthwhile (in terms of cost) to have a commercial mill prepare your own feeds to your formula?
Never.

Do you feel seasonal changes affect the value of feeding sweet feed?
No.

Are pelleted feeds advantageous to feed?
No.

Are pelleted forages an adequate substitute for loose forage?
No, they don't have enough bulk or fiber.

What are the advantages and disadvantages of feeding hay cubes?
I don't feel there is an advantage. They are very difficult to feed.

Are horses that are fed pelleted feeds more prone to choke, crib, or chew wood?
Yes.

Are there any advantages to feeding extruded feeds?
No.

Forages

Hay

What hays do you feed?
Alfalfa and Coastal Bermuda.

Why do you feed these?
Because alfalfa is the best, and coastal is available.

Are there other hays you would prefer if they were available locally?
No.

Which cutting do you prefer?
Second and third cutting of alfalfa, and any good cutting of coastal.

How do you judge the quality of hay?
I judge it by the protein content.

From what parts of the country do you like your hay to come?
I like my alfalfa to come from New Mexico.

What is the best method of feeding hay?
A manger, because it is the most convenient.

Do you recommend feeding hay free-choice or in measured amounts?
I recommend free-choice.

What types of problems can arise if a horse does not receive adequate forage (hay or pasture)?
They may start cribbing, and they'll be more likely to have impaction related colics.

What proportion of hay to concentrate is generally best?
A proportion of ¾ hay to ¼ concentrate.

Pasture

How much time do you allow your horses to graze?
I allow my horse to graze all day.

Do you keep any horses on pasture 24 hours a day?
Yes, I do.

What special care do these horses need?
They need plenty of clean water and shade.

What kind of pasture grass do you prefer?
Coastal bermuda.

How many acres per horse is minimal for pasture in your area?
Five acres is minimal.

Is there a danger from toxic weeds if pastures are well cultivated?
No.

Classes of Horses
Broodmares

Do you prefer that broodmares be in fleshy or thin condition prior to the onset of the breeding season?
Thin condition

How much concentrate do you feed your broodmares per day
    A. during pregnancy? 2½ gallons of oats a day

    B. during lactation?   3 to 3½ gallons of oats a day

    C. when open?   1 gallon of oats a day

Stallions

Do you feel more research is needed in the area of stallion nutrition?
No.

How much exercise do your stallions get on a daily basis, and what method do you use to exercise them?
They are turned loose in paddocks for about ten hours a day.

Do you feed stallions certain supplements specifically to enhance their reproductive performance?
No.

Foals

Do you creep feed foals?
No.

What do you feed them?
They eat alongside their dam until they are weaned.

At what age do you wean?
I wean at six months of age.

When do you deworm foals for the first time and what do you use?
I deworm for the first time at seven days of age, and then every thirty days thereafter. I feel that most deworming medicines are good, and we rotate the use of them.

Weanlings

What method do you use to wean foals?
I put the foal in a stall, and the mare at a distance so that the foal cannot hear her.

How much do you feed weanlings?
I feed my weanlings ½ a gallon a day.

What types of supplements do you provide weanlings?
A good vitamin supplement.

Yearlings

How do you manage yearlings? (Are they stalled, pastured or a combination?)
My yearlings are pastured.

What do you feed sales yearlings?
I feed them the same as the other yearlings.

When do you begin prepping yearlings for the sales?
About three months prior to the sale.

Management
Feeding

What factors do you think are most important in planning and preparing a balanced ration?
Cost and protein level.

What can be done to increase the palatability of a ration?
First, make sure there is no mold present in the feed. Molasses can be added to increase the palatability.

Do you feed bran mashes?
No.

What are the most common problems that can cause a horse to be a "hard keeper"?
Having bad teeth or the age of the horse.

Are there any special feeds or supplements you feed "hard keepers"?
I feed them a commercial feed mix.

How many times a day do you feed?
I feed two times a day.

At what times of the day do you feed?
7:00 A.M. and 6:00 P.M.

Do you feed equal portions at each feeding?
Yes, I do.

Is it is better to change feed rations routinely, or is it better to stick with a proven formula?
It is better to stick with a proven formula.

If a horse does not eat, how long do you leave the feed in front of him?
I leave the feed in front of them for eight hours.

What management practices would you recommend to avoid colic and laminitis?
Feeding the same time and feeding the same amount each day will help to avoid these problems.

Do you alter your ration with the changing of the seasons?
No.

How do you encourage a horse to drink more water if it is consuming inadequate amounts?
You can add table salt to the water.

Supplements

Is supplemental salt important in the horse's diet?
If the horse does not have free-choice salt available to it, then yes, it is important in the diet.

Do you recommend using trace mineralized salt blocks?
Yes.

Do you feed any supplements?
I feed a vitamin supplement to stallions during the breeding season.

Do you supplement vitamin E?
Vitamin E is contained in the vitamin mixture.

Is the use of commercial protein supplements worthwhile?
No.

Can excesses of protein be harmful and negatively affect performance?
Yes.

Does protein supplementation increase muscle mass?
No.

What percentage of protein do you think is necessary in the ration of foals? 14% – 16%, *yearlings?* 14%, *two year-olds?* 12%, *mature horses?* 12%.

Do you feed any of your horses a source of added fat such as corn oil?
No.

Basic Care

What type of bedding do you prefer in stalls?
Pine shavings.

How often do you have your horses' teeth checked and floated?
Twice a year.

What types of inoculations do you have done on your horses?
Rhino, Fluvac, Distemper, Eastern and Western Encephalomyelitis, and Tetanus toxoid.

How often do you have these done?
Rhino and fluvac twice a year, the rest once a year.

Do you have any blood analyses done?
Yes.

When do you have these performed?
I have them performed twice a month on the stallions during the breeding season.

What do you look for in a blood test?
I look for any abnormalities.

Parasite Control

How frequently do you recommend deworming?
I recommend it every thirty days.

Would you recommend dewormers that are fed on a daily basis?
Yes, I feel it is a good practice.

Do you think there is a danger of parasites building up a resistance to these dewormers?
No.

Is it essential that horses get tube dewormed at least once a year, or are there other methods that are just as effective?
Yes, I feel they should be tube dewormed at least once a year.

What is the most practical method for preventing the spread of parasites in pastures?
Harrowing the pasture.

General

What areas of equine nutrition do you feel most need further research?
The cause of Osteochondritis dissecans (OCD), lesions in young horses.

What are the danger signs that show an inadequate feeding program?
A poor quality hair coat.

Do you think most horse people have a good knowledge of equine nutrition?
No.

If there are any comments on the care or feeding of horse that you would like to add, please feel free to do so.
You should always feed at the same time each day.

Carol Lavell

Carol Lavell, a former event rider from Fairfax, Vermont, has made a name for herself as a talented dressage rider and trainer. Since 1985, she has represented the United States, both as a team member and individually, at the North American Dressage Championships, the United States Equestrian Team National Championships, the World Championships, the Pan American Games, the Olympic Sports Festival, and the World Equestrian Games. Horses she has trained to Grand Prix titles are **In the Black, Lilak, and Gifted.**

In 1989, on her impressive bay Hanoverian, **Gifted,** Ms. Lavell was named Dressage Champion of North America. She spent 1990 training and competing in Europe, and she was the highest placed American at the World Equestrian Games in Stockholm, Sweden. That year, she was also named Athlete of the Year in Equestrian Sports by the United States Olympic Committee. 1991 saw her become the United States National Grand Prix Champion, as well as the United States Equestrian Team's National Champion at Grand Prix.

Ms. Lavell has degrees in biochemistry from Vassar College and the Massachussetts Institute of Technology.

The interview...

Grains

Would you recommend using processed grains (such as rolled or steamed) as opposed to whole natural grains?

This depends on the age of the horse, the appearance of undigested grains in the manure, the horse's preference of one type of processing over another, and whether or not the grain will have to be stored for a long period of time.

What method of processing would you recommend for oats and corn?

For oats, crimping or rolling. For corn, rolling or steaming.

What are the advantages and disadvantages of corn and oats?
Corn has the highest caloric value per pound. It keeps weight on thin horses that won't consume much feed. Also, it is generally cheaper than oats and mixed feed in my area. The disadvantages of corn are that it molds dangerously in humid weather, some horses find it unpalatable, and if processed, it has a poor storage life during much of the year.
Oats are more palatable than corn, and they store better. The disadvantage is that they are always expensive because they are for horses. Also, some unscrupulous dealers sell inferior quality oats.

Are there any particular geographic regions that excel in the production of certain grains?
I feel Canadian oats are the best.

Commercially Prepared Horse Feeds

Have you found commercial feed mixes from reputable companies to be consistently high in quality?
No.

What is the best method for horsemen to judge the quality and usefulness of a commercial horse feed?
By the size and weight of the grains in the mix, and by the smell– moldy molasses has a distinctive odor. Unfortunately, it is impossible to judge the nutritional value of the feed by looking at it, particularly vitamin quality. Therefore, the successful use of the product by other horsemen should be considered.

When is it worthwhile to have a commercial mill prepare your feeds to your own formula?
When you have a barn full of highly specialized equine athletes such as endurance horses or racehorses, that may be on high fat diets, or if you are producing your own grains.

Are pelleted feeds advantageous to feed?
Yes, if the horse doesn't clean up "fines," or if he sorts out certain inclusions. Also, if long storage of the feed is required, pelleting may help prevent oxidation of some nutrients.

Are pelleted forages an adequate substitute for loose forage, such as pasture or hay?
No! Horses that eat fast have nothing to do for hours. Pellets are good for supplementing hay that is poor in nutritional quality.

What are the advantages and disadvantages of feeding hay cubes?
They require less storage room, and there is less oxidation of vitamins. However, "speed eaters" with "time on their hands" develop

bad habits. There is also the possibility of the inclusion of animal matter in the cubes.

Are horses that are fed pelleted feeds more prone to choke, crib, or chew wood?

I don't think they are more prone to choke, but I do think they are more prone to crib and chew wood.

Forages

Hay

What hays do you feed?

Alfalfa and timothy at home. When we are in Florida, coastal-bermuda is fed.

Why do you feed these?

Availability, palatability, nutritional value, and cost.

Are there other hays you would prefer if they were available locally?

Grass hays are available sometimes; they're very good if green.

Which cutting do you prefer?

I prefer the second cutting because it can be cut earlier, before it's mature, so it has a higher nutrient content. It can also be dried better after cutting.

How do you judge the quality of hay?

I look at the color, leafiness, and size of the stalks. It should smell fresh, and when shaken out, it should be dust free.

From what parts of the country do you like your hay to come?

Canada and New York.

What is the best method of feeding hay?

I feed my horses in a manger on the ground because of less waste.

Do you recommend feeding hay free-choice or in measured amounts?

Free-choice, except for the "fatties."

What are the advantages of mixing grasses and legumes together in pastures and in hay?

I've never seen horses on a 100 percent legume pasture; it's too valuable as hay. The advantages of mixing legumes and grasses together in hay is that you can adjust the protein content. A legume hay provides more protein than a mature or older horse needs, so by adding a grass hay, the protein content can be reduced. Adding alfalfa to grass hay is a good way to increase the protein in the diet of a young horse. Also straight alfalfa needs a phosphorous supplement because of its high calcium level.

What types of behavioral and gastric problems can arise if a horse does not receive adequate forage (hay or pasture)?

Every kind of boredom vice can appear. As far as gastric goes, when the ratio of pounds of grain fed to pounds of fiber fed approaches, or exceeds 1:1, problems with colic are likely to occur. This is due to gas produced during fermentation of feedstuffs and low motility of the gut. Loose stools may also be a problem.

Pasture

How much time do you allow your horses to graze?

My competition horses are lucky if they are able to get out for two hours a day.

Do you keep any horses on pasture 24 hours a day?

No.

What special care do pasture horses need?

They need to have adequate shelters with clean dry floors, clean water, and salt or mineral blocks. Young horses will need a protein supplement. They need safe fencing, constant foot care and group deworming. They should also be provided with fly wipe rubbers. (These dispense fly–spray on horses when they walk under them.)

What kind of pasture grass do you prefer?

Timothy.

Is there a danger from toxic weeds if pastures are well cultivated?

Not here, but yes, there can be.

Supplementation

Vitamin and Mineral

If a horse is receiving a high quality, well balanced diet, is vitamin or mineral supplementation necessary?

This depends on the physical demands placed on the horse, but normally most horses don't need it. However, if the horse is working, it may need a supplement. Of course, if the calcium to phosphorus ratio is unbalanced, supplementation is necessary.

Do horses need a trace mineralized salt source or just a salt source?

A trace mineralized salt source. I prefer feeding trace mineralized salt in a block form for the noncompetitive horses. For the competitive horses, I prefer to add it to the feed in measured amounts.

Can vitamin E supplementation enhance performance and fertility, and benefit the highly stressed horse?

I have used it, unsuccessfully, to prevent tying-up. I have also used it in conjunction with medicine to aid the tied up horse. I found that if I used this medicine without the vitamin E, it took longer for the horse to recuperate.

Do you supplement vitamin E?
Yes.

Are there any supplements particularly beneficial to a dressage horse?
I feel the B vitamins and iron are beneficial.

Are injectable supplements superior to oral supplements?
NEVER!

What are the risks and disadvantages of administering injectable supplements routinely?
There can be severe reactions to injectable vitamins. Horses get sore necks, abscesses, and may even suffer anaphylactic shock.

Do you feel most horsemen oversupplement or undersupplement their horses?
Most oversupplement their horses. They tend to duplicate nutrients because they do not know the nutrient content of what they are feeding. They also don't know what the nutrients are needed for.

Electrolytes

Is electrolyte supplementation helpful before and/or after competition?
It is helpful if done after a competition. Electrolytes are not stored in excess. If they are not needed, they are rapidly excreted from the body. If they are needed, they will be selected from the bloodstream. The need for electrolytes in my horses arises after work. I don't work a horse immediately after feeding it, so supplementing beforehand would not be helpful.

If you use them, how do you provide your horses with electrolytes?
I use a homemade mix and mix it into the grain. If I'm on the road showing, I'll dose syringe a horse that is a poor eater.

Can electrolyte supplementation ever be harmful?
It can if you destroy your horse's mineral balance.

What steps can be taken to prevent any harmful effects of electrolyte supplementation?
Don't overfeed any supplement, and don't duplicate.

Protein and Protein Supplements

Is the use of commercial protein supplements worthwhile?
Yes.

Which oilseed meal protein supplement do you prefer?
I prefer soybean meal because it contains all the amino acids necessary for equine nutrition. Cottonseed meal and linseed meal are incomplete supplements, and peanut meal is unavailable here.

Can excesses of protein be harmful and negatively affect performance?
Yes, definitely.

Does protein supplementation increase muscle mass?
It's not as simple as that. Protein is a building block of muscle, but the horse must have the genetics, hormones, enzymes, and exercise in order for the protein to increase the muscle mass.

Added Fat

Do you feed added fat?
I have fed between four and five cups of corn oil to keep weight on my horse Gifted when he simply wouldn't eat. We just poured it on his grain.

How can a horse benefit from having fat added to the diet?
Fat is the highest calorie supplement, with the lowest volume and weight. It doesn't fill up the stomach. Fat is beneficial to poor eaters that are being shipped for over 24 hours. It helps to keep them from losing weight.

Management

Feeding

Does training stress placed on a dressage horse greatly increase its need for protein, energy, or vitamins and minerals?
Dressage is a high stress activity—mentally and physically. Because much of the muscle activity is isometric in nature, it is possible for the horse to use up more energy stores, vitamins, and minerals than it can replace through normal feeding. This is especially true if the horse is travelling a lot and not receiving its 4 or 5 meals a day, or if the horse is a picky eater.

How do you provide the extra energy that a dressage horse needs?
Corn oil and straight grains.

Does a proven upper level (above fourth level) horse require a different ration than a horse that is just beginning training?
Yes. An upper level horse will usually require less protein than a horse just beginning training. A younger horse doesn't necessarily need as much food because it isn't working as hard or as long. Also they do less travelling and are under less stress.

What factors are most important in planning and preparing a balanced ration?
> The availability of nutrients, the forage versus grain ratio, supplements, the work load placed on the horse, the cost, and knowledge of equine nutrition.

What can be done to increase the palatability of a ration?
> Molasses or apple cider can be poured over the feed.

Do you feed bran mashes?
> Yes. Since it is a wet feed, it is fed after long truck trips in order to improve hydration. It is also fed for its laxative effects. It has a large volume of fiber, so it keeps the gut motile.

*What **correctable** problems can cause a horse to be a "hard keeper"?*
> Having another horse close by that covets its feed, causing it anxiety, flies on the feed, moldy or spoiled feed, and dirty feed tubs. It may be that the horse has become bored with the ration, or the volume of feed may be too large–meals should be small and spread out over time. Also, minimize the stress placed on the horse through the type and timing of work.

Are there any special feeds or supplements you feed "hard keepers"?
> Yes, oil and straight grain with or without molasses.

How many times a day do you feed?
> Usually between three and six times a day. Even a fat horse will be fed this many times, but it will just be smaller amounts.

At what times of the day do you feed?
> The first feeding is in the early A.M. Then throughout the day till late evening, about 10:00 P.M.

What changes should be made in the horse's diet when its activity level is increased or decreased, and when it is ill or injured?
> When the horse's activity level increases, the calories fed should increase. When its activity level decreases, the amount of fiber in the diet should increase and the grain level should decrease. If the horse is ill or injured it needs a low calorie diet high in vitamins. The diet also needs to have a good fiber content to keep the gut motile.

Is it better to change the feed ration routinely, or is it better to stick with a proven formula?
> I do change my ration, but not routinely. I change only when the nutrient availability changes, or if the horse gets bored with the ration.

If a horse does not eat, how long do you leave the feed in front of him?
> Not very long. Two hours at the most.

How can one encourage the horse to drink more water if it is consuming inadequate amounts?

Clean the water bucket, add electrolytes to the diet, use apple cider in the water.

What management practices would you recommend to avoid colic and laminitis?

Provide a high volume of good quality fiber. Do not feed a large volume of grain at one meal, and do not stress the horse close to meals. Provide plenty of water. Store the feed where horses cannot get into it on their own, and feed consistently—the same time each day, and the same ration. Don't make radical changes. Deworm regularly and rotate the type of dewormer.

Are there special times when water should be withheld from the horse?

Yes, when it's heavily tranquilized for some medical procedure.

Basic Care

How often do you have your horses' teeth checked and floated?

All the time.

What types of inoculations do you have done on your horses?

They receive flu and rhino shots every ninety days. Tetanus and Eastern and Western Equine Encephalomyelitis shots are given twice a year.

Do you have any blood analyses done?

Yes,when I feel the horse isn't okay.

What do you look for in a blood test?

Anemia, the white blood cell count (infections), and red blood cell volume versus plasma.

Parasite Control

How frequently do you recommend deworming, and by what method?

I deworm eight to ten times a year. I rotate between febendazole, pyrantel, and ivermectin. I also never have the same number of weeks between deworming.

Would you recommend the dewormers that are fed on a daily basis?

I don't know yet.

Is it essential that horses get tube dewormed or are there other methods as effective?

There are other methods that are just as effective.

What is the most practical method for preventing the spread of parasites in pastures?
Manure should be picked up. All horses should be dewormed at the same time, and no new horses should be turned out until they have been dewormed.

Training

Are your horses worked every day?
Yes, if possible.

How does this affect their attitude?
It keeps it healthy.

Do you recommend that horses be rested prior to competition?
No.

General

What areas of equine nutrition do you feel most need further research?
Vitamin and mineral deficiencies due to stress, management of stress and appetite. The side effects of steroid use due to the tendency of some trainers to use them for body building.

What physical characteristics does a well fed horse display?
Well fed horses will have a glossy hair coat, good skin quality, strong hoof wall, good muscle tone, energy to perform, a good appetite, clear, watery sweat, and the ability to dissipate heat through the skin.

What are the danger signs that show an inadequate feeding program?
These horses will be either excessively fat or excessively thin, have a poor quality hoof wall, poor respiratory recovery after exercise, poor heat transfer through the skin, low energy level, poor appetite, a coarse or dull hair coat, frequent lameness problems, skin infections.

Do you think most horse people have a good knowledge of equine nutrition?
Not at all.

If there are any comments on the care or feeding of horse that you would like to add, please feel free to do so.
Not all supplements are what they say they are, or do what they say they do. People need to learn about proper nutrition, and not go for gimmicks.

Jack Van Berg

Jack Van Berg was born and raised in Thoroughbred racing. Van Berg's father, the late Hall of Fame trainer Marion H. Van Berg, started his son in the stable at age eight. By the time he was 16, Van Berg had his trainer's license.

In 1955, when Van Berg was in his early twenties, he saddled his first stakes winner, Dagazha. Since that time, Van Berg has sent out 160 other stakes winners. Those include Horse of the Year Alysheba, the leading money-winning Thoroughbred of all time. Van Berg also sent out classic winner Gate Dancer, which challenged him to overcome many obstacles, including dislike of crowd noise. (Gate Dancer was equipped with ear muffs when he won the 1984 Preakness Stakes in track record time.)

In 1976, Van Berg won a record 496 races. In 1985, he followed in his father's footsteps and was inducted into the Racing Hall of Fame in Saratoga Springs, New York. Van Berg in 1987 became the first trainer to surpass the 5,000 win mark. That year, he was named the "Big Sport of Turfdom" by the Turf Publicists of America. Van Berg led the nation in number of wins for eight years, and was the nation's third-leading trainer by purses won every year from 1985 – 88. Horsemen around the country look up to Jack Van Berg as one of the top in his profession.

The interview...

Grains

How do you prefer to feed oats and corn?

I prefer either to roll or crack corn just prior to feeding. If you buy corn that is already processed (steamed or rolled), you lose a great deal of the oils and nutrient content. Oats should be treated in the same manner. I think crushing them just before feeding is the best. I don't like to buy rolled oats (they are too dry), and I think you lose a lot of the nutrient content.

What is the minimum weight per bushel for a good quality oat?
I feel it should be 45 pounds.

Are there any particular geographic regions that excel in the production of certain feeds?
Canada is the best for oats, then Colorado and Montana. Washington is the best for grass hays, California and Arizona for alfalfa.

Commercially Prepared Horse Feeds

How do you feel about commercial mixes from reputable companies?
Most commercial feeds are high in quality, but I prefer to feed the whole grains that are raised in good growing country.

What is the best method to judge the quality of a commercial horse feed?
By close, visual examination.

Is the addition of sweet feed more advantageous in winter months?
No, corn or barley is a better addition.

Is sweet feed a poor feed in summer months?
No, I don't think so.

Are pelleted feeds advantageous to feed?
No, I don't think so.

Are pelleted forages an adequate substitute for loose forage, such as pasture or hay?
I don't think pelleted forages should replace regular forage sources, such as hay and pasture. I think you lose nutrients when heat is applied to the forage during the pelleting process.

Are horses that are fed pelleted feeds more likely to crib or chew wood if adequate forage is provided?
No, I don't think so.

Are there any advantages to extruded feeds?
No, not really.

Forages

Hay

What hays do you feed?
Alfalfa and timothy.

And why do you feed these?
I believe they have the highest nutritional value.

Are there other hays you would prefer if they were available locally?
Colorado or Montana prairie hay.

Which cutting do you prefer?
The third cutting for alfalfa and the second cutting for prairie hay.

How do you judge the quality of hay?
Visual examination.

What is the best method of feeding hay?
I prefer a hay net, because there is less waste.

Do you recommend feeding hay free-choice or in measured amounts?
I like to feed my hay free-choice.

Pasture

Do you ever turn your racehorses out on pasture?
Yes, I do.

What kind of pasture grass do you prefer?
Bermuda grass and clover.

How many acres per horse is minimal for pasture?
This depends on the season and what part of the country you are in.

Is there a danger from toxic weeds if pastures are well cultivated?
No, not if you manage them properly.

Supplementation
Vitamin and Mineral

If a horse is receiving a high quality, well balanced diet, do you think vitamin or mineral supplementation is necessary?
No, I don't think it would be necessary.

Do horses need a trace mineralized salt source or just a salt source?
I prefer feeding trace mineralized salt free-choice.

Are any supplements particularly beneficial to the racehorse?
If you feed a well-balanced, high quality diet, you don't need any extra supplements.

Do you feel injectable supplements are superior to oral supplements?
Yes, I do.

What are the risks of administering injectable supplements routinely?
There are some risks associated with injecting iron compounds.

Electrolytes

Are electrolytes helpful?
Yes, in hot weather, when the horses are sweating a lot.

How do you provide your horses with electrolytes?
In their water or grain.

Can electrolyte supplementation ever be harmful?
No, I don't believe so.

Protein and Protein Supplements

Which oilseed meal protein supplement do you prefer?
I prefer peanut meal.

Can excesses of protein be harmful and negatively affect performance?
Yes, on young, growing horses, excesses of protein can negatively affect performance.

Added Fat

Do you think feeding added fat is beneficial?
Yes, and I think corn oil is the best source to add to the ration.

Drugs

Are drugs being abused in horse racing?
No, I do not feel they are.

Does Lasix really help bleeders?
Yes, it does.

Management

Feeding

How can one keep a horse in good shape nutritionally?
The best feed you can buy will keep a horse healthy nutritionally.

In what ways do you provide the extra energy that a racehorse needs as compared to a horse doing light work or no work?
I feed them more grain.

Do you feed bran mashes?
I feed a bran mash every night.

What is the most common type of problem that can cause a horse to be a "hard keeper"?
Nervousness.

How many times a day do you feed?
I feed three times a day.

At what times of the day do you feed?
3:30 A.M., 11:00 A.M., and 5:00 P.M.

Do you change your feed rations routinely or is it better to stick with a proven formula?

I think it's important to stick with a proven formula.

How can one encourage a horse to drink more water if it is consuming inadequate amounts?

By increasing the salt content of its feed.

What management practices would you recommend to avoid colic and laminitis?

Feed good quality hays and grains that are free of mold and toxins.

Are there special times when water should be withheld from the horse?

Two hours before running a race, and small amounts at a time when they are hot.

Basic Care

What type of bedding do you prefer in your stalls?

I prefer wood shavings.

How often do you have your horses' teeth checked and floated?

Every 60 days.

Do you have blood analysis done on your horses?

Sometimes, when their appearance becomes poor or they have a decrease in performance. We check the white and red blood cell counts.

Parasite Control

How frequently do you deworm?

I deworm every 60 to 90 days.

What is the most practical method for preventing the spread of parasites in pastures?

I like to rotate my pastures with cattle; I've found it to be very helpful.

Training

Do you use a scientific training program?

No, I use traditional training methods.

Do you recommend that racehorses be ridden in a track atmosphere every day for training?

Yes, I do.

Do you recommend that horses be rested prior to a race?

No, I don't rest my horses prior to a race.

General

What are the physical characteristics that a well fed horse displays?
Sharp, clear eyes, and a glossy, healthy looking hair coat.

What are the danger signs that show an inadequate feeding program?
A rough, poor looking hair coat.

Do you think most horse people have a good knowledge of equine nutrition?
Yes, I believe so.

Dan Rosenberg

Dan Rosenberg has been around horses most of his life. He has worked for Glade Valley Farms, and also Clovelly Farms, and in1975, he became the broodmare manager at Calumet Farm.

In 1978, he became general manager at Three Chimneys Farm, one of the leading Thoroughbred farms in America. In addition to holding this prestigious position, he is the vice-president and a member of the board of directors of the Kentucky Equine Institute. He is also a member of the Advisory Committee for the Midway College Equine Studies program, and

is the Director of the Keeneland Pony Club. He is the past president of the Kentucky Thoroughbred Farm Managers.

The interview...

Grains

Would you recommend using processed or whole grains?
I recommend whole natural grains. There is a potential for loss of nutrients when grains are heated or processed. In clinical trials, there seems to be little difference between the digestibility of processed grain and whole grain.

What are the advantages and disadvantages of corn and oats?
Corn is high in energy, however it can contribute to intestinal problems due to microtoxins. Oats are advantageous because horses like them and do well on them. There are no disadvantages.

What is the minimum weight per bushel for a good quality oat?
Forty-two pounds.

Are there any regions that are best for the production of grains?
I don't care where they come from as long as they are high quality.

Commercially Prepared Horse Feeds

Have you found commercial feed mixes from reputable companies to be consistently high in quality?
Yes, the key being reputable companies.

What is the best method for judging the quality and usefulness of a commercial horse feed?
Successful use of it by others, good appearance and performance of the horses on the feed, and independent lab testing.

When is it worthwhile to have a commercial mill prepare feeds to your own formula?
When they don't manufacture a particular feed that is desired.

Are pelleted feeds advantageous to feed?
They may be, under some circumstances.

Are pelleted forages an adequate substitute for loose forage (such as pasture or hay)?
No, because pelleted forages decrease the time spent eating, and that can lead to boredom in the horse.

What about feeding hay cubes?
They are an advantage if good quality hay is not available. But they do not allow enough eating time and the horse may become bored.

Are horses fed pelleted feeds more prone to choke, crib, or chew wood?
They are more prone to choke, but not crib or chew wood.

Are there any advantages to feeding extruded feeds?
They have a good shelf life.

Forages

Hay

What hays do you feed?
Alfalfa, alfalfa/timothy, and timothy.

Why do you feed these?
They are high in protein and minerals.

Are there other hays you would prefer if they were available locally?
Timothy/clover.

Which cutting do you prefer?
I prefer the second or third cutting, because there is less stem.

How do you judge the quality of your hay?
Maturity, color, smell, and taste.

From what parts of the country do you prefer to purchase your hay?
Anywhere if it's of good quality—mostly Ohio, Indiana, and Michigan.

What is the best method of feeding hay?
I prefer feeding it on the ground, because horses naturally eat off the ground, and they experience less trouble with dust and eye problems. Also, without careful management, hay in mangers can become moldy.

Do you recommend feeding hay free-choice or in measured amounts?
In general, I recommend free-choice, except for horses whose weight must be controlled.

What types of behavioral and gastric problems can arise if a horse does not receive adequate forage?
In terms of behavioral problems—boredom. In terms of gastric problems—they lose gut motility, which can lead to colic.

What proportion of hay to concentrate is generally best?
That varies with age and use of the horse.

Pasture

How much time do you allow your horses to graze?
That varies, depending on the time of year and the status of the horse. In general, as much as possible.

Do you keep any horses on pasture 24 hours a day?
Yes, during the summer and fall, mares without foals, including those in early gestation, barren, and maiden mares.

What special care do these horses need?
Close attention.

What kind of pasture grass do you prefer?
For central Kentucky, predominantly bluegrass with some orchardgrass and rye.

How many acres per horse is minimal for pastures?
Four acres per horse in central Kentucky.

Is there danger from toxic weeds if pastures are well cultivated?
I have never had a problem.

Classes of Horses

Broodmares

Do you prefer broodmares be in fleshy or thin condition prior to the onset of the breeding season?
I would prefer perfect condition all year long.

Will "flushing" (bringing them into the breeding season in a thin condition and then feeding them to gain) mares enhances their fertility?
I have not seen it make a great deal of difference.

How many pounds of concentrate do you feed broodmares per day
A. *during pregnancy?*   8 – 12 lbs.
B. *during lactation?*   10 – 12 lbs.
C. *when open?*   Depends on body condition and time of year.

Stallions

How much exercise do your stallions get on a daily basis, and what method do you use to exercise them?
Our stallions are ridden at an easy canter two or three miles a day, six days a week, all year long.

Do you feed stallions supplements to enhance reproductive performance?
No.

Foals

What do you feed foals?
16% (protein) sweet feed.

At what age do you wean?
Five to six months.

When do you worm foals for the first time, and what type of wormer do you use?
Two months, TBZ and piperizine.

Weanlings

What method do you use to wean foals?
We wean from the field a few mares at a time. Mares and foals are turned out at the normal time. Some hours later, we will return, pick up two mares, lead them onto a van, and haul them to another part of the farm.

Do you change their ration, or do they remain on the creep ration?
We don't change the ration.

How much do you feed weanlings?
4½ to 5½ lbs.

Yearlings

> *How do you manage yearlings? (Are they stalled, pastured, or a combination?)*
> Combination.

> *How does this management style affect their nutritional needs?*
> It allows them a lot of free access to forage.

> *What do you feed sales yearlings?*
> 14% (protein) sweet feed.

> *When do you begin preparing yearlings for the sales?*
> Sixty days prior to the sale.

Management

Feeding

> *What factors are most important in planning a balanced ration?*
> Know the nutrient profile of the forage (pasture and hay) and balance accordingly with concentrate.

> *How can you ensure the palatability of a ration?*
> Provide good quality ingredients.

> *Do you feed bran mashes?*
> Yes, to mares after foaling.

> *What is the most common cause of a horse being a "hard keeper"?*
> Bad teeth.

> *Are there any special feeds or supplements you feed "hard keepers"?*
> Not really, just feed more, more often.

> *How many times a day do you feed?*
> Twice daily.

> *At what times of the day do you feed?*
> Early morning and late afternoon.

> *Do you feed equal portions at each feeding?*
> Yes, usually.

> *If the horse does not eat, how long do you leave the feed in front of it?*
> One hour.

> *What management practices would you recommend to avoid colic and laminitis?*
> Frequent small feedings, free access to forage.

> *Are there special times when water should be withheld from the horse?*
> No, unless the horse is overheated or has just had a long van ride. They should then be watered slowly.

Supplements

Is supplemental salt important in the horse's diet?
Yes, free-choice salt.

Do you recommend using blocks to supplement salt?
Yes.

Do you feed any supplements?
No. They are not needed if the ration is properly balanced.

Do you supplement vitamin E?
No.

Do you think commercial protein supplements are valuable and worthwhile?
Yes, if used to properly balance a concentrate.

Which oilseed meal protein supplement do you prefer?
I prefer soybean meal because it has a good amino acid profile.

Can excesses of protein be harmful and negatively affect performance?
No.

Does protein supplementation increase muscle mass?
Not beyond the potential for muscle mass.

What percentage of protein is necessary in the ration of (a) foals? 16% *(b) yearlings?* 14% *(c) two-year-olds?* 12% *(d) mature horses?* 10% *?*

Do you feed any horses a source of added fat, such as corn oil?
I feed the sales yearlings 4 ounces of carron oil (mixture of slaked lime, water, raw linseed oil).

Basic Care

What type of bedding do you prefer in stalls?
Straw.

How often do you have horses' teeth checked and floated?
Annually.

What types of inoculations do you have done?
Tetanus, flu, rabies, botulism, rhino pneumonitis, and EWE.

Do you have any blood analyses done?
When necessary, if I suspect a health problem.

Parasite Control

How frequently do you recommend deworming?
Every 60 days.

Would you recommend dewormers which are fed on a daily basis?
I have not used them.

Is it essential that horses be tube dewormed?
It makes me feel better to tube deworm, but other methods can be effective if administered properly.

What is the most practical method for preventing the spread of parasites in pastures?
Mowing, chain harrowing, not overgrazing, and a regular deworming program.

General

What areas of equine nutrition do you feel most need further research?
The influence of pasture on nutritional intake.

What are the physical characteristics that a well fed horse displays?
Good flesh, healthy coat, bright eye, and a good attitude.

What are the danger signs that show an inadequate feeding program?
Underweight, poor condition, poor performance, stunted growth, and poor health.

Do you think most horse people have a good knowledge of equine nutrition?
No.

Bill Brown

Bill Brown became interested in Standardbreds at an early age. He worked first as a groom, then as a second trainer to Hall of Famer Frank Ervin in the early to mid-1950's. Mr. Brown "retired" from the race circuit in 1958 to embark upon a career in the Standardbred breeding industry by becoming manager of Castleton Farm's Standardbred Nursery in Lexington, Kentucky. At the time, the farm comprised over 3,000 acres. During the twelve and a half years that Mr. Brown managed the nursery, he gained valuable knowledge and experience in the area of feeding and raising young horses.

In 1970, Mr. Brown was offered the management of Blue Chip Farms in Wallkill, New York. This farm, started in 1968 by the Kimelman family, has become the largest commercial Standardbred breeding farm in New York.

Blue Chip regularly raises 90 – 100 yearlings each year. Their current stallion roster includes On The Road Again, New York's leading pacing stallion in 1990 and 1991. Also residing at Blue Chip is the international trotting sire Meadow Road.

Mr. Brown is a board member of the Goshen-Historic Track, which is a national landmark, and The Harness Horse Youth Foundation, which awards college scholarships to young people interested in equine careers. He is also a member of the Cornell Equine Advisory Committee which develops equine programs and policies for New York State.

The interview...

Grains

Would you recommend using processed grains, such as rolled or steamed, as opposed to whole natural grains?
I prefer whole oats for the average horse, and rolled or crimped oats for the older horse with digestive problems.

What are the advantages and disadvantages of corn and oats?
Corn is a good supplement to feed with oats. However, in this area, the Northeast, corn is of poor quality. Its moisture content is too high and it is difficult to get a consistent grade. Most horses will eat oats without any problems.

What should the minimum weight be for a good quality oat?
It should be greater than 42 pounds per bushel.

Are there geographic regions that excel in the production of grains?
For oats, northern Minnesota, Michigan, and Canada. For corn, the Midwest.

Commercially Prepared Horse Feeds

Have you found commercial feed mixes from reputable companies to be consistently high in quality?
Yes.

What is the best method for horsemen to judge the quality and use-fulness of a commercial horse feed?
The oats in the feed should have a good berry. The feed should not be overburdened with molasses. There should be a minimum of residue ("fines") left in the feed trough after the horse eats.

When is it worthwhile (in terms of cost) to have a commercial mill prepare your own feeds to your formula?
When it is a large operation. For us, it is cost effective to have a mill prepare our feeds to our own formulas because we have over 300 horses (depending on the season) on our farm.

Is sweet feed a poor feed in summer months?
No. However, it must be kept cool to prevent spoilage.

Are pelleted feeds advantageous to feed?
Yes.

Are horses fed pelleted feeds more prone to choke, crib, or chew wood?
They are not more prone to choke, especially if they are raised on pelleted feeds, but if adequate hay is not provided, they will be more likely to crib and chew wood.

Forages
Hay

What kinds of hay do you feed?
Depends on the age and the status of horse. Mares: Alfalfa, timothy and clover mix. Yearlings: Good clover and timothy mix, or straight alfalfa. Sale yearlings: timothy. Barren mares: timothy.

Are there other hays you would prefer if they were available locally?
No.

Which cutting do you prefer?
The first cutting.

How do you judge the quality of hay?
By its texture and the stage at which it was cut.

From which parts of the country do you like your hay to come?
Northern New York and Canada.

What is the best method of feeding hay?
I prefer on the ground, but the manger or rack is more economical.

Do you recommend feeding hay free-choice or in measured amounts?
I recommend feeding it in measured amounts.

What types of problems can arise if a horse does not receive adequate forage (hay or pasture)?
If they don't receive adequate hay, they may begin cribbing. Also, too much grain and too little hay will result in intestinal problems.

What proportion of hay to concentrate is generally best?
Depends on condition, but roughly 3½ pounds of hay to 1 pound of grain.

Pasture

How much time do you allow your horses to graze?
For older horses: in the winter—7hours, in the summer—18 hours; and for yearlings and mares with older foals: 24 hours a day, with access to sheds.

Do you keep any horses on pasture 24 hours a day?
Yes, yearlings.

What special care do these horses need?
Shelter. Feed-wise, they are evaluated twice a day. They are inspected for condition four times a day.

What kind of pasture grass do you prefer?
I prefer a variety—orchardgrass, bluegrass, and legumes (clover).

How many acres per horse is minimal for pasture in your area?
Minimum is one acre under the best conditions, but you can never have enough ground.

Is there a danger from toxic weeds if pastures are well cultivated?
Not if they are mowed regularly and chain harrowed.

What are the advantages of mixing grasses and legumes together in pastures and hay?
The legumes help return nitrogen to the ground and they are a good grazing supplement. As far as hay goes, in the first cutting, legumes are fine. However, I find that in the second cutting, legumes have a tendency to cause slobbering.

Classes Of Horses

Broodmares

Do you prefer that broodmares be in fleshy or thin condition prior to the onset of the breeding season?
Medium covering over the ribs is most preferable.

Does "flushing" mares (bringing them into the breeding season in a thin condition and then feeding them to gain) enhance their fertility?
I do not practice this method, but spring grass could probably be considered a natural flushing agent.

Do you change broodmares' ration just before and after foaling?
Yes, just prior to foaling we increase the rations; just after foaling, we put them on plain oats until the foal heat.

How many pounds of concentrate do you feed your broodmares per day during pregnancy, lactation, and when open?
For all stages, it depends on the condition of the mare.

Stallions

Is more education needed in the area of stallion nutrition?
Yes, I feel that most people overfeed their stallions.

How much exercise do your stallions get on a daily basis?
Each stallion has his own paddock, and they exercise freely for about four hours a day. If one has a tendency to keep too much weight on, we ride him prior to and during the breeding season.

Do you feed stallions certain supplements specifically to enhance their reproductive performance?
Not really. They receive wheat germ oil and a blood tonic along with their regular rations throughout the year.

Foals

Do you creep feed foals?
Yes.

What do you feed them?
Small pellets containing 18% protein.

At what age do you begin creep feeding?
They first learn to eat pellets while they are in a stall (the mare is tied up). At about one month of age, they are put in pastures with sheds, where they have access to the creeps.

At what age do you wean?
At five months.

When do you deworm foals for the first time and what do you use?
Foals are dewormed for the first time at ten days with thiabendazole. They are tube dewormed at four weeks of age. Dewormings are repeated every four to five weeks thereafter.

Weanlings

What method do you use to wean foals?
While they are out on pasture, we take two or three mares away from the group every couple of days. We leave one docile mare in with the group until they are moved to the yearling sheds.

Do you change their ration, or do they remain on the creep ration?
The protein level is decreased to 15% and the pellets are larger.

How much concentrate do you feed weanlings?
They are fed twice a day. The amount fed depends on the condition of the group and the amount of hay they are eating.

What types of supplements do you provide weanlings?
Copper salt, Vigertone®, and Biophos®.

Yearlings

How do you manage yearlings? (Are they stalled, pastured or a combination?)
They are shed raised in groups of ten to fifteen, according to age and sex.

How does this management style affects their nutritional needs?
Occasionally, one has a tendency to get heavy, but overall, shed raising is the best way to raise a yearling. Plus, it is economical.

What do you feed sales yearlings?
After sales yearlings are brought back into the barn for preparation, they are fed oats and a prepared sweet feed twice a day. They receive a bran mash once a day.

When do you begin prepping yearlings for sales?
Seven to eight weeks prior to the sale.

Management

Feeding

What factors are most important in planning and preparing a balanced ration?
The age and the condition of the horse in question.

What can be done to increase the palatability of a ration?
Don't make pellets too hard. However, they need to be firm enough to cut down on waste and pellet dust.

Do you feed bran mashes? If so, how often?
Stallions and sales yearlings–once a day.

What common problems can cause a horse to be a "hard keeper"?
Teeth that need floating, being wormy, and placing too much stress on the horse. Also, the horse may not like the ration. Try to find a ration he favors.

Are there any special feeds or supplements you feed "hard keepers"?
Crimped or rolled oats with a light coating of molasses, and soft palatable hay.

How many times a day do you feed?
Two times a day.

At what times of the day do you feed?
Stalled horses: 4:00 A.M. and 3:00 P.M. Shed horses: 7:00 A.M. and 3:00 P.M.

Do you feed equal portions at each feeding?
Not always. Weanlings and yearlings usually get a larger portion in the evening.

If a horse does not eat, how long do you leave the feed in front of him?
30 to 45 minutes.

What management practices would you recommend to avoid colic and laminitis?
Feed according to the condition of the horse, and keep your horse parasite-free.

Do you alter your ration with the changing of the seasons?
No, but we may decrease the amount given if there is good pasture.

Supplements

Is supplemental salt important in the horse's diet?
Yes.

Do you recommend using trace mineralized salt blocks?
Yes.

Do you feed any supplements?
Copper salt, Biophos®, and Vigortone®.

What benefits do they provide?
Biophos® reduces occurrences of epiphysitis. For adequate bone development, mineral supplements are important.

Is the use of commercial protein supplements worthwhile?
They are not necessary if you have a good balanced ration.

Which oilseed meal protein supplements do you prefer?
Soybean meal. We give it to mares that have a tendency to be light milkers.

Can excesses of protein be harmful and negatively affect performance?
Yes.

What percentage of protein is necessary in the ration of foals? 18% , *yearlings?* 15% , *two year-olds?* 12% – 14% , *and mature horses?* 12% – 14%.

Do you feed any of your horses a source of added fat such as corn oil?
Sometimes we give sales yearlings corn oil–about 2 ounces a day.

Basic Care

What type of bedding do you prefer in stalls?
Straw.

How often do you have horses' teeth checked and floated?
Once a year.

What types of inoculations do you have done on your horses?
Flu-Vac, Rhino, Strangles, Eastern and Western Encephalomyelitis, Tetanus Toxoid, Botulism, Rabies, and Potomac Fever.

How often do you have these done?
Rhino, every 60 days, the rest according to schedule recommended by my veterinarian.

Do you have any blood analyses done?
Yes, if sickness or condition warrants it.

Parasite Control

How frequently do you recommend deworming?

Mares are dewormed every five weeks; weanlings and yearlings are dewormed every four weeks.

Do you think there is a danger of parasites building up a resistance to dewormers when low doses are fed on a daily basis?

I think this is a possibility with any dewormer. Fecals should be run on a regular basis to check for parasite eggs, the presence of which may indicate a resistance.

Is it essential that horses get tube dewormed at least once a year, or are there other methods as effective?

It's not essential to tube deworm, but I feel that it is an effective practice towards controlling parasites.

What is the most practical method for preventing the spread of parasites in pastures?

Chain harrowing of fields and regular mowing.

General

What areas of equine nutrition do you feel most need further research?

Effects of growth, nutrition, and stress on joint development.

What are the physical characteristics that a well fed horse displays?

Good hair coat, no excessive weight, alert appearance.

What are the danger signs that show an inadequate feeding program?

Dull hair coat, hay belly, depressed look, unhealthy hooves, joint problems.

Do you feel most people have a good knowledge of equine nutrition?

No, everyone seems to have his own methods. There does not seem to be a consensus on the proper feeding of horses.

If there are any comments on the care or feeding of horse that you would like to add, please feel free to do so.

In general, I feel we "push" the growth process on our young stock by overfeeding. This, coupled with the stresses of training in two-year olds, has been very detrimental to the racing breeds. Joint problems abound. However, the market place (i.e., owners) demands that sale yearlings have a certain "look" in order to be commercially viable. Few commercial breeders can afford to ignore this demand, even though it goes against their better judgment. There is some indication, at least in the Standardbred industry, that attitude changes are taking place. "Bigger" is not always better, and pushing two-year olds to the race track may someday become an option, not a necessity.

Rodney Reed

Rodney Reed, currently based in Wapanuka, Oklahoma, has been training horses at major tracks since 1978. Since that time, his horses have won over 400 times, placed second over 300 times, and third over 200 times. Reed is a member of the silent partnership known as the Super Select Partners.

As an example of Reed's knack for success, in1991 Reed had the first three finishers in the Ross Meadows Poor Boy Quarter Horse Futurity. Two months later, at Blue Ribbon Downs in Sallisaw, Oklahoma, Reed qualified four horses for the Blue Ribbon Futurity (Grade I Quarter Horse). Three of those four qualifiers finished first, second and third, and then he sent out the Blue Ribbon Derby winner, Masters Go Man.

In 1992 he won the Blue Ribbon Futurity again with Bugged Thoughts, and also won the Blue Ribbon Derby with First Down Kelly.

Rodney Reed's excellent results are only possible through skillful training and a sound management and feeding program.

The interview...

Grains

How do corn and oats fit into your feeding program?

Corn has a great deal of energy, more than oats. I feed a mix of both of them. In the summer, I'll back off on the corn, but in the winter I always feed cracked corn.

What about processing these grains?

Right now, I'm feeding cracked corn; it seems as if horses can eat it a little better. I have fed whole corn with no problems—it's good for their teeth. As far as oats go, I'd rather feed a whole oat. The horses don't seem to have any trouble with them.

Is the weight of the oat an important quality factor?

I like a good heavy oat. Generally, the heavier they weigh per bushel, the better oat they are.

Are there any particular geographic regions that excel in the production of grains?

The Dakotas.

Commercially Prepared Horse Feeds

Have you found commercial feed mixes from reputable companies to be consistently high in quality?

Yes.

What is the best method to judge the quality and usefulness of a commercial horse feed?

By looking at all the grains, the percentage of molasses, and the consistency from batch to batch.

Is sweet feed more advantageous to feed in winter months?

Yes, I use sweet feed mainly in the winter.

Are pelleted feeds advantageous to feed?

No, and I don't use any pelleted feeds.

Are horses fed pelleted feeds more prone to choke, crib, or chew wood?

Yes, I think horses that are fed pelleted feed are more likely to choke and have stable vices.

Forages

Hay

What hays do you feed?

I like to feed a good quality coastal hay or prairie hay/alfalfa mix.

Which cutting do you prefer?

I prefer the second or third cutting.

What geographical areas do you prefer your hay to come from?

I get coastal hay from Oklahoma, and alfalfa from Colorado.

What is the best method of feeding hay?

At my ranch, I feed in big hay bunks, and I feed all the hay they want. I never take hay away from them, not even before a race.

What are the advantages of mixing grasses and legumes?

It gives them more protein and variety in their hay.

What problems can arise if a horse doesn't receive adequate forage?

Colic, stress founder, and twisted intestine. Also stable vices, and they don't do as well as a horse that is receiving enough forage.

Pasture

Do you turn your racehorses out on pasture?

Yes, I graze them a lot, and whenever I rest them, I turn them out in the pasture.

What kind of pasture grass do you prefer?
Coastal bermuda.

Supplementation
Vitamin and Mineral

In a high quality well balanced diet, is vitamin or mineral supplementation necessary?
Supplementation—to make sure they're getting what they need, especially with minerals—won't hurt them if the diet stays balanced.

Do you use a trace mineralized salt source or just a salt source?
I prefer a trace mineralized salt source, which I add to their feed.

Can vitamin E supplementation actually enhance performance?
Yes, and it sure helps a nervous horse.

Do you feel injectable supplements are superior to oral supplements?
Yes.

What are the risks and disadvantages of administering injectable supplements routinely?
None for the type of injections I give, like B_{12}, vitamin E, and blood builders.

Do you think most horsemen oversupplement or undersupplement their horses?
I'd have to say many of them oversupplement.

Electrolytes

Are electrolytes helpful?
Yes, definitely.

How do you provide electrolytes?
I've used them every way possible , but I prefer to add them to water.

Protein and Protein Supplements

Is using commercial protein supplements worthwhile?
Yes, I feed Calf Manna® on a regular basis. I don't use any soybean meal, or anything like that.

Can excesses of protein be harmful and negatively affect performance?
Yes, it can.

Drugs

Do you think drugs are being abused in horse racing?
Not any more.

Does Lasix really help bleeders?
Yes.

How do stimulants affect a horse's health and appetite?
Just like a human, it will make him go off his feed.

Management

Feeding

Does training stress increase need for protein, energy, and vitamins?
Yes, I feed a protein supplement, corn oil to increase the energy content of the ration, and also a vitamin supplement.

Is there a difference in rations between a horse that is "racing fit" and one that is just entering training?
Yes, I'd feed a horse that's been running hard a lot more—just to get him to eat all he can. I might feed him three or four times a day—all he'll clean up. The horse just entering training will be fed twice a day.

Do you change your feeding program as a race draws near?
I may feed them more, but I don't change ingredients.

What can be done to increase the palatability of a ration for a finicky or picky eater?
You need to find something he'll eat. However, it is possible to train one to eat. Start out feeding him an amount he will clean up. Gradually increase this amount so that he's eating larger amounts each time, and give him a certain period of time to clean it up. When the time is up, pull his feed tub until the next feeding. This will usually straighten a horse out. Sometimes a horse will be burnt out because someone has overfed him.

Do you feed bran mashes?
No, I mix bran into the ration sometimes, but not as a mash.

What correctable problems can cause a horse to be a "hard keeper"?
Bad teeth and being wormy can both cause him a great deal of trouble. Also, a horse that's sore can be a hard keeper because he's in pain.

What do you recommend feeding them?
I recommend feeding a hard keeper alfalfa and a good sweet feed mixed with oats and corn. They also need good bedding. I think clean proper bedding is very important. A horse needs to be comfortable and be able to lie on a soft bedding.

How many times a day do you feed?
I prefer to feed three times a day.

At what times of the day do you feed?
5 A.M., noon, and 5 P.M.

Do you ever change your horses' diet?
The only time I change their diet is when their exercise level decreases. I'll feed a little bit less when that happens.

If a horse does not eat, how long do you leave the feed in front of him?
I give them an hour to eat.

Are there special times when water should be withheld from the horse?
I never withhold water, neither before nor after a race.

Basic Care

What about having blood analyses done?
I do recommend a blood analysis for the racehorse.

What do you look for?
I look at the blood count to see if everything is balanced properly.

Parasite Control

How frequently do you deworm?
I'll tube worm a horse when I first get it in. I'll deworm again in 30 days. After that, I deworm every 60 days.

Training

Do you recommend that racehorses be ridden in a track atmosphere every day for training?
No, I prefer some variety in terms of where they are trained.

Do you recommend that horses be rested prior to a race?
Yes, two days—but remember I train Quarter Horses.

General

What areas of equine nutrition do you feel most need further research?
I'd say the area of supplementation, i.e. vitamin and mineral.

What are the physical characteristics that a well fed horse displays?
Carry some weight, be fit and stout looking, with no ribs showing.

What are the danger signs that show an inadequate feeding program?
A depressed horse and poor performance.

Do most horsemen have a good knowledge of equine nutrition?
Many people do, but some don't know how to feed a horse.

Comments

Provide a well balanced feed, and feed exactly on time every day. You need to be consistent over a period of time to get, and keep, the horse as healthy as you can.

Mike Robbins

Mike Robbins began his racing career as a groom and exercise rider. He made his debut at the major tracks in 1977, and in the early 1980's he convinced Tom Neff to allow him to train some horses that Neff did not have time to train. Mike Robbins established himself as a leading trainer and never looked back.

The horses Robbins has trained include Sgt. Pepper Feature, which won the Golden State Futurity, and as a three-year-old, won the Golden State, Dash For Cash, and Los Alamitos Derbies and was named Champion Three-year-old. Robbins brought him back as a four-year-old, and with wins in the Los Alamitos Championship and the Champion of Champions, Sgt Pepper Feature was named World Champion, Champion Aged Horse, and Champion Aged Gelding. The filly Dashs Dream won several major races for Robbins, including the All American Derby, and was named World Champion, Champion Three-year-old, and Champion Three-year-old Filly. At four, she was named Champion Aged Mare. Robbins also trained First Down Dash, which had several major wins, and Special Leader, which won the All American Gold Cup in 1991 and the 1991 Champion of Champions at Los Alamitos, and was named the 1991 World Champion, Champion Aged Horse, and Champion Aged Stallion.

Robbins' ability as a horseman is clearly illustrated by the fact his horses stay sound, healthy, and winning year after year.

The interview...

Grains

Do you use processed grains, such as rolled or steamed, as opposed to whole natural grains?

Yes, my horses seem to digest processed grains better.

What method of processing would you recommend for oats and corn?
I recommend rolled oats and cracked corn.

What are the advantages and disadvantages of corn and oats?
Corn helps to keep the unwanted points of the teeth worn down
and it's high in nutrition. However, it may mold during storage.
Oats are high in nutrition and a good source of fiber. The only disadvantage of oats would be buying an inferior oat.

*Are there any particular geographic regions that excel in the produc-
tion of grains?*
We prefer that ours come from the northern regions.

Commercially Prepared Horse Feeds

*Have you found commercial feed mixes from reputable companies to
be consistently high in quality?*
Yes.

*What is the best method to judge the quality of a commercial horse
feed?*
Percent protein in the feed, and the overall look, smell, and feel of it.

*When is it worthwhile to have a commercial mill prepare feeds to
your formula?*
When you have a large number of horses in your care.

Is sweet feed more advantageous to feed in winter months?
Yes.

Is sweet feed a poor feed in summer months?
No.

Are pelleted feeds advantageous to feed?
Not in my opinion.

*Are pelleted forages an adequate substitute for loose forage (such as
pasture or hay)?*
No, I think you lose a certain amount of nutrition by processing
any type of forage.

What are the advantages and disadvantages of feeding hay cubes?
I just don't like them. Some horses won't eat cubes.

*Are horses that are fed pelleted feeds more prone to choke, crib, or
chew wood?*
I have had no experience with these problems.

Forages
Hay

What hays do you feed?
Alfalfa and coastal.

Why do you feed these?
Alfalfa is high in protein and energy. Coastal provides fiber.

Are there other kinds you would prefer if they were available locally?
Timothy.

Which cutting do you prefer?
Any cutting besides the first one. The first cutting is likely to be more weedy and have higher traces of fertilizer than later cuttings.

How do you judge the quality of hay?
By the way it feels and smells, and the overall look.

From where do you like hay to come?
New Mexico.

What methods do you use to feed hay?
We feed alfalfa on the ground, and coastal in a hay bag.

Do you recommend feeding hay free-choice or in measured amounts?
I like to feed hay in measured amounts.

What are the advantages of mixing grasses and legumes together?
More variety in nutrition.

What problems can arise if a horse doesn't receive adequate forage?
Besides providing nutrition, adequate hay tends to prevent boredom in the stall. Also, horses can survive on hay or grass alone. They probably would not survive on oats or corn alone.

Pasture

Do you have "rest periods" where you turn your racehorses out on pasture?
Yes.

How much time do you allow them to graze?
All day.

What kind of pasture grass do you prefer?
Coastal.

Is there a danger from toxic weeds if pastures are well cultivated?
The danger in this situation is minimal.

Supplementation
Vitamin and Mineral

> *If a horse is receiving a high quality, well balanced diet, do you think vitamin or mineral supplementation is necessary?*
> No.

> *Do horses need a trace mineralized salt source?*
> Yes. I like trace mineralized salt added to the feed.

> *What is the advantages of supplementing vitamin E to the racehorse?*
> It's advantageous for horses that have been stressed.

> *Can vitamin E supplementation enhance performance and fertility?*
> It can benefit them.

> *Do you supplement vitamin E?*
> It's in the supplement that I feed.

> *Are injectable supplements superior to oral supplements?*
> No.

> *Do you feel most horsemen oversupplement or undersupplement their horses?*
> I think most oversupplement.

Electrolytes

> *Are electrolytes helpful if given before and/or after a race?*
> I have had better results after racing.

> *How do you provide electrolytes?*
> I add them to the feed and water.

Protein and Protein Supplements

> *Can excesses of protein be harmful and negatively affect performance?*
> Excess protein tends to dull them, as does excessive vitamin supplementation.

> *Does protein supplementation increase muscle mass?*
> Not to my knowledge.

Added Fat

> *Do you think adding fat to feed rations is beneficial?*
> Yes, I add corn oil to the ration.

> *How can a horse benefit from having fat added to the diet?*
> They tend to burn off a lot of body fat, so it helps them maintain their body condition better.

Drugs

Are drugs being abused in horse racing?
No.

Does Lasix really help bleeders?
Yes.

How do stimulants affect a horse's health and appetite?
They can make the horse go off its feed.

Management

Feeding

Does the training stress placed on racehorses increase their need for protein, energy, or vitamins and minerals?
Yes, because training and racing depletes the body of those nutrients.

How do you provide the extra energy that a racehorse needs as compared to a horse doing light work or no work?
I add more energy, vitamins and minerals to the rations of the horses that are working harder.

Do you change your feeding program as a race draws near?
No.

What factors do you think are most important in planning and preparing a balanced ration?
Having a good ratio of grains, minerals, and additives in the ration.

What can be done to increase the palatability of a ration?
More molasses or less, and any other flavor that they like.

Do you feed bran mashes?
Sometimes, because some horses don't digest dry feed as well as others.

What is the major reason that causes a horse to be a "hard keeper"?
Mainly nervousness.

Are there any special feeds or supplements you feed "hard keepers"?
No.

How many times a day do you feed?
I feed three times a day.

At what times of the day do you feed?
5:00 A.M., 11:00 A.M., and 5:00 P.M.

Do you feed equal portions at each feeding?
No, I feed half the ration at the 11:00 A.M. feeding.

If a horse does not eat, how long do you leave the feed in front of him?
As long as it takes; some eat slower than others.

How do you encourage a horse to drink more water if it is consuming inadequate amounts?
By adding more salt to the ration.

What management practices would you recommend to avoid colic and laminitis?
A good diet of high quality feed and hay. We also have very close supervision of the horses by experienced people.

Are there special times when water should be withheld from the horse?
I prefer to give them smaller amounts prior to racing.

Basic Care

What type of bedding do you prefer in stalls?
I prefer wood shavings.

How often do you have horses' teeth checked and floated?
Twice a year.

What types of inoculations do you have done on your horses?
I vaccinate my horses for Rhino, Venezuelan equine encephalomyelitis, and anything else recommended by my veterinarian.

Do you have any blood analyses done?
Yes

When do you have these performed?
After racing or when one is down (has a depressed performance).

What do you look for in a blood test?
A balanced overall result.

Parasite Control

How frequently do you recommend deworming, and by what method?
We tube worm about every ninety days.

Would you recommend the dewormers that are fed on a daily basis?
Not really, because when we tube worm them, we know they are getting all the medicine.

Is it essential that horses get tube dewormed, or are there other methods that are just as effective?
I feel they should be tube dewormed at least twice a year.

What is the most practical method for preventing the spread of parasites in pastures?
Rotating the pastures.

Training

Do you use a scientific training program?
I use my own scientific training program, which is the old fashion way updated.

Do you recommend that racehorses be ridden in a track atmosphere every day for training?
No.

Do you recommend that horses be rested prior to a race? If so, how long?
Some, one to two days, but I train Quarter Horses.

General

What areas of equine nutrition do you feel most need further research?
I would like to see more research with vitamins and minerals.

What are the physical characteristics that a well fed horse displays?
A good hair coat, good feet, and overall good health.

What are the danger signs that show an inadequate feeding program?
A failing appearance.

Do you think most horse people have a good knowledge of equine nutrition?
No.

If there are any comments on the care or feeding of horses that you would like to add, please feel free to do so.
I think many horsemen tend to feed too many supplements. A good balanced ration should contain all the nutrients the horse needs.

Tom Ivers

 Tom Ivers, of Vevay, Indiana, is an alumnus of the pre-med program at Ohio Wesleyan University and is a member of the American College of Sportsmedicine, the American Association for Equine Sportsmedicine, and the Second and Third International Conferences on Equine Exercise Physiology. He is also the physiology lab director at Celestial Acres, in Oklahoma City, and the Thoroughbred sportsmedicine lab director at Westerly training Center in Santa Ynez, California.

Mr. Ivers has made a significant contribution to the field of equine sportsmedicine. He has written several books on this subject, including *The Fit Racehorse, Equine Sportsmedicine News, The Science of Arabian Racing*, and *The Racehorse Owner's Survival Manual*, and he was a contributing author to *Equine Sportsmedicine*. He has also produced several popular videos on race training. *(Contact Equine Research, Inc. for information on obtaining Mr. Ivers' books and videos.)*

Mr. Ivers has also written columns for *Equine Practice, Horse and Rider, Horse Care*, and *Modern Horse Breeder*. Articles by or about Mr. Ivers have appeared in *Equus, Hoof Beats, The Blood-Horse, The Quarter Horse Journal, The Thoroughbred Record*, and many others.

In the role of consultant, Mr. Ivers has used his expertise in exercise design and implementation, sportsmedicine laboratory design, racehorse nutrition, shoeing/biomechanics, gait analysis, infrared thermography, Standardized Exercise Testing, high speed treadmill testing and exercise, and bone density analysis. He has also done hundreds of consultations on winning racehorses, and horses conditioned with his interval training techniques have won more than eight million dollars.

In addition to these accomplishments, Mr. Ivers has fourteen years of experience training Standardbreds, Thoroughbreds, and Quarter Horses. He is also the owner of Equine Racing Systems, Inc., which sells hi-tech scales, heartrate monitors, high speed treadmills, and other sportsmedicine products for the horse racing market.

The interview...

Grains

What method of processing would you recommend for oats and corn?
I recommend rolled oats and cracked corn.

What are the advantages and disadvantages of feeding corn?
Corn has a more concentrated carbohydrate. You can feed less
weight per bulk for the equivalent nutrient value of oats. As a disadvantage, corn can be difficult to chew for horses with bad teeth.

What are the advantages and disadvantages of oats?
Oats are universally palatable—I have never seen a horse refuse
oats. But, in general, oats are low in energy value, and the quality
varies greatly—some oats are all husk. However, the new Pennuda
variety (naked oats) has a high nutrient value.

What is your biggest concern when feeding the racehorse?
My biggest concern, in the hard-working horse, is that energy intake support the workload. One of the easiest ways to improve racing performance of just-claimed Thoroughbreds is to increase
their energy intake. We've found that most are underfed soluble
carbohydrates and go into a race glycogen deficient. Under these
circumstances, the horse tends to "fade" at the end of even a short
sprint. In a near all-out one to two minute race, the horse doesn't
have time to mobilize fuels that are stored remotely; only fuels
packed into muscle cells or circulating in the blood can provide
racing energy. The job of the conditioner/nutritionist is to ensure
as many racing muscle cells as possible are packed with glycogen.

How can you obtain a quick performance improvement?
A quick performance improvement can be had simply by increasing the energy in the ration, either by feeding more pounds of
grain each day, or by changing the mix toward more energy dense
grains such as corn, barley, or Pennuda oats.

An additional, longer term improvement can be achieved by increasing the day-to-day race-specific workload so that larger numbers of
muscle cells are recruited during exercise, resulting in an eventual
supercompensation that will enable the horse to maintain high
speeds for longer distances. This additional exercise must be supported with additional carbohydrate intake.

Can the additional energy intake be provided by oats?
We have found that at a certain point you simply cannot stuff enough
oats into a horse in a day to supply the necessary energy.

Without adequate energy supplies, the hard-working racehorse not only tires in competition, but becomes progressively muscle-sore. Unfortunately, the damaged muscle cells are those the horse uses for racing, so it becomes weaker and loses firepower. Once a racehorse goes into training, it should never lose weight, but gain, instead. If the appropriate exercise is being delivered, the weight gained will be lean muscle mass—the racing motor and its fuel.

Are there problems with feeding an energy-rich diet?

Certainly there are problems associated with feeding energy-rich diets. Changes in diet must be effected gradually in order that the digestive system accommodate them. Otherwise, loose bowels, scours, and digestive tract acidity develop–one reason for free-choice grass hay. Feeding must be spread out over the day–perhaps four feedings of equal portions. No huge meal at night unless colic is the goal.

How do you deal with high-energy racehorses?

Racehorses full of energy can be a handful. Because we do so little work with racehorses in training, trainers tend to dislike the energized horse, the "hot" horse, and want to starve him back into submission. The better solution is to burn that excess energy daily, through exercise.

How important is protein in the diet of the racehorse?

Protein is an important nutritional concern for racehorses. Equine research is beginning to catch up to human research in this area, with excellent equine research teams investigating the impact of feeding different configurations of protein. Feeding protein is not just a matter of adding soybean meal to a feed. Protein is made up of amino acids, and these must be properly balanced.

It is becoming clear in my mind that feeding more protein, *of precisely the right kind,* is going to be important in the years to come–at least in racehorses.

By what means do you think this added protein will be provided?

While it's the job of science to be conservative and exhaustively analytical in its pronouncements, the job of the horse trainer and the athletic coach is to innovate, often through the use of sometimes obscure scientific knowledge. Today, amino acid concoctions are being administered to many racehorses via the needle. This approach is certainly more expensive and more dangerous than if adequate nutritional information about these substances were available to all and more commercial feed manufacturers were formulating better protein supplements.

According to the research group at the Swedish University in

Uppsala, proteins, in particular certain amino acids, "steer" muscle cell metabolism. It appears that feeding certain ratios of amino acids prior to exercise can affect the way muscle cells burn fuel, which fuels are burned, and the dynamics of lactic acid and ammonia production.

Amino acids are the building blocks of proteins; when protein is digested, it is broken down into amino acids. When protein is digested, the body produces the amino acids it needs and keeps a balance. When amino acids are fed separately, a temporary imbalance can be created. Such an imbalance, properly implemented, may be beneficial on race day.

There is a lot of research being conducted throughout the world on the uses of specific amino acids. What does all this mean? Nothing, yet. Someday, though, I think amino acid intake is going to be a very important part of race preparation, probably training as well. Keep your eye on alanine.

Commercially Prepared Horse Feeds

Have you found commercial feed mixes from reputable companies to be consistently high in quality?

Yes—but that depends on the regional mill manufacturing the feed.

What is the best method for judging the quality and usefulness of a commercial horse feed?

Total Digestible Nutrients. Laboratory analysis (down to micronutrients and trace minerals) to compare against the label. You're looking for a solid basic ration—not one that tries to cover all the bases. From that point you can supplement.

When is it worthwhile to have a commercial mill prepare feeds to your own formula?

I doubt that it is worthwhile. Unless you're an equine nutritionist, you'll miss important details. The basic ration must be properly balanced. Savings are not worth the potential for error.

Is sweet feed more advantageous to feed in winter months?

No. Sweet feed is equally important year round.

Are pelleted feeds advantageous to feed?

They can be. In general, they are highly digestible. But you can't "hide" supplements as well in them (after pelleting), and some horses refuse them, or take a mouthful over to the water bucket and slosh it around for moisture—this mucks up the water bucket.

Are pelleted forages an adequate substitute for loose forage (such as pasture or hay)?

My experience is that they are.

What are the advantages and disadvantages of feeding hay cubes?
The advantages are that there is less waste, they are easier to handle, and there is less spoilage. The disadvantages are inconsistencies in quality and processing.

Are horses fed pelleted feeds more prone to choke or crib?
Choke, no; cribbing, yes.

Are there any advantages to extruded feeds?
Yes, they contain more Total Digestible Nutrients per pound.

Forages

Hay

What hays do you feed?
Alfalfa and timothy. Alfalfa has a higher protein/mineral value, and timothy has bulk value. In racehorses, I try to obtain my basic ration constituents from grain, using hay more as a supplement and digestive aid. Unless you test several bales from each load of hay, nutrient contents are quite variable and therefore unknown.

How do you judge the quality of hay?
Hay should be green, with no dust, weeds, mold, or foreign material; the stems should have moisture and be chewable.

What is the best method of feeding hay?
Feed hay on the ground. This keeps resulting dust low, out of circulation, and out of the horse's lungs.

Do you recommend feeding hay free-choice or in measured amounts?
Free-choice.

What types of problems can arise if a horse does not receive adequate forage (hay or pasture)?
Stable vices: cribbing, stall walking, grain gobbling. Gastric disturbances: colic, acid buildup, and ulcers. Saliva is a buffer, and chewing hay moves buffer into the digestive system. Gut flora is maintained at normal levels. Bulk keeps the digestive tract moving.

Grazing and Turn-out

How important is pasture to the equine of today?
It is extremely important for the mental well-being of horses.

How much time do you allow your horses to graze?
As much as possible—minimum, 2 hours.

Do you keep any horses on pasture 24 hours a day?
Yes. But be careful in the spring, when rich new grass can overwhelm the digestive tract and cause founder.

Vitamin and Mineral Supplementation

If a horse is receiving a high quality well balanced diet, is vitamin or mineral supplementation necessary?
The scientific advice would be a conservative "adequately balanced ration and no supplements." But the high performance athlete's needs differ from the ordinary animal's. Because little has been published in the lay press other than the conservative view, most racehorses are receiving their vitamin supplements the expensive and dangerous way: via the needle.

Whether these injections are beneficial is a relatively unexplored question, but it is clear from basic research that there is a place for supplementation of free-radical scavengers, like vitamins E and C, in hard-working horses. Vitamin B complex seems to increase appetite in some horses. There are hundreds of vitamin, mineral, and micro-nutrient concoctions for sale, each with claims that may determine which, if any, are useful in improving and maintaining peak performance in a money-earning athlete.

There is reason to believe that nutritional supplementation can result in a wide variety of performance-affecting consequences, some beneficial, others not.

Drugs

How do you feel about drug use and regulation for racehorses?
Drug regulations and enforcements vary from jurisdiction to jurisdiction. Recently, "milkshakes" have been banned in some racing locales which allow Lasix, Bute, and other pre-race preparations that are obviously designed to improve racing performance. In my mind, there is a difference between milkshakes and medications that should be universally banned for the safety of horses and riders, as well as for the level playing field the betting public would like to see.

What about the "ergogenic aids" mentioned in some of the sports-medicine literature?
In human sport, there are some drugs, and some nutrients, that are known as "ergogenic aids," performance enhancing chemicals. For example, corn is an ergogenic aid for most Thoroughbreds and Quarterhorses attempting to survive on straight oats and a dozen different additives. Not only that, but extra corn, fed four days out from a race, will give an added boost to the racehorse in a process known as "glycogen loading." This is legal and it should be.

Blood buffering is another ergogenic technique that has made its way from human athletics to equine competition. Essentially, buffers, like sodium bicarbonate, are fed in enough quantity that the blood pH is affected by perhaps a tenth of a point rise by racetime. Fatigue during the race will be delayed slightly, as with glycogen loading, and the horse may gain a few lengths on the competition at the finish. In both cases, nutrients are being used to improve racing performance.

There are dozens of other nutrients being sold with the idea that they are ergogenic aids, from bee pollen to DMG. While tubing a horse with large quantities of bicarbonate and sugar on race day may be a bit draconian when a 4-day regimen of carbohydrate loading and blood buffering through the feed could easily be accomplished, it still represents the delivery of nutrients, not drugs. If milkshakes are banned, then so should all the other supposed nutritional perfor-mance enhancers out there, including corn, which will make a far bigger difference than milkshakes.

General Comment

The most promising vitamin and mineral supplements now being studied extensively are the anti-oxidants. These accelerate healing and tend to help alleviate sorenesses and inflammations. Horse-men must be careful mixing a variety of vitamin and mineral supplements with an already adequate basic ration. In general, there is too much overall supplementation going on in racing stables, with various products adding together to deliver megadoses of the wrong chemicals.

The nutritional marketplace is populated with exotic nutritional supplements. These include DMG, MSM, Bee Pollen, Royal Jelly, DMSO, Chondroitin Sulfate, digestive enzymes, gut flora, blood buffers, glycogen loaders, and many others. There are dozens of exuberant stories that go with each. Most are harmless. If you are going to try these substances, do so as scientifically as possible. Se-lect a group of horses, use one additive at a time, change no other factors, take appropriate steps to test the results, and draw your own conclusions until better scientific evidence is available.

My advice is to get in touch with a knowledgable, up-to-date equine nutritionist and formulate a complete basic ration, with supplements available for certain circumstances you're likely to encounter in a stable of high performance athletes. If every horse in the barn is being fed the same thing every day, you're not really paying attention to the actual needs of your athletes. And you're probably wasting money.

Darolyn Butler

Darolyn Butler, of Humble, Texas (Houston area) is a highly competitive and successful endurance rider. She has ridden 184 races, 72 of which she has won, and her horses have been awarded Best Condition 45 times. She has accumulated nearly 12,000 miles of riding.

After years of competing in western shows and rodeos, Darolyn's introduction to endurance riding came in 1981 when she entered and rode in the Tevis Cup. Since then, Darolyn has won four National Championships (including the 1991 Family Championship, awarded to the family who rides the most miles together in sanctioned American Endurance Ride Conference competitions). She rides with her husband, Pat French, and her two daughters Ceci and Rima. Darolyn has also successfully completed four international endurance competitions, including Austria in 1985 and Carson City, Nevada in 1991. In 1987, she won the individual bronze medal and was a member of the gold medal team at the North American Championship in Front Royal, Virginia.

Since 1983, Darolyn has produced numerous equestrian training videos and event coverages. She and her husband produce and market the *Horseman Video,* a quarterly video magazine. They also produce a 30-minute nationally broadcast television show, called *The Horse Show.*

Darolyn also holds endurance clinics, writes training articles, and has produced a screenplay on the ultimate endurance race. She is also preparing an endurance training book.

The interview...

Grains

Do you recommend using processed grains or whole natural grains?
I recommend using processed grains.

What method of processing would you recommend for oats and corn?
I recommend rolled or steamed oats and chopped corn.

What are the advantages and disadvantages of oats and corn?
Oats are readily available, and are reasonably priced in most areas. Oats have the lowest digestible energy concentration and the lowest weight per volume of all common grains. This makes oats safe because they are less likely to be overfed. A complication is the quality of oats vary more compared to other grains, with the result that energy yield can vary from region to region depending on the crop and the year of harvest.

It is important that a horse not be fed by giving X amount of oats for energy and Y amount of hay for protein. Each part of the ration contributes to nutritional categories. So, although oats may have lower energy than corn, they have a higher and better quality protein content. Crimped or roiled oats can improve their energy availability by 7–10%, thus there is more nutritional value derived.

Corn has a higher digestible energy content than oats, and so needs more care in its feeding. Instead of being the "hot" feed that some people consider it, corn will actually produce less heat than oats when the weights of the two are adjusted so that similar amounts of digestible energy are being fed. This is because the higher fiber content of oats can also be utilized to produce heat.

Are there regions that excel in the production of certain grains?
The Midwest states, Iowa, Nebraska, and Kansas, are the primary producers of the best corn, while oats range over the U.S.

Commercially Prepared Horse Feeds

Have you found commercial feed mixes from reputable companies to be consistently high in quality?
Commercially prepared feeds by reputable companies have proven to be adequate for day to day feeding or off season feeding. However, during heavier months of endurance competition, I prefer to mix my own feed, which is a combination of oats and corn and perhaps a small amount of sweet feed for palatability.

What is the best method for judging the quality and usefulness of a commercial horse feed?
The best way to judge sweet feed is simply to read the ingredients and watch your horse's weight gain and bloom. A great deal of protein is not needed in the diet of a long distance horse. Carbohydrates are more important.

Is it worthwhile to have a mill prepare feeds to your own formula?
It would be worth having your own formula milled if you were

feeding as many as 5 to 10 competition horses. However, most people seldom have more than 3 or 4 distance horses in training, and it is economical to simply feed a proper balance of oats and corn yourself. I like the freedom to increase corn on heavy work days, and back off during the lighter days. You can only back off or increase **quantity** if you are feeding a pre-mixed commercial feed. Feeding your own combination really makes sense at those times.

Is sweet feed more advantageous to feed in winter months?
Winter months are probably the time I'm most apt to feed sweet feed. In hot, humid climates, one must be cautious that the feed doesn't spoil. Again, with endurance horses, you do not need this type of feed except a little bit as an occasional appetite enhancer.

Are pelleted feeds advantageous to feed?
I feel pelleted feeds are an absolute "no-no" for endurance horses. Distance horses need a tremendous amount of roughage in their system. Feeding a compact high volume feed like pellets is asking for trouble. It has been suggested that pelleted feeds may produce gas in an equine, and any kind of gastronomical distress for a competing distance horse can be debilitating, if not deadly.

Are pelleted forages an adequate substitute for loose forage?
Pelleted feeds are not close to being an adequate substitute for loose forage such as pasture or hay. Horses need roughage to keep the gut hydrated and moving during competition day. One of the criteria strictly monitored in endurance competition is gut sounds. If these are substantially decreased, the horse is observed and possibly delayed from continuing competition. If the gut sounds don't return to normal, the horse isn't allowed to continue. Riders depend on soupy grain mashes, good medium protein hay, and natural grass to keep a horse going for 50 to 100 miles in one day.

What are the advantages of and disadvantages of feeding hay cubes?
Hay cubes have an advantage as far as storing, both at home and traveling. I still feel that the athletic horse needs the natural roughage which he misses by eating the compacted hay cubes.

Are horses fed pelleted feeds more prone to crib or chew wood?
I believe that without adequate roughage in the diet, horses have more of a tendency to crib, chew wood, or pick up other stable vices. They need that chewing behavior for psychological reasons.

Are there any advantages to extruded feeds?
The new extruded feeds are very interesting, but I still think the endurance athlete needs natural grains and roughage in its diet to perform at maximum level.

Forages

Hay

What kind(s) of hay do you feed?

In Texas, our primary competition feed is improved bermuda or prairie hay. The west coast is fortunate to have oat hay, and many areas have an abundance of alfalfa. The high calcium content of alfalfa may be good for race day, but I believe some experts when they say a constant alfalfa diet inhibits natural production of calcium. They also don't need the excessive protein of alfalfa either.

Are there other kinds you would prefer if they were available locally?

I would use oat hay if it were available, as I think it is an excellent hay for our long distance horses. Timothy in other parts of the country would be acceptable as well.

Which cutting do you prefer?

There are many factors that play on the cuttings, such as weather, both preceding and at the time of cutting. We usually try to avoid the first cutting, as it may be weedier and stemmier than the second and third cuttings.

How do you judge the quality of hay?

I smell it, feel it, and take a good look at it. If it's dusty, smells, or looks moldy, you don't want any part of it. Baling hay is a science in itself, so be sure your hay supplier delivers properly cured, sweet smelling hay. The horses certainly can be credited with being good judges, too. Do they like it, eat it cheerfully , and seem to thrive on it? If so, chances are that it is good.

One word of warning, however. In certain parts of the U.S., mainly in Oklahoma, Texas, and Kansas, the blister beetle may be found in alfalfa hay. We have lost three good horses to this insect from different loads of hay, from different states. Less than a tablespoon of the beetles ingested can kill a 1,000 pound horse.

From what parts of the country do you like hay to come?

If I were to buy alfalfa, I would certainly prefer it to come from Colorado or areas that had not experienced the blister beetles. As far as bermuda and prairie grass hay, local is fine, as long as it is fertilized and baled under good conditions.

What is the best method of feeding hay?

There are pros and cons for several accepted ways. Haysacks are a necessary evil when travelling, both in the trailer and in stalls without hayracks. They work fine, but a certain amount of hay still ends up on the ground, and there's the chance that a pawing hoof can get tangled in a haysack that was not tied high enough or properly. Endurance riders contend with this often as their horses spend many nights tied to the trailer or in a small portable corral. Feeding on the ground at an endurance ride, providing the horse is free to move around, seems to be the safest method. If the horse is tied or on a tether, tie the haysack securely and high for the night.

Mangers and feed troughs, especially with pasture horses, seem to be ideal to cut down on trampled hay. However, one must be alert to water and rotten or moldy hay collecting in the trough.

Do you recommend feeding hay free-choice or in measured amounts?
Before, during, and after a long distance competition, our horses are offered free-choice hay. Normally, they don't eat that well on the road anyway, so I am anxious for them to keep as much roughage in their system as possible. At home after a particularly tough competition or trip, they are offered hay free-choice for a few days and then cut back to a measured amount morning and night.

What proportion of hay to concentrate is generally best for the endurance horse?
By weight, we feed a little over twice as much hay as grain, plus the pasture forage they are getting daily.

Grazing and Turn-out

How important is pasture to the equine of today?
I can't say enough about the advantages of allowing a competition horse to live and graze on good pasture. It's great for his psyche and his digestive tract. When possible at a competition, we pick a good grassy spot to park and corral the horses so they may continually graze. Be aware of different grasses or legumes like clover and alfalfa. Grazing on something that rich, or any really abundant green grass can produce a case of colic if the horse is not used to it.

The more time a horse is allowed to spend in pasture, the fewer stable vices he will develop. I truly believe a horse is much happier and healthier roaming over a few acres instead of caged in a box stall. Not everyone has ideal conditions to do that, but even a small area to roam in is better for the horse than being stalled.

Statistics have proven that the stalled horse has many more times the cases of colic than pastured horses. I attribute this to the constant movement of the gut of pastured horses, as well as to their being content about where they are.

Do you keep any horses on pasture 24 hours a day?
All our competition horses stay on pasture 24 hours a day.

What kind of pasture grass do you prefer?
In winter we normally have good rye grass, and in summer a fertilized bermuda. Any good native grass makes a great pasture and it certainly doesn't hurt to fertilize it regularly, either.

Is there a danger from toxic weeds if pastures are well cultivated?
There's always a danger of toxic weeds and a horse owner should visit with the county agent in his area to acquaint himself with what may be in his pasture that could be a problem.

Supplementation

Vitamin and Mineral Supplementation:

If a horse is receiving a high quality, well balanced diet, is vitamin or mineral supplementation is necessary?
I believe most serious horse owners over-supplement their horses, and most casual owners under-supplement. I believe a well balanced diet supplies most of the minerals and vitamins needed, unless they are depleted through competition and training. We are subjecting the long distance horse to maximum performance, and in many parts of the country the soil is deficient in some necessary minerals such as selenium. If that is indicated in your area, then get a reading on it from your county agent and administer the proper supplemental amounts. Overdoses of vitamin E can be especially harmful, so be cautious if you decide to supplement.

How do you feel about salt and mineral blocks?
All horses, and especially long distance competition horses, should have free access to salt and mineral blocks. We keep blocks out continually, but often break them off into small pieces or put loose salt out after long, hot competitions.

Can vitamin E supplementation actually enhance performance?
I don't feel oversupplementation of vitamin E will enhance a horse's performance, but a deficiency could certainly inhibit maximum performance and perhaps cause death by related maladies like tying up (azoturia) during or after competition.

Are any supplements particularly beneficial to an endurance horse?
We pre-load our horses on electrolytes starting 24 hours prior to major competitions, and dose them immediately before, throughout, and after the race. If it is especially hot and grueling, we may continue oral electrolyting for the next 24 to 48 hours. Then the horse should take up at the salt block where you left off.

Biotin is another supplement that has proven very helpful for weak hooves, but my ongoing favorite supplement is the Solid Gold®

brand of yucca and sea meal. I have been told to use a half table-spoon morning and night of each of these for the best results, and I use them faithfully on horses in tough competitive use, older horses, or horses with old injuries that may affect their performance. YeaSac® is a brewers yeast product that I have found very useful for good energy reserves on top competition horses as well.

Are injectable supplements superior to oral supplements?

Horse owners should stay away from injectable supplements. There is always a risk associated with invading the body with a needle and risking infections or abcesses. If the same effect can be produced with an oral supplement, that is the safest route.

Electrolytes

How do you provide electrolytes?

The best homemade recipe is a third/third/third mixture of Mortons table salt, lite salt, and calcium carbonate, or crushed limestone (**not lime**). This is relatively inexpensive and very effective. In humid areas, you might find it necessary to increase the calcium carbonate portion, especially if your horse has a tendency toward "thumps" (Synchronous Diaphragmatic Flutter).

Amounts given need to balance with the length of the competition, the temperature, humidity, toughness of the course, and the particular horse's needs. Some horses need twice to three times the amount of calcium carbonate as others.

If we mix these dry ingredients with peanut oil, it does three things: it makes the dose more palatable; it lubricates the inside lining of the mouth so it doesn't become so irritated after several hours or possibly days of intense electrolyting; it moistens these dry ingredients so they may be administered with a large syringe.

Recently, I have added dry animal fat to this mixture. It seems to give the horse an extra energy kick on race days. In addition, it makes the salt mixture a little creamier and it gives the horses an incredible shot of energy along with the peanut oil.

Not quite so expensive, but useful just as well, is regular vegetable cooking oil. This not only adds fat to the horse's diet, but it encourages good gut motility. This is especially needed on a tough race day. Many times a horse with slow gut sounds can be brought around by a few ounces of corn oil from a syringe.

Speaking of corn, if my horse will tolerate it in the summer, I prefer to feed corn as my best fat source throughout the year. However, some horses react with a high respiration rate during competition, so I may have to pull them off of it during the hot months.

Can electrolyte supplementation ever be harmful?

I've been told you can "pickle" a horse's stomach with too many electrolytes, but I have yet to see a horse suffering from an overdose. However, I have seen many who are suffering from dehydration due to not having enough electrolytes.

General Management

Feeding Horses

Do the conditioning stresses of endurance horses greatly increase their need for protein, energy, vitamins, or minerals?

Endurance conditioning and competition do put an inordinate amount of stress on the endurance athlete. When you are "draining the well" you must resupply it with what you are depleting. Protein is not a major concern, as they seem to get ample protein from the feedstuffs that afford them the fat and energy. However, a good commercial supplement is an excellent idea for a horse in heavy training or competition.

Do you change your feeding program as a ride draws nearer?

As the ride draws near, and the electrolyte loading starts, one really can't do a lot about feed loading without risking the animal's health, but one thing I found works well at the race sight is to keep hay in front of the horses at all times. I give them several small meals throughout the day prior to a big race, and one more feeding between 10:00 P.M. and 12:00 A.M., so they can snack through the evening and early morning hours if they like. The purpose is to keep them from getting hungry and eating a huge amount, which may encourage colic or over-fullness during the initial competition. If you keep the edge off their appetite and let them eat casually 12 to 24 hours before the race, they will have moderately full guts to pull energy and fluid from during the competition.

Do you feed bran mashes?

In many cases, getting the horse to eat may be a real problem at a competition. I'm convinced they should be eating as wet a bran mash as possible. I mix their normal feed ration, which for a top racer is usually two-thirds oats and one-third corn, with about the same amount of bran as corn. Add to this: slices of apples and carrots, one or two cups of sweet feed, about a half cup of vegetable oil, and water, until it's the consistency of soupy oatmeal. Try this at home, because some horses will need some introduction to this "souper grog" as I call it.

Now if you get to a ride and they refuse to eat any of this wonderfully prepared mixture, maybe go back to their normal dry or slightly damp ration. However, you won't be able to give him as much ration if it's dry or different than his normal food, or you will be asking for trouble. You may have to lead him to graze on green grass, as he needs something in his gut prior to competition.

Many people are surprised we feed our horses grain during competitions. They may not eat much during a quick (less than 4 hour) 50 miler, but at slower paces, or for a 100 miler, horses have been known to eat up to 20 pounds during the course of the competition. They need this energy and roughage in their gut to encourage gut motility, energy replacement, and continued re-hydration.

One of the advantages of the "souper grog" is that the horse uses none of his precious body fluids to re-hydrate the grain you may be feeding at the stops. Likewise, let them eat all the green grass they would like. There is no better natural hydrater and electrolyte source than good, green grass. You will see many experienced endurance riders allowing—even encouraging—their mounts to snatch bites of green as they move down the trail. They know those nibbles of grass at 40 miles will pay off 85 or 90 miles into the race.

One additional benefit we may be experiencing with the "souper grog" is that it seems to keep the sand cleansed out of our horses' systems. We occasionally have a case of sand colic in non-competition horses, but almost never in the horses that regularly compete and get the "souper grog."

How do you feed "hard keepers"?

I try to increase consumption of corn, perhaps moving it up to nearly half the ration. I also believe brewers yeast will put some extra body fat on them, or at least help utilization of their daily feed. Making sure their teeth are regularly floated is also important.

If nerves are the problem, one answer is to arrive at the ride sight a day or two early and let them settle down. Try to feed them relatively the same as at home, maybe even feed them in the same bucket. If the horse isn't drinking, bring water from home as well.

Saltiness from the electrolytes for 12 to 24 hours should encourage a horse to drink while traveling and at the ride sight. However, the old adage, "You can lead a horse to water, but you can't make him drink" was never more true. Many a horse has been pulled from competition because he wasn't drinking enough to stay hydrated.

There are horses that refuse to eat or drink for some time after electrolytes are administered. If so, I suggest rinsing the electrolyte residue from the mouth. Another method for starting them eating and drinking is to give them their most favorite snack, like an apple, carrot, or a bit of sweet feed. Once they start eating and rid themselves of the electrolyte taste, they will be ready to drink.

In an endurance competition you should allow the horse all the water he wants, as often as he wants it, as long as you're continuing to move. That is the key. The only exception would be after a fast finish when you may have an extremely hot horse. You might want to limit his initial drinking, but over the next 30 minutes to an hour he should be able to drink as much as he likes.

How do you arrange your feeding schedule?

We normally feed an equal portion twice a day, but as mentioned before, when traveling or at a ride site, I believe in giving several small meals so they have the gut filled up more evenly. Even though a tight schedule may be a problem when traveling, it's a good idea to stop at least every four hours for a stretch break for the horses and allow them to have a meal outside the trailer as close to their normal eating time as possible.

What changes should be made in the horse's diet after a competition?

The first 24 hours after a competition is the most effective time to re-energize, reload, and refuel a horse. People might think after he's through working it's time to back off. Not so, especially on a hard keeper. We continually keep the "souper grog" and good hay in front of them, as well as additional treats such as carrots and apples. If they don't eat the "souper grog" within a few hours, it seems to sour if it's warm, so you throw it away. With this in mind, it's wise to mix small increments and offer it again later.

In a few days, you may want to reduce the quantity of feed or perhaps just the ration of corn to oats, since the horse is now well on his way to bouncing back and you are not doing any heavy training for a few weeks. The same if he is ill or injured and must be laid up for a few weeks. He will keep his conditioning intact for up to six weeks, but you don't want to build a layer of blubber.

Basic Care

How do you bed stalls?

Our farm primarily uses shavings for stall bedding and trailer bedding. We seldom stall horses unless they are being kept up due to injury or illness. When stalled, about six to ten inches of shavings seem most satisfactory, and they are cleaned once or twice daily.

Putting shavings in the trailer has two benefits. It gives additional padding to the horse from the road jarring, and it eliminates the mess horses make when they urinate and defecate. The shavings absorb the urine and make the manure easier to remove.

How often do you have your horses' teeth checked and floated?
Once a year.

What vaccination program do you use?
Our horses are inoculated once a year. They are inoculated against Rhino, flu, VEE, tetanus, and occasional rabies and strangles if we feel it is necessary. The traveling competition horses receive all of the above on a yearly schedule or on our veterinarian's recommendation. All horses on the property are Coggins tested at least once a year.

Do you have any blood analyses performed?
We only run blood analyses if we have an undiagnosable problem or if a horse has tied up and we want to see how much tissue damage has taken place.

What do you look for in a blood test?
In the case of a horse that has tied up, we look for waste products in the form of muscle enzymes which are produced when tissue breaks down. In other cases, such as listlessness, poor hair coat, or poor behavior, we check the red and white blood cell count.

Parasite Control

How frequently do you deworm, and by what method?
The Gulf Coast area is so moist and warm that parasite control is a serious problem. Until Strongid C® (a daily fed dewormer) came on the market, we tube dewormed once a year and paste dewormed four to six times a year. Now we feel confident to tube deworm once a year and paste, perhaps once, six months later.

Would you recommend the daily fed dewormer?
We are sold on the daily dewormer and have seen excellent results in the 18 months we have used it. The horses seem to thrive on it, and they utilize their feed much better.

Is it essential to tube deworm?
I believe that a good daily dewormer and rotating two different paste dewormers twice in a year is quite adequate.

What is the most practical method for preventing the spread of parasites in pastures?
Good pasture rotation, allowing a pasture to rest, and picking up the manure in a pasture are the best methods of preventing the spread of parasites.

Training

Are your horses worked every day?

I feel long distance horses are many times the victims of over training. When initially conditioning a horse, three times a week at
around 5 to 10 miles a day is plenty of riding. Eventually build the
mileage up to at least one 20-mile ride per week. At that point, you
could start competition.

Do you recommend that horses be rested prior to competition?

If a horse is doing at least one 50-mile competition every 4to 6
weeks, a week's rest after a competition is suggested. A person
could ride the horse three times a week, but twice would probably
be adequate to maintain condition, and to build endurance.

Experts have said that once a horse reaches peak condition, he
loses very little for six weeks if he does nothing at all. We have
found this to be true of our seasoned horses and are amazed at
how little continual conditioning they need if brought along correctly and competed on regularly.

We do rest them slightly the week before a competition, but give
them a bit of a ride the day prior to the race after arriving at the
ride site. They get about a week's rest upon completing the race.

General

What areas of equine nutrition do you feel need further research?

It would be interesting to see controlled research on energy producing foods and supplements.

What are the physical characteristics that a well fed horse displays?

A well fed horse displays a shiny coat, smooth muscling, strong
healthy hooves, clear eyes, and a good disposition.

What are the danger signs that show inadequate feeding?

If I notice a horse whose ribs are beginning to show, yet he's not
being ridden that hard, or if he has a dull and lifeless hair coat, I
know I have some sort of feeding problem. Perhaps he is just not
getting enough or is deficient in something.

Do you think most people have good knowledge of equine nutrition?

I feel most people still have a lot to learn about nutrition for their
horses. The commercial feed companies with their glamour ads
and their "Easy to Feed XYZ Brand" attitudes have spoiled people
into letting them do their thinking and ration planning for them.
Granted, they are much better equipped to do so, and their products are excellent, but the bottom line is most of the American
public is taking their word for it.

Clark Bradley

Clark Bradley has been a professional horse trainer since 1966, and has exhibited horses in almost every type of Quarter Horse competition. He has won the National Reining Horse Association Futurity twice, the All-American Quarter Horse Congress Versatility four times, the Congress Jr. and Sr. Reining twice, the Congress Team Roping three times, the Congress Two-year-old Pleasure Futurity, and many other awards, too numerous to list.

Mr. Bradley now operates a training stable in Richmond, Virginia, where he offers a program for open and futurity horses. He also holds very successful horsemanship schools for amateurs and youth.

Mr. Bradley serves as honorary director of the Ohio Quarter Horse Association. He is past president and now a board member of the National Reining Horse Association, and is a member of the Show and Contest Committee of the American Quarter Horse Association. He is also an A.Q.H.A. and N.R.H.A. judge and has judged throughout the United States and Europe.

The interview...

Grains

Would you recommend using processed grains (such as rolled or steamed) as opposed to whole natural grains?

Yes, because they are more easily digested.

What method of processing would you recommend for oats and corn?

For oats, crimping. For corn, coarse cracking or steam rolling

What are the advantages of processing oats and corn?

Processing improves digestibility by cracking the kernel.

Are there any particular geographic regions which excel in the production of certain grains?

Oats–northern United States and Sweden.

Commercially Prepared Horse Feeds

Have you found commercial feed mixes from reputable companies to be consistently high in quality?
Yes.

What is the best method for judging the quality and usefulness of a commercial horse feed?
Read the feed tag. Or if the feed is not pelleted, quality can be determined by visually examining the grains.

When is it worthwhile (in terms of cost) to have a commercial mill prepare your own feeds to your formula?
If you have a good formula, you can study costs (corn vs. oats) and change the ratio of grains to make it cheaper per ton.

Is sweet feed more advantageous to feed in winter months?
Not necessarily. Molasses is good for controlling dust and for some horses it is more appetizing, but it doesn't produce more heat.

Are pelleted feeds advantageous to feed?
They may be more digestible and cause less waste and sifting with some horses.

Are pelleted forages an adequate substitute for loose forage?
When forages are pelleted, the hay is harvested earlier, so there is a higher moisture, protein, and vitamin content. However, you cannot look at the pellet or cube and determine the quality of the hay used.

Forages
Hay

What hays do you feed?
Alfalfa and alfalfa/grass mix.

Why do you feed these?
It is available, the horses eat it well, and they stay in excellent condition.

Are there other kinds you would prefer if they were available locally?
No.

Which cutting do you prefer?
I prefer the second, third, or fourth cutting, because there is less stem and fewer weeds.

How do you judge the quality of your hay?
Color, smell, and lab analysis.

From what parts of the country do you like to purchase your hay?
We feed locally grown hay because of availability, and it is very good quality.

What is the best method of feeding hay?
Any common sense method is fine, but I normally feed it on the ground.

Do you recommend feeding hay free-choice or in measured amounts?
Measured amounts.

What are the advantages of mixing grasses and legumes for stabled horses?
Straight legumes may be too high in protein and other nutrients.

What types of behavioral and gastric problems can arise if a horse does not receive adequate forage (hay or pasture)?
The horse may start to crib, weave, or kick. In terms of gastric problems— colic.

Pasture

How much time do you allow your horses to graze?
Horses in training and show horses are turned out for about an hour a day, but it is more to keep them mentally happy than for nutrition.

Do you keep any horses on pasture 24 hours a day?
Yes.

What special care do these horses need?
Nutritionally, older horses need no special care, but colts and yearlings need some grain.

What kind of pasture grass do you prefer?
Bluegrass.

How many acres per horse is minimal for pasture?
That depends on the location.

Is there a danger from toxic weeds if pastures are well cultivated?
No, not in my area.

Supplementation
Vitamin and Mineral

If a horse is receiving a high quality, well balanced diet, is vitamin or mineral supplementation necessary?
I think so.

Do horses need a trace mineralized salt source or just a salt source?
Both.

Do you prefer to feed trace mineralized salt free-choice or in measured amounts?
Free-choice.

Can vitamin E supplementation enhance performance and fertility, and benefit the highly stressed horse?
Yes.

Do you supplement vitamin E?
Yes.

Can excesses of vitamin E be harmful?
Yes.

Are there any supplements you feel are particularly beneficial to a performance horse?
No.

Are injectable supplements superior to oral supplements?
The only advantage is that you know that the horse received the supplement and did not sort it out of the feed.

Are there risks in administering injectable supplements routinely?
Abcesses.

Do most horsemen oversupplement or undersupplement their horses?
Show horse owners oversupplement; non-show horse owners undersupplement.

Electrolytes

Are electrolytes helpful?
Only if they are needed. I only use them on long trips, in very hot weather, or when the horses are not drinking well.

How do you provide your horses with electrolytes?
I add it in powder form to the water or feed. If the horse is really stressed, I have a veterinarian administer them intravenously.

Protein and Protein Supplements

Do you think the use of commercial protein supplements is worthwhile?
Yes.

Which oilseed meal protein supplement do you prefer?
I prefer soybean meal because of availability and cost.

Can excesses of protein be harmful and negatively affect performance?
Yes.

Management
Feeding

How do training stresses affect performance horses?
It increases their need for energy, vitamins, and minerals.

In what ways do you provide the extra energy that a performance horse needs as compared to a horse doing light work?
I feed more grain.

Do you feed bran mashes?
No.

What types of problems, which are correctable, *are most likely to cause a horse to be a "hard keeper"?*
Being wormy or having bad teeth.

Are there any special feeds or supplements you feed "hard keepers"?
No.

How many times a day do you feed?
Normally twice a day. Three times a day for horses needing more weight.

At what times of the day do you feed?
8 A.M. and 4:30 P.M.

Do you feed equal portions at each feeding?
Yes.

What changes should be made in the horse's diet when its activity level is increased or decreased, or when it is ill or injured?
More grain as training increases, less as they are rested. Ill or injured horses–feed them enough to allow them to feel good.

Is it better to change the feed ration routinely, or is it better to stick with a proven formula?
Stick with the same one, but be sure that it is a good formula.

If the horse does not eat, how long do you leave the feed in front of it?
Half a day.

What management practices would you recommend to avoid colic and laminitis?
Feed adequate amounts of quality forage, feed on a regular schedule, and use good quality feed.

Are there any special times when water should be withheld from horses?
Only when they are really hot; then they should be allowed only a few sips at a time.

Basic Care

What type of bedding do you prefer in your stalls?
Sawdust/shavings mix.

How often do you have horses teeth checked and floated?
Every six months.

What types of inoculations do you have done on your horses?
Flu, rhino—every 60 days. Tetanus, Potomac fever, Eastern and
Western Encephalomyelitis—annually.

Do you have blood analyses done?
Only if the horse has a problem.

Parasite Control

How frequently do you recommend deworming, and by what method?
Every 60 days–we tube deworm twice a year and use ivermectin the
rest of the time. We recently tried Strongid C® with good results.

Would you recommend Strongid C®?
Yes. I have used it on six horses (three growing and three in heavy
training) for the last four months. All of them look great and I have
been able to decrease their grain intake.

*Is it essential that horses be tube dewormed periodically, or are there
other methods which are just as effective?*
Yes, we do tube deworm because you are sure that all the medicine
gets into the stomach.

*What is the most practical method for preventing the spread of para-
sites in pastures?*
Only put recently dewormed horses on pasture and do not over-
graze the pasture.

Training

Are your horses worked every day?
No, five days a week.

Should horses be rested occasionally from competition?
We try to rest all of our horses every 60 to 90 days.

General

What are the physical characteristics that a well fed horse displays?
He is bright, alert, and his hair coat is in good condition.

What are the danger signs that show an inadequate feeding program?
Dull hair coat, dull expression, pot belly.

Do you feel most horsemen have a good knowledge of equine nutrition?
No.

Al Dunning

Al Dunning, of Scottsdale, Arizona, has been showing Quarter Horses, Appaloosas, Paints, and Arabians for many years. He owns and operates Almosta Ranch, a Quarter Horse training facility. Among his show ring successes, Mr. Dunning has trained and shown eight American Quarter Horse Association World Champions, eight A.Q.H.A. Reserve World Champions, a National Reining Horse Association World Champion, and more than 300 Arizona Year End Champions. He has also trained three A.J.Q.H.A. World Champions, five A.Q.H.A. Amateur World Champions, and eleven All- American Quarter Horse Congress winners. Mr. Dunning has won the Tropicana Cutting Futurity, the Pacific Coast Cutting Horse Association Derby, the Las Vegas Classic/Challenge, and numerous other cutting competitions.

Since 1975, Mr. Dunning has been on the Arizona Quarter Horse Breeders Association board of directors, and he is the current Drug Committee Chairman. He is also the 1991 vice-president of that organization. From 1984 – 1986, he was president of the Arizona Cutting Horse Association. Mr. Dunning is involved in many other organizations, including the A.Q.H.A., National Cutting Horse Association, and American Horse Show Assocition. He is also an approved judge for the A.Q.H.A. and National Snaffle Bit Association.

Mr. Dunning is involved in many clinics and seminars, in the U. S. and abroad, and has had several articles published in leading horse magazines. His book, *Reining,* is a top seller, and he has also made several highly useful instructional video tapes. *(The reader may contact Equine Research, Inc. for information on locating these items.)*

The interview...

Grains

Would you recommend using processed grains (such as rolled or steamed) as opposed to whole natural grains?

A whole oat or a whole grain is better than rolled or steamed. Most of the time, rolled or steamed oats are lower in quality, even before

425

processing. If we feed corn (we don't feed much), it is cracked.

What are the advantages and disadvantages of corn and oats?
Corn is high in energy and promotes good hair condition. Basically, you can condition a horse fast on corn. A disadvantage is it sometimes can be harder to digest. If we do feed corn, it's in a sweet feed. Oats are easy to digest and have good protein and energy content. Also, it is hard to overfeed straight oats in most cases, although if you feed a lot of oats and don't exercise a horse enough, it can cause the horse to become fat and hyperactive.

What should the minimum weight per bushel be for a quality oat?
We don't have a minimum weight. We get the fattest ones we can.

From what area do you prefer to get your grain?
Most of the oats we feed are from Minnesota and Colorado.

Commercially Prepared Horse Feeds

Have you found commercial feed mixes from reputable companies to be consistently high in quality?
No, many of the feed companies cut corners in terms of quality, to save money. They use a lesser quality grain and forage source. When they grind and mix it up, nobody knows the difference.

What is the best method for horsemen to judge the quality and usefulness of a commercial horse feed?
Buy from a company that is consistent in quality. Visually inspect the grain to make sure the kernel is good and fat. Feed it to the horses and see how they like it, and how they respond condition wise. Also, make sure the feed is cost efficient.

So you use a lot of visual appraisal of your grains?
Yes, the same way with hay, too. We don't send it to the laboratory.

When is it worthwhile (in terms of cost) to have a commercial mill prepare your own feeds to your formula?
Never, I would say, because of the high cost and problems in terms of storage and keeping it. Most mixed feeds have additives in them to keep them moist, and if you buy them in bulk, they may mold. You also need bulk tanks to store it.

Do you feed sweet feed?
I only feed sweet feed as a supplement. If I get a horse that doesn't really assimilate its feed, and it looks as if it needs to put on some weight, then we'll supplement it with some sweet feed and another conditioner. This horse basically needs something more than good quality alfalfa hay, bermuda grass hay and a good whole oat can supply. I would say we need to feed sweet feed more in the winter.

Do you feed sweet feed in summer months?
Our summers are so hot, and since sweet feed provides more energy than oats, we avoid feeding it. Excess energy can make horses become hot, dehydrated, and hyperactive. They'll also need to drink a lot and, consequently, need to urinate more.

Are there advantages to pelleted feeds?
I fed a pelleted feed before and I didn't like it. There are some pelleted supplements that are okay, but only to use as a supplement. However, pellets are clean to feed and can be weighed easily.

Are pelleted forages an adequate substitute for loose forage?
No. We find that when you substitute a pellet, such as a hay pellet or alfalfa pellet, for a forage source, it causes problems. Basically, this is because the horse doesn't spend enough time eating. They get bored and find other things to do.

Are horses fed pelleted feeds more prone to choke, crib, or chew wood?
I had a horse that choked when eating pellets. The vet had to run a tube down its throat and break the pellets loose. Also, a friend of mine had a horse choke and die right before a show. So I guess that does happen, but I don't think it's a huge problem. I do feel they are more inclined to crib and chew wood.

What do you think about feeding hay cubes?
They tend to be cheap, and they're cheap because the hay that is ground up and cubed may not be as high in quality as it should be. Also when they scoop up all that stuff in the field there's a chance that rodents and trash can be included in the cubes.

Forages
Hay
What hays do you feed?
Alfalfa and bermuda grass hay.

Why do you feed these?
They are the best hays in terms of nutritional value.

Are there other hays you would prefer if they were available locally?
I have fed timothy in the past, and the horses seemed to get along very well on it. But it's not a grass that's available in our area.

Which cutting do you prefer?
We feed third, fourth, and sometimes even fifth cutting hay. There's less stem, and the fields are a whole lot cleaner by then. These cuttings also have a lower protein content than the first, second, and third cuttings, so they cost less. They are also a better quality hay to feed horses.

How do you judge the quality of your hay?
We judge our hay first by visual inspection. We look at the color, the size of the stem, and the quality of the leaf. We make sure that it's a good clean baling, and that there's no thistles or grass combined with the alfalfa hay. Also, many times, we'll take a piece of the hay and taste it. Good, clean hay tastes good—dirty, low quality hay does not. Also, we judge it by the way our horses accept it.

From what parts of the country do you like to get your hay?
I can get both alfalfa and bermuda grass hay from right here in Arizona, in the Colorado River basin area (Yuma and Parker, Arizona). This river runs between the border of Arizona and California.

What is the best method of feeding hay?
I like to feed it on the ground. It's the best way for horses to eat. Most of the time, if you have it in a hay manger, they'll pull a lot of it out and eat it off the ground anyway.

Do you recommend feeding hay free-choice or in measured amounts?
We regulate the amount of hay we feed our horses, depending on the condition of the horse.

What are the advantages of mixing grasses and legumes together in pastures and in hay?
We don't have any alfalfa pasture because it's too rich for grazing. We have bermuda grass in the summer, and in the winter, a mix of bermuda, oats, barley, and rye. It's a mild feed, so most of the time we have to feed alfalfa hay along with it, but only a small amount.

What types of behavioral or gastric problems occur when horses don't receive adequate forage (hay or pasture)?
If horses have time to graze, they seem to be more settled. They don't want to crib, weave, or kick, because they can graze in the pasture and relax. It helps their attitude to be turned out on pasture. The only time we ever have problems with gastric disturbances in our area is when horses eat off the ground in a pasture and ingest sand. They get what we call sand colic. But that's only in extreme cases. We just don't see many problems like that.

Pasture

Do you keep any horses on pasture 24 hours a day?
Yes, we have young and also some older horses on pasture.

What kind of care do your pastured horses need?
All of our pastures have shade and sprinkler systems. The horses will get under the sprinklers to cool off. We give our pastured horses a great deal of care. The colts are brought in frequently to be cared for.

Their feet are cleaned, they're watched very carefully for thrush, they're dewormed, and we keep salt in the pasture, free-choice.

What kind of pasture grass do you prefer?
Most of our pastures are bermuda grass in the summer, and in the winter, a mix of bermuda grass, barley, rye and oats ("winter mix").

How many acres per horse is minimal for pasture?
Well, it all depends on the kind of pasture you have. Some places in Arizona are heavily irrigated and fertile, and can handle five horses per acre. However, in general, I would say one horse per five acres, even though I have a two acre pasture that I put two or three horses in, and they do fine on it year round.

Is there a danger from toxic weeds if pastures are well cultivated?
We don't have that here in Arizona. We have so much heat that it basically knocks out the weeds. There is some loco weed in northern Arizona, but the people who are cultivating alfalfa hay clean that up.

Supplementation
Vitamin and Mineral

If a horse is receiving a high quality, well balanced diet, is vitamin or mineral supplementation necessary?
No, only in an extreme case such as with a horse that's weak or lethargic.

Do horses need trace mineralized salt or just a salt source?
We feed trace mineralized salt, free-choice.

Do you supplement vitamin E?
No.

Are there any supplements beneficial to a performance horse?
If they need it, yes. If not, the excess nutrients will be excreted in the sweat and urine. I think a lot of the stuff about supplements is basically hype. When you can feed a high quality, well balanced diet, I don't think supplementation is necessary.

Are injectable supplements better than oral supplements?
No. It's bad for the horse's attitude and a real pain to do.

Is there a problem with people oversupplementing horses?
Yes. They'll feed the horse several different supplements at the same time. I think that the horse's kidneys and digestive tract can do without all that stuff.

Electrolytes

Are electrolytes helpful before and/or after competition?
We feed electrolytes both prior to and after competition. We do this because it returns their system to metabolic stability a whole lot quicker after stress. Horses here lose their fluids very quickly.

How do you provide your horses with electrolytes?
We feed the electrolytes both in the feed and in the water.

Can electrolyte supplementation ever be harmful?
The only problem we've had is some horses don't like the way electrolytes taste in the water, and they'll stop drinking for a day or two. In the heat, this situation can really cause some problems.

Protein and Protein Supplements

Do you use commercial protein supplements?
We don't feed any protein supplements at all.

Can excesses of protein be harmful and negatively affect performance?
Excessive protein can cause skin problems and colic. It can also cause a horse to be unreceptive to training.

Does protein supplementation increase muscle mass?
I think it's a misuse of supplementation, and I'm not into that.

Management

Feeding

Does training stress placed on performance horses greatly increase their need for protein, energy, or vitamins and minerals?
If you feed a good balanced diet, you normally shouldn't need any increases in those nutrients. If a horse starts to show some stress or some wear and tear from training, or if it is a nervous horse, supplementation may help. Sometimes we will supplement vitamins by feeding wheat germ oil or the B-vitamins, particularly thiamin.

In what ways do you provide the extra energy that a performance horse needs, as compared to a horse doing light work?
Feeding more oats is the best way to provide a horse with more energy without making it fat. Also, oats don't cause hyperactivity or any attitude changes in the horse.

Does a proven horse require a different ration than a horse just beginning training?
The older horse or the horse that's already trained takes less feed than the horse that's beginning training, mainly because the horse beginning training requires more riding.

What factors are important in preparing a balanced ration?
Good hay, good oats, and watching the horses carefully to make
sure that they are getting what they need. If they do need any extra
supplementation, it should be provided.

What can be done to increase the palatability of a ration?
First of all, the quality of the feed makes a real difference. Most of
our horses won't readily eat a lower quality hay. If we change to a
higher quality hay, they'll eat it right up. Another thing we try to do
to get a horse to eat a little more is change the feed. For instance,
we'll switch from a bermuda grass hay to alfalfa. If necessary, we'll
mix a little molasses in the feed.

Do you feed bran mashes?
The only time I'll feed a bran mash is when we're on the road, or if
the horse has a digestive problem, we'll put him on a bran mash
before he returns to eating hay. Also, if we bed a horse on straw at a
show, I'll feed a bran mash.

What correctable problems can cause a horse to be a "hard keeper"?
First, make sure you are really feeding a high quality feed. If you
are, then I'd say the most likely problem would be their teeth.
Many people don't pay attention to the horse's teeth. Our horse's
teeth are floated regularly. We also have the caps, wolf teeth and
bridle teeth removed. I think this really makes a difference in how
they eat. Also, proper parasite control is needed.

Are there any special feeds or supplements you feed "hard keepers"?
No, we just feed these horses more of the ration ingredients. We'll
also feed a hard keeper three times a day instead of twice. And depending on the horse, it may be fed more oats or just more hay.

How many times a day do you feed?
We feed our horses twice a day.

At what times of the day do you feed?
5:00 A.M. and 5:00 P.M. I think it's important to feed horses at the
same time every day.

*What changes should be made in the horse's diet when its activity
level is increased or decreased, or when it's ill or injured?*
This will depend on the horse's condition. Our horses get ridden
quite a bit, so we don't decrease or increase their rations too
much. Usually an ill horse will require less feed, but this depends
on the illness. There are some illnesses where it's important to
keep a horse on feed, and there are others where it is better not to.

Do you change your feed rations occasionally or do you stay with a proven formula?
We stick to a proven formula that we've been using for a long time.

If a horse does not eat, how long do you leave the feed in front of him?
Only half a day. If they haven't cleaned up their feed by the next feeding, we remove it and take note of the amount left over. Then we put new feed in and see how the horse reacts.

How can one encourage a horse to drink more water if it is consuming inadequate amounts?
Use of electrolytes encourages the horse to drink more water. Also, I find that thiamin will make a difference when hauling horses. If we get to a show and the horse really doesn't like the taste of the water, we'll take Coca Cola® or something like that and put it in the water. It just sweetens the taste up a little bit.

What management practices would you recommend to avoid colic and laminitis?
Regulation of the feed and feeding a quality feed.

Are there special times when water should be withheld from the horse?
Only for a health reason or something like that. Since horses need at least 12 gallons of water a day, we don't withhold water from them for any performance reasons. Horses out here in this heat need a lot more, maybe up to 20 gallons.

Basic Care

What type of bedding do you prefer in your stalls?
Pine shavings.

How often do you have horses' teeth checked and floated?
We check our horses twice a year and most of the time all the horse's teeth are floated at least once a year.

What types of inoculations do you have done on your horses?
In the spring, we give a flu shot, eastern and western encephalomy-elitis, and tetanus. We also give a flu shot in the fall. I don't give my horses rhino or rabies. We don't have many rabies problems here.

Do you have any blood analyses done?
Only if there is a problem. If we know a horse well, and all of a sudden there's a drastic change in condition (i.e., the way they're eating, or their performance), we'll do a blood work-up to check for any problems that we can't visually detect.

Parasite Control

How frequently do you recommend deworming, and by what method?
We tube deworm our horses four times a year, and we paste them twice a year with an ivermectin product.

Would you recommend the dewormers that are fed on a daily basis?
We don't use them.

Do you think there is a danger of parasites building up a resistance to these dewormers when low doses are fed on a daily basis?
Yes, and that's why we switch off and paste our horses twice a year.

What is the most practical method for preventing the spread of parasites in pastures?
We rotate some, keep our pastures mowed, and we deworm all of our horses routinely. We clean our pastures with a flat drag, and keep them harrowed. There's basically no manure piles left in them and there's no build up of moisture in any one area. However, routine deworming of the horse is the best way to control parasites in pasture horses.

Training

Are your horses worked every day?
Mostly, though some of the older horses get turned out and aren't worked every day. But I'd say if I have 20 horses in training, 15 get ridden every day.

Do you recommend that horses be rested prior to competition?
Our horses are in such good condition that resting really doesn't make a lot of difference. As a matter fact, exercise is better for them. Sometimes, if you haul a horse for a long distance, it helps to give him a little time off to avoid overstressing him. But most of the time, in routine horse show events, there's no need to rest a horse before competition.

General

What areas of equine nutrition do you feel most need further research?
Well, I'm a little concerned about some of the research going on. You read one thing and pick up a magazine six months later and read just the opposite opinion by another outstanding veterinarian. Some of the things I've seen in publications really baffle me. These inconsistencies force me to take it all with a grain of salt. Our program here is fairly basic. We believe in a balanced diet, high quality feed, and good maintenance of the horses. I think that takes care of just about everything.

Ron McAnally

Trainer Ron McAnally began his racing career as a teenager, rubbing horses for his uncle, trainer Reggie Cornell. Since saddling his first stakes winner in 1960, McAnally has travelled many miles across the country with his stable.

McAnally sent out his 100th stakes winner in 1991, one year after being inducted into the Racing Hall of Fame, along with his outstanding runner, John Henry (the leading money earning Thoroughbred for many years). In 1981, McAnally received an Eclipse Award as outstanding trainer, as John Henry won his first Horse of the Year and was voted champion handicap and turf male. John Henry was champion turf male in 1983 and 1984, and was again voted Horse of the Year in 1984. In 1989 and 1990, another runner from McAnally's stable, Bayokoa, was named champion turf female.

From his base in Southern California, McAnally has been a very successful and popular trainer and conditioner. In 1991 the quality of his efforts was again recognized when he won the Eclipse Award as outstanding trainer for the second time!

The interview...

Grains

Would you recommend using processed grains, such as rolled or steamed, as opposed to whole grains?
No.

What method of processing would you recommend for oats and corn?
I recommend using whole oats and cracked corn.

What are the advantages?
Cracked corn is easier for a horse to eat and digest. Whole oats don't lose nutrients.

Are there particular regions that excel in the production of oats?
Canada.

Commercially Prepared Horse Feeds

Have you found commercial feed mixes from reputable companies to be consistently high in quality?
Yes.

Are there any advantages to pelleted feeds?
No.

Are pelleted forages an adequate substitute for loose forage (such as pasture or hay)?
There is less waste, but there is also less nutrition.

What are the advantages and disadvantages of feeding hay cubes?
The advantage is there is less waste, but they are also lower in nutritional quality.

Forages

Hay

What hays do you feed?
Alfalfa and timothy, because of the nutrition they provide.

Are there other hays you would prefer if they were available locally?
Good clover.

Which cutting do you prefer?
I prefer the second cutting.

How do you judge the quality of hay?
By smell and the overall look.

From what parts of the country do you like hay to come?
Nevada.

What is the best method of feeding hay?
Either in a hay net because less effort is involved, or on the ground because it is more natural.

Do you recommend feeding hay free-choice or in measured amounts?
I like to feed hay free-choice.

What are the advantages of mixing grasses and legumes together in pastures and in hay?
More variety in nutrition.

Pasture

How much time do you allow pastured horses to graze?
10 hours.

What kind of pasture grass do you prefer?
Mixed.

How many acres per horse is minimal for pasture in your area?
Around five acres.

Is there a danger from toxic weeds if pastures are well cultivated?
Yes, there still is a danger.

Supplementation
Vitamin and Mineral

If a racehorse is receiving a high quality, well balanced diet, do you think vitamin or mineral supplementation is necessary?
Yes.

Do horses need trace mineralized salt or just a salt source?
Just a salt source.

How do you prefer feeding salt?
I prefer to add it to the feed in measured amounts.

Do you supplement vitamin E?
Not by itself. I supplement multi-vitamins which includes E.

Are injectable supplements superior to oral supplements?
No.

Do most horsemen oversupplement or undersupplement racehorses?
I think most oversupplement.

Electrolytes

Are electrolytes helpful if given before and/or after a race?
Yes, before and after.

If you use them, how do you provide your horses with electrolytes?
I use them once in a while, and they are provided by a veterinarian.

Is electrolyte supplementation ever harmful?
No.

Protein and Protein Supplements

Which oilseed meal protein supplement do you prefer?
Linseed meal, because it helps with digestion.

Can excesses of protein be harmful and negatively affect performance?
No.

Does protein supplementation increase muscle mass?
No, I don't think so.

Added Fat

Is feeding added fat beneficial?
No.

Drugs

Are drugs being abused in horse racing?
Not where they are controlled, as in California.

Does Lasix really help bleeders?
Yes.

Management

Feeding

Does the training stress placed on racehorses greatly increase their need for protein, energy, vitamins, or minerals?
Yes, the more stress that is put on a horse, the more vitamins, minerals, and protein are needed to replace what has been depleted.

In what ways do you provide the extra energy that a racehorse needs as compared to a horse doing light work or no work?
I provide a lot of food and more vitamins.

Is there a difference in rations between a horse that is "racing fit" and one that is just entering training?
Yes.

Do you change your feeding program as a race draws near?
Sometimes feed is taken away the day of a race.

What factors do you think are most important in planning and preparing a balanced ration?
Provide them with all the needed nutrients.

What can be done to increase the palatability of a ration?
Add sweet feed or Red Glow®.

Do you feed bran mashes? If so, how often, and for what reason?
I feed them every night. They help keep the horse healthy.

Are there any special feeds or supplements you feed "hard keepers"?
Red Glow®.

Is it better to change the feed ration routinely, or is it better to stick with a proven formula?
You should change the ration only if it is needed.

How can one encourage a horse to drink more water if it is consuming inadequate amounts?
By adding more salt to the ration.

Are there special times when water should be withheld from the horse?
Just prior to racing.

Basic Care

> *What type of bedding do you prefer in your stalls?*
> I prefer straw.

> *How often do you have your horses' teeth checked and floated?*
> Every two months.

> *What types of inoculations do you have done on your horses?*
> Flu vac and rhino.

> *How often do you have these done?*
> Every three months.

> *Do you have any blood analyses done?*
> Not often. Only when needed.

Parasite Control

> *How frequently do you recommend deworming, and by what method?*
> At the track, every three months with a paste dewormer. At the
> farm they are tube dewormed every month.

General

> *What areas of equine nutrition do you feel most need further research?*
> I'd like to see more research in the area of maintaining soundness.

> *What are the physical characteristics that a well fed horse displays?*
> They feel good and look good.

> *Do you feel most horsemen have a good knowledge of equine nutrition?*
> Yes.

Brooks Thompson

Brooks Thompson received a B.S. degree in Animal Science from Texas A&M University in 1983. While attending college, he worked for Stallions Unlimited in Brenham, Texas. Since his graduation from Texas A&M, he has been employed by the Phillips Ranch in Frisco, Texas, where he is currently Ranch Manager. Phillips Ranch has been famous from its inception as one of the most highly productive Quarter Horse operations in the world. It has produced hundreds of high quality performance and halter horses, but is best known for its successes in the Quarter Horse racing world.

The legendary Phillips Ranch is the home of Dash For Cash, winner of back-to-back Champion of Champions races, as well as being named World Champion two years in a row. He is also the All Time Leading Sire of Money Earners, and his offspring have won stakes races, championships and awards too numerous to list.

Dash For Cash and many other highly valuble Quarter Horses are under the respected care and management practices of Brooks Thompson.

The interview...

Grains

Would you recommend using processed grains as opposed to whole grains?
Yes. Processed grains are more digestible.

What method of processing would you recommend for oats and corn?
For oats, I would recommend steam rolling. For corn, flaking.

What are the advantages and disadvantages of corn and oats?
The advantage of corn is that it has a high amount of energy. The disadvantage is that it has poor digestibility and palatability. Oats are advantageous because they are high in palatability, but they have a lower source of energy.

What should the minimum weight be for a good quality oat?
Thirty-two pounds per bushel.

Are there any geographic regions which excel in the production of grains?
Grains from the midwest seem to be the most desirable.

Commercially Prepared Horse Feeds

Have you found commercial feed mixes from reputable companies to be consistently high in quality?
Yes.

What is the best method for judging the quality and usefulness of a commercial horse feed?
The feed tag is useful for finding out the composition of the feed. Feeding trials are a good indicator of its usefulness.

When is it worthwhile to have a commercial mill prepare feeds to your own formula?
If your particular geographic location presents nutrient deficiencies, or if you have other special needs.

Is sweet feed more advantageous to feed in winter months?
We feed sweet feed year-round.

Are pelleted forages an adequate substitute for loose forage (such as pasture or hay)?
No, the digestive tract requires more bulk.

What are the advantages and disadvantages of feeding hay cubes?
The advantage is that they are easier to handle. However, it is hard to judge the quality of the hay used.

Are horses that are fed pelleted feeds more prone to choke, crib, or chew wood?
I don't think so.

Forages
Hay

What hays do you feed?
Alfalfa and coastal bermudagrass.

Why do you feed these?
We feed alfalfa because it is a superior horse hay. Coastal is fed because it is readily available.

Are there other hays you would prefer if they were available locally?
No, alfalfa and coastal are sufficient for our program.

Which cutting do you prefer?
The second or third cutting, because they are usually cleaner.

How do you judge the quality of your hay?
The stage of maturity, texture, leafiness, amount of foreign material, and color.

From what parts of the country do you prefer to purchase hay?
Coastal—locally. Alfalfa—New Mexico.

What is the best method of feeding hay?
I prefer to feed hay in a manger because there is less waste and it is usually more sanitary.

Do you recommend feeding hay free-choice or in measured amounts?
I recommend measured amounts.

What types of behavioral and gastric problems can arise if a horse does not receive adequate forage (hay or pasture)?
In terms of behavioral problems—chewing wood, cribbing, weaving, etc. As for gastric problems—there is a real need to feed horses roughage because some bulkiness in the ration is required to prevent colic and founder.

What proportion of hay to concentrate is generally best?
Roughly 2:1 is best.

Pasture

How much time do you allow your horses to graze?
Some of our horses have pasture available all the time, others never graze.

What kind of pasture grass do you prefer?
Coastal bermuda.

Is there a danger from toxic weeds if pastures are well cultivated?
Rarely.

What are the advantages of mixing grasses and legumes together on pasture and in hay?
Mixing them together allows you to get the benefits from both types of forages.

Classes of Horses

Broodmares

Do you prefer broodmares be in a fleshy or thin condition prior to the breeding season?
Fleshy.

Do you believe that "flushing" (bringing them into breeding season in a thin condition, then feeding to gain) mares enhances their fertility?
No.

Do you change the broodmares' ration just before and after foaling?
During late gestation and after foaling, mares require more nutrients.

How many pounds of concentrate do you feed broodmares per day
 A. during pregnancy? About 6 lbs.
 B. during lactation? About 11 lbs.
 C. when open? About 4 lbs.

Stallions

Do you feel that more research is needed in the area of stallion nutrition?
No.

How much exercise do your stallions get on a daily basis, and what method do you use to exercise them?
They are put on a walker for 30 to 45 minutes.

Do you feed your stallions supplements to enhance reproductive performance?
No.

Foals

Do you creep feed foals?
No.

At what age do you wean?
We wean at four and a half to five months of age.

When do you deworm your foals for the first time and what do you use?
The first deworming is done at 30 days of age. We typically use a strongid paste.

Weanlings

What method do you use to wean foals?
Our foals are weaned "cold turkey."

What do you feed weanlings?
We feed them a concentrate with 16% protein three times a day.

How much do you feed weanlings?
Roughly 8 pounds of concentrate, and 4 to 5 pounds of alfalfa.

What types of supplements do you provide weanlings?
Salt.

Yearlings

How do you manage yearlings? (Are they stalled, pastured or a combination?)
Combination. Our sale horses are stalled.

How does this management style affect their nutritional needs?
The horses on good pasture need less hay.

What do you feed sales yearlings?
A 14% crude textured feed and alfalfa.

When do you begin prepping yearlings for sales?
At least 90 days prior to the sale.

Management

Feeding

What factors are most important in planning and preparing a balanced ration?
The total digestible nutrients, calcium/phosphorus ratio, percent of digestible protein, and percent crude fiber.

What can be done to increase the palatability of a ration?
Increasing the percentage of oats, or adding molasses.

Do you feed bran mashes?
Occasionally, for mares that may need their stool softened.

What common problems can cause a horse to be a "hard keeper"?
Having teeth that need to be floated, needing to be dewormed, and how the horse is housed or pastured.

Are there any special feeds or supplements you feed "hard keepers"?
Calf Manna® is a good supplement.

How many times a day do you feed?
The mares and stallions are fed twice a day and the young horses are fed three times a day.

At what times of the day do you feed?
Mares and stallions—7 A. M. and 5 P. M. Young horses—7 A. M., 1 P. M., and 5 P. M.

Do you feed equal portions at each feeding?
Yes.

Is it better to change the feed ration routinely, or is it better to stick with a proven formula?
The fewer changes you make, the better.

If a horse does not eat, how long do you leave the feed in front of it?
Until the next feeding.

What management practices would you recommend to avoid colic and laminitis?
Consistency in quality, amounts, and schedule.

Do you alter your ration with the changing of the seasons?
We alter the ration of the pasture horses to adjust to seasonal changes that affect the nutrition of the grasses.

How do you encourage a horse to drink more water if it is consuming inadequate amounts?
By feeding more salt.

Are there special times when water should be withheld?
If the horse is hot, or has been on a trailer without available water, they need to be "watered out" (given water in small amounts, not allowed free access).

Supplements

Is supplemental salt important in the horse's diet?
Yes.

Do you recommend using salt or trace mineralized salt?
Salt.

Do you feed any supplements?
Occasionally, if they are needed.

Do you supplement vitamin E?
No.

Is the use of commercial protein supplements worthwhile?
In some cases, if they are needed.

Which oilseed meal protein supplement do you prefer?
Soybean meal, because of its digestibility and palatability.

Can excesses of protein be harmful and negatively affect performance?
No, but it is a waste of money, as protein supplements are expensive.

What percentage of protein is necessary in the ration of
(a) foals? 16%   *(b) yearlings?* 14%   *(c) two year-olds?* 12%
(d) mature horses? 10% *?*

Do you feed any horses a source of added fat such as corn oil?
Our sale horses usually receive corn oil in small amounts.

Basic Care
What type of bedding do you prefer in stalls?
Wood shavings.

What types of inoculations do you have done?
Rhino, flu, VEWT.

How often do you have these done?
Every three months.

Do you have any blood analyses done?
Coggins, CBC, Thyroid, etc.

When do you have these performed?
Coggins, annually; other tests, as needed.

Parasite Control

How frequently do you recommend deworming, and by what method?
Every three months, by tube.

Would you recommend the new dewormers which are fed on a daily basis, and why?
I have not used any.

Is it essential that horses get tube dewormed?
I believe it is essential, but there are also good paste wormers available.

What is the most practical method for preventing the spread of parasites in pastures?
Regular deworming.

General

What areas of equine nutrition do you feel most need further research?
The causes and prevention of colic.

What are the physical characteristics that a well fed horse displays?
Bright eyes, glossy hair coat, a great deal of energy, and a certain amount of fat over the ribs.

What are the danger signs that show an inadequate feeding program?
Small foals, abortions in pregnant mares, poor hair coats, etc.

Do you feel most horse people have a good knowledge of equine nutrition?
No.

Bill Lanning

Bill Lanning and his wife, Ann, have managed Edgewood Farms, Inc., in Pilot Point, Texas, for the past thirteen years.

The beautiful full service facility offers much to the Quarter Horse industry...from a complete breeding operation to training, showing, and selling halter and performance horses. Edgewood Farms is the home of Mr. Conclusion, the 1991 American Quarter Horse Association leading Sire of Halter Horses and Halter Point Earners in the nation.

Bill began his work with horses 29 years ago, at the age of 16. Not only did this set the course of his life, but it also introduced him to his wife, Ann. They have combined their love for each other, along with their love for horses and their work, into a combination which has proven successful over the years.

The interview...

Grains

Would you recommend using processed grains (such as rolled or steamed) as opposed to whole natural grains?
No.

If processed, what methods would you recommend for oats and corn?
For oats, I would recommend crimped. For corn— cracked.

What are the advantages and disadvantages of corn and oats?
A disadvantage of corn is that it is a "hot" (high energy) feed, and as a result it can produce excess gas. The advantage with oats is that they are very palatable and consistent in protein. I don't feel that oats have a disadvantage.

What is the minimum weight per bushel for a good quality oat?
38 to 42 pounds.

Are there any geographic regions that excel in the production of grains?

Northern oats are big and pretty and usually weigh about 42 pounds to the bushel.

Commercially Prepared Horse Feeds

Have you found commercial feed mixes from reputable companies to be consistently high in quality?

I have the majority of the time.

What is the best method for horsemen to judge the quality and usefulness of a commercial horse feed?

Examine the feed and see how much trash or fillers are in it. Also, try it and see how well your horses do on it according to your program.

When is it worthwhile to have a commercial mill prepare feeds to your own formula?

I don't think it is cost effective to have a mill prepare your own feed formula.

Does sweet feed play a part in your feeding program?

I only use sweet feed in the creep feeders to get my foals to start eating well.

Are there any advantages to feeding pelleted feeds?

No! !

Are pelleted forages an adequate substitute for loose forage (such as pasture or hay)?

No, horses that are kept stalled become easily bored during periods of time in which they have nothing to do. Providing loose forage such as hay will occupy their time longer.

What are the advantages and disadvantages of feeding hay cubes?

I personally don't feel there is an advantage to feeding hay cubes. I don't like the idea of feeding cubes. It's hard to determine the quality of the hay that was used to make the cube, or how much trash was in it.

Are horses that are fed pelleted feeds more prone to choke, crib or chew wood?

They're not necessarily more likely to choke, but they are more likely to crib and chew wood.

Are there advantages to extruded feeds?

Not in my opinion.

Forages

Hay

> *What hays do you feed?*
> Alfalfa.
>
> *Why?*
> It is easily digested and has a high protein level.
>
> *Are there other hays you would prefer if they were available locally?*
> No.
>
> *Which cutting do you prefer?*
> The third and fourth cutting for the show horses, as it has more leaf and smaller stems. The first, second, and third cuttings are fine for the broodmares.
>
> *How do you judge the quality of hay?*
> By examining its color, smell, texture, and appearance.
>
> *From what parts of the country do you like hay to come?*
> West Texas–Vernon, Wichita Falls
>
> *What is the best method of feeding hay?*
> I like the manger, because a horse can eat all the hay out of it, probably with less waste.
>
> *Do you feed hay free-choice or in measured amounts?*
> Broodmares and pasture horses receive hay free-choice. Horses in stalls are fed controlled amounts.
>
> *What types of problems can arise if a horse does not receive adequate forage (hay or pasture)?*
> Wood chewing, cribbing, and colic.

Pasture

> *How much time do you allow your horses to graze?*
> Show horses are turned out to play and relax but not for grazing reasons.
>
> *Do you keep any horses on pasture 24 hours a day?*
> Yes, the broodmares.
>
> *What special care do these horses need?*
> Good alfalfa hay and clean water.
>
> *What kind of pasture grass do you prefer?*
> Bermuda.
>
> *Is there a danger from toxic weeds if pastures are well cultivated?*
> No.

What are the advantages of mixing grasses and legumes in a pasture?
Mixing forages in a pasture allows you to have good grazing available at different times of the year.

How about mixed hay for stabled horses?
I prefer straight alfalfa hay for the stabled horses.

Classes of Horses

Broodmares

Do you prefer that broodmares be in fleshy or thin condition prior to the onset of the breeding season?
Fleshy.

How many pounds of concentrate do you feed broodmares a day
A. *during pregnancy?*   2 pounds (about 60 days prior to foaling).
B. *during lactation?*   2 pounds.
C. *when open?*   None.

Stallions

How much exercise do your stallions get?
One stallion is turned out 2 to 3 hours a day in a large area. The other stallion is still being shown, and he is worked 6 days a week for 20 minutes each time.

Do you feed stallions certain supplements specifically to enhance their reproductive performance? If so what are they?
Lexotinic® and wheat germ oil.

Foals

Do you creep feed foals?
Yes.

What do you feed them?
A sweet feed containing 12% protein mixed with crimped oats and Calf Manna®.

At what age do you begin creep feeding them?
Two weeks old.

At what age do you wean?
Four months of age.

When do you deworm foals for the first time and what do you use?
We begin deworming them at two months of age and we tube worm them.

Weanlings

What method do you use to wean foals?
We wean our foals according to the phases of the moon, and we

separate the foals from the mares at that time. It is an old fashioned method but one that works very well for us. The mares and foals take it easier than methods we have tried previously. We also have had better results. We have used this method for several years now and are completely satisfied with it. In fact, many people consult us regarding weaning.

Do you change their ration, or do they remain on the creep ration?
They remain on the creep ration.

What types of supplements do you provide weanlings?
Epiphy Stop®, calcium Carbonate, and Select I®.

Yearlings

How do you manage yearlings? (Are they stalled, pastured or a combination?)
Those being shown are stalled; others are pastured.

What do you feed sales yearlings?
They're fed the same as the others.

Management

Feeding

What factors are most important in planning and preparing a balanced ration?
Meeting the nutritional requirements of the horses I am feeding in relation to their age, work programs, and usage.

What can be done to increase the palatability of a ration?
Use of high quality ingredients.

Do you feed bran mashes?
No.

What common problems can cause a horse to be a "hard keeper"?
Bad teeth, poor health, and being a picky eater.

Are there any special feeds or supplements you feed "hard keepers"?
I just try to find the problem with the hard keepers and correct it so that they, too, can thrive on my feeding program.

How many times a day do you feed?
Twice.

At what times of the day do you feed?
7 A.M. and 5 P.M.

Do you feed equal portions at each feeding?
Yes, unless a particular individual is having an adjustment in its feeding program.

If a horse does not eat, how long do you leave the feed in front of it?
Twelve hours.

Do you alter your ration with the changing of the seasons?
No, I adjust the ration of my horses according to their work program and/or as an individual needs to gain or lose weight.

What steps do you take to minimize gastric disturbances and laminitis?
I feed a well planned, balanced feed ration, and am consistent with my feeding program and times of feeding.

How do you encourage a horse to drink more water if it is consuming inadequate amounts?
Provide salt blocks and mineral blocks free choice.

Are there special times when water should be withheld from the horse?
Yes. If a horse is too hot, or water has been withheld for several hours for some reason or another, the horse should not be allowed to drink too much, too fast.

Supplements

Is supplemental salt important in the horse's diet?
Yes.

Do you recommend using trace mineralized salt blocks to supplement the horse?
Yes.

Do you feed any supplements? If so, what type?
Select Nu-Image®.

What benefits do you feel it provides?
It helps condition hair coats.

Do you supplement vitamin E?
Yes, part of the year, for the breeding stallions.

Is the use of commercial protein supplements worthwhile?
Some of them are.

Can excesses of protein be harmful and negatively affect performance?
Yes.

Does protein supplementation increase muscle mass?
No.

Do you feed any of your horses a source of added fat such as corn oil?
No.

Basic Care

What type of bedding do you prefer in stalls?
Wood shavings.

How often do you have horses' teeth checked and floated?
We check our horses' teeth approximately every two months and they are floated when needed, based on this evaluation.

What types of inoculations do you have done on your horses?
VEWT, Strep, Rhino, Flu.

How often do you have these done?
Once a year.

What proportion of grooms per horses do you prefer?
I prefer one groom for ten horses.

Do you have any blood analyses done?
Yes.

When do you have these performed?
When we feel the horses aren't looking the way they should in actions or appearance (i. e., bad hair coats, etc.).

What do you look for in a blood test?
We look at the WBC (white blood cell count), RBC (red blood cell count), and hemoglobin.

Parasite Control

How frequently do you recommend deworming, and by what method?
We deworm every 60 days. All show horses, weanlings, and yearlings are tubed each time. The broodmares are tubed one time and paste dewormed the next, on a rotation basis.

Would you recommend the new dewormers that are fed on a daily basis?
No, I don't feel that they get the job done.

Is it essential that horses get tube dewormed, or are there other methods that are just as effective?
I think tubing is the best way to go in preventive deworming programs.

What is the most practical method for preventing the spread of parasites in pastures?
Have an effective deworming program and drag your pastures often.

General

What are the physical characteristics that a well fed horse displays?
A good shiny hair coat, alert look, and good physical appearance.

What are the danger signs that show an inadequate feeding program?
Thin horses, a dull and depressed appearance, and a dead hair coat.

Do you think most horse people have a good knowledge of equine nutrition?
No.

Are there any comments on the care or feeding of horses that you would like to add?
Pay close attention to each horse and feed on an individual program to meet each horse's needs. Follow a deworming program that will be effective and help you utilize the full nutritional value of the feed and supplements you are providing your horses.

John Lyons

John Lyons, of Parachute, Colorado, has been conducting training seminars and clinics across the U.S., Australia, and Canada since 1981. His training methods stress safety and response, and his techniques are easily understood and applied. Mr. Lyons teaches the rider to communicate with the horse, and provides steps toward achieving the desired response. His symposiums and clinics attract over 10,000 horsemen and women each year.

Mr. Lyons' training techniques have been profiled in such magazines as *Western Horseman, Horse & Rider, Horse Illustrated, Horseman,* and *Equus.* His book, *Lyons on Horses,* describes in detail the training methods that he teaches in his symposiums and clinics. He also has made excellent instructional videos, including *"Round Pen Reasoning," "Leading and Loading Safely,"* and the *"John Lyons Symposium Video Collection."* (The reader may contact Equine Research, Inc. for information on locating these items.)

The interview...

Grains

Would you recommend using processed grains (such as rolled or steamed) as opposed to whole natural grains?

I prefer whole grains as opposed to processed grains. You gain only about 5% digestibility by rolling grains. However, you can lose a considerable amount of quality when the grain is cracked and exposed over a period of time. Another factor when deciding between whole or processed grains is the age of the horse. The older the horse is, the more tempted I would be to use cracked grains for easier digestibility.

What method of processing would you recommend for oats and corn?
For oats, rolled and steamed. For corn, cracked.

What are the advantages and disadvantages of corn and oats?
The advantage of feeding corn is the higher level of digestible energy it provides. It is also less expensive per volume of energy needed. The same is true for barley.

The disadvantage of corn is that it is a more dangerous feed in terms of the risk of colic due to mistakes in feeding. Additionally, in high humidity areas, there is the risk of corn mold poisoning.

An advantage of using oats is that it works well as a dilute for corn or barley, allowing them to be fed more safely. Oats reduce starch in the hindgut, which in turn reduces the potential for colic.

The disadvantage of grains is that they are not a natural feed for horses. If the horse is not being worked, it does not require the high energy level that is provided by grains. A good quality hay can better meet the energy needs of the average horse.

What is a minimum weight per bushel for a good quality oat?
The minimum for a good quality oat is roughly 33 lbs per bushel.

Are there any geographic regions which excel in the production of feed grains?
The northern midwest states along with Colorado, New Mexico, Kansas, and Oklahoma.

Commercially Prepared Horse Feeds

Have you found commercial feed mixes from reputable companies to be consistently high in quality?
Yes.

What is the best method for horsemen to judge the quality and usefulness of a commercial horse feed?
Horsemen can typically judge the quality of their feed by using their own powers of observation. If the grain looks dusty or old, or doesn't smell fresh, then you can bet that the quality is not going to be as high as it should be. Of course, you would also want to look at the feed label for the breakdown or analysis of the feed.

When is it worthwhile to have a commercial mill prepare feeds to your own formula?
It can be worthwhile when you are located in an area where you have easy access to the mill and can buy and safely store large amounts of corn, barley, and oats. The advantage comes from being able to mix the grains to your own specification. When you consider that corn and barley typically cost less, yet yield a higher

level of digestible energy, you can formulate a ration that is not only more economical, but also more efficient. In essence, you can feed smaller quantities of corn and barley, receive more digestible energy, and pay less money to do so.

Is sweet feed more advantageous to feed in winter months?

I personally try to stay away from feeds that are sticky and heavy with molasses. The molasses is often added to keep the dust down, but like any form of sugar, it gives no nutritional benefit to the horse. And in winter, the molasses tends to freeze in our part of the country, making it even less desirable. Sweet feed, in my opinion, is not the "best" feed at any time.

Are pelleted feeds advantageous to feed?

The advantage is that it is less dusty, easier to handle, more consistent in nutrient quality, and it is less likely to spoil. However, they are not necessarily good when fed by themselves for any long period of time without a form of roughage being fed as well.

Are pelleted forages an adequate substitute for loose forage (such as pasture or hay)?

Pelleted forages are an adequate substitute during short periods. You have to be careful, though, that the complete feed pellet does not have too high a level of energy. It could result in the horse colicking from too much high protein and starch in the hindgut. This is especially true if the horse is suddenly switched from pasture to pellets without adequate time to adjust.

How do you feel about feeding hay cubes?

Though cubed hay is a better source of roughage than pellets, they are not the best source of food for your horse. Hay cubes, in my opinion, can actually be dangerous to a horse. For one reason, the machine that cubes the hay does not use a magnet. It collects the hay much like a vacuum and indiscriminately picks up anything and everything in the field, even wire or other dangerous objects. These objects may then get chopped up, cubed, and fed to your horse without you knowing it. Another danger lies in the fact that the hay is left in the field until it is extra dry. When these dry cubes are fed to the horse, the cubes absorb moisture in the stomach and expand, creating a potentially dangerous situation for the horse. The best way to prevent this from happening is to soak the cubes in water 20 – 30 minutes before feeding them to the horse.

Are horses fed pelleted feeds more prone to choke, crib, or chew wood?
Horses are more likely to choke on this type of feed because it is so
hard and dry. However, horses that are fed pellets are not any
more prone to crib or chew wood than ones who aren't, if they are
provided with adequate forage (hay or pasture).

Are there any advantages to extruded feeds?
One advantage would be their consistency.

Forages
Hay
What hays do you feed?
I feed an alfalfa and grass hay mixture.

Why do you feed this kind?
To feed straight alfalfa, with the grain that I am feeding my stallion
Zip, would cause a buildup of too much starch and protein in his
diet. Not only would it be more difficult for him to digest, it would
cause his manure to be abnormally sticky and smelly. The grass
hay acts to dilute the alfalfa, alleviating these problems.

Are there other hays you would prefer if they were available locally?
Timothy.

Which cutting do you prefer?
Selecting a specific cutting would depend on the circumstances,
such as the time of year and what I am feeding my horse in addition to the hay. For example, if it was winter and no grain was being fed, I would prefer the third alfalfa cutting. The first cutting
would have more grass mixed in it, diluting the alfalfa. The third
cutting, in contrast, would have the greatest concentration of alfalfa, making it the highest in protein content and the most beneficial to my horse in this circumstance.

How do you judge the quality of hay?
I check the stems for size, color, and brittleness; they should be
large, green, and flexible. Additionally, I look for a hay that has a
large percentage of leaves in proportion to stems. Other important
factors are cleanliness and freshness. I avoid any hay that contains
trash, weeds, mildew, or dirt.

From what parts of the country do you like your hay to come?
Colorado, New Mexico, California, and Arizona.

What is the best method of feeding hay?
Feeding a horse on the ground is the most natural position for

him. It produces more saliva in his mouth, which aids in digestion. Eating from the ground also stretches the horse's muscles out, which is better for his back. In addition, feeding in this manner causes fewer chances of lung problems and eye trauma, which typically result from feeding a horse at eye level, where he can get poked in the eye by stems.

Do you recommend feeding hay free-choice or in measured amounts?
I recommend free-choice.

What are the advantages of mixing grasses and legumes?
It provides a more balanced diet.

What behavioral and gastric problems can arise if a horse does not receive adequate forage (hay or pasture)?
There are several things that can possibly be the result of your horse not receiving adequate forage. It is always best to consult a veterinarian or someone who is an expert in these areas to determine if, in fact, forage deficiency is the reason for your horse's problems.

What proportion of hay to concentrate is generally best for the performance horse?
You should feed enough hay for the horse to receive adequate roughage to keep his hindgut working well. For a horse that is being put through rigorous training, you want to feed as much high energy as you can, but you have to temper that with enough roughage to ensure good digestion.

Pasture

How important is pasture to the equine of today?
Pasture has become of little importance, as far as feed value to today's equine. Most people do not depend on pasture to meet the nutritional needs of their horses. Instead, they rely on the research and development of commercial feeds. However, if given the option, I feel the pasture is still the best way to feed, because it is the most natural way for the horse. And in most cases, what is natural to him will usually benefit him physically and mentally.

How much time do you allow your horses to graze?
Ideally, I like to let them graze 24 hours a day.

Do you keep any horses on pasture 24 hours a day?
Yes.

What special care do these horses need?
None.

What kind of pasture grass do you prefer?
Mixed grass.

How many acres per horse is minimal for pasture?
It depends on the condition of the pasture.

Is there a danger from toxic weeds if pastures are well cultivated?
There should be little, if any, danger from toxic weeds in pastures that are well cultivated.

Supplementation
Vitamin and Mineral
If a horse is receiving a high quality, well balanced diet, is vitamin or mineral supplementation necessary?
No.

Do horses need a trace mineralized salt source or just a salt source?
I prefer a trace mineralized salt source.

How do you prefer feeding trace mineralized salt?
I prefer to feed it in a loose form, free-choice.

Can vitamin E supplementation actually enhance performance and fertility, or benefit the highly stressed horse?
Yes.

Do you supplement vitamin E?
Yes.

Can excesses of vitamin E be harmful?
I think an excess of anything can be harmful.

Are there any supplements particularly beneficial to a performance horse?
I think a balanced diet is the most beneficial.

Are injectable supplements superior to oral supplements?
I don't give injectables. I believe needles should be used by veterinarians.

Electrolytes
Are electrolytes helpful if done before and/or after a competition?
Yes, both before and after. In correct amounts, electrolytes help to maintain a stable water balance in the horse's system, which helps it recover from abnormal amounts of activity that could cause fluid loss.

If you use them, how do you provide your horses with electrolytes?
I prefer to use a paste electrolyte that comes in a tube.

What steps can be taken to prevent any harmful effects of electrolyte supplementation?
To prevent harmful effects, don't overuse the product. If you are ever in doubt whether to use it, don't.

Protein and Protein Supplements

> *Is the use of commercial protein supplements worthwhile?*
> Yes, if needed.

> *Which oilseed meal protein supplement do you prefer?*
> I prefer soybean meal.

> *Can excesses of protein be harmful and negatively affect performance?*
> Yes.

> *Does protein supplementation increase muscle mass?*
> I would assume that providing adequate protein in addition to exercise would be apt to increase muscle mass.

Added Fat

> *Is feeding added fat beneficial?*
> Yes, to a certain degree.

> *What sources of fat would you recommend?*
> I use corn oil.

> *How can a horse benefit from having fat added to the diet?*
> It provides additional energy and it gives the horse's coat a shiny, well-conditioned look.

Management

Feeding

> *Do the training stresses of performance horses increase their need for protein, energy, vitamins, and minerals?*
> Yes. The increased stress and expenditure of energy during training requires additional amounts of these nutrients be fed.

> *In what ways do you provide the extra energy that a performance horse needs?*
> I supply a working horse with grain and feed supplements when he is performing and needs the extra energy. During light work, I prefer to feed just good quality hay.

> *Does a proven horse require a different ration than a horse just beginning training?*
> Yes. The mental stress and energy expenditure will be greater for the horse beginning training.

> *What factors do you think are most important in planning and preparing a balanced ration?*
> When planning or preparing a balanced ration, you should consult the experts: veterinarians, feed companies, agricultural universities, and books such as this one.

What can be done to increase the palatability of a ration?
The method I use to increase palatability for my stallion Zip is to
soak his feed in water. Because I travel so much putting on the
John Lyons Symposiums, Zip is constantly subjected to water that
he is not accustomed to drinking. Soaking his feed in water also
ensures that he gets the fluids he needs, no matter what the water
tastes like. Other methods of increasing the palatability would be
to choose more naturally digestible feeds, cooking or processing
the feed, and feeding in smaller amounts over an extended period.

Do you feed bran mashes?
In certain regions where sand colic is likely, I might feed bran mash.

*What types of correctable problems can cause a horse to be a "hard
keeper"?*
There are numerous problems that can cause a horse to be a "hard
keeper": teeth, stomach problems, stabling problems, etc.

Are there any special feeds or supplements you feed "hard keepers"?
I would feed a more digestible feed, one that would be higher in fat
and starch for more energy to make him feel better.

How many times a day do you feed?
Two.

Do you feed equal portions at each feeding?
Yes.

If a horse does not eat, how long do you leave the feed in front of him?
As long as the feed doesn't spoil, I leave it in front of him until he
cleans it up.

*How do you encourage a horse to drink more water if it is consuming
inadequate amounts?*
As I mentioned earlier, because Zip and I travel, we are subject to
different tasting water everywhere we go. Zip may not be inclined
to drink the water if given the choice, so I put the water in his feed
to ensure he gets enough fluid.

*What management practices would you recommend to avoid colic
and laminitis?*
I try to maintain a well balanced, routine feeding program to avoid
problems.

Basic Care

What type of bedding do you prefer in stalls?
Wood shavings.

How often do you have horses' teeth checked and floated?
Once a year.

What types of inoculations do you have done on your horses, and how often do you have them done?
I follow my veterinarian's recommendations on all inoculations.

Do you have any blood analyses done?
Yes, when I think something is wrong with the horse.

Parasite Control

How frequently do you recommend deworming, and by what method?
Deworming frequency depends on the area and environment, but when I do deworm my horse, I like to use a paste.

Would you recommend the dewormers that are fed on a daily basis?
I personally cannot recommend this type of deworming. To me, any dewormer is a poison, and I'm not sure continued feeding on a daily basis is a proper method for my horse.

Should horses be tube dewormed, or are there other methods which are just as effective?
I think there are other methods that can be just as good.

What is the most practical method for preventing the spread of parasites in pastures?
Being from Colorado, I would have to say snow! I would suggest you talk to experts in your area to find out what is most practical for you in your locale.

Training

Are your horses worked every day?
No.

How does this affect their attitude?
They love it.

Do you recommend that horses be rested prior to competition?
Like any athlete, a light workout the day or two before a heavy competition is the most beneficial.

General

What areas of equine nutrition do you feel most need further research?
It is great research has brought us this far, but ongoing study is important in all areas if we want to continue to improve the care of our horses.

What are the physical characteristics that a well fed horse displays?
A horse that is properly fed and in good health will be alert and active, moving with energy. He will have bright, clear eyes, adequate flesh and muscle tone for his frame, and have a good hair coat.

What are the danger signs that show an inadequate feeding program?
The most obvious signs of an inadequate feeding program are a thin, lifeless horse with a poor coat.

Do most horse people have a good knowledge of equine nutrition?
I think that horse people have more opportunity today to develop a strong knowledge of equine nutrition through publications like this book and other research material that is available.

Are there any comments on the care or feeding of horses that you would like to add?
Anyone willing to pick up a book like this to learn about the needs of their horse is already making strides to improve the quality of their horse's life, and they should be commended.

Richard Shrake

Richard Shrake is an internationally known and highly regarded judge, lecturer, instructor, and trainer. He has judged World Shows for Quarter Horses, Arabians, Paints, Appaloosas, and Pintos. His students have won at major shows, including the All-American Quarter Horse Congress, the American Quarter Horse Association and American Junior Quarter Horse Association World Championship Shows, Arabian Nationals, Santa Barbara Nationals, and Cow Palace.

He is well known for his Resistance Free Training and Riding Methods, which stress total communication between horse and rider during ground work and while mounted.

Mr. Shrake is the owner of A Winning Way, Ltd., a video production company that produces the series of Richard Shrake training videos. He has had several articles published in leading horse magazines, among them *The Quarter Horse Journal, Performance Horseman, Appaloosa World, Equus,* and *Arabian Times.* He is also the author of the popular book *Horsemanship. (The reader may contact Equine Research, Inc. for information on purchasing Mr. Shrake's book and videos.)*

The interview...

Commercially Prepared Horse Feeds

Have you found commercial feed mixes from reputable companies to be consistently high in quality?

Yes, I have.

What is the best method to judge the quality and usefulness of a commercial horse feed?

By the quality of research that went into developing the feed, and by how the horse does on the feed.

Is it worthwhile to have a commercial mill prepare feeds to your own formula?
I don't feel that it is.

Do changes in the seasons affect the usefulness of sweet feeds?
No.

Are there advantages in using hay cubes?
Hay cubes are easier to store, and they take up less space than baled hay.

Are horses who are fed pelleted feeds more prone to choke, crib, or chew wood?
I don't feel that they're more likely to choke, but they are more likely to crib or chew wood.

Forages

Hay

What hays do you feed?
Alfalfa.

Why?
Because good quality alfalfa has a higher nutritional value, and is all around better than other hays.

Which cutting do you prefer?
I prefer the third or fourth cutting.

How do you judge the quality of hay?
I judge by the smell. It should smell fresh, not musty.

What is the best method of feeding hay?
I prefer feeding hay on the ground. As the horse eats off the ground, it stretches its back and lengthens the top line.

Do you recommend feeding hay free-choice or in measured amounts?
I recommend feeding it in measured amounts.

What types of behavioral problems can arise if a horse does not receive adequate forage?
They are likely to develop stable vices such as cribbing and wood chewing.

What ratio of hay to concentrate, by weight, is generally best for the performance horse?
A 50:50 ratio is best.

Pasture

How important is pasture to the equine of today?
It is very important for winter let-down after the show season.

How much time do you allow your horses to graze?
Those being let down are out 90% of the time. Horses in training are out 10% of the time.

Do you keep any horses on pasture 24 hours a day?
Breeding stock and foals.

What special care do these horses need?
Adequate shelter.

Is there a danger from toxic weeds if pastures are well cultivated?
No.

Supplementation
Vitamin and Mineral

If a performance horse is receiving a high quality, well balanced diet, is vitamin or mineral supplementation necessary?
Yes.

Do horses need supplemental salt?
Yes. I feed trace mineralized salt free-choice.

Can vitamin E supplementation enhance performance?
Yes.

Do you supplement vitamin E?
Yes.

Are injectable supplements superior to oral supplements?
No.

Electrolytes

When are electrolytes helpful?
They are helpful both prior to and after a competition.

Protein and Protein Supplements

Is the use of commercial protein supplements worthwhile?
Yes.

Which oilseed meal protein supplement do you prefer?
I prefer soybean meal and linseed meal.

Added Fat

Is feeding added fat beneficial?
Yes, I would recommend vegetable oil.

Management
Feeding

Does a proven horse require a different ration than a horse just beginning training?
A proven horse should be on a diet closer to maintenance levels.

What can be done to increase the palatability of a ration?
Add molasses to the feed.

Do you feed bran mashes?
I'll feed them if I have a horse that has colicked.

What is the most common problem that causes a horse to be a "hard keeper"?
Being a hard keeper is usually caused by the condition of their teeth. Often floating the teeth will improve the situation.

How many times a day do you feed?
I feed equal portions three times a day.

What changes should be made in the horse's diet when the activity level is changed?
The ration should be increased if the activity level is increased, and it should be decreased when activity is decreased.

Is it advantageous to change feed rations routinely?
It is better to stick to a proven formula.

If a horse does not eat, how long do you leave the feed in front of it?
I'll leave it for twelve hours.

How do you encourage a horse to drink more water if it is consuming inadequate amounts?
Add more salt to the diet.

What management practices would you recommend to avoid colic and laminitis?
Feed small amounts at regular intervals.

What type of bedding do you prefer in stalls?
Straw.

How often do you have horses' teeth checked and floated?
Twice a year.

Parasite Control

How frequently do you deworm, and by what method?
I deworm once a month with a paste.

Is it essential that horses get tube dewormed periodically?
No, pasting is just as effective.

What is the most practical method for preventing the spread of parasites in pastures?
I believe that rotating pastures, along with regular dragging and mowing, helps prevent the spread of parasites.

Training

Are your horses worked every day?
No, but on the days they aren't worked, they are turned out or groomed.

Do you recommend that horses be rested prior to competition?
No.

General

What are the physical characteristics that a well fed horse displays?
Good muscle tone and coat, and a bright eye.

What are the danger signs that show an inadequate feeding program?
A dull coat, dull eye, and a large stomach.

Do you think most horse people have a good knowledge of equine nutrition?
No.

If there are any comments on the care or feeding of horses that you would like to add, please do so.
I feel that Purina Mills, Inc. spends more on research and nutrients than all commercial companies combined. We should take more advantage of what they have to offer.

John Sosby

John Sosby has been at Claiborne Farm almost all his life, since moving there with his family at the age of three. Clairborne Farm has for many years been one of the most famous and successful Thoroughbred farms in the world. John Sosby has played a significant role in making this possible. He was made yearling manager in 1967, and in 1975 he took on the duties of general manager.

In 1991, Kentucky Thoroughbred Media, an organization of writers and broadcasters of Thoroughbred matters in Kentucky, awarded Sosby the Ambassador of Racing Award. This award honors those who have worked tirelessly to promote Thoroughbred racing.

The interview...

Commercially Prepared Horse Feeds

Have you found commercial feed mixes from reputable companies to be consistently high in quality?
Yes.

What is the best method for judging the quality and usefulness of a commercial horse feed?
The condition of the horse and how the horse eats the feed.

Is it worthwhile to have a commercial mill prepare feeds to your own formula?
They are responsible for quality and preparation. The cost of the equipment is too great for a farm to own and maintain.

Is sweet feed more advantageous to feed in winter months?
Yes.

Is sweet feed a poor feed in summer months?
No.

Forages
Hay

What hays do you feed?
Clover.

Are there other hays you would prefer if they were available locally?
No.

Which cutting do you prefer?
I prefer the first, because it is the best cutting.

How do you judge the quality of hay?
Mostly by its appearance.

From what parts of the country do you prefer to purchase hay?
Ohio and Michigan.

Which is the best method to feed hay?
On the ground.

Do you recommend feeding hay free-choice or in measured amounts?
We feed 14 to 18 pounds a day in the winter; less in the summer.

Pasture

How much time do you allow your horses to graze?
Yearlings, stallions, and foaling mares are out for six hours a day in the winter and eighteen hours in the summer.

Do you keep any horses on pasture 24 hours a day?
Yes, in the summer, maiden and barren mares are out 24 hours a day.

What special care do these horses need?
They need to be checked every four hours day and night.

What kind of pasture grass do you prefer?
Bluegrass-clover.

In your area, how many acres per horse is minimal for pasture?
Two.

Classes of Horses
Broodmares

Should broodmares be in fleshy or thin condition prior to the onset of the breeding season?
I prefer them to be in thin condition.

Does "flushing" (bringing them into breeding season in a thin condition and then feeding them to gain) mares enhances their fertility?
I do not practice this method.

Do you change broodmares' rations just before and after foaling?
Very little.

How much concentrate do you feed broodmares per day
A. *during pregnancy?*   8 qts.
B. *during lactation?*   6 qts.
C. *when open?*   6 qts.

Stallions

Do you feed stallions any supplements specifically to enhance their reproductive performance?
No

Foals

Do you creep feed foals?
No.

What do you feed foals?
Sweet feed with 14% protein—up to 5 lbs. per day for older foals.

At what age do you wean?
All foals are weaned on the same day—the first Tuesday of October.

Weanlings

What method do you use to wean foals?
All foals are removed from their dams on the same day.

Do you change their ration or do they remain on the creep ration?
They get the same feed, except that it is increased to 16% protein.

How much do you feed weanlings?
Roughly 10 lbs. of grain per day, spread over three feedings.

What types of supplements do you provide weanlings?
A vitamin premix is added to the feed.

Yearlings

How do you manage yearlings? (Are they stalled, pastured, or a combination?)
In the summer, they are out all night and part of the day. In the winter, they are out during the day and in at night.

How does this management style affect their nutritional needs?
The longer that they are on bluegrass pasture, the better.

When do you begin preparing yearlings for sales?
April 1.

Management

Feeding

What factors are most important in planning and preparing a balanced ration?
Good oats—41 pounds to the bushel or more.

What can be done to increase the palatability of a ration?
Add molasses.

Do you feed bran mashes?
No.

How many times a day do you feed?
Twice a day.

At what times of the day do you feed?
7:00 A.M. and 3:00 P.M.

Do you feed equal portions at each feeding?
Yes.

Supplements

Is supplemental salt important in the horse's diet?
Yes, fed free-choice.

Do you feed any supplements?
In the feed—vitamins A, D, and E, copper, selenium, and biotin.

Which oilseed meal protein supplement do you prefer?
I prefer adding soybean meal to the feed.

Can excesses of protein be harmful and negatively affect performance?
Yes.

What percentage of protein do you think is necessary in the ration of (a) foals? 14%   *(b) yearlings?* 16%   *(c)mature horses?* 14%?

Basic Care

What type of bedding do you prefer in stalls?
Rye and wheat straw.

What types of inoculations do you provide?
We give inoculations for botulism, tetanus, flu, and rhinopnemonitis.

Do you have blood analyses done?
Only if a horse is sick.

What do you look for in a blood test?
Infection and dehydration.

Parasite Control

Should horses be tube dewormed or are there other methods as effective?
There are other methods that have proven successful.

What is the most practical method for preventing the spread of parasites in pastures?
Use ivermectin or Strongid C®.

General

What are the physical characteristics that a well fed horse displays?
Dapples in the hair coat.

What are the danger signs that show an inadequate feeding program?
Long, dry coats.

Are there any comments on the care or feeding of horses you would like to add?
Keep pregnant mares off fescue and don't overfeed. With ivermectin, it is possible to have better looking, healthier horses on less feed.

APPENDIX

Weights and Measures Conversion Tables

Abbreviations

g = gram
lb = pound
mg = milligram
kg = kilogram
ppm = parts per million
kcal = kilocalorie
Mcal = megacalorie
mm = millimeter
cm = centimeter
km = kilometer

Weight

1 mg = 0.001 g
1 mg/g = 453.6 mg/lb
1 mg/lb = 0.002 mg/g
1 mg/g = 0.1%
1 mg/kg = 0.4536 mg/lb
1 mg/lb = 2.20 mg/kg
1 mg/lb = 2.0 g/ton
1 mg/lb = 2.20 ppm
1 mg/g = 1,000 ppm
1 mg/kg = 1 ppm
1 ppm = 0.45 mg/lb
1 ppm = 0.91 g/ton
1 ppm = 0.001 mg/g
1 ppm = 1.0 mg/kg
1 ppm = 0.4536 mg/lb
1 ppm = 0.0001%
1 gram = 0.002 pounds
1 gram = 0.04 ounces
1 g/ton = 0.5 mg/lb
1 g/lb = 2,000 g/ton

1 g/ton = 0.0005 g/lb
1 g/ton = 0.002 lb/ton
1 g/ton = 1.10 ppm
1 g/ton = 0.0001%
1 g/kg = 0.1%
1 ounce = 28.35 grams
1 pound = 453.62 grams
1 pound = 0.4536 kilograms
1 lb/ton = 453.6 g/ton
1 kilogram = 2.20 pounds
1 kcal = 1,000 calories
1 kcal/kg = 0.4536 kcal/lb
1 kcal/lb = 2.20 kcal/kg
1 kcal = 0.001 Mcal
1 Mcal = 1,000 kcal
1% = 10 mg/g
1% = 10,000 g/ton
1% = 10 g/kg
1% = 10,000 ppm

Length

1 mm = 0.04 inch
1 cm = 0.4 inch
1 cm = 0.033 foot
1 inch = 25.4 mm
1 inch = 2.54 cm
1 foot = 30.5 cm
1 foot = 0.305 meter
1 yard = 0.914 meter
1 meter = 3.3 feet
1 meter = 1.1 yards
1 mile = 1.609 km
1 mile = 5,280 feet
1 mile = 8.0 furlongs
1 furlong = 0.13 mile
1 furlong = 220.0 yards
1 km = 0.6 mile

Volume

1 milliliter = 0.5 pint
1 milliliter = 473.0 ounces
1 ounce = 0.002 milliliter
1 ounce = 0.13 cup
1 cup = 8.0 ounces
1 pint = 2.0 milliliters
1 pint = 29.41 quarts
1 quart = 0.034 pint
1 quart = 0.95 liter
1 quart = 0.25 gallon
1 liter = 1.057 quarts
1 liter = 0.264 gallon
1 gallon = 3.79 liters
1 gallon = 4.0 quarts

Temperature

°F to °C—subtract 32 and multiply by 0.556
°C to °F—multiply by 1.8 and add 32

examples....

0°F = -17.8° C	0°C = 32°F
10°F = -12.2°C	10°C = 50°F
20°F = -6.7°C	20°C = 68°F
30°F = -1.1°C	30°C = 86°F
40°F = 4.4°C	40°C = 104°F
50°F = 10.0°C	50°C = 122°F
60°F = 15.6°C	60°C = 140°F
70°F = 21.1°C	70°C = 158°F

TABLE 1– Daily Nutrient Requirements of Stallions During Breeding Season

	Mature Weight (kgs)	Digestible Energy (Mcal)	Crude Protein (g)	Lysine (g)	Calcium (g)	Phosphorus (g)	Magnesium (g)	Potassium (g)	Vitamin A (10³ IU)
Metric units	200	9.3	370	13	11	8	4.3	14.1	9
	400	16.8	670	23	20	15	7.7	25.5	18
	500	20.5	820	29	25	18	9.4	31.2	22
	600	24.3	970	34	30	21	11.2	36.9	27
	700	26.6	1,064	37	32	23	12.2	40.4	32

	Mature Weight (lbs)	Digestible Energy (calories)	Crude Protein (oz)	Lysine (oz)	Calcium (oz)	Phosphorus (oz)	Magnesium (oz)	Potassium (oz)	Vitamin A (10³ IU)
English units	440	9,300	13.05	0.46	0.39	0.28	0.15	0.50	9
	880	16,800	23.63	0.81	0.71	0.53	0.27	0.90	18
	1,100	20,500	28.92	1.02	0.88	0.63	0.33	1.10	22
	1,320	24,300	34.22	1.20	1.06	0.74	0.40	1.30	27
	1,540	26,600	37.53	1.31	1.13	0.81	0.43	1.43	32

Daily Nutrient Concentrations for Stallions During Breeding Season (90% Dry Matter Basis)

Digestible Energy (Mcal/kg)	(Mcal/lb)	Crude Protein (%)	Lysine (%)	Calcium (%)	Phosphorus (%)	Magnesium (%)	Potassium (%)	Vitamin A (IU/kg)	(IU/lb)
2.15	1.00	8.6	0.30	0.26	0.19	0.10	0.33	2,370	1,080

Adapted from *Nutrient Requirements of Horses.*

TABLE 2– Daily Nutrient Requirements of Pregnant Mares

Mature Weight (kgs)	Month of Pregnancy	Digestible Energy (Mcal)	Crude Protein (g)	Lysine (g)	Cal- cium (g)	Phos- phorus (g)	Magne- sium (g)	Potas- sium (g)	Vitamin A (10³ IU)
200	9	8.2	361	13	16	12	3.9	13.1	12
	10	8.4	368	13	16	12	4.0	13.4	12
	11	8.9	391	14	17	13	4.3	14.2	12
400	9	14.9	654	23	28	21	7.1	23.8	24
	10	15.1	666	23	29	22	7.3	24.2	24
	11	16.1	708	25	31	23	7.7	25.7	24
500	9	18.2	801	28	35	26	8.7	29.1	30
	10	18.5	815	29	35	27	8.9	29.7	30
	11	19.7	866	30	37	28	9.4	31.5	30
600	9	21.5	947	33	41	31	10.3	34.5	36
	10	21.9	965	34	42	32	10.5	35.1	36
	11	23.3	1,024	36	44	34	11.2	37.2	36
700	9	23.6	1,039	36	45	34	11.3	37.8	42
	10	24.0	1,058	37	46	35	11.5	38.5	42
	11	25.5	1,124	39	49	37	12.3	40.9	42

Metric units

Mature Weight (lbs)	Month of Pregnancy	Digestible Energy (cal)	Crude Protein (oz)	Lysine (oz)	Cal- cium (oz)	Phos- phorus (oz)	Magne- sium (oz)	Potas- sium (oz)	Vitamin A (10³ IU)
440	9	8,200	12.73	0.46	0.56	0.42	0.14	0.46	12
	10	8,400	12.98	0.46	0.56	0.42	0.14	0.47	12
	11	8,900	13.79	0.49	0.60	0.46	0.15	0.50	12
880	9	14,900	23.07	0.81	0.99	0.74	0.25	0.84	24
	10	15,100	23.49	0.81	1.02	0.78	0.26	0.85	24
	11	16,000	24.97	0.88	1.09	0.81	0.27	0.91	24
1,100	9	18,200	28.25	0.99	1.23	0.92	0.30	1.03	30
	10	18,500	28.75	1.02	1.23	0.95	0.31	1.05	30
	11	19,700	30.55	1.06	1.31	0.99	0.33	1.11	30
1,320	9	21,500	33.40	1.16	1.45	1.09	0.36	1.22	36
	10	21,900	34.04	1.20	1.48	1.13	0.37	1.24	36
	11	23,300	36.12	1.27	1.55	1.20	0.39	1.31	36
1,540	9	23,600	36.58	1.27	1.59	1.20	0.40	1.33	42
	10	24,000	37.32	1.31	1.62	1.23	0.41	1.36	42
	11	25,500	39.65	1.38	1.73	1.31	0.43	1.44	42

English units

Daily Nutrient Concentrations for Pregnant Mares (90% Dry Matter Basis)

Month of Preg.	Digestible Energy (Mcal/kg)	(Mcal/lb)	Crude Protein (%)	Lysine (%)	Calcium (%)	Phosphorus (%)	Magnesium (%)	Potassium (%)	Vitamin A (IU/kg)	(IU/lb)
9	2.00	0.90	8.9	0.31	0.39	0.29	0.10	0.32	3,330	1,510
10	2.00	0.90	9.0	0.32	0.39	0.30	0.10	0.33	3,280	1,490
11	2.15	1.00	9.5	0.33	0.41	0.31	0.10	0.35	3,280	1,490

Adapted from *Nutrient Requirements of Horses.*

478

TABLE 3– Daily Nutrient Requirements of Lactating Mares

Mature Weight (kgs)	Time Period	Dig. Energy (Mcal)	Crude Protein (g)	Lysine (g)	Cal- cium (g)	Phos- phorus (g)	Magne- sium (g)	Potas- sium (g)	Vitamin A (10³ IU)
200	Foaling to 3 months	13.7	688	24	27	18	4.8	21.2	12
	3 months to weaning	12.2	528	18	18	11	3.7	14.8	12
400	Foaling to 3 months	22.9	1,141	40	45	29	8.7	36.8	24
	3 months to weaning	19.7	839	29	29	18	6.9	26.4	24
500	Foaling to 3 months	28.3	1,427	50	56	36	10.9	46.0	30
	3 months to weaning	24.3	1,048	37	36	22	8.6	33.0	30
600	Foaling to 3 months	33.7	1,711	60	67	43	13.1	55.2	36
	3 months to weaning	28.9	1,258	44	43	27	10.4	39.6	36
700	Foaling to 3 months	37.9	1,997	70	78	51	15.2	64.4	42
	3 months to weaning	32.4	1,468	51	50	31	12.1	46.2	42

Metric units

Mature Weight (lbs)	Time Period	Dig. Energy (cal.)	Crude Protein (oz)	Lysine (oz)	Cal- cium (oz)	Phos- phorus (oz)	Magne- sium (oz)	Potas- sium (oz)	Vitamin A (10³ IU)
440	Foaling to 3 months	13,700	24.27	0.85	0.95	0.63	0.17	0.75	12
	3 months to weaning	12,200	18.62	0.63	0.63	0.39	0.13	0.52	12
880	Foaling to 3 months	22,900	40.25	1.41	1.59	1.02	0.31	1.30	24
	3 months to weaning	19,700	29.59	1.02	1.02	0.63	0.24	0.93	24
1,100	Foaling to 3 months	28,300	50.34	1.76	1.98	1.27	0.38	1.62	30
	3 months to weaning	24,300	36.97	1.31	1.27	0.78	0.30	1.16	30
1,320	Foaling to 3 months	33,700	60.35	2.12	2.36	1.52	0.46	1.95	36
	3 months to weaning	28,900	44.37	1.55	1.52	0.95	0.37	1.40	36
1,540	Foaling to 3 months	37,900	70.44	2.47	2.75	1.80	0.54	2.27	42
	3 months to weaning	32,400	51.78	1.80	1.76	1.09	0.43	1.63	42

English units

Dig – Digestible

Daily Nutrient Concentrations for Lactating Mares (90% Dry Matter Basis)

	Digestible Energy (Mcal/kg) (Mcal/lb)		Crude Protein (%)	Lysine (%)	Calcium (%)	Phos- phorus (%)	Magnesium (%)	Potassium (%)	Vitamin A (IU/kg) (IU/lb)	
Foaling to 3 months	2.35	1.10	12.0	0.41	0.47	0.30	0.09	0.38	2,480	1,130
3 months to weaning	2.20	1.05	10.0	0.34	0.33	0.20	0.08	0.30	2,720	1,240

Adapted from *Nutrient Requirements of Horses.*

TABLE 4– Daily Nutrient Requirements of Weanlings

Metric units

Est. Mat. Wt. (kgs)	Age in Months	Growth Rate	Daily Gain (kg)	Dig. Energy (Mcal)	Crude Protein (g)	Lysine (g)	Cal-cium (g)	Phos-phorus (g)	Mag-nesium (g)	Potas-sium (g)	Vi-tamin A (10³ IU)
200	4		0.40	7.3	365	15	16	9	1.6	5.0	3
	6	Moderate	0.30	7.6	378	16	13	7	1.8	5.7	4
		Rapid	0.40	8.7	433	18	17	9	1.9	6.0	4
400	4		0.85	13.5	675	28	33	18	3.2	9.8	7
	6	Moderate	0.55	12.9	643	27	25	14	3.4	10.7	8
		Rapid	0.70	14.5	725	30	30	16	3.6	11.1	8
500	4		0.85	14.4	720	30	34	19	3.7	11.3	8
	6	Moderate	0.65	15.0	750	32	29	16	4.0	12.7	10
		Rapid	0.85	17.2	860	36	36	20	4.3	13.3	10
600	4		1.00	16.5	825	35	40	22	4.3	13.0	9
	6	Moderate	0.75	17.0	850	36	34	19	4.6	14.5	11
		Rapid	0.95	19.2	960	40	40	22	4.9	15.1	11
700	4		1.10	19.7	986	41	44	25	4.8	14.6	10
	6	Moderate	0.80	20.0	1,001	42	37	20	5.1	16.2	12
		Rapid	1.00	22.2	1,111	47	43	24	5.4	16.8	12

English units

Est. Mat. Wt. (lbs)	Age in Months	Growth Rate	Daily Gain (lbs)	Dig. Energy (cal.)	Crude Protein (oz)	Lysine (oz)	Cal-cium (oz)	Phos-phorus (oz)	Mag-nesium (oz)	Potas-sium (oz)	Vi-tamin A (10³ IU)
440	4		0.88	7,300	12.88	0.53	0.56	0.32	0.06	0.18	3
	6	Moderate	0.66	7,600	13.33	0.56	0.46	0.25	0.066	0.20	4
		Rapid	0.88	8,700	15.27	0.64	0.60	0.32	0.07	0.21	4
880	4		1.87	13,500	23.81	0.99	1.16	0.64	0.117	0.35	7
	6	Moderate	1.21	12,900	22.68	0.95	0.88	0.49	0.127	0.38	8
		Rapid	1.54	14,500	25.57	1.06	1.06	0.56	0.13	0.39	8
1,100	4		1.87	14,400	25.40	1.06	1.20	0.67	0.13	0.40	8
	6	Moderate	1.43	15,000	26.46	1.13	1.02	0.56	0.14	0.45	10
		Rapid	1.87	17,200	30.34	1.27	1.27	0.71	0.15	0.47	10
1,320	4		2.20	16,500	29.10	1.24	1.41	0.78	0.15	0.46	9
	6	Moderate	1.65	17,000	29.98	1.27	1.20	0.67	0.16	0.51	11
		Rapid	2.09	19,200	33.86	1.41	1.41	0.78	0.17	0.53	11
1,540	4		2.43	19,700	34.78	1.45	1.55	0.88	0.17	0.52	10
	6	Moderate	1.76	20,000	35.31	1.48	1.31	0.71	0.18	0.57	12
		Rapid	2.20	22,200	39.19	1.66	1.52	0.85	0.19	0.59	12

Dig. – Digestible

Daily Nutrient Concentrations for Weanlings (90% Dry Matter Basis)

Age in Months	Growth Rate	Digestible Energy (Mcal/kg)	(Mcal/lb)	Crude Protein (%)	Lysine (%)	Cal-cium (%)	Phos-phorus (%)	Mag-nesium (%)	Potas-sium (%)	Vitamin A (IU/kg)	(IU/lb)
4		2.60	1.25	13.1	0.54	0.62	0.34	0.07	0.27	1420	650
6	Moderate	2.60	1.25	13.0	0.55	0.50	0.28	0.07	0.27	1680	760
	Rapid	2.60	1.25	13.1	0.55	0.55	0.30	0.07	0.27	1470	670

Adapted from *Nutrient Requirements of Horses.*

TABLE 5– Daily Nutrient Requirements of Yearlings

Est. Mat. Wt. (kgs)	Age in Months		Daily Gain (kg)	Dig. Energy (Mcal)	Crude Protein (g)	Lysine (g)	Cal- cium (g)	Phos- phorus (g)	Mag- nesium (g)	Potas- sium (g)	Vitamin A (10³ IU)
200	12	Mod. growth	0.20	8.7	392	17	12	7	2.4	7.6	6
		Rapid growth	0.30	10.3	462	19	15	8	2.5	7.9	6
	18	Not in training	0.10	8.3	375	16	10	6	2.7	8.8	8
		In training	0.10	11.6	522	22	14	8	3.7	12.2	8
400	12	Mod. growth	0.40	15.6	700	30	23	13	4.5	14.5	12
		Rapid growth	0.50	17.1	770	33	27	15	4.6	14.8	12
	18	Not in training	0.25	15.9	716	30	21	12	5.3	17.3	15
		In training	0.25	21.6	970	41	29	16	7.1	23.4	15
500	12	Mod. growth	0.50	18.9	851	36	29	16	5.5	17.8	15
		Rapid growth	0.65	21.3	956	40	34	19	5.7	18.2	15
	18	Not in training	0.35	19.8	893	38	27	15	6.4	21.1	18
		In training	0.35	26.5	1,195	50	36	20	8.6	28.2	18
600	12	Mod. growth	0.65	22.7	1,023	43	36	20	6.4	20.7	17
		Rapid growth	0.80	25.1	1,127	48	41	22	6.6	21.2	17
	18	Not in training	0.45	23.9	1,077	45	33	18	7.7	25.1	21
		In training	0.45	32.0	1,429	60	44	24	10.2	33.3	21
700	12	Mod. growth	0.70	26.1	1,176	50	39	22	7.2	23.1	19
		Rapid growth	0.85	28.5	1,281	54	44	24	7.4	23.6	19
	18	Not in training	0.50	27.0	1,215	51	37	20	8.5	27.8	24
		In training	0.50	36.0	1,615	68	49	27	11.3	36.9	24

Dig.– Digestible
Mod.– Moderate

Daily Nutrient Concentrations for Yearlings (90% Dry Matter Basis)

Age in Months		Digestible Energy (Mcal/kg)	Crude Protein (%)	Lysine (%)	Cal- cium (%)	Phos- phorus (%)	Mag- nesium (%)	Potas- sium (%)	Vitamin A (IU/kg)
12	Moderate growth	2.50	11.3	0.48	0.39	0.21	0.07	0.27	1,950
	Rapid growth	2.50	11.3	0.48	0.40	0.22	0.07	0.27	1,730
18	Not in training	2.30	10.1	0.43	0.31	0.17	0.07	0.27	2,050
	In training	2.40	10.8	0.45	0.32	0.18	0.08	0.27	1,620

Adapted from *Nutrient Requirements of Horses.*

TABLE 5– Daily Nutrient Requirements of Yearlings

Est. Mat. Wt. (lbs)	Age in Months		Daily Gain (lbs)	Dig. Energy (cal.)	Crude Pro-tein (oz)	Lysine (oz)	Cal-cium (oz)	Phos-phorus (oz)	Mag-nesium (oz)	Potas-sium (oz)	Vitamin A (10³ IU)
440	12	Mod. growth	0.44	8,700	13.83	0.60	0.42	0.25	0.09	0.27	6
		Rapid growth	0.66	10,300	16.30	0.67	0.53	0.28	0.09	0.28	6
	18	Not in training	0.22	8,300	13.23	0.56	0.35	0.21	0.10	0.31	8
		In training	0.22	11,600	18.41	0.78	0.49	0.28	0.13	0.43	8
880	12	Mod. growth	0.88	15,600	24.69	1.06	0.81	0.46	0.16	0.51	12
		Rapid growth	1.10	17,100	27.16	1.16	0.95	0.53	0.16	0.52	12
	18	Not in training	0.55	15,900	25.26	1.06	0.74	0.42	0.19	0.61	15
		In training	0.55	21,600	34.22	1.45	1.02	0.56	0.25	0.83	15
1,100	12	Mod. growth	1.10	18,900	30.02	1.27	1.02	0.56	0.19	0.63	15
		Rapid growth	1.43	21,300	33.72	1.41	1.20	0.67	0.20	0.64	15
	18	Not in training	0.77	19,800	31.50	1.34	0.95	0.53	0.23	0.74	18
		In training	0.77	26,500	42.15	1.76	1.27	0.71	0.30	1.00	18
1,320	12	Mod. growth	1.43	22,700	36.09	1.52	1.27	0.71	0.22	0.73	17
		Rapid growth	1.76	25,100	39.75	1.69	1.45	0.78	0.23	0.75	17
	18	Not in training	0.99	23,900	37.99	1.59	1.16	0.64	0.27	0.89	21
		In training	0.99	32,000	50.41	2.12	1.55	0.85	0.36	1.18	21
1,540	12	Mod. growth	1.54	26,100	41.48	1.76	1.38	0.78	0.25	0.82	19
		Rapid growth	1.87	28,500	45.19	1.91	1.55	0.85	0.26	0.83	19
	18	Not in training	1.10	27,000	42.86	1.80	1.31	0.71	0.30	0.98	19
		In training	1.10	36,000	56.97	2.40	1.73	0.95	0.40	1.30	24

Dig. – Digestible
Mod. – Moderate

Daily Nutrient Concentrations for Yearlings (90% Dry Matter Basis)

Age in Months		Digestible Energy (Mcal/lb)	Crude Pro-tein (%)	Lysine (%)	Cal-cium (%)	Phos-phorus (%)	Mag-nesium (%)	Potas-sium (%)	Vitamin A (IU/lb)
12	Moderate growth	1.15	11.3	0.48	0.39	0.21	0.07	0.27	890
	Rapid growth	1.15	11.3	0.48	0.40	0.22	0.07	0.27	790
18	Not in training	1.05	10.1	0.43	0.31	0.17	0.07	0.27	930
	In training	1.10	10.8	0.45	0.32	0.18	0.08	0.27	740

Adapted from *Nutrient Requirements of Horses.*

TABLE 6– Daily Nutrient Requirements of Two-Year-Olds

Est. Mat. Wt. (kgs)		Daily Gain (kgs)	Dig. Energy (Mcal)	Crude Pro- tein (g)	Lysine (g)	Cal- cium (g)	Phos- phorus (g)	Mag- nesium (g)	Potas- sium (g)	Vitamin A (10³ IU)
200	Not in training	0.05	7.9	337	13	9	5	2.8	9.4	8
	In training	0.05	11.4	485	19	13	7	4.1	13.5	8
400	Not in training	0.15	15.3	650	26	19	11	5.7	18.7	16
	In training	0.15	21.5	913	37	27	15	7.9	26.2	16
500	Not in training	0.20	18.8	800	32	24	13	7.0	23.1	20
	In training	0.20	26.3	1,117	45	34	19	9.8	32.2	20
600	Not in training	0.30	23.5	998	40	31	17	8.5	27.9	24
	In training	0.30	32.3	1,372	55	43	24	11.6	38.4	24
700	Not in training	0.35	26.3	1,117	45	35	19	9.4	31.1	27
	In training	0.35	36.0	1,529	61	48	27	12.9	42.5	27

Metric units

Est. Mat. Wt. (lbs)		Daily Gain (lbs)	Dig. Energy (cal.)	Crude Pro- tein (oz)	Lysine (oz)	Cal- cium (oz)	Phos- phorus (oz)	Mag- nesium (oz)	Potas- sium (oz)	Vitamin A (10³ IU)
440	Not in training	0.11	7,900	11.89	0.46	0.32	0.18	0.10	0.33	8
	In training	0.11	11,400	17.11	0.67	0.46	0.25	0.15	0.48	8
880	Not in training	0.33	15,300	22.93	0.92	0.67	0.39	0.20	0.66	16
	In training	0.33	21,500	32.21	1.31	0.95	0.53	0.28	0.92	16
1,100	Not in training	0.44	18,800	28.22	1.13	0.85	0.46	0.25	0.82	20
	In training	0.44	26,300	39.40	1.59	1.20	0.67	0.35	1.14	20
1,320	Not in training	0.66	23,500	35.20	1.41	1.09	0.60	0.30	0.98	24
	In training	0.66	32,300	48.40	1.94	1.52	0.85	0.41	1.36	24
1,540	Not in training	0.77	26,300	39.40	1.59	1.24	0.67	0.33	1.10	27
	In training	0.77	36,000	53.93	2.15	1.69	0.95	0.46	1.50	27

English units

Dig. – Digestible

Daily Nutrient Concentrations for Two-Year-Olds (90% Dry Matter Basis)

	Digestible Energy (Mcal/kg)	(Mcal/lb)	Crude Protein (%)	Lysine (%)	Cal- cium (%)	Phos- phorus (%)	Mag- nesium (%)	Potas- sium (%)	Vitamin A (IU/kg)	(IU/lb)
Not in training	2.20	1.00	9.4	0.38	0.28	0.15	0.08	0.27	2,380	1,080
In training	2.40	1.10	10.1	0.41	0.31	0.17	0.09	0.29	1,840	840

Adapted from *Nutrient Requirements of Horses.*

TABLE 7– Daily Nutrient Requirements of Working Horses

Mature Weight (kgs)		Digestible Energy (Mcal)	Crude Protein (g)	Lysine (g)	Calcium (g)	Phosphorus (g)	Magnesium (g)	Potassium (g)	Vitamin A (10³ IU)
200	Light work	9.3	370	13	11	8	4.3	14.1	9
	Moderate work	11.1	444	16	14	10	5.1	16.9	9
	Intense work	14.8	592	21	18	13	6.8	22.5	9
400	Light work	16.8	670	23	20	15	7.7	25.5	18
	Moderate work	20.1	804	28	25	17	9.2	30.6	18
	Intense work	26.8	1,072	38	33	23	12.3	40.7	18
500	Light work	20.5	820	29	25	18	9.4	31.2	22
	Moderate work	24.6	984	34	30	21	11.3	37.4	22
	Intense work	32.8	1,312	46	40	29	15.1	49.9	22
600	Light work	24.3	970	34	30	21	11.2	36.9	27
	Moderate work	29.1	1,164	41	36	25	13.4	44.2	27
	Intense work	38.8	1,552	54	47	34	17.8	59.0	27
700	Light work	26.6	1,064	37	32	23	12.2	40.4	32
	Moderate work	31.9	1,277	45	39	28	14.7	48.5	32
	Intense work	42.6	1,702	60	52	37	19.6	64.7	32

Metric units

Mature Weight (lbs)		Digestible Energy (cal.)	Crude Protein (oz)	Lysine (oz)	Calcium (oz)	Phosphorus (oz)	Magnesium (oz)	Potassium (oz)	Vitamin A (10³ IU)
440	Light work	9,300	13.05	0.46	0.39	0.28	0.15	0.50	9
	Moderate work	11,100	15.66	0.56	0.49	0.35	0.18	0.60	9
	Intense work	14,800	20.88	0.74	0.64	0.46	0.24	0.79	9
880	Light work	16,800	23.63	0.81	0.71	0.53	0.27	0.90	18
	Moderate work	20,100	28.36	0.99	0.88	0.60	0.33	1.08	18
	Intense work	26,800	37.81	1.34	1.16	0.81	0.43	1.44	18
1,100	Light work	20,500	28.93	1.02	0.88	0.64	0.33	1.10	22
	Moderate work	24,600	34.71	1.20	1.06	0.74	0.40	1.32	22
	Intense work	32,800	46.28	1.62	1.41	1.02	0.53	1.76	22
1,320	Light work	24,300	34.22	1.20	1.06	0.74	0.39	1.30	27
	Moderate work	29,100	41.06	1.45	1.27	0.88	0.47	1.56	27
	Intense work	38,800	54.75	1.91	1.66	1.20	0.63	2.08	27
1,540	Light work	26,600	37.53	1.31	1.13	0.81	0.43	1.43	32
	Moderate work	31,900	45.05	1.59	1.38	0.99	0.52	1.71	32
	Intense work	42,600	60.67	2.12	1.83	1.31	0.69	2.28	32

English units

Daily Nutrient Concentrations for Working Horses (90%Dry Matter Basis)

	Digestible Energy (Mcal/kg)	(Mcal/lb)	Crude Protein (%)	Lysine (%)	Calcium (%)	Phosphorus (%)	Magnesium (%)	Potassium (%)	Vitamin A (IU/kg)	(IU/lb)
Light work	2.20	1.05	8.8	0.32	0.27	0.19	0.10	0.34	2,420	1,100
Moderate work	2.40	1.10	9.4	0.35	0.28	0.22	0.11	0.36	2,140	970
Intense work	2.55	1.20	10.3	0.36	0.31	0.23	0.12	0.39	1,760	800

Adapted from *Nutrient Requirements of Horses.*

TABLE 8– Daily Nutrient Requirements for Maintenance

	Mature Weight (kgs)	Digestible Energy (Mcal)	Crude Protein (g)	Lysine (g)	Calcium (g)	Phosphorus (g)	Magnesium (g)	Potassium (g)	Vitamin A (10³ IU)
Metric units	200	7.4	296	10	8	6	3.0	10.0	6
	400	13.4	536	19	16	11	6.0	20.0	12
	500	16.4	656	23	20	14	7.5	25.0	15
	600	19.4	776	27	24	17	9.0	30.0	18
	700	21.3	851	30	28	20	10.5	35.0	21

	Mature Weight (lbs)	Digestible Energy (calories)	Crude Protein (oz)	Lysine (oz)	Calcium (oz)	Phosphorus (oz)	Magnesium (oz)	Potassium (oz)	Vitamin A (10³ IU)
English units	440	7,400	10.44	0.35	0.28	0.21	0.11	0.35	6
	880	13,400	18.91	0.67	0.56	0.39	0.21	0.71	12
	1,100	16,400	23.14	0.81	0.71	0.49	0.27	0.88	15
	1,320	19,400	27.37	0.95	0.85	0.60	0.31	1.06	18
	1,540	21,300	30.02	1.06	0.99	0.71	0.37	1.24	21

Daily Nutrient Concentrations for Maintenance (90%Dry Matter Basis)

Digestible Energy (Mcal/kg)	(Mcal/lb)	Crude Protein (%)	Lysine (%)	Calcium (%)	Phosphorus (%)	Magnesium (%)	Potassium (%)	Vitamin A (IU/kg)	(IU/lb)
1.80	0.80	7.2	0.25	0.21	0.15	0.08	0.27	1,650	750

Adapted from *Nutrient Requirements of Horses.*

TABLE 9– Composition of Common Forages

Forage	Dry Matter (%)	Digestible Energy (Mcal/kg)	Digestible Energy (Mcal/lb)	Crude Protein (%)	Lysine (%)	Ether Extract (%)	Fiber (%)	Ash (%)
ALFALFA								
Pasture, late vegetative	23.2	0.68	0.31	5.1	0.29	0.7	5.6	2.4
Pasture, full bloom	23.8	0.55	0.25	4.6	---	0.6	7.2	2.6
Hay, early bloom	90.5	2.24	1.02	18.0	0.81	2.6	20.8	8.4
Hay, midbloom	91.0	2.07	0.94	17.0	---	2.4	25.5	7.8
Hay, full bloom	90.9	1.97	0.89	15.5	0.79	1.8	27.3	7.1
BAHIAGRASS								
Pasture	28.7	0.61	0.26	3.6	---	0.5	8.7	3.2
Hay	90.0	1.75	0.79	8.5	---	1.8	28.1	5.7
Hay, late vegetative	91.0	1.70	0.77	8.9	---	2.1	29.7	7.1
Hay, early bloom	91.0	1.61	0.73	6.4	---	1.4	30.9	8.5
BARLEY								
Hay	88.4	1.78	0.81	7.8	---	1.9	23.6	6.6
BERMUDAGRASS, COASTAL								
Pasture	30.3	0.72	0.33	3.8	---	1.1	8.6	2.4
Hay, 15-28 days' growth	88.4	1.92	0.87	10.6	0.38	2.4	26.7	6.7
Hay, 29-42 days' growth	93.0	1.96	0.89	10.9	---	2.4	28.0	6.2
Hay, 43-56 days' growth	93.0	1.74	0.79	7.3	0.28	2.5	30.4	7.5
BLUEGRASS, KENTUCKY								
Pasture, early vegetative	30.8	0.64	0.29	5.4	---	1.1	7.8	2.9
Pasture, milk stage	42.0	0.75	0.34	4.9	---	1.5	12.7	3.1
Hay, full bloom	92.1	1.58	0.72	8.2	---	3.0	29.9	5.4
BROME, SMOOTH								
Pasture, early vegetative	26.1	0.66	0.31	5.6	---	1.0	6.0	2.7
Pasture, mature	54.9	0.89	0.40	3.4	---	1.3	19.1	3.8
Hay, midbloom	87.6	1.87	0.85	12.6	---	1.9	28.0	9.5
Hay, mature	92.6	1.57	0.71	5.6	---	1.8	29.8	6.7
CANARYGRASS, REED								
Pasture	22.8	0.58	0.26	3.9	---	0.9	5.6	2.3
Hay	89.3	1.78	0.81	9.1	---	2.7	30.2	7.3
CLOVER, ALSIKE								
Pasture, early vegetative	18.9	0.47	0.21	4.5	---	0.6	3.3	2.4
Hay	87.7	1.71	0.78	12.4	---	2.4	26.2	7.6
CLOVER, LADINO								
Pasture, early vegetative	19.3	0.48	0.22	5.0	---	0.9	2.7	2.3
Hay	89.1	1.96	0.89	20.0	---	2.4	18.5	8.4
CLOVER, RED								
Pasture, early bloom	19.6	0.50	0.22	4.1	---	1.0	4.6	2.0
Pasture, full bloom	26.2	0.66	0.27	3.8	---	0.8	6.8	2.0
Hay	88.4	1.96	0.89	13.2	---	2.5	27.1	6.7
FESCUE, KENTUCKY								
Pasture	31.3	0.70	0.32	4.7	0.18	1.7	7.7	2.2
Hay, full bloom	91.9	1.89	0.86	11.8	---	5.1	23.9	7.6
Hay, mature	90.0	1.76	0.80	9.8	---	4.2	28.1	6.1
LESPEDEZA, COMMON								
Pasture, late vegetative	25.0	0.55	0.25	4.1	---	0.5	8.0	3.2
Hay, midbloom	90.8	1.93	0.88	11.4	---	2.3	26.2	4.5
LESPEDEZA, KOBE								
Hay, midbloom	93.9	1.96	0.89	10.0	---	2.8	26.2	3.8

(continued)

TABLE 9– Composition of Common Forages

Forage	Dry Matter (%)	Digestible Energy (Mcal/kg)	(Mcal/lb)	Crude Protein (%)	Lysine (%)	Ether Extract (%)	Fiber (%)	Ash (%)
MEADOW PLANTS, INTERMOUNTAIN								
Hay	95.1	1.60	0.73	8.2	---	2.4	31.2	8.2
OATS								
Hay	90.7	1.75	0.79	8.6	---	2.2	29.1	7.2
ORCHARDGRASS								
Pasture, early bloom	23.5	0.54	0.24	3.0	---	0.9	7.5	1.9
Pasture, midbloom	27.4	0.55	0.25	2.8	---	1.0	9.2	2.1
Hay, early bloom	89.1	1.94	0.88	11.4	---	2.6	30.2	7.6
Hay, late bloom	90.6	1.72	0.78	7.6	---	3.1	33.6	9.1
PANGOLAGRASS								
Pasture	20.2	0.39	0.10	1.8	---	0.5	6.6	1.5
Hay, 15-28 days' growth	91.0	1.72	0.78	9.2	---	2.2	29.1	7.7
Hay, 29-42 days' growth	91.0	1.62	0.74	6.7	---	1.8	29.5	7.3
Hay, 43-56 days' growth	91.0	1.41	0.64	5.7	---	1.6	29.3	6.9
PRAIRIE PLANTS, MIDWEST								
Hay	91.0	1.48	0.67	5.8	---	2.1	30.7	7.2
REDTOP								
Hay, midbloom	92.8	1.83	0.83	11.1	---	2.4	29.0	6.0
RYEGRASS, ITALIAN								
Pasture	22.6	0.51	0.23	4.0	---	0.9	4.7	3.9
Hay, late vegetative	85.6	1.57	0.71	8.8	---	2.1	20.4	9.4
SORGHUM, JOHNSONGRASS								
Hay	90.5	1.50	0.68	6.7	---	2.0	30.4	7.7
TIMOTHY								
Pasture, late vegetative	26.7	0.70	0.29	3.3	---	1.0	8.6	2.0
Pasture, midbloom	29.2	0.58	0.27	2.7	---	0.9	9.8	1.9
Hay, early bloom	89.1	1.83	0.83	9.6	---	2.5	30.0	5.1
Hay, midbloom	88.9	1.77	0.80	8.6	---	2.3	30.0	5.4
Hay, full bloom	89.4	1.73	0.78	7.2	---	2.6	31.5	4.6
Hay, late bloom	88.3	1.59	0.72	6.9	---	2.4	31.5	4.8
TREFOIL, BIRDSFOOT								
Pasture	19.3	0.42	0.19	4.0	---	0.8	4.1	2.2
Hay	90.6	1.99	1.19	14.4	---	1.9	29.3	6.7
WHEAT								
Pasture, early vegetative	22.2	0.64	0.29	6.1	---	1.0	3.9	3.0
Hay	88.7	1.68	0.76	7.7	---	2.0	25.7	7.0
WHEATGRASS, CRESTED								
Pasture, early vegetative	28.5	0.72	0.33	6.0	---	0.6	6.2	2.9

Note: All hay is sun-cured. All values are on an as fed basis. --- indicates data is unavailable.
Adapted from *Nutrient Requirements of Horses.*

TABLE 10– Composition of Common Concentrate Components

Component	Dry Matter (%)	Digestible Energy (Mcal/kg)	(Mcal/lb)	Crude Protein (%)	Lysine (%)	Ether Extract (%)	Fiber (%)	Ash (%)
ALFALFA MEAL								
15% protein, dehydrated	90.4	2.00	0.91	15.6	0.63	2.2	26.2	8.9
17% protein, dehydrated	91.8	2.16	0.98	17.4	0.85	2.8	24.0	9.8
BARLEY								
Grain	88.6	3.26	1.49	11.7	0.40	1.8	4.9	2.4
Grain, Pacific coast	88.6	3.17	1.48	9.7	0.27	2.0	6.0	2.4
BEET, SUGAR								
Pulp, dehydrated	91.0	2.33	1.06	8.9	0.54	0.5	18.2	4.9
BREWERS GRAIN								
Dehydrated	92.0	2.53	1.15	23.4	0.88	5.9	13.7	4.4
BREWERS YEAST								
Dehydrated	93.1	3.07	1.40	43.4	3.23	1.0	3.2	6.7
CANOLA MEAL								
Seeds, solvent extracted	90.8	2.83	1.28	37.1	2.08	2.8	11.0	6.4
CARROT								
Roots, fresh	11.5	0.43	0.20	1.2	---	0.2	1.1	1.0
CORN								
Dried distillers grain	92.0	3.21	1.46	27.8	0.81	6.6	11.3	3.1
Ground ears	86.2	2.83	1.29	7.8	0.17	3.2	8.1	1.6
Grain	88.0	3.38	1.54	9.1	0.25	3.6	2.2	1.3
COTTON								
Seeds, solvent extracted	91.0	2.74	1.25	41.3	1.68	1.5	12.2	6.5
FATS AND OILS								
Hydrolyzed animal fat	99.2	7.94	3.61	---	---	98.4	---	---
Vegetable oil	99.8	8.98	4.08	---	---	99.7	---	---
FLAX, COMMON								
Seeds	93.6	3.40	1.54	21.1	0.86	36.0	6.2	4.9
Meal, solvent extracted	90.2	2.74	1.25	34.6	1.16	1.4	9.1	5.9
MOLASSES and SYRUP								
Beet sugar molasses	77.9	2.65	1.20	6.6	---	0.2	0.0	8.9
Citrus, syrup	66.9	2.27	1.03	5.7	---	0.2	0.0	5.1
Dried sugarcane molasses	94.4	3.21	1.46	9.0	---	0.8	7.1	12.0
Sugarcane molasses	74.3	2.60	1.18	4.3	---	0.2	0.4	9.9
OATS								
Grain, grade 1	89.0	2.99	1.36	12.5	0.44	5.1	10.8	3.0
Grain, Pacific coast	90.9	2.91	1.32	9.1	0.33	5.0	11.2	3.8
PEANUT MEAL								
Seeds, solvent extracted	92.4	3.00	1.36	48.9	1.45	2.1	7.7	5.8
RICE								
Bran with germs	90.5	2.62	1.19	13.0	0.57	13.6	11.7	10.4
Grain, ground	89.0	3.38	1.54	7.5	0.24	1.6	8.6	5.3
RYE								
Grain	87.5	3.36	1.53	12.0	0.41	1.5	2.2	1.6
SORGHUM (MILO)								
Grain	90.1	3.21	1.46	11.5	0.26	2.7	2.6	1.7

(continued)

TABLE 10– Composition of Common Concentrate Components

Component	Dry Matter (%)	Digestible Energy (Mcal/kg)	(Mcal/lb)	Crude Protein (%)	Lysine (%)	Ether Extract (%)	Fiber (%)	Ash (%)
SOYBEAN MEAL								
Seeds, solvent extracted	89.1	3.14	1.43	44.5	2.87	1.4	6.2	6.4
Seeds without hulls, solvent extracted	89.9	3.36	1.53	48.5	3.09	1.0	3.5	6.0
SUNFLOWER								
Seeds without hulls, solvent extracted	92.5	2.59	1.17	45.2	1.68	2.7	11.7	7.5
WHEAT								
Bran	89.0	2.94	1.33	15.4	0.56	3.8	10.0	5.9
Grain, hard, red winter	88.9	3.43	1.56	13.0	0.40	1.6	2.5	1.7
Grain, soft, red winter	88.4	3.41	1.55	11.4	0.36	1.6	2.4	1.8
Grain, soft, white winter	90.2	3.54	1.61	10.6	---	1.5	2.2	1.5
Mill-Run	89.9	3.12	1.42	15.6	0.57	4.1	8.2	5.1

Note: All values are on an as fed basis. --- indicates data is unavailable. Adapted from *Nutrient Requirements of Horses.*

TABLE 11– Approximate Feed Consumption (based on % body weight)
(Mature Weight–200 kgs or 440 lbs)

	Weight		% Body Weight			Total kgs or lbs					
				Con-		Forage		Concentrate		Total Feed	
Class	(kgs)	(lbs)	Forage	centrate	Total	(kgs)	(lbs)	(kgs)	(lbs)	(kgs)	(lbs)
Maintenance	200	440	1.5-2.0	0.0-0.5	1.5-2.0	3-4	7-9	0-1	0-2	3-4	7-9
Mares											
Late gestation	200	440	1.0-1.5	0.5-1.0	1.5-2.0	2-3	4-7	1-2	2-4	3-4	7-9
Early lactation	200	440	1.0-2.0	1.0-2.0	2.0-3.0	2-4	4-9	2-4	4-9	4-6	9-13
Late lactation	200	440	1.0-2.0	0.5-1.5	2.0-2.5	2-4	4-9	1-3	2-7	4-5	9-11
Light work	200	440	1.0-2.0	0.5-1.0	1.5-2.5	2-4	4-9	1-2	2-4	3-5	7-11
Moderate work	200	440	1.0-2.0	0.75-1.5	1.75-2.5	2-4	4-9	2-3	3-7	4-5	8-11
Intense work	200	440	0.75-1.5	1.0-2.0	2.0-3.0	2-3	3-7	2-4	4-9	4-6	9-13
Nursing foal 3 months	75	165	0.0	1.0-2.0	2.5-3.5	0.0	0.0	.75-2	2-3	2-3	4-6
Weanling 6 months	95	209	0.5-1.0	1.5-3.0	2.0-3.5	.48-.95	1-2	1-3	3-6	2-3	4-7
Yearling 12 months	140	309	1.0-1.5	1.0-2.0	2.0-3.0	1-2	3-5	1-3	3-6	3-4	6-9
Long Yearling 18 months	170	375	1.0-1.5	1.0-1.5	2.0-2.5	2-3	4-6	2-3	4-6	3-4	8-9
Two-year-old 24 months	185	408	1.0-1.5	1.0-1.5	1.75-2.5	2-3	4-6	2-3	4-6	3-5	7-10

Note: Figures are rounded off to the nearest kilogram or pound. Adapted from *Nutrient Requirements of Horses.*

TABLE 11– Approximate Feed Consumption (based on % body weight)

(Mature Weight–400 kgs or 880 lbs)

Class	Weight (kgs)	(lbs)	% Body Weight Forage	Con-centrate	Total	Forage (kgs)	(lbs)	Concentrate (kgs)	(lbs)	Total Feed (kgs)	(lbs)
Maintenance	400	880	1.5-2.0	0.0-0.5	1.5-2.0	6-8	13-17	0-2	0-4	6-8	13-18
Mares											
Late gestation	400	880	1.0-1.5	0.5-1.0	1.5-2.0	4-6	9-13	2-4	4-9	6-8	13-18
Early lactation	400	880	1.0-2.0	1.0-2.0	2.0-3.0	4-8	9-18	4-8	9-18	8-12	18-26
Late lactation	400	880	1.0-2.0	0.5-1.5	2.0-2.5	4-8	9-18	2-6	4-13	8-10	18-22
Light work	400	880	1.0-2.0	0.5-1.0	1.5-2.5	4-8	9-18	2-4	4-9	6-10	13-22
Moderate work	400	880	1.0-2.0	0.75-1.5	1.75-2.5	4-8	9-18	3-6	7-13	7-10	15-22
Intense work	400	880	0.75-1.5	1.0-2.0	2.0-3.0	3-6	7-13	4-8	9-18	8-12	18-26
Nursing foal											
3 months	145	320	0.0	1.0-2.0	2.5-3.5	0.0	0.0	1-3	3-6	4-5	8-11
Weanling											
6 months	180	397	0.5-1.0	1.5-3.0	2.0-3.5	0.9-2	2-4	3-5	6-12	4-6	8-14
Yearling											
12 months	265	584	1.0-1.5	1.0-2.0	2.0-3.0	3-4	6-9	3-5	6-12	5-8	12-18
Long Yearling											
18 months	330	728	1.0-1.5	1.0-1.5	2.0-2.5	3-5	7-11	3-5	7-11	7-8	15-18
Two-year-old											
24 months	365	805	1.0-1.5	1.0-1.5	1.75-2.5	4-5	8-12	4-5	8-12	6-9	14-20

(Mature Weight–500 kgs or 1,100 lbs)

Class	Weight (kgs)	(lbs)	% Body Weight Forage	Con-centrate	Total	Forage (kgs)	(lbs)	Concentrate (kgs)	(lbs)	Total Feed (kgs)	(lbs)
Maintenance	500	1,100	1.5-2.0	0.0-0.5	1.5-2.0	8-10	17-22	0-3	0-6	8-10	17-22
Mares											
Late gestation	500	1,100	1.0-1.5	0.5-1.0	1.5-2.0	5-8	11-17	3-5	6-11	8-10	17-22
Early lactation	500	1,100	1.0-2.0	1.0-2.0	2.0-3.0	5-10	11-22	5-10	11-22	10-15	22-33
Late lactation	500	1,100	1.0-2.0	0.5-1.5	2.0-2.5	5-10	11-22	3-8	6-17	10-13	22-28
Light work	500	1,100	1.0-2.0	0.5-1.0	1.5-2.5	5-10	11-22	3-5	6-11	8-13	17-28
Moderate work	500	1,100	1.0-2.0	0.75-1.5	1.75-2.5	5-10	11-22	4-8	8-17	9-13	19-28
Intense work	500	1,100	0.75-1.5	1.0-2.0	2.0-3.0	4-8	8-17	5-10	11-22	10-15	22-33
Nursing foal											
3 months	175	386	0.0	1.0-2.0	2.5-3.5	0.0	0.0	2-4	4-8	4-6	10-14
Weanling											
6 months	215	474	0.5-1.0	1.5-3.0	2.0-3.5	1-2	2-5	3-6	7-14	4-8	9-17
Yearling											
12 months	325	717	1.0-1.5	1.0-2.0	2.0-3.0	3-5	7-11	3-7	4-6	14-22	8-10
Long Yearling											
18 months	400	880	1.0-1.5	1.0-1.5	2.0-2.5	4-6	9-13	4-6	9-13	8-10	18-22
Two-year-old											
24 months	450	992	1.0-1.5	1.0-1.5	1.75-2.5	5-7	10-15	5-7	10-15	8-11	17-25

Note: Figures are rounded off to the nearest kilogram or pound. Adapted From *Nutrient Requirements of Horses*.

(continued)

TABLE 11– Approximate Feed Consumption (based on % body weight)

(Mature Weight–600 Kgs or 1,320 lbs)

Class	Weight (kgs)	(lbs)	% Body Weight Forage	Con-centrate	Total	Total kgs or lbs Forage (kgs)	(lbs)	Concentrate (kgs)	(lbs)	Total Feed (kgs)	(lbs)
Maintenance	600	1,320	1.5-2.0	0.0-0.5	1.5-2.0	9-12	20-26	0-3	0-7	9-12	20-26
Mares											
Late gestation	600	1,320	1.0-1.5	0.5-1.0	1.5-2.0	6-9	13-20	3-6	7-13	9-12	20-26
Early lactation	600	1,320	1.0-2.0	1.0-2.0	2.0-3.0	6-12	13-26	6-12	13-26	12-18	26-40
Late lactation	600	1,320	1.0-2.0	0.5-1.5	2.0-2.5	6-12	13-26	3-9	7-20	12-15	26-33
Light work	600	1,320	1.0-2.0	0.5-1.0	1.5-2.5	6-12	13-26	3-6	7-13	9-15	20-33
Moderate work	600	1,320	1.0-2.0	0.75-1.5	1.75-2.5	6-12	13-26	5-9	10-20	11-15	23-33
Intense work	600	1,320	0.75-1.5	1.0-2.0	2.0-3.0	5-9	10-20	6-12	13-26	12-18	26-40
Nursing foal 3 months	200	440	0.0	1.0-2.0	2.5-3.5	0.0	0.0	2-4	5-9	5-7	11-15
Weanling 6 months	245	540	0.5-1.0	1.5-3.0	2.0-3.5	1-2	3-5	4-7	8-16	5-9	11-19
Yearling 12 months	375	827	1.0-1.5	1.0-2.0	2.0-3.0	4-6	8-12	4-8	8-17	8-11	17-25
Long Yearling 18 months	475	1,047	1.0-1.5	1.0-1.5	2.0-2.5	5-7	10-16	5-7	10-16	10-12	21-26
Two-year-old 24 months	540	1,190	1.0-1.5	1.0-1.5	1.75-2.5	5-8	12-18	5-8	12-18	9-14	21-30

(Mature Weight–700 Kgs or 1,540 lbs)

Class	Weight (kgs)	(lbs)	% Body Weight Forage	Con-centrate	Total	Total kgs or lbs Forage (kgs)	(lbs)	Concentrate (kgs)	(lbs)	Total Feed (kgs)	(lbs)
Maintenance	700	1,540	1.5-2.0	0.0-0.5	1.5-2.0	11-14	23-31	0-4	0-8	11-14	23-31
Mares											
Late gestation	700	1,540	1.0-1.5	0.5-1.0	1.5-2.0	7-11	15-23	4-7	8-15	11-14	23-31
Early lactation	700	1,540	1.0-2.0	1.0-2.0	2.0-3.0	7-14	15-31	7-14	15-31	14-21	31-46
Late lactation	700	1,540	1.0-2.0	0.5-1.5	2.0-2.5	7-14	15-31	4-11	8-23	14-18	31-39
Light work	700	1,540	1.0-2.0	0.5-1.0	1.5-2.5	7-14	15-31	4-7	8-15	11-18	23-39
Moderate work	700	1,540	1.0-2.0	0.75-1.5	1.75-2.5	7-14	15-31	5-11	12-23	12-18	27-39
Intense work	700	1,540	0.75-1.5	1.0-2.0	2.0-3.0	5-11	12-23	7-14	15-31	14-21	31-46
Nursing foal 3 months	225	496	0.0	1.0-2.0	2.5-3.5	0.0	0.0	2-5	5-10	6-8	12-17
Weanling 6 months	275	606	0.5-1.0	1.5-3.0	2.0-3.5	1-3	3-6	4-8	9-18	6-10	12-21
Yearling 12 months	420	926	1.0-1.5	1.0-2.0	2.0-3.0	4-6	9-14	4-8	9-19	8-13	19-28
Long Yearling 18 months	525	1,157	1.0-1.5	1.0-1.5	2.0-2.5	5-8	12-17	5-8	12-17	11-13	23-29
Two-year-old 24 months	600	1,320	1.0-1.5	1.0-1.5	1.75-2.5	6-9	13-20	6-9	13-20	11-15	23-33

Note: Figures are rounded off to nearest kilogram or pound. *Adapted from Nutrient Requirements of Horses.*

Table 12– Mineral Composition of Common Forages

(All hay is sun-cured, all values are on an "as fed" basis)

	Dry matter (%)	Macrominerals						Microminerals						
		Cal-cium (%)	Mag-nesium (%)	Phos-phorus (%)	Potas-sium (%)	Sodium (%)	Sulfur (%)	Cobalt (mg/kg)	Copper (mg/kg)	Iodine (mg/kg)	Iron (mg/kg)	Man-ganese (mg/kg)	Selen-ium (mg/kg)	Zinc (mg/kg)
ALFALFA														
Pasture, late vegetative	23.2	0.40	0.08	0.07	0.53	0.05	0.08	0.04	2.5	---	26	9	---	---
Pasture, full bloom	23.8	0.28	0.10	0.06	0.86	0.04	0.07	0.12	3.6	---	70	10	---	8
Hay, early bloom	90.5	1.28	0.31	0.19	2.32	0.14	0.27	0.26	11.4	0.15	205	33	0.50	27
Hay, midbloom	91.0	1.24	0.32	0.22	1.42	0.11	0.26	0.36	16.1	0.15	204	25	---	28
Hay, full bloom	90.9	1.08	0.25	0.22	1.42	0.06	0.25	0.21	9.0	0.12	141	38	---	24
BAHIAGRASS														
Pasture	28.7	0.13	0.08	0.09	0.44	---	---	---	2.1	---	24	21	0.02	8
Hay	90.0	0.45	0.17	0.20	---	---	---	---	---	---	54	---	---	---
Hay, early bloom	91.0	0.24	0.23	0.18	1.46	---	---	---	---	---	---	---	---	---
BARLEY														
Hay	88.4	0.21	0.14	0.25	1.30	0.12	0.15	0.06	3.9	---	265	35	---	---
BERMUDAGRASS, COASTAL														
Pasture	30.3	0.15	---	0.08	---	---	---	---	---	---	---	---	---	---
Hay, 15-28 days' growth	88.4	0.35	0.18	0.24	1.90	---	---	---	---	---	---	---	---	---
Hay, 29-42 days' growth	93.0	0.30	0.11	0.19	1.58	---	---	---	---	---	---	---	---	---
Hay, 43-56 days' growth	93.0	0.24	0.12	0.17	1.21	---	---	---	---	---	---	---	---	---
BLUEGRASS, KENTUCKY														
Pasture, early vegetative	30.8	0.15	0.05	0.14	0.70	0.04	0.05	---	---	---	92	---	---	---
Pasture, milk stage	42.0	---	---	---	---	---	---	---	---	---	---	---	---	---
Hay, full bloom	92.1	0.24	---	0.25	1.40	---	---	---	---	---	---	---	---	---
BROME, SMOOTH														
Pasture, early vegetative	26.1	0.14	0.08	0.12	0.82	---	0.05	---	---	---	---	---	---	6
Pasture, mature	54.9	0.14	---	0.09	---	---	---	---	1.2	---	---	---	---	---
Hay, midbloom	87.6	0.25	0.09	0.25	1.74	0.01	---	0.51	21.9	---	80	35	---	26
Hay, mature	92.6	0.24	0.11	0.20	1.71	0.01	---	0.17	9.6	---	74	68	---	22
CANARYGRASS, REED														
Pasture	22.8	0.08	---	0.08	0.83	---	---	---	---	---	---	---	---	---
Hay	89.3	0.32	0.19	0.21	2.60	0.01	0.12	---	10.6	---	134	82	---	16
CLOVER, ALSIKE														
Pasture, early vegetative	18.9	0.22	0.06	0.08	0.44	0.08	0.03	---	1.1	---	86	13	---	---
Hay	87.7	1.14	0.39	0.22	1.95	0.40	0.17	---	5.3	---	228	61	---	---
CLOVER, LADINO														
Pasture, early vegetative	19.3	0.25	0.08	0.07	0.50	0.02	0.03	---	---	---	---	---	---	4
Hay	89.1	1.20	0.42	0.03	2.17	0.12	0.19	0.14	8.0	0.27	419	110	---	15
CLOVER, RED														
Pasture, early bloom	19.6	0.44	0.10	0.07	0.49	0.04	0.03	0.03	1.7	0.05	59	10	---	4
Pasture, full bloom	26.2	0.26	0.13	0.07	0.51	0.05	0.04	0.03	2.6	0.07	79	12	---	4
Hay	88.4	1.22	0.34	0.22	1.60	0.16	0.15	0.14	9.7	0.22	211	95	---	15

FESCUE, KENTUCKY												
Pasture	31.3	0.16	0.09	0.12	0.72	---	0.06	---	---	---	---	7
Hay, full bloom	91.9	0.40	0.16	0.29	2.17	---	0.24	25.7	---	174	95	35
Hay, mature	90.0	0.37	0.14	0.27	1.76	0.02	---	19.8	---	119	87	32
LESPEDEZA, COMMON												
Pasture, late vegetative	25.0	0.30	---	0.07	0.32	---	---	---	---	---	---	---
Hay, midbloom	90.8	1.07	0.22	0.17	0.94	---	---	---	---	282	211	---
LESPEDEZA, KOBE												
Hay, midbloom	93.9	1.11	0.27	0.32	0.89	---	---	---	---	291	193	---
MEADOWPLANTS, INTERMOUNTAIN												
Hay	95.1	0.58	0.16	0.17	1.50	0.11	---	---	---	---	---	---
OATS												
Hay	90.7	0.29	0.26	0.23	1.35	0.17	0.21	4.4	0.07	369	90	41
ORCHARDGRASS												
Pasture, early bloom	23.5	0.06	0.07	0.09	0.80	0.01	0.06	7.8	0.03	185	24	7
Pasture, midbloom	27.4	0.06	0.09	0.05	0.57	0.07	---	13.7	0.38	19	37	---
Hay, early bloom	89.1	0.24	0.10	0.30	2.59	0.01	0.23	16.9	0.27	83	140	36
Hay, late bloom	90.6	0.24	0.10	0.27	2.42	0.01	---	18.1	18.0	76	151	34
PANGOLAGRASS												
Pasture	20.2	0.08	0.04	0.04	0.29	---	---	---	---	---	---	---
Hay, 15-28 days' growth	91.0	0.53	0.18	0.19	1.55	---	---	---	---	---	---	---
Hay, 29-42 days' growth	91.0	0.42	0.14	0.21	1.27	---	---	---	---	---	---	---
Hay, 43-56 days' growth	91.0	0.35	0.13	0.16	1.00	---	---	---	---	---	---	---
PRAIRIE PLANTS, MIDWEST												
Hay	91.0	0.32	0.24	0.12	0.98	---	---	---	---	80	---	31
RYEGRASS, ITALIAN												
Pasture	22.6	0.15	0.08	0.09	0.45	0.00	0.02	---	---	226	---	---
Hay, late vegetative	85.6	0.53	---	0.29	1.34	---	---	---	---	274	---	---
SORGHUM, JOHNSONGRASS												
Hay	90.5	0.80	0.31	0.27	1.22	0.01	0.09	---	---	534	---	---
TIMOTHY												
Pasture, late vegetative	26.7	0.11	0.04	0.07	0.73	0.03	0.03	2.4	0.04	35	34	10
Pasture, midbloom	29.2	0.11	0.04	0.09	0.60	0.06	0.04	3.3	---	52	56	---
Hay, early bloom	89.1	0.45	0.11	0.25	2.14	0.01	0.12	9.8	---	181	92	55
Hay, midbloom	88.9	0.43	0.12	0.20	1.61	0.01	0.12	14.2	---	132	50	---
Hay, late bloom	88.3	0.34	0.08	0.13	1.42	0.06	0.14	---	---	203	---	38
TREFOIL, BIRDSFOOT												
Pasture	19.3	0.33	0.08	0.05	0.63	0.02	0.05	2.5	0.09	34	16	6
Hay	90.6	1.54	0.46	0.21	1.74	0.06	0.23	8.4	0.10	206	26	70
WHEAT												
Pasture, early vegetative	22.2	0.09	0.05	0.09	0.78	0.04	0.05	---	---	22	---	---
Hay	88.7	0.13	0.11	0.18	0.88	0.19	0.19	---	---	177	---	---
WHEATGRASS, CRESTED												
Pasture, early vegetative	28.5	0.12	0.08	0.09	0.09	---	---	---	---	---	---	---

--- indicates data is unavailable.

Adapted from Nutrient Requirements for Horses

493

Table 13– Mineral Composition of Common Concentrate Components

(All values are on an "as fed" basis)

	Macrominerals							Microminerals						
	Dry matter (%)	Calcium (%)	Magnesium (%)	Phosphorus (%)	Potassium (%)	Sodium (%)	Sulfur (%)	Cobalt (mg/kg)	Copper (mg/kg)	Iodine (mg/kg)	Iron (mg/kg)	Manganese (mg/kg)	Selenium (mg/kg)	Zinc (mg/kg)
ALFALFA MEAL														
15% protein, dehydrated	90.4	1.25	0.26	0.23	2.22	0.07	0.19	0.17	9.5	0.12	280	28	0.28	19
17% protein, dehydrated	91.8	1.38	0.29	0.23	2.40	0.10	0.22	0.30	8.6	0.15	405	31	0.33	19
BARLEY														
Grain	88.6	0.05	0.13	0.34	0.44	0.03	0.15	0.17	8.2	0.04	73.5	16	0.18	17
Grain, Pacific coast	88.6	0.05	0.12	0.34	0.51	0.02	0.14	0.09	8.1	---	86.1	16	0.10	15
BEET, SUGAR														
Pulp, dehydrated	91.0	0.62	0.26	0.09	0.20	0.18	0.20	0.07	12.5	---	267	34	0.11	1.0
BREWERS GRAIN														
Dehydrated	92.0	0.30	0.15	0.50	0.08	0.21	0.29	0.07	21.2	0.06	245	37	0.70	28
BREWERS YEAST														
Dehydrated	93.1	0.14	0.24	1.36	1.68	0.07	0.44	0.51	38.4	0.36	83	6	0.91	39
CANOLA MEAL														
Seeds, solvent extracted	90.8	0.63	0.55	1.18	1.22	0.01	1.23	---	77.0	---	85	49	0.91	73
CARROT														
Roots, fresh	11.5	0.05	0.02	0.04	0.32	0.06	0.02	---	1.0	---	14	3.6	---	---
CORN														
Dried distillers grain	92.0	0.10	0.06	0.41	0.17	0.09	0.42	0.08	44.2	0.05	205	21	0.24	32
Ground ears	86.2	0.06	0.13	0.23	0.44	0.02	0.16	0.27	6.9	0.03	78	20	0.06	12
Grain	88.0	0.05	0.11	0.27	0.32	0.03	0.11	0.13	3.7	---	31	5	0.12	19
COTTON														
Seeds, solvent extracted	91.0	0.17	0.54	1.11	1.30	0.04	0.26	0.48	19.5	---	188	21	0.90	61
FATS AND OILS														
Hydrolyzed animal fat	99.2	---	---	---	---	---	---	---	---	---	---	---	---	---
Vegetable oil	99.8	---	---	---	---	---	---	---	---	---	---	---	---	---
FLAX, COMMON														
Seeds	93.6	0.22	0.40	0.54	0.74	---	0.23	---	---	---	90	61	---	---
Meal, solvent extracted	90.2	0.39	0.60	0.80	1.38	0.14	0.39	0.19	25.7	---	319	38	0.82	---

494

MOLASSES AND SYRUP														
Beet sugar molasses	77.9	0.12	0.23	0.02	4.72	1.16	0.46	0.36	16.8	---	68	4	---	14
Citrus, syrup	66.9	1.18	0.14	0.09	0.09	0.28	0.14	0.11	72.2	---	339	26	---	92
Dried sugarcane molasses	94.4	1.03	0.44	0.14	3.39	0.19	0.43	1.14	74.9	---	236	54	---	31
Sugarcane molasses	74.3	0.74	0.31	0.08	2.98	0.16	0.35	1.18	48.8	1.56	196	44	---	15
OATS														
Grain, grade 1	89.0	0.05	0.12	0.34	0.38	---	---	---	5.8	---	83	37	0.20	35
Grain, Pacific coast	90.9	0.10	0.17	0.31	0.38	0.06	0.20	---	---	---	73	38	0.08	---
PEANUT MEAL														
Seeds, solvent extracted	92.4	0.29	0.15	0.61	1.18	0.03	0.30	0.11	15.0	0.06	143	27	---	33
RICE														
Bran with germs	90.5	0.09	0.88	1.57	1.71	0.03	0.18	1.38	11.0	---	207	358	0.40	30
Grain, ground	89.0	0.07	0.13	0.32	0.44	0.06	0.04	0.04	2.7	0.04	50	18	---	15
RYE														
Grain	87.5	0.06	0.11	0.32	0.45	0.02	0.15	---	7.6	---	63	72	0.38	28
SORGHUM (MILO)														
Grain	90.1	0.04	0.15	0.32	0.37	0.01	0.13	0.27	5.4	---	57	12	0.41	27
SOYBEAN MEAL														
Seeds, solvent extracted	89.1	0.35	0.27	0.63	1.98	0.03	0.41	0.11	19.9	---	165	31	0.45	50
Seeds without hulls, solvent extracted	89.9	0.26	0.29	0.64	2.12	0.01	0.44	0.11	20.2	0.11	130	37	0.19	57
SUNFLOWER MEAL														
Seeds without hulls, solvent extracted	92.5	0.42	0.65	0.94	1.17	0.03	0.31	---	3.7	---	31	19	2.12	97
WHEAT														
Bran	89.0	0.13	0.56	1.13	1.22	0.05	0.21	0.07	12.6	0.07	145	119	0.51	98
Grain, hard, red winter	88.9	0.04	0.13	0.38	0.43	0.02	0.13	0.14	4.9	---	36	35	0.25	33
Grain, soft, red winter	88.4	0.03	0.12	0.36	0.35	0.01	0.13	0.10	5.7	---	40	32	0.04	34
Grain, soft, white winter	90.2	0.06	0.10	0.30	0.39	0.02	0.12	0.14	7.0	---	36	36	0.05	27
Mill-Run	89.9	0.10	0.47	1.02	1.20	0.22	0.17	0.21	18.5	---	95	104	0.63	---

Adapted from *Nutrient Requirements for Horses*   --- indicates data is unavailable.

Table 14– Vitamin Composition of Common Forages

(All hay is sun-cured, all values are on an "as fed" basis)	Dry matter (%)	Caro- tene (mg/kg)	A equiv- alent (IU/kg)	D (IU/kg)	E (mg/kg)	Biotin (mg/kg)	Choline (mg/kg)	Folate (mg/kg)	Niacin (mg/kg)	Panto- thenic acid (mg/kg)	Ribo- flavin (mg/kg)	Thia- min (mg/kg)	B6 (mg/kg)	B12 (µg/kg)
ALFALFA														
Pasture, late vegetative	23.2	---	---	51	39.7	---	---	---	---	---	---	---	---	---
Pasture, full bloom	23.8	---	---	---	---	---	---	---	---	7.5	---	---	---	---
Hay, early bloom	90.5	126.5	50,608	1,806	23.5	---	---	---	---	---	---	---	---	---
Hay, midbloom	91.0	30.3	41,900	1,810	10.0	---	---	---	---	---	9.6	---	---	---
Hay, full bloom	90.9	59.1	23,631	1,810	10.0	---	---	---	---	---	---	---	---	---
BAHIAGRASS														
Pasture	28.7	52.4	20,973	---	---	---	---	---	---	---	---	---	---	---
Hay	90.0	---	---	---	---	---	---	---	---	---	---	---	---	---
Hay, late vegetative	91.0	---	---	---	---	---	---	---	---	---	---	---	---	---
Hay, early bloom	91.0	---	---	---	---	---	---	---	---	---	---	---	---	---
BARLEY														
Hay	88.4	46.4	18,574	975	---	---	---	---	---	---	---	---	---	---
BERMUDAGRASS, COASTAL														
Pasture	30.3	100.0	39,993	---	---	---	---	---	---	---	---	---	---	---
Hay, 15-28 days' growth	88.4	---	---	---	---	---	---	---	---	---	---	---	---	---
Hay, 29-42 days' growth	93.0	---	---	---	---	---	---	---	---	---	---	---	---	---
Hay, 43-56 days' growth	93.0	---	---	---	---	---	---	---	---	---	---	---	---	---
BLUEGRASS, KENTUCKY														
Pasture, early vegetative	30.8	148.5	59,420	---	47.8	---	---	---	---	---	---	---	---	---
Pasture, milk stage	42.0	---	---	---	---	---	---	---	---	---	---	---	---	---
Hay, full bloom	92.1	---	---	---	---	---	---	---	---	---	---	---	---	---
BROME, SMOOTH														
Pasture, early vegetative	26.1	152.1	60,854	---	---	---	---	---	---	---	---	---	---	---
Pasture, mature	54.9	---	---	---	---	---	---	---	---	---	---	---	---	---
Hay, midbloom	87.6	---	---	---	---	---	---	---	---	---	---	---	---	---
Hay, mature	92.6	---	---	---	---	---	---	---	---	---	---	---	---	---
CANARYGRASS, REED														
Pasture	22.8	---	---	---	---	---	---	---	---	---	---	---	---	---
Hay	89.3	16.9	6,762	---	---	---	---	---	---	---	8.5	3.57	---	---
Pasture, early vegetative	18.9	72.4	28,977	---	---	---	---	---	---	---	---	---	---	---
Hay	87.7	163.2	65,285	---	---	---	---	---	---	---	15.1	4.21	---	---
CLOVER, LADINO														
Pasture, early vegetative	19.3	68.1	27,249	---	---	---	---	---	---	---	---	---	---	---
Hay	89.1	143.7	57,475	---	---	---	---	---	9.8	1.0	15.2	3.74	---	---
CLOVER, RED														
Pasture, early bloom	19.6	48.5	19,402	---	---	---	---	---	---	---	---	---	---	---
Pasture, full bloom	26.2	54.4	21,744	---	---	---	---	---	---	---	---	---	---	---
Hay	88.4	24.3	9,727	1,700	---	0.09	---	---	37.7	9.9	15.7	1.97	---	---

Feed								
FESCUE, KENTUCKY								
Pasture	31.3	68.2	27,279	---	---	---	---	---
Hay, full bloom	91.9	---	---	---	---	---	---	---
Hay, mature	90.0	---	---	---	---	---	---	---
LESPEDEZA, COMMON								
Pasture, late vegetative	25.0	---	---	---	---	---	---	---
Hay, midbloom	90.8	---	---	---	---	---	---	---
LESPEDEZA, KOBE								
Hay, midbloom	93.9	---	---	---	---	---	---	---
MEADOWPLANTS, INTERMOUNTAIN								
Hay	95.1	31.9	12,744	---	---	---	---	---
OATS								
Hay	90.7	27.0	10,792	1,400	---	---	---	---
ORCHARDGRASS								
Pasture, early bloom	23.5	---	---	---	---	---	---	---
Pasture, midbloom	27.4	---	---	---	---	---	---	---
Hay, early bloom	89.1	33.4	13,366	---	---	---	---	---
Hay, late bloom	90.6	18.1	7,247	---	---	---	---	---
PANGOLAGRASS								
Pasture	20.2	---	---	---	---	---	---	---
Hay, 15-28 days' growth	91.0	---	---	---	---	---	---	---
Hay, 29-42 days' growth	91.0	---	---	---	---	---	---	---
PRAIRIE PLANTS, MIDWEST								
Hay	91.0	---	---	865	---	---	---	---
REDTOP								
Hay, midbloom	92.8	4.6	1,856	---	---	---	---	---
Pasture	22.6	---	---	---	---	---	---	---
Hay, late vegetative	85.6	248.2	99,287	---	---	---	---	---
SORGHUM, JOHNSONGRASS								
Hay	90.5	35.3	14,102	---	---	---	---	---
TIMOTHY								
Pasture, late vegetative	26.7	62.6	25,028	---	---	---	---	---
Pasture, midbloom	29.2	56.7	22,672	---	---	---	---	---
Hay, early bloom	89.1	46.8	18,719	11.6	---	---	---	---
Hay, midbloom	88.9	47.4	18,964	1,763	---	---	---	---
Hay, full bloom	89.4	42.5	17,000	---	---	---	---	---
TREFOIL, BIRDSFOOT								
Pasture	19.3	---	---	1,398	---	---	---	---
Hay	90.6	130.6	52,250	---	---	---	---	---
WHEAT								
Pasture, early vegetative	22.2	115.4	46,180	---	12.6	4.7	14.6	6.16
Hay	88.7	75.8	30,304	1,370	---	---	6.1	15.1
WHEATGRASS, CRESTED								
Pasture, early vegetative	28.5	123.4	49,377	---	---	---	---	---

--- indicates data is unavailable

μ = micrograms.

Adapted from Nutrient Requirements for Horses

497

Table 15— Vitamin Composition of Common Concentrate Components

(All values are on an "as fed" basis)

	Dry matter (%)	Carotene (mg/kg)	A equivalent (IU/kg)	D (IU/kg)	E (mg/kg)	Biotin (mg/kg)	Choline (mg/kg)	Folate (mg/kg)	Niacin (mg/kg)	Pantothenic acid (mg/kg)	Riboflavin (mg/kg)	Thiamin (mg/kg)	B_6 (mg/kg)	B_{12} (µg/kg)
ALFALFA MEAL														
15% protein, dehydrated	90.4	74.5	29,787	---	81.9	0.25	1,573	1.56	41.6	20.7	10.6	2.99	6.28	---
17% protein, dehydrated	91.8	120.3	48,132	---	105.9	0.33	1,349	4.37	37.0	29.8	12.9	3.39	7.19	---
BARLEY														
Grain	88.6	2.0	817	---	23.2	0.15	1,037	0.57	78.5	8.1	1.6	4.52	6.48	---
Grain, Pacific coast	88.6	---	---	---	26.2	0.15	976.3	0.50	46.7	7.1	1.5	4.19	2.89	---
BEET, SUGAR														
Pulp, dehydrated	91.0	0.2	88	580	---	---	820.9	---	16.8	1.4	0.7	0.39	---	---
BREWERS GRAIN														
Dehydrated	92.0	---	---	---	26.7	0.63	1,652	0.20	44.0	8.2	1.5	0.6	0.7	0.004
BREWERS YEAST														
Dehydrated	93.1	---	---	---	2.1	1.04	3,847	9.69	443.3	81.5	33.6	85.21	36.66	1.1
CANOLA MEAL														
Seeds, solvent extracted	90.8	---	---	---	---	0.82	6,082	2.09	183.1	12.4	3.0	4.72	---	---
CARROT														
Roots, fresh	11.5	77.9	31,160	---	6.9	0.01	---	0.14	6.7	3.5	0.6	0.67	1.39	---
CORN														
Dried distillers grain	92.0	2.8	1,104	---	---	0.48	1,161	0.86	36.8	11.5	5.2	1.66	7.17	---
Ground ears	86.2	3.4	1,379	---	17.2	0.03	355.1	0.24	17.2	4.1	0.9	2.84	5.95	---
Grain	88.0	5.4	2,162	---	20.9	0.07	496.0	0.31	22.5	5.1	1.1	3.73	6.16	---
COTTON														
Seeds, solvent extracted	91.0	---	---	---	14.6	0.56	2,783	2.55	40.9	13.7	4.7	7.32	5.41	---
FATS AND OILS														
Hydrolyzed animal fat	99.2	---	---	---	---	---	---	---	---	---	---	---	---	---
Vegetable oil	99.8	---	---	---	57.0	---	---	---	---	---	---	---	---	---
FLAX, COMMON														
Seeds	93.6	---	---	---	---	---	---	---	---	---	---	---	---	---
Meal, solvent extracted	90.2	---	---	---	7.5	---	1,393	1.26	33.0	14.7	2.9	7.54	8.60	---

MOLASSES AND SYRUP													
Beet sugar molasses	77.9	--	--	4.0	--	827.5	--	41.0	4.5	2.3	--	--	--
Citrus, syrup	66.9	--	--	--	--	--	--	26.9	12.7	6.2	--	--	--
Dried sugarcane molasses	94.4	--	--	5.2	--	--	--	--	--	--	--	--	--
Sugarcane molasses	74.3	--	--	5.4	0.69	763.4	0.11	36.4	37.4	2.8	0.86	4.21	--
OATS													
Grain, grade 1	89.0	--	--	--	--	--	--	13.6	6.3	1.6	6.19	1.94	--
Grain, Pacific coast	90.9	--	--	20.2	--	916.9	--	14.4	11.7	1.2	--	--	--
PEANUT MEAL													
Seeds, solvent extracted	92.4	--	--	2.9	0.33	1,893	0.65	177.5	36.8	9.1	5.70	5.95	--
RICE													
Bran with germs	90.5	--	--	85.3	0.42	1,243	1.60	305.9	25.0	2.6	21.94	16.21	--
Grain, ground	89.0	--	--	14.0	0.80	926.5	0.25	40.0	7.1	0.7	2.90	4.40	--
RYE													
Grain	87.5	0.1	35	14.5	0.05	419.1	0.58	14.1	7.2	1.8	4.51	2.97	--
SORGHUM (MILO)													
Grain	90.1	1.2	468	10.0	0.26	692.5	0.22	46.6	10.2	1.2	4.52	5.40	--
SOYBEAN MEAL													
Seeds, solvent extracted	89.1	--	--	3.0	0.36	2,704	0.69	26.1	13.8	3.0	6.59	5.90	--
Seeds without hulls, solvent extracted	89.9	--	--	3.3	0.32	2,746	0.74	21.5	14.8	2.9	3.10	4.92	--
SUNFLOWER MEAL													
Seeds without hulls, solvent extracted	92.5	--	--	11.1	--	3,627	--	242.1	40.6	3.5	3.10	13.67	--
WHEAT													
Bran	89.0	2.6	1,048	14.3	0.38	1,201	1.77	196.7	27.9	3.6	8.36	10.33	--
Grain, hard, red winter	88.9	--	--	11.1	0.11	1,007	0.38	53.0	10.2	1.3	4.52	3.02	--
Grain, soft, red winter	88.4	--	--	15.6	--	891.7	0.41	53.4	10.1	1.5	4.71	3.21	--
Grain, soft, white winter	90.2	--	--	18.0	0.11	978.0	0.40	53.0	11.1	1.2	4.70	4.77	--
Mill-Run	89.9	--	--	31.9	0.31	1,004	1.08	115.6	13.7	2.1	15.25	11.09	--

Adapted from *Nutrient Requirements for Horses*

-- indicates data is unavailable

μ = micrograms.

BIBLIOGRAPHY

Ambrosiano, N. "The Best Way To Feed Horses." *Equus,* Vol. 156 (October 1990), pp. 81–84, 120–121.

Ambrosiano, N. "Designer Feeds—Are They For Your Horse?" *Equus,* Vol. 161 (March 1991), pp. 57–60, 128–131.

Asquith, R.L. "Injectable Wormer." *The Blood-Horse* (February 18, 1984), pp. 1371, 1376–1377.

Asquith, R.L., E.L. Johnson, J. Kivipelto, and C. Depew. "Erroneous Weight Estimation of Horses by Veterinarians and Lay Horsemen." *Proceedings of the 36th Annual Convention of the American Association of Equine Practitioners* (December 2-3, 1990), Lexington, Kentucky, pp 599607.

Asquith, R.L. and J. Kivipelto. "The Efficiency and Acceptability of Ivermectin Liquid Compared to that of Oral Paste in Horses." *Journal of Equine Veterinary Science,* Vol. 7, No. 6 (1987), pp. 353–355.

Bailey, H. *Vitamin E—Your Key to a Healthy Heart.* Arco Books, Inc., 1971.

Bello, T.R. "Anthelmintic Effects of Injectable and Oral Paste Formulations of Ivermectin Against 28–day Infections of Parascaris Equorum." *Journal of Equine Veterinary Science,* Vol. 9, No. 6 (November/December 1989), pp. 307–309.

Bertone, J.J., J.L. Traub-Dargatz, R.W. Wrigley, D.G. Bennett and R.J. Williams. "Diarrhea Associated With Sand in the Gastrointestinal Tract of Horses." *Journal of the American Veterinary Medical Association,* Vol. 193, No. 11 (December, 1988), pp. 1409–1411.

Biasatti, H. "Fat: Food for Athletes—An Interview with Dr. Gary Potter." *The Quarter Racing Journal* (June 1991), pp. 30–32.

Biles, D.B. "Protection Against Shaker Foals." *The Blood-Horse* (December 7, 1985), pp. 8816–8817.

Biles, D.B. "When The Grass Is Not Greener." *The Blood-Horse* (February 15, 1986), pp. 1274–1278.

Biles, D.B. "Avoiding Avocados." *The Blood-Horse* (April 5, 1986), p. 2442.

Boraski, Edward A. "Ivermectin Kills Ascarids but not Rumors." *Equine Veterinary Journal* (1988), 7(1):44-45.

Bratcher, J. "Undernourished Horses." *Horse & Rider,* Vol. XXIX, No. 2 (February 1990), pp. 22–25, 54–55, 57, 59.

Bratcher, J. "Winter is Coming—It's Hay Time!" *HorsePlay,* Vol. 18, No. 11 (November 1990), pp. 38–39.

Breuer, L.H. *Proceedings of the Maryland Nutritional Conference* (1974), p. 102.

Briggs, K. "Stressed Out!" *Canadian Horseman* (May/June 1991), pp. 18–21.

Brown, J.H., and V. Powell-Smith. *The Systems of The Horse.* Howell Book House Inc., 1984.

Buechner, V. "Feeding The Patient That Can't Eat." *Horse Care* (April 1991), pp. 24–25.

Butler, Doug. *The Principles of Horseshoeing II.* Doug Butler Publisher, 1985.

Byers, D. "Colic—With 66 Causes A Plethora of Problems." *The Blood-Horse* (March 17, 1984), pp. 2135–2138.

Carmel, Douglas K. Tapeworms in Horses. *Equine Veterinary Journal* (1988), 8(4):343.

Chaitow, L. *Thorsons Guide To Amino Acids.* Thorsons 1991.

Cunha, T. "Feed Stuff—Feeding The Weanling." *Horse & Rider*, Vol. XXIX, No. 1 (January 1990), p. 8.

Cunha, T. "Feed Stuff—Update on Vitamin D." *Horse & Rider*, Vol. XXIX, No. 2 (February 1990), p. 16.

Cunha, T. "Feed Stuff—Update on Vitamin A." *Horse & Rider*, Vol. XXIX, No. 3 (March 1990), pp. 12, 50.

Cunha, T. "Feed Stuff—Update on Thiamin." *Horse & Rider*, Vol. XXIX, No.6 (June 1990), p. 14.

Cunha, T. "Feed Stuff—Is Excess Protein Harmful?" *Horse & Rider*, Vol. XXIX, No. 7 (July 1990), pp. 26–27.

Cunha, T. "Feed Stuff—Alfalfa, An Asset?" *Horse & Rider*, Vol. XXIX, No. 8 (August 1990), p. 18.

Cunha, T. "Feed Stuff—The Role of Fiber." *Horse & Rider*, Vol. XXIX, No. 9 (September 1990), p. 12.

Cunha, T. "Feed Stuff—How Much Is Enough?" *Horse & Rider*, Vol. XXIX, No. 10 (October 1990), pp. 16–17.

Cunha, T. "Feed Stuff—The Growth Dilemma." *Horse & Rider*, Vol. XXIX, No. 11 (November 1990), p. 16.

Cunha, T. "Feed Stuff—Body Condition And Reproduction." *Horse & Rider*, Vol. XXIX, No. 12 (December 1990), pp. 14–15.

Cunha, T.J. *Horse Feeding and Nutrition*. Second Edition. Academic Press, Inc., 1991.

Cymbaluk, N.F. "Effects of Dietary Energy Source and Level of Feed Intake on Growth of Weanling Horses." *Equine Practice*, Vol. 11. No. 9 (October 1989), pp. 29–33.

Daurio, C.P., and W.H.D. Leaning. "The Effect of Oral Ivermectin on Immature Ascarids in Foals." *Journal of Equine Veterinary Science*, Vol. 9, No. 6 (November/December 1989), pp. 312–315.

Davison, K.E., G.D. Potter, L.W. Greene, J.W. Evans, and W.C. McMullan. "Lactation and Reproductive Performance of Mares Fed Added Dietary Fat During Late Gestation and Early Lactation." *Journal of Equine Veterinary Science*, Vol. 11, No. 2 (March/April 1991), pp. 111–115.

Depew, C.G. "Grains For Horses." *Southern Horseman*, Vol. XXX, No. III (March 1991), pp. 44, 48

DiPietro, J.A., and K.S. Todd. "Anthelmintics Used in Treatment of Parasite Infections in the Horse." *Equine Practice* (1989), 11(4):5-15.

Drudge, J.H., and E.T. Lyons. "Internal Parasites of Equids with Emphasis on Treatment and Control." Hoechst-Roussel Agri-Vet Company, Somerville, New Jersey 08876, 1986.

Drudge, J.H., and E.T. Lyons. "Tapeworms in Horses." *Equine Data Line: A Horse Research Newletter*, University of Kentucky, College of Agriculture, Lexington, Kentucky, September 1987, pp. 9-10.

Dugan, B. "Common Sense Feeding." *Horseman*, Vol. 34, No. 8 (March 1990), pp.52, 56.

Eades, S. C. and J. N. Moore. "The Importance of Endotoxin in Horses With Colic." *The Quarter Horse Journal* (June 1991), pp. 62–63.

Eades, S.C. and J.N. Moore. "Improving Intestinal Blood Flow in Horses." *The Quarter Racing Journal* (July 1991), pp. 60–61.

Eddy, V. "Extruded Feed—Some Food For Thought." *Hoof Beats* (June 1991), p. 105.

Editorial Staff. "Colic Risk Factors." *Companion Animal News* (Winter 1990), p. 7.

Editorial Staff. "Facts and Questions." *The Blood-Horse* (June 29, 1991), pp. 3207–3210.

Editorial Staff. "Horse Care in the News—AAEP Takes Stand on Steroids." *Horse Care* (July 1991), pp. 6–7.

Editorial Staff & Jackson, S. "Feeding Your Horse—Form Fosters Function." *Performance Horseman*, Vol. 9, No. 11 (October 1990), pp. 22–27, 55.

Editorial Staff and Michel,S. DVM. "Colic: What to Do Until the Vet Comes." *Practical Horseman*, Vol. 19, No. 6 (June 1991), p. 80.

Editorial Staff & Morris, D.D. "The Truth About Tired Blood." *Performance Horseman*, Vol. 8, No. 1 (December 1989), pp. 36–45.

Editorial Staff & Potter, G.D. "Getting Your Horse To Eat More." *Practical Horseman*, Vol. 18, No. 3 (March 1990), pp. 30–38.

Editorial Staff, Practical Horseman. *The Complete Guide To Feeding Your Horse*. Practical Horseman, 1979.

Editorial Staff. "Up Front—Banking Colostrum For A Rainy Day." *Modern Horse Breeding*, Vol. VII, No. 10 (December 1990), p. 5.

Eiselt, D. "Stones in the Large Intestine—Enterolith-Related Colic." *HorsePlay*, Vol. 18, No. 4 (April 1990), pp. 50–51.

Ensminger, M.E. *Horses and Horsemanship*. Sixth Edition. Interstate Publishers, Inc., 1990.

Evans, J.W. *Horses, A Guide to Selection, Care, and Enjoyment*. Second Edition. W.H. Freeman and Company, 1989.

Evans, J.W., A. Borton, H.F. Hintz and L.D. Van Vleck. *The Horse*. Second Edition. W.H. Freeman and Company, 1990.

Fitzgerald, W.J. "The Mechanics of Stress." *Horse & Rider*, Vol. XXIX, No. 6 (June 1990), pp. 18–19.

Fraser, P. "Dietary fat: That Edge for Performance." *Canadian Horseman* (March/April 1991), pp. 48–50.

Gager, E.R., and B. Rhodes. *Sound Mouth-Sound Horse, The Gager Method of Equine Dental Care*. Emerson Publishing Company, 1983.

Georgi, Jay R. "*Parasitology for Veterinarians*." W.B. Saunders Company, Philadelphia/London/Toronto, 1980.

Glade, M.J., and M. Campbell-Taylor. "Effect of Dietary Yeast Culture Supplementation During the Conditioning Period on Equine Exercise Physiology." *Journal of Equine Veterinary Science*, Vol. 10, No. 6 (November/December 1990), pp. 434–443.

Glade, M.J., and N.K. Luba. "Benefits to Foals of Feeding Soybean Meal to Lactating Broodmares." *Journal of Equine Veterinary Science*, Vol. 10, No. 6 (November/December 1990), pp. 422–428.

Goater, L.E., T.N. Meacham, F.C. Gwazdauskas, and J.P. Fontenot. "The Effect of Feeding Excess Energy to Mares During Late Gestation." *Proceedings of the 7th Equine Nutrition and Physiology Symposium* (1981), pp. 111–116.

Goody, P.C. *Horse Anatomy, A Pictorial Approach To Equine Structure*. J.A. Allen & Company Limited, 1990.

Graffis, D.W., E.M. Juergenson, and M.H. McVickar. *Approved Practices In Pasture Management*. The Interstate Printers and Publishers, Inc., 1985.

Green, J.T. "Suggestions For Horse Pasture Management." *Southern Horseman*, Vol. XXX, No. III (March 1991), pp. 28–21.

Greene, D.S., and J.V. Davies. "Abstract: Colic From a Gallstone—A Large Gallstone was Removed from the Common Bile Duct." *Veterinary Update*, Vol. 5, No. 3–4 (May/April 1990), p. 36.

Hagerbaumer, J. "A Stable Environment, Abuse or Asylum?" *Horse Care* (June

1991), pp. 43–47, 61.

Hale, P. "New Wormer Offers Many Benefits." *The Texas Thoroughbred* (April 1991), p. 8.

Harper, Frederick. "Knowing Weight of Your Horse is Vital." *The Florida Horse* (January 1990), p 58.

Harper, F. "Creep Feeding." *Horseman*, Vol. 34, No. 8 (March 1990), p. 50.

Harper, F. "Do Midterm Mares Need More Groceries?" *Modern Horse Breeding*, Vol. VII, No. 10 (December 1990), pp. 15–21.

Harper, F. "Not Too Fat, Not Too Thin." *Modern Horse Breeding*, Vol. VII, No. 2 (February 1991), pp. 9–12.

Henneke, D.R., G.D. Potter, and J.L. Kreider. "Rebreeding Efficiency In Mares Fed Different Levels Of Energy During Late Gestation." *Proceedings of the 7th Equine Nutrition and Physiology Symposium* (1981), pp. 101–103.

Henneke, D.R., G.D. Potter, and J.L. Kreider. "A Condition Score Relationship To Body Fat Content Of Mares during Gestation And Lactation." *Proceedings of the 7th Equine Nutrition and Physiology Symposium* (1981), pp. 105–110.

Henneke, D.R., G.D. Potter, J.L. Kreider, and B.F. Yeates. "Relationship Between Condition Score, Physical Measurements and Body Fat Percentage in Mares." *Equine Veterinary Journal* (1981), pp. 371–372.

Herbert, K.S. "They are What They Drink." *The Blood- Horse* (March 20, 1982), pp. 2125–2126.

Herbert, K.S. "Improving Hay." *The Blood-Horse* (January 12, 1985), p. 206.

Herbert, K.S. "Moldy Corn Causes Deaths." *The Blood-Horse* (February 23, 1985), p. 1376.

Herbert, K.S. "Making Hay Without Sunshine." *The Blood-Horse* (April 13, 1985), pp. 2562–2563.

Herbert, K.S. "Drought and the Horse Industry." *The Blood-Horse* (July 5, 1986), pp. 4621.

Herbert, K.S. "That Creeping Feeling," *The Blood-Horse* (July 26, 1986), pp. 5386.

Herbert, K.S. "A Bovine Solution." *The Blood-Horse* (August 30, 1986), pp. 6233–6234.

Herbert, K.S. "Getting Out the Bugs." *The Blood-Horse* (October 4, 1986), p. 7173.

Herbert, K.S. "Hay for Horses—It Has to be the Best." *The Blood-Horse* (October 18, 1986), pp. 7558–7561.

Herbert, K.S. "FDA Concerned With Clenbuterol Use." *The Blood-Horse* (July 6, 1991), p. 3314.

Herd, R.P., and G.J. Kociba. "Effects of Ivermectin on Blood Constituents." *Equine Veterinary Journal* (May/June 1991), 17(2):142-144.

Hintz, H.F. *Horse Nutrition, a Practical Guide.* Arco Publishing, Inc., 1983.

Hintz, H.F. "The 1989 NRC Estimates of Protein Requirements." *Equine Practice*, Vol. 11, No. 10 (November/December 1989), pp. 5–6.

Hintz, H.F. "Weight Gains Of Mares During The Last Trimester Of Gestation." *Equine Practice*, Vol. 12, No. 7 (July/August 1990), pp. 6–10.

Hintz, H.F. "Legume Management." *Equine Practice*, Vol. 13. No. 1 (January 1991), pp. 8–9.

Hintz, H.F. "Oxalic Acid and Millet." *Equine Practice*, Vol. 13. No. 2 (February 1991), pp. 5–6.

Hintz, H.F. "Cholelithiasis in Horses." *Equine Practice*, Vol. 13. No. 4 (April 1991), pp. 13–16.

Hintz, H.F. "Moldy Corn, Megacolon, and Hyperlipidemia." *Equine Practice*,

Vol. 13. No. 5 (May 1991),pp. 23–24.

Hintz, H.F., B. Morrison, J. Williams, and T. Hernandez. "Evaluation of Naked Oats." *Equine Practice*, Vol. 13. No. 7 (July/August 1991), pp. 6-8.

Hobby, L. "Because Worms Adapt, So Must Deworming Methods." *Hoof Beats* (June 1991), pp. 97–98.

Hopfer, A.M., et al. "Abstract: The Elimination of Equine Strongyles and Hematological and Pathological Consequences Following Larvacidal doses of Thia-benzadole." *Veterinary Parisitology*, Vol. 14 (1984), pp. 21–32.

Householder, D.D., and G.D. Potter. "*Horse Nutrition and Feeding.*" 1984.

Huston, R., and B.A. Lee. "How to Feed Protein—More is Not Always Better." *HorsePlay*, Vol. 18, No. 8 (August 1990), pp.38–41.

Jackson, S.G. "The Science of Nutrition." *The Blood-Horse* (December 10, 1983), pp. 9204–9218.

Jackson, S.G. "Nutrition of Young Horses—Balanced Ration for Growth." *The Blood-Horse* (November 23, 1985), pp. 8398–8402.

Johnson, S. "Using The Proper Tools." *The Blood-Horse* (March 24, 1984), pp. 2292–2296.

Jones, W.E. "The Benefits of MP (Mucopolysaccharide) Supplements." *The Horseman's Journal*, Vol. 42, No. 3 (March 1991), pp. 26–27.

Jones, W.E. *Sports Medicine For The Racehorse*. Veterinary Data, 1991.

Kalsbeek, H.C. "Abstract: Nonsurgical Correction of the Left Colon—Rolling Often Precludes Surgery." *Veterinary Update*, Vol. 5, No. 3–4 (May/April 1990), pp. 42–43.

Kelley, L.J. "Grazing With Gusto." *Modern Horse Breeding*, Vol. VII, No. 8 (September/October 1990), pp. 13–19.

Kelley, L.J. "The Scoop On Concentrates—Selecting Feeds For Specific Needs." *Modern Horse Breeding*, Vol. VII, No. 8 (September/October 1990), pp. 22–26.

Kelley, L.J. "Feeding The Stressed Horse." *Modern Horse Breeding*, Vol. VII, No. 8 (September/October 1990), pp. 26, 48.

Kellon, E.M. *The Older Horse—A Complete Guide to Care and Conditioning for Horses 10 and Up*. Breakthrough Publications, Millwood, New York, 1986.

Kivipelto, J. "A Comparison of Some Effects of Ivermectin and Certain Conventional Anthelmintic Drugs on Parasitologic and Physiologic Values in Young Horses." Master's Thesis, University of Florida, Department of Animal Science Gainesville, Florida 32210, 1986.

Kivipelto, J., and R.L. Asquith. "Duration of Efficacy of Ivermectin and Various Other Anthelmintics When Used in the Young Horse." (unpublished data) Department of Animal Science, University of Florida, Gainesville, Florida, 1990-1091.

Lane, T.J. "Blister Beetle Poisoning." *The Blood-Horse* (November 5, 1983), pp. 8036–8042.

Lee, B.A., K. Thompson, and R. Huston. "Fundamentals of Feed—Protein." *Horse Care* (January 1990), pp. 24–28.

Lee, B.A., K. Thompson, and R. Huston. "Fundamentals of Feed—Carbohydrates and Fats." *Horse Care* (February 1990), pp. 19–22.

Lee, B.A., K. Thompson, and R. Huston. "Fundamentals of Feed—Water-Soluble Vitamins." *Horse Care* (March 1990), pp. 24–29.

Lee, B.A., K. Thompson, R. Huston, and J. Pagan. "Fundamentals of Feed—Fat-Soluble Vitamins." *Horse Care* (April 1990), pp. 42–46.

Ley, W.B., C.D. Thatcher, W.S. Swecker, and P.N. Laesard. "Chelated Mineral Supplementation in the Barren Mare—A Preliminary Trial." *Journal of*

Equine Veterinary Science, Vol. 10, No. 3 (May/June 1990), pp. 176–181.

Lichtenfels, J. Ralph. "Helminths of Domestic Equids." *Proceedings of the Helminthological Society of Washington* (December 1975), Volume 42.

Loving, N.S. "The Abyss Of Starvation." *Horse Care* (February 1990), pp. 46–51.

Loving, N.S. "The Long Haul." *Horse Care* (May 1991), pp. 45–49, 60–62.

Loving, N. S. "Horse Care Update—Copper and Developmental Bone Disease." *Horse Care* (July 1991), pp. 38–41.

Lynch, S.A. "The Urge To Drink." *Equus*, Vol. 165 (July 1991), p. 40–43, 108–111.

Lyons, E.T. "Long-Term Parasite Control." *The Blood-Horse* (April 28, 1984), pp. 3143–3145.

Lyons, E.T., J.H. Drudge, and S.C.Tolliver. "On the Life Cycle of *Strongyloides westeri* in the Equine." *The Journal of Parasitology* (1973), 59(5):780-787.

Mackay-Smith, M. "Colic—Roll Away the Pain." *Equus*, Vol. 152 (June 1990), pp. 83–85.

Mal, M.E., T.H. Friend, D.C. Lay, S.G. Vogelsang, and O.C. Jenkins. "Physiological Responses of Mares to Short Term Confinement and Social Isolation." *Journal of Equine Veterinary Science*, Vol. 11, No. 2 (March/April 1991), pp. 96–101.

"*Martin's The Edge.*" Martin Feed Mills LTD, Vol.1, No. 2 (1991).

McBane S. "Stressed Out, Part VI—How the Horse's Body is Affected by, and Deals With, the Stress of Disease." *Horse Care* (November/December 1989), pp. 50–53.

McBride, G. "What's in Your Hay?" *Canadian Horseman* (March/April 1991), pp. 42–43.

McCarthy, G. *Pasture Management For Horses And Ponies.* Howell Book House Inc., 1987.

McDonald, L.E. *Veterinary Endocrinology and Reproduction.* Lea & Febiger, 1975.

McKenzie, R.A., and O.P. Brown. "Avocado Poisoning." *Veterinary Update*, Vol. 6, No. 5–6 (May/June 1991), p. 82.

McKissick, G.E., I.H. Sutherland, J. Foix, and G. Olson. "The Safety of Ivermectin Administered Orally to Pregnant Mares." *Journal of Equine Veterinary Science*, Vol. 7, No. 6 (1987), pp. 357–367.

Milbert, N. "Illinois Horsemen Say 'No, Thanks' To Milkshakes." *Hoof Beats* (July 1991), pp. 27–32.

Miller, M. "Mold and More Mold." *Equus*, Vol. 155 (Sept. 1990), pp. 51–54.

Miller, R. "The Limited Value of Bran." *Equi Aide Products, Inc.* (Sept. 10, 1990), p. 3.

Morrison, F.B. *Feeds and Feeding*, abridged, ninth edition. The Morrison Publishing Company, 1961.

Myers, G. "How To Control Your Horse's Internal Parasites." *Horse Illustrated*, Vol. 15, No. 5 (May 1991), p. 7.

Oklahoma State Cooperative Extension Service. "The Effect of Cold Temperatures on Horse Nutrient Needs." *The Quarter Horse Journal* (February 1991), p. 29.

Pagan, J.D. "The Feeding of the Horse." *The Blood-Horse* (May 27, 1989), pp. 2904–2908.

Paul, J.W. "Veterinary Update—How To Avoid the Dangerous Effects of Migrating Parasitic Larvae." *Horse Illustrated*, Vol. 15, No. 7 (July 1991), p 1.

Potter, G.D., S.P. Webb, J.W. Evans, and G.W. Webb. "Digestible Energy

Requirements For Work and Maintenance of Horses Fed Conventional and Fat-Supplemented Diets." *Journal of Equine Veterinary Science*, Vol. 10, No. 3 (May/June 1990), pp. 214–218.

Powell, D.G. "Dealing with Heat Stress." *The Thoroughbred Times* (June 21, 1991), p. 23.

Redmond, L. M., D. L. Cross, T. C. Jenkins, and S. W. Kennedy. "The Effect of Acremonium Coenophialum on Intake and Digestibility of Tall Fescue Hay in Horses." *Journal of Equine Veterinary Science*, Vol. 11, No. 4 (July/August 1991), pp 215–219.

Reinemeyer, Craig, R. "Anthelmintic Resistance in the Horse." *Equine Veterinary Science* (1987), 7(6):390-391.

Riley, M. "The Grass-Kept Horse." *Canadian Horseman* (May/June 1991), pp. 12–15.

Rodiek, A. "Horse Care Forum—Speaking Out, Feeding For Performance." *Horse Care* (April 1991), pp. 11–15.

Rook, J.S., and J.V. Marteniuk. "It Must Have Been Something They Ate." *Equus*, Vol. 158 (December 1990), pp. 61–64.

Rook, J.S., J.V. Marteniuk, A. Warwick, R. Hammer, and G. Poppy. "An Outbreak of Impaction Colic Due to Ingestion of Cockspur Hawthorn Fruit." *Equine Practice*, Vol. 13. No. 2 (February 1991), pp. 28–32.

Rooney, J.R. "Some Thoughts on Colic." *Journal of Equine Veterinary Science*, Vol. 9, No. 6 (November/December 1989), p. 296.

Seanor, J.W., et. al. "Abstract: Renal Disease Associated With Colic in Horses." *Modern Veterinary Practice*, Vol. 65, A26–A29 (1984), p. 223.

Sellers, R. "Proven! Effective! Increases Stamina!" *The Backstretch* (June-July 1991), pp. 20-21,67.

Sellnow, L. "Solving a Tall Problem." *The Blood-Horse* (November 24, 1984), pp. 8676–8677.

Sellnow, L. "Good Grazing." *The Blood-Horse* (February 2, 1985), pp. 852–854.

Sellnow, L. "Man vs. Weevil." *The Blood-Horse* (March 9, 1985), p. 1773.

Sellnow, L. "Coping With Confinement." *The Blood-Horse* (September 7, 1985), p. 5158.

Sellnow, L. "Deadly, But Safe." *The Blood-Horse* (October 5, 1985), p. 6883.

Sellnow, L. "Linking Breakdowns and Diet." *The Blood- Horse* (May 3, 1986), pp. 3162–3164.

Sellnow, L. "Cultured Horse Feed." *The Blood-Horse* (May 5, 1990), pp. 2368–2369.

Sellnow, L. "Maintaining The Athlete." *The Blood-Horse* (March 23, 1991), pp. 1640–1641, 1664–1665.

Smith, C.A. "Equine Nutrition—Part I, Is Your Horse Getting All The Nutrients It Needs From Its Hay and Pasture?" *Horse Illustrated*, Vol. 14, No. 10 (October 1990), pp. 32–34.

Smith, C.A. "Equine Nutrition—Part II, Kernels of Truth About Grain." *Horse Illustrated*, Vol. 14, No. 11 (November 1990), pp. 84–87.

Smith, C.A. "Equine Nutrition—Part III, Supplementing Your Horse's Hay and Grain is a Balancing Act That Requires You to Know When Less is More." *Horse Illustrated*, Vol. 14, No. 12 (December 1990), pp. 26–30.

Smith, C.A. "The Deworming Dilemma." *Horse Illustrated*, Vol. 15, No. 6 (June 1991), pp. 72–75.

Sprinkle, F.P. "Basic Principles of Stallion Management." *The Blood-Horse* (December 21, 1985), pp. 9240–9241.

Squires, E.L., G.E. Todter, W.E. Berndtson, and B.W. Pickett. "The Effect of Anabolic Steroids on Reproductive Function in Young Stallions." *Journal of Animal Science*, Vol. 54 (1982), p. 576.

Squires, E.L., J.M. Maher, and J.L. Voss. "The Effect of Anabolic Steroids on Reproductive Function in Young Mares." *Proceedings of the 8th Equine Nutrition and Physiology Symposium* (1983), p. 279.

Stricklin, J.B. "Three-Year Summary of Equine Colic Cases in the Abilene Area—Abstract." *Equine Practice*, Vol. 13. No. 5 (May 1991), p. 37.

Stull, C.L. "Nasty and Noxious Plants." *Horse Care*, (April 1990), pp. 53–58.

Subcommittee on Horse Nutrition, Committee on Animal Nutrition, Board of Agriculture, National Research Council. *Nutrient Requirements of Horses*. Fifth Revised Edition. National Academy Press, 1989.

Swann, P. *Performance Drugs In Sport*. Forty-first Yeneb Pty Ltd., 1990.

Thomas, H.S. "Feeding Concentrates—A Guide To Oats & Corn, Wheat, Barley, Meals, Molasses, 7 Commercial Mixes." *HorsePlay*, Vol. 18, No. 8 (August 1990), pp. 32–35.

Tobin, T. *Drugs and the Performance Horse*. Charles C. Thomas, Publisher, Springfield, Illinois, 1981.

Toby, M.C. "Parasite Research." *The Blood-Horse* (February 19, 1983), p. 1441.

Tyznik, W.J. "About Feeding Horses." *Hoof Beats* (June 1990), pp. 82–87.

Uhlinger, Christine. "Effects of Three Anthelmintic Schedules on the Incidence of Colic in Horses." *Equine Veterinary Journal* (1990), 22(4):251-254.

Varner, D.D., J. Schumacher, T.L. Blanchard, and L. Johnson. *Diseases and Management of Breeding Stallions*. American Veterinary Publications, 1991.

Wagoner, D.M. (Ed.). *The Illustrated Veterinary Encyclopedia for Horsemen*. Equine Research Publications, 1977.

Wagoner, D.M. (Ed.). *Veterinary Treatments and Medications for Horsemen*. Equine Research Publications, 1977.

Wagoner, D.M. (Ed.). *Breeding Management and Foal Development*. Equine Research Publications, 1982.

Watkins, B.E. "Fundamentals of Feed—The Trace Elements." *Horse Care* (June 1990), pp. 38–42.

Watkins, B.E. "Fundamentals of Feed—Mineral Supplements." *Horse Care* (July 1990), pp. 48–51.

Watkins, B. "Hay: A Guide to Evaluation." *Horse Care* (July 1991), pp. 27–33.

Williams, W. "Abstract: Enterolithiasis—It Caused Recurrent Colic." *Veterinary Update*, Vol. 5, No. 3–4 (May/April 1990), p. 39.

Winter, M. "Does Giving Lasix Stress a Racehorse?" *Hoof Beats* (July 1991), pp. 129–130.

Wood, C.H. "Take Care of the Old Timer—Management of the Geriatric Horse." *Hoof Beats* (May 1991), pp. 101–104.

Wooden, G.R. "Vitamin and Trace Mineral Supplements—Evaluating Adequacy or Excesses." *Equine Practice*, Vol. 12. No. 3 (March 1990), pp. 15–22.

Zicker, S.C., M.S. Spensley, Q.R. Rogers, and N.H. Willits. "Protein-Calorie Malnutrition in Sick Foals." *Horse Care* (April 1991), pp. 23–24.

FIGURE CREDITS

Figure 1–1. J. Noye.

Figure 2–1. J. Noye.

Figure 2–3. Cappy Jackson.

Figure 2–7. Cappy Jackson.

Figure 2–8. Safe Upper Limit of Minerals in Water. Adapted from *Nutrient Requirements of Horses* © 1989, by the National Academy of Sciences, published by the National Academy Press, Washington, D.C.

Figure 2–9. Safe Levels of Soluble Salts in Water. Adapted from Shirley, R. L., C. H. Hill, J. T. Maletic, O. E. Olsen, and W. H. Pflander, "Nutrients and Toxic Substances in Water For Livestock and Poultry." National Academy of Sciences-National Research Council, 1974.

Figure 3–1. J. Noye.

Figure 3–5. J. Noye.

Figure 3–6. J. Noye.

Figure 3–8. Courtesy of H. F. Hintz, Cornell University and *The Horse* © 1977, 1990, by J. W. Evans, A. Borton, H. F. Hintz, and L. D. Van Vleck, published by W. H. Freeman and Company, New York, New York.

Figure 3–10. Courtesy of H. F. Hintz, Cornell University.

Figure 3–11. Courtesy of *The Quarter Horse Journal.*

Figure 3–13. Bracken Fern illustration © 1979, courtesy of Lucretia Breazeale Hamilton. From *Plants That Poison,* © 1979 by Ervin M. Schmutz, Ph.D., published by Northland Publishing, Flagstaff, Arizona.

Figure 3–14. Courtesy of *Hoof Beats.*

Figure 3–15. Don Shugart.

Figure 3–18. J. Noye.

Figure 3–19. Courtesy of *The Quarter Horse Journal.*

Figure 4–1. J. Noye.

Figure 4–10. Daily Phosphorus Requirements of 1,100-pound Mares. Adapted from *Nutrient Requirements of Horses* © 1989, by the National Academy of Sciences, published by the National Academy Press, Washington, D.C.

Figure 4–11. Calcium to Phosphorus Ratios. Compiled from *Nutrient Requirements for Horses* © 1989, by the National Academy of Sciences, published by the National Academy Press, Washington, D.C., *Horse Feeding and Nutrition,* © 1980, 1991 by Tony J. Cunha, published by Academic Press, Inc., San Diego, and *Horse Nutrition: A Practical Guide,* © 1983 by Harold F. Hintz, published by Arco Publishing, Inc., New York, New York.

Figure 4–17. Don Shugart.

Figure 4–21. Courtesy of Charles H. Bridges, Texas A&M University and the Journal of the American Veterinary Medical Association, volume 193, page 215, 1988.

Figure 4–24. J. Noye.

Figure 4–26. J. Noye.

Figure 4–27. J. Noye.

Figure 4–29. Cappy Jackson.

Figure 5–6. Body Condition Score Chart developed at Texas A&M University by Dr. Gary Potter and co-workers.

Figure 5–15. Courtesy of the National Cutting Horse Association.

Figure 5–16. J. Noye.

Figure 5–18. J. Noye.

Figure 5–19. Information from *Thorsons Guide to Amino Acids,* by Leon Chaitow.

Figure 5–21. J. Noye.

Figure 6–1. J. Noye.

Figure 6–2. Adapted from the *Official United States Standards for Grain,* United States Department Of Agriculture–Federal Grain Inspection Service.

Figure 6–4. Adapted from the *Official United States Standards for Grain,* United States Department Of Agriculture–Federal Grain Inspection Service.

Figure 6–6. Adapted from the *Official United States Standards for Grain,* United States Department Of Agriculture–Federal Grain Inspection Service.

Figure 6–7. From *Manual of the Grasses of the United States,* by A. S. Hitchcock, May 1935, revised by Agnes Chase 1951, published by the United States Department of Agriculture, miscellaneous publication No. 200, United States Government Printing Office, Washington D.C.

Figure 6–8. From *Manual of the Grasses of the United States,* by A. S. Hitchcock, May 1935, revised by Agnes Chase 1951, published by the United States Department of Agriculture, miscellaneous publication No. 200, United States Government Printing Office, Washington D.C.

Figure 6–9. Adapted from the *Official United States Standards for Grain,* United States Department Of Agriculture–Federal Grain Inspection Service.

Figure 6–10. Adapted from the *Official United States Standards for Grain,* United States Department Of Agriculture–Federal Grain Inspection Service.

Figure 6–12. J. Noye.

Figure 6–13. J. Noye.

Figure 7–1. Courtesy of *The Blood-Horse.*

Figure 7–2. Courtesy of the National Cutting Horse Association.

Figure 7–3. J. Noye.

Figure 7–5. Courtesy of *Hoof Beats.*

Figure 7–8. Cappy Jackson.

Figure 8–3. J. Noye.

Figure 8–5. J. Noye.

Figure 8–6. Courtesy of *The Blood-Horse.*

Figure 8–7. J. Noye.

Figure 9–3. From *Manual of the Grasses of the United States,* by A. S. Hitchcock, May 1935, revised by Agnes Chase 1951, published by the United States Department of Agriculture, miscellaneous publication No. 200, United States Government Printing Office, Washington D.C.

Figure 9–4. From *Manual of the Grasses of the United States,* by A. S. Hitchcock, May 1935, revised by Agnes Chase 1951, published by the United States Department of Agriculture, miscellaneous publication No. 200, United States Government Printing Office, Washington D.C.

Figure 9–5. From *Manual of the Grasses of the United States,* by A. S. Hitchcock, May 1935, revised by Agnes Chase 1951, published by the United States Department of Agriculture, miscellaneous publication No. 200, United States Government Printing Office, Washington D.C.

Figure 9–8. J. Noye.

Figure 9–10. White clover, from Wasser, C. H. 1982. Ecology and Culture of Selected Species Useful in Revegetating the West. U. S. Department of the Interior, Fish and Wildlife Services, FWS/OBS-82/56.

Figure 9–14. J. Noye.

Figure 9–16. J. Noye.

Figure 9–17. From *Manual of the Grasses of the United States,* by A. S. Hitchcock, May 1935, revised by Agnes Chase 1951, published by the United States Department of Agriculture, miscellaneous publication No. 200, United States Government Printing Office, Washington D.C.

Figure 9–18. From *Manual of the Grasses of the United States,* by A. S. Hitchcock, May 1935, revised by Agnes Chase 1951, published by the United States Department of Agriculture, miscellaneous publication No. 200, United States Government Printing Office, Washington D.C.

Figure 9–19. From *Manual of the Grasses of the United States,* by A. S. Hitchcock, May 1935, revised by Agnes Chase 1951, published by the United States Department of Agriculture, miscellaneous publication No. 200, United States Government Printing Office, Washington D.C.

Figure 9–21. J. Noye.
Figure 9–22. J. Noye.
Figure 10–10. J. Noye.
Figure 10–17. J. Noye.
Figure 10–19. Courtesy of *The Quarter Horse Journal.*
Figure 10–20. Courtesy of Darolyn Butler.
Figure 10–21. J. Noye.
Figure 10–23. Courtesy of W.L. Anderson, D.V.M.
Figure 10–30. J. Noye.
Figure 11–4. Courtesy of W. L. Anderson, D. V. M.
Figure 11–9. Courtesy of Don Sustaire.
Figure 12–1. J. Noye.
Figure 12–2. Courtesy of the Shell Chemical Company, Agricultural Division.
Figure 12–3. Courtesy of the Shell Chemical Company, Agricultural Division.
Figure 12–5. Courtesy of the Shell Chemical Company, Agricultural Division.
Figure 12–7. Courtesy of the Shell Chemical Company, Agricultural Division.
Figure 12–12. Courtesy of the Shell Chemical Company, Agricultural Division.
Figure 12–13. Courtesy of the Shell Chemical Company, Agricultural Division.
Figure 12–20. J. Noye.
Figure 12–21. J. Noye.
Chapter 14
Jack Van Berg, courtesy of *The Blood-Horse.*
Rodney Reed, courtesy of *Quarter Week.*
Mike Robbins, courtesy of *Quarter HorseTrack* .
Ron McAnally, courtesy of *The Backstretch.*
John Sosby, courtesy of *The Blood-Horse.*

GLOSSARY

abdominal tap, process by which fluid is removed from the abdomen for laboratory analysis

absorption efficiency, efficiency of absorption of vitamins, minerals, and other nutrients

acute deficiency, deficiency characterized by a short and relatively severe course

adenosine diphosphate, product of the decomposition of the energy reserve of the muscles

adenosine triphosphate, represents the energy reserve of the muscle

aflatoxins, toxins produced by fungi; cause of poisoning in animals eating contaminated grains; cause damage to brain and liver

agalactia, failure of the secretion of milk

Agropyron, scientific name for wheat grass, which stores high concentrations of selenium and can produce selenium toxicity

alkali, a substance which neutralizes an acid to form a salt

alkali disease, selenium toxicity

alkaline, having the reactions of an alkali

alkaloids, very bitter, basic organic substances found in plants

alkalosis, increased alkalinity of blood and tissues, increased blood bicarbonate

alkalotic, characterized by alkalosis

allele, one of two or more contrasting genes

ambient, surrounding

amino acid, any of a class of organic compounds containing nitrogen; forms the building blocks of protein

analgesic, drug that relieves pain without causing loss of consciousness

analog, any organ having the same function as another, but of a different evolutionary origin

anaphylactic shock, condition caused by anaphylaxis, an unusual allergic reaction to a foreign protein or drug

anemia, condition in which the blood is deficient in either quality or quantity; characterized by paleness of mucous membranes, loss of energy, rapid heartbeat

aneurysm, sac formed by the dilation of the walls of an artery, or a vein filled with blood

annual, plant that completes its life cycle in one growing season

anterior pituitary, lobe at the base of the brain which secretes and stores hormones that regulate most of the basic body functions

antibodies, substances in blood serum or other body fluids formed to restrict or destroy bacteria, toxins, or foreign proteins

antigens, substances which cause formation of antibodies

antioxidant, substance which hinders oxidation

antithiamin, compound which affects thiamine absorption; destroys thiamine

arteriole, minute arterial branch

arteriovenous shunting, formation of a blood vessel that allows blood from arteries to bypass veins, cutting off circulation

articular, pertaining to a joint

ascarid, intestinal parasite of young horses

associative effect, occurs when large amounts of concentrate overwhelm the foregut and cause most of the ingesta to move into the hindgut; causes simple carbohydrates to be converted into volatile fatty acids, which are not as efficient an energy source as glucose, which is the form into which simple carbohydrates are converted in the foregut

Aster xylorrhiza, scientific term for woody aster, which collects and stores selenium for its own use; unpalatable to the horse

Astragaluses, scientific term for milk vetch, which collects and stores selenium for its own use; unpalatable to the horse

ataxia, inability to coordinate voluntary muscular movements

Atriplex, scientific term for four-winged salt brush, which collects and stores, but does not use, high concentrations of selenium; can produce selenium toxicity in the horse if ingested

atrophy, decrease in size or wasting away of a body part or tissue

azoturia, condition characterized by sudden attack of sweat and paralysis of hindquarters; caused by accumulation of glycogen in muscles, releasing excessive lactic acid during exercise

bactericidal, having properties of a bactericide

bactericide, agent that destroys bacteria

bacteriostatic, inhibiting the growth or multiplication of bacteria

banamine, flunixin meglumine; nonsteroidal anti-inflammatory drug useful for treating cases of colic; rapidly alleviates pain and discomfort associated with colic

beta carotene, precursor of vitamin A

bicarbonate, basic component of some salts; sharp increase may cause elevation of blood pH

biennial, occurring once in two years

bioflavonoids, yellow plant pigment; anti-hemorrhagic

biopsy, removal and examination of tissue or other material from a living animal for diagnostic purposes

blood doping, practice of withdrawing and reinfusing red blood cells so oxygen may be carried to the cells more quickly; makes blood too thick to flow freely

blood serum, clear liquid which separates from the blood when it clots

blood solids, red and white blood cells, platelets

bolt, ingest feed rapidly without sufficiently chewing

bolus, large pill or mass of feed ready to be swallowed; mass passing along the intestines

bomb calorimeter, instrument for measuring heat change in a system

botulism, infection with Clostridium botulinium, type of food poisoning caused by a toxin produced by Clostridium botulinium

bracken fern, plant containing thiaminase and antithiamin, which

destroy thiamine
bradycardia, abnormal slowness of the heartbeat
buffer, decreases or prevents the reaction that a chemotherapeutic
agent would produce if administered alone
bute, see phenylbutazone
calcitonin, hormone secreted when excesses of phosphorus are fed;
prevents absorption of calcium by the bone; normally secreted when
calcium levels are high in the blood
calcium bentonite, material added to pelleted feeds to assist in pelleting
process
calcium hydroxide, stabilizer added when potassium iodide is
administered as a supplement
calcium iodate, compound used to supplement iodine; does not
require a stabilizer
calcium oxalate, insoluble compound formed when calcium binds to
oxalic acid, causing oxalate poisoning and calcium deficiency
calcium pantothenate, vitamin of the B complex
calorie, unit of heat; amount of heat required to raise one gram of water
one degree Celcius
calorimeter, instrument for measuring heat change in a system
cantharidin, produces blistering of the skin
carbohydrase, any one of a group of enzymes which break down
carbohydrates
carbohydrate, term used to include organic compounds containing
carbon, hydrogen, and oxygen
carotene, pigment in carrots and other foodstuffs; precursor of vitamin
A; converted into vitamin A in the liver and stored there
casein, principal protein of milk
cast, situation in which a horse rolls and is unable to rise because its
legs are folded up against a fence or wall
catalytic enzymes, enzymes that help trigger reactions within the body
cecum, intestinal pouch that the ileum and colon open into
cellulose, carbohydrate that appears only in plants and is digested by
microorganisms in horse's hindgut; also referred to as fiber
cerebrospinal fluid, fluid containing salts, proteins, and sugar, which
surrounds the spinal cord and brain stem
chelated minerals, make minerals more available to the horse by
increasing intestinal absorption and utilization
chlorophyll, green pigment of plants by which photosynthesis occurs
choke, condition in which ingesta becomes blocked in esophagus
cholelithiasis, presence or formation of gallstones
cholesterol, fat-like substance found in all animal fats and oils, bile, blood,
brain tissue, milk, nerve fiber sheaths, liver, kidneys, and adrenal glands
choline chloride, used in treatment of fatty infiltration of liver
choroid, dark brown vascular coat of the eye; nourishes retina and lens,
darkens the eye; consists mainly of blood vessels
chronic deficiency, long term, continued deficiency

Clostridium botulinium, organism that causes botulism

coccidia, parasites that consume dietary thiamine in the intestinal tract, making it (thiamine) less nutritionally available to the horse

coenzyme, simpler portion of an enzyme which is necessary for digestion

coffin bone, pedal bone surrounded by the hoof

colic, any abdominal pain; can be caused by twisted, distended, or impacted intestine, excessive gas formation, interruption of blood supply to any part of the intestine

collagen, main supportive protein of skin, tendon, bone, cartilage, and connective tissue

colostrum, milk secreted by mare immediately after giving birth; clears foal's intestines of fecal matter (meconium); supplies foal with first antibodies

complex carbohydrate, includes starches and celluloses; must be broken down into simpler sugars by bacterial and protozoal action and by digestion before it can be used in horse's system

concentrate, mixture of feedstuffs, including grains and non-grain components

congenital, existing at, and usually before, birth

conjunctivitis, inflammation of the delicate membrane that lines the eyelid

connective tissue, fibrous tissue that binds and supports various body structures

crenate, shrunken, scalloped, or notched

cribbing, vice that arises from boredom or lack of long roughage, in which horse grasps edge of stall door, fence, etc., and sucks in air

crude protein, percentage of protein contained in a feed

cuticle, outer layer of the skin

cyanosis, bluish discoloration of the skin and mucous membranes due to deficient oxygenation of the blood

cystitis, inflammation of the bladder

Day-blooming Jessamine, noxious weed; ingestion of causes symptoms similar to vitamin D toxicity; also known as Wild Jasmine, Day Cestrum

Day Cestrum, noxious weed; ingestion of causes symptoms similar to vitamin D toxicity; also known as Wild Jasmine, Day-blooming Jessamine

deciduous, not permanent; lost at maturity

dermatitis, inflammation of the skin

dermatophilosis, fungus which causes mycotic dermatitis, an inflammation of the skin

desiccation, act of drying up

developmental orthopedic diseases (DOD), diseases of the bone in growing horses, including epiphysitis, osteochondrosis, osteochondritis dissecans

dicoumarol, anticoagulant

digestible energy, portion of the gross energy in a feedstuff that the animal is able to digest and absorb

digestion trials, tests that determine the amount of energy produced by an animal

digestive tract, tract through which food passes; where nutrients are absorbed; consists of mouth, pharynx, esophagus, stomach, small intestine, cecum, large colon, small colon, rectum

dimethylglycine (DMG), anti-stress nutrient, cell antioxidant, immune system enhancer; reduces levels of lactic acid produced during work

dipyrone, mild anti-spasmodic, analgesic

disaccharide, class of carbohydrate

diuretic, agent that causes the secretion of urine

DNA, deoxyribonucleic acid; found in nucleus of every cell; carries coded information for reproducing cells of same kind; basis of heredity

dopamine, neurohormone that stimulates the horse

drench, dose of medicine given to a horse by pouring it into the horse's mouth

duodenum, first portion of the small intestine; extends from pylorus to jejunum

dystocia, abnormal labor or birth

elastin, essential constituent of yellow elastic tissue

electrolyte, substance present in body fluids which is capable of conducting electricity in various body functions, such as nerve impulses, oxygen and carbon dioxide transport, and muscle contractions

emaciated, condition of being excessively thin, in a wasted condition

embolus, clot brought by the blood from another vessel and forced into a smaller one, obstructing circulation

encapsulate, enclose within a capsule

encyst, enclose within a sac, bladder, or cyst

endocarp, bony inner covering of seed structure within fruit

endogenous, growing from within

endophyte, parasitic organism growing within the body of the host

endotoxin, toxic substance formed by bacteria found within the cell

enteritis, inflammation of the intestine, usually the small intestine

enterolith, stone that develops in the intestine, formed by salt deposits around a hard object

enzyme, organic compound which produces or accelerates change in a substance

epidermis, outermost layer of the skin

epinephrine, powerful vasopressor that increases blood pressure and stimulates the heart muscle

epiphysis, piece of bone that is separated by cartilage from the long bone in early life, but later becomes a part of the larger bone; it is at the cartilage joint that growth of the long bone occurs

epiphysitis, inflammation of the end of a long bone or of the cartilage that separates it from the long bone

epistaxis, hemorrhage from the nose; nosebleed

epithelial, pertaining to epithelium

epithelium, layer of cells of which skin and mucous membranes are formed

ergosterol, sterol synthesized in plants; becomes vitamin D when irradiated with UV rays; preventative of rickets

ergot, elongated black-purple mass of fungus that replaces rye grain; ingestion causes uterine muscle contractions, precipitating abortion

erythrocyte transketolase, thiamine-containing enzyme

esophagus, canal extending from pharynx to stomach

estrous, pertaining to estrus

estrus, period of sexual receptivity in the female; heat

Ethoxyquin, antioxidant added to feeds to reduce chances of rancidity

ethylene diaminedihydroiodide (EDDE), compound used to supplement iodine

fatty acids, key components of lipids; determine many of the physical characteristics of lipids

ferrous fumarate, supplemental iron found in oral doses of digestive inocula administered to foals

float, to file down the teeth in order to remove sharp edges

fluoride, compound that contains flourine, which is essential for proper tooth and bone formation

folic acid, one of the vitamins of the B complex; necessary for cell metabolism and normal red blood cell formation

fusarium, toxin found in moldy grain; can cause brain damage

gamete, mature germ cell; ovum or sperm

gastric mucosa, mucous membrane of the stomach

gastrointestinal tract, digestive tract

gelatinization, process in manufacture of extruded feeds; may increase availability of carbohydrates; promotes conversion of complex carbohydrates into absorbable simple sugars in the digestive tract

genera, taxonomic categories

genotoxic, deadly to genes

gestation, pregnancy

ginseng, plant root that contains many vitamins and minerals

glucocorticoid, hormone that raises concentration of liver glycogen and blood sugar

glutathione peroxidase, antioxidant enzyme; aids in detoxification of peroxides, which are toxic to the cells

gluten, protein of wheat that gives dough its tough, elastic character

glyceride, organic acid ester of glycerol

glycerol, clear, colorless, odorless, thick, sweet tasting liquid obtained from decomposition and distillation of fats; dissolves many substances

glycogen, animal starch found in the liver; the form in which carbohydrates from feeds are stored before being converted to glucose

glycoprotein, any of a class of proteins consisting of a compound of protein with a carbohydrate group

goiter, enlargement of the thyroid gland

gonad, ovary or testis; gamete-producing gland

gossypol, yellow pigment found in cotton seed; may be detrimental to horses when fed at higher than recommended levels

grass tetany, hypomagnesaemia; caused by magnesium deficiency

grease heel, chronic inflammation of the skin of the fetlocks and pasterns

Grindelia squarrosa, scientific name for gum weed, a plant that collects and stores, but does not use, high concentrations of selenium; can produce selenium toxicity if ingested by the horse

Gurierrezia saraothral, scientific name for broomweed, snakeweed, match weed; collects and stores, but does not use, high concentrations of selenium; can cause selenium toxicity if ingested by the horse

heart rhythm, pattern of heart beats

heaves, respiratory disturbance characterized by forced expiration of breath; caused by allergies and dust; results from reduced elasticity in and rupture of respiratory bronchioles and pulmonary alveoli

hematopoiesis, formation and development of blood cells

hemicellulose, general name for group of carbohydrates that resemble cellulose but are more soluble and more easily decomposed

hemicellulose extracts, materials added to pelleted feeds to assist in the pelleting process

hemoglobin, oxygen-carrying red pigment of the red blood cells

hemolytic disease, condition in which mare produces antibodies which destroy red blood cells of the foal

hemolytic icterus, hemolytic disease

hemorrhage, excessive bleeding

hepatic, pertaining to the liver

hermaphrodite, organism possessing gonads of both sexes

heterogenesis, reproduction that differs in character in successive generations

heterogonic, pertaining to heterogenesis

hexosan, class of polysaccharide

hexose, class of monosaccharide

hindgut, portion of the digestive tract, including the cecum and large intestine

histamine, capillary dilator; stimulates gastric secretion

homogenic, homozygous

homozygous, possessing an identical pair of genes in regard to a given character

hordenine, chemical alkaloid compound; used for treating diarrhea, typhoid fever; its detection by urine testing can cause disqualification of performance horses

horsetail, plant which contains thiaminases and antithiamin, which destroy thiamine

hybrid, animal or plant produced from parents that are different in kind

hydrochloric acid, major constituent of the gastric juices

hypercalcitonism, caused by excess calcium intake

hyperirritability, pathological responsiveness to slight stimuli

hyperkalemia, abnormally high potassium content of the blood

hyperkalemic periodic paresis, muscle weakness associated with hyperkalemia

hyperlipidemia, excess of lipids in the blood

hyperparathyroidism, abnormally increased activity of parathyroid gland

hypocalcemia, reduction of blood calcium below normal; calcium deficiency

hypochromia, abnormal decrease in the hemoglobin content of the erythrocyte; characterized by loss of pigment in red blood cells

hypochromic, pertaining to hypochromia

hypocupremia, copper deficiency

hypothermia, abnormally low body temperature

hypothyroidism, deficiency of thyroid activity; may result in aborted, stillborn, or weak foals

icterus, jaundice; yellowish discoloration of visible mucous membranes of the body

ileocecal valve, allows ingesta to travel from the ileum to the cecum, but not in the opposite direction

ileum, last section of the small intestione

immunoglobulins, group of proteins, including antibodies

in vitro digestion system, test used to analyze hay

incubation, period between the implanting of an infectious disease and its clinical manifestation

insulin, hormone produced by the pancreas; secreted into the blood to regulate carbohydrate metabolism

iris, muscular and fibrous curtain which hangs behind cornea of the eye and regulates the amount of light allowed to reach inner parts of the eye

iron dextran, supplemental iron

jaundice, icterus; yellowish discoloration of the visible mucous membranes of the body

jejunum, central section of the small intestine

jugging, intravenous supplementation of electrolytes, amino acids, vitamins, and minerals

juglone, antibiotic derived from the leaves and husks of the black walnut tree

kilocalorie, calorie used in the study of metabolism; amount of heat required to raise 1 kg water from 15° C to 16° C

Kjeldahl protein test, test used to analyze hay

lacrimation, secretion and discharge of tears

lactic acid, organic acid normally present in muscle tissue, produced by anaerobic muscle metabolism

Lactobacillus, bacteria that produces very large amounts of lactic acid from fermentable carbohydrates

laminae, thin plates or layers

laparotomy, surgical opening of the abdominal cavity; performed when diseased conditions of organs in the abdomen or pelvis require surgical treatment, for purposes of diagnosis or for removal of structures

lasix, drug used to stop exercise-induced pulmonary hemorrhage; also a diuretic, causing increased urine excretion

lecithin, lipid found in animal tissues, especially nerve tissue, semen, bile, and blood; used in treatment of rickets, anemia, and diabetes

leptospira, bacteria that invade the cornea, causing periodic blindness

lignin, compound that forms, in connection with cellulose, the cell wall of plants

lignin sulfonate, material added to pelleted feeds to aid in the pelleting process

lipid, any one of a group of organic substances which are insoluble in water, but soluble in alcohol, ether, chloroform, and other fat solvents

lumen, cavity or channel within a tube or tubular organ

lysine, amino acid; essential for growing horses

Machaeranthera, scientific name for aster; collects and stores, but does not use, high concentrations of selenium; ingestion of could cause selenium toxicity

malnourished, suffering from insufficient nutrient intake

megacalorie, equal to 1,000,000 calories; used to express Digestible Energy

melanin, dark pigment of the body

menadione, used for vitamin K supplementation; has physiological properties of vitamin K

menaquinone, same as menadione

mesentery, tissue that supports the small intestine

metabolic, pertaining to metabolism

metabolic bone diseases, interrelated growth disorders of the bone; linked to deficiencies of calcium and phosphorus, along with deficiencies of copper and zinc

metabolism, chemical changes in a cell which provide energy for vital bodily processes and activities

metabolite, any substance produced by metabolism

methionine, amino acid necessary for young, growing animals

methylsulfolnylmethane (MSM), sulfur-rich organic compound; metabolic end product of DMSO; helps prevent muscle soreness

microcytic, characterized by shrinkage of the red blood cells

microfilaria, minute, prelarval stage of some parasites

microflora, microorganismal bacteria

microgram, one millionth of a gram

molt, shedding of outer covering and development of new one

monosaccharide, simple sugar; carbohydrate that cannot be decomposed by hydrolysis

mucin, chief constituent of mucus

mucosa, mucous membrane

mucous membrane, membrane that lines the hollow organs, air passages, digestive tract, urinary passages, and genital passages

mycotoxin, bacterial toxin

mylo-hyoid, pertaining to molar teeth and hyoid bone

myocitis, muscular inflammation

myoglobin, hemoglobin of muscle; stores oxygen

near-infrared reflectance, method of analyzing hay

necropsy, post mortem examination

neonatal isoerythrolysis, hemolytic disease

nitrogen fixing bacteria, bacteria which remove nitrogen from the air for plant use; found in nodules on roots of legumes

nitrogen-free extract, percentage of soluble carbohydrates which remains after crude fiber, crude fat, crude protein, dry matter, and ash are removed from a feed

nodule, small node or knot which is solid and can be detected by touch

norepinephrine, stimulant that affects the brain and heart; present in the adrenal galnds

nucleic acid, component of genes necessary for heredity

oocyst, encysted or encapsulated ookinete in wall of stomach

ookinete, fertilized form of malarial parasite in body of mosquito

Oonopsis, scientific term for goldenweed, a plant that collects and stores selenium for its own use; unpalatable to the horse

organic, pertaining to substances derived from living organisms

oribatid, free living pasture mite found on established pastures; necessary intermediate host of tapeworms

osmotic pressure, fluid pressure within and outside the cells

osteochondritis dissecans, one of the metabolic bone diseases; results in splitting of pieces of cartilage into the joint, particularly the knee or shoulder joint; linked to a calcium/phosphorus deficiency

osteochondrosis, one of the metabolic bone diseases; disease of one or more of the growth centers which begins as degeneration, followed by recalcification

osteomalacia, occurs in foals; equivalent of rickets in adult horses; bones soften as a result of absorption of the salts they contain; may be associated with deficiency of vitamin D; causes deformity of softened bones

oxalate, any salt of oxalic acid

oxalic acid, compound found in several species of plants; continued ingestion of may result in a calcium deficiency

oxide, any compound of oxygen with an element or radical

pancreatitis, inflammation of the pancreas; can be caused by fat infiltration in the liver

parathormone, trade name for the hormone of the parathyroid glands; secreted when excesses of phosphorus are fed or when calcium levels are low in the blood

parrot mouth, congenital defect; condition in which lower jaw is too short or upper jaw is too long

parthenogenetic, reproducing by developing own unfertilized egg; no male sperm is required

pathogenetic, pathogenic; giving origin to disease

pathogenicity, ability of a microorganism to produce disease

pathological, pertaining to pathology

pathology, branch of medicine that treats the nature of disease; study of the causes, development, and results of disease processes

pentacalcium orthoperiodate (PCOP), compound used to supplement iodine

pentosan, class of polysaccharide

pentose, class of monosaccharide

pepsinogen, digestive enzyme secreted by gastric mucosa; breaks down into pepsin, a protein-digesting enzyme

perennial, lasting throughout the year or for several years

perilymph, fluid contained in the space between the osseous and membranous labyrinth of the inner ear

periodic opthalmia, inflammatory disease of the eye which is the most common cause of blindness in the horse

peripheral, situated near the periphery, or edge

peristalsis, worm-like movement by which tubular organs (intestines, digestive tract, etc.) propel their contents

peristaltic, having the actions of peristalsis

peristaltic action, pertaining to peristalsis

peritoneal lining, lining of the abdomen

peritoneum, membrane which lines the abdominal cavity

peritonitis, inflammation of the peritoneum

peroxide, toxin which impairs cell membrane's permeability, making the cell very fragile

phagocyte, any cell which ingests microorganisms or other cells and foreign particles

pharynx, sac between the mouth and esophagus

phenylbutazone, most common non-steroidal anti-inflammatory drug; blocks formation of prostaglandins; commonly called "bute"

phospholipid, lipid containing phosphorus which, on hydrolysis, yields fatty acids, glycerin, and a nitrogenous compound

phosphoprotein, compound that contains phosphorus and protein

photophobia, abnormal aversion to light

photosynthesis, chemical combination caused by action of light; formation of carbohydrates from carbon dioxide and water in the chlorophyll tissue of plants under the influence of light

phylloquinone, source of vitamin K

phytate, salt of phytic acid; organic form of phosphorus found in plants

phytin, substance that is antagonistic to calcification of bone; linked to rickets; organic phosphate compound found in plants

placenta, organ which joins the fetus to the uterus of the mare and allows for exchange of substances through the blood

plasma, liquid portion of the blood

polycythemia, excess of red corpuscles in the blood

polysaccharide, one of a group of carbohydrates which contain more than four molecules of simple carbohydrates combined with each other

polyunsaturated, many unsaturated fats bonded together

postparturition, period after delivery of a foal

potassium iodate, compound used to supplement iodine

potassium iodide, substance used to supplement iodine; requires a stabilizer to prevent iodine from being destroyed

potassium permanganate, used as an oxidizing agent, antiseptic, and disinfectant; used to remove lignin from acid detergent fiber in feed analysis

precursor, substance from which another substance is formed

probiotic, feed additive; helps establish desirable balance of gastrointestinal organisms

progesterone, hormone which prepares uterus for reception and development of fertilized egg

proline, an amino acid

proprioception, receiving stimulation within the tissues of the body

prostaglandin, stimulant to intestinal and uterine muscles

prothrombin, precursor of thrombin; essential for clotting of blood

protozoa, primitive organism consisting of a single cell

proximate analysis, method of hay analysis

Pseudomonas, motile bacteria found in soil and water

pupate, process of forming an outer covering, inside which larva develops into adult insect

pyloric sphincter, tight band of muscle that regulates the juncture of the stomach with the small intestine

pylorus, aperture by which stomach contents enter duodenum

rancid, term applied to fats that have undergone decomposition

rendered fat, fat derived from animal sources and processed for animal consumption

reserpine, substance that lowers blood pressure, slows heart rate, causes diarrhea

resin, lipid that is found in and provides energy to the growing plant; related to fats in structure

rhizome, root stock of a plant

ruminant, animal which has a stomach with four complete cavities through which food passes during digestion; includes oxen, sheep, goats, deer, antelope

saturated fat, type of fatty acid; most are solid at room temperature; obtained from animal sources; less digestible than unsaturated fatty acids

serum, clear portion of any animal liquid separated from its more solid elements; clear liquid which separates in the clotting of blood

serum ferritin, indicator of horse's iron level

shear mouth, congenital defect; condition in which horse's upper jaw is wider than normal; results in extremely sharp edges on molars

shipping fever, disease related to stress of transport; symptoms include weakness, nasal discharge; discharge from eyes; distressed breathing, coughing

Sideranthus, plant which collects and stores, but does not use, high concentrations of selenium; ingestion of may cause selenium toxicity

sod, soil

sodium bentonite, material added to pelleted feeds to aid in the pelleting process

sodium bicarbonate, used as an antacid; administered with other medications to produce alkalinity of urine; reduces effects of acidic environment in the exercising muscle; administered to animals suffering from azoturia

sodium chloride, salt

sodium iodide, compound used to supplement iodine
sodium thiosulfate, compound which stabilizes the iodine supplement potassium iodide, so that iodine is not destroyed
sow mouth, congenital defect; condition in which lower jaw is too long; lower incisors protrude past the uppers
sphincter, tight band of muscle that surrounds opening of an organ
spinous processes, upward projections of the vertebrae
spontaneous combustion, self-ignition of material through chemical action of its constituents
Stanleya, scientific name for prince's plume, plant which collects and stores selenium for its own use; usually unpalatable to the horse
stolon, horizontal branch from base of a plant that produces new plants from buds at its tip
stomate, hole on leaves of plants through which water evaporates
Streptococcus fecium, bacteria in bowel
strongylids, roundworms
subcutaneous, beneath the skin
superoxide dismutase, intracellular enzyme that is part of body's defense against toxic oxides
syndronous diaphragmatic flutter, "hiccup" caused by spasm of diaphragm in rhythm with heartbeat; also called thumps
synovial fluid, transparent fluid contained in joint cavities, bursae, and tendon sheaths for lubrication
synthesis, production of a substance by combining its elements or compounds
tannin, tannic acid; used externally as an astringent and to treat burns
tetany, localized spasmodic contractions of muscles; may cause twitching or convulsions; caused by subnormal levels of blood calcium
theobromine, has physiologic properties similar to caffeine; used as a diuretic and coronary artery dilator
thiaminase, enzyme that destroys thiamine
threonine, one of the essential amino acids
thrombus, clot in a blood vessel or in one of the cavities of the heart; caused by coagulation of blood and remaining at the point of formation
thrush, degenerative condition of the frog of the horse's hoof
thumps, syndronous diaphragmatic flutter; repeated contraction of the diaphragm in rhythm with the heart beat; caused by low blood levels of calcium and potassium
thyroid gland, organ that secretes the hormone thyroxin, which increases the rate of metabolism
thyroxine, thyroid hormone; regulates metabolic rate; essential for growth and reproduction; influences lactation
tocopherol, alcohol with the properties of vitamin E
trachea, windpipe
transverse processes of lumbar vertebrae, side projections of the vertebrae
triglyceride, fat containing three fatty acids
trisaccharide, class of carbohydrate

tryptophan, amino acid; necessary for synthesis of niacin

tyrosine, non-essential amino acid; forms thyroxine when combined with iodine

unsaturated lipids, highly digestible fats; liquid at room temperature; obtained from vegetable sources

urea, chief waste product discharged in the urine; formed in the liver and carried to the kidneys by the blood

vascular, pertaining to vessels

vasoconstriction, diminution of blood vessels; leads to decreased blood flow to a specific area

vasodilator, causing enlargement of blood vessels

vertebrae, bone components of spinal column

Vinca herbacea, Vinca rosea, plants that contain reserpine, which lowers blood pressure, slows the heart rate, and causes diarrhea

viscosity, quality of being viscous

viscous, sticky or gummy

viviparous, producing living young from within the body

volatile oil, lipid related in structure to fat

wax, lipid related in structure to fat

Weende System, method of determining carbohydrate level in a feed sample

white line, margin of horn between the sole and the hoof wall; acts as soft cementing material between the wall and sole; line through which nails should be driven when shoeing

white muscle disease, muscular degeneration; results from vitamin E deficiency

Wild Jasmine, noxious weed; ingestion of causes symptoms similar to vitamin D toxicity; also known as Day-blooming Jessamine, Day Cestrum

wobbler's syndrome, disease that affects cervical spinal cord and vertebrae of young horses; marked by incoordination; linked to vitamin E deficiency

wolf teeth, small teeth that erupt in upper jaw, usually in front of the molars

xanthurenic acid, product of metabolism of tryptophan

yellow star thistle, toxic plant that contains thiaminases and antithiamin, which destroy thiamine

INDEX